Integrating the Language Arts

SECOND EDITION

David Yellin
OKLAHOMA STATE UNIVERSITY

Mary E. Blake
UNIVERSITY OF CHARLESTON

Beverly A. DeVries
SOUTHERN NAZARENE UNIVERSITY

Holcomb Hathaway, Publishers
Scottsdale, Arizona 85250

Dedication

David Yellin: I dedicate this book to Pamela, Lindsay, and Aubree.

Mary Blake: I dedicate this edition to my students and colleagues, who have taught me so much.

Beverly DeVries: I dedicate this book to my husband Merlyn, who encouraged me through each step of this endeavor.

Library of Congress Catologing-in-Publication Data

Yellin, David
    Integrating the language arts / David Yellin, Mary E. Blake, Beverly A. DeVries.—2nd ed.
      p.   cm.
    Includes bibliographical references and index.
    ISBN 1-890871-23-0
    1. Language arts (Elementary)—United States.   2. Language experience approach in education—United States.   3. Interdisciplinary approach in education—United States.   I. Blake, Mary E.   II. DeVries, Beverly A.   III. Title.

LB1576.Y45 2000
372.6—dc21   99-089314

Holcomb Hathaway, Publishers
6207 North Cattle Track Road, Suite 5
Scottsdale, Arizona 85250
(480) 991-7881
www.hh-pub.com

10 9 8 7 6 5 4 3

ISBN 1-890871-23-0

Printed in the United States of America.

Contents

CHAPTER 4

Language Origins, Acquisition, and Development   109

CHAPTER 5

Listening and Speaking   151

CHAPTER 6

Language and Literacy: The Reading Factor   207

CHAPTER 10
Reading and Writing Across the Curriculum   413

CHAPTER 11
Working with a Diverse Population   465

APPENDIX
Self-Diagnostic Instrument   505

Preface

This new edition of *Integrating the Language Arts* reflects the authors' belief that learning the language arts involves higher mental processes than mere skill memorization and cuts across all the subject content areas. This second edition offers a balanced approach between direct instruction in the communication arts and integrating listening, speaking, reading, writing, viewing, and visual representing with other content areas such as music, art, mathematics, social studies, and science. Our discussions reflect the latest research in the language arts areas as well as research in cognitive development and advances in technology. This edition addresses the important topics of community and parental involvement in the education process and offers thoughtful coverage of multiculturalism and diversity in the schools.

This textbook is intended for both undergraduate and graduate students, who plan to teach the language arts in the primary, intermediate, and middle grades (K–8). Whether students will teach all of the subjects in a self-contained second-grade class or the language arts exclusively in a departmentalized seventh-grade setting, this textbook provides the background and practical teaching suggestions to help readers become successful teachers. Please take a moment now to read through the table of contents to familiarize yourself with the depth and breadth of coverage included within.

This revised edition includes a number of important new discussions. For example, we have added a concise overview describing the similarities and differences among the various approaches to teaching the language arts, including the separate skills, whole language, integrated, and balanced approaches. Current information on brain research and multiple intelligences is described as it relates to the language arts. Discussions of students with special needs are designed to help classroom teachers work effectively with an increasingly diverse student population. Updated examples of lesson plans, thematic units, children's literature, assessment tools, and book award lists are found throughout the text. You will also find suggestions for direct instruction in specific skill areas of the language arts.

We believe in incorporating real-life activities and experiences into the classroom, and as a result, this new edition is more interactive—it encourages readers to become actively involved in their own learning, to move beyond the textbook and apply what they learn through real-life teaching experiences. Throughout the book, students will encounter the following special features:

■ Each chapter includes one or more *"In the Classroom"* vignettes, illustrating how real teachers teach the language arts using techniques included in the textbook.

- The recurring boxed feature *"In & Beyond the Classroom"* offers suggestions for assignments and projects that will move your students beyond their textbook into the community and its classrooms for valuable field experiences.

- *Meaningful quotations*, appearing in the text margins throughout the book, will stimulate thinking and in-class discussions.

- Our *"With Children"* feature offers practical and fun language arts activities for your students to use in their field-based teaching.

- The end-of-chapter feature *"Technology"* provides important information about the great variety of software and hardware options available to today's teachers.

- In each chapter, *"E-learning"* offers an annotated list of Websites that will enable your students to access the most current information about a topic and to explore topics of special interest.

- Finally, each chapter closes with *"Related Readings"* and *"References,"* ensuring that students will have at their fingertips the resources they need to do further research on a topic.

We hope readers will use this textbook in an interactive manner, as we have designed it to be used. Encourage your students to discuss each chapter openly in class and to complete as many of the *In & Beyond the Classroom* suggestions as possible. Have them access websites and do field observations of children and teachers in order to learn from others in the field. Encourage students to keep a journal of reflections about their readings, their observation experiences in classrooms, and other field experiences. Have them share journal reflections with you and with their peers. Each person gets something different out of a textbook and a college course. Teaching is truly a collaborative undertaking—through sharing with others we all grow in our understanding of how to teach.

Acknowledgments

We would like to thank the following reviewers, who read the manuscript for this new edition and offered constructive suggestions for its improvement. The book is better as a result of their efforts: M. Priscilla Myers, Plattsburgh State University of New York; Sherron Killingsworth Roberts, University of Central Florida; Gail J. Gerlach, Indiana University of Pennsylvania; and Charles E. Matthews, College of Charleston.

In addition, David Yellin would like to acknowledge the following people for their support and encouragement in this textbook project: his wife, Pamela Gold Yellin; his early mentor at Arizona State University, Nicholas Silvaroli; his colleagues at Oklahoma State University, especially David England; and the many classroom teachers around the state of Oklahoma, particularly Diane Moser. A special thanks to Ora Sedhaphak and Nancy Brooks Thompson for helping with the final details of the book.

Mary Blake wishes to thank all her students, past and present. She also wishes to thank her former advisors at the University of Connecticut: Donald Protheroe, Judith Meagher, and the late William Page. A special thanks goes to Rebecca Shuler for gathering much of the research for this edition.

Beverly DeVries wishes to thank the other two authors for inviting her to join them in writing this edition of the textbook. Also, special thanks to Linda Jones, Tammy McGee, and Shari Kimbro for providing research on the gifted programs, to Jo Dorhout for providing information for the technology sections, and to Natasha Moore for editing the addresses of the websites.

Introduction to the Language Arts

1

IN THIS CHAPTER

This chapter introduces some of the broad concepts necessary to help you learn about and teach the language arts. As you read the first section on planning, note the relationship between what a teacher believes and what she or he practices in the classroom. Next, think about the different ways to view the language arts curriculum.

Four major topics are addressed in this chapter. First we discuss the new *Standards for the English Language Arts* established by the International Reading Association and the National Council of Teachers of English. Viewing and visual representing have been added to the original four components of the language arts—reading, writing, listening, and speaking. Figure 1.1 is a diagram of the six components. Next we discuss two learning theories: Jerome Bruner's Learning Experiences Ladder and Brian Cambourne's Learning Theory. Third, we define the four approaches to the language arts: separate skills, whole language, integrated, and balanced. Finally we discuss the ways in which today's teachers and schools are changing and evolving.

The Class Vignette in this chapter and those throughout the book exemplify how effective teachers integrate the six components of the language arts in all subject areas throughout the entire day. The distinctions among listening, speaking, reading, writing, viewing, and visual representing are blurred or eliminated in favor of using the communication arts to enable students to learn about content areas. The focus is always on communication, learning, and meaning, regardless of the activity.

Figure 1.1

Integrated language arts wheel.

quiz

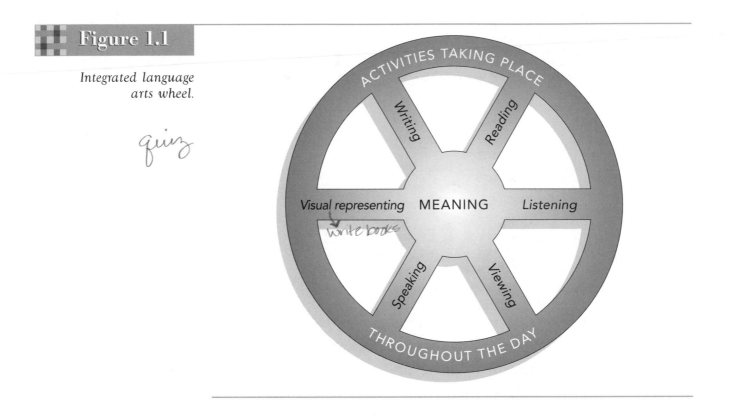

Teaching the Language Arts

Traditionally in the primary, elementary, and middle grades (kindergarten through grade 8), the term **language arts** is defined in terms of four curriculum areas: listening, speaking, reading, and writing. In some school districts, this is referred to as the communication arts block; in other districts, it is called the English curriculum, although the term English as a subject area is more often used at the high school level. In this text, we will use the most common term, language arts, to refer to the English communication skills taught in kindergarten through grade 8 (K–8).

Recently the two major professional organizations concerned with teaching the language arts, the **International Reading Association (IRA)** and the **National Council of Teachers of English (NCTE),** met together to create the new *Standards for the English Language Arts* (1996). This was a significant accomplishment. Classroom teachers from all over the United States working in small groups and large, over a number of years, pooled their expertise, their knowledge, and their experiences and were able to agree on certain fundamental concepts that should guide the teaching/learning of the language arts. It is their work and wisdom that form the foundation of this new edition, *Integrating the Language Arts.*

One of the significant contributions of the IRA and NCTE committees that created the new *Standards* was the addition of two components to the traditional four language arts components: viewing and visually representing have been added to listening, speaking, reading, and writing. **Viewing** refers to the communication processes involved when children view videos, computer simulations, and computer games; comprehend book illustrations; and interpret charts, tables, maps, and other print media. **Visually representing** is the other side of viewing, namely, illustrating books; producing home pages on the Internet; creating murals, dioramas, collages, and other works of art such as sculpture; dancing; and doing mime. Both the IRA and the NCTE acknowledge the importance of these two areas as we begin the twenty-first century by giving them equal weight with the more familiar listening, speaking, reading, and writing.

BEYOND THE CLASSROOM

Write, phone, or e-mail either the IRA (IRA, 800 Barksdale Road, P.O. Box 8139, Newark, DE 19714-8139; 1-800-336-7323; http://www.reading.org) or the NCTE (NCTE, 111 W. Kenyon Road, Urbana, IL 61801-1096; 1-800-369-6283; http://www.ncte.org) and request your own complete copy of the new *Standards for the English Language Arts.*

In addition, the NCTE/IRA *Standards for the English Language Arts* identifies 12 major tenets that should guide the teaching/learning process at all grade levels. Figure 1.2 presents these tenets for your discussion and reflection. As you read this chapter and the rest of the textbook, refer back to these 12 standards often. They are the structure that guides this textbook and should provide you with material to reflect on as you enter the teaching profession.

1. Students read a wide range of print and nonprint texts to build an understanding of texts, of themselves, and of the cultures of the United States and the world; to acquire new information; to respond to the needs and demands of society and the workplace; and for personal fulfillment. Among these texts are fiction and nonfiction, classic and contemporary works.

2. Students read a wide range of literature from many periods in many genres to build an understanding of the many dimensions (e.g., philosophical, ethical, aesthetic) of human experience.

3. Students apply a wide range of strategies to comprehend, interpret, evaluate, and appreciate texts. They draw on their prior experience, their interactions with other readers and writers, their knowledge of word meaning and other texts, their word identification strategies, and their understanding of textual features (e.g., sound–letter correspondence, sentence structure, context, graphics).

4. Students adjust their use of spoken, written, and visual language (e.g., conventions, style, vocabulary) to communicate effectively with a variety of audiences and for different purposes.

5. Students employ a wide range of strategies as they write and use different writing process elements appropriately to communicate with different audiences for a variety of purposes.

6. Students apply knowledge of language structure, language conventions (e.g., spelling and punctuation), media techniques, figurative language, and genre to create, critique, and discuss print and nonprint texts.

7. Students conduct research on issues and interests by generating ideas and questions, and by posing problems. They gather, evaluate, and synthesize data from a variety of sources (e.g., print and nonprint texts, artifacts, people) to communicate their discoveries in ways that suit their purpose and audience.

8. Students use a variety of technological and information resources (e.g., libraries, databases, computer networks, video) to gather and synthesize information and to create and communicate knowledge.

Figure 1.2

The Standards for the English Language Arts.

(continued)

9. Students develop an understanding of and respect for diversity in language use, patterns, and dialects across cultures, ethnic groups, geographic regions, and social roles.
10. Students whose first language is not English make use of their first language to develop competency in the English language arts and to develop understanding of content across the curriculum.
11. Students participate as knowledgeable, reflective, creative, and critical members of a variety of literacy communities.
12. Students use spoken, written, and visual language to accomplish their own purposes (e.g., for learning, enjoyment, persuasion, and the exchange of information).

As you study, reflect on, and discuss the *Standards for the English Language Arts* in your class, pay attention to the following. First, note that these standards reflect the wisdom and consensus of veteran teachers throughout the nation regarding what is most important to know about the English language arts. Second, most of the standards are general and straightforward enough that you should feel comfortable with them as you prepare to teach the language arts in grades K–8. For example, standards 1, 2, and 3 refer to the need for students to read widely and apply their reading as they interact with other readers and writers. Standards 4 and 5 refer to the ability to use language flexibly in a variety of ways and to meet a variety of situations. Standard 6 addresses the notion of language structures, conventions, and genres. Standard 7 speaks to the relatively new notion of students (and teachers) as researchers; not only are you expected to be consumers of research, but teachers today are expected to do research in their classrooms and share their findings with other teachers. Standard 8 emphasizes the need for students to be familiar with and use advanced technology. Standards 9, 10, and 11 speak to the broad issue of diversity within and outside the classroom. It calls for respect and understanding of others who may be different from you. And finally, standard 12 is concerned that students use language, in all its forms, to accomplish their own goals and needs.

DEVELOPING A PHILOSOPHY OF EDUCATION

When the classroom teachers met to discuss and eventually formulate the new *Standards for the English Language Arts*, they were not only pooling their wisdom based on experience but were also collaborating and articulating their philosophies regarding children, the content and materials of the language arts, and the nature of the teaching/learning process. Successful teachers also act on the basis of a personal teaching philosophy, a set of beliefs that guides their practices with children.

As you continue reading this text, you should gradually begin to shape your own philosophy of education, particularly as it relates to how you will teach students about the language arts. In 1916, the famous educator–philosopher John Dewey said that every teacher brings to the classroom a philosophy about education, about how children learn best. It is this philosophy that allows you to make decisions each day—from how you will arrange the furniture in the classroom to how you will evaluate your students' skills in reading or writing to which methods and materials you will use to teach spelling and handwriting to how you will maintain classroom control and

You cannot teach a person anything—you can only help him find it in himself.

GALILEO

discipline. In short, all of the choices regarding how, when, and what you teach are ultimately dependent on your personal philosophy.

Reflect on the following quote for a moment: "Teaching without developing one's own philosophy of education would be analogous to building a house on sand instead of on a firm foundation, or taking a trip without a road map" (Hessong & Weeks, 1987, p. 144).

Just as you would not embark on a long vacation trip without a road map, so too you need a map to guide you as you prepare to teach. The constant decisions you will be called upon to make throughout the school year must be based on a consistent set of beliefs if your students are to trust you as their guide in the learning process.

Acquiring such a philosophy is a slow and sometimes arduous process; it requires that you be open to the views of others but strong enough in your own convictions to resist being led by others. In *The Lonely Crowd* (1961), a classic sociological study of the American character, David Riesman describes two types of individuals: The **other- or outer-directed** person conforms, follows, and looks for the approval of others before acting; the **inner-directed** person follows an inner set of beliefs and values that guides his or her decision making. Psychologist Jerome Bruner (1962) saw individual mental growth and development in terms of how people move from a state of outer-directedness to one of inner-directedness. As you become more inner-directed as a person, your personal philosophy as a teacher will become more evident. Eventually you will see yourself as a decision maker whom others look to for advice and guidance.

To help you in this process, the remainder of this chapter describes some other learning theories that affect teachers and a number of different ways of viewing the language arts. Each language arts approach has its own strengths and possible weaknesses. Analyze them and reflect on them in conjunction with other learning theories that you have studied. Since every child is different and every child also possesses unique strengths and weaknesses, no one approach will be suitable for all students all of the time. For that reason, we ask you to pick and choose the best from many options to find your own way. Cunningham put it this way: "When a teacher provides more routes to the goal of literacy, more children will find a route that will take them there" (1995, p. 19).

Examine the following approaches to viewing the language arts critically. Compare them to your own experiences and observations in the classroom. Your ability to analyze this text, other research literature in the language arts, other learning theories, and your observations in the classroom is part of the process of becoming a reflective teacher with your own personal philosophy of education. As you reflect critically on what you see, hear, and read, you will become a more responsible decision maker in the classroom, which is the hallmark of the professional educator (Zeichner & Liston, 1987).

> ### BEYOND THE CLASSROOM
>
> As you read this text in conjunction with the course you are taking, keep a weekly journal of your thoughts, observations, and experiences. Keeping a regular written journal is one of the best ways to clarify and develop your own philosophy of education.

RELATED LEARNING THEORIES

Before examining the various approaches to teaching the language arts, consider two learning theories that greatly affect teaching in general, and thus the teaching of the language arts. One theory is Bruner's Learning Experiences Ladder and the other is Cambourne's Learning Theory.

Jerome Bruner's Learning Experiences Ladder

While researching children, Bruner (1966) found that children learn best from personal experiences and learn least from verbal explanations. See Figure 1.3 for Bruner's **Learning Experiences Ladder.** Since the most effective way a student learns is through direct experiences, the base of the ladder, a teacher should provide as many direct experiences as possible. Obviously, not all teaching can be through direct experiences; therefore, the teacher should provide many simulated experiences that demand students use more than one sense. Some of these experiences can be playing simulated games, constructing models, or role playing. If direct or simulated experiences are not available, the next experience, though not as effective because it does not engage as many senses, is vicarious experiences. Many of these experiences, such as computer programs and videos, are readily available today. Visual experiences, which only include the visual sense, are better than just a verbal explanation, which is the least effective way to learn. Many textbooks provide pictures, charts, and graphs to explain a concept.

Rupley et al. (1998/1999) support Bruner's theory when they stress the importance of nurturing vocabulary development in the elementary school.

Figure 1.3

Bruner's Learning Experiences Ladder.

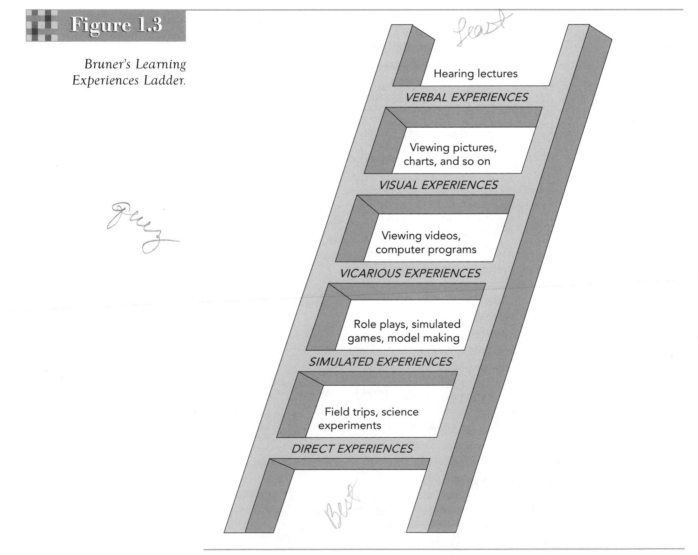

Source: Adapted from Bruner (1966), as cited in Kellough & Roberts (1991).

show the meaning of a word!

They state that a teacher who merely verbalizes a definition of a word or attempts to get students to understand the word's meaning from the context of the passage does not help students to fully comprehend or understand the new word.

An example of a teacher putting Bruner's theory into practice is Mr. Lopez. When he was preparing to study popular children's author Tomie dePaola with his second-graders, he decided that the least effective way for his students to learn about dePaola's life and books would be if he prepared a lecture about the author. He knew it was necessary to bring in pictures of Tomie dePaola and some of his books. He knew that an even more effective way for them to appreciate Tomie dePaola would be for him to show a video of Tomie dePaola working in his studio, explaining how he gets his ideas. Mr. Lopez also planned for his students to become actively involved and act out some of their favorite stories they would be reading. The last and the best learning experience he planned for the students was for Tomie dePaola to visit the classroom, tell about himself, and read some of his books out loud to students. Mr. Lopez not only put Bruner's theory into practice but also integrated the six components of the language arts. Although not every teacher will be fortunate enough to have well-known authors visit the classroom, many other learning experiences are equally effective.

Brian Cambourne's Learning Theory

Another theory that emphasizes the importance of students' direct involvement for effective learning is Brian Cambourne's **Learning Theory.** Cambourne (1988) posits that eight conditions are necessary for learning to take place;

Teaching means helping a child realize his potential.

ERICH FROMM

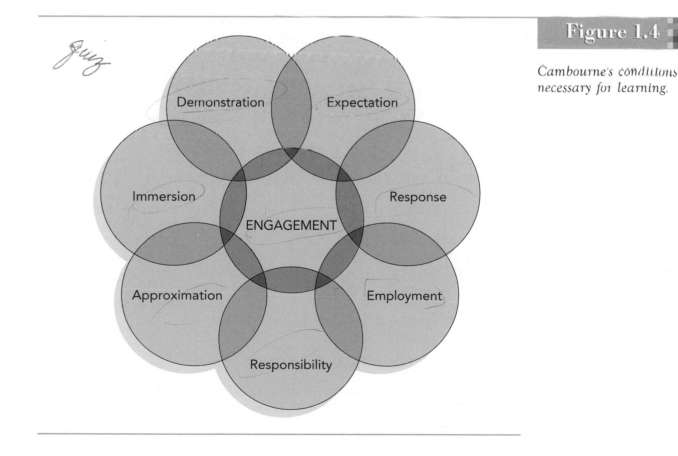

Figure 1.4

Cambourne's conditions necessary for learning.

these are immersion, demonstration, expectation, response, employment, responsibility, approximation, and engagement. Figure 1.4 shows how the eight conditions are interrelated, with student engagement being at the center of the learning process.

Immersion, demonstration, expectation, and response are led by the teacher. It should be the teacher's goal to set up a classroom that immerses students in worthwhile, authentic learning tasks. There should be (1) numerous opportunities to read about topics that interest the individual student; (2) varied opportunities to learn how to effectively articulate information, stories, poems, etc., either verbally or in written communication; and (3) many opportunities for students to express themselves through the visual or performing arts. The teacher must demonstrate the new concept to the students and demonstrate how to use the information in real-life settings. Also, the teacher must set high but realistic standards for all students and expect all students to be successful in learning the concept or task. It is then the teacher's responsibility to respond to the students with encouraging feedback that praises the students' approximations or attempts and that does not criticize them. This feedback should be verbal and occur while students are engaged in the task.

Employment, responsibility, and approximation are the conditions that the students bring to the learning process. The students must apply themselves when given the opportunities to immerse themselves in reading, writing, and other learning activities; they cannot be mere spectators. Students must assume responsibility for their learning; therefore, they must be willing to spend more time on tasks that are difficult for them. They also need to assume responsibility for the final results of their learning. As students learn, there will be times when their work is a mere approximation of their best work; the learning process does not always result in perfect understanding the first or second time students encounter a new idea or task. However, during the process, students must be willing to take risks and experiment with new ideas because that is when growth takes place.

When you read Chapter 8, you will see how Brian Cambourne's Learning Theory applies to writing.

BEYOND THE CLASSROOM

Interview a teacher, principal, or parent regarding theoretical orientation to learning and the language arts. See how different the viewpoints are within a school building, across a school district, and among districts.

Four Ways to View the Language Arts

There are many ways of looking at an entire curriculum area such as the language arts. In this section, four different approaches to teaching the language arts are presented for you to reflect on and discuss in your class: the separate skills approach, the whole language approach, the integrated approach, and the balanced approach. By clarifying some of the similarities and differences among these approaches, we hope you will avoid some of the confusion that occurs in education when similar terms are used interchangeably or without clear definitions.

SEPARATE SKILLS APPROACH

The separate skills approach is one of the most commonly observed approaches in the elementary grades due to the way most schools are presently organized. In the **separate skills approach,** each language arts subskill area (reading, spelling, handwriting, grammar) is viewed as a unique entity, separate from other subject areas. Often these separate skills are taught during distinct times of the day (Tompkins, 1997). The school day is divided into specific subject areas and regulated according to strict time periods. For example, reading might be taught every day from 8:40 to 9:30 A.M., followed by spelling from 9:40 to 10:30 A.M., and grammar from 10:40 to 11:30 A.M. Within these time periods, each subject area is further broken down into smaller and smaller subskills, such as a lesson on the long vowel sound of /a/ in reading, the adding of "ing" to words in spelling, and contrasting nouns and pronouns in grammar. Such an approach is based on behavioristic principles of part-to-whole learning (Goodman, 1986).

By emphasizing separate skills in isolation from one another, teaching becomes a dissection process; that is, listening, speaking, reading, writing, viewing, and visual representing are all broken down and divided into myriad subskills, following an elaborate predesignated scope and sequence. Textbooks and curriculum guides further support this dissection process. By implication, the teacher is to follow the chapters in the textbook, in sequential order, teaching one subskill after another. Again we see here the part-to-whole sequencing of instruction and learning most characteristic of behavioral psychology. Figure 1.5 shows the separate skills approach in diagram fashion.

Note in this diagram that each language arts subject area and the subskills within each area are isolated from one another. This is a major characteristic of the separate skills approach. Learning is compartmentalized; course content in one area is taught separately from all other areas. Since a certain amount of subject matter must be covered within each specific time block, the class tends to be teacher-dominated, relying on whole-group lecture. Direct, intensive, systematic instruction controlled by the teacher is another characteristic of this approach (Strickland, 1998). The emphasis of this approach is on covering content through skills lessons. Critics of the separate skills approach (Goodman, 1986; Kohl, 1967; Kozol, 1967; Weaver, 1996) have argued that such an approach treats teachers and children as things to be manipulated, leaves little room for active student involvement, and

isolated from each other

Figure 1.5   *Separate skills approach charts.*

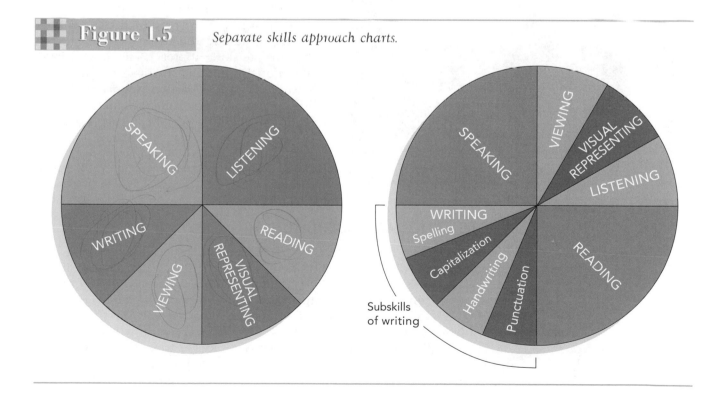

Subskills
of writing

assumes that knowledge of the separate parts will eventually lead the student to an understanding of the greater whole of literacy.

If the separate skills approach has so many drawbacks, why is it still widely employed in the K–8 curriculum? There are several reasons. First, the separate skills approach is an old and time-honored view of what school should be like. This is the way it has been for many years, and many people seem satisfied with it. The schools are basically a conservative institution in our society; change occurs very slowly, as John Goodlad (1997) noted in his study of American education.

Second, the separate skills approach, from a principal's view, serves administrative purposes well. For example, it allows the school principal to know exactly what children and teachers are working on at a particular time of the day. The entire school can be organized around subject areas, fitting into specific time slots and specific rooms. This makes for an efficient use of people, building, and material resources. It is also relatively easy to evaluate such an approach. Evaluation can be done on a mass scale, periodically, through group-administered standardized tests.

A third reason for the longevity of the separate skills approach is the powerful influence of commercial textbook publishers. Many schools rely heavily on basal readers and other standardized textbooks to teach subject matter. Since these are organized into chapters and subheadings along separate subskills, teachers are encouraged to instruct in a similar manner. Joel Spring (1988), another critic of American education, has argued that the primary purpose of the textbook industry is to make a profit; therefore, innovation and creativity in the industry are discouraged.

Another support for the separate skills approach relates to the public's concerns about schools in general. A widely held belief, according to public opinion polls, is that classroom management or discipline should be a primary objective of the schools (Rose & Gallup, 1998). Therefore, for some people the use of bell systems, separate time periods for separate subjects, direct lecture, and systematic instruction implies a more managed, orderly approach to schooling.

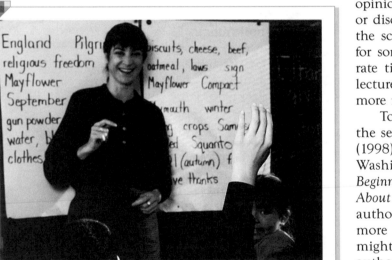

> *A great teacher makes hard things easy.*
>
> RALPH WALDO EMERSON

Today, among the strongest advocates of the separate skills approach are G. Reid Lyon (1998) of the National Institute of Health in Washington, D.C.; Marilyn Adams, author of *Beginning to Read: Thinking and Learning About Text* (1990); and Lisa Delpit (1995), an authority on minority education. To learn more about the separate skills approach you might want to read any one of these three authors' works.

WHOLE LANGUAGE APPROACH

Standing in sharp contrast to the separate skills approach is the whole language approach. Advocates, such as Ken Goodman (1992, 1996), Carol Edelsky (Edelsky, Altwerger & Flores, 1991), and Constance Weaver (1994) contend, first, that the **whole language approach** is a philosophy of language education that looks at the whole child learning language within the natural environment of the home, community, and school. Second, it is a child-centered philosophy that favors giving students choices as to what they will read and write. Third, language arts subjects, such as reading and writing, are not taught separately but instead are inextricably linked together. Finally, whole language advocates argue that the skills of language arts are best learned through indirect means by authentic reading, writing, listening, speaking, viewing, and visually representing activities, based on children's interests (Goodman, 1996; Veatch, 1992; Watson, 1989).

Let's elaborate briefly on some of the major points associated with the whole language approach, remembering that this and other approaches will be addressed more specifically in the chapters on reading and writing.

The whole language approach to teaching is based on students' needs, interests, and experiences as opposed to a predetermined curriculum or teacher-controlled scope and sequence of skills. It believes in intrinsic motivation rather than extrinsic rewards. The language arts are viewed as a whole. Children are encouraged to choose entire books to read, to write complete stories, and to discuss their reading and writing with the teacher and their peers. Figure 1.6 represents the whole language approach. Note that a slice from the whole language "pie" includes all aspects of the language arts.

In the whole language classroom, children use language to learn about language. This means that the teacher begins at whatever point in learning the student feels comfortable. For most young children, this means starting with listening and speaking activities. Listening either to the teacher read books aloud or at the listening center, engaging in discussions about picture books, chatting with one another over their drawings at the art centers, and conducting puppet shows help give young children confidence in using language that later they will apply as they learn to read and write.

Such classrooms look different from separate skills classrooms in that much in-class time is devoted to free reading and writing. Whole language

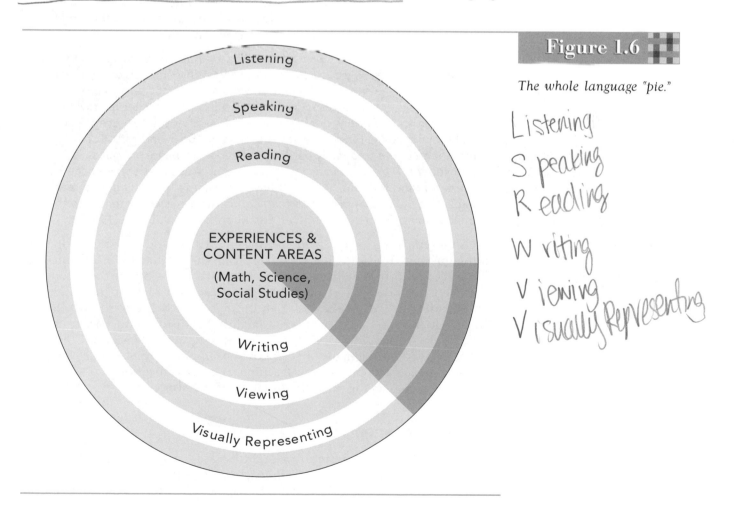

Figure 1.6

The whole language "pie."

teachers believe that only by reading and writing can students become readers and writers. Children's literature books rather than basal readers are at the heart of these classrooms. The students are treated as authors themselves and encouraged to talk about books they have read and share stories they have written (Short, Harste, & Burke, 1996).

Authentic literacy is another term applied to the whole language classroom (Krashen, 1993). This means first that children get to choose what they read and write. Second, they are encouraged to talk about their reading and writing. Using language freely, exploring with language, and experimenting as part of the learning experience are other aspects of authenticity (Goodman, 1996). Examples of authentic literacy activities include reading, writing, and sharing songs, letters, recipes, jokes, lists, directions for playing games, food labels, and cartoons.

The following two classroom examples exemplify the child-centered, indirect instructional approach characteristic of whole language:

Teaching is the art of assisting discovery.

MARK VAN DOREN

> A young child is writing her first story. She does not know how to spell most of the words she wants to use. "How do you spell *house*?" she asks her teacher. Depending on the nature of the writing activity or the teacher's understanding of the child's needs at the time, the teacher might simply spell the word for her or else say something like: "What do you think it begins with? Now sound out the rest. That's a good spelling of *house*." Note that while the student may not have spelled the word correctly, her attempt to invent or construct a spelling based on her knowledge of sounds and symbols is important. Children use their temporary self-constructed spellings as they gradually attain spelling awareness through much reading and writing. The work of Donald Graves (1994) in the area of process writing expands on this notion and will be discussed further in the chapter on writing.

> In another classroom, a student is reading silently. He moves his finger along the page slowly; his lips keep moving. When he comes to a really difficult word, he raises his hand and waits for the teacher to help him. There are other hands raised in the classroom. The teacher is moving about the room rapidly, but it is obvious she cannot get to every single child immediately. Finally she stops and says, "Boys and girls, listen to me. If you come to a really hard word in your book, take a guess at it and see if it makes sense as you read further. Another thing you can do is ask a friend for help. You don't have to wait for me to continue reading." This indirect approach to reading instruction is consistent with the philosophy of whole language as described by Frank Smith (1997).

Using temporary or invented spelling in writing and making predictions (taking guesses) in reading are encouraged in whole language classrooms and will be discussed further in later chapters in this text. Both of these concepts reflect the central focus of the whole language approach on meaning and understanding as well as the use of an indirect approach toward skill instruction. If you would like to read more about the history and background of whole language, see Julia DeCarlo's *Perspectives in Whole Language* (1995).

The classroom vignette that follows exemplifies the whole language approach, which emphasizes the teaching of communication skills in a natural manner, in keeping with the interests of the students.

INTEGRATED APPROACH

The term **integrated curriculum** or **integrated approach** is often associated with the whole language approach (Tompkins, 1997). In fact, some authors use the terms interchangeably or include the integrated approach

Vignette *in the classroom*

Miss Allison teaches second grade in a small town in eastern Oklahoma. Her students are interested in studying about animals, so this becomes the first unit of the year. She begins by reading some simple fiction books about animals. However, she quickly discovers that the children are more interested in facts, so she introduces them to nonfiction. She brings three books to class: *Elephants* by Anthony Fredericks (1998), *Wild Cats: Cougars, Bobcats and Lynx* by Deborah Hodge (1996), and *Llamas* by Emilie Lepthien (1996). Some students begin drawing and writing about their favorite animals; they use the three reference books. Some decide to make clay figures of the animals. Others go to the library to find still more books about animals. As the enthusiasm of the children builds, the teacher decides that this would be an ideal opportunity to take a field trip to the zoo in Oklahoma City. She enlists the help of a few parent volunteers. The students write letters home explaining when the trip will be and what they will need to bring (paper bag lunch).

Miss Allison: Today I want to read you a book that has something to do with our field trip tomorrow.

June: I know, it's about the zoo.

Miss Allison: That's right. This book is called *One Day at the Zoo* (1968) by Dick Snyder. Let's listen and look at the photographs of the animals. (She reads aloud from the book.) Now that we've heard this story, what do you think we will see at the zoo tomorrow?

Hands fly up all over the room; many responses are given. A lively discussion about zoo babies begins and continues throughout the period. Miss Allison writes the children's responses on the board.

The field trip proves to be a great success. For many of the students, this is their first visit to a real zoo. During follow-up discussion of what they saw and did at the zoo, Miss Allison draws three columns on the board and asks, "What do you remember hearing, seeing, and doing at the zoo?" She writes their brainstorming responses in the three columns.

Next, Miss Allison asks, "How many of you would like to write your own stories about a visit to the zoo?" A few hands go up. "Perhaps the rest of you would like to draw your stories first and then write about them later." More hands go up. The writers go to the writers' corner to get paper and pencils. They occasionally glance at the three columns on the board. The artists work hard on their drawings of animals at the zoo. Some of them put titles at the top or bottom of their drawings. As she walks about the room, Miss Allison encourages each of them to write a sentence about the drawing.

A few of the parent volunteers come to visit the room while the students are working on their stories. Miss Allison decides to enlist the volunteers' help in making bound books of the children's stories. As the students finish writing their books, the parent volunteers help create hard covers for them. For these young authors, seeing their own writings bound like real books is as exciting as the trip to the zoo!

under the whole language philosophy (Bromley, 1998). There are many similarities between the whole language and integrated approaches; however, for the sake of clarification, we will distinguish between the two as follows.

The focus of an integrated approach is on content; it attempts to combine or integrate various subject areas within a single class period. As such, it views all subject matter disciplines (listening, speaking, reading, writing, viewing, and visually representing as well as math, science, social studies, etc.) as related in terms of the way students approach learning (Bosma & Guth, 1995). Historically, the concept of integration can be traced back to John Dewey in the

1930s, who argued for linking children's experiences with the new knowledge they were acquiring in the classroom; Dewey also believed in incorporating real-life activities in the classroom (Bosma & Guth, 1995). The term *integration* appeared in the 1980s when literacy scholars began linking reading and writing instruction together (Tierney & Pearson, 1983). This then led to the linking of oral language with reading and writing as literacy researchers sought a broader view of their field (Au, Mason, & Scheu, 1995). This linkage among the various subject matter disciplines is also in keeping with what has come to be known as **brain-based learning;** brain-based theories of learning argue that the human brain naturally seeks to make connections among the various pieces of information provided by the environment (Caine & Caine, 1994).

Raphael and Hiebert (1996) contend that this linking or integrating among aspects of the communication arts content reflects the **social constructivist** perspective toward language. This view holds that learners use language as a primary means to construct their knowledge of the world. Learning to read and write involves higher mental processes than mere skill memorization and cuts across all the subject content areas. For instance, students read and write in social studies class as a way of learning about history and geography. Through talking and sharing with their teachers and peers, children gradually construct anew their understanding of specific content.

One of the primary ways that teachers attempt to integrate subject matter content across the various disciplines is through thematic literature units. By having children read books (across all genres) on a particular theme (say, animals) and doing a variety of activities related to that theme (for example, research writing, mural construction, graphing facts learned), the concept of integration is achieved.

Another type of integration, found most often in the upper elementary, middle, and secondary school grades, is the notion of **reading and writing across the curriculum** (Lapp, Flood & Farnan, 1996). This is the specific use of reading and writing activities in subject discipline areas (such as history, math, earth science) to aid the student in learning the specific content of that subject. Teaching students how to peruse a textbook in terms of an author's purpose, how to use subheadings, how to outline and take notes—these all fall under the heading of reading and writing across the curriculum. Expanding students' reading beyond the textbook in biology by encouraging them to read a biography of Charles Darwin is another use of reading across the curriculum. Having students in a middle-grade American history class write a diary entry from the point of view of Meriwether Lewis incorporates writing across the curriculum. Figure 1.7 depicts the integrated approach and demonstrates how the six components of the language arts are woven into the study of all subject areas as one theme is studied.

BALANCED APPROACH

The newest among the four terms discussed here is the **balanced approach.** The term itself only appears in the literature to any great extent after 1995. Why a new term in the field of literacy? The best way to first understand the balanced approach is to see it from a political perspective. Throughout the 1980s and into the 1990s, advocates for the separate skills approach and advocates for the whole language approach repeatedly clashed in the news media: Jeanne Chall (separate skills) debated Ken Goodman (whole language) on the stage of the International Reading Convention; professional articles on both approaches talked about the great reading wars; state legislatures across the country, from California to North Carolina, got into the fray, with some demanding more holistic approaches to schooling and others arguing for

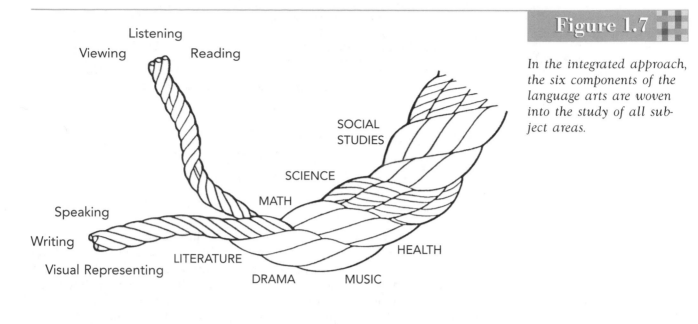

Figure 1.7

In the integrated approach, the six components of the language arts are woven into the study of all subject areas.

more separate systematic skills instruction. Blame for students' low standardized test scores was laid equally at the feet of whole language and separate skills. The education profession was politicized and polarized over the issue of literacy instruction (Strickland, 1998).

In an effort to reconcile the factions and, more important, to reflect what actual classroom teachers were doing in their classrooms under the heading of literacy instruction, the term *balanced approach* was born. In its simplest definition, the balanced approach to literacy instruction allows teachers to select both from holistic, indirect instructional methods and from the separate skills approach. The teacher selects whichever is most appropriate for each student at a particular point in that child's learning process. As such, "balanced" means broad and flexible and is inclusive enough to move between the two approaches, which were previously thought to be opposites (Baumann & Ivey, 1997; Spiegel, 1998).

Known as comprehensive

Dixie Spiegel, a literacy authority, contends that for too long educators were looking for the "silver bullet"—that single answer to the debate between phonics and whole language, that one solution to resolve the direct instruction versus indirect instruction controversy. In her own state of North Carolina, the politicians argued for holistic practices as the solution one year and then a few years later switched their position to phonics and separate skills instruction. Everyone was seeking the "silver bullet," the quick fix, the one-program-fits-all solution. It didn't happen. Instead, Spiegel and others (Allington & Walmsley, 1995; Baumann & Ivey, 1997; McIntyre & Pressley, 1996) suggest the balanced approach that permits the teacher to choose among strategies as the need arises and the occasion demands. Teachers, as reflective decision makers, cannot be restricted to a single approach for all students all of the time. A balanced view of literacy is a comprehensive view, broad and flexible enough to accommodate separate skills and holistic practices. Figure 1.8 depicts the balanced approach, which requires a "balance" between both ends to make it work.

BEYOND THE CLASSROOM

Research your state's legislation or interview a state legislator regarding the phonics/whole language controversy. Verify which theory the stance is based on.

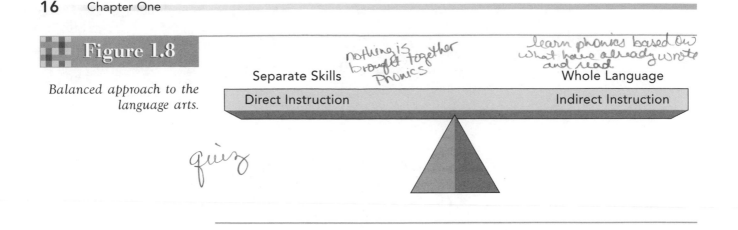

Figure 1.8

Balanced approach to the language arts.

quiz

It is obvious that approaches to teaching the language arts have changed throughout this past century. If one were to visit classrooms throughout the United States, virtually every conceivable approach would be encountered. Some teachers who are slow to embrace change may still use the same method in which they were taught. Other teachers may embrace new trends quickly, making frequent changes without really understanding the theories behind new approaches. All teachers must study theories and become reflective, flexible teachers. We must remember that we are teaching students, and not teaching a particular method. One approach to teaching language arts may work with some students; however, another group of students may need a different approach. A good teacher always meets the needs of individual students and understands why he or she uses a particular approach.

Teachers and Schools Undergo Change

In 1997, President Bill Clinton challenged America's parents and teachers to ensure that every child would be reading by the end of grade 3. To facilitate this goal, he proposed the training of 1 million volunteer tutors throughout the nation who would work in school and after school with youngsters in need of special help. The program is known as **America Reads.** In support of this nationwide effort, the National Council of Teachers of English has published *Volunteers Working with Young Readers*, written by Lester Laminack (1998). Laminack lays out some of the common pitfalls encountered by new volunteers working with beginning readers and stresses the expert role of the classroom teacher as the guiding force behind such a program. Successful tutoring of at-risk children depends on the tutors and teachers working closely together (Flannigan, 1998).

Laminack was encouraged to write this text as more and more inexperienced volunteers were entering the field of literacy training. In his book, Laminack describes five different students and how each approaches learning to read from a slightly different perspective and consequently has different tutorial needs. The kind of backgrounds children come from and the type of errors they make in reading should suggest the variety of approaches that tutors take.

LEGISLATIVE INVOLVEMENT IN EDUCATION

The America Reads initiative has spurred many state legislatures to get involved in reading instruction. From New York to Oklahoma to California, state legislatures have passed bills that essentially mandate reading proficiency for all children by the end of grade 3—as if it were that simple. In the state of Oklahoma, for example, in 1977 the legislature passed what has come to be known as the Reading Sufficiency Act. This act requires that all children in grades 1 and 2 be tested in reading to determine if they are reading at grade level and if they should be promoted to grade 3. If it is determined that the student's reading comprehension scores are not up to grade level, an individual instructional plan, similar to the IEPs used with learning-disabled children, will be created. The plan utilizes additional in-school instructional time (tutoring in some cases) as well as after-school, Saturday, and even summer instruction. How the additional instructional time in school and out is to be paid for by the district is not specified in the legislation. This is often the case with well-meaning politicians who devise plans before appropriating funds. Oklahoma's Reading Sufficiency Act also tests all third-graders on nationally standardized reading tests. Those students who do not score at grade level or above will receive an additional plan of improvement, including specialized tutoring; in some cases, they may be held back for another year of third grade (Benson, 1998). Furthermore, the act suggests specific teaching methods be used to enhance students' reading skills. These methods generally come under the heading of "phonemic awareness" or phonics. This too has caused concern among teachers, as it implies that one method is superior to all others and must be used by all teachers.

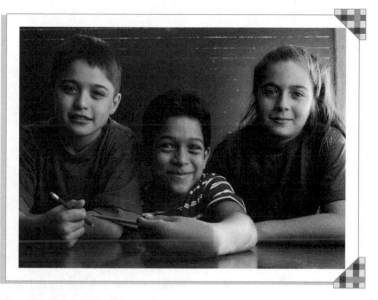

The state of California has passed similar legislation aimed at reading instruction and reading improvement. Essentially the California law mandates that "phonemic awareness" be taught in grades 1, 2, and 3 to the exclusion of other reading methods such as whole language (Tompkins, 1998). California has gained particular notoriety as its state's reading scores have plummeted. Whereas California once ranked among the top 3 states in the nation in reading, California now ranks 48. The press and politicians blamed the whole language approach to reading, which focuses on reading and writing complete texts with phonemic awareness addressed indirectly within the context of reading and writing activities. Ignored by the press and politicians alike was the fact that California's classrooms are grossly overcrowded and that many new immigrants, speaking dozens of different languages, now dominate its school districts. Given these changing demographic, social, and cultural conditions, it is no wonder that test scores declined.

Denny Taylor, one of the preeminent literacy researchers in America, takes issue with the movement toward legislating early reading instruction based on a handful of "questionable" research studies. In her book *Beginning to Read and the Spin Doctors of Science* (1998), Taylor states that it is an exercise in political persuasion and not a scientific fact that phonemic awareness must be taught. She believes that what years of research and classroom observations of young children have shown is that reading and writing are social and purposeful activities where children continually move back and forth "between function and form, meaning and abstraction."

It is important for readers of this text to be aware of the various sides in the reading debate. It is also important to keep up with the latest legislation in your own state as it affects reading instruction, particularly when one method is mandated over another by legislation. However, the position taken here is that there must be a balance among the different approaches to teaching reading, based on research findings, as well as a respect for different teaching styles and approaches. We agree with the International Reading Association's position statement on phonemic awareness, which states that "phonemic awareness should not be overemphasized to the point that other important aspects of a balanced literacy curriculum are left out or abandoned" (International Reading Association, 1998, p. 8).

Today, most of the leading researchers in the field of reading (for example, G. Reid Lyon, P. David Pearson, and Keith Stanovich) agree that early reading instruction should not be viewed as an either-or choice between phonics and whole language but should be seen as a blend or mix between direct and indirect approaches, between systematic lessons and wide daily reading. In the end, we believe that such commonsense approaches, based on sound research, will prevail over the hurried push to legislate literacy in the schools.

In this book, you will find methods and strategies that reflect the separate skills, whole language, integrated and balanced approaches. Teachers need to develop a repertoire of teaching techniques based on the multiple approaches to teaching the language arts in order to adapt their teaching to the individual needs of their students. The primary focus of this textbook, however, is the integrated approach. The book advocates not only the integration of the six communication arts areas but also holds that these areas serve as the foundation blocks for learning about other content areas such as math, social studies, and science. For example, in the upper elementary, middle, and senior high grades, all students are required to listen to class lectures, take written notes, engage in oral discussions, read from their subject matter textbooks, and view videos and computer screens. The higher the grade level, the greater is the demand placed on the communication skills for mastering content matter. This idea is developed further in later chapters.

Who dares to teach must never cease to learn.

JOHN COTTON DANA

Summary

Good teaching involves constant and continuous decision making. This is at the heart of what it means to be a reflective teacher. To achieve this, a teacher must possess a philosophy of education in general, as it relates to children, teaching, and learning, and must apply this philosophy specifically to the teaching of language arts.

There are at least four main approaches to teaching the language arts. In the separate skills approach, the language arts curriculum is broken down into many separate subskills, which are taught in isolation from one another. This is more of a managerial system than an instructional approach, with the teacher as the prime manager and students assuming passive roles. The whole language approach is more student-centered because students are given a choice of which books to read and what types of genre to write in. The whole language approach integrates all six of the language arts areas. It focuses on the needs, experiences, and interests of the individual child; uses authentic texts to develop literacy awareness; and tries to make learning language a natural extension of using language. In the integrated approach, the six areas of the language arts are used as the students study broad themes that encompass other content areas such as math, science, social studies, and the arts. The balanced approach, a relatively new term, uses the whole language approach with a balance of teacher-taught skills that are part of the reading and writing activities.

activities *With Children*

These activities are designed to be used with students in an elementary classroom. They reflect the variety of approaches—separate skills, whole language, integrated, and balanced—discussed in this chapter. It is important that you get a chance to work with students in real classroom learning situations so you can determine for yourself what does and does not work. Such experience also gives you an opportunity to reflect on how children learn.

BRAINSTORMING

Teach a group of students the rudiments of brainstorming, which is often used in the whole language approach. Select a topic with which they are familiar, such as school or sports or favorite items. Then brainstorm in a small group, recording the children's ideas. Your list should form the basis for a later writing lesson.

GROUP EXPERIENCE

The following activity is one way to use the Language Experience Approach in the classroom. After returning from a field trip, encourage your students to talk about it. Record their statements on a large language-experience chart and have them read the chart. Then they may wish to illustrate some of the sentences or develop their own stories.

SPELLING HUNT

In the whole language approach, peers help each other with the mechanics of writing. As part of the students' ongoing writing activities, have them pair off and become peer editors for spelling. One of their jobs is to hunt for misspelled words, circle them, and help write them correctly.

THE JOURNAL

Share with your students the journal you are keeping; perhaps read them an entry or two. Then discuss with them why people keep journals. Suggest that they begin to keep a journal for the school year to record their experiences. Try to give students some time each day to write in their journal.

ACTION RESEARCH

Become involved in action research. Within a one- or two-week period, try the combination of reading/writing activities in Activity 1 or Activity 2 with the same group of students. Each activity includes two different approaches to teaching the language arts. While you do the research and after you complete the activities, reflect on the following: How did the students as a group and as individuals react to each activity? How comfortable did you feel doing each activity?

Activity 1

After choosing a story from the class reading list, find out from the classroom teacher which vocabulary words may be new to the students. Introduce the new words to the students before they read the story. Then have the students silently read the story and answer some literal, inferential, and evaluative questions at the end of the reading. Check the papers and reflect on how many literal questions were answered correctly and how in-depth the answers of the other questions were.

One week later, introduce a new story to the same class by having them predict from the title and pictures what will happen in the story. Read the story together, having the students follow along on their copy or with you holding the text so they can see the picture. As you read, have the students predict and discuss the story. Permit them to raise questions about the characters and action. At the end of the reading, give them some literal, inferential, and evaluative questions and again check for correct answers and the depth of understanding.

Activity 2

With a group of second graders, assign a writing topic (e.g., My Favorite Food or My Favorite TV Program). Give them time in class to write and edit their own work. Grade the papers by checking for content and mechanical errors.

One week later with the same group of students, read Kevin Henke's *Lily and the Purple Plastic Purse*. As you read it, discuss the story with the students. At the end of the reading, permit students to relate some of the "frustrating" times they have had at school or their favorite school snack or their favorite school activity. As you are discussing, make a word map of key words the students may want to use later in their writing. Instruct the students to write about any one of their school experiences. Give students time to write and confer with peers as they write. Instruct them to have peers edit their work by circling misspelled words or other mechanical errors. Collect the papers and compare this second set of papers to the first set, checking for content and mechanical errors.

Internet Videos technology

Each chapter in this book includes a section called Technology. Throughout this past century, technology, both in general and in schools, has changed and with it the educational paradigm. At one time, the teacher was the center of the classroom and the main source of information. However, since many schools today have computers connected to the Internet, cyberspace is becoming an important source of information.

Many teachers have learned how to use the Internet by surfing the Net. However, some of these same teachers may not feel comfortable attempting to teach their young students how to effectively use the Internet. In this section, we share some videos that are available to schools that will help elementary students learn how to use the Internet. Of course, viewing the videos will not in itself permit the students to become proficient on the Internet; they must be given time to use it.

> "Kids on the Internet" (from FUTUREKIDS Computer Learning Center)
> Michael Wiese Productions
> 11288 Ventura Blvd., Suite 821
> Studio City, CA 91604
> Telephone: 1-800-833-5738

Children on this commercial video explain how to get connected to the Internet, how to surf the Internet, and how to send e-mail.

Three free videos from NASA help bring science and the space program into the classroom:

1. "Global Quest: The Internet in the Classroom" promotes the use of the Internet in the classroom.
2. "Global Quest II: Teaching with the Internet" explains how to use the Internet in all subject areas.
3. "Connecting to the Future" explains how to include the entire community on the Internet.

To receive these free videos, write to:

Jennifer Sellers
NASA Ames Research Center
Mail Stop 322-18
Moffett Field, CA 94035-1000

Telephone: 501-615-9788
E-mail: sellers@quest.arc.nasa.gov

websites   *E-learning*

nces.ed.gov/pubsearch/

The National Center for Education Statistics releases the statistical reports for education in the United States. They include such topics as academic achievement and assessment, elementary education, parental involvement, students at risk, and technology and access to the Internet.

www.negp.gov/Reports/20nelson.htm

This is the home page for National Education Goals Benchmarks and Standards as Tools for Science Education Reform.

www.nctm.org/standards2000/

This is the home page for National Council of Teachers of Mathematics: Standards 2000.

www.gsh.org/NSTA_SSandC/nses_home.htm

This is the home page for the National Science Teacher Association Standards.

www.accesseric.org/

This is the Educational Resources Information Center home page, which provides resources on education for teachers.

discoveryschool.com/schrockguide/edref.htm

This is Kathy Schrock's link for education reform, research, and professional development.

putwest.boces.org/St/StUSGov.html#NEGP

This site has the national standards.

nces.ed.gov/pubsearch/pubsinfo.asp?pubid=98464XXXXX

This site from NCES gives long-term trends in student reading performance.

www.schooledu.swt.edu/Whole_Language.html
This site contains several articles about whole language and reading.

home.okstate.edu/homepages.nsf/toc/internet
This site is designed for teachers interested in utilizing the Internet in the classroom.

www.edbriefs.com
The US Ed.Net Briefs and Washington Ed.Net Briefs are free weekly newsletters sent to subscribers via e-mail. They summarize interesting education news stories.

www.edbriefs.com/resource.html
This site lists the newest and most useful online resources pertaining to education.

www.edcen.ehhs.cmich.edu/
This site is a resource center for educators to exchange views and experiences.

clearinghouse.com
This site reviews and supplies purchasing information for numerous software titles for K–12 language arts application.

Related Readings

Select one or more of the articles and books listed below. Find the work in the library or on the Internet, read it, and write a brief summary. Share your summary with other members of your class. Becoming a reader of research will help you become a more reflective practitioner in the language arts.

Goodman, K. (1996). *Ken Goodman on reading: A common-sense look at the nature of language and the science of reading.* Portsmouth, NH: Heinemann.

This book is an easy-to-understand text about the characteristics of language and how it works. It explains how proficient reading works and how written texts are organized. It also discusses the reading process and how to teach reading and writing.

Graves, D. H. (1994). *A fresh look at writing.* Portsmouth, NH: Heinemann.

This book helps a teacher understand the writing process and how to establish a classroom of writers. Graves gives many practical examples of how to organize the classroom and what to do in various situations. Especially helpful are the ways to conduct mini-lessons, organize portfolios, and work with different genres.

Guthrie, J. T., & Wigfield, A. (1997). *Reading engagement: Motivating readers through integrated instruction.* Newark, DE: International Reading Association.

This book is a collection of works by reading experts. Each chapter emphasizes a different way to motivate students to read by engaging them in meaningful activities. The goal is self-efficacy in literacy.

Smith, F. (1997). *Reading without nonsense* (3rd ed.). New York: Teacher's College Press.

This is an excellent text on the reading process. Smith looks at what happens when the eye meets the page and how the brain plays an intricate part in the reading process. He believes that using whole texts makes reading easy; separating it into parts makes reading very difficult. In Chapter 11, he gives some rules teachers should never follow and some rules all teachers should follow if they want to help students as they begin to read.

Trussell-Cullen, A. (1996). *Inside New Zealand classrooms.* Katonah, NY: Richard C. Owen Publishers.

This book explains how the New Zealand schools are organized. A child enters school on his or her fifth birthday. The levels of progression are different from those of the United States. Classroom organization is also discussed, based on a child-centered philosophy.

References

Adams, M. (1990). *Beginning to read: Thinking and learning about text.* Cambridge, MA: MIT Press.

Allington, R., & Walmsley, S. (eds.) (1995). *No quick fix: Rethinking literacy programs in America's elementary schools.* New York: Teacher's College Press.

Au, K. H., Mason, J. M., & Scheu, J. A. (1995). *Literacy instruction today.* New York: Harper-Collins.

Baumann, J., & Ivey, G. (1997). Delicate balances: Striving for curriculum and instructional equilibrium in second grade literature/strategy based classrooms. *Reading Research Quarterly, 32,* 244–273.

Benson, L. (1998). Reading sufficiency act set to benefit kids' education. *Tulsa World,* March 1998.

Bosma, B., & Guth, N. D. (1995). *Children's literature in an integrated curriculum.* New York: Teacher's College Press.

Bromley, K. (1998). *Language arts: Exploring connections.* Boston: Allyn & Bacon.

Bruner, J. (1962). *On knowing.* Cambridge, MA: Harvard University Press.

Bruner, J. S. (1966). *Toward a theory of instruction.* Cambridge, MA: Harvard University Press.

Caine, R., & Caine, G. (1994). *Making connections: Teaching and the human brain.* Palo Alto, CA: Addison-Wesley Publishers.

Cambourne, B. (1988). *The whole story: Literacy in the classroom.* Jefferson City, MO: Scholastic.

Cunningham, P. (1995). *Phonics they use: Words for reading and writing* (2nd ed.). New York: Harper-Collins College Publishers.

DeCarlo, J. (ed.) (1995). *Perspectives in whole language.* Boston: Allyn & Bacon.

Delpit, L. (1995). *Other people's children: Cultural conflict in the classroom.* New York: The New Press.

Edelsky, C., Altwerger, B., & Flores, B. (1991). *Whose language: What's the difference?* Portsmouth, NH: Heinemann.

Flannigan, A. (1998). Volunteers need to be reading mentors. *The Council Chronicle, 7*(5), 12.

Goodlad, J. (1997). *In praise of education.* New York: Teacher's College Press.

Goodman, K. (1986). *What's whole in whole language?* Portsmouth, NH: Heinemann.

Goodman, K. S. (1992). I didn't found whole language. *The Reading Teacher, 46*(3), 188–199.

Goodman, K. (1996). *Ken Goodman on reading: A common-sense look at the nature of language and the science of reading.* Portsmouth, NH: Heinemann.

Graves, D. H. (1994). *A fresh look at writing.* Portsmouth, NH: Heinemann.

Hessong, R., & Weeks, T. (1987). *Introduction to education.* New York: Macmillan.

International Reading Association (1998). Convention tackles the big issues. *Reading Today, 15*(6), 20.

International Reading Association (1998). IRA Board issues position statement on phonemic awareness. *Reading Today, 14*(6), 26.

Kellough, R., & Roberts, P. (1991). *A resource guide for elementary school teaching: Planning for competence* (2nd ed.). New York: Macmillan.

Kohl, H. (1967). *36 children.* New York: Signet Press.

Kozol, J. (1967). *Death at an early age.* Boston: Houghton Mifflin.

Krashen, S. (1993). *The power of reading: Insights from the research.* Englewood, CO: Libraries Unlimited.

Laminack, L. (1998). *Volunteers working with young readers.* Urbana, IL: NCTE.

Lapp, D., & Flood, J. (1994). Integrating the curriculum: The steps. *The Reading Teacher 47,* 416–419.

Lapp, D., Flood, J., & Farnan, N. (1996). *Content area reading and writing* (2nd ed.). Boston: Allyn & Bacon.

Lyon, G. R. (1998). Why reading is not a natural process. *Educational Leadership, 55*(6), 14–18.

McIntyre, E., & Pressley, M. (eds.) (1996). *Balanced instruction: Strategies and skills in whole language.* Norwood, MA: Christopher-Gordon.

Raphael, T., & Hiebert, E. (1996). *Creating an integrated approach to literacy instruction.* Ft. Worth, TX: Harcourt, Brace College Publishers.

Riesman, D. (1961). *The lonely crowd.* New Haven, CT: Yale University Press.

Rose, L., & Gallup, A. (1998). The 30th annual Phi Delta Kappa/Gallup poll on the public's attitudes toward public schools. *Phi Delta Kappan, 80*(1), 41–58.

Rupley, W., Logan, J., & Nichols, W. (1998/1999). Vocabulary instruction in a balanced reading program. *The Reading Teacher, 52*(4), 336–346.

Short, K., Harste, J., & Burke, C. (1996). *Creating classrooms for authors: The reading-writing connection* (2nd ed.). Portsmouth, NH: Heinemann.

Smith, F. (1997). *Reading without nonsense* (3rd ed.). New York: Teacher's College Press.

Spiegel, D. (1998). Silver bullets, babies and bathwater: Literature response groups in a balanced literacy program. *The Reading Teacher, 52*(2), 114–124.

Spring, J. (1988). *Conflicts of interest: The politics of American education.* New York: Longman.

Strickland, D. (1998). What's basic in beginning reading? *Educational Leadership, 55*(6), 6–10.

Taylor, D. (1998). *Beginning to read and the spin doctors of science.* Urbana, IL: NCTE Publications.

Tierney, R., & Pearson, P. D. (1983). Toward a composing model of reading. *Language Arts, 60*(5), 568–589.

Tompkins, G. (1997). *Literacy for the 21st century: A balanced approach.* Upper Saddle River, NJ: Merrill Publishing.

Tompkins, G. (1998). Reading comprehension. From a speech given at Oklahoma State University, Stillwater, OK, June 25, 1998.

Vacca, R. (1996). The reading wars: Who will be the winners? Who will be the losers? *Reading Today, 14*(2), 3.

Veatch, J. (1992). Whole language and its predecessors. *Journal of Reading Education, 18,* 69–77.

Watson, D. (1989). Defining and describing whole language. *The Elementary School Journal, 90,* 129–141.

Weaver, C. (1994). *Reading process and practice.* Portsmouth, NH: Heinemann.

Weaver, C. (1996). *Teaching grammar in context.* Portsmouth, NH: Heinemann.

Zeichner, K., & Liston, D. (1987). Teaching student teachers to reflect. *Harvard Educational Review, 57*(1), 23–48.

Language Arts Integration Beyond the Classroom

2

IN THIS CHAPTER

overview

In this chapter, you will learn about the importance of home and community influences on children's language arts abilities. The significance of parent–child interaction, the influence of the home, the role of play, and the influence of the community are all areas in which teachers need to have knowledge if they are to work with children as individuals. As you read this chapter, think about how you will acquire this type of personal knowledge about your students.

From a teacher's perspective, development of the communication arts occurs long before children ever enter school. Teachers know this, yet often their actions don't reflect an understanding of the significance of parental, home, and community influences on children's performance in school. As you read this chapter, think seriously about the outside forces that affect children and their language arts abilities. Also reflect on how you can alter your teaching strategies as you acquire more and more information about your students' personal backgrounds and home environments.

In the past, schools gave lip service to the importance of parental involvement in school affairs: an occasional parent–teacher meeting; a few open-school nights for parent conferences; occasional letters or phone calls home (usually commenting on a child's negative behaviors). In general, schools kept a posture of separateness from the home. Today this attitude is considered a mistake that must be corrected. This is especially true if schools are to ever really meet the needs of children from minority and low socioeconomic backgrounds, whose parents often view the school as an alien environment.

The following four statements should guide your thinking as you read and reflect on the content of this chapter:

1. Teachers need to know parents as people.
2. Parents need to know teachers as people.
3. Both parents and teachers need to experience each other's environments.
4. From this mutual knowledge come empathy, understanding, and support.

Parental Influences and the Language Arts

Parents are the first and primary language model an infant encounters. Young children, for example, often unconsciously imitate the speech and mannerisms of their parents. In fact, all aspects of oral language acquisition and development are influenced enormously by parents. Not only the actual language spoken (French, Spanish, English) but also the form of that language (standard or nonstandard) is the result of parental influence. The language skills of reading and writing are also tremendously affected by parental behaviors (Enz & Searfoss, 1996). The social interaction between parent and child and the attitudes generated about oral language and literacy form the basis of teachers' concerns for much closer cooperation between school and home (Heath, 1983).

Many researchers, beginning with Lev Vygotsky (1976), have stressed the importance of parent–child talk in the home for the child's later cognitive development and success in socialization with peers. Vygotsky's theory about the importance of social interaction for specific language growth and general cognitive development is one of the foundations upon which whole language philosophy is based. Vygotsky believed that two important things occur when parents and children interact verbally in social settings. First, children learn to express ideas in words. All of the stimuli and experiences of childhood need the outlet of language. The feedback children receive confirms their notions of themselves as persons. Second, words help children clarify their thinking. According to Vygotsky's theory, language and thought are closely linked. Children use language to solve real-world problems, assisted by adult learners. Eventually adults give less and less assistance as children begin to learn and discover on their own.

Scholars have also linked this early parent–child talk and cognitive growth to later achievement in school learning (Finn, 1998; Metsala, 1996; Zellman & Waterman, 1998). The nature and quality of the verbal exchanges between parent and child affect the child's later academic performance. This impact can be either negative or positive. Clearly, then, teachers need to have some understanding of what is occurring in the home to foster children's growth in school.

Similarly, once children enter school, it is crucial that their parents stay involved. This has not always been the case. A 1998 survey by *Weekly Reader* magazine found that 78 percent of sixth-graders responded that they wished their parents were more involved in their school education. Only 3 out of 10 students reported their parents attending any school program or making a classroom visit (*Reading Today*, 1997/1998).

PARENTS AND LANGUAGE

One of the first things teachers need to know is that language learning in the home occurs easily and naturally because it is part of the normal social interaction between parent and child. This confirms Vygotsky's belief in the importance of social interaction for learning. Research on the interaction of preschool children with parents and siblings at home (Snow, 1983) concluded that four main factors make this a most positive beginning for the child:

1. Language in the home is always situation-specific.
2. Home language focuses on meaning rather than form.
3. Parent–child language is based on mutual trust.
4. Both parent and child are affected by each other's speech.

Language is situation-specific. Observations of children interacting with their parents and siblings at home show that language is always used in a purposeful manner that is comprehensible to the child. This is because the language relates to objects, events, and actions in the immediate environment of the youngster. For example, a mother may tell her child, "Stop climbing on that sofa." Another time she might say, "You can have only one cookie before dinner." In *Piagetian* terms (see Chapter 4 for a discussion of Piaget), this environment is said to be highly concrete. Abstract language, if used at all, is always clarified by reference to the physical environment so familiar to the child. For example, a father may tell his child, "You have to be careful with electrical appliances. If we plug too many into one outlet . . . there, did you see that spark?" One result of this use of situation-specific language is that the child begins using language with a sense of its place in her or his real world.

Language focuses on meaning rather than form. In parent–child interaction, language is always used for some meaningful purpose. As long as meaning is conveyed, the language flow is not interrupted. Corrections of a child's pronunciation and grammar do occur in the home, but infrequently and generally only when a parent cannot comprehend what the child is saying. More often than not, however, parents respond to the content of their children's speech. If it is meaningful—that is, if the parent can understand the message—the dialogue continues.

Contrast this situation with one that can occur in school. Individual students sometimes find their speech interrupted by a teacher more concerned with the grammar the child is using than the message he or she is trying to convey. What does such behavior teach children about the value of their own ideas?

that there question is not important- that they are dumb!

Language is built on trust. Language is one of the primary ways in which parent and child are bonded to each other. The language they use is both purposeful and meaningful; therefore, it is carefully attended to by both parties. Language is also the primary way in which children share with their parents and receive important information, a process crucial for the harmonious functioning of the family. Without the proper information regarding

> **BEYOND THE CLASSROOM**
>
> With a small group of your peers, make a list of all the ways you can think of in which a teacher can acquire information about a student's home and community life. Select one of these ways and try it. For example, you might visit a playground or some other area in the community after school and observe children to learn about the other influences on the learning of the language arts in your classroom.

what is expected of each member of the household, misunderstandings arise; and when language breaks down between parent and child, physical action takes its place. Finally, children use language to express their deepest feelings and emotions. This actually begins with an infant's first cries and the attention these receive from the child's parents.

Collectively, the bonding nature of language between parent and child, the exchange of important information, and the expression of deep feelings among family members establish the sense of trust and security that characterizes the family.

Parents who know their children's teachers and help with the homework and teach their kids right from wrong—these parents make all the difference.

PRESIDENT BILL CLINTON

Parents and children are affected by language. Language is powerful in both its spoken and written forms. When a child first uses speech to control the actions of an adult, a sense of this power begins to emerge. For example, when the child says "Gimme juice" and then receives the desired object, a powerful message is conveyed. This is because language is the primary way in which people act upon others; the child first comes to understand this in the supportive, familiar setting of the home. And just as the child is able to affect the actions of adults, parents use language to affect children's behavior. The power works both ways and signifies for the child the enormous importance of language in social situations.

Language Development in the Home

Observational studies of parent–child interaction have identified three specific ways in which oral language is developed in the home (Snow, 1983). Classroom teachers can learn from such research and apply the findings to teaching.

First, parents spend a great deal of time answering children's questions: "How long before we get to Grandma's?" "Why can't I go to Janey's house?" "When will Daddy be home?" Even nonparents are familiar with this "Why?" stage of child language. Furthermore, when children talk, parents don't just give simple responses. Almost automatically, adults add on to or expand the child's speech, sometimes with grammatical elaboration, other times with additional information or facts. This is how dialogue between parent and child is sustained over long periods of time. Snow termed this the semantic contingency of language. **Semantic contingency** refers to adults focusing on the meaningful intent of a child's statements rather than on the form it takes (i.e., grammatical or limited vocabulary).

A second characteristic of parent–child language interaction is **scaffolding,** a term used by Jerome Bruner (1983) to describe how adults structure dialogues with children to ensure communicative success. That is, parents subtly lead children's talk back and forth in a way that maintains a sense of meaningful direction. The adult provides the scaffolding, or structure, upon which the child builds language competence. This is particularly important for young children, whose minds and speech tend to flit from topic to topic. Scaffolding is thus a gentle way of supporting young children's early attempts to sustain dialogue with their parents in significant ways.

Accountability is a third term associated with parent–child interaction; it too enhances language growth (Snow, 1983). Here are some examples: A mother insists that her child answer the question asked before going on to another topic; a child old enough to speak properly lapses into baby talk, and her mother tells her to speak correctly; a child begins a lengthy explanation of something and

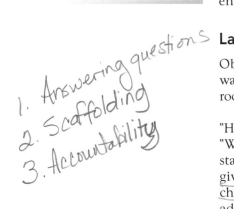

1. Answering questions
2. Scaffolding
3. Accountability

BEYOND THE CLASSROOM

Identify one student in an elementary classroom. Record a sample of the child's language in school using either a tape recorder or written notes. Then visit the child's home and make a similar language-sample recording either in the home or in the community. What similarities and what differences can you discover between the two samples?

switches in midsentence to another topic, so the parent brings him back to the original topic with a question or two. In each of these instances, the child is held accountable to the sole standard of meaningful communication.

sole standard of meaningful conversation

PARENTS AND READING

In school, reading is probably the most important subject in terms of parent, teacher, and child concerns, and the most time is devoted to this area. Frank Smith (1997) has argued that parent–child interaction involving print exerts enormous influence on the later development and interest of children in school-based reading activities. As with oral language, therefore, the more teachers of young children know about the home as a reading environment, the better they are able to help children in their classes (Koskinen et al., 1999; Metsala, 1996).

Metsala (1996) found that the characteristics that contribute to positive reading outcomes in a child are the following:

1. Access to children's books
2. Frequently being read to
3. Special areas for reading
4. Parents' positive attitude toward reading
5. Frequent visits to library
6. Conversations with caregiver about books

Metsala and associates (1995/1996) state that if caregivers cannot read, they should be encouraged to view the pictures with the child and ask higher-level questions such as "Why?" while they discuss the pictures.

In her study of children who learn to read at a very early age, Karen Thomas (1985) applied the concepts of semantic contingency, scaffolding, and accountability to understand the influence of parents and home environment on reading. In comparing the homes of children who learned to read early with those of children who did not, Thomas noted that the significant difference lay in the *type* of social interaction between adult and child. For example, parents, grandparents, and older siblings who answer a child's questions regarding the print or pictures in books and magazines provide examples of the concept of semantic contingency as applied to reading. Other examples of semantic contingency come from adults who read aloud often to young children, reread a child's favorite story over and over again, and tell stories from memory. In all cases it is the quality of the adult–child interaction involving print that makes the difference in the child's later reading interests and abilities.

When parents structure conversations with children around the books they have read, they become examples of the notion of scaffolding as applied to reading. The back-and-forth dialogue between child and adult, in which the adult offers support when needed by providing information or asking questions, focuses the child on the meaning of print in a most positive way. Thomas also found that children living in such an environment eventually begin to model the verbal behaviors of their parents; that is, they ask and answer questions about stories in a way that reveals an internalized sense of what a story is and what books are all about. In kindergarten and first grade, teachers often spend weeks trying to teach these same concepts under the heading of general readiness for reading. Imagine the head start that the children described by Thomas have when they first enter school!

Other researchers have echoed the importance of the earliest parent–child interaction as preparation for school (Enz & Searfoss, 1996). Glenda Bissex (1980), Marie Clay (1979), and Don Holdaway (1979), all leading authorities on early literacy acquisition, stressed the importance of having parents read aloud to their preschoolers. Children whose parents read aloud to them on a regular basis are better prepared to deal with the processes of reading and writing when they arrive in school. They can relate print to sound, have a grasp of the structure of language, understand the concept of story, and have been exposed to adults as reading models. In short, they are motivated to want to read and write upon entering the school building for the first time.

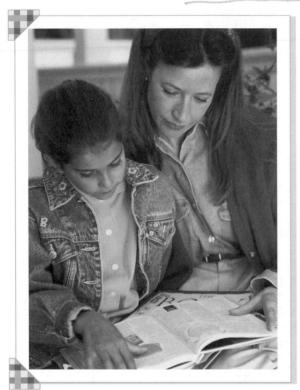

An interesting research project involving parents, children, and reading was conducted in Haringuey (a section of London), England, over a two-year period (Tizard, Schofield, & Hewison, 1982). Six- and 7-year-olds were encouraged to take books home and "read" them to their parents each week. The parents did not attempt to teach their children to read. In fact, some of the parents were illiterate or did not speak English. The experiment simply involved young children reading aloud each evening to their parents from books of their own choosing—and the results were extraordinary. The children who read aloud to their parents were more motivated to learn to read in school, enjoyed reading, and scored higher on reading tests than did matched groups who did not read aloud to their parents but had received special remedial help from their teachers in school. In addition, the parents of the first group of children enjoyed participating in the project. They honestly believed that their children would learn to read because they thought of themselves as readers.

The significance of parents reading to and with young children cannot be overemphasized. Federal research studies, such as the National Indicators of Well Being and the National Household Education Survey done in 1996, clearly showed a correlation between preschool children who were read to by their parents and later achievement in reading (*Reading Today*, 1997/1998). These studies found, for instance, that 57 percent of children in the United States ages three to five were read aloud to every day. Other interesting statistical findings from the federal research surveys included "critical aspects of children's lives," which affected later school achievement. For example, as a mother's education level rises, the more likely she is to read to her child on a daily basis: 77 percent of children were read to by mothers with a college degree compared to 37 percent of children whose mothers had not completed high school. A breakdown of the data regarding reading and the home shows the following:

- 64 percent of white children, 44 percent of black children, and 39 percent of Hispanic children were read to every day in 1996.
- 46 percent of children in families below the poverty line were read to every day compared to 61 percent above the poverty line.
- 61 percent of children living in two-parent homes were read to every day compared to 46 percent of children who live with one or no parent (*Reading Today*, 1997/1998).

Research studies such as these confirm something teachers probably intuitively know—namely, that learning to read is an active social process. Simply creating a pleasant environment with a variety of print samples is important, but more important is the positive social interaction that must take place between adult and child within that environment. The implication of these studies for the classroom teacher of language arts is clear: Reading instruction should take place in a warm social setting in which children feel comfortable and have easy access to adults as models, guides, and resources for the reading process.

PARENTS AND WRITING

In the past, not as much attention was paid to writing as to reading. Today educators do not separate the two literacy skills. For example, it has already been noted that children whose parents read to them and talk about books with them tend to also be more successful in writing activities in school. This is true because the underlying principles of language (the sound–symbol relationship, syntactic rules, focus on meaning) apply equally well to both reading and writing. The two are twin aspects of communication.

One educator who has stressed parental involvement in preschoolers' writing experiences is Linda Lamme of the University of Florida. Lamme bemoans the fact that writing in the home has been ignored and argues that the consequences are serious. In her book *Growing Up Writing* (1984), she stated:

> There are both educational and social reasons for the decline in writing ability. Writing at home is less common that it was in the days before the telephone. Today, fewer family members keep journals or diaries than in the days before television. (p. 15)

To correct this problem, Lamme makes specific suggestions for parents in order to encourage them to write in the home with their children. First, parents too often dismiss the scribblings of their youngsters as unimportant. Scribbling, however, is the foundation for writing. Therefore, parents should value their children's scribbles and talk about them. Lamme urges parents to tell their children what they like about their writing rather than asking them, "What is it?"

To further encourage home writing, Lamme suggests providing time, space, and materials for writing. Designating some time during the day for encouraging writing also implies monitoring the amount of time spent watching television. Space for writing can be created in a number of ways. Stand-up writing places can be created with newsprint or butcher-block paper taped to a refrigerator, door, or wall. With sturdy cardboard and chalkboard paint, parents can create their own chalkboards. Sit-down places can include a small desk, a dining table, or the floor. Finally, materials for writing can include any type of inexpensive paper, lined or unlined: newsprint, butcher-block paper, paper bags, old magazines—literally anything will work. To write or draw, children need a variety of pencils, pens, crayons, magic markers, paints, and brushes.

The key element, according to Lamme, is to get families to spend time writing together. For instance, in the Lamme household, notes are constantly exchanged between parents and children. There is also a memo board on which family members can write messages to one another as they come and go throughout the day. All family members keep scrapbooks and diaries. Older children write stories and learn how to do simple bookbinding. And all of this takes place in the natural social setting of the home, where the child feels most comfortable. Figure 2.1 gives some suggestions for writing activities at home.

When families do engage in various writing activities, the benefits for children are enormous. Youngsters begin to recognize print in the environment beyond their homes, such as the O in the stop sign on the corner. They recognize other letters on food packages in the grocery store, such as the D in

Figure 2.1	Scribbling on large paper
	Writing on slate boards
Suggestions for writing at home.	Water painting on newsprint
	Drawing with pencils and crayons
	Finger painting
	Creating collage cutouts and written words
	Labeling family photographs
	Writing or drawing notes to grandparents
	Exchanging family notes

Scribbling on large paper

Writing on slate boards

Water painting on newsprint

Drawing with pencils and crayons

Finger painting

Creating collage cutouts and written words

Labeling family photographs

Writing or drawing notes to grandparents

Exchanging family notes

Posting a home memo board

Using sticky notes

Writing holiday cards

Writing about vacations

Keeping scrapbooks

Writing in journals

Keeping diaries

Labeling trip photographs

Doritos. Eventually they begin to recognize whole words in print, such as *Wal-Mart* and *McDonald's.* This is called **environmental print.** Denny Taylor's studies (1983) of young children demonstrated that many youngsters are aware of print in their homes and communities and begin to associate words with meaning before they enter school. These environmental-print experiences and this print awareness are what teachers should build upon when young children enter school. However, this was not always the case.

In the past, according to Carolyn Burke (1985), the nature of the child–parent–teacher relationship was too often hierarchical. That is, it was based on the assumption that one person should dominate the others. The result was either little cooperation between home and school or an adversarial relationship that generated little respect among the parties involved. The newer view is one of collaboration, in which each person is equal and respected, problem solving involves consensus, and all responsibilities are shared. If teachers truly have the best interests of children at heart, they must work closely with parents. Teachers and parents must view each other as partners.

BEYOND THE CLASSROOM

Interview the parents of a young child. Determine what, if any, activities they engage in with their child that relate to reading and writing. Also, see if you can determine the attitudes of these parents toward reading and writing at home. Finally, ask them how they remember learning to read and write.

The Importance of Play

Child psychologists and educators agree that play serves an important role in human development. Child psychologist Jerome Bruner (1976, 1983), for example, has stressed that it is mainly through play that young children develop both early physical skills and cognitive abilities. Physical development is enhanced through the use of simple tools and toys and by engaging in activities such as running, jumping, and throwing. When children play pretend games with blocks, their cognitive abilities are likewise developed, for they are learning about the properties of blocks. Play thus becomes a chance to explore spatial relationships, speed, weight, and sequence, depending on how creatively the blocks are used.

STAGES OF PLAY

Other educators have stressed the importance of child play for social development (Sarafino & Armstrong, 1986). With very young children, there appears to be a progression in the social involvement of early play experiences. At first, the child plays alone; this is known as *solitary play*. In some instances, young children create imaginary playmates with whom they carry on lengthy conversations. Singer (1973) contended that this type of imaginative play is very stimulating for cognitive growth and the development of creativity in young children. Next the child engages in *parallel play*, in which two children play independently in the same room. Later comes *associative play*, in which children share toys but continue playing on their own. Eventually comes *cooperative play*, in which two or more children engage in a common task. Although every type of play is important, associative and cooperative play provide the best opportunities for children to learn through social interaction by using language in purposeful settings. Figure 2.2 outlines the stages of play.

TYPE	DESCRIPTION
Solitary play	Single child and a toy or imaginary playmate
Parallel play	Two or more children engaged in separate activities
Associative play	Two or more children sharing toys but without real interaction
Cooperative play	Joint task pursued; sharing; following rules

Figure 2.2

Stages of play.

Playing together in a social setting also leads to another important type of learning. Rule learning, so crucial to later success in school, is almost always developed first through the preschool child's engagement in play. When children play cooperatively, one of the first requirements is that certain rules or guidelines be established. This is done quickly and the rules followed literally. Violations of the rules of a game lead to quarrels but also to revisions of the rules. Such a revision can be both a powerful learning experience and an excellent vehicle for verbal and cognitive development (Sarafino & Armstrong, 1986).

In addition to rule learning, play among young children utilizes extensive *symbolic representation*, which is another excellent example of creativity developed through play. As the term implies, symbolic representation occurs when, for example, children agree to call a stick a horse, to be ridden in a particular game. Such representation also follows carefully designated rules, which children are quick to point out to one another when violated. The large amount of time children spend utilizing symbolic representation in these make-believe games forms the foundation for the development of abstract thinking and problem-solving skills, again so crucial for later success in school (Fein, 1981).

DRAMATIC PLAY

Perhaps the best example of play that brings together cooperative activity, social skills, rule learning, symbolic representation, and verbal abilities is **dramatic play.** Dramatic play is "central to human experience" (Cox, 1988). It is one of the first and primary ways in which all people—but particularly children—communicate with their peers about their environment, their culture, and themselves. Jean Piaget believed that it is the most natural way for young children to communicate, since it allows for sound, gesture, and movement to complement speech. This is evident when young children dress up to play house, doctor, or teacher. Rules have to be established regarding who will play each of the roles and what each will say and do. The complex negotiations involved lead to the development of sophisticated communication skills. In addition, such situations teach children a most important lesson, namely, that verbal negotiation is a viable alternative to physical violence for resolving conflicts (Sarafino & Armstrong, 1986).

Educators have long recognized the importance of dramatic play as a link to later school dramatic activities (McCaslin, 1996). Children who enter school with years of cooperative-play experiences are prepared to use those skills to learn about content areas such as science, social studies, and of course language arts. For example, teachers can engage their students in little skits to drive home important points. In the classroom, a child, table, and chair can become—for one exciting moment—George Washington crossing the Delaware River during the War of Independence. The physical involvement of dramatics can help many children to understand and remember difficult concepts and to learn new facts for later application. It's also fun.

Neuman (1995) stressed the importance of including literacy in the child's play. Within the family and with friends, children can play Post Office so they learn the importance of writing letters, notes, invitations, etc., and the importance of the envelope with a stamp (which can be a sticker). They can play Let's Eat and look at old ads for grocery specials, write grocery lists, look up recipes, and read labels on empty boxes.

Barnitz and Barnitz (1996) also encourage literacy play at birthday parties. Caregivers can pick a child's favorite book and all the invitations, home decorations, games, and treats can be based on the story. For example, if a first-grader loves Eric Carle's *The Very Hungry Caterpillar*, the invitations can be a plain piece of paper with the child's drawing of a caterpillar or a butterfly. At the party, the caregiver can read the story, have props so the children can act out the story, or play Pin the Food on the Caterpillar's Face.

LANGUAGE PLAY

There is another realm of play called **language play.** Children of all ages delight in playing with or using language in creative, often humorous ways. There are silly rhymes—actually poems taken from playground games—that all children can recite: "I scream, you scream, we all scream for ice cream." There are also challenging tongue twisters such as "Peter Piper picked a peck of pickled peppers." And who doesn't have a favorite "knock, knock" joke based on a play on words? Then there are the hundreds of children's jump-rope rhymes, such as "A my name is Alice and I come from Alabama; my husband's name is Allan and we sell apples." In a classic work entitled *A Rocket in My Pocket* (1948), Carl Withers collected hundreds of such rhymes and playground games. Don and Alleen Nilsen (1978) have even written a college text on linguistics that incorporates the notion of using word play, games, advertising jingles, and place names as a means of teaching about the creative nature of language.

In summary, children's play is much more than mere play: It is a learning experience; it is a social experience; it is a language experience. The discerning teacher capitalizes on all the students' social and language experiences in the classroom.

BEYOND THE CLASSROOM

Observe some preschool children on a playground or at a park. Better yet, volunteer to supervise some neighbor's or relative's children in a play situation. Record their language and actions. What kinds of play can you identify? What skills, verbal and nonverbal, are being learned and practiced? Reflect on how this observation experience could be applied to a learning experience for older students in a language arts classroom.

Home Differences and the Hidden Curriculum

Sociologists have long known that there are significant differences in the home life and child-rearing practices among different cultures, races, and ethnic groups. Research has shown that children's attitudes toward schooling and school achievement are affected by many social, cultural, and economic factors (Hayden & Fagan, 1995; Ogbu & Simons, 1994). Therefore, to be an effective teacher in the classroom for all students, you will need to have knowledge about the homes and communities of the children you teach.

The effect of home–community life on students' academic achievement, or the social dimension of schooling, is also known as the **hidden curriculum**—what students are taught by inference or learn indirectly (McInerney & McInerney, 1998). Similarly, Koppman in 1989 referred to the home as "the child's first teacher." Study the two examples below of the hidden curriculum of the home in terms of the potential influences on the child as student.

ONE HOME WHERE . . .

- Parents and children eat dinner together and discuss their day at work and school.
- Parents question children about their activities and expect answers.
- Children ask questions and receive answers.
- Parents and children watch TV and play computer games together.
- Parents read books, magazines, and newspapers regularly.
- Family members write letters and e-mail messages to friends and relatives.
- Bedtime stories are part of the nightly routine.

A SECOND HOME WHERE . . .

- Family members come and go, eating dinner at separate times.
- The TV is on all day, including meal times, discouraging conversation.
- Parents communicate with each other but believe children are to be seen and not heard.
- Few books or magazines are present in the home.
- The telephone, rather than writing, is the main means of communication.
- Adults often leave children unattended with the TV as babysitter.

In the first home, communication skills are valued and used. Listening, speaking, reading, and writing are natural parts of the child's environment. This is called a *language-rich environment* (Auten, 1985; Britton, 1986; Wells, 1986). Oral and written language are used in various functional and familiar ways. The sharing of experiences is valued. And while meaningful communication is the primary focus, the adult language models—spoken and written—also exemplify the accepted form of language, which is what schools stress (Graves, 1994). Finally, the presence and use of books, magazines, and newspapers in the home mirror the literate environment that these children encounter upon entering the classroom. Clearly, then, children from such homes have a big advantage when they begin school.

In the second home, there is neither opportunity nor encouragement for oral communication. This is not to say that the second home is nonverbal but rather that the language environment is substantively different from that which the child will encounter upon entering school. In such homes, the dominance of the television set (unsupervised by adults), the absence of a variety of print material, and the low value placed on reading and writing by adults present a negative but nonetheless powerful hidden curriculum.

What different messages do these two homes convey to children about the importance of schooling, language, and literacy? Which environment is more similar to that which children encounter when they enter school?

MINORITY STUDENTS AND ACADEMIC ACHIEVEMENT

Many researchers have long noted the achievement gap (as measured primarily by standardized tests) that exists between white middle-class students and minority students from low socioeconomic backgrounds (Applebee, Langer, & Mullis, 1986; Shade & New, 1993; Singham, 1998). A myriad of explanations have been offered to explain this gap, including culturally biased tests (Salvia & Ysseldyke, 1998); differences among child-rearing practices (White, 1988); the different ways various minorities are socialized toward school (Banks, 1993); inappropriate teaching practices (Delpit, 1995); language and cultural factors (Rumberger & Larson, 1998); the effects of poverty on achievement (Rumberger & Larson, 1998); and differences in perceptions of the relationship between academic success and effort (Singham, 1998).

John Ogbu, one of the leading authorities on minority children and academic achievement, has long argued that the issues are more complex than most educators realize (Ogbu, 1974; Ogbu & Simons, 1994). In the 1990s, Ogbu and his colleagues (Ogbu & Gibson, 1991; Ogbu & Simons, 1994) surveyed thousands of minority students, including African-Americans, Asian-Americans, Native Americans, and Mexican-Americans, with regard to their home lives and their attitudes toward school and academic achievement. Through this research, they sought to explain why certain minority groups do better than others in school. According to Ogbu, some minority children, particularly from low socioeconomic backgrounds, get negative signals regarding schooling in general and literacy in particular. Such children may not expect school to make a difference in their lives and consequently see little point in studying or striving to achieve (Ogbu & Simons, 1994; Rumberger & Larson, 1998; Singham, 1998; Yellin & Koetting, 1990).

Clearly it is important for teachers to recognize the diversity that exists within their classrooms. Cultural, racial, ethnic, and economic differences must be viewed positively for their richness. The research data argue for a new approach to teaching literacy, one that builds on the experiences and interests of each child while at the same time provides direct skills instruction when necessary. By balancing and selecting the most appropriate practices to meet the needs of all students, teachers can help to narrow the academic achievement gap (Benning & Nakashima, 1998; Singham, 1998).

Language Arts and the Community

Parents and the home environment thus exert powerful influences on children's language development and literacy attainment. But there are still other influences beyond the home that must be taken into account in order to truly make school a place where each child's individual potential is developed. One of these influences is the community in which the child lives.

Frank Smith (1975), a psycholinguist and reading authority, has argued that children learn about the world through three primary modes: experience, observation, and language. In the home, language is primarily developed through social interaction between parent and child. What the child sees and does in the home is crucial for his or her development as a learner. In the broader environment of the community and neighborhood, experience, observation, and language are enormously expanded and influenced by various forces, many of which cannot be controlled by the parent. These forces, too, exert a powerful influence on the child as learner.

ORAL LANGUAGE DEVELOPMENT AND THE COMMUNITY

Next to the parent and home, the neighborhood community is the most important influence in a child's early life as it relates to later school achievement (Taylor, 1983). The clearest example of this influence is in oral language usage. Although most people in the United States speak English, there are different forms, or dialects, of English. Courtney Cazden (1981) found that there are many myths associated with dialects. For example, some people believe that a dialect is a substandard language. Not so: Everyone speaks a dialect. In the United States, people refer to the Southern drawl, the Midwest twang, and the New England clipped tongue, to name just three of the larger dialect regions. Furthermore, within each of these large dialect regions, there are hundreds of subdialects, such as the Bostonian ("pahk the cah") and Brooklynese ("toity-toird street"). A **dialect,** therefore, is simply a language variation influenced by communal and geographic factors. No one dialect is superior or inferior to another.

The dialects spoken by other children and adults in the community partially shape every child's language long before he or she enters the classroom. And this shaping affects more than mere language usage: It also serves, in Jerome Bruner's (1983) view, as "a linguistic model of reality" that the child carries to school. This means that the child's language, influenced by the community, has major implications for how the child performs in school. To better understand this notion of a linguistic model of reality, it is important to consider a bit of language history, beginning with the Whorfian hypothesis.

> ### BEYOND THE CLASSROOM
>
> Visit a neighborhood different from your own. Shop in some of the stores. Observe children in the parks or on the playgrounds. Record your observations in your journal. As a teacher, what aspects of this community life could you build on to develop in your students a more positive attitude toward school and literacy attainment? Share your findings with other members of the class.

Whorfian Hypothesis

Benjamin Whorf was an anthropologist and linguist who worked in the early part of the twentieth century. Some of his observational research was carried out among the Hopi and other Native American tribes in the southwestern United States. Whorf noted that in comparison to English, the Hopi language has restricted concepts of time and space. He also noted that the Hopi have a view of the world quite different from that of other peoples. Whorf (1956) suggested that the structure of the Hopi language influenced their worldview and cultural values. That is, the language of the community influences the individual's cognitive processing of experiences. Although linguists and educators have argued about the degree of influence that language exerts over the way people view the world, most agree that Whorf was correct. Each person's language is not neutral; rather it shapes, to some extent, the way that person experiences and sees the world, which in turn affects the way that person learns.

Dialect and Academic Achievement

For many years educators, linguists, sociologists, and politicians have argued about the relationship between dialect and academic achievement. This debate has centered around the high failure rate of youngsters from minority backgrounds who do not speak standard English.

The significance of Benjamin Whorf's theory for educators becomes clear when looking at language differences (dialects) within the same culture. In the 1960s, Basil Bernstein (1971) collected language samples from working-class and middle-class children in England. He noted that the linguistic differences between these two groups were specific enough to constitute two different language dialects, or codes: the restricted code spoken by working-class children and the elaborated code spoken by middle-class children. Bernstein concluded that children from the lower classes speak a form of the language substantially different from that spoken in school. These differences between children's language and school language might partially explain the poor academic performance of children of lower socioeconomic status (Ogbu & Simons, 1994).

In the United States, Bernstein's writings and their implications for schools refocused attention on the issue of nonstandard dialect and academic achievement during the late 1960s and early 1970s. Since most poor

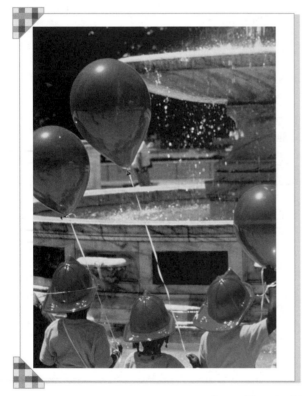

minority children in the schools who were experiencing serious academic difficulties were also nonstandard-dialect speakers, some educators jumped to the conclusion that nonstandard dialect must be the culprit. The reasoning went something like this: Compared to standard English (the language of schools), nonstandard English appears to be deficient in its ability to communicate thoughts and ideas. Thus the linguistically different child who speaks nonstandard English in the classroom is at a great disadvantage. The implied solution is to change the child's language to meet the standards of the school. This belief is referred to in the literature as the **Deficit Theory of Language** (Blank & Solomon, 1972).

In the United States, perhaps the strongest critic of the Deficit Theory is William Labov, the linguist from the University of Pennsylvania who in 1985 first showed that nonstandard speech, though different, is nevertheless a viable speech form. Labov's central argument is that dialect speech is logical and systematic, contains its own grammar, and is fully capable of meaningful communication. The problem is that most white, middle-class teachers don't understand it and therefore label it as inferior, deficient, or something requiring remediation.

Joan Tough (1985) is another well-known linguist and educator who is sharply critical of the Deficit Theory and the negative approaches taken toward speakers of nonstandard English in the classroom. She has argued that language is not a mere set of skills to be memorized through extensive drills. In real language situations, there are no prescribed answers. Instead language must be used, experienced, and recognized as a primary means of expression. Above all, language must be accepted as long as it communicates meaning effectively, regardless of its style or form.

Salinger (1988) has suggested the following five guidelines for working with linguistically different students:

1. In the early grades, children should be encouraged to acquire standard English in addition to their own dialect.

2. The process of acquiring a second "language code" is difficult and requires practice over long periods of time.

3. Modeling standard English construction, rather than overcorrecting, is the preferred teaching strategy.

4. Oral reading miscues caused by dialect differences should not be corrected as long as the deviations do not change the meaning of the text.

5. Dialect speakers should be encouraged to write extensively and to work out their own sense of grammar. In time, with more exposure to standard English forms in books, their writing will approximate standard grammar.

The Ripkin Learning Center in inner-city Baltimore, Maryland, is a different kind of classroom. Adolescents and young adults come and go throughout the day. Children drop by for after-school help with their homework. One wall lists the names of students with perfect attendance. There is a lending library of books, free for the taking. Homemade posters show learners who have achieved their personal goals. One poster shows a photograph of a young man holding a driver's license and saying "What a feeling!"

The Ripkin Learning Center is named after Cal Ripkin, Jr., star infielder of the Baltimore Orioles baseball team. Ripkin and his wife, Kelly, donated $250,000 to Baltimore's citywide literacy program known as Baltimore Reads. This organization coordinates a multitude of community literacy efforts. The present mayor of Baltimore, Kurt L. Schmoke, is a major supporter of Baltimore Reads, as are the *Baltimore Sun* newspaper, prominent Baltimore businessmen, and other sports figures.

What began as an adult literacy program has spread to include all segments of the Baltimore community. Parents were encouraged to attend the various after-school programs and work with their children. Soon other programs were developed to address the parents' own literacy needs. In a subtle way, the program's focus shifted toward family literacy to include children, teens, and adults. Today, Baltimore Reads is a model for the rest of the nation of what can be done when all the forces of a city come together to focus on improving the literacy of its entire population.

> ## BEYOND THE CLASSROOM
>
> Interview some minority college students about their early schooling experiences. Do they recall any conflicts between school and community? How did they deal with these conflicts? What have been their experiences at college? Also, try to read some articles in the *Journal of Negro Education* or a popular magazine such as *Ebony* to learn more about a culture that you will encounter when you teach and that may be foreign to you. The classic text in this area is J. L. Dillard's *Black English* (1973, New York: Random House).

THE OTHER LANGUAGE ARTS IN THE COMMUNITY

In addition to oral language, the community environment also has an enormous influence on the other language arts areas of listening, reading, writing, viewing, and visual representing. For example, listening skills that are taught in the classroom should be based initially on some understanding of the listening skills of the community. The child of the city grows up amid the sounds of automobile horns blasting, fire engine bells clanging, rock music blaring from the upstairs apartment, the pneumatic drill jarring the pavement and deafening the ears. The child of the country hears church bells in the distance, the lonesome whistles of freight trains passing through in the night, the mooing of cows, the cock-a-doodle-do of the rooster at sunrise, the wind rustling through tree branches on a stormy night. Such sounds and many others can be brought to the classroom in the form of tape recordings or commercial records. By building lessons on that which is already familiar to children, teachers not only forge a link between school and community but also have a greater chance of success with these lessons.

The child's neighborhood community also serves as an introduction to environmental print. Words from the Tony's Pizza sign or the Stop sign at the corner of Main Street and Third Avenue are easily recognized by the young child after repeated visits to these areas. Similarly, McDonald's hamburger bags, Wheaties billboards, Mobil gas stations, and Ford neon signs bombard students every day of their lives with words, words, words. These words are learned at sight rather than being decoded phonetically; therefore educators call them *sight words.* Since so many sight words are learned naturally and easily by children merely from living in their community, teachers need to build on this knowledge when it comes to creating reading and writing activities. Letting children write on topics of their own choice and employing words and experiences children are already familiar with just make good common sense.

If the community is such an important influence on children's language arts abilities, it also makes sense for teachers to view their community as both a laboratory and a resource center with which to teach about the language arts. Right now, in your own community, there are dozens of excellent field trip possibilities that can add to the language arts curriculum. There are also many other adults in your community with talents and skills related to what you are teaching about in your classroom. There are businesses that can provide materials (in most cases, for free) that you can use in class projects. But first you must make the effort to acquaint yourself with these many resources and then determine how best to use them to support your academic program in the language arts.

One of the characteristics of the most effective teachers is their ability to make classroom lessons relevant to the lives of students. When children recognize their own community as a source of information, as a sort of living chalkboard, education takes on a new and more powerful meaning. The Classroom Vignette that follows shows how one teacher decided to make better use of her community as a teaching resource.

Vignette *in the classroom*

Mrs. Boltman, a fifth-grade teacher in a medium-size rural community, is dissatisfied with the way some of her lessons are going. Her students seem less than enthused with the language arts textbook. Furthermore, they complain that they can't see the point in what they are being asked to study. Many of the students say they already know what they want to be once they finish school (which for many will be when they turn 16 and can legally drop out).

In search of a new approach to teaching the language arts, Mrs. Boltman turns to the yellow pages of the telephone book. She begins by listing the names and addresses of businesses and organizations that might relate to her language arts curriculum for the year. Then she contacts these resources. After doing field research in her community and interviewing some key people, she decides what to do. With the permission of her principal, she arranges for a series of mini–field trips, interviews, guest speakers, and other educational experiences in her community. These will be ongoing trips, conducted throughout the school year, and related to the course content taught in class. Figure 2.3 shows a partial sample of her list.

YELLOW PAGES LISTINGS	LANGUAGE ARTS IDEAS
Antique Repairing and Restoring	Examine old objects, relate to history, stimulate creative writing from unusual object.
Aquarium and Pet Shop	Choose a pet, name it, describe it.
Cessna Pilot Center	Interview pilots, read about planes from the past, create instructional manual.
Farm Animal Auction Center	Visit and later act out an auction scene.
Holiday Travel Agency	Use dozens of colorful brochures to stimulate imaginations about faraway places, acting, reading, writing.
Lie Detection and Security Service	Initiate mystery reading, writing, play acting.
South Community Hospital	Interview doctors and nurses, follow-up reading, writing (compare with soap operas about hospitals), discussion.

Figure 2.3

Community resources for the language arts.

The Community and Functional Literacy

The acquisition of literacy (the ability to read and write) has long been considered solely within the domain of the schools. But certain aspects of literacy associated with home and community go beyond what takes place in most classrooms. Learning to read the label on a medicine bottle and using a repair manual to fix a bicycle are examples of this type of literacy, often called *functional literacy* (Luke, 1988). Functional literacy links reading and writing skills to performance in the world beyond the classroom. Therefore, it is also referred to as *real-world literacy* or *survival literacy*.

Today, the teaching of functional literacy in the schools is controversial. First, there still is not complete agreement on a definition of functional literacy (Ehringhaus, 1990). For years the term was strictly associated with adults learning vocational reading and writing skills required of specific jobs. The federal government created the program Right to Read, which hired tutors for illiterate adults and focused on job-related reading and writing skills.

BEYOND THE CLASSROOM

Make an analysis of your own community similar to the one in the Classroom Vignette. List potential resources in the yellow pages that relate to the language arts; then brainstorm ideas for each resource. Next, share your list with a classroom teacher. What is the teacher's reaction? Does he or she see any impediments to implementing these ideas? If so, how can you work around these?

The U.S. Bureau of the Census has still another definition of functional literacy: It considers anyone over the age of 14 who has completed the sixth grade to be literate. Obviously this definition is unacceptable to educators (Ehringhaus, 1990).

Only recently have educators begun to recognize functional literacy skills as a part of the secondary curriculum. But since some students—particularly the minority poor—drop out before high school graduation, it is increasingly important that elementary teachers also concern themselves with providing students with the survival skills in reading and writing that they need in today's society. Thus functional literacy can be defined as follows: **Functional** literacy includes the specific reading and writing skills necessary to participate successfully in the world of work, to be intelligent consumers of products, and to serve as effective citizens.

FUNCTIONAL LITERACY AND THE SCHOOLS

Education takes place in the combination of the home, the community, the school, and the receptive mind.

ARRY EDWARDS

David Bloome (1985) has contended that in order for the schools to play a real role in providing functional reading and writing skills, educators must learn from the homes of students. In the home and the community, reading and writing skills are viewed as relevant only in terms of what they can do for the individual; this attitude is particularly true for students of lower socioeconomic status. Yet in classrooms, reading and writing are often still taught as skills in the abstract. Thus there exists a built-in conflict of values between what the home teaches and what the school preaches. To change this situation, teachers need to begin to view literacy as a social process. Learning to read and write should be not only exciting but also relevant to the lives of students.

Teachers in elementary school, particularly language arts teachers, have a great opportunity to relate school activities to the world of children beyond the classroom. For example, reading skills taught in classrooms should also be applied to helping students read neighborhood street signs, labels on boxes and cans, restaurant menus, bicycle repair manuals, the telephone directory, newspaper articles and advertisements, recipes for cooking, and job applications. Similarly, writing skills in class should be reinforced with functional lessons on writing personal and business letters, filling out checks, completing simple forms (such as applying for a library card), and completing more complex forms (such as job and credit applications).

Linking the school with the home and the community is practiced by some of the most well-known classroom teachers in the United States. In the small community of Boothbay Harbor, Maine, Nancie Atwell has her middle school students share about their lives and go out into the community for reading and writing ideas. Her language arts curriculum is based on the real world of her students: the community of Boothbay Harbor and the state of Maine (Atwell, 1998). In Rabun's Gap, Georgia, Eliot Wigginton teaches traditional English grammar and composition skills to his high school students by having them venture out into the community to tape-record interviews of people, particularly craftspeople and folk artists, as a way of researching the history of their mountain homeland. The students then transcribe and edit the tapes, write and revise articles, and finally publish their work each semester as a magazine. The results of their efforts eventually find their way into a book. Known as the Foxfire project, Wigginton's approach to teaching about literacy through community interviews has been adopted by other teachers across the country (Wigginton, 1972, 1985).

BEYOND THE CLASSROOM

Get together with a fellow student and take a walk through your community. Note the aspects of community life (signs, billboards, window displays, and so on) that could be utilized to teach about functional literacy. Make a list of all the potential functional literacy materials you find. Discuss your findings in class and relate them to the language arts. Then visit some classrooms in your community to discover which teachers are incorporating this type of information into their lessons.

Teachers Working with Parents

This chapter concludes with a brief discussion of what you can and should do as teachers to forge closer links with parents, students' homes, and the community. This is not meant as an extra activity in addition to all your other school responsibilities; rather, your involvement with parents, homes, and communities should form the core of how you approach your students and the classroom learning environment.

Begin by recognizing that before a child enters your classroom, he or she has had at least six years of language learning that should not be ignored. The school is only one learning environment; equally important are the environments of home and community and, particularly, the influence of parents. This appears to be obvious, yet it is the obvious that is so often overlooked. For example, Wells and Wells (1984) concluded that many teachers ignore the richness of the home as a language learning environment and teach as though the school were the first language learning experience for the child.

Next, learn as much as possible about the homes and communities of the children you teach. Start at the beginning of the school year. One way to begin is by surveying your students about some basic information about themselves and their home lives. You can do this by creating your own Home Background Inventory for each child to complete in class. Figure 2.4 is an example of such a survey instrument used by one teacher. You might wish to add other incomplete sentences to gather more information.

WHO ARE YOU?

Figure 2.4

Home background inventory.

My name is _____ .

I live at _____ .

I have _____ brothers and _____ sisters.

Their names are _____ .

My father works at _____ .

My mother works at _____ .

After school, I go _____ .

For supper, my favorite food is _____ .

In the evening, I like to _____ .

The best thing about my neighborhood is _____ .

When I grow up, I want to be _____ .

An even more powerful method of gathering information about students' homes and communities involves spending some time after school and on weekends just wandering around the neighborhood, discovering your students as people beyond the classroom. You will also want to make visits to the homes of your students. Remember, one goal of the integrated approach is to have parents and teachers get to know each other as people. A home visit is an ideal way to break down some of the artificial barriers that professional educators have inadvertently placed between themselves and parents. If it sounds strange to expect already overburdened teachers to make regular home visitations, consider the following.

In Texas, parents of low-income, disadvantaged neighborhoods have joined together with teachers to improve the schools. For example, Zavala Elementary School in Austin and Ysleta Elementary School in El Paso are part of the Alliance Model, funded by the Texas Education Agency, which brings teachers, parents, and community leaders together to address the most serious school problems. The results: academic achievement, as demonstrated by standardized test scores in reading and math, rose dramatically (Hatch, 1998).

Some states—for example, Florida—already require Chapter One (remedial skills) teachers to make and report on home visits for every child in their classrooms. In Rochester, New York, public school teachers are responsible for making personal home contact, particularly for those students identified as being "at risk" of failing or dropping out of school. This is part of each teacher's contract (Urbanski, 1988).

As a whole, the teaching profession has not done a good job of joining hands with parents. This is difficult to admit but nevertheless true, despite the existence for years of parent–teacher organizations. Patricia Koppman, past president of the International Reading Association (IRA), one of the largest professional organizations for elementary school teachers, has long argued that membership in the IRA should be opened to parents. How, Koppman wonders, can teachers "place emphasis on children without emphasizing the parent as well" (1989, p. 3)? To strengthen the links between school and home, the IRA has produced several booklets specifically designed for parents:

- *You Can Help Your Young Child with Writing* by Marcia Baghban
- *How Can I Prepare My Young Child for Reading?* by Paula C. Grinnell
- *You Can Help Your Child Connect Reading to Writing* by Nicholas P. Criscuolo

Professional educators need to know about these and other materials. Teachers can recommend them to parents who ask, "How can I help my child to do better in school?" Many teachers have copies of these materials available to hand out to parents. Generally such publications are distributed free or at a minimal cost by educational organizations such as the IRA or the National Council of Teachers of English (NCTE).

Another point that teachers must remember in working with parents is to respect the linguistic and cultural differences of the family. Parents must be made to feel welcome, particularly minority parents who may have had negative school experiences during their own education and may harbor resentment toward the schools. This means accepting the parents' (and children's) language.

In the classroom, teachers also need to value linguistic diversity among children. This does not mean teaching only what the children want to learn or accepting gross deviations from school standards; it does mean being flexible and open enough to learn from others. In certain cases, it means acquiring new knowledge about nonstandard dialects, foreign languages (in the case of bilingual students), and special ethnic holidays and customs. Teachers should encourage students to talk about themselves, their families, their special customs and holidays. Such knowledge enhances classroom lessons, increases empathy toward parent and child alike, and is the best motivator of otherwise unmotivated children.

Encouraging parents to become involved in all aspects of the school is another must if school and home are to work closely together. Zellman and Waterman (1998) reported that parental "school involvement was associated with better test scores in reading and teacher ratings of fewer learning problems" (p. 374). The involvement was divided into two categories: positive school-site involvement (e.g., attending scheduled events, serving on school board or advisory committees, attending PTA meetings and volunteering for a regular activity) and homework involvement. Because school involvement plays a positive role in students' achievement, it is important for teachers to communicate often to parents to encourage them to become involved with school-site activities and their child's homework.

There are many ways in which teachers can communicate with parents on a regular basis. One of the simplest is a class newsletter written by the teacher and sent home to parents on a weekly or monthly basis. Judy Collins, a sixth-grade teacher in Tryon, Oklahoma, has written such a newsletter for years. In it, she includes information about current class projects and upcoming class and school events that are of interest to parents. Occasionally she adds suggestions for working with children at home to complement class projects. Figure 2.5 is an example of another teacher's newsletter.

The key to communicating with parents—be it by letter, by phone, or in person—is to be both positive and specific in making suggestions (see Figure 2.6). It is always easy to find things to criticize about young children, but this will not help your case with parents. On the other hand, if you can first identify some good things about a student, there is a better chance that parents will listen to some of the problem areas (with which they are probably already familiar).

September 20, 2000

Figure 2.5

Teacher newsletter to parents.

Dear Parent,

This past week has been a good one at Foothills Elementary School. We have had a number of exciting events. On Tuesday, a special assembly program featured a demonstration of CPR techniques by qualified paramedics from our local hospital. You might wish to ask your son or daughter about it.

Next week we will begin our special unit on Mexico. The children are gathering pictures and articles about Mexico from newspapers and magazines. We are also writing to the Mexico Chamber of Commerce as well as to travel agencies requesting maps and tourist information. We are excitedly awaiting their response. Each child is also working on a small research project about life in Mexico. Your daughter or son will be bringing home library books to do research.

As a culmination of our unit on Mexico, we will have a "Mexican Fiesta Day" in class. If you would like to help with this project, please contact me. Also, if you have any questions about your child's work, please call me at school or at home.

Sincerely,

Mrs. Lupino

Figure 2.6

Ways teachers can include parents in the child's school experience.

1. Prepare a monthly classroom newsletter and include the following:
   - "Dear Teacher" section where parents can write in questions of concern (not about individual children, but about general situations)
   - "Teacher's Expertise" section where the teacher shares information about developmental stages of writing/reading and information about the reason for some classroom practices
   - Report on special classroom projects where involvement from home is needed
   - One or two collaborative classroom writings (poems, stories, etc.)
   - Special invitation for parents to come on a specific day for a special lesson, such as science experiment or other demonstration
   - Appropriate books for the month (Halloween, Thanksgiving, Christmas traditions, Valentine's Day, etc.)
   - Hints on how to help the child at home
2. Conduct parent workshops on specific areas.

Source: Adapted from Enz (1995), "Strategies for Promoting Parental Support for Emergent Literacy Programs." *The Reading Teacher, 49(2),* 168–170. Copyright © 1995 by the International Reading Association. All rights reserved.

Next, remember that parents want to know how to assist their children. However, simply recommending that parents help children at home is too vague, and telling them to assist with homework assignments smacks of teachers passing the buck. This is where your ability to make concrete, simple, but practical suggestions comes in. Following are six basic yet effective suggestions you can make to parents:

1. Read aloud each night for 5 or 10 minutes from a storybook that your child has selected. Afterward, discuss the book with your child. What does he like about the story? What does he think will happen next? Keep it simple, short, and fun.
2. Tell your child you want to hear her read to you. Then listen to your child read without correcting or criticizing her reading. You can help if she asks for it, but primarily be a listener. Afterward, praise her reading efforts.
3. Do a paired reading activity with your child. Again, let the child choose the reading material. Next, both parent and child, seated together comfortably, read aloud simultaneously. If the child wishes to read aloud alone after a while, you can easily shift to becoming a listener. Again, corrections should only be made if requested or if the meaning of the story is altered by the error.
4. Ask to read what your child has written for school (stories, essays, compositions, letters). Comment on and praise the ideas and content of the written work. Discuss the writing with your child as you would with any author; your child is indeed an author and should feel proud of that accomplishment.
5. Encourage your child to write notes or letters to friends, relatives, or business companies that sell children's products. Make letter writing a monthly family affair.
6. Once a week, help your child to organize his or her school notebook. Remove old and messy pages. Perhaps recopy important papers that need to be saved. This is also a good opportunity to inquire about what transpired in school on a particular day.

Note that each of these recommendations to parents avoids discussion of specific language arts skills. This is intentional. The purpose of these suggestions is to help parents work with their children in a positive manner. Teachers can encourage parents to read and write with their children and to discuss school as part of the daily routine. Teachers can also help parents establish (or reinforce) some important learning habits or routines for their children. For example, finding a time and place for homework to be done without too many distractions is important for success as the child moves into the upper grades, in which each subject matter teacher may give some homework assignment.

Teachers have lives after school, too. Build on this in your teaching. To form links between the classroom and students' home and community environments, teachers need to be willing to share about their own lives. Tell children about your home and your after-school interests, hobbies, and activities. Perhaps bring objects from your home (in the tradition of "show and tell") that will give your students a better picture of who you are as a person. This should in turn encourage your students to want to share more openly about their lives and their homes and communities.

Volunteerism or Service Learning in the Schools

"Service learning is a way to help our young people grow individually and as members of society. It is about helping our young people grow up to understand the connection between living and learning, what it means to be an adult, what it means to live as a citizen in a free and 'civil' society, and what it means to live as a truly compassionate and caring human being" (Carol Kinsley, executive director of the Community Service Center, Springfield, MA)

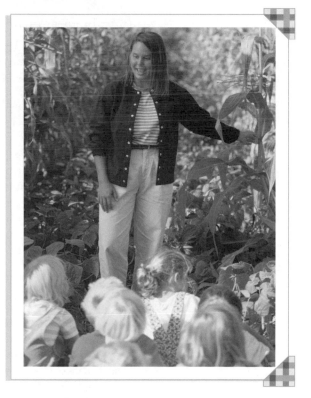

More and more communities are involving adults and school-age children in the concept of service learning. Service learning benefits the students who provide the service as well as the people in the community who are directly affected by the service. Although service learning has been focused at the high school level, it is also prevalent in many middle and elementary schools. In Springfield, Massachusetts, for example, teachers utilize service experiences at every grade level and in every curriculum area (Kinsley, 1997).

The service learning concept has been around for many years on an informal basis under the heading of volunteerism. For example, individual classroom teachers or school clubs ask their students to volunteer for a particular service project, such as cleaning up around the school grounds, reading books to younger children, or visiting with the elderly in nursing homes. But such projects were dependent on individual teachers and small groups of motivated students. Today the term service learning is conceived more broadly, encompasses more students, and has taken on a more formal structure.

In 1993, President Bill Clinton, the Congress, and various community organizations nationwide helped create the Corporation for National Service. This is a public–private partnership that helps administer major national service initiatives such as AmeriCorps, VISTA, Learn and Serve, and the National Civilian Community Corps (Kinsley, 1997).

Service learning involves students in community activities that complement their classroom studies and are part of the curriculum; being an integral part of the school curriculum is one of the things that makes service learning different from mere volunteerism. Service learning programs engage young people in community activities that show how skills acquired in school can be used to solve real-life problems. At the same time, these program activities help students understand their ability to address the quality of life and address real needs in their communities (Alt, 1997).

For example, students might visit a homeless shelter on a weekly basis and read and write with the children there. Visiting with these children, they establish relationships with people different from themselves and gain an understanding of the conditions that lead to homelessness. A good program design or framework can help students act out of a desire to meet a genuine human need. Conscious planning and purposeful thinking can maximize the potential outcomes of the service learning experience.

Service learning planning includes the following elements (Berkas & Maland, 1993). *Preparation* consists of the learning activities that take place prior to the service learning itself. Students must first understand what is expected of them as well as what they can expect from the service learning project. Preparation components include the following:

- Identify and analyze the problem to be addressed
- Select and plan the project
- Conduct training and orientation sessions with the students

The next phase of service learning is the *action* phase. This is the actual service itself, and it too must meet certain criteria. Primarily it must:

- Be meaningful
- Have academic integrity
- Have adequate supervision
- Provide for student ownership
- Be developmentally appropriate

Reflection is the third phase of service learning. Reflection enables students to think critically about their service learning experience. When students reflect on their experiences, they thing about them, read about them, write about them, discuss them with others, and learn from their experiences. Reflection time is structured time, built into the overall plan of service learning and is a real learning experience for children. Reflections can be enhanced through the following:

A teacher is the child's third parent.

HYMAN MAXWELL BERSTON

- Discussion
- Reading
- Writing
- Projects

The final phase is the *celebration* component of service learning. Celebration is the way in which students are recognized for their service contributions. It also provides closure to a sometimes lengthy (a full semester) ongoing service activity. Celebration is one way adults let children know that their service efforts are valued. The following are examples:

- School assemblies
- Certificates
- Special media coverage

- Pizza parties
- Joint party celebration with the service recipients (e.g., cookies and punch with the preschoolers)

If you would like to learn more about service learning in the schools and communities, contact the University of Minnesota at 1-800-808-SERVE or e-mail them at www.NICEL.COLED.UNMN.edu.

Summary

Teachers need to acquaint themselves with the educational environment beyond the classroom if they are to help their students more effectively. This means meeting parents, learning about home environments, and visiting the community. It also means that teachers should incorporate into their classroom instruction the new knowledge they glean from interacting with parents and experiencing firsthand students' homes and communities.

Social interaction is an important learning force for children. Parents who interact with their children in the areas of oral language, reading, and writing are preparing their children for the world of school. The nature of social interaction, however, varies considerably in both the home and the community, particularly according to socioeconomic level. Children from low-income backgrounds do not have the same types of home and community experiences to draw upon as middle-class children. This fact must be taken into consideration by the teacher, and certain adjustments must be made.

A close working relationship between school and community, between teachers and parents, is also crucial. Home and community must be understood by teachers as learning environments and utilized in the classroom. The first step in this process involves gaining knowledge of these environments; the second demands reassessment of the working relationship between school and home—or the lack of such a relationship. The powerful potential of schools working closely with parents and the community has yet to be tapped.

activities *With Children*

These activities are designed to be used with students in an elementary classroom. They reflect the variety of approaches discussed in this chapter. It is important that you get a chance to work with children in real classroom learning situations so you can determine for yourself what does and does now work with children. It also gives you an opportunity to reflect on how children learn.

COMMUNITY INTERVIEW

Teach the children about interviewing, and then role-play an interview in class. Have each student select a person in the community whom he or she knows well and interview that person about the job she or he does. They should try to find out specifically what types of reading and writing skills the job requires.

COMMUNITY LITERACY HUNT

Have each student in your classroom spend a half hour on a main local street examining signs, store windows, advertisements, and the like. Ask them to make a list of the different types of reading materials people encounter daily on this street.

DAILY SCHEDULE

Most young people do not know how to schedule their time. Ask each student to keep an account of his or her after-school activities on an hourly basis. They should do this for one week. Then have them make charts to determine the best time for them to schedule their daily homework.

SURVEY YOUR HOME

Ask the students to survey their homes. What kinds of books, magazines, and newspapers can they find? Have them make a list of their findings and share it with the rest of the class.

BRAINSTORMING

Teach a group of children the rudiments of brainstorming. Select a topic with which they are familiar, such as school or sports or favorite goods. Then brainstorm in a small group, recording the children's ideas. Your list should form the basis for a later writing lesson.

Protective Programs technology

When connecting to the Internet, one concern of parents and educators is the accessibility of information that is objectionable for elementary students. However, teachers and parents do not need to keep students off the Internet entirely just because it includes sites that are unsuitable for children. Parents and educators can purchase and install on their computers software programs designed to protect youngsters from offensive material. Following is a list of sample programs with the mailing address and Web address so one can download the program and receive additional information on how the particular program works:

"Cyber Patrol"
Microsystems Software, Inc.
600 Worcester Road
Framingham, MA 01701
Telephone: 1-800-489-2001
info@microsys.com
www.cyberpatrol.com/

"CYBERSitter"
Solid Oak InterGo and KinderGuard
Software, Inc.
PO Box 6826
Santa Barbara, CA 93160
Telephone: 1-800-388-2761
sales@solidoak.com
www.solidoak.com/cyrsitter.htm

"InterGO"
TeacherSoft, Inc.
903 East 18th Street, Suite 230
Plano, TX 75074
Telephone: 214-424-7882
TeacherSoft@teachersoft.com
www.teachersoft.com/

Another safety net to use on the Internet is an Internet filter, which monitors all Internet activity. The programs permit the adult to block certain hosts. "Version Zero" is a free program on the Internet but is somewhat limited. It is available from ftp.coast.net. "Version One," a more extensive, commercial package, is available from:

Turner Investigation, Research and Communications
Box 151-3456 Dunbar Street
Vancouver, BC V65 2C2 Canada
Telephone: 604-733-5095
bturner@direct.ca
www.xmission.com/~seer/jdksoftware/netfilt.html

websites   *E-learning*

www.pbs.org/rogers
This is Mister Roger's website, which includes articles for parents and a booklist of stories that correlate with the TV program's themes.

www.parentsplace.com/readroom/childnew/index.html
This site is a newsletter that has resources for parents to work with the children.

www.kn.pacbell.com/wired/bluewebn/index.html
This site promotes Internet projects and is a terrific general resource that is sorted by topic.

ole.net/ole
This site is a browsing place for lesson ideas. It is sorted by grade level and subjects.

www.gsh.org.wce
This is a publishing center and forum about using technology successfully. It is geared for teachers and parents.

www.creativegood.com/help/
This is a site for parents about making the Internet easy to use.

www.parentsjournal.org/
This site provides parents with information about today's problems in the schools.

www.macconnect.com/~jrpotter/train.spml
This site has early literacy activities for parents that they can use to foster child development in the early years.

npin.org/
This site gives parents suggestions on helping their child.

www.ed.gov/pubs/parents
This site has government documents for parents.

www.magmacon.com/~dsleeth/sitetoc.htm
This site teaches children how to use computers.

scholastic.com/inschool/
This is the site for the *Instructor* magazine.

indiana.edu/~eric_rec/fl/pcto/
This site contains stories for parents to read to their children. They are arranged by grade level.

www.puzzlemaker.com/
This site permits you to create mazes, word searches, crosswords, math squares, etc., for any lesson.

www.pta.org/
This site gives the national standards for parent and family involvement in schools. It gives tips on helping with homework.

www.parenttime.com
This site is sponsored by Time Warner and provides ways parents can help their children in school.

www.publicagenda.org/index.html
Public Agenda Online is a nonpartisan organization devoted to public opinion, such as what adults think about kids these days, and public policy reports.

familyeducation.com/community.asp
This site provides teachers and parents with the opportunity to vote in opinion polls, such as "Should tax money be used to fund public preschool programs?"

www.americaspromise.org.
This site gives information on how to become one of Colin Powell's Schools of Promise.

Related Readings

Barnitz, J., & Barnitz, C. (1996). Celebrating with language and literature at birthday parties and other childhood events. *The Reading Teacher, 50(2),* 110–117.

    This article gives in-depth details on how to plan a birthday party on a child's favorite book and gives a list of books to use for other holidays.

Baumann, J., & Thomas, D. (1997). "If you can pass Momma's tests, then she knows you're getting your education": A case study of support for literacy learning within an African American family. *The Reading Teacher, 51(2),* 108–120.

    A teacher and parent give perspective about the bias some teachers may have about African American children. Just because children are a minority or from a low socioeconomic class does not mean that the parents are illiterate or do not care about their child's education.

Educational Leadership (1998), 55(8).

    This entire issue, titled Engaging Parents and the Community in Schools, has articles on involving parents in their child's education. The articles give practical programs that have been tested in a number of schools across the United States.

Enz, B., & Searfoss, L. (1996). Expanding our views of family literacy. *The Reading Teacher, 49(7),* 576–579.

    This article contains an extensive list of home literacy ideas that teachers can share with parents. The list includes literacy ideas for everyday activities and special play activities.

Fox, B., & Wright, M. (1997). Connecting school and home literacy experiences through cross-age reading. *The Reading Teacher, 50(5),* 396–403.

    This article describes Storymates, a cross-age reading program that connects school and home literacy experiences for 9- to 11-year-olds through storybook reading to younger children.

Lazar, A., & Weisberg, R. (1996). Inviting parents' perspective: Building home–school partnerships to support children who struggle with literacy. *The Reading Teacher, 50(3)*, 228–237.

> This study explains how children's reading improved when the parents were asked to share their knowledge and insight about their children's reading habits.

Neuman, S. (1995). Reading together: A community-supported parent tutoring program. *The Reading Teacher, 49(2)*, 120–129.

> This article describes the parent volunteer program, which provides opportunities for adults to read with children. The article lists specific books and activities to use for everyday happenings such as going to the doctor or dentist.

References

Alt, M. N. (1997, October). How effective an educational tool is student community service? *NASSP Bulletin: Service Learning: Leaving Footprints on the Planet*, 8–16.

Applebee, A., Langer, J., & Mullis, J. (1986). *The writing report card national assessment of educational progress* Report No. 15-W-02. Princeton, NJ: Educational Testing Services.

Atwell, N. (1998). *In the middle* (2nd ed.). Upper Montclair, NJ: Boynton/Cook Publishers.

Auten, A. (1985). Building a language-rich environment. *Language Arts, 62*, 95–100.

Banks, J. (1993). Multicultural education: Characteristics and goals. In J. Banks & C. Banks (eds.), *Multicultural education: Issues and perspectives.* Boston: Allyn & Bacon.

Barnitz, J., & Barnitz, C. (1996). Celebrating with language and literature at birthday parties and other childhood events. *The Reading Teacher, 50(2)*, 110–117.

Baumann, J., & Thomas, D. (1997). "If you can pass Momma's tests, then she knows you're getting your education": A case study of support for literacy learning within an African American family. *The Reading Teacher, 51(2)*, 108–120.

Benning, V., & Nakashima, E. (1998, September 16). Schools strive to raise scores of minorities. *The Washington Post*, p. 7.

Berkas, T., & Maland, J. (1993). Excellence in action: The community service learning program. St. Paul: University of Minnesota, Center for Experiential Education and Service Learning, Department of Vocational and Technical Education.

Bernstein, B. (1971). *Class, codes and control.* London: Routledge and Kegan Paul.

Bissex, G. L. (1980). *GNYS at work: A child learns to write and read.* Cambridge, MA: Harvard University Press.

Bloome, D. (1985). Reading as a social process. *Language Arts, 62(2)*, 134–142.

Britton, J. (1986). *Language and learning.* Hammondsworth, England: Penguin.

Bruner, J. (1983). *Child's talk: Learning to use language.* New York: W. W. Norton.

Bruner, J., Jolly, A., & Sylva, K. (1976). *Play: Its role in development and evolution.* London: Penguin Books.

Burke, C. (1985). Parenting, teaching, and learning as a collaborative venture. *Language Arts, 62(8)*, 836–843.

Cazden, C. (1981). *Language in early childhood education.* Washington, DC: National Association for the Education of Young Children.

Clay, M. (1979). *Reading: The patterning of complex behavior* (2nd ed.). Auckland, New Zealand: Heinemann.

Cox, C. (1988). *Teaching language arts.* Boston: Allyn & Bacon.

Delpit, L. (1995). *Other people's children: Cultural conflict in the classroom.* New York: The New Press.

Ehringhaus, C. (1990). Functional literacy assessment: Issues of interpretation. *Adult Education Quarterly, 40(4)*, 187–196.

Enz, B. (1995). Strategies for promoting parental support for emergent literacy programs. *The Reading Teacher, 49(2)*, 168–170.

Enz, B., & Searfoss, L. (1996). Expanding our views of family literacy. *The Reading Teacher, 49(7)*, 576–579.

Fein, G. (1981). Pretend play in childhood: An integrative review. *Child Development, 52(4)*, 1059–1118.

Finn, J. (1998). Parental engagement that makes a difference. *Educational Leadership, 55(8)*, 20–24.

Graves, D. (1994). *A fresh look at writing.* Exeter, NH: Heinemann Educational Books.

Hatch, T. (1998). How community action contributes to achievement. *Educational Leadership, 55(8)*, 16–19.

Hayden, R., & Fagan, W. (1995). Literacy learning outside the classroom. *The Reading Teacher, 49(3)*, 260–262.

Heath, S. (1983). *Ways with words: Language, life and work in communities and classrooms.* New York: Cambridge University Press.

Holdaway, D. (1979). *The foundations of literacy.* New York: Scholastic.

International Reading Association. Parents and reading: Reading to young children: Statistics to consider. (1997/1998, December/January). *Reading Today, 15(3)*, 25.

Johnston, K. (1989). Parents and reading: A U. K. perspective. *The Reading Teacher*, 72(6), 332–357.

Kinsley, C. W. (1997, October). Service learning: A process to connect learning and living. *NASSP Bulletin: Service Learning: Leaving Footprints on the Planet*, pp. 1–7.

Koppman, P. (1989). Recognizing the importance of parents. *Reading Today*, 6(4), 3.

Koskinen, P., Blum, I., Bisson, S., Phillips, S., Creamer, T., & Baker, T. (1999). Shared reading books and audiotapes: Supporting diverse students in school and at home. *The Reading Teacher*, 52(5), 430–444.

Labov, W. (1985). The logic of non-standard English. In P. P. Giglioli (ed.), *Language and social context*. New York: Viking Press.

Lamme, L. (1984). *Growing up writing: Sharing with your children the joys of good writing*. Washington, DC: Acropolis Books.

Luke, A. (1988). Functional literacy in the classroom. *Australian Journal of Reading*, 11(1), 4–10.

McCaslin, N. (1996). *Creative dramatics in the classroom* (6th ed.). New York: Longman.

McInerney, D., & McInerney, V. (1998). The goals of schooling in culturally diverse classrooms. *The Clearinghouse*, 71(6), 363–366.

Metsala, J. (1996). Early literacy at home: Children's experiences and parents' perspectives. *The Reading Teacher*, 50(1), 70–75.

Metsala, J., Brody, G., Stoneman, Z., & McCoy, J. (1995/1996). How caregivers support literacy development of Head Start graduates in a rural setting. *The Reading Teacher*, 49(4), 340–342.

Neuman, S. (1995). Reading together: A community-supported parent tutoring program. *The Reading Teacher*, 49(2), 120–129.

News of the profession: The city that reads. (1997/1998, December/January). *Reading Today*, 15(3), 27.

Nilsen, D., & Nilsen, A. (1978). *Language play: An introduction to linguistics*. Rowley, MA: Newbury House Publishers.

Ogbu, J. (1974). *The next generation*. New York: Academic Press.

Ogbu, J. (1978). *Minority education and caste*. New York: Academic Press.

Ogbu, J. (1985). Research currents: Cultural-ecological influences on minority school learning. *Language Arts*, 62(8), 860–869.

Ogbu., J., & Gibson, M. (eds.) (1991). *Minority status and schooling*. New York: Garland Press.

Ogbu, J., & Simons, H. (1994). *Cultural models of literacy: A comparative study*. Berkeley, CA: National Center for the Study of Writing and Literacy.

Rumberger, R., & Larson, K. (1998). Toward explaining differences in educational achievement among Mexican-American language-minority students. *Sociology of Education*, 71(1), 68–92.

Salinger, T. (1988). *Language arts and literacy for young children*. Columbus, OH: Merrill.

Salvia, J., & Ysseldyke, J. (1998). *Assessment* (7th ed.). Boston: Houghton Mifflin.

Sarafino, E., & Armstrong, J. (1986). *Child and adolescent development* (2nd ed.). St. Paul, MN: West Publishing Co.

Shade, B., & New, C. (1993). Cultural influences on learning: Teaching implications. In J. Banks & C. Banks (eds.), *Multicultural education: Issues and perspectives*. Boston: Allyn & Bacon.

Singer, J. L. (1973). *The child's world of make-believe: Experimental studies of imaginative play*. New York: Academic Press.

Singham, M. (1998). The canary in the mine: The achievement gap between Black and White students. *Phi Delta Kappan*, 80(1), 8–17.

Smith, F. (1975). *Comprehension and learning*. New York: Holt.

Smith, F. (1997). *Reading without nonsense* (3rd ed.). New York: Teacher's College Press.

Snow, C. E. (1983). Literacy and language: Relationships during the preschool years. *Harvard Educational Review*, 53(2), 165–189.

Taylor, D. (1983). *Family literacy*. Portsmouth, NH: Heinemann Books.

Thomas, K. (1985). Early reading as a social interaction process. *Language Arts*, 62(5), 469–475.

Tizard, J., Schofield, W., & Hewison, J. (1982). Collaboration between teachers and parents in assessing children's reading. *British Journal of Educational Psychology*, 52(1), 1–15.

Tough, J. (1985). *Listening to children talk*. London: SCDC Publications.

Urbanski, A. (1988). The Rochester contract: A status report. *Educational Leadership*, 46(3), 48–52.

Vygotsky, L. (1976). *Thought and language*. Cambridge, MA: MIT Press.

Wells, G. (1986). *The meaning makers: Children learning language and using language to learn*. Portsmouth, NH: Heinemann.

Wells, G., & Wells, J. (1984). Learning to talk and talking to learn. *Theory into Practice*, 23(3), 190–197.

White, B. (1988). *Educating the infant and toddler*. Lexington, MA: Lexington Books.

Whorf, B. (1956). *Language, thought, and reality*. Cambridge, MA: MIT Press.

Wigginton, E. (1972). *The Foxfire Book*. New York: Anchor Press.

Wigginton, E. (1985). *Sometimes a shining moment: The Foxfire experience*. Garden City, NY: Anchor Press.

Withers, C. (1948). *A rocket in my pocket*. New York: Scholastic Book Services.

Yellin, D., & Koetting, R. (1990). Literacy instruction and children raised in poverty. *Journal of Curriculum Theorizing*, 8(4), 101–114.

Zellman, G., & Waterman, J. (1998). Education-Parent participation. *Journal of Educational Research*, 91(6), 370–381.

Planning and Delivering Language Arts Instruction

3

IN THIS CHAPTER

This chapter deals with the importance and nature of planning for and delivering the language arts content from an integrated perspective. First, you will read about some of the general principles of learning that guide teachers. As you read, think about the factors that affect motivation in the classroom, particularly for at-risk students, those children who often encounter difficulty in the traditional classroom setting.

Next, you will learn to apply the general principles of teaching and learning to specific situations in the language arts. You will find suggestions and activities to help you learn more about your students, to become a "kidwatcher," to use an interest inventory, and to incorporate time for real reading and writing during the school day.

Teachers use many different types of plans. As you read this chapter, you will become familiar with yearly, unit, weekly, daily, and mini-lesson plans. The mini-lesson plan is described in detail, as it fits best with the integrated philosophy.

The chapter concludes with a discussion of four learning domains, children's varied learning styles, and various teaching strategies. As you read the last section, reflect on your own strengths as a learner and your preferred teaching style.

Planning for Learning

Regardless of the perspective they bring to teaching (separate skills, whole language, integrated, or balanced), all teachers plan carefully for instruction. Planning requires an understanding of the general principles of learning. It also forces the teacher to consider how individual or daily lessons fit within larger learning units of a week or longer. Planning can include grading students' papers and planning next week's skill sheets, as well as evaluating students' journals and reflecting on the class and individual student needs.

GENERAL PRINCIPLES FOR TEACHING AND LEARNING

In theory, education is based on sound philosophical concepts. Teachers approach their job with certain beliefs or principles regarding children, learning, and teaching. Marzano (1992) described these under five dimensions of learning, which focus on the learner.

Dimension 1—Positive attitude and perceptions about learning. A student's attitude and perceptions of a situation play a powerful role in learning. To a teacher, the classroom environment may appear positive, engaging, and safe; however, if a student perceives it differently, learning may not occur. For example, Jane, a third-grader, just came in from the playground where she had had a dreadful fight or disagreement with Molly without the teacher's knowledge. When Molly gives her creative dramatic presentation about Betsy Ross, Jane may not accept or understand any of it because her attitude toward Molly is very negative. In fact, Jane may even develop a negative attitude about Betsy Ross.

Dimension 2—Thinking involved in acquiring and integrating knowledge. Learning does not come from teachers passing out information to be memorized; instead, each learner needs to construct his or her own meaning from the situation. For example, when a first-grade teacher in rural North Dakota starts talking about a city's skyscraper without showing pictures, Peter (who never has been anywhere but to his small town) may imagine an object that resembles an ice cream dipper. However, as the teacher compares a skyscraper to 36 grocery stores stacked on top of each other, Peter begins to have a better image of a skyscraper.

Dimension 3—Thinking involved in extending and refining knowledge. Learners are always refining what they know as they encounter new experiences. The most effective learning occurs when one attempts to challenge what one already knows or attempts to see the old concept in a new way. One example of this type of learning is to ask students at the end of the year to classify 15 authors they studied into three or four groups and to justify their reasons for classifying them as they did. In order to do this, the students must not only recall the facts they learned about each author, the types of literature the authors wrote, and the style of each author but must also begin to compare and contrast the authors in order to classify them. It is likely that the students will make lists that are totally different from each other's.

Dimension 4—Thinking involved in using knowledge meaningfully.
Knowledge is remembered when a student can apply the information to his or her personal life; skills are developed and refined when they are used. For example, many young students enjoy learning about snakes. The knowledge becomes important when the class goes on a nature hike in the woods in eastern Oklahoma where some poisonous snakes live. The knowledge becomes very meaningful if one of the students is bitten by a snake and the class needs to apply their knowledge in order to treat the bite.

Dimension 5—Productive habits of mind. True learning occurs when the learner is sensitive to feedback; desires precision; keeps seeking solutions even when they are not apparent; uses creative, divergent thinking to find solutions; and reflects instead of making snap judgments. Students cannot possibly learn everything there is to know; therefore, it is important for students to acquire thinking skills. One way an elementary teacher can help students acquire thinking skills is to give the class a whodunit story at the beginning of the week and play Yes–No Questions for five minutes at the beginning of the afternoon classes. One great collection of short mystery cases is *The Case of the Red Herring*, published by Creative Thinking Press and Software (P.O. Box 448, Pacific Grove, CA 93950).

Be Guided by Child Development Theory

Effective teaching should reflect an understanding of child development theory. Just as children's physical growth takes place in stages and steps, learning is also developmental (DeHaven, 1983). This means that although children occasionally have intellectual spurts or make intuitive leaps of understanding, the process is in general slow; it unfolds gradually and is enhanced by a positive environment.

Another way of understanding this principle is to take the long view. Your job is not to fill empty heads with facts for the present but—more important—to excite children about learning for the many years to come, in school and out. Furthermore, your effectiveness is measured not by the number of chapters in the textbook you cover or the number of worksheets your students complete but by the attitude toward learning and work habits children acquire. Remember, schooling is a long-term process and learning is forever. You may not get through every lesson or accomplish all of your daily goals. In teaching, you must expect the unexpected; that's why there is always tomorrow. So relax and enjoy the experience of participating in young children's growth.

Establish a Positive Learning Environment Early

To do your best and to be most effective, you must feel comfortable teaching in your classroom. Similarly, the children must feel comfortable learning. These conditions result in a positive learning environment. The *emotional tone* of a room is measured by the quality of human interactions (Wong & Wong, 1991). You have observed classrooms that were cold, rigid, and formal; you have also seen rooms in which warmth and a natural friendliness prevailed. The unspoken messages that these contrasting learning environments convey are what John Goodlad (1984) called the *implicit curriculum*. Your goal, as you begin to think and plan, is to create the best possible learning environment for yourself and your students.

Of course, creating a positive learning environment is easier said than done. Obviously every teacher wants to create a pleasant classroom atmosphere in which students work and learn, in which everyone succeeds. One way to begin is by personalizing your teaching. This means being yourself and being open with your students. Share your experiences, your feelings, your beliefs about teaching and learning. Tell children about the kinds of books you like to read and the things you write about in your journal. Your openness is a first step toward establishing a classroom climate based on trust and personal interaction, the hallmarks of humanism and the integrated approach (Wong & Wong, 1991). In turn, this encourages your students to be more open and honest with you and with their classmates. Together you can build the elusive positive learning environment.

Maintain High Academic Standards for All Students

For years, research into learning achievement has consistently shown that when teachers set high expectations for their students, both personally and academically, they get better results (Wong & Wong, 1991). This means that early in the school year you must let your students know what you expect from them: proper headings on all their papers, neatness, pride in their work, and so on. Encourage them to push themselves, to set their own high standards, and to be proud of their accomplishments. The effort they expend in meeting reasonable challenges is what ultimately leads to personal growth.

Therefore, one of your tasks as an effective teacher is to carefully structure activities that stretch children to their utmost without frustrating them by repeated failures. It also involves being very conscious of the different needs and abilities of your students and constantly adjusting your teaching to meet those needs. Wang, Reynolds, and Walberg (1995) have referred to this as "serving students at the edges." Some students learn at a slower rate than their peers, use language differently from the teacher, or have personal problems that affect their school performance. Although such children may require more time or assistance to complete various learning activities, you must not lessen your expectations of them. All students can and do want to learn.

Ultimately your goal as a teacher is to step back and let go. Removing your overt support from the learning process allows children to grow, to take responsibility for their own learning. Eventually every child must discover that he or she is indeed competent, that he or she can succeed and experience that "I can do it" feeling. Helping children to assume more and more responsibility for their own learning is, however, dependent on a teacher's careful planning.

Planning Should Be Cooperative

Teachers who believe in children and understand the implications of humanistic philosophy for learning want students to participate in planning their own learning experiences. Allowing children to participate is one way to motivate students to put forth maximum effort in their work.

For example, selecting topics for units of study can be done cooperatively. The teacher and students would first identify some units of study within the language arts. A class might choose to focus on the history of language, to study a favorite author in depth, to explore poetry, or to read and study a single novel. After a number of topics have been chosen, the class would either vote to select one unit or divide into small groups to do a number of the projects independently.

Teachers and students together can also identify themes for reading and writing activities. Reading themes might include mysteries, informational books, animal books, and science fiction. Each child would read a few books within the selected theme. Related to the reading theme would also be appropriate writing activities that the teacher and students could agree upon in advance. For example, students might write radio commercials to publicize their books, write letters to the authors, or create a scene for a play based on one of their books.

Choosing and creating learning centers is another important part of cooperative planning. Learning centers are a popular teaching approach, particularly in the primary grades. In deciding what learning centers to create, a teacher should consider not only the curriculum demands but also the interests of the students. Asking children about the kinds of centers they would like to participate in, and getting their help in creating the centers, is a great learning experience as well as a motivator. Children treat the centers better knowing they had a stake in their creation.

Success is also built by encouraging independent projects. Not all children enjoy working in groups all the time. Sometimes children should work alone on projects of their own choosing. Often during a lesson, some issue, topic, project, or activity strikes a positive chord with a particular student. This is the chance for the teacher to encourage that child to pursue an independent project. If class time, appropriate materials, and some supportive guidance are provided, even young children can work on independent projects that interest them. For example, one fifth-grade student became fascinated with the origins of certain English words and wanted to explore this area further by doing library research. Although this was not part of the fifth-grade language arts curriculum, the teacher was flexible enough to permit this learning experience for a single student.

Alternative evaluation methods and student self-checking form another important aspect of cooperative learning. Most classrooms are dominated by tests: end-of-the-week spelling tests, grammar quizzes, unit tests over the chapters in the basal reader, and so on. When teachers and children talk to each other honestly about evaluation, they discover that there are alternatives to the testing syndrome. And often the alternatives are a lot more interesting than filling in blanks on a paper. One teacher tests using a buddy system, in which each child finds a friend to review material taught during the week. Another teacher has a file that children can use to check their work at their own convenience. A third teacher employs oral panel discussions over material taught instead of written exams. And more and more teachers are using folders of children's actual work over the course of a semester or a year as the ultimate measure of what a child has accomplished (Farr & Tone, 1998).

> ### IN & BEYOND THE CLASSROOM
>
> Observe a classroom with these five general principles of education in mind. What evidence can you find to support or refute them? Record your observations in the form of a list that you can share with your fellow students.

Planning Should Reflect the Principles of Motivation

Learning, especially self-directed learning, is closely tied to the concept of motivation. According to Lauren Resnick, past president of the American Educational Research Association, the real key to a child's success in school lies not just in the teacher's ability to teach the subject content effectively. More important, it is inextricably linked to how children feel about themselves as learners (Marzano, 1992). This includes such things as the child's self-concept, self-esteem, self-worth, and perceived competence as a learner. All of these factors are included under the heading of motivation; because of the importance of this topic, there is a separate section devoted to it later in this chapter. Suffice it to say for now that how well *you* are able to motivate children **(extrinsic motivation)** and how well you are able to create conditions under which *they* motivate themselves **(intrinsic motivation)** determine in large part the success you feel as a teacher.

AT-RISK STUDENTS: YOUR RESPONSIBILITY

Today's schools are different from the schools your parents attended, perhaps even different from the elementary school you attended. The primary difference lies in the makeup of the school population. Statistics tell the story:

Nearly one-quarter of the children in schools in the United States live in poverty; approximately 50 percent of African-American students come from poverty-stricken homes, as do 40 percent of Hispanic students; 9.5 million households are headed by single females, half of whom are unemployed (Chafel, 1997).

What is the significance of this for you as a language arts teacher? Public education is based on the belief that all children are entitled to an education, that all can learn and are worthy of respect. Yet by dropping out of school by the thousands each year, young people are signaling that something is drastically wrong. The relationship between impoverished home background and school failure is well documented. Poor kids from overcrowded homes and crime-ridden neighborhoods simply don't do well in school.

In the past, the subject of school failure among poor and minority children has been given only peripheral attention in teacher education programs. Yet in most elementary classrooms, these are the very students who, because of their negative behavior, command the majority of a teacher's attention. Though controversial and complex, this topic is too important to ignore or minimize.

First, who are these at-risk children? You probably have already seen them in classrooms during your observations. When they constitute the majority in a classroom, as they do in many inner-city schools, they are highly visible, to the extent that their behavior sometimes makes headlines in the newspapers. (Jonathan Kozol's book *Savage Inequalities* [1991] paints a disturbing picture of inner-city children attending schools with falling plaster, no textbooks, drug abuse in the bathrooms, and gang violence on the playgrounds.) When they are only a minority in the classroom, they are often ignored, placed in an isolated corner, repeatedly punished, or removed from the room. These are the children with the lowest academic achievement; usually this means they are reading and writing two or more years below grade level. These are also the children with the poorest attendance records, which compounds the initial problem of academic weakness. They may have already been held back one or two grades out of the misguided notion that having them repeat the same grade will improve their behavior and raise their academic performance (Shepard & Smith, 1985, 1990). Often they come from low socioeconomic and ethnic minority backgrounds. These are the children of poverty (Chafel, 1997).

Although such children have been given many labels, the term **at-risk** is preferable because it signifies that these students face the greatest risk of leaving school without having acquired the skills, knowledge, and attitudes necessary to function successfully in society. At present, they make up a disproportionately high percentage of the children in Chapter One, special education, and remedial reading classrooms (Slavin, Kerweitt, & Madden, 1989). Unless schools and classrooms change, these youngsters will grow up to become a burden on society, filling up the prisons, halfway houses, and welfare rolls. In short, their problems are teachers' problems.

How closely teachers are linked to the success or failure of such youngsters has been well documented. This is an instance of a self-fulfilling prophecy: What teachers expect is often what they get. This concept originated in the 1960s when a number of learning experiments were conducted, first in the animal laboratories at Harvard University and then in one California school district. The latter experiment was deliberately set up to mislead teachers into believing that certain children in their classroom would "bloom," or make great academic spurts during the school year. The children selected by the experimenters were in fact at-risk students, who typically would not make great academic gains. By the end of the school year, these children achieved at a level significantly greater than expected, and the experimenters concluded that only the teachers' attitudes could account for the children's unusual academic success. The prophecy had been fulfilled.

The book that describes this early research, and which first used the term *self-fulfilling prophecy*, is *Pygmalion in the Classroom* by Robert Rosenthal and Lenore Jacobson (1968). Though considered a classic in educational circles, this work was not without its critics. The authors' main conclusion—that teachers' expectations can influence student performance positively or negatively—created a major controversy in 1968; it also stimulated a great deal of additional research in the area of teacher attitudes and student performance. Much of the research focused on low-achieving minority students. Cooper and Good (1983) have summarized much of that research and concluded that despite the criticisms against Rosenthal and Jacobson, their conclusions regarding the influence of teachers' attitudes on student achievement are still relevant today.

> ### IN & BEYOND THE CLASSROOM
>
> Observe one at-risk child over a period of three weeks. Describe in as much detail as possible the child's actual behaviors in class. What characteristics do you notice? What evidence of the self-fulfilling prophecy can you identify in the classroom or school?

The task before teachers is therefore clear: The needs of at-risk children must be addressed in school, particularly in the primary and intermediate grades and specifically in the language arts classroom, which focuses on basic language and literacy abilities. Rather than ignoring, failing, or removing such children, teachers must work even harder to assure these children of some degree of success as learners. The basis for success is already well known. It includes such teacher behaviors and practices as the following (Bickel, 1983; Brophy, 1982).

- Providing a supportive, positive environment
- Personalizing instruction with a variety of teaching strategies
- Planning for in-class time to practice new skills
- Involving students in planning new learning experiences
- Maintaining high expectations for all students

PRINCIPLES FOR EFFECTIVE INSTRUCTION

Whatever your philosophy of education or preferred approach to teaching the language arts, all teachers plan and prepare carefully for effective instruction. Here are some general principles to keep in mind.

Get to Know Your Students

Effective teachers begin with children in mind: their experiences, their abilities, their interests, their needs. With children as the focus of your planning, you must first spend time getting to know your students. Four ways to do so are show-and-tell activities, autobiographies, interest inventories, and kidwatching.

Show-and-tell is one of the oldest and most popular activities in the primary grades. It is also used successfully with older students, who call it "sharing." In either case, show-and-tell consists of a student bringing some object from home and preparing a brief talk about it to present to the whole class or to a small group. The teacher questions the child about the object and thereby perhaps learns more pertinent information about the student's home, parents, siblings, and interests. All of this information eventually helps the astute language arts teacher prepare more personalized and motivating lessons.

A second means of acquiring information about your students is by having them write their own life stories, or autobiographies. To get the students started on this, write your own autobiography and share it with them. This helps them to better understand what an autobiography consists of, while at the same time giving you a chance to demonstrate your openness and thereby to start creating links between yourself and the children. Once your students get the idea, they will be excited about telling their stories. Even young children can write autobiographies. Often they rely on pictures as much as words. Combining pictures and words is a good creative activity even for older students. Other types of autobiographies include photographic exhibits, collages, and three-dimensional displays. Show or model a few of these options and then let your students choose.

A third popular way to get to know your students is through the use of interest inventories. These are written forms completed by the students. They are teacher-made and generally utilize a fill-in-the-blank format, a checklist, or a combination of the two. They can be administered early in the school year, even on the first day, to give you some idea of the children's interests regarding home, school, particular subjects, sports, television, books, travel, and so on. Figure 3.1 is an example of one type of inventory suitable for use with upper elementary and intermediate students.

Figure 3.1

Sample interest inventory.

Name _____ Date _____

School _____ Age _____

1. How much do you like to read? (Check one answer.)
   ____ A little   ____ A lot   ____ Not at all

2. What newspapers do you read?
   _____

3. What are your favorite comic strips in the newspaper?
   _____

4. What magazines do you read?
   _____

5. What three living women do you admire most?
   A. _____ B. _____ C. _____

6. What three living men do you admire most?
   A. _____ B. _____ C. _____

7. Who are your heroes (men or women)?
   _____

8. What hobbies do you have?
   _____

9. What are your favorite television programs?
   _____

10. How many television programs do you watch each day?
    _____

11. How many hours each day do you usually spend watching television?
    _____

12. How many hours a day do you spend on the computer?
    Do you use the computer to play games or to search web sites?
    _____

(continued)

13. What are your favorite movies?

_____

14. Who are your favorite movie, television, and music stars?

_____

15. What are the three best fiction books you have ever read?
    A. _____ B. _____ C. _____

16. What are the three best nonfiction books you have ever read?
    A. _____ B. _____ C. _____

17. What men or boys from fiction or nonfiction do you remember best?

_____

18. What women or girls from fiction or nonfiction do you remember best?

_____

19. What books have you read that you disliked very much? Why?

_____

20. Check the kinds of things you like to see, read, or hear about. (You may check as many as you wish.)

____ Love stories	____ Criminals	____ Horses
____ Baseball	____ Murder mysteries	____ Basketball
____ War stories	____ Jokes	____ Space travel
____ Mathematics	____ Famous people	____ Cowboy stories
____ Historical tales	____ How to make things	____ Travel articles
____ Mythology	____ Football	____ Encyclopedias
____ Real-life adventures	____ Teenagers' problems	____ Politics
____ Poetry	____ Nature stories	____ Health
____ Movie stars	____ Scientific experiments	

21. What is your favorite subject in school?

_____

22. What subject do you like least?

_____

Figure 3.1

Continued.

The term *kidwatching* was coined by Yetta Goodman in an article in *The National Elementary Principal* (1978). Since that time, it has been widely discussed and associated with the whole language approach to the language arts. Goodman, like so many other educators, argued against the proliferation of standardized testing and the dominance of commercial textbooks and learning kits in education. She contended that a professionally trained teacher possesses skills of observation that, when applied properly, are an alternative form of evaluating teacher instruction and pupil learning. For it is through time spent watching children in learning situations, that teachers can best evaluate the successes and failures of previously taught lessons and can plan appropriately for upcoming lessons. Without such **kidwatching** time, teachers either operate in the dark or blindly follow the dictates of the basal reader manual or some other prepackaged curriculum material.

All teachers spend some time during class simply watching their students work. These periods of casual observation subtly confirm or refute the standardized test results of individual children, influence teacher planning of future lessons, and serve as a major source of information for conferences with parents. But in the past, observing children was not considered a serious part of a professional educator's job, nor was it legitimized by administrators or curriculum planners as a valuable way for teachers to spend class time. Today that has changed. Observing students is respected as a valuable part of what teachers do, especially in terms of meeting the individual needs of all their students.

For example, The Awakening Seed, an alternative elementary school in Tempe, Arizona, uses a whole language approach. Teachers at this school spend a good deal of time watching kids. Observation is part of their professional duties. They know that what they observe influences their beliefs about learning and their practices as teachers. These teachers are learning from watching their students. By reflecting on what they have observed, these teachers can adapt their teaching to the needs of their children. In short, kidwatching is central to the philosophy of The Awakening Seed school and is a serious part of what teachers do there (Mersereau, Glover, & Cherland, 1989).

If you are to become an effective teacher, you will have to spend some time each day in class really looking at and listening to children. Some of your kidwatching time will be brief and informal and utilize mental note taking. At other times, however, you may wish to sit at length with notebook by your side, carefully observing a single child or group of children.

Plan for In-Class Reading Time

Teachers need to have large blocks of reading time during the day—not time for teaching reading skills but time for kids to read in school. In a 1985 study titled *Becoming a Nation of Readers*, Anderson and several colleagues found that in the primary grades the average daily amount of time that children actually spent reading was only 7 minutes. Then in most reading classes, "reading time" consisted of the teacher talking about reading and the children filling in worksheets. However, in 1998 Baumann and Hoffman found that "teachers, on average, spent 2 hours and 23 minutes each day on reading and literacy" (p. 636), and teachers used only 55 of these minutes for teacher-directed skill or strategy instruction lessons.

Mrs. Bowker, a second-grade teacher who has been teaching for a number of years, recently adopted a whole language teaching approach. Her classroom is a *print-rich environment*. There are books, hardback and paperback, everywhere: on bookshelves, lining the windowsills, in children's cubbyholes. There are also magazines, newspapers, maps, brochures, and posters. The room is saturated with reading materials of all kinds. Real reading is in evidence throughout the daily routine.

The day's activities begin with quiet time for journal writing; each child writes in his or her personal journal and then reads it silently. For the next 15 minutes, the teacher reads aloud to the class from a lengthy book, one that not all of the children might tackle on their own: *From the Mixed-Up Files of Mrs. Basil E. Frankweiler* by E. L. Konigsburg. When she finishes reading, the children all take out their own books and begin reading; their reading period lasts for 1 hour, a technique called **sustained silent reading (SSR)**.

Despite the variety of activities going on, the room seems quiet and calm. The teacher is seated at a table surrounded by a group of children. These are her slowest readers. Each child has selected her or his own book from a list of books by Bernard Waber: *An Anteater Named Arthur; Ira Sleeps Over; Lyle Finds His Mother; Lyle, Lyle, Crocodile;* and *A Firefly Named Torchy*. The class theme for this month involves reading a number of books by the same author. One child at a time reads aloud as Mrs. Bowker listens. Undisturbed, the other children in the group continue their silent reading in their own books until they are called on to read aloud.

Some of the other children in the class are stretched out on a rug reading. Four little girls are seated around a small table; occasionally they whisper to each other about parts of their books. They are all reading different books by Beverly Cleary, the second author selected by the class for intensive study. The list of books by this author includes *Beezus and Ramona, Ellen Tibbits, Henry and the Clubhouse, Henry and Ribsy, Dear Mr. Henshaw, Henry and Beezus, Henry and the Paper Route,* and *Henry Huggins.*

The reading group around the teacher breaks up. One boy goes to the tape recorder and puts on a headset. Then he opens his book and reads silently as he listens to the tape. Another boy takes out drawing paper and begins to copy an illustration from his book. Other members of the group return to their desks or favorite corners of the room to continue their reading, this time silently. While the Waber group is dispersing, the Cleary group gathers around one child who has brought a special pen/pencil case from home. These students put their reading books aside to talk about it. The teacher notices this but doesn't say anything. A few moments later they break up, giggling, and go back to their reading.

Over in the corner, two girls are sitting by themselves softly reading aloud to each other. They have both selected Beverly Cleary's *Ramona the Pest.* They hold hands as they enjoy the book together.

The teacher now calls one little girl to her desk. They begin conferencing about the book she is reading: *Little House on the Prairie* by Laura Ingalls Wilder, the third author chosen as part of the theme. Wilder's books also include *Little House in the Big Woods, Little Town on the Prairie,* and *On the Banks of Plum Creek.* This literature conference lasts about 10 minutes. The child is obviously enthused by the book as she explains a favorite passage. The teacher, too, listens with interest; she asks the child questions, trying to draw out still more information about the book.

Still other students go to the class library to use the large dictionary or work on activities in their reading folders. There is a pleasant hum in the room, but it is not so loud as to interfere with the conference or small-group activities.

Later in the same day, after lunch, the class engages in sustained silent reading (SSR) for 20 minutes: Some of the children continue reading their books from the morning during this free reading time; others select different free reading books; still others thumb through favorite magazines. By the end of the day, the children in this class have been reading or listening to someone else reading for a total of 95 minutes!

Plan for In-Class Writing Time

Effective teachers plan for large blocks of time devoted specifically to writing. Additional writing activities are incorporated into mathematics, social studies, and science lessons.

Recall that in Mrs. Bowker's class the very first activity in the morning is journal writing. Every child keeps a journal in a spiral-bound notebook. Journal writing is a time for putting thoughts down quickly. Some children want to share their journals with the teacher immediately; others do not. Later in the day, the children may refer to their journals as a source of creative writing ideas. Journal writing is discussed later in this text.

In addition to journals, all of the children in Mrs. Bowker's class keep writing folders in which they place their creative writings. They work on writing for one hour a day, following the hour of reading: Some of the children are writing short stories; others continue longer works begun the previous week; a few are involved in collaborative group creations. Again the teacher spends part of this time conferencing with individual students about the progress of their writing.

Although in theory this teacher spends one hour on reading and another on writing, in actual practice reading, writing, and talking about literature flow naturally back and forth throughout the two-hour period. Research indicates that reading, writing, and literature are "interdependent aspects of literacy" that cannot be separated by artificial time periods or separate subject designations (Routman, 1996).

Create an Environment Conducive to Language Development

An earlier section in this chapter discussed the importance of creating a positive, supportive learning environment. In the language arts, this means creating and sustaining an atmosphere conducive to language use and development. Children need to be encouraged to use language in its various forms, both oral and written. Oral language presents certain problems because some teachers still believe that "silence is golden." But classrooms in which students' talk is forbidden or hindered are not appropriate language environments. Some research even suggests that such classrooms may be hindering children's language development (Dillon & Searle, 1981).

The real voyage of discovery consists not in seeking new landscapes, but in having new eyes.

MARCEL PROUST

Effective teachers place oral language use at the heart of all lessons. During reading and writing activities, children converse with the teacher, ask for help from friends, and share their work in small groups. There is usually a low hum in the room, but it is not so loud as to be distracting to other students engaged in silent work.

Children must be taught to converse in low tones while working in small groups. In fact, training children to work cooperatively, to modify their voice levels, and to monitor their own movement around the classroom is a crucial part of the teacher's job. Language arts teachers need to take time at the beginning of the school year to teach children the behaviors necessary to work independently, to cooperate in small groups, to make choices, and to ask for help from other students when the teacher is busy.

A final note about children's language is in order. When students are permitted and encouraged to converse naturally as a part of the learning process, their talk is not aimless but meaning-focused. That is, children talk about the meaningful activities they are engaged in. For example, one study found that before and during writing activities children talk to one another in order to clarify their ideas and test new techniques (Wells, 1986). Another study found that children use oral conferencing with both teachers and peers to further clarify their own thought processes before writing (Graves, 1994). Finally, Savage (1998) found that children use language to reflect on the significance of literature read in class for their personal lives. Relating events in one's own life to stories read in class sometimes results in overly exuberant students and a too-noisy classroom. However, the increased appreciation for literature and the enthusiasm for reading are well worth it.

Educators have long known that language develops and improves only through regular use in a variety of settings and for a variety of purposes. The more children use oral language and interact with print, the more confident they become of their language abilities. It is thus a major responsibility of the language arts teacher to plan for and provide a literate environment in which students flourish as language users and learners.

Facilitate Independent Working and Learning

Finally, it is important to develop in children the skills necessary to work independently. If children are to grow as readers, writers, and oral language users, they must develop a sense of competence in their own communication abilities. This can only happen when teachers stop pushing learning and instead trust children as learners (Comber, 1987). This is another benefit of kidwatching because it forces the teacher to stand back and observe from a distance. When teachers do this, they observe some children getting started on their own almost immediately, others requiring teacher assistance, and still others going to their friends for help or feedback about work they've completed. Teachers also witness how children reflect on the choice of activities, ponder which book to read for free reading, or chew on a pencil while trying to resolve a writing problem. These things only happen when teachers provide time and choices for students. In this manner, competence ultimately develops from independence.

Facilitating the development of this sense of competence in independent work again necessitates careful teacher planning. Reutzel and Hollingsworth (1988) have suggested three ways in which teachers can lead children to learn both independent work habits and decision-making skills: learning centers, units of study, and in-class projects. All three of these topics are discussed in greater detail later in this text, so for now it will suffice to briefly define and describe them.

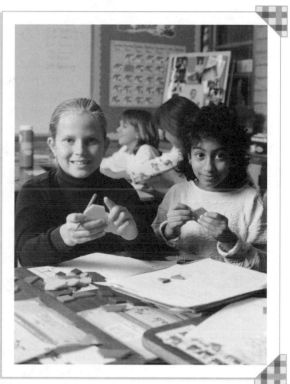

A **learning center** is a place in a classroom containing the materials and directions for completing a series of related activities, usually in a brief period of time. Generally the center provides children with a choice of activities and a means of self-checking before moving on to the next activity. Small groups may work at the center together, or students may perform their tasks independently of one another.

A **unit** is a series of related activities focused on a single topic or theme; it is usually completed over a longer period of time, perhaps a few days or weeks. Although a unit may center on a specific content area, such as dinosaurs, it always includes listening, speaking, reading, writing, and art activities. Children are required to share their expertise, work cooperatively on a joint venture, and work independently of others.

A **project** is a physical creation related to a curriculum area. It can result from a lengthy unit or stand alone. Small projects (such as book reports) can be completed individually, but most larger projects require a small group of students, working cooperatively, to create something (a class newspaper or puppet show, for example). Projects contain separate parts, which require a division of labor. Children can contribute to the project in the area in which they are most skilled or have a particular interest. In a newspaper project, for example, one student might focus on illustrations, a second child might interview classmates, and a third could be responsible for editing the written work.

A cautionary note about planning. The approach to planning described here is based on three major premises:

1. The central focus of the teacher and the instruction should be on the individual student and his or her development.
2. Humanistic, child-centered practices better motivate children to work hard at learning tasks more effectively than punitive threats.
3. The communication arts form an integrated whole and should be presented as such.

However, unless teachers are consciously aware of how their practices in the classroom match their beliefs about children and learning, both long- and short-term planning can, as DeHaven put it (1983), "degenerate into a mere listing of skills." This is because the larger educational units of school and community usually remain skill- and product-oriented. Therefore, despite the best intentions, it is very easy for teachers—particularly new teachers—to slip into a skill-and-drill mode without realizing it.

That caution given, the discussion now turns to the different types of plans that teachers use. You may find some of these plans more to your liking than others. That is normal. But keep an open mind to the strengths behind the various types of plans before deciding which one to use.

Types of Plans Teachers Use

Effective teachers of the language arts rely on a variety of plans. Careful and consistent planning is also one of the marks of the reflective teacher. Keep this in mind as you read about the following types of plans: yearly or semester, unit, weekly, daily, and mini-lessons.

THE YEARLY OR SEMESTER PLAN

The new school year is only a few weeks away. You have many things on your mind: What will the children be like? Who are their parents? How should you arrange the classroom? What materials do you need to order from the school? These and many other questions are swirling around in your mind as the excitement builds. But this is also the time to give some thought to your long-range goals for the coming year or semester. Take some time to reflect on what you expect from your students and yourself over the course of the year. Now make one list of all the questions you have and another of your general goals and expectations. This is how you further the process of reflection and make it something concrete.

Using your lists, you can begin to sketch out a long-range plan. Keep in mind that you are creating a broad outline, a general plan of goals to be achieved later with the help of more specific unit, weekly, and daily plans. There are a number of ways to approach long-range planning. Such plans usually do not contain many specific details; often there are spaces left to be filled in as the year progresses. Figure 3.2 is one teacher's yearly plan.

In this particular plan, the teacher begins by thinking about the children and their parents. She knows she will be having individual conferences with them, but what else can she do to establish the kind of relationship and atmosphere she wants? She also realizes that she will need to create group and individual projects if the students are to learn cooperation and independence. She thinks of possible field trips and in-class activities that could further help the class come together as a group. She sees that such activities allow some of the parents to involve themselves with the class as well.

One of the first things this teacher should do is get addresses and phone numbers of parents and make early contact with the families of the students she is teaching. She may inquire about their home and work schedules and learn about their particular interests in helping in the class. Since it is just the beginning of the school year, her plans in this area remain open and heavily dependent on the children and parents themselves.

In her plan, this teacher has resisted the temptation to list a scope and sequence of skills, giving instead just major headings. After all, what if the children are not ready for a particular skill lesson? What if they have already mastered it? How can the teacher tie subjects to students' personal interests? School-provided textbooks and curriculum guides are just that: guides. They cannot be allowed to totally dictate what and how a teacher teaches. Plan-

MY GOALS	ACTIONS I TOOK TO ACHIEVE GOALS	HOW SUCCESSFUL WAS I?
Children		
Establish rapport		
Establish trust		
Establish cooperation		
Establish independence		
Encourage creativity		
Parents		
Make contacts	Letters sent home	
Recruit aides	Phone calls made	
Encourage support with homework		
Subjects		
Listening	Tape recordings	
Speaking		
Reading	SSR	
Writing		
Math		
Science		
Social Studies		
Resources		
Other classroom teachers		
Reading/speech specialists		
Librarian	Once-a-week visits	
Principal		
Audiovisual equipment		
Community		

Figure 3.2

Sample yearly plan.

ning should also be guided by diagnostic testing, classroom inventories, the children's writing folders, and hours of careful student observation.

The final section of this sample plan, Resources, is crucial to effective teaching yet often ignored in teachers' plans. There are many resources that teachers utilize. For example, at the beginning of the school year, the teacher may inventory the available audiovisual equipment in the school in order to plan future units and projects. These are material resources. People are also resources: teachers, administrators, staff, and members of the community who can contribute a wealth of information, abilities, ideas, and support.

The point is that no single teacher, regardless of how talented he or she may be, can ever meet the needs of all the students all the time without depending on others. No one knows it all. Good teachers see all those around them as resources. Talking with colleagues in the lounge or at recess is one way to discover the people resources in your school. Perusing the local telephone directory, especially the yellow pages, provides immediate ideas regarding community resources. As each school year progresses, you will discover more about the resources you can call upon to make your teaching more exciting and relevant to the needs of the children.

Another way of viewing a yearly or semester plan is in terms of the school calendar. Most schools publish a calendar that lists special events on a month-by-month basis. The school secretary can provide you with the dates of field trips, special auditorium programs, holidays, early dismissal, open house, standardized testing, and so on. Noting important school dates on your own calendar in September can assist you in your planning throughout the school year.

THE UNIT PLAN

According to Jerome Bruner (1961, 1983), knowledge is structured and ordered into large concepts or patterns. A unit is one way of concretely structuring new knowledge and skills for children. Although the teacher should begin the year with some general themes in mind, units often arise naturally from the needs and interests of students. For example, students in one second-grade classroom became enthralled with dinosaurs because of a few books they had read. This led the teacher and her pupils to search for more information about dinosaurs and to plan some art activities and an original dramatization around the single theme of dinosaurs. Another class decided to design a series of activities around a study of weather following a visit by a local meteorologist. In both cases, the teacher and pupils jointly planned the unit and the related activities. And in the course of each unit, there was ample opportunity to integrate other subject areas—such as social studies, science, art, and music—with the language arts.

Creating units through integrated planning is not easy. One common mistake that teachers make is assuming that units automatically correspond to chapters in a textbook that can be used in their entirety. Another mistake is believing that all theme units should be given equal time and emphasis; this happens because typically textbook chapters are of approximately the same length, implying that equal amounts of time should be devoted to each.

How, then, should a unit be created? To begin, the teacher must recognize that units do not exist in books; they must be created. This means starting with textbooks but also using additional reading and reference materials related to the unit topic. Materials that may not be present in the school building should be collected. Finally, the teacher must assess the skill needs and abilities of the students in determining the kinds of listening, speaking, reading, and writing activities to organize. Clearly unit planning requires a teacher to make many decisions. Here are 10 questions to keep in mind to help you venture into unit planning:

1. What is the major concept I wish to develop?
2. What are the related subsidiary concepts?
3. What background information and experiences should I provide for my students?
4. Where can the students go to find additional information?
5. Are there sufficient resources within the classroom and school, or must I provide supplementary materials?
6. What resources are available in the community?

7. What specific activities will the children engage in? Individual? Small group?

8. How will I integrate listening, speaking, reading, viewing, visual representing, and writing into this unit?

9. How will I evaluate the unit? A test? A class project? Group or individual reports? Portfolios?

10. How much time does this unit warrant?

For example, one teacher initiated a unit on poetry suitable for fifth or sixth grade intended to last two to three weeks. The teacher's literature book contained a few good poems, and the grammar textbook suggested some poetry writing assignments. A few students brought in favorite poems from previous classes; other students suggested activities involving poetry. The unit began to take shape. Figure 3.3 shows the teacher's initial outline for the poetry unit; more detailed planning was reserved for the weekly and daily lesson plans.

RESOURCES	ACTIVITIES	EVALUATION
Class library	Reading aloud	Individual poetry
School library	Choral speaking	Group reports
Home resources	Illustrating poems	
Public library	Writing original poems	
Recordings of poems	Research on the lives of poets	
Web sites		

Figure 3.3

Sample unit outline: Poetry.

A unit plan can also be conceptualized with a schematic diagram. A **schematic diagram** is a visual means of organizing vocabulary terms related to a unit. It also helps students to better conceptualize the overall content of the unit. Although originally designed to support vocabulary development within content-area reading lessons (Early & Barron, 1969), the schematic diagram can be used to introduce key terms in any unit. To construct a schematic diagram, a teacher must first decide on the major concepts to be taught in a unit and identify the important related terms. This material is presented to the class in the form of a diagram on an overhead transparency or ditto handout. Figure 3.4, for example, compares poetry with prose.

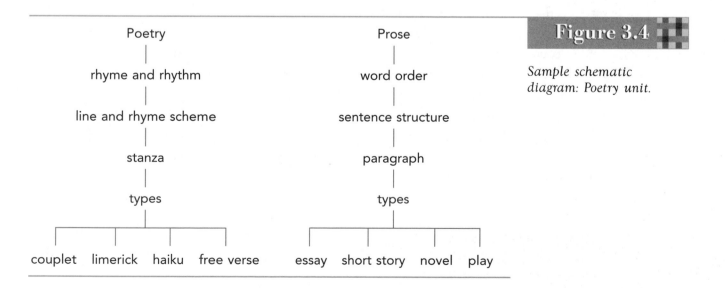

Figure 3.4

Sample schematic diagram: Poetry unit.

Another type of unit can be created around a single book. Study the Classroom Vignette and Figure 3.5 that follow describing how one fifth-grade teacher responded to the needs and interests of her class and created an integrated unit.

Vignette in the classroom

One day an impromptu discussion about fear begins among a group of fifth-grade children.

"I know someone who won't walk in the woods because he's afraid of snakes," Bobby says.

"Heck, I once saw a water moccasin jump into a boat," Paul says.

"I'd be scared of snakes too if it had been my boat," Ralph says.

"Yeah, but you wouldn't be afraid of going out in a boat again, would you?" Bobby asks.

"Snakes aren't that scary, but I know someone who's afraid of crowds and small rooms. He won't even ride in an elevator," Margie says.

The talk continues like this, with students sharing about other fears they or people they know have: fear of heights, fear of spiders, fear of the dark.

"What about comic book heroes like Superman and Batman?" Lindsay asks. "They are so powerful they probably aren't afraid of anything."

"How would you like to read a book about a boy who had a fear of the water and discovered his own source of courage?" their teacher, Ms. Whitecloud, asks. She shows them a copy of the book *Call It Courage* by Armstrong Sperry, the story of a young boy in Polynesia who must prove his bravery against many odds and overcome his fear of the sea.

Once the actual unit begins, it grows; it stretches from two weeks into a month. The children read the novel in and out of class. They also spend hours making toothpick constructions of traps and huts and balsa wood carvings of canoes as well as doing library research reports. From paper and other art supplies, they make replicas of South Sea islands, huts, and canoes. An entire scene of Polynesia is painted on butcher-block paper and then placed on the classroom walls as a background mural. As the unit comes to an end, the student committees share their reports and posters.

Finally, all of the constructions are combined to make one gigantic scene that the students share with the primary grades. As the younger children are escorted into the room, they marvel at the mural on the wall and the floor. Then the fifth-graders begin a dramatic retelling of the entire story. As they speak, they point to the places where specific events have occurred. The primary-grade children are spellbound by the story and also by the three-dimensional illustrations.

Afterward some of the parents wish to see this extravaganza for themselves; they agree to help put on a little Polynesian celebration for the children. Fruit punch, bananas, breadfruit pudding, mangoes, coconut milk, and other exotic foods are brought in for the children to sample while Hawaiian music and recordings of the ocean play in the background. What began a month ago as a simple class discussion has become a gala event that the children will remember for years to come.

Figure 3.5 shows the outline this teacher and her students created for the unit on the book *Call It Courage*.

Figure 3.5

CONCEPTS TAUGHT

1. Legends
2. Fiction vs. nonfiction
3. Characteristics of the novel
4. How fears develop
5. The nature of courage
6. Survival skills

Sample unit outline: Call It Courage.

BACKGROUND INFORMATION

1. Read aloud other legends
2. Map study of Pacific and Polynesia
3. History of Polynesia

MATERIALS

1. 30 copies of the book
2. Other library books by Armstrong Sperry
3. Maps and books on Polynesia
4. Glue
5. Toothpicks
6. Balsa wood
7. Construction paper

ACTIVITIES

1. In-class reading
2. Home reading
3. Chapter discussion
4. Projects:
    A. Individual paper-and-toothpick construction
    B. Small-group boat and village making
    C. Whole-class wall mural
5. Group reports on food, clothing, shelter of Polynesia
6. Dramatization and celebration

THE WEEKLY PLAN

The weekly plan is probably the most commonly used type of plan in the elementary grades. It is also the one you are most likely familiar with from your school days. Generally it is contained in a plan book that looks like an ordinary spiral notebook, with each page divided into squares representing the days of the week and the subject periods within each day. Traditionally a teacher lists in each box the period, the subject, the subskill, and the chapter or page number in the textbook or workbook. Figure 3.6 shows one teacher's plan book.

Note that this weekly plan book illustrates the separate skills model, in which time periods correspond to separate subjects, and these subjects are approached as skills to be taught, usually in conjunction with chapters in a textbook or workbook. This is an efficient way of managing time, subjects, and materials, but it is also unnaturally fragmented and ignores opportunities for unit integration. Contrast this weekly plan with the one shown in Figure 3.7, which was taken from the plan book of a second-grade teacher from Gainesville, Florida, who was moving toward a more integrated approach.

Figure 3.6   *Sample traditional weekly plan.*

	1	2	3	4	5	6	7
Monday	Reading Ginn Ch. 3 bring pictures	Spelling pretest correct in class	Grammar nouns & pronouns (Ch. 6)	Lunch Recess	Math Fractions (Ch. 5)	Soc. Studies The First Colonies (Ch. 4) bring maps	Science The Cell (Ch. 10) borrow charts
Tuesday							
Wednesday							
Thursday							
Friday							

This is an interesting weekly plan from a number of perspectives. This school relies heavily on the textbooks and curriculum guides of a major publishing company. Every language arts teacher is required to provide the skill lessons contained in the guides—primarily phonics lessons. The teachers are also required to give the end-of-term tests contained in the basal reader series, and to prepare students for the FCAT and Florida Writes administered in third grade. (Florida is not alone among states in using multiple standardized tests.) The pressures on this second-grade teacher are therefore enormous.

In her classroom, the day begins with dialogue journals: children's personal writings, to which the teacher responds. This is followed by the Morning Challenge, a few short quiz questions over skill areas she knows the students will be tested on. For instance, she includes a decoding question on the long vowel sound of /a/, a coin-recognition math problem, and a clock-reading problem. These skills are not taught as whole-class, full-period skill lessons; instead they are group-checked at the end of the day. The teacher then decides which students need more practice in a particular area for the next day or week. Three times during the day, she devotes time to reading aloud to the class: once from a short picture book, then from a resource book

Figure 3.7   *Sample integrated plan.*

Monday	Tuesday	Wednesday	Thursday	Friday
7:50–8:05	**7:50–8:05**	**7:50–8:20**	**7:50–8:05**	**7:50–8:05**
Dialogue Journal Morning Challenge Independent Work	Dialogue Journal Morning Challenge Independent Work	Dialogue Journal Morning Challenge Independent Work	Dialogue Journal Morning Challenge Independent Work	Dialogue Journal Morning Challenge Independent Work
8:10–8:40	**8:10–8:40**	**8:25–9:10**	**8:10–8:40**	**8:10–8:40**
Music	P. E.	Art	Music	P. E.
8:45–9:20	**8:45–9:20**	**9:10–9:30**	**8:45–9:10**	**8:45–9:20**
Read Aloud: Book _____ Poem _____ Song _____ Poetry Person _____	Read Aloud: Book _____ Poem _____ Song _____ Poetry Person _____	Read Aloud: Ch. 1-Krystal Book _____ Poem _____ Song _____ Poetry Person _____	Read Aloud: Book _____ Poem _____ Song _____ Poetry Person _____	Read Aloud: Ch. 1-Krystal Book _____ Poem _____ Song _____ Poetry Person _____
9:25–10:30	**9:25–10:30**	**9:30–10:30**	**9:10–9:25**	**9:25–9:40**
Theme Study Ch. 1-Ki, Byron ESL-Gabriel	Theme Study Ch. 1-Ki, Byron ESL-Gabriel	Theme Study Ch. 1-Ki, Byron ESL-Gabriel	Ch. 1-Krystal Finish: Dialogue Journals Morning Challenge Independent Work	Finish: Dialogue Journals Morning Challenge Independent Work Theme Study Ch. 1-Ki, Byron ESL-Gabriel
10:30–11:00	**10:30–11:00**	**10:30–11:00**	**9:25–10:30**	**9:40–10:30**
Independent Reading	Independent Reading	Independent Reading	Theme Study Ch. 1-Ki, Byron ESL-Gabriel	Theme Study
11:00–11:30	**11:00–11:30**	**11:00–11:30**	**10:30–11:00**	**10:30–11:00**
Process Writing Block	Process Writing Block—Gifted	Process Writing Block	Independent Reading—Gifted	Independent Reading
11:30–12:00	**11:30–12:00**	**11:30–12:00**	**11:00–11:30**	**11:00–11:30**
Math: Ch. 2 Enrichment:	Math:	Math: Enrichment:	Process Writing Block	Process Writing Block
12:00–12:30	**12:00–12:30**	**12:00–12:30**	**11:30–12:00**	**11:30–12:00**
Lunch	Lunch	Lunch	Math:	Math: Enrichment:
12:30–1:00	**12:30–12:45**	**12:30–12:40**	**12:00–12:30**	**12:00–12:30**
Media	Free Play	Free Play	Lunch	Lunch
1:00–1:15	**12:45–1:00**	**12:45**	**12:30–1:00**	**12:40–1:00**
Free Play	Read Aloud Chapter Book	Early Dismissal	Computer Lab	Process Writing Block
1:15–1:30	**1:00–1:30**		**1:00–1:15**	**1:00–1:15**
Read Aloud Chapter Book	Check Morning Challenge		Free Play	Free Play
1:30–2:00	**1:30–2:00**		**1:15–1:30**	**1:15–1:30**
Check Morning Challenge Take-Home Folders Ready	Sharing _____ Old Story _____ Old Poem _____ Old Song _____		Read Aloud Chapter Book	Read Aloud Chapter Book
			1:30–2:00	**1:30–2:00**
			Check Morning Challenge Sharing	Check Morning Challenge

related to the weekly or monthly theme, and finally from a longer chapter book. Thus the bulk of the morning is spent on independent work related to an integrated theme, in this case an environmental science/social studies exchange project with a second-grade class in Salem, Oregon. Every day includes free reading, writing folders, and math work.

THE DAILY LESSON PLAN

Although the weekly plan may look thorough, it is more of a guide or out-line. The details underlying each subject lesson are omitted. Unless you have taught the same subject and grade for many years, it is difficult to teach directly from such a plan. Determining the structure, sequence, and materials you need for each subject lesson requires a daily lesson plan. A daily lesson plan is a detailed written explanation of what a teacher will do and what students are expected to learn during a single subject period. The plans shown in Figures 3.8 and 3.9 describe and give an example of a skill lesson for a 45-minute period.

Figure 3.8

Components of a full-form daily lesson plan.

1. **Curriculum Area**

   The curriculum area is a brief identification or title for the subject area being taught and the specific subskill within the subject. The teacher must therefore decide which concept within each subject area to teach that day.

2. **Aim or Goal**

   The aim or goal is the introduction to any lesson. It may be written on the chalkboard in explicit terms. A question related to the aim should be placed on the board, as in the guided discovery approach.

3. **Motivation**

   Motivation is whatever the teacher does to stimulate student interest in the topic before beginning formal instruction. This might mean asking a provocative question, beginning a discussion, showing a film, reading a passage from a book, or playing a tape recording. Regardless of the nature of the motivational technique employed, it must be clearly understood that motivation comes before, and is separate from but related to, the actual teaching steps.

4. **Materials Needed**

   Each separate lesson requires the teacher to identify the materials needed for that lesson and to acquire them beforehand.

5. **Teaching Procedures/Steps**

   In this section of the plan are listed the actual things involved in teaching the lesson. This includes giving oral directions, writing examples on the chalkboard, questioning students, distributing handouts, and so on.

6. **Practice Activity**

   The teaching steps should not take the entire class period. If they do, then the teacher has dominated the lesson. Some time must be allowed for student practice to ensure learning.

7. **Follow-Up Activity**

   The follow-up or conclusion of the lesson should adequately summarize the teaching and learning that took place during the period. The teacher might provide the summary or call on a child to do so. Second, follow-up includes assigning a related activity, generally done at home, to reinforce classroom learning.

Source: D. Yellin (1985), *Integrating the Elementary Language Arts.*

1. **Curriculum Area:** Listening, speaking, writing
2. **Aim/Goal**
   A. Cognitive: The children will be able to improve listening skills while listening to the teacher read a story and while listening to descriptions given by their classmates.
   B. Affective: The children will enjoy using their mind's eye as they listen to a story.
   C. Physical: The children will use their senses to enrich their learning.
   D. Intuitive: The children will use guided fantasy to enrich their learning.
   E. Social: The children will respect their classmates as they in turn describe the "hidden treasure" they found.
3. **Motivation:** Questions/discussion
   A. "When we read a story, what do we use?"
   B. "When we listen to a story, what do we use?"
   C. "Today we are going to use only our ears, so let's close our mouths and eyes and listen carefully to the story I'm going to read. As I read it, try to image the story in your mind."
4. **Materials Needed**
   A. *Show and Tell* by Elvira Woodruff (1991). New York: *The Trumpet Club.*
   B. One hidden treasure (small object, such as old potato masher, meat thermometer, pot holder, salt/pepper shaker, or broken small toy, wrapped as a present for each child with his/her name on it). The teacher hides them around the room while the children are at recess.
5. **Teaching Procedures/Steps**
   A. Direct students to close their eyes and mouths and listen carefully.
   B. Read *Show and Tell* with as much expression as possible.
   C. After the reading, ask the students to imagine what would happen next if the story continued.
6. **Practice Activity** (whole class or small groups)
   A. Tell the children to look around the room and find the package with their name on it. They are not to open the treasure until everyone is back in the circle on the floor.
   B. When everyone returns to the circle, have all the children but one close their eyes while the one student opens the treasure.
   C. The child who unwraps the treasure is to explain the object without telling what it is. The children get three guesses. If no one can guess what it is, the children open their eyes to see the treasure. (If the teacher is concerned about children peeking, have the child who is opening and describing his/her treasure hide behind some object.)
   D. Permit all children to open and explain their treasure, with the classmates guessing.
   E. After everyone has had a turn, ask the children to write a sequel to the story *Show and Tell*, using their new treasure as the item used for show-and-tell.
7. **Follow-Up Activity**
   A. Discuss the importance of carefully listening to the story and the descriptions of others.
   B. Share the stories that the students wrote.

Figure 3.9

Sample daily lesson plan for grade 1 or 2.

THE MINI-LESSON

The daily lesson plan is an example of a traditional lesson plan. However, it has a serious drawback: It can take too much time to complete all the activities outlined, and consequently students do not have enough time to practice on their own. This is especially true for students who are anxious to get started on their work while other students hold up the class asking questions. For this reason, many teachers are shifting to the mini-lesson as an alternative approach to daily lesson planning.

The mini-lesson was originally described by Lucy Calkins (1986, 1994) in her discussion of process writing. Calkins was looking for an alternative to the "maxi-lesson" (45-minute skill period) that would allow more time for students to actually write during class yet still provide them with the skills knowledge they need. Nancie Atwell (1998), another well-known process writing advocate, also uses the mini-lesson each day to get the writer's workshop started with her middle school students. When carefully planned, the mini-lesson is a viable alternative to the full-period daily lesson plan. Furthermore, a lesson plan such as one combining a writer's workshop with a mini-lesson reflects the balanced approach to teaching. It is authentic and contextually driven yet provides direct instruction on a specific, needed skill.

The mini-lesson, as discussed by Calkins (1994) and Atwell (1998), is directed at process writing lessons, but the concept of the mini-lesson can be applied to any subject area. It first requires that the teacher understand the immediate needs of the students. Next, the teacher should analyze the skill or behavior to be taught. Finally, the lesson derived from this analysis must be presented without lengthy explanation or theoretical justification.

As an observant, reflective, kidwatching teacher, you will soon get a sense of your students' interests, strengths, weaknesses, and needs. From this knowledge, your own mini-lessons will emerge naturally. Basically there are three types of mini-lessons: classroom management, specific skills, and techniques or tips.

Classroom Management Mini-Lessons

Early in the school year, one third-grade teacher creates a number of interesting learning centers for her students. She hopes these will liven up some lessons and also teach the children how to work responsibly without constant teacher supervision. A few weeks into the semester, however, problems arise over how the centers, particularly the listening center, are to be used. The teacher therefore calls the class together for a mini-lesson on how to use a learning center.

She restates the specific instructions for using the listening center with a brief lecture. "Class, we are having some difficulties using the listening center properly. I want to review the rules with you again so we won't have to stop in the middle of the lesson. I'll demonstrate this with the Orange Group. Everyone in the Orange Group, take your seats at the listening center table and put on your headsets."

She waits until the children are seated and ready. Allowing time for children to get settled is important. "Everyone ready? Now Brenda will pass out the paper you will need to write your responses. Carlos will be in charge of turning on the tape recorder. Good. Did everyone see how they did it? Let's let the Blue Group try." Again she waits while the two groups trade places. Learning how to get organized takes time, particularly with young children.

"See if they remember the rules for using the center. Watch to see how the helpers do their jobs so there is no arguing or wasted time at the center. Watch carefully as they demonstrate how to adjust the headsets, distribute the papers, and turn on the tape recorder."

The class observes the Blue Group go through a mock version of the center. The children are now paying attention. "Does everyone understand how we work at the listening center? Good. Now let's get back to work, and I'll watch to see how you do." This mini-lesson is over.

A second example of a classroom management mini-lesson occurs later in the week. This one centers around how to choose a book for free reading time. Again the mini-lesson takes the form of a brief lecture and demonstration.

The teacher uses the *think aloud* technique to show the students how she solves problems in her head. "Class, today I want to talk to you about how I go about choosing a book for free reading time. First, let's walk over here to the class library. There are lots of good books. How shall I decide? Well, here's an interesting title, *The Witch of Blackbird Pond.* The paper cover on the book is called the book jacket. On the inside of the book jacket, there is a brief summary of the story." She reads silently for a few moments. "Hum, this sounds interesting. Here's another book with an interesting title, *James and the Giant Peach,* but it doesn't have a book jacket. I'll just sit here and read the first two pages to see how I like the beginning of the story." She sits and reads for a minute. "I'm not sure about this book. I think I'll put it back. You know it is OK to choose a book, start reading it, and then later decide to put it back on the shelf and try another. It's your choice. Now, let's all practice for a few minutes selecting a book from the library that we might want to read later."

The point of this mini-lesson is to help children get started in their free reading. Some children like to read but just can't seem to find a book. They choose books to read on the basis of their size. Perhaps their parents or teachers always selected books for them in the past; now they must choose for themselves. This is hard. As they procrastinate in choosing a book, such children may wind up disrupting the free reading time of other students in the class. This mini-lesson on how to select a book is important if free reading time is to be successful.

Specific Skills Mini-Lessons

The students in one fourth-grade class have been writing reviews of their favorite books. The reviews are to be published in the school newspaper. In reviewing the rough drafts, the teacher notices that there seems to be some confusion over how book titles should be written in the narrative of a report. Therefore, the teacher decides to conduct a mini-lesson on underlining titles and capitalizing important words in a book title.

Her lesson takes the form of a brief lecture with examples. "I've prepared an overhead transparency with some of the book titles you've used in your writing. First, notice that titles of books are always underlined. I know that in the books you read, you may see titles written with a funny kind of print, known as italics. But since we can't do this in our handwriting, we simply underline the words in the title. This tells the reader that this is the name of the book and not part of the discussion. Are there any questions?" A few students raise their hands.

"Now study the different examples of book titles on this poster."

<u>Book Titles Underlined</u>

<u>Anne Frank: The Diary of a Young Girl</u>
<u>Julie of the Wolves</u>
<u>The Wind in the Willows</u>
<u>And Then What Happened, Paul Revere?</u>
<u>To Kill a Mockingbird</u>
<u>A Wrinkle in Time</u>
<u>Ira Sleeps Over</u>

"Now we need to talk about capitalization in book titles. Do you see that not every single word is capitalized? Little words like *a*, *of*, and *the* are usually not capitalized because they are not the most important words in the title. However, we always capitalize the first word of a book title even if it is *a*, *the*, or *to*, as the examples show. In short titles, every single word may be capitalized. Now let's look at a few more titles from the books you are reading."

Another mini-lesson focuses on the different uses of the comma and the period in writing. Again, this lesson originates when the teacher reviews the children's story writing and notices the same types of errors appearing on a number of different students' papers. One way to teach skill mini-lessons about punctuation is to show the children paragraphs taken from their favorite books and reproduced on overhead transparencies. The teacher and students can discuss how the periods and commas are used by referring to the example on the overhead transparency. Then the students can copy the example into their notebooks for future reference. Having an actual example to refer to is often more helpful than memorizing a complicated rule. The final step is for the students to take out a rough copy of their own writing and reexamine how they used commas and periods. The teacher then can move about the room helping individual children edit their stories.

Techniques and Tips Mini-Lessons

Another kind of mini-lesson can be even briefer than the ones already described. For example, one teacher notices from the students' writings that certain words are often misspelled: *receive, piece, believe, deceive, achieve.*

Her mini-lesson consists of a brief spelling tip to help the children in the future. "Class, let me have your attention. I've noticed that many of you have made a particular kind of spelling error involving the letters *i* and *e*. Here is a little rhyme you can remember that may help you in your spelling: '*i* comes before *e* unless after *c* or when it sounds like *a* as in *neighbor* and *weigh*.'" The rhyme is written on the board, and the students copy it into their notebooks. They spend a few minutes brainstorming other words that fit the rule. Then the children go back to their writing.

The teacher is well aware that there are some common exceptions to this little rule, but those will come later. Identifying all the examples that fit the rule plus all of the exceptions would take half the period. Also, she wisely does not attempt to teach any other spelling rules in this mini-lesson. That would mean spending a full 45-minute lesson on spelling and would leave no time for actual writing.

Two weeks later in this same classroom, the teacher notices another common spelling error in the children's writing. This time it concerns words ending with the (/uh/ + r) sound. She decides to give them another little spelling tip rather than teaching a full-blown lesson. It is brief and to the point. "Boys and girls, when I have to decide how to spell a word with the /ur/ ending sound, I remember this rule: Most two-syllable words in English with that ending sound are spelled *-er*. Therefore, when in doubt, use *-er*. Only a few words are spelled with *-ar* or *-or*. Can you think of some *-ar* or *-or* examples?" The class comes up with *dollar, collar, doctor,* and *tractor*. They also discover how many more *-er* endings there are. After a brief discussion, the children return to their writing.

A third example of a mini-lesson employing a writing technique or tip is described by Calkins (1994). In it Shelly Harwayne, a master teacher, teaches her sixth-graders a technique to get started quickly in their writing folders each day instead of staring into space, waiting for inspiration. Harwayne explains that many writers, even professionals, have trouble gearing up to write. She then suggests a way to help her students get the writing period off to a good start. Her mini-lesson technique includes three steps:

1. First, reread what you've written the day before.
2. Next, ask yourself how you feel about it.
3. Then decide where you can make it better.

By beginning with what they have done previously, the students are able to get back into the flow of writing.

Although most mini-lessons are directed at the entire class, the teacher may decide to do one for just a few students. The skill taught might be something these students alone need, or it may just be more efficient at the moment to teach the skill to a small group rather than stopping the entire class. In any case, language arts teachers know that the skill or information covered in such a small-group mini-lesson will eventually spread to the rest of the class. This is because in the cooperative model of learning, the children are encouraged to conference together, to share and help one another as a regular part of the learning process. Lucy Calkins (1994) views small-group mini-lessons as a way of adding new information "to the class pot" without spending a lot of valuable time repeating instruction to every student in the class individually.

When you use mini-lessons, keep these points in mind:

- Teach what is most immediately relevant.
- Make it useful and generalizable to students' work.
- Keep the session brief—10 minutes maximum.
- Allow time for questions.
- Don't expect mastery of the skill immediately; that will come later, after considerable practice.

Meeting Learning Objectives

When teachers plan for learning experiences, they must keep many factors in mind: the abilities and interests of their students, the materials available, and the nature of learning. The last of these is probably the most misunderstood. This section discusses four domains of learning: cognitive, affective, psychomotor, and socialization.

Often school curriculums, and particularly standardized tests, artificially separate these equally important aspects of learning. Even worse, the affective, psychomotor, and socialization aspects of learning may be omitted entirely from the curriculum because they are not as frequently tested by standardized instruments. The result is a curriculum based exclusively on one type of learning: cognitive. However, studies in child psychology, brain development, and academic achievement have demonstrated that all four learning domains are equally important for the complete development of young people (Sarafino & Armstrong, 1986). Figure 3.10 summarizes the four learning domains.

COGNITIVE LEARNING

Almost all schools in the United States emphasize the **cognitive learning** domain, the area of learning that stresses the mental or intellectual processes. Jean Piaget's theory of the stages of cognitive development (sensorimotor, preoperational, concrete operations, formal operations) provides one way of describing the mental development of children and is probably the most influential theory in the schools today. In his *Taxonomy of Educational Objectives: The Cognitive Domain* (1956), Benjamin Bloom delineated the

Figure 3.10   *Four learning domains.*

	COGNITIVE	AFFECTIVE	PSYCHOMOTOR	SOCIALIZATION
Type	Intellectual	Emotional	Physical	Interactive
Activities	Memorizing phonics rules	Observing the class gerbil	Pantomiming	Preparing a class newscast
	Defining parts of speech	Listening to poetry	Hitting a baseball	Creating a group social studies mural
	Correcting punctuation errors in workbooks	Displaying *all* children's work in the classroom	Writing and illustrating poetry	Preparing Reader's Theatre presentation
			Drawing, cutting, pasting, and sewing bookbindings (publishing)	

cognitive domain as a hierarchical arrangement, from low-level memorization to higher-level reasoning abilities. Bloom's taxonomy has also had enormous impact on the curriculum, particularly on the scope and sequence of skills found in basal reader series and curriculum guides.

The emphasis on cognitive learning in the schools can be attributed in part to teachers' overreliance on textbooks. Textbooks generally present factual material, which requires student memorization rather than discussion or inquiry. Teachers using textbooks as their primary instructional resource usually require students to listen to lengthy lectures (which are particularly inappropriate for young children), define specific terms, recall the names of people and places, and memorize dates and specific rules. In part, this instructional approach is a response to the increasing pressures on teachers to prepare students for standardized tests at the national, state, and district levels, all of which emphasize cognitive abilities and are evaluated with multiple-choice, machine-graded instruments (Clay, 1990; Goodman, 1978).

Today most educators agree that the stress placed on cognitive learning to the exclusion of other types of learning in the elementary grades is too narrow and inappropriate for educating the whole child (Brandt, 1997; McCarthy, 1997; Pool, 1997). First of all, learning is complex and multifaceted; it includes more than IQ scores and test-taking abilities. Research on how the brain operates and how learning occurs has also shown that all learning is holistic: It requires both halves of the brain, analytic/logical reasoning as well as intuitive/emotional responses (Clark, 1986). In short, cognitive learning cannot be truly separated from the other learning domains. To exclude the affective, psychomotor, and socialization aspects of learning is to ignore the reality of how children learn and to hamper the very cognitive abilities teachers try so hard to develop.

AFFECTIVE LEARNING

The **affective learning** domain includes feelings, emotions, attitudes, and appreciation of aesthetics (sense of beauty). For example, teachers know that if a student does not like school, she or he will not do well in it, regardless of how high the child's IQ may be. Furthermore, all children like certain subjects and activities more than others. These preferences are reflected in achievement: Students perform better in subjects they enjoy. Finally, children's attitudes toward school in general and toward particular subjects very often reflect their parents' attitudes (Draper, Ganong, & Goodell, 1987). Parents who express negative attitudes about school or speak disparagingly of a teacher in front of their children make it much more difficult for those children to adjust to the school environment.

Of greater concern is what teachers do to create positive attitudes toward school and learning in their students. An overemphasis on basic skills, drill exercises, and memorization of facts has resulted in a neglect of the affective domain of learning in many classrooms (Sternberg, 1997). This imbalance has created some serious negative consequences. For example, students often leave school without having attained any appreciation of art, music, literature, or history (Jarolimek & Foster, 1985). Despite 12 years in supposedly integrated school systems, many high school graduates also remain closed-minded to views that differ from their own and to people who talk, look, or act differently.

In the integrated, whole language, and balanced approaches to language arts, the affective domain is inextricably tied to cognitive learning. The language arts teacher has the opportunity to create an atmosphere, design activities, and encourage active student participation in learning that links the affective to the cognitive. This is done in part by building lessons and units based on students' interests as well as their needs. For example, reading conferences and small-group discussions of books focus on students' emotional reactions to and feelings about what they have read rather than on the facts they remember. In a reading conference, a teacher might begin by asking a child, "Why did you choose this book to read?" Follow-up questions could include: "What was your favorite part?" "Is there anything about the book you didn't like?" "How did the book make you feel?"

Teachers can include the affective learning domain in the curriculum in the following ways:

- Relate school subjects to students' lives by personalizing the curriculum.
- Give students a choice of subjects to read and write about.
- Encourage small-group discussions about the content of lessons.
- Build on the honest feelings of students toward the material they are asked to learn.
- Incorporate student suggestions for making subject-matter lessons more interesting (for example, after expressing dislike for labeling the parts of speech for each word within a sentence, one fifth-grade class came up with several alternative games to learn the parts of speech).

PSYCHOMOTOR LEARNING

Psychomotor learning is defined as the use of physical movement to enhance general understanding of school concepts. It includes such varied activities as facial expressions used in pantomime; tactile and manipulative skills required for constructing, drawing, cutting, pasting, and sewing; and bodily movements used in dramatics and play activities. Unfortunately, for a long time psychomotor learning was associated only with the very young child and with the learning-disabled child. Today it is recognized as equally important as and supportive of the other learning domains, and it should be an integral part of the school day (Carbo, Dunn, & Dunn, 1986). Even older students learn best when they have a chance to participate physically in the learning experience.

Basic to all child development theories since the 1950s and the publication of Jean Piaget's works in the United States, this concept is not always practiced in the classroom. Often in primary, intermediate, and middle school classrooms, there is still too much emphasis placed on long periods of silent listening and seatwork. This reflects the still-prevalent view that talk and movement are disruptive to intellectual pursuits.

The work of William Glasser (1984), among others, has shown that higher levels of cognitive growth occur when psychomotor aspects of learning are incorporated into the classroom. Allowing children to move around the room, to manipulate objects, and to use their bodies as well as their minds actually increases learning. For example, formal grammar lessons in the elementary grades are among the most abstract and obtuse for young children to learn. Here are three psychomotor activities that serve as alternatives to rote memorization:

1. Teach children to pantomime the meaning of certain phrases within sentences, such as *under the bed, above the ground, around the tree,* and *into the barn.*
2. Ask children to act out the difference between a *blind Venetian* and a *venetian blind.*
3. Have students work in small groups to arrange word and phrase cards demonstrating the relationship between sentence structure and meaning.

Other psychomotor activities in the language arts classroom include illustrating, cutting, pasting, stapling, and sewing as part of bookmaking to share written work. Presentations of finished research projects or theme units can incorporate songs, dances, posters, dramatic acting, and the use of original props.

Another important aspect of the psychomotor domain of learning is *attention span,* the ability to concentrate on a task. In general, the younger the child, the shorter is the attention span (Sarafino & Armstrong, 1986). For example, while a fifth-grader may sit and work on a composition for 30 minutes without getting up, a first-grader may need to walk around after 5 minutes of intense, concentrated writing. Teachers who understand the relationship between attention-span limits and psychomotor learning try to break up longer lessons with special time-outs for stretching, water breaks, peer discussions, or rounds of Simon Says. It makes little sense for a teacher to plow along in a lecture, even the best lecture, when students' heads are drooping and yawns fill the room. Such signs mean the children need a break. Physical activities can be used to make any lesson more enjoyable and appropriate to the attention-span limitations of their students.

SOCIALIZATION LEARNING

Socialization learning is defined as the physical and verbal communication skills needed to sustain human relations and to function effectively in our society. The process of socialization begins at home and is furthered in the community. However, it is in school that this process really broadens to include contact with diverse religious, racial, and ethnic groups. The notion of the school as a melting pot, a place for broadening horizons and relationships, is an old one. However, the socialization process is too often taken for granted; this is a mistake because, like any other important aspect of learning, it must be planned.

According to Jarolimek and Foster (1985), there are actually three aspects to socialization learning: social interaction skills, cooperative group skills, and conflict resolution skills. *Social interaction* skills begin with the establishment of a positive self-image in each individual student. A teacher can foster this development by designing activities that allow students to experience success and a sense of competence in the classroom. Success and competence are the key ingredients in a positive self-image. Only when children feel good about themselves and believe they are worthy of respect and praise can they be taught the appropriate behaviors for interacting with others in different situations. Some simple activities that promote social interaction through success and competence include the following:

- Appointing students to distribute and collect class papers
- Appointing monitors to assist with attendance taking
- Rotating leadership roles during group activities
- Allowing students to help with bulletin board preparations

Using *cooperative groups* allows children to experience specific situations that require them to use their individual social skills. Johnson and Johnson (1987) have written extensively on the topic of cooperative learning. Their central argument is that too many classrooms are organized around either a competitive or an individualistic model. The result is that many children pass through years of schooling without having developed the cooperative social skills required for participation in society. Since the classroom is the one place where diverse groups of children are brought together on a regular basis, it is also the ideal place for cooperative learning.

One way to teach cooperative learning skills is through role playing and dramatics. Through play acting, children have a chance to act out the skills they will need later to function in a group. These important skills include taking turns speaking and listening, sharing materials among the group members, dividing various tasks so that all contribute, and ensuring that all children can assume leadership roles when appropriate. Such important behaviors cannot be learned working alone in a corner of the room (Johnson & Johnson, 1987).

The final aspect of socialization learning is *conflict resolution*. Young children typically resolve conflicts by physical means: the fight-or-flight response. In school, they learn the rules of behavior and how to communicate their feelings, wants, and needs verbally rather than physically. Here are three positive alternatives for conflict resolution that teachers can give students:

1. *Chatter groups.* Informal talk sessions about topics of immediate concern to a particular group of children or the entire class. These groups can meet early in the morning or late in the afternoon.

2. *Brainstorming.* The technique of generating ideas through brainstorming that can be applied to social as well as academic problems.

3. *Role playing.* Simple skits in which children act out their feelings regarding problems that have arisen in class, on the playground, between friends, and so on.

BEYOND THE CLASSROOM

Survey students in an elementary classroom about their likes and dislikes about school in general and certain subjects in particular. Chart or graph your findings. Are there any patterns? What do you think explains the patterns? Compare your results with those of your fellow students.

Language arts teachers recognize that all these activities involve the use of oral language ability. Thus, they not only help in resolving potential classroom conflicts but also enhance students' verbal skills by giving them an opportunity to practice communication about real-life issues.

Learning Styles

Each child has a unique or preferred manner for approaching a learning situation, called a **learning style.** (Similarly, every teacher has a preferred way or method of teaching certain concepts called a teaching method or strategy.) A teacher who can identify a child's preferred learning style also understands that child's strengths in learning and can teach to those strengths.

For example, traditional whole-class instruction is generally not successful with children with specific learning disabilities. Instead, special education teachers try to match their instructional approaches to the specific learning styles and strengths of their students (Hodgin & Wooliscroft, 1997). In recent years, more and more educators have taken the position that all teachers should be able to identify the learning styles of their students and then teach using the most appropriate instructional techniques (Dunn, 1996). This is a complex and controversial area; the purpose of this section is merely to acquaint you with the idea of student learning styles and to get you thinking about utilizing a variety of teaching strategies. This section should also help you reflect on your kidwatching experiences in classroom or laboratory settings.

Everyone has a learning style. Some people learn best in highly structured settings, guided by written directions, moving step-by-step in a logical, analytical fashion. Such people have been called left-brain–oriented because the left hemisphere of the brain is associated with visual and analytic information processing. Other people take a more global approach to learning, making intuitive guesses, utilizing tactile methods, and preferring more informal settings; these people are called right-brain–oriented (Dunn, Cavanaugh, Eberle, & Zenhauser, 1982; Levy, 1982). During the 1980s, many educators became enamored of brain research as it applied to instruction. However, merely labeling people as right- or left-brain thinkers is misleading. Research clearly shows that although individuals have preferred learning styles, both the right and left hemispheres of the brain are involved in all aspects of learning (Yellin, 1983).

The more one investigates the topic of learning style, the more complex it appears. For instance, an individual's preferred learning style is affected by such variables as temperature and time of day. Are you a morning person who prefers a cool room or a night owl who likes a warmer setting for studying? Do you learn best in an absolutely quiet setting, or do you need music in the background? Does snacking help you concentrate, or is it a distraction? These factors are also part of learning style. Interestingly enough, some evidence suggests that while most teachers have their big burst of intellectual energy early in the morning, more than half of elementary-age children concentrate best in the late morning or early afternoon (Dunn, Beaudry, & Klavas, 1989). Figure 3.11 summarizes some of the factors that affect learning style.

Figure 3.11

Learning style factors.

Environment: sound, light, temperature, room arrangement

Emotionality: interest, persistence, responsibility

Sociological needs: learning alone, learning with others, learning with media aids

Physical characteristics: child growth rates, perceptual strengths, mobility needs

Psychological inclinations: hemispheric preference, inductive/deductive preference, impulsive/reflective preference

Source: Adapted from M. Carbo, R. Dunn, & K. Dunn (1986), *Teaching Students to Read Through Individual Learning Styles.*

There are many ways to classify learning styles. This section identifies just a few of the most common and presents them in a dichotomous model based on the work of Claxton and Ralston (1978). A dichotomous approach contrasts two opposite learning style descriptions along a continuum. Although some children may appear to fit one of the two extremes, most children exhibit some of the characteristics of both learning styles and thus fall somewhere along the continuum between the two extremes. Figure 3.12 lists some common learning styles.

Figure 3.12

Student learning styles.

Impulsivity ←——————→	Reflectivity
Global ←——————→	Analytic
Visual ←——————→	Auditory
Visual-Auditory ←——————→	Kinesthetic

IMPULSIVE–REFLECTIVE

The learning style dimension characterized by impulsivity or reflectivity is associated with the work of Jerome Kagan (1965, 1987; Kagan & Kagan, 1970). Kagan's Matching Familiar Figures Test is still used to assess this dimension of learning.

In the classroom, the impulsive learner is most easily recognized. This is the child whose hand always flies up even before the teacher has finished asking the question. Such children have little fear of failure and appear to be more concerned with responding than with giving the correct answer. Often they are easily distracted by irrelevant material and miss the main idea or central theme of a book. On spelling and grammar tests, they rush to finish but often make many careless errors. Speed rather than accuracy drives the impulsive student.

The reflective child is slow and deliberate. Such children consider all alternatives before responding and approach problem solving in a highly systematic, critical way. This is the little perfectionist in your classroom. A favorite of teachers, the reflective child may nonetheless be one who is overly inhibited and anxious about schoolwork. These children may freeze up during test situations. They also respond very negatively when their written assignments are returned with red marks for grammar, punctuation, and spelling errors. In short, these are the students who need to be taught that making mistakes is part of learning, that taking risks is allowed.

GLOBAL–ANALYTIC

Marie Carbo, Rita Dunn, and Kenneth Dunn (1986) have done extensive work in applying the notion of learning styles to reading behavior and instruction. They contended that despite the many approaches to teaching reading, "every reading method emphasizes either an essentially global or analytic approach to reading" (p. 60).

A global reading style is one in which the student learns best when presented with whole texts. These children respond to the story itself rather than to individual details. They learn as they read, processing information in large patterns despite making individual errors. Though they enjoy reading stories, such children often dislike memorizing dates, places, and names. Analytic readers, on the other hand, learn information best when it is presented in bits and pieces. They are more concerned with remembering individual details than with subjectively responding to the story as a whole.

According to Carbo (1997), most primary-grade children are global learners; that is, they learn to read best when given the opportunity to listen to and read entire stories.

VISUAL–AUDITORY

Visual and *auditory* are the two most common terms applied in the teaching of reading. Although all children utilize both auditory and visual processing while learning to read, it is nonetheless possible to identify individual children who appear to process information more readily when it is presented auditorily in a teacher lecture or on a listening tape. Phonics instruction, which predominates in the primary grades, is an auditory approach to teaching reading because it stresses the learning of isolated sounds and symbols. Recent research suggests that young children, who have very limited attention spans, are less likely to be successful learners using a strictly auditory approach. Thus teachers who utilize auditory approaches should supplement their lessons with visuals on the chalkboard or on overhead transparencies (Carbo, Dunn, & Dunn, 1986).

Visual learners, on the other hand, learn best when material is presented in a format they can see: on the chalkboard, on large charts, on overhead transparencies, and in books. Such students respond to whole texts, sight-word vocabulary, and other global reading activities. Since young children are more likely to have visual acuity skills superior to their auditory discrimination abilities, whole-text and sight-word approaches are more likely to be successful (Carbo, Dunn, & Dunn, 1986).

VISUAL-AUDITORY–KINESTHETIC

Most approaches to reading today combine aspects of auditory and visual learning. The teacher usually spends some time teaching phonics as well as sight-word vocabulary. This eclectic approach seems appropriate because most children utilize both auditory and visual styles in learning to read. However, for primary-grade children, even this combined approach leaves much to be desired. In a summary of the research on reading styles, Carbo, Dunn, and Dunn (1986) concluded that "many students do not develop full visual acuity until third grade and full auditory acuity until fifth grade."

The implications of these findings are important for all teachers of reading. Because perceptual strengths (visual and auditory) mature more slowly than other physical abilities, many primary-grade students are frustrated by their inability to remember the material taught. The problems such young children encounter suggest the need for an alternative approach to teaching reading.

The kinesthetic learning style utilizes all of the senses, not just sight and hearing. It incorporates tactile and bodily movement along with the manipulation of materials. Learning by physically doing characterizes this approach. Research has shown that most young children, as well as underachieving older children, tend to be kinesthetic learners. In the language arts classroom, these youngsters learn best when given opportunities to manipulate letters and words and to engage in reading games, pantomiming, tracing, book illustrations, and dramatics. Ironically, many remedial reading programs, which are designed for poor readers, focus on students' weaknesses in the visual and auditory areas rather than capitalizing on learning style strengths in the tactile/kinesthetic area (Carbo, Dunn, & Dunn, 1986).

Multiple Intelligences Theory

In recent years, researchers and educators have studied Howard Gardner's **Multiple Intelligences Theory.** Even though it was not written as an educational theory, the theory has greatly impacted education. While studying

Figure 3.13   *Howard Gardner's Multiple Intelligences Theory.*

INTELLIGENCE	DEFINITION	PERSONALITY TRAITS
Linguistic	Mastery of language	Loves to read, writes well, enjoys jokes, has well-developed vocabulary, speaks well
Musical	Superb musical competence	Sings well, plays instruments well, has ability to compose and hear environmental sounds as music
Logical–Mathematical	Ability to calculate easily and think abstractly	Computes complicated problems in head, enjoys brainteasers, enjoys games such as chess
Spatial	Ability to form spatial images	Able to create models and sculptures and use maps and compasses
Bodily–Kinesthetic	Ability to use one's body for expressive or athletic goals	Excels in sports and drama, enjoys tactile materials
Intrapersonal	Ability to understand oneself	Is able to express oneself well, possesses high self-esteem
Interpersonal	Ability to understand and "read" others	Loves to socialize, is a natural leader, possesses empathy for others
Naturalist	Ability to classify plants, minerals, and rocks	Loves to study the outdoors, quickly sees things in nature that others do not see

Source: Adapted from Gardner (1993) and Checkley (1997).

the human brains of stroke victims, Gardner became interested in the various parts of the human brain that controlled different physical functions. He realized that even though a person lost his speech after a stroke, that same person might still be able to sing. In *Frames of Mind*, Gardner (1993) described his theory of seven intelligences. Later he recognized an eighth intelligence (Checkley, 1997). See Figure 3.13 for a description of the eight intelligences.

Gardner believes that all humans possess some degree of all eight intelligences, but each human does not have the same strength in each intelligence. It is the nurturing and the importance of a single intelligence within one's culture that will develop that one intelligence over the others. Gardner posits that each intelligence must be nurtured in order for it to develop properly and more fully and that many people have a dominant intelligence at birth.

How does this theory relate to the teaching of language arts? Teachers need to recognize that each child's mind is different and that any subject material can be taught in more than one way. Study Figure 3.13 to understand the personality traits that accompany each intelligence. As you study it, reflect on how the personality traits would affect a student's approach to the reading, writing, listening, speaking, viewing, and visual representing activities that you would do in your classroom. The Classroom Vignette that follows explains the activities that Mrs. Bee does with her class in order for her to understand her students. Notice how Mrs. Bee uses Gardner's Multiple Intelligences Theory to help provide a wide variety of language arts activities through the use of learning centers and activity cards. See Figure 3.14 for the activity cards for each center.

Vignette in the classroom

After studying Gardner's Multiple Intelligences Theory, Mrs. Bee, a fourth-grade teacher, decided to set up centers based on the eight intelligences in order to do a little classroom research. She wanted to find out which type of activity each of her students preferred in order to see if that activity might correlate with his or her dominant intelligence.

She set up eight centers with the activity cards found in Figure 3.14. She gave the students three and a half weeks to complete all the centers. They were instructed to write in their journals after they completed each center. They were to explain if they liked or disliked the activity and to give their reasons. After the centers were completed, Mrs.

Bee collected the journals and read them. She made a list of children who enjoyed each center. Then in small groups, she discussed the activities in each center and asked which center they enjoyed most and why. She found it interesting that all the students stated their likes and dislikes just as they did in the journal; however, as they discussed the activities with their classmates, they elaborated more on the reasons for their likes and dislikes. Because of her findings, Mrs. Bee attempted throughout the year to give a large variety of activities for each thematic unit she taught. She wanted to give each student an opportunity to learn in his or her dominant intelligence.

| **Figure 3.14** | Following are the activity cards that Mrs. Bee used in each center, as discussed in the Classroom Vignette. |

Activity cards for eight learning centers.

1. *Linguistic.* You remember the familiar song "Old MacDonald Had a Farm." Your task is to write a poem about Old MacDonald. You may imagine new information about him that the rest of us do not know. Your poem can be any type; it does not have to rhyme or have rhythm. After you have revised it, edited it, and have it ready for publication, share it with a small group.

2. *Musical.* Compose a new version of the song "Old MacDonald Had a Farm." When you are ready, sing it into the tape recorder that is provided. Be very creative with a new tune and a new text!

Figure 3.14

Continued.

3. *Logical–Mathematical.* Following is a list of livestock that Old MacDonald has to sell. Each day that the market is open, the prices change. Each day that he goes to market, it costs him $250 (gas, meals, rent of truck, etc.). You must decide which day he should sell his livestock. Of course, he desires the greatest profit possible. His livestock that are ready for market are listed, and the prices are given for each day that the market is open.

OLD MACDONALD'S LIVESTOCK
    7 cows, 15 sheep, 10 pigs, and 20 ducks
MARKET DAY

Livestock	Monday's Price	Friday's Price
Cows	$950 each	$900 each
Sheep	$800 each	$975 each
Pigs	$800 each	$825 each
Ducks	$45 each	$40 each

4. *Bodily–Kinesthetic.* You may do one of the following activities:

    A. Create a dance that fits your rendition of "Old MacDonald" or the original song of "Old MacDonald." Be sure to practice it so you can perform it for the entire class at the end of the three weeks.

    B. Create a new game that Old MacDonald or his children would enjoy playing on the farm during the day or during the long winter evenings. It can be a game that is played with a ball or some other object, or it may be a new board game. Be creative!

5. *Intrapersonal.* By yourself, do one of the following activities:

    A. Write about the type of farm and animals you would have if you lived on a farm. Describe your farm, explaining where it would be located and what your main source of income would be.

    B. Draw a mural or a diagram of the type of farm you would like to have. Include the surroundings, buildings, animals, etc.

Figure 3.14

Continued.

6. *Interpersonal.* Do this activity with six other classmates. When you find six other classmates, each of you must become one of the following people—Old MacDonald, George, Tom, Joe, Hank, Al, and Jim. When you have decided who each of you will be, do the following activity.

Old MacDonald and his neighbors are planning a neighborhood park. Presently the land is a grassy area with no sidewalks or streetlights. All neighbors have donated equal amounts of money except Old MacDonald, who donated a larger amount of money and donated all the land. There is $50,000 to spend on the equipment, lighting, and sidewalks for the park. Your group must decide what equipment to purchase and then draw a plan. All neighbors want it to be a beautiful, safe place during the day and night.

Following is a list of possible equipment with the price of each, and a list of the neighbors with their preferences.

EQUIPMENT	PRICE
Wading pool	$9,000
Swimming pool	$35,000
1-mile jogging trail	$20,000
Swing set	$500
Tennis court	$35,000
Streetlight	$300 each
Slide	$200
Bench	$65 each
Shuffleboard court	$1,700
Basketball court	$1,000
Basketball hoop	$250 each

NEIGHBORS

A. Old MacDonald and his wife are retired and are too old for jogging. They love to swim and play shuffleboard. Their grandchildren, who visit often, are toddlers.

B. George and his wife are young with two toddlers. They cannot swim but love to play tennis.

C. Tom and his wife have three teenage daughters, who are on the swim team but who pay big dollars to use the city pool during the summer. Tom is willing to donate $2,000 extra for the swimming pool.

D. Joe and his wife have three teenage sons, who are basketball stars. Joe's wife loves to jog.

E. Hank and his wife have one teenage daughter and a toddler. The teenage daughter is on the track team and the swim team.

F. Al and his wife have three teenage sons. One is on the track team and the other two play tennis. Al is willing to donate $2,000 extra for the tennis court.

G. Jim and his wife are also retired. Jim's wife jogs to maintain her health; Jim loves to play shuffleboard with his brother, Old MacDonald.

Figure 3.14

Continued.

7. *Naturalist.* Go outside to the back playground. If this was Old MacDonald's land, what do you think he would do with it? Be creative as you write or draw your plan!

8. *Spatial.* In the ziplock bags, you find toothpicks, straws, noodles, labels, rubber bands, Q-tips, craft sticks, waxed paper, and clear contact paper. Using any of these materials, construct something that would be useful to Old MacDonald. Display your project on the shelf in the back of the room.

Teaching Strategies

A **teaching strategy** is a specific set of organized teacher behaviors designed to facilitate student learning. Though the goal for the student remains the same—learning new material—the strategy or strategies employed by a teacher to reach that goal vary considerably. The plural term *strategies* is perhaps more appropriate because it reflects the actual classroom practice of teachers, who rarely use a single approach for all children in all learning situations. And this is as it should be. Good teachers are eclectic strategists: They pick, choose, and adapt various methods to meet specific conditions and students' specific learning needs. Similarly, the research on teaching methods does not support any one teaching strategy for all children at all times. Rather, it shows that good teachers adapt methods to their personal style and the idiosyncrasies of the teaching/learning situation (Jarolimek & Foster, 1985; Joyce & Weil, 1980).

IN & BEYOND THE CLASSROOM

Analyze the materials in an elementary-grade classroom. What evidence can you find that these materials are geared to a particular style of learning? Next observe some students in this same room. What evidence can you find that these children exhibit a particular learning style preference? Record your observations and share them with your peers.

Three teaching strategies—direct lecture, guided discovery, and learning centers—are general approaches to teaching. More specific teaching strategies related to language arts content are discussed in later chapters.

DIRECT LECTURE

The direct lecture is the most traditional and still the most popular of teaching strategies. Separate surveys of kindergarten teachers, graduate students, elementary teachers, and preservice teachers revealed that most preferred the whole-group direct lecture approach (Kagan, 1987). Why is this so?

First, many teachers believe that the direct lecture approach is the most efficient way to get information across to students in a clear, concise, and relatively rapid manner. Given the fact that most school systems are dominated by fixed time periods during which specific subject matter must be covered, it is not surprising that so many teachers rely on the direct lecture strategy.

A second major reason for the popularity of direct lectures relates to teacher control. In the direct lecture approach, almost all the learning variables can be controlled: the amount of information presented, the manner of presentation, the time allotted for the lesson, the questions and answers. Furthermore, the direct lecture allows a teacher to face the entire class all the time, which at least theoretically ensures a certain amount of classroom control.

There are also a number of disadvantages to the direct lecture. The biggest disadvantage is that it tends to make students passive listeners rather than active learners. Without active student involvement, it is also difficult for the teacher to assess student progress. Since lengthy lectures allow little time for discussion, student understanding is tested almost exclusively by written exams. The more time a teacher must spend testing and grading tests, the less time is available for teaching. Finally, the teacher-dominated lecture allows little time in class for children to interact with one another concerning the material to be learned; thus the affective domain of learning and the development of social learning skills are largely ignored.

GUIDED DISCOVERY

The guided discovery strategy is most often observed in the science and social studies areas, yet it is equally applicable to the language arts (Rotherman, 1987). It begins with the presentation of a problem or question. Facts are gathered, past experiences are recalled, and discussion ensues. Then the data are organized and hypotheses formulated. The latter are tested and either accepted, rejected, or revised. Finally, conclusions are drawn that relate to the original question or problem. Throughout this process, the teacher serves as a guide and resource when needed, but the discussion and investigation are student-led.

The obvious advantage of guided discovery is the active involvement of students in the learning process. There is constant peer interaction, small-group discussion, questions and answers. Social interaction skills and sharing of information characterize this strategy, which focuses on children "learning how to learn" (Morine & Morine, 1975). The guided discovery approach also allows the teacher to evaluate student progress and learning through kid-watching in addition to the standardized test instruments that the school system may require. Evaluation through observation allows the teacher to identify those students who are having difficulty mastering a new concept or utilizing critical thought processes or who lack vocabulary knowledge to express themselves effectively. Once these students are identified, mini-lessons or personal conferences can be arranged to help them immediately.

The major criticism of the guided discovery strategy concerns the effective use of time. Since the lesson is dependent on student involvement, there is no guarantee that the teacher's intended goal can be met within the time limits of a single period. What if the students develop unusual hypotheses that lead them down false trails? Is this a valuable use of class time? This is one of the risks of the guided discovery strategy. Teachers must constantly make decisions regarding the quality of the student discussion and investigation. Then, if necessary, they can always step in and redirect the lesson.

The other criticism and possible disadvantage of this strategy relates to classroom control. By its very nature, the guided discovery lesson results in more student movement and talking than the direct lecture approach. Some teachers and administrators do not feel comfortable with movement and talking in the classroom because they believe those interfere with learning. Obviously, excessive amounts of movement and noise by a class of 30 or more children can be potentially chaotic. In this sense, the guided discovery strategy places great demands on the teacher's organizational skills and ability to teach children to work independently and cooperatively.

In terms of the actual content learned in a lesson, research has shown that the direct lecture and guided discovery strategies are equally effective (Jacka, 1985). The Classroom Vignette on the following page is an example of how a specific third-grade skill lesson in the language arts might be taught using each of these approaches.

LEARNING CENTERS

The use of learning centers is a third teaching strategy. Unlike a direct lecture or even a guided discovery strategy, both of which begin with whole-group activities, a learning centers strategy is based on the philosophy that children learn best in small groups working with their peers (Vermette, 1998). Many elementary-grade teachers utilize a learning centers strategy to some extent.

There are four major components to a learning centers strategy:

1. Physical rearrangement of the room
2. Control of student movement
3. Teacher as resource person
4. Evaluation of individual student progress

The physical rearrangement of the room is an important step of the learning centers strategy. Chairs and desks can be moved to form separate learning areas. Bookcases and cardboard partitions can also divide up the room into special centers. The new space arrangement is one that allows children to sit face-to-face rather than in rows, looking at the backs of heads. Figure 3.15 shows a sample room arrangement.

Another aspect of the learning centers strategy is student movement. How can you get students to move from one center to another in an orderly fashion? How long should a group remain at a particular center? Do the children move as groups or individuals? These are some things you must think through before sending students to the centers. Here are three ways to manage movement in the learning centers approach:

1. First, make a bulletin board display showing the various learning centers and their locations. Next, place colored tags on this display to represent your different student groups. When you move the tags from one center to another, the children know that they should move as well.
2. Each day create a schedule for the use of the learning centers. Post this schedule for the groups to read, and go over it in class. The schedule tells the class groups how to move throughout the day.

Vignette *in the classroom*

DIRECT LECTURE EXAMPLE

A teacher writes on the chalkboard the following definition: *A noun is the name of a person, place, or thing.* Then he says, "Today we are going to learn about nouns. Copy this definition into your notebooks." The class copies.

When all the students are finished, the teacher continues. "Here are some examples of nouns," he says. He writes on the board the words *man, New York,* and *apple.* Then he makes three columns on the board: *People, Places,* and *Things.* Next he writes the nouns in the appropriate columns and asks the students to copy the chart into their notebooks.

"Nouns are all around us," he says. "Can anyone think of a noun you see in this room?" A few hands go up, and the teacher calls on one student.

Student: I see pencils, books, and chairs.
Teacher: Good, Bobby. Let's write those on our list.

As the list grows, the teacher explains, "Some nouns are always written with a capital letter. These are called proper nouns." He writes some proper nouns on the board and directs the students to copy them into their notebooks. The lesson continues in this manner, with the teacher lecturing and the students copying.

GUIDED DISCOVERY EXAMPLE

A teacher writes on the chalkboard, *The _____ raced across the street.* She then turns to the class and asks, "Who can read this sentence?" Hands go up to volunteer. After calling on one student, the teacher asks, "What's wrong with this sentence?"

Student: There's a word missing.
Teacher: OK, who can give us the missing word?
Student: Car.
Teacher: Good. Is there another word we could use?
Student: Dog.
Student: How about *camel?* (The class laughs, but the teacher writes down all the responses.)

Teacher: Now I want you to work in your groups and see how many more words you can come up with.

The students begin whispering among themselves and writing down their ideas. The brainstorming gets lively. Some of the students notice that some words can be used as nouns in certain sentences but as verbs in others. Their lists grow as each group tries to outdo the others. The teacher walks around the room observing the groups.

Teacher: OK, let's add all your words to our list. Now study the list on the board. What do these words have in common?
Students: There are some people. There are some animals. Most of the words begin with consonants. And they're all one- or two-syllable words.
Teacher: That's very good.

The teacher did not anticipate the last two responses; nevertheless she writes them on the board, even though they are not characteristics of nouns. To get students back on track, she asks, "Can anyone think of a three-syllable word that begins with a vowel but would still fit in our sentence?"

Student: Elephant.
Teacher: Good. Now let's try some more sentences in our groups.

The students work in their groups, filling in the blanks in the new sentences with nouns. As they brainstorm, more and more of the groups discover that the same word can be either a verb or a noun, depending on how it is used in a sentence. For example: Don't *toy* with your food./My brother brought me a *toy.* The lesson continues in this manner until the teacher feels the children are ready to generate their own definition of a noun based on their discoveries.

Figure 3.15   *Sample room arrangement with learning centers.*

3. Use a "post office" delivery system. Every child has a cubbyhole in which to store personal books. Each morning the teacher delivers a short letter telling the child what to do during the day and stressing the sequence of movement from center to center. Such a procedure also reinforces the functional nature of reading skills, as each child must read his or her own schedule.

In the learning centers strategy, the teacher assumes a variety of roles, most of which involve interacting with small groups or individual students. Instead of lecturer, the teacher becomes resource person and problem solver. The following are some of the things that the teacher does throughout the day when using a learning centers strategy:

- Conducts mini-lessons for groups of children
- Tutors individual students in skill areas
- Answers questions from individual students at the centers
- Observes and evaluates individual children at work
- Directs the movement between centers
- Conferences with individual students about personal matters that are interfering with schoolwork

The learning centers strategy can employ many traditional ways of evaluating students. These include end-of-the-week tests, unit exams, and standardized tests. In addition, other types of evaluation are associated with the learning centers strategy; two of the most common are observation and work portfolios.

Kidwatching, or careful observation of individual students, is one of the most important forms of evaluation a teacher can perform in the classroom (Goodman & Goodman, 1989). The teacher observes in order to accurately describe a child's actual behaviors. How well does the student work in a small group? What kinds of cooperative learning skills does the student exhibit? How well does the student perform a task when left alone? Does the student show initiative? Can the student handle responsibility? Only through careful, intensive observation can teachers determine the answers to these questions and effectively help each child as an individual. This is the way teachers individualize instruction.

The use of portfolios or folders to evaluate students' performance during the course of a school year is growing in popularity (Farr & Tone, 1998). Portfolios have been widely used in the past to evaluate secondary students on artistic production, and they are now being used to assess progress in writing skills. Portfolios (or folders for younger students) can also be used in conjunction with the learning centers strategy as a record of the child's work during a period of time. The portfolio or folder contains work samples that the student has completed at each center during the course of a week or more. Some children's folders will contain more than others. But over the course of a few months, every child will accumulate work that is representative of her or his accomplishments during that time; the teacher can assess the work accordingly. The portfolio or folder should contain evidence of what the student has accomplished and in which skill areas the child has grown.

There is always one moment in childhood when the door opens and lets the future in.

GRAHAM GREENE

Types of Learning Centers

Learning centers take on many different looks, depending on the physical setup of the classroom and the teacher's preferences. One type of center—a grammar center, for example—might consist of worksheets that students complete and check. The worksheets could be either made by a teacher or taken from a grammar textbook, workbook, or actual classroom work; in any case, they should all be focused on a single topic, such as adverbs. Since no one source has enough practice activities on adverbs, the teacher might use pages from several books or actual examples from the children's writing. The purpose of such a center is to give additional practice in a skill area to those students who need it.

A second type of learning center could be a reading center, an area of the room set aside for free reading. It might include comfortable chairs or soft pillows for children to lie on and books, magazines, newspapers, brochures, and other reading materials for children to choose from. This is generally a quiet area where students can read silently on their own.

A third center might be a listening center, as described in more detail in Chapter 5. It would contain worksheets for children to write their answers on, a tape recorder, and headsets. The students would sit on chairs around the center. At the end of a center session, they could either check their papers or turn them in to the teacher, depending on the organizational structure that the teacher created.

Still another type of center could be a space set aside for small-group instruction by the teacher. At this center, any subject area could be reviewed, depending on the needs of the students as determined by the teacher. The teacher could work with a small group of children for a set, uninterrupted amount of time. The other children in the room would know not to disturb the teacher or the students at the instruction center.

Another important center would be the creative writing center. This could consist of a table, chairs, and the materials to facilitate creative writing: paper, extra pencils, and perhaps a picture file or idea folder to get students started on their writing. As the end of a particular project neared, the center might be turned into a publishing center that would include the materials necessary for simple bookbinding.

Although the learning centers strategy is generally associated with younger students, older students also benefit from working in small groups on their own, using the teacher as a resource as needed. Strickland and Morrow (1988) have suggested that the following centers in the language arts are appropriate for upper elementary and middle school students: a fiction writing center, a nonfiction writing center, a poetry writing center, a newspaper writing center, and a report writing center. As with the other centers described, these centers would need the appropriate materials and directions to allow students to work without teacher assistance.

Regardless of the type of center used, the most effective centers involve self-checking whenever possible. One of the goals of the learning centers strategy is for the teacher to be free to give individual attention to students who need the help or to work with small groups of students in a remedial situation. The teacher cannot do this while constantly running from center to center checking students' work.

One way to achieve student independence and encourage self-evaluation is through the use of activity cards. Activity cards can help children become responsible for their own learning and engage in self-evaluation. Some commercial companies sell activity cards, but teachers still need to accumulate the materials necessary for each center. Teachers who instead create their own activity cards for each center can truly individualize their language arts program according to the needs and interests of the students. These cards also tend to be more creative and useful than anything teachers could purchase.

Teaching Strategies and At-Risk Students

Earlier in this chapter, there was a discussion of the unique problems of at-risk children, the potential dropouts who without special attention are not likely to survive in the present school system. This chapter concludes with a discussion of the special teaching strategies required to meet the needs of these students. Special strategies are needed because the traditional practices just have not worked with at-risk students in the past (Slavin, Kerweitt, & Madden, 1989). The sad conclusion of recent research is that "even the best instructional programs cannot ensure success for every child" (Slavin, 1996, p. 5).

In short, research has shown that at-risk students require a radically different approach to schooling and the use of much more innovative teaching strategies than those currently being practiced. Ironically, these radical approaches are often the hallmark of the most effective schools in the United States, which have few at-risk students. They focus on motivating individual students, not groups, and they stress learning how to learn rather than the memorization of facts in isolation from application. The key concepts associated with motivating and teaching the at-risk student in the language arts are summarized in the following paragraphs.

SELF-MONITORING

The slowest or academically weakest students are often the ones who don't recognize their own difficulties in learning. They tend to plod along, period after period, absorbing little but somehow believing that learning is magically taking place. Such students need to be taught to monitor their own learning and specifically to recognize when learning breaks down (Brandt, 1997). **Self-monitoring** is a term describing the ability of a student to recognize when learning is not taking place, to identify the cause of the problem, and to make the proper adjustments.

Self-monitoring strategies are most easily taught in the area of reading. Reading is a search for meaning, a problem to be solved, an answer to be discovered, a concept to be understood. The act of reading, either for pleasure or for information, is the reconstruction of the author's intended meaning in light of the reader's experience. Therefore, when understanding is blocked or meaning interfered with, the reader is signaled to stop and adjust his or her reading behavior. Some adjustment strategies include rereading a difficult passage; seeking key or clue words (nouns or adjectives); reading beyond the difficult passage in search of more clues to meaning and then returning to the passage; formulating questions while reading and trying to answer those questions; and asking help of the teacher or a friend.

These self-monitoring strategies are used almost automatically by good readers. However, the weakest readers in a classroom—those ultimately at risk of dropping out—do not utilize such strategies because they do not recognize when the comprehension process has broken down. The errors they make and the confusion they encounter while reading are not seen as signals to alter their reading strategies. Instead, such readers passively read on, expecting understanding to come to them miraculously.

Thus the teaching strategy for such students should be twofold. First, the teacher must explain the notion of self-monitoring, particularly how to recognize when the comprehension process has broken down. Once students grasp the notion of reading as an active, meaning-focused process, they are no longer satisfied with mere word calling or page turning. Then they can be taught some of the specific strategies to help them focus on comprehension and understanding.

RISK TAKING AND LEARNING

There is a strong correlation between school achievement and motivation to learn. Typically, the at-risk student is not motivated in school and subsequently experiences failure, which discourages effort toward achievement. It is a predictable pattern. One of the best theoretical models to address this issue is known as the Risk Taking Theory, first described by John W. Atkinson (1974; Atkinson & Birch, 1978). In summary, Atkinson has argued that in all learning situations there are two separate and contending forces to be dealt with. On the one hand, there is the need to achieve success in order to receive praise, rewards, and recognition; on the other is the real fear of failure as well as the ridicule, condemnation, and punishment it may bring. There is thus a psychological dilemma facing the child, who must weigh the chances of success against the chances of failure. Risk taking is therefore an integral part of learning and must be taught as such.

SUCCESS BREEDS SUCCESS

The most successful students are those who have experienced the most success in the past and therefore are willing to take more risks in difficult learning situations (Kolesink, 1978). The weakest students, the potential dropouts, have years of failure behind them. Their school experiences have often taught them not to try, not to take chances, because they will meet failure anyway. Thus they are not willing to risk failure, which (according to Atkinson) is a prerequisite for achieving success.

Teachers who work with at-risk students therefore need to create situations in which these students will experience success. They can shorten work activities so that students can complete assignments; provide study guides and vocabulary sheets to make reading assignments easier; and document small successes with graphs, written comments, and letters to parents. All these activities are necessary to encourage students to take risks in the more difficult learning situations ahead.

MOTIVATION AND TASK DIFFICULTY

What makes an activity motivating? Surprisingly, research has shown that a task that is challenging is also motivating (Atkinson, 1974; Weiner, 1972). This is because students exert their greatest efforts when they perceive a task to be of moderate difficulty—not so difficult as to frustrate any chance for success but not so easy as to make success meaningless. For example, losing a close tennis match with your friend would be more satisfying than winning against your younger brother. That's because a person who engages in an activity seeks not only success but also knowledge about her or his competencies in a particular area (Weiner, 1972). When the situation is so easy that success is guaranteed, such as playing tennis against a child, a person learns little about her or his ability. The same is true when the task is so difficult that success is impossible, such as playing tennis against Pete Sampras. Only the moderately challenging task provides self-knowledge, which is the key element in motivating achievement. In other words, only when there is balance between the chances for success and the risk of failure is the individual truly motivated to try his or her best.

THE IMPORTANCE OF SUBGOALS

For the weakest students in the classroom, most school tasks seem insurmountable; these students see only an interminable string of activities ahead. One way to help them is to model how to analyze a task into smaller, more attainable subgoals. In this way, students encounter small successes on the way toward accomplishing the larger task of a project (Levin, 1986).

In the language arts, this can be accomplished in a number of ways. For example, students can be taught how to make outlines for each of their assignments. A reading assignment might include the following tasks: identify the purpose for reading; formulate questions to guide your reading; read the passage while keeping these questions in mind; and write an answer for each question formulated. In a writing assignment, an outline of subtasks might include the following: brainstorm with a friend for ideas to write about; jot down ideas and select one you like; complete an outline or rough idea of what you want to write about; and get together with a friend to discuss your rough idea before making changes. In both of these examples, the focus is on several small subtasks. The larger task—reading the book or writing the composition—is completed gradually in a series of small steps; thus it does not seem so overwhelming to the student with a history of failure or incomplete assignments.

COOPERATIVE LEARNING STRATEGIES

One theory suggests that the dominant models in school, competitive and individualistic, work against the poorest students (Johnson & Johnson, 1987). For example, in a classroom set up to emphasize competition through spelling bees, timed exercises, and handwriting awards, the weakest students invariably fail. An alternative model is one that emphasizes cooperative learning activities that require individuals to work in groups toward a single group goal. Cooperative learning thus provides a chance for success for students who may not achieve it on their own. Following are the six characteristics of such a learning model:

1. A group goal means all share the success attained.
2. Achieving a mutual goal requires a division of labor.
3. Interdependence among group members is positive and supportive.
4. Rewards are linked to interdependence and cooperation.
5. Individual accountability is reduced but still important.
6. Interpersonal and socialization skills are learned and practiced along with content knowledge.

Changing Teacher Roles

According to some research studies, teachers relate to students in one of two ways: They either exercise control over student behavior or support student autonomy (Ryan, Connell, & Deci, 1985). Controlling student behavior makes for orderly classrooms but also results in passive students who lack the incentive to do independent creative work. As discussed earlier in this chapter, research shows that students perceive themselves as most competent when given some autonomy in a learning experience. This is particularly true of at-risk students who have experienced much control, little autonomy, and still less success in school, to the extent that their self-esteem is at rock bottom.

To change this attitude, teachers need to reassess their own roles. First, they must relinquish some of their controlling behaviors. For example, instead of lecturing to students, some teachers now see themselves as leading and encouraging students in independent and group work. Serving as a resource, answering questions, and coaching students on a one-to-one basis allow teachers to maintain order and discipline while permitting greater student autonomy. This additional autonomy leads the at-risk student with low self-esteem to take more risks, exercise choices, and tolerate uncertainty in learning situations without frustration. Only in such a free atmosphere can students come to believe in their own abilities and become motivated to exert the effort necessary for academic success (Brophy, 1982; Peters & Blue, 1978).

One-to-One Tutoring

Perhaps the most controversial conclusion regarding at-risk children is that for them to be successful in the traditional classroom, some time each day must be spent in one-to-one tutoring. Individual tutoring is not a new idea. However, in the past most educators rejected the notion of individual tutoring as a solution to the high dropout rate among at-risk students because it was unrealistic: Too much money and too many people would be required to implement such a program on a large scale in most schools.

Despite the cost and difficulty of implementation, experts in this field, such as Robert Slavin (Slavin, 1996; Slavin & Madden, 1989; Slavin, Kerweitt, & Madden, 1989) and Benjamin Bloom (1981, 1984) have concluded that only one-to-one tutoring makes a difference with at-risk students. This means that schools must make a serious commitment to recruiting the volunteers and hiring the paraprofessionals necessary for such a large-scale tutoring program.

Approximately 1,000 school districts in the United States have approached the problem of potential dropouts among at-risk students by adopting Communities in Schools (CIS), which was founded in 1977. CIS is committed to connecting community resources with schools and their students and families in order to help students who are at risk of dropping out of school. It begins in the elementary schools and continues through high schools.

This program has been highly successful in Charlotte-Mecklenburg, North Carolina, where CIS is now in 21 of its public schools, serving more than 6,000 students. These 21 schools use a wide variety of programs. Volunteers from the community and civic organizations become tutors and mentors for at-risk students; dentists provide free dental exams; and volunteers from the Junior League become involved with service projects with these students to help them learn the joy of giving to others. One of Charlotte-Mecklenburg's elementary schools is open year-round and for extended hours during the school year in order to provide classes in dance, art, and computers (Lewis & Morris, 1998).

In El Paso, Texas, one of its 53 CIS sites works with former gang members. The focus of this CIS is to provide these students who have dropped out of school with strategies to resolve conflict without fighting. These students may also attend classes so they can earn a GED. Another CIS site in El Paso provides summer programs for younger students on a college campus, while other sites provide literacy classes for adults who speak Spanish (Lewis & Morris, 1998).

The new electronic interdependence recreates the world in the image of a global village.

MARSHALL MCLUHAN

The Communities in Schools program has been successful in providing at-risk students personal attention from a caring adult, a safe learning environment, life-long skills, and opportunities to serve others. The primary mission of the CIS program is to keep at-risk students from dropping out of school.

No educator likes to admit that the schools have failed to educate some children. Yet for many at-risk children, this is the reality. Such students thus require a radically different approach and new strategies (Slavin, 1996). This is why programs such as Communities in Schools should be examined carefully and considered seriously as alternatives to the present educational system when working with at-risk children.

Summary

Planning for a successful language arts program takes time, but it is time well spent. Among the various types of plans used by teachers are the yearly or semester plan, the unit plan for a single book or subject area, the weekly plan book, the individual daily plan, and the mini-lesson plan.

Related to planning are the concepts of students' diverse learning styles, multiple intelligences, and teachers' varied instructional strategies. All students exhibit varied learning styles, including visual, auditory, tactile, and kinesthetic. All students possess the eight intelligences—linguistic, musical, logical–mathematical, bodily–kinesthetic, intrapersonal, interpersonal, naturalist, and spatial—with one intelligence being dominant. Teacher knowledge of both students' learning styles and the multiple intelligences helps in the task of individualizing lessons. Teachers' instructional strategies include the direct lecture, guided discovery, and learning centers. The strengths and weaknesses of these various strategies should be considered before being employed in a given teaching situation.

Finally, at-risk children pose unique problems for the classroom teacher. Such children, often from disadvantaged backgrounds and lacking in basic academic skills, require alternative teaching strategies if they are to acquire the skills of literacy. Placing such children in traditional classroom settings is not the answer: programs such as CIS should be considered.

With Children activities

LEARNING STYLES LESSON

Create a reading comprehension lesson. Tape record a short story. Have students read the story while they listen to it through headsets. Use kinesthetic activities involving paper, paint, yarn, cardboard, and miscellaneous objects to create a three-dimensional representation of a scene from the book.

MAP MAKING

Teach the whole class the rudiments of map making using the classroom as your subject. After each student has created a map of the classroom, discuss the alternative uses of learning space. Then let them create a map of their ideal classroom.

CLASS CALENDAR

Show the class a copy of the school calendar and discuss the importance of planning in school. Then create your own class calendar. List important class activities such as students' birthdays, holidays, tests, parties, and field trips.

Acceptable Use Policy technology

While teachers plan for the delivery of language arts and other subjects, they must also think about the rules that students must follow in the classroom, in the halls, and on the playground to provide a safe environment for all. Today teachers and administrators must also post the rules that students will follow while in the computer lab and while using any classroom computer. Many schools have an "Acceptable Use Policy" (AUP) that must be signed by a legal guardian before the child is permitted to use the computers (Kehoe & Mixon, 1997). Kehoe and Mixon (1997) give the following sets of rules concerning courtesy, safety, and general basics:

RULES CONCERNING COURTESY

1. Save only on floppy disks.
2. Do not waste paper.
3. Log off when leaving the computer.
4. Speak softly in the lab.
5. Remember that your e-mail can be read by others.
6. Don't be a "pig" and take too much time on the computer.

RULES CONCERNING SAFETY

1. Do not give your real name, home address, or telephone number on the Internet.
2. Do not meet privately with someone you met on the Internet.

3. Do not share your password with anyone.

4. If you have "strange" feelings about someone you met on the Internet, tell an adult.

BASE RULES

1. Do not sell or exchange or buy illegal items on the Internet.

2. Do not exchange sexually explicit material on the Internet.

3. Do not send threatening messages on the Internet.

4. Do not plagiarize; give credit to the source.

5. Do not forge any e-mail.

6. Do not post defaming messages.

Teachers and administrators can download a variety of templates for AUPs by contacting one of the following:

1. http://www.erehwon.com/k12aup/

2. gopher://eric.syr.edu/11/Guides/Agreements

3. http://www.gsn.org/web/issues/aup/home.html

websites   *E-learning*

www.ed.gov/free

This site has hundreds of free educational resources from federally sponsored programs.

www.educate.si.edu

This site contains lessons, activities, and nearly 500 educational products.

www.col-ed.org/cur#Lang

This site has lesson plans for elementary language arts, math, science, and social studies.

weber.u.washington.edu/~chudler/neurok.html

This site is sponsored by the National Center for Research Resources. It is a rich resource of graphics, information, and interactivity for children.

Related Readings

RELATED BOOKS

Guthrie, J., & Wigfield, A. (eds.) (1997). *Reading engagement: Motivating readers through integrated instruction.* Newark, DE: International Reading Association. This book is a collection of essays from reading experts on how to teach reading so children are actively engaged instead of passive learners.

Marzano, R. (1992). *A different kind of classroom: Teaching with dimensions of learning.* Alexandria, VA: Association for Supervision and Curriculum Development. Marzano bases his five dimensions on the learning theories of Piaget, Bruner, and Vygotsky. The text has class scenarios in order for the reader to connect the theory with an everyday situation.

Roller, C. (1996). *Variability not disability: Struggling readers in a workshop classroom.* Newark, VA: International Reading Association. This book is especially helpful for teachers who desire to use the reading workshop. Roller explains how to ensure that readers of all abilities and learning styles succeed.

RELATED JOURNAL ARTICLES

The following issues of *Educational Leadership* devote the entire journal to the topic that is listed. All articles are by leading experts in the field of education; many have been cited in this chapter.

Educational Leadership 52(4). This December 1994/January 1995 issue, titled "The Inclusive School," discusses the various types of special needs.

Educational Leadership 53(5). This February 1996 issue, titled "Students with Special Needs," discusses topics such as attention deficit, ESL, and the gifted.

Educational Leadership 54(6). This March 1997 issue, titled "How Children Learn," discusses the brain, learning styles, multiple intelligence, and neural branching.

References

Anderson, R., Hiebert, E., Scott, J., & Wilkerson, I. (1985). *Becoming a nation of readers.* Washington, DC: National Institute of Education.

Atkinson, J. W. (1974). Motivational determinants of intellectual performance and cumulative achievement. In J. W. Atkinson & J. O. Raynor (eds.), *Motivation and achievement.* Washington, DC: Winston Publishers.

Atkinson, J. W., & Birch, D. (1978). *An introduction to motivation* (2nd ed.). New York: D. Van Nostrand Co.

Atwell, N. (1998). *In the middle: New understandings about writing, reading and learning* (2nd ed.). Portsmouth, NH: Heinemann.

Baumann, J., & Hoffman, J. (1998). Where are teachers' voices in the phonic/whole language debate? Results from a survey of U.S. elementary classroom teachers. *The Reading Teacher, 51*(8), 636–651.

Bickel, W. (1983). Effective schools. *Educational Researcher, 12*, 3–31.

Bloom, B. (1956). *Taxonomy of educational objectives: The cognitive domain.* New York: David McKay Publishers.

Bloom, B. (1981). *All our children learning.* New York: McGraw-Hill.

Bloom, B. (1984). The search for methods of group instruction as effective as one to one tutoring. *Educational Leadership, 41*(8), 4–18.

Brandt, R. (1997). On using knowledge about our brain: A conversation with Bob Sylwester. *Educational Leadership, 54*(6), 16–19.

Brophy, J. (1982). Successful teaching strategies for the inner city child. *Phi Delta Kappan, 63*, 527–530.

Bruner, J. (1961). *The process of education.* Cambridge, MA: Harvard University Press.

Bruner, J. (1983). *Child's talk: Learning to use language.* New York: W. W. Norton.

Calkins, L. (1986). *The art of teaching writing.* Portsmouth, NH: Heinemann.

Calkins, L. (1994). *The art of teaching writing.* (2nd ed.). Portsmouth, NH: Heinemann.

Carbo, M., Dunn, R., & Dunn, K. (1986). *Teaching students to read through individual learning styles.* Englewood Cliffs, NJ: Prentice Hall.

Carbo, M. (1997). Reading styles times twenty. *Educational Leadership, 54*(6), 38–42.

Chafel, J. (1997). Children's views of poverty: A review of research and implications for teaching. *The Educational Forum, 61*(1) 360–371.

Checkley, K. (1997). The seven . . . and eighth. *Educational Leadership, 55*(1), 8–13.

Clark B. (1986). *Optimizing learning: The integrated education model in the classroom.* Columbus, OH: Merrill.

Claxton, C., & Ralston, Y. (1978). *Learning styles: Their impact on teaching and administration.* Washington, DC: George Washington University. AAE-ERIC Research Paper No. 10.

Clay, M. (1990). What is and what might be in evaluation. *Language Arts, 67*(3), 288–298.

Comber, B. (1987). Celebrating and analyzing successful teaching. *Language Arts, 64*(2), 182–195.

Cooper, H., & Good, T. (1983). *Pygmalion grows up.* New York: Longman Co.

DeHaven, E. (1983). *Teaching and learning the language arts* (2nd ed.). Boston: Little, Brown & Co.

Dillon, D., & Searle, D. (1981). The role of language in one first grade classroom. *Research in the Teaching of English, 15,* 311–328.

Draper, T., Ganong, M., & Goodell, V. (1987). *See how they grow: Concepts in child development and parenting.* Mission Hills, CA: Glencoe Publishing Co.

Dunn, R. (1996). *How to implement and supervise a learning styles program.* Alexandria, VA: Association of Supervision and Curriculum Development.

Dunn, R., Beaudry, J., & Klavas, A. (1989). Survey of research on learning styles. *Educational Leadership, 46*(6), 50–58.

Dunn, R., Cavanaugh, D., Eberle, B., & Zenhauser, R. (1982). Hemispheric preference: The newest element of learning style. *The American Biology Teacher, 44*(5), 291–294.

Early, M., & Barron, R. (1969). Use of the structured overview in mathematics classes. In H. Herber & P. Sanders (eds.), *Research in reading in the content areas: First year report.* Syracuse, NY: Syracuse University.

Farr, R., & Tone, B. (1998). *Portfolio and performance assessment: Helping students evaluate their progress as readers and writers* (2nd ed.). Fort Worth, TX: Harcourt Brace College Publishers.

Gardner, H. (1993). *Frames of mind* (10th anniversary ed.). New York: Basic Books.

Glasser, R. (1984). Education and thinking: The role of knowledge. *American Psychologist, 39*(3), 93–104.

Goodlad, J. (1984). *A place called school.* New York: McGraw-Hill Book Co.

Goodman, Y. (1978). Kidwatching: An alternative to testing. *The National Elementary Principal, 57*(2), 41–45.

Graves, D. (1994). *A fresh look at writing.* Portsmouth, NH: Heinemann.

Hodgin, J., & Wooliscroft, C. (1997). Eric learns to read: Learning styles at work. *Educational Leadership, 54*(6), 43–45.

Jacka, B. (1985). The teaching of defined concepts: A test of Gagne and Briggs' model of instructional design. *Journal of Educational Research, 78*(4), 224–227.

Jarolimek, J., & Foster, C. (1985). *Teaching and learning in the elementary school.* New York: MacMillan.

Johnson, D., & Johnson, R. (1987). *Learning together and alone: Cooperative, competitive and individualistic learning.* Englewood Cliffs, NJ: Prentice Hall.

Joyce, B., & Weil, M. (1980). *Models of teaching.* Englewood Cliffs, NJ: Prentice Hall.

Kagan, J. (1965). Impulsive and reflective children: Significance of conceptual tempo. In J. Krumboltz (ed.), *Learning and the education process.* Chicago: Rand McNally.

Kagan, J. (1987). Cognitive style and instructional preferences: Some influences. *Educational Forum, 51*(4), 393–403.

Kagan, J., & Kagan, N. (1970). Individual variation in cognitive process. In P. H. Mussen (ed.), *Carmichael's manual of child psychology: Vol. 1.* New York: Wiley and Co.

Kehoe, B., & Mixon, V. (1997). *Children and the internet.* Upper Saddle River, NJ: Prentice Hall.

Kolesink, W. (1978). *Motivation: Understanding and influencing human behavior.* Boston: Allyn & Bacon.

Kozol, J. (1991). *Savage inequalities: Children in America's schools.* New York: Crown Publishers.

Levin, J. (1986). Four cognitive principles of learning-strategy innovation. *Educational Psychologist, 21*(1–2), 3–17.

Levy, J. (1982). Children think with whole brains. In *Student learning styles and brain behavior.* Reston, VA: National Association of Secondary School Principals.

Lewis, R., & Morris, J. (1998). Communities for children. *Educational Leadership, 55*(8), 34–36.

Manning, M., Manning, G., & Long, R. (1994). *Theme immersion inquiry-based curriculum in elementary and middle schools.* Portsmouth, NH: Heinemann.

Marzano, R. (1992). *A different kind of classroom: Thinking with dimensions of learning.* Alexandria, VA: Association of Supervision and Curriculum Development.

McCarthy, B. (1997). A tale of four learners: 4Mat's learning styles. *Educational Leadership, 54*(6), 46–53.

Mersereau, I., Glover, M., & Cherland, M. (1989). Dancing on the edge. *Language Arts, 66*(2), 28–32.

Morine, H., & Morine, G. (1975). *Discovery: A challenge to teachers.* Englewood Cliffs, NJ: Prentice Hall.

Peters, W. H., & Blue, A. G. (1978). Teacher intellectual disposition as it relates to student openness in written response to literature. *Research in the Teaching of English, 12*(8), 127–136.

Pool, C. (1997). Maximizing learning: A conversation with Renate Nummela Cain. *Educational Leadership, 54*(6), 11–15.

Reutzel, D., & Hollingsworth, P. (1988). Whole language and the practitioner. *Academic Therapy, 23*(4), 405–416.

Rosenthal, R., & Jacobson, L. (1968). *Pygmalion in the classroom.* New York: Holt, Rinehart & Winston.

Rotherman, K. (1987). Guided investigation. *School Science Review, 68*(2), 631–634.

Routman, R. (1996). *Literacy at the crossroads: Crucial talk about reading, writing and other teaching dilemmas.* Portsmouth, NH: Heinemann.

Ryan, M. (1989, July 23). We can turn our schools around. *Gainesville Sun, Parade Magazine,* pp. 10–11.

Ryan, R., Connell, J., & Deci, E. (1985). A motivational analysis of self-determination and self-regulation in education. In C. Ames & R. Ames (eds.), *Research on motivation in education: The classroom milieu.* New York: Academic Press.

Sarafino, E., & Armstrong, J. (1986). *Child and adolescent development* (2nd ed.). St. Paul, MN: West Publishing Co.

Savage, J. (1998). *Teaching reading and writing: Combining skills, strategies and literacy* (2nd ed.). Boston: McGraw-Hill.

Seely, A. (1995). *Integrated thematic units.* Westminster, CA: Teacher Created Materials.

Shepard, L., & Smith, M. (1985). *Boulder Valley kindergarten study: Retention practices and prevention effects.* Boulder: University of Colorado Laboratory of Educational Research.

Shepard, L., & Smith, M. (1990). Synthesis of research on grade retention. *Educational Leadership, 47*(8), 84–88.

Slavin, R. (1996). Neverstreaming: Preventing learning disabilities. *Educational Leadership, 53*(5), 4–7.

Slavin, R., Kerweitt, N., & Madden, N. (1989). *Effective programs for students at risk.* Boston: Allyn & Bacon.

Slavin, R., & Madden, N. (1989). What works for students at risk: A research synthesis. *Educational Leadership, 46*(5), 4–13.

Smith, F. (1997). *Reading without nonsense* (3rd ed.). New York: Teacher's College Press.

Sternberg, R. (1997). What does it mean to be smart? *Educational Leadership, 54*(6), 20–25.

Strickland, D., & Morrow, L. (1988). Creating a print rich environment. *Language Arts, 42*(2), 156–157.

Vermette, P. (1998). *Making cooperative learning work.* Upper Saddle River, NJ: Merrill.

Wang, M., Reynolds, M., & Walberg, H. (1995). Serving students at the margins. *Educational Leadership, 52*(4), 12–17.

Weiner, B. (1972). *Theories of motivation.* Chicago: Rand McNally.

Wells, G. (1986). *The meaning makers: Children learning language and using language to learn.* Portsmouth, NH: Heinemann.

Wong, H., & Wong, R. (1991). *The first days of school: How to be an effective teacher.* Sunnyvale, CA: Harry K. Wong Publishers.

Yellin, D. (1983). Left brain, right brain, super brain: The wholistic model. *Reading World, 23*(1), 36–43.

Yellin, D. (1985). *Integrating the elementary language arts.* Dubuque, IA: Eddie Bowers Publishers.

Yellin, D., & Koetting, R. (1990). Literacy and poverty. *Journal of Curriculum Theorizing, 8*(4), 101–114.

Language Origins, Acquisition, and Development

4

IN THIS CHAPTER

In this chapter, you will learn about the field of linguistics. **Linguistics** is the scientific study of language. Linguistics is a broad field, and linguists study many different aspects of language. Linguists also aid teachers by suggesting a working definition of language, one that teachers can use as a guide in their instructional practices.

Some linguists focus their attention on the history of language. If you teach the upper elementary and middle school grades, you will probably want to explore how the English language developed and changed over time. The study of word origins is another fascinating aspect of the history of language.

Reading further in this chapter, you will encounter the controversy surrounding the relationship between language and thought. For example, how do verbal and written language activities enhance thought processes? As a classroom teacher, you will be expected to incorporate oral and written activities into your instruction to enhance children's critical thinking.

Later in this chapter, you will read about the controversies surrounding language acquisition, the relationships between language and thought, and some of the latest research regarding how young children's brains develop and the effect on later learning. As classroom teachers, you will be expected to keep up with these developments as you try to make your classroom a place where language abilities and critical thinking are enhanced.

Language Study

The study of language has fascinated humans for hundreds of years. Scholars throughout the world have sought to trace the origins of words in their own particular language. Some have even sought to identify the single perfect language. One bizarre experiment even involved placing an infant in an isolated environment devoid of language in an attempt to discover which, if any, language the child would produce naturally. Sadly, the child died and the project was abandoned. Today it is recognized that all languages are equally perfect for their own communicative purposes.

Linguists and teachers alike are interested in the relationship between thought and language. Does speech influence the thought processes? Can thinking be improved through verbal activities? Or are the two entities immune to each other's influence? It is important because the newest research contends that listening, speaking, reading, and especially writing enhance learning in all content areas (Tierney, 1990; Fulwiler, 1987).

The study of language is also one of the keys to understanding the theory that underlies various teaching practices, such as author's chair, literature conferences, reciprocal questioning, and process writing. Teachers need to be aware of how children use language for learning. Chapter 3 described the role of the teacher as kidwatcher; this chapter stresses the importance of observing children particularly as language users. The information you gain from watching and listening to students in turn influences the kinds of materials you use and the manner in which you teach. This is how teachers individualize instruction. This is also the key to becoming a reflective teacher.

DEFINITION OF LANGUAGE

There are many ways of defining language. The definition used in this text comes from the linguist Ronald Wardhaugh (1972): "Language is a system of arbitrary vocal symbols used for human communication (p. 14)." Breaking this definition down into its component parts provides a better understanding of the nature of language.

Language Is Systematic

Anyone who has ever head a nonsense rhyme and chuckled, seen a sign with a word intentionally misspelled (such as *Kountry Kitchen*), or corrected a child who said "That mines" intuitively recognizes that language has an organization. It is governed by certain rules. Language is also systematic. When a person violates the system or breaks the rules, language begins to dissolve; it no longer communicates clearly.

Language actually contains three systems: The phonological system deals with sounds; the semantic system deals with meaning; and the syntactic system deals with word order in sentences. It is important to note that in speaking, reading, and writing, all three systems interact to produce meaningful communication.

Language Is a System of Sounds

Phonology is a systematic study of speech sounds. It is a broad field that encompasses many aspects related to the sounds of a language (Lass, 1984). When linguists study a language, one of the first things they do is analyze the speech sounds of that language. For example, some linguists want to know exactly how certain sounds in a language are produced by the vocal chords and the placement of the tongue, teeth, and lips. Such knowledge is helpful in learning a foreign language or correcting a speech impediment. This particular branch of phonology is known as *phonetics*. The speech therapist in your school or district has studied phonetics intensively and can help you work with children who have speech difficulties. Articulation problems are one common example of a childhood speech problem. A student in your class may pronounce the /th/ sound as /d/. Through specific speech exercises, the speech therapist can help the child correct this problem.

Any language can be broken down phonetically into the distinct, separate sounds that make up words; such an individual sound is known as a phoneme. A *phoneme* is the smallest significant unit of sound in a language. To represent the significant sounds in a word, linguists place each symbol for a sound between two slash marks like this: /c/ /a/ /t/. This tells people to pronounce the sounds "cuh," "ah," and "tuh" rather than the names of the letters. Although the human voice is capable of making many different sounds, the English language is based on only about 44 phonemes.

These 44 sounds in turn are represented by 26 letters, or graphemes. *Graphemes* are written symbols that represent phonemes or sounds. As a teacher of reading, you can easily see that one of the first problems all young children face in learning to read is how to decide which sound a particular letter or combination of letters makes in a given word. If there were the same number of letters in the alphabet as there are sounds in the English language, reading could be taught as the mere memorization of the match between sound (phoneme) and symbol (grapheme). In fact, there have been some efforts in the past to create new alphabet programs for teaching English that employ this one-to-one match. None of these efforts, however, has caught on with teachers to any large extent. This is because the programs approach the sound system of English in isolation from its system of word arrangement and meaning, which is contrary to the way people communicate.

Although there is not a perfect one-to-one match between the sounds and symbols of the English language, it is nonetheless important for students to understand that there are certain conventions or rules they must follow as speakers, readers, and writers. In writing, for example, *fl, th, cr, ab, ot,* and *er* are systematic arrangements of letters that form parts of English words; however, combinations such as *bc, pk, qr, uu,* and *tp* are not. As children use language orally, experiment with writing, and see print in books, on posters, and on signs, they gradually become accustomed to and internalize the common patterns in English. As a result, they use language correctly according to its rules long before coming to school. These rules are imbedded in the brain through exposure to and practice with language. Four-year-old Aubree can tell her sister "I'll help you with that after I've finished my pudding" long before she hears about dependent clauses and prepositions.

The notion that internalized language patterns follow systematic rules is the foundation upon which classroom instruction should be based. This is implied by the hierarchical description of the functions of language given by Halliday (1982) as well as by research showing that young children learn and acquire knowledge through active participation and manipulation of concrete materials in language-rich settings (Kantrowitz & Wingert, 1985).

Language Is a System of Meaning

Semantics is the general term given to the study of meaning in a language (Miller, 1985). A person who is speaking does not use sounds randomly; such talk would sound nonsensical and would serve no purpose. Even very young children recognize this. Nor do people use sounds in isolation; instead they string phonemes together into meaningful patterns to form words. Words are not used randomly either. They are strung together in meaningful units to build sentences. Finally, sentences must be arranged in meaningful patterns to form paragraphs and extended discourse (speeches, novels, plays, and so on). All these levels are included under the heading semantics.

Linguists generally begin their study of meaning at the word level; they use the term *morphology* for the study of word meanings. When a group of phonemes is arranged to produce a meaningful unit, that unit is called a *morpheme*. Any word in the English language can be considered a morpheme: *ball, house, run, blue,* and so on. Some words, however, contain more than one morpheme. In the compound word *baseball,* there are two distinct units of meaning, *base* and *ball;* therefore, there are two morphemes in this one word. Compound words are easily recognized, but what about the word *uncovering?* There are actually three separate morphemes in this word. : the prefix *un-,* the root or base word *cover,* and the suffix *-ing.* Prefixes and suffixes are known as *bound morphemes* because they only take on meaning when they are bound or attached to words. Words such as *cover* are *free morphemes* because they contain meaning even when they are free, or standing alone. Identify the free and bound morphemes in the following words: *boys, softly, rebuild, unfriendly.*

Vocabulary lessons about root words, prefixes, and suffixes are examples of lessons in morphology. Studying about synonyms (words that have the same meaning), antonyms (words that have opposite meanings), and homonyms (words that sound alike but are spelled differently and have different meanings) is also part of morphology lessons.

Language Is a System of Arrangement

Syntax provides the rules or system for arranging words into orderly and meaningful sentences (Miller, 1985). This is true in both written and spoken language. To understand the importance of the syntactic system, consider the following example:

> The dog bit the man.
> The man bit the dog.

Although the two sentences contain the same words, the new arrangement of words in the second sentence obviously alters its meaning. Other times the words in a sentence can be rearranged without altering its underlying meaning. Though the word order is different, the following sentences express the same meaning:

> The girl gathered the flowers.
> The flowers were gathered by the girl.

If there were no rules for the ordering of words, any random arrangement could constitute language. But this is not the case. *The by gathered flowers girl* is clearly nonsense or a nonsentence. In school, the rules of syntax are taught under the heading of *grammar;* sentences that do not make sense or are missing a word are considered *ungrammatical.*

It should be apparent by now that the semantic system for meaning is related to the syntactic system of word order. The two are parallel and dependent on one another, as demonstrated by the research done on the language behaviors of young children (Lindfors, 1985). Children simply and naturally use language in meaningful ways. Even very young children who are just acquiring language do not go around creating nonsensical sentences, at least not for long. And even though they may not be able to define the terms *adverb* and *preposition,* they still can recognize what is and is not a meaningful sentence.

The systematic nature of language at the phonological, semantic, and syntactic levels is also what makes language predictable. When presented with an oral sentence such as "The young ——— ran across the street," very young children can make meaningful predictions based on their intuitive knowledge of language. Similarly, when shown the letter *q* followed by a blurred mark (perhaps a printing error), school-age children who have had a few years experience with print can predict what letter will follow. All readers predict on the basis of their desire to make sense out of what they see on the printed page. Making sense out of print is what drives the reading comprehension process. Reading authority Robert Tierney (1990) has put it this way:

> Readers use their background knowledge in conjunction with their expectations to develop meanings by continuously relating their views and experiences to the ideas, characters, and events suggested by the text. They visualize people and events, tie together ideas, anticipate outcomes, ask themselves questions, assess the plausibility of understandings, and revise their ideas as they mentally revise the text or replace it with others. (p. 38)

BEYOND THE CLASSROOM

Collect oral language samples from preschool children. Transcribe these samples and then analyze them. Are they meaningful? Do they contain grammatical errors? Discuss how they relate to the notions of the three systems of language. What evidence can you see of a positive language environment and the interrelationship between speech and print?

Vignette *in the classroom*

Joan Warren is a teacher consultant in South Brunswick, New Jersey. She believes that young children learn best through "active, hands-on teaching methods like games and dramatic play," that "youngsters' social growth is as essential as their academic achievement," and that teaching "should fit the child instead of making the child fit the school" (Kantrowitz & Wingert, 1985, p. 50).

Observers of the Greenbrook school in South Brunswick see youngsters scattered throughout the room, working in small groups on cooperative projects of their own choosing. The children talk as they work. They use language to interact with their peers, to ask questions, to request things, to direct others. As they play with geometric puzzles, shape blocks, dolls, and trucks, they continue to talk. They also use language to learn about language. Every day for about a half-hour, they listen to a story read by their teacher. During story time, they ask questions about the words they see in print; later they act out parts of the book. Their

knowledge of print grows as they begin to recognize familiar words in other books and magazines and on boxes and candy wrappers. Print is as natural to the learning environment as talking. Children also ask about words and use words in their writing as naturally as they speak to one another. Their focus is on meaningful communication; the teacher serves as a guide, resource, and helper as needed.

In another school, children are seated at separate desks. The desks are arranged in rows, one child behind the other, with the teacher at the front of the room. All eyes are on the teacher. The students chant in unison a rule from their workbook; then they bend their heads over their papers and carefully copy the rule into their notebooks. There is no talking in the class. The teacher walks up and down the aisle to check that everyone has copied the rule correctly. Some children are having difficulty and must start over again; others have finished early and look toward the clock on the wall, waiting for recess.

Language Is Arbitrary and Symbolic

Though the three systems of language can be used to predict certain word spellings and word arrangements, the individual meanings of words cannot be predicted from the sound or appearance of those words. This is because meaning must be assigned, and each language assigns meaning in a slightly different way, using different sounds and different symbols. For example, there is no inherent connection among the sounds /d/ /o/ /g/, the symbols *d-o-g*, and the furry, tail-wagging animal that barks. This is what is meant by the idea that language is arbitrary. Figure 4.1 shows some common words written in five different languages.

Figure 4.1	Common words in five languages.			
ENGLISH	FRENCH	SPANISH	GERMAN	CHINESE
dog	chien	perro	Hund	狗 *gŏu*
cat	chat	gato	Katze	猫 *mūo*
one	un	uno	eins	一 *yī*
two	deux	dos	zwei	二 *èr*
boy	garçon	muchacho, niño	Junge	男孩 *nán hái*
girl	fille	muchacha, niña	Madchen	女孩 *nŭ hái*
book	livre	libro	Buch	書 *shū*
green	vert(e)	verde	grun	綠 *lù*
apple	pomme	manzana	Apfel	苹果 *píng gŭo*

It is obvious that objects and ideas can be represented in many different ways through language. But no one way is more effective than another. This means that no single language is either superior or inferior to any other language. However, throughout history people have believed—and fought bloody wars over their belief—that their own language was superior to that of their neighbors. The language issue becomes even more complex because of the multiple variations, or dialects, within a single language (discussed in Chapter 2). For example, the New England dialect, the Southern dialect, and the Midwestern dialect are just a few of the speech variations used in the United States. Again, as with separate languages, no one dialect is superior or inferior to another; they are all merely variations within a language.

When spoken languages take on written form, the use of symbols also comes into play; in this sense language is also symbolic. The phonological system must be represented graphically for there to be a written system of language. Once again, every language chooses its own symbols. Thus speakers of English use an alphabet of 26 letters to represent their language, while the Chinese employ 3,000 characters (Bromley, 1988). Written languages differ in other ways. Israeli children learning Hebrew read and write from right to left; Chinese children read their language from top to bottom. Thus the symbols and arrangement of symbols can vary greatly from one language to another. This is another example of the arbitrary nature of language.

Taken together, the arbitrary and symbolic nature of language is what makes learning a new language both challenging and fascinating. Because "words create images of objects and things" (DeHaven, 1983, p. 10), language has a tremendous creative capacity. Language can be used to tell stories, make up jokes, persuade, and surprise people. This creative capacity of language should form the essence of what goes on in the language arts classroom.

> ### BEYOND THE CLASSROOM
>
> Symbols that represent meaning do not have to be letters or words. In advertising, for example, symbols are used to represent entire products. Collect examples of symbols used on television, in magazines and newspapers, on billboards, and on T-shirts. How can these symbols be used to teach children about the symbolic nature of language?

Language Is Vocal

For linguists, speech is primary. In all societies, speech precedes the written form of language development. This is not to minimize the importance of writing but rather to put it in its historical perspective. Writing systems developed only as a means to give permanence to spoken sounds; not all societies, even in modern times, have a written language. Therefore, oral language forms the foundation for later literacy instruction.

One way of understanding the importance of speech for later literacy development involves studying the vocal patterns or rhythmic nature of speech. *Intonation* is a term describing how a speaker expresses emotion and feeling with words. This is a primary way or conveying a message with words. The three main aspects of intonation are *stress*, *pitch*, and *juncture*, which are also aspects of the phonological system.

Stress is a term meaning "accent." It refers to the degree of emphasis placed on certain syllables, words, or phrases within sentences. Stress influences meaning, as the following examples demonstrate:

Will John *really* be at the party?
Will *John* really be at the party?

By emphasizing one word more than another in a sentence, a speaker conveys a slightly different meaning. Accenting different syllables within the same word can even produce new words with different meanings:

Margie was *present* at the concert.
Margie will pre*sent* the award to the winner.

The term *pitch* refers to the rise-and-fall patterns in voices, particularly at the ends of sentences. By altering the level of his or her voice, a person can also slightly alter the meaning of the sentence. Pitch is represented in print with punctuation, as in the following examples:

Alice is beautiful.
Alice is beautiful!
Alice is beautiful?

The first sentence is read in a normal tone of voice. The second sentence causes a speaker to raise the pitch of her or his voice. And the third sentence alters the pitch still more to ask a question. Skilled writers use punctuation, varied spellings (such as *we gonna go*), and slang expressions to mimic different speech patters. When children are encouraged to do the same in their writing, they begin to see some of the relationships between spoken and written language.

The term *juncture* refers to the way speakers pause or terminate the flow of speech, particularly within and between sentences. Notice how the varying use of punctuation causes you to pause at different places in the following sentences and subsequently to alter the meaning of the sentences, though the words are exactly the same:

Woman without her man is nothing.

Woman: without her, man is nothing.

BEYOND THE CLASSROOM

Tape-record some speech samples of children and adults. Listen to the intonation patterns and try to represent them in writing. Transcribing vocal speech into written form is a good way to understand the importance and function of punctuation. What differences do you notice between the patterns in adult and child language?

Understanding the vocal intonation patterns of the English language provides a better appreciation of punctuation. It is not uncommon for two different writers to punctuate the same sentence differently depending on the emphasis and meaning they are striving for. Although there are certain restrictions on the use of punctuation, there is also a great degree of literary license. Children learn this by experimenting with language.

There are certain aspects of vocal language that cannot be represented by punctuation. These are the nonverbal gestures, or body language, that often accompany speech; linguists call these *paralinguistic* features of language. Body language is important, particularly in dramatic presentation, because it too conveys meaning. Among the more common examples of body language that accompany vocal speech are postures, hand gestures, and facial expressions. Squared shoulders, a chest thrust forward, a pointed finger gesture, and eyes narrowed into a glare imply something about a speaker.

Vignette in the classroom

Mr. Baron's third-grade classroom is located in a large city in the Southwest. The school population is a mixture of white, African-American, Hispanic, Native American, and, most recently, Vietnamese and Cambodian children. In Mr. Baron's class alone, there are children who speak English, Spanish, Navaho, Apache, French, Vietnamese, and Cambodian. On the walls of the room are posters and signs that reflect all the different languages spoken. Throughout the day, children use their native tongues as well as English. Mr. Baron regularly asks the students, "How do you say that in English?" If the child does not know, he or she goes to one of the many bilingual paraprofessionals in the building to get the translation. These students are learning English, but there is no stigma attached to the use of their native language. In fact, being bilingual or even trilingual in this school is valued and seen as something very positive.

Language Is Used for Human Communication

The ending of the definition of language has two parts. First is the notion that language exists for the purpose of communication: The content of the message is more important than the style of the delivery. This is true of spoken as well as written language. Second, language distinguishes humans from other animal species. Though they may communicate in various ways—lion's roar, whale's song, bee's dance—animals come nowhere close to the communication abilities of humans.

HALLIDAY'S SEVEN FUNCTIONS OF LANGUAGE

The purpose of language is communication. A well-known description of language by the British linguist Michael Halliday is enlightening on this point. Halliday's study of the language used by his son Nigel and his writings on grammar, the social significance of language, and the role of language and meaning have influenced the work of many scholars in the fields of linguistics and language teaching (Halliday, 1975, 1976, 1977, 1978, 1982).

Halliday proposed that a child defines language in terms of its meaning potential and its usefulness. The more the child hears and uses language, the more she or he becomes aware of the power of language. Halliday described the child's growing awareness of the significance of language as a series of stages leading to adult language. The stages are described in terms of the different functions that language serves. This is similar to the sociolinguistic view that children's language functions develop through a process of interaction with others, primarily adult language users. Study Figure 4.2 and consider the same three questions that Halliday asked himself in formulating his model: How is language used by the young child? What purposes does language serve? How are these purposes achieved through listening, speaking, reading, and writing? Following is a discussion of the seven language functions.

Figure 4.2 *Halliday's seven functions of language.*

FUNCTION	CHILD'S LANGUAGE EXAMPLE	ENHANCING EXPERIENCES
1. Instrumental (satisfy needs)	"I want that cookie."	Simple problem solving; business letters
2. Regulatory (instrument of control)	"Do this first."	Role playing; games
3. Interactional (social maintenance)	"Let's do this together."	Conversational play; friendly letters; chatter groups
4. Personal (express individuality)	"I like this the best."	Journals; discussions; tape recordings; show-and-tell
5. Heuristic (explore outside environment)	"Why is it snowing?"	Interviews; discussions; question-and-answer games
6. Imaginative (create own environment)	"Let's pretend that we're lost and . . . "	Make-believe; dress-up; dramatic acting
7. Representational/Informative (convey information to others)	"This is my new Barbie."	Show-and-tell; sharing discussions

Source: Adapted from M. Halliday (1977), *Explorations in the Functions of Language.* Copyright © Elsevier Science Publishers BV.

1. Instrumental. The *instrumental function* is seen quite early in life when a child discovers that language is a way of satisfying basic needs. When a child is hungry and cries, his mother nurses him. When he falls and screams in pain, someone comforts him. When he actually begins to use meaningful words, he further discovers that language can be a tool or an instrument to satisfy a need, state a wish, or obtain some basic object, such as food. The child has discovered that language can be useful.

Halliday gives the following example to make this point. In the 1960s, zoologists studying animal intelligence were amazed that when a chimpanzee was given three short sticks, it was able to construct one long stick to poke at a bunch of bananas hanging from the roof of its cage. Halliday contends that faced with the same problem, the human child constructs the sentence "I want a banana." At that point, the child is aware that language is a powerful tool for meeting needs.

Halliday surmises that the child subconsciously understands that if language can be used to meet his or her needs, it can also be used to control the behavior of others. This awareness leads to the next level.

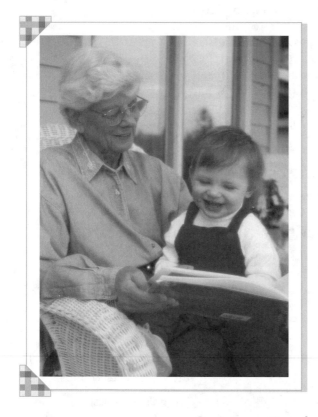

2. Regulatory. The *regulatory function* occurs once a child realizes the power of language to control others. There is no end to the demands that this child makes of adults and peers: "Pick me up." "Tie my shoe." "Give me that toy." The discovery of the regulatory function of language leads the child to give instructions and orders. This is particularly evident in the play of young children, especially when they are learning and then changing the rules of a new game. Halliday calls this the "do as I tell you" stage.

Basil Bernstein, another well-known British linguist, described an incident between a mother and child that exemplifies how language can be used to control behavior (Halliday, 1976). Upon leaving the supermarket, the mother discovered that her little darling had taken something without telling her. A series of regulatory uses of language followed: "You mustn't ever take anything without paying for it." "I'm so disappointed in you." "You should know better than to take things." "If you ever do that again, I'll . . . " (p. 5). By itself, this one incident has little significance, but over time the child internalizes these rules to control her or his behavior. Later the child uses similar language to control the behavior of younger siblings and peers.

3. Interactional. The *interactional function* occurs as a result of awareness of the regulatory function of language and opportunities to play with other children. It eventually leads the child to understand that language is the way people maintain relationships with others. Halliday refers to this as the "me and you" or "let's do this together" function. It is the way in which young children form friendships and adolescents bond into close-knit groups. Teenage cliques are defined by their way of talking among themselves; newcomers are automatically outsiders until they learn the language of the group.

4. Personal. The *personal function* is closely tied to the interactional function. In addition to being a way to bond with a group, language is also the way to stand out. It is a way to form and express individuality: "I like vanilla fudge ripple the best." "I love to swim, but I'm afraid of water snakes." "I think fast cars are great." Through language, people express their opinions, feelings, attitudes, and emotions. In responding to others, a child is also becoming a unique individual. Thus language also serves a very important role in the development of personality and in answering the question, "Who am I?"

5. Heuristic. The *heuristic function* literally concerns seeking information. Halliday terms this the "tell me why" function of language. "Why is the sky blue?" "Why do I have to go to bed at eight o'clock?" "Why do I have to eat my vegetables?" Through the heuristic function of language, the child grows intellectually by acquiring new knowledge. Growing awareness of the larger environment leads to growing appreciation of the value of language in asking questions of others. Without language as a guide, everything would have to be experienced firsthand, often with disastrous consequences. ("Why can't I touch the stove, Mommy?")

All children engage in this extensive questioning behavior with parents and other significant adults. It is the primary way in which they learn about the world. However, not all parents respond to children's questions in the same manner. It is significant to note that the question–answer routine begun at home is also a characteristic of school learning. Halliday suggests that the extent of the "parent's linguistic attention to the child" correlates positively with success in school, particularly during the first grade. For example, at home the child learns the meaning of words such as *question*, *answer*, *knowing*, and *understanding*. These are important terms to know and use; without them, it is difficult to be successful in school. Halliday refers to this as the "language for talking about language" (1977).

6. Imaginative. The *imaginative function* occurs when children discover that language can also be used to create one's own environment. This is the world of make-believe, or "let's pretend that . . . " It is the basis of solitary and eventually group play. Imaginative language can also function to maintain an internal world, carried around by talking to oneself, humming a favorite sound, or smiling over a riddle. Through language, the child creates a unique world, a world of fantasy, of princesses and dragons, of dreams and poetry. Words such as *make-believe* and *pretend* enter the vocabulary. The imaginative function is thus also a primary way for the child to express creativity.

7. Representational/Informative. The *representational/informative function* is the function of language in which information is conveyed to others. In one sense, it completes the communication cycle that begins with the child using language to satisfy basic needs. Sending messages, giving reports, describing objects, and helping others are all part of the representational or informative function of language. This more complex and sophisticated use of language characterizes adult language. No longer is language used just to satisfy basic needs, ask questions of others, or socialize. These are all very important functions in themselves, but now language takes on the role of conveying important information to others who require it. The child is becoming an adult. Furthermore, the representational function of language is most often called upon in school settings. Without question, the school is a language environment that demands much of a youngster's language ability.

Halliday's seven functions of language have influenced many scholars because they provide a useful way for grouping and talking about language. This model can also be used to describe some of the ways in which children learn about language in school. For example, Frank Smith (1977) and Gay Pinnell (1985) have developed approaches to language instruction in the

Not the school, nor the teachers, but the student is the preponderant factor in education.

JAMES WELDON JOHNSON

schools based upon Halliday's original model. Laminack (1990) used Halliday's functions of language to describe the language growth of his son Zachary from 13 months to 2½ years, as shown in Figure 4.3.

Figure 4.3   *Language use and the seven functions of language.*

INSTRUMENTAL
Language for getting things done and for satisfying one's needs

"Dad, I want my pencil to write down a few things I need." After hearing his mom say she would make a list before shopping. (3 years, 5 months)

REGULATORY
Language for controlling the behavior of others

While playing with a Fisher-Price Main Street, Zachary moved the dog off the sidewalk outside the pet shop. When asked if someone had bought the dog, he responded, "The dogs have to go. I wrote a sign: No dogs allowed on the streets." (4 years, 3 months)

INTERACTIONAL
Language for maintaining and establishing relationships

Today Zachary wrote his first message for an audience other than himself. He scribbled across a church bulletin, then looked at me and said, "Daddy, I wrote you a letter. It says, I love mine Dad." (2 years, 5 months)

PERSONAL
Language for expressing personality or individuality

On Sunday mornings Zachary frequently climbs into our bed and snuggles up until he can get one of us to wake up and talk to him. I asked upon his arrival, "Who will get up and make our breakfast?" He responded, "Not I, said the pig." Then he giggled. (1 year, 4 months)

HEURISTIC
Language for finding things out and for exploring the environment

Today in the parking lot of a shopping center Zachary asked, "What do these big yellow words say?" *"Fire lane,"* I responded. "What means *fire lane?*" he asked. I explained as we walked into the store. (3 years, 10 months)

IMAGINATIVE
Language as a means of creating a world of one's own

Recently at preschool Zachary and one of his friends, Melissa, have begun to play McDonald's. He and Melissa hold hands and walk around the playground. If asked, they were going to McDonald's and would be back on Sunday. Occasionally, they took orders and made deliveries. (1 year, 9 months)

REPRESENTATIONAL/INFORMATIVE
Language for conveying information

Glenda, Zachary, and I were sitting around the table nearing the end of the evening meal. I said to Glenda, "Do you plan to have any i-c-e-c-r-e-a-m or p-o-p-c-o-r-n later?" Zachary beamed and announced, "I want some p-o-p-k-o-y." When I questioned what he thought that was, he grinned and said, "Candy." (2 years, 1 month)

Halliday's model can also be considered as a description of how language develops. The four major conclusions that can be drawn from this model are:

1. Learning to talk is inextricably tied to meaning.
2. Language develops primarily in a social setting.
3. Language is both a personal tool and a social instrument.
4. Language development from childhood to adulthood is dependent on social interaction with other language users.

> ## IN & BEYOND THE CLASSROOM
>
> After studying and discussing Halliday's seven language functions, observe a classroom of young children. Listen and tape-record their language. Try categorizing the language samples according to Halliday's seven functions. What implications for instruction does this model have?

A Brief History of the English Language

Linguists and foreign language specialists are continually noting the vitality, vicissitudes, and creativity of language. Scholars use language as one window onto the pageant that is the history of humankind, for language helps partially answer the questions, Who am I? and Where have I come from? A brief look at the history of the English language provides a better understanding of the history and linguistic roots of Anglo-American culture and an additional appreciation for the importance of language study.

Any study of American English must first look toward Britain; the British in turn look to all of Europe and Asia for their linguistic roots. Indeed all of the world's languages, no matter how different they may sound and look, are related (Meyers & Hoffman, 1979). English, for example, is one branch of the Indo-European family of languages, which also includes Iranian, Armenian, Slavic, Indian, and Germanic languages.

This study of the English language begins nearly 5,000 years ago, when hundreds of small nomadic tribes roamed the plains of central Europe and Asia. As these tribes came in contact with one another, they often fought, perhaps in part because they could not understand each other's language. Of central importance was the migration of one of those tribes, the Teutons, to the area that today includes Germany and parts of Scandinavia. From a single Teutonic dialect grew the modern languages of German and Dutch, which later greatly influenced the English language. Figure 4.4 shows a linguistic map of Europe.

Linguists and historians alike divide the history of the English language into three major periods: Old English (449–1066), Middle English (1066–1500), and Modern English (1500 to the present).

OLD ENGLISH

Around 600 B.C. the Celts, one of many European tribes, invaded and eventually settled in the British Isles. Thus the first language of England was Celtic. Although the linguistic impact of the Celts was minimal, the names of the river Thames and the city of London can be traced to the original Celtic tongue. However, the real linguistic invasion did not occur until 55 B.C., when Julius Caesar, at the head of the armies of Rome, conquered the still-scattered and disorganized Celtic tribes. For the next 500 years, the Romans remained in England, exercising enormous influences on life in the British Isles, not the least of which was linguistic. Such common words as *colony, village,* and *agenda* come directly from Latin, the language of the Romans. So too does the word *circus*, from the horse and chariot races held at Circus Maximus. But eventually conflicts closer to Rome forced the Romans to withdraw their troops from England.

Figure 4.4

Indo-European family of languages.

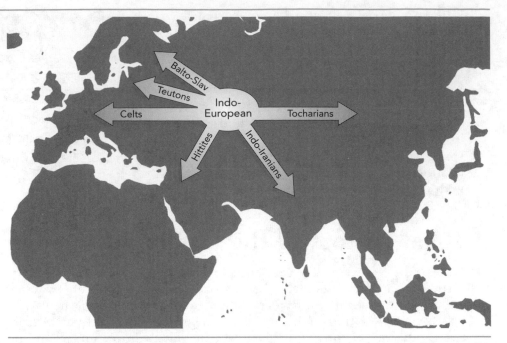

Source: D. Yellin (1983a), "Learning to Spell." Reprinted with permission of David Yellin and the *Daily Oklahoman.*

The withdrawal of the Roman camps (*castra* is the Latin for *camp*, as in such English place-names as *Lancaster*) produced a power vacuum, and a new series of invasions occurred. Beginning in the sixth century A.D., more Germanic tribes, each speaking its own dialect, crossed the English Channel in hopes of dominating a part of the British Isles. Among the more successful of these tribes were the Saxons, the Angles, and the Jutes. The battles of these tribes are described in the King Arthur legends and form a part of British literary history. The Angles even gave their name to England, which was originally Angleland (Yellin, 1983a).

During this period the Saxons, Angles, and Jutes adopted many of the Roman terms used by the Celtic tribes, such as *inch, mile,* and *street.* This process of word changes and exchanges among various languages, called *borrowing,* is one of the most fundamental concepts of language development. Word borrowing is the raw material for the study of language. Borrowings from foreign tongues also explain some of the spelling demons that bedevil young children learning to write English. But most of all these borrowings are what enliven a language and tie it to the great family of languages.

The Old English period is also significant for the most famous early written work, the epic poem *Beowulf.* This poem, written in the Saxon dialect during the eighth century, is studied today not only as a great work of literature but also as a source of clues about the changes that the English language has undergone in morphology (word meanings) as well as orthography (writing system). Some Old English words are still recognizable in their modern forms, such as *tun/town* and *boc/book,* but many words from this period look quite strange to the modern reader.

MIDDLE ENGLISH

The Old English period ended and the Middle English period began in 1066 when William, duke of Normandy, invaded England. William the Conqueror crowned himself the new king of England and insisted that his language, Norman French, be accepted as the official language in the English royal court.

Later he made French the sole medium of instruction in the English school system. Thus with a single stroke, the English language was greatly altered once again. For the next 400 years, French remained the elite language in England, although the masses continued to speak their Anglo-Saxon dialect.

During this period of French occupation, many French words became Anglicized or altered, including *preach, beef, baron,* and *crime.* Other words adopted from the French include *literature, liquor, servant,* and *science.* At the same time, significant changes were taking place in the spelling and meaning of English words, in part because of word borrowings but also because of the influence of the great writers of the time. Geoffrey Chaucer's *Canterbury Tales,* written during this period, is another good example of how the English writing system has changed over time.

MODERN ENGLISH

The current period in the history of the English language was ushered in by one of the most prolific writers of all time, William Shakespeare (1564–1616). Shakespeare lived in an age in which new ideas were spreading rapidly across Europe and throughout England. This cultural rebirth, or Renaissance, was a period of reverence and support for literature, art, and music. Today Shakespeare's plays and sonnets are well known and studied in high schools across the country. Less well known is the fact that Shakespeare was also a great inventor of words, perhaps the greatest of all time. Some scholars credit him with inventing over 1,700 words, including *assassination, castigate, critical, misplaced, monumental,* and *impartial.* This is another beautiful example of the vitality of language: It not only includes borrowings from other languages but also allows for the creation of new words.

Another great influence on the English language was William Caxton's invention of the printing press in 1476. Before the widespread use of machine printing, handwritten works employed variant spellings for the same words, depending on who was doing the copying. But with the printing press came a new consistency to the spelling of written language, which in turn influenced literacy instruction. And the influence of printed books was also felt beyond the shores of England. The early colonists of the New World established a printing press in Cambridge, Massachusetts, as early as 1683.

As more and more books were printed in England and the colonies, a comprehensive reference work to aid the spelling, pronunciation, and precise meaning of English words was needed. Samuel Johnson's *Dictionary of the English Language,* first published in 1775, became the forerunner of the great dictionaries that further aided in establishing consistent standards for the language of a rapidly growing society.

ENGLISH IN THE UNITED STATES

In the United States, the English language continued to change. Words from other languages became part of American English through borrowings and alterations. For example, European place-names such as *Hamburg, Frankfurt, Tangiers,* and *Turkey* were applied to items of cuisine: *hamburger, frankfurter, tangerine,* and *turkey.* Contact with Native Americans led to the incorporation of other new words: *raccoon, squaw, pecan, chipmunk, moose, skunk, canoe, moccasin,* and *succotash.* French fur trappers added words such as *chowder, rapids, pioneer,* and *prairie.* In the Southwest, settlers adopted such Spanish terms as *fiesta, parade, siesta, rodeo, lasso,* and *ranch.*

Today many place-names in the United States reflect the concepts of borrowing and altering. They also give young people a feel for the origins of their country as well as for the English language. Figure 4.5 shows some common place-names borrowed from other languages.

Figure 4.5	NATIVE AMERICAN	Yakima, WA	Tallahassee, FL
		Ottawa, KS	Massachusetts
Origins of place-names in the United States.		Tahlequah, OK	Connecticut
		Shawnee, OK	Oklahoma
		Chickasha, OK	Missouri
		Omaha, NE	Kansas
		Mandan, ND	
	EUROPEAN	Moscow, ID	Florence, AL
		Geneva, NY	Athens, GA
		Rome, NY	Dublin, GA
	FRENCH	Des Moines, IA	Eau Claire, WI
		Baton Rouge, LA	Montpelier, VT
		New Orleans, LA	
	SPANISH	San Antonio, TX	Las Cruces, NM
		San Diego, CA	Las Vegas, NV
		Los Angeles, CA	San Francisco, CA
		El Paso, TX	Pueblo, CO

Another aspect of American English relates to one of the most tragic periods in U.S. history, that of slavery. Around 1630, the British started trading for slaves in Africa and bringing them to the New World to serve the colonists. Later, with the development of the great plantations in the South, the slave trade increased enormously. The many Africans brought across the ocean spoke dozens of different languages. Thrown together in horrible slave quarters, the Africans had to develop a common language to communicate; later they had to develop a means of communicating with their English-speaking masters. The language that developed is what linguists call pidgin. A *pidgin language* occurs when speakers of different languages use the grammar and pronunciation of one language along with the vocabulary of another language to form a composite language (Malmstrom, 1977). Eventually the pidgin language of the first slaves was passed on to the next generation, who in turn passed it on to their children. Such a mixture of language forms is called a *creole*, or mixed, language. Today the Sea Islands off the coast of South Carolina are inhabited primarily by slaves' descendants, who speak a unique creole dialect known as Gullah.

BEYOND THE CLASSROOM

Create an outline wall map of the United States. On the map, add interesting place-names and their origins. Note how many different countries contribute to the many English-sounding names you may take for granted. Encourage your students to select a place-name they are familiar with and trace its origins. Perhaps begin with the name of the state in which you live. Figure 4.6 lists some references to begin your study of word origins.

Figure 4.6	Alexander, H. (1969). *The Story of Our Language.* Garden City, NY: Doubleday.
	Asimov, I. (1968). *Words from History.* Boston: Houghton Mifflin.
Sources for origins of place-names.	Morris, W., & Morris, M. (1967). *Dictionary of Word and Phrase Origins.* New York: Harper & Row.
	Pizer, V. (1976). *Ink, Ark, and All That: How American Places Got Their Names.* New York: G. P. Putnam's Sons.

Vignette *in the classroom*

Mrs. Hightower teaches language arts and social studies to the fifth-graders in a small, rural school in eastern Oklahoma. In the past, she has used separate textbooks for each subject and has taught them during separate times of the day. This year she has decided to experiment with a unit approach that encompasses content and skills from both the language arts and social studies curriculums. First she combines the periods to give her one large block of time for language arts and social studies. Then she asks her students what they would like to study that combines these two subject areas. The students decide to study their own state, from settlement to statehood.

They begin their unit by studying the map of Oklahoma and identifying specific place-names that they recognize. Many of the names are of Native American origin, as this part of the Midwest was once designated by the government as Indian Territory, an area of settlement for the tribes displaced from the eastern portion of the

United States. Some of the students in Mrs. Hightower's room are Native Americans and have heard family stories of the Trail of Tears and the Oklahoma Land Run. They share their grandparents' exciting firsthand accounts of life in the early Oklahoma settlements. From studying the map further, the students discover place-names, such as *Stroud*, whose origins can be traced back to cities in Europe. The study of word origins is also a lesson in geography and history.

As the unit grows, the students clamor for visits to the school and public libraries to do research to supplement the firsthand interviews with members of the community. Mrs. Hightower is amazed at how rapidly her students' research skills improve through using the Internet, encyclopedia, dictionary, atlas, and other reference materials. Classroom textbook lessons on how to do research have always met with great resistance in the past; now the students can't wait to get to the library to look up unusual place-names.

Language and Cognition

How does the brain actually work? What is the role of language in thought? For example, does the way people speak influence the way they think? The question of the relationship between thought and language is an old one. Aristotle believed that a person's perception of the world was transmitted as sensations throughout the body as well as the mind. The cognitive processes were viewed as intrinsic to the brain and immune from environmental influences such as language. Thus Aristotle concluded that there was no connection between thought and language. This classical Greek view persisted unaltered until the seventeenth century, when the philosopher John Locke theorized that internal mental activities were composed of individual ideas, which in turn had been derived from external sensations. Therefore, Locke argued, internal thought must be related to external stimuli such as language. But the nature of this relationship remained to be determined by later scholars (Carroll, 1972; Vinacke, 1974).

Eventually psychologists also began to investigate observable body movements as a clue to understanding the mechanism of thought. Early behavioral psychologists, such as J. B. Watson, believed that movements of the tongue, lips, and vocal chords responded to the thought processes in some manner. For Watson, thought was inseparable from speech. The physical movements of the speech mechanism he viewed as the overt manifestation of covert thinking (Carroll, 1972; Vinacke, 1974).

The purpose of education is to awaken joy in creative expression and knowledge.

ALBERT EINSTEIN

THREE COGNITIVE THEORISTS

More recently, the nature of the relationship between language and thought has been crystallized through the work of three psychologists: Lev Vygotsky, Jerome Bruner, and Jean Piaget. The research and theories of these individuals have contributed to knowledge about language and thought, which in turn has greatly affected the latest developments in language arts instruction.

Lev Vygotsky

Lev Vygotsky (1962) observed young children in Russia as they used language in play and other social situations. Based on these observations, Vygotsky argued that thought development was partly determined by language development. According to his theory, when children talk, either to themselves or to others, they are shaping their internal thought patterns. The development of the child's ability to think out loud is thus the key to the development of complex thought processes (Hennings, 1989). One significant aspect of this development is the notion of **egocentric speech:** talk not directed to another object or person. Egocentric speech, Vygotsky argued, is the key transition period leading toward true thought as characterized by inner speech. Inner thought processes, he believed, are structured by inner speech and later by overt speech. Viewing speech and thought in this deterministic manner, Vygotsky argued that improving the linguistic abilities of children also improves their overall cognitive abilities.

Central to Vygotsky's views is the influence of adults on children. His observations led him to conclude that children's interactions with adults not only shape their language patterns but also influence their thought patterns. At first, children can understand adult language but cannot reproduce it or generate complex ideas. Later, as speech is internalized, it is used to control thinking. In this sense Vygotsky, like Halliday, believed that verbal interactions between children and adults help children "learn how to mean." Meaningful social interactions with adults spur cognitive as well as verbal development in the child. This theory, called the **Social Interaction Theory of Development,** has greatly influenced the current whole language movement (Bayer, 1990).

Another key concept of Vygotsky's theory is the notion of the *zone of proximal development*. This refers to the gap between what the child knows and can express on her or his own and what the adult must provide in terms of information and language structures. Children need adults to grow linguistically and cognitively. In a sense, the child is always one step behind the adult, straining to keep up. With the proper adult models, the child's language and thought continue to develop; without them, the child's thought processes are severely limited.

Jerome Bruner

Jerome Bruner (1961, 1962, 1978) saw language as a tool of the intellect and a cognitive instrument capable of transforming experience. Language, in Bruner's view, aids reasoning powers by freeing the mind from total dependence on the appearance of reality. For example, the child who can verbalize a situation is not easily fooled by a parent who hides a ball and claims it has disappeared. Thus, according to Bruner, one role of language is to activate thought and concept development. Concept development involves the creation of **schemata,** or models in the brain, which store information necessary for higher-level thinking. The older the child, the greater the role language plays in the creation of these schemata. In one experiment, children were asked to sort pictures into categories. The experimenter noted that children ages two to six categorize only on the basis of color, shape, or size. Around age seven, there is a shift from reliance on perceptual appearances to reliance on symbolic representation. Consequently, older children can explain their grouping strategy by saying, "They're all tools." The term *tools* permits a form of classification higher than color, shape, or size, all of which are grounded on physical perception.

Bruner also believed in the importance of social interaction for a child's linguistic and cognitive growth. Building on Vygotsky's earlier work, Bruner argued that the child uses the language of adults to move from one stage of language development to another; thus the child's language leans and builds upon the adult's. This process Bruner termed *scaffolding* (1978, 1987). The linguistic scaffold, or structure provided by the adult, allows the child to construct language and internalize the rules of language through experience.

Bruner's theories on thought development and schema formation can be seen in the classroom when teachers use schematic diagrams, semantic maps, and web diagrams. Though these terms are used slightly differently, the processes they represent all include similar steps: A verbal brainstorming session leads to a visual representation, which eventually creates a mental picture that the student uses to store information suitable for later problem solving. In the elementary classroom, diagramming, mapping, and webbing are used to help children better comprehend text structures they have read, lectures they will hear, and written work they wish to produce (Pearson & Johnson, 1985).

Jean Piaget

Jean Piaget (1952, 1959, 1964, 1965, 1967) observed children in Geneva, Switzerland, over a period of many years, during which time he formulated his theories on learning and development. Piaget's central theory is that a human is a biological system, structured by laws of growth and development that can only be modified within limits. Thought and language are also rooted in this sequential development. Though Piaget granted that language may reflect and to an extent facilitate cognitive development, he stressed that language cannot account for thought. Unlike Vygotsky, Piaget argued that thought precedes and is separate from language.

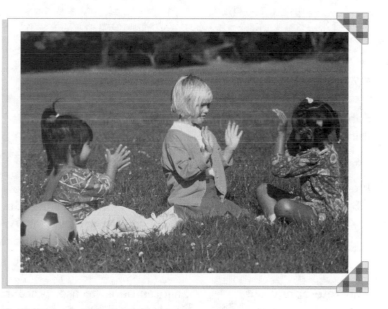

Recall from Chapter 2 that Piaget took a developmental view of cognitive growth and language development. He saw mental growth occurring parallel to physical growth. It begins with the newborn infant listening to the sounds of the environment and continues as the child imitates sounds and creates new sounds while exploring language. With increased age also comes vocabulary growth. Joan Tough (1984) found that children on average use about 3 words at 12 months, 20 words at 18 months, 300 words at 24 months, 900–1,000 words at 36 months, at least 2,000 words by the age of 5, and 4,000 words by the age of 7.

Piaget described child language in terms of egocentric speech and socialized language. Egocentric speech only takes into account the child's view. In communication settings, this means failing to listen to others or respond to others effectively. Egocentricity also helps explain young children's limitations in projecting beyond immediate, concrete situations (Tough, 1984).

Both language and thought are constrained by egocentricity initially, but as children grow older and become more aware of others, they need to give and receive information; peers become more important. Children's speech and thought therefore adapt through interactions with other speakers and thinkers. Eventually this leads to the socialized speech so important for Vygotsky's view of cognitive growth.

Three terms are associated with Piaget's view of language development: assimilation, accommodation, and equilibrium. **Assimilation** occurs when new information and perceptions are organized into already existing schemata. Assimilation is therefore a continuous process through which an individual integrates new information into older or established patterns of thought. But what happens when the child encounters a new piece of information or engages in a new experience unrelated to previous ones? Since this new information cannot be structured into an existing pattern, a new pattern must be created. This process Piaget called **accommodation,** a continuous process through which new informational patterns are created in the mind to store and utilize new objects, facts, or experiences. **Equilibrium** is a continuous process involving the harmonious interplay between assimilation and accommodation.

Another of Jean Piaget's famous theories contends that the interaction among assimilation, accommodation, and equilibrium, in combination with environmental forces, leads children to pass through a series of distinct stages of mental development. These stages in turn are influenced by and correspond to stages of language development. Figure 4.7 summarizes Piaget's stages of mental growth.

Figure 4.7 *Piaget's stages of cognitive development.*

STAGE	CHARACTERISTICS
Sensorimotor (birth to 18 months)	Children act upon real objects to learn about the world. By learning through the five senses, concepts of cause and effect and of object permanence develop.
Preoperational (18 months to 7 years plus)	Children use words as symbols to represent objects and ideas. Learning through play becomes more important; real and imaginary objects are incorporated into activities. As the concept of "word" develops, the power of egocentrism declines. Egocentrism must again be overcome when learning to read and write in school.
Concrete operations (7 to 11 years plus)	Children begin to use logical reasoning and are able to classify and perform simple operations. Concrete, manipulable objects are important for learning abstract concepts. Mental processes, in addition to trial and error, are utilized in problem solving. Learning becomes internalized.
Formal operations (12 years plus)	Children's verbal and logical reasoning is not restricted to physical objects or concrete situations. As language abilities develop, abstract reasoning becomes easier. Wide reading, extensive writing, and small-group oral language activities expand children's cognitive growth.

Source: Adapted from J. Piaget (1965), *The Language and Thought of the Child;* E. Sarafino & J. Armstrong (1986), *Child and Adolescent Development;* J. Tough (1984), "How Young Children Develop and Use Language"; L. Calkins (1983), *Lessons from a Child.*

Piaget's theory of mental development and its relationship to language can be useful to a teacher if viewed judiciously. Piaget never meant to suggest that the age levels are fixed and absolute. For example, the concrete operations stage of learning persists long into adulthood as a primary way of learning new things. Imagine trying to understand the workings of an automobile engine without having an actual engine to study and greasy parts to handle!

PSYCHOLINGUISTIC VIEW OF LANGUAGE AND THOUGHT

The most recent views concerning the relationship between language and thought come from the psycholinguists. The psycholinguists in turn built their theories on the constructivist views of Piaget and Vygotsky. Essentially **Psycholinguistic Theory** states that the sound system (phonology), the system for word meanings (morphology), and the system for arranging words into sentences (syntax) cannot be separated from the larger system of meaning (Norton, 1989).

Goodman and Burke (1988) have described the development of the psycholinguistic position as follows:

> Psychologists have emphasized the use that people make of language, the ways that language relates to learning and thinking, and how language controls people's behavior. Linguists have analyzed the structural components of language, explored the meaning of words and sentences in different settings, and described how language changes are based on historic, economic, age, geographic, or racial differences. (p. 93)

In the 1960s and 1970s, the fields of psychology and linguistics came together. Communication theory, the sociology of group interaction, brain research, and the grammatical theories of Noam Chomsky all combined into psycholinguistic research, which attempted to show the "interrelationship

Vignette in the classroom

Ralph, a fifth-grader, is studying about plants and flowers. He comes across a new word, *chrysanthemum,* which he cannot pronounce. His teacher helps him with the pronunciation; together they look up the word in the dictionary. Ralph discovers that a chrysanthemum is a type of brightly colored flower. He is already familiar with roses, so he can easily assimilate this new piece of information into his existing concept of flowers. In a later science lesson about the root system of plants, Ralph is confused about how water and minerals travel through a plant. His teacher takes time to briefly explain the concept of plant vessels. Ralph must develop a new schema in his cognitive system to accommodate this information, which he will later use in assimilating higher-level information about the physical properties of matter.

Ralph thus maintains a healthy balance between assimilation and accommodation. However, if Ralph had an imbalance in favor of assimilation, he would know only a few broad categories, so crammed with facts as to be cognitively useless. If he had an imbalance in favor of accommodation, he would know too many narrow categories without establishing clear relationships among them, which would also inhibit problem solving. The key, in Piagetian terms, is to maintain equilibrium between assimilation and accommodation.

between thought and language processes . . . how people use language, how language affects human behavior and how language is learned" (Goodman & Burke, 1988, p. 94).

Today the impact of the psycholinguistic view can be seen most clearly in the area of reading. Psycholinguists such as Frank Smith (1988) have argued that reading is not a passive act but rather one that involves an active, complex interaction between experiences, thought processes, and language. This theory of reading is termed *meaning-centered*.

The psycholinguistic view states that reading involves the use of three separate cue systems: graphophonic, semantic, and syntactic. The *graphophonic system* allows the reader to pick up visual symbols (graphic system) and translate them into sounds (phonological system). The *semantic system* draws on the cognitive schema of the reader, which are stored in the brain as meaningful units relating words, clauses, and sentences to functions and ideas. Finally, the *syntactic system* links the graphophonic and semantic systems through a system of grammatical rules (Goodman & Burke, 1988). Figure 4.8 shows the relationship among the three cue systems.

Whole Language Theory of the 1980s and 1990s takes the Psycholinguistic Theory one step further by stating that just as reading development cannot be separated from language and experience, so writing cannot be separated from reading (Flower & Hayes, 1980; Tierney, 1990).

Figure 4.8

Cue systems linking thought and language.

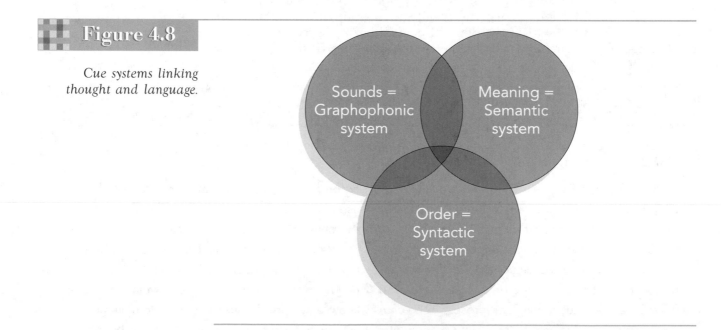

BRAIN RESEARCH AND LANGUAGE AND THOUGHT

The phenomenal breakthroughs in brain research that allow neurobiologists and neurosurgeons to study the living brain with microscopic cameras have altered our view of learning. Educators particularly are gaining a greater appreciation for the incredible amount of learning that takes place in the first few years of life. At birth, a baby's brain is a bundle of millions of neurons, each emitting an electrical impulse to other neurons. Every time a neuron is used, activated by an experience in the environment, it becomes part of the giant electric circuitry that is the human brain. If not used, the neurons may die and permanently affect future learning (Begley, 1996).

The relationship between language and thought can also be examined in terms of the functioning of the brain. Most of the current knowledge about the brain comes from neurological reports of brain-injured persons. The portion of the brain studied most during these medical operations is the cerebral cortex. The cerebral cortex is divided into twin hemispheres—left and right—which are joined by the corpus callosum, a bundle of interconnecting fibers. The hemispheric, or lateral, specialization of the brain is unique to the human species and accounts in part for the unique evolutionary development of language in humans (Ornstein, 1977).

The concept of lateral specialization of the brain has been the subject of extensive study, much speculation, and still more controversy. Research has found that the left side of the brain controls the right side of the body, and the right side of the brain controls the left side of the body. It is more difficult to pinpoint the locus of specific functions such as analytic reasoning, spatial processing, musical talent, and verbal abilities.

In the late 1970s and early 1980s, a dichotomous view of the brain's functions was popularized by many educators. For example, Lee and Rubin (1979) stated:

> Now we know that left brain thinking is logical and symbolic, the right comparative and relational; the left verbal and mechanical, the right spatial, musical and integrative; the left analytic, sequential, logical and linear, the right, imaginative, holistic and intuitive. (pp. 32–33)

Figure 4.9 shows this division.

LEFT HEMISPHERE	RIGHT HEMISPHERE	Figure 4.9
Analytic reasoning	Synthetic reasoning	*Hemispheric division of the brain.*
Logical thought	Intuitive reasoning	
Verbal skills	Spatial orientation	
Math skills	Artistic endeavors	
Linear operations	Part–whole relationships	
Sequential processing	Diffuse processing	
Phonics, syntax, semantics	Visual, spatial, emotional perceptions	
Sequential ordering	Holistic, relational ordering	
Mediated intellect	Patterned intellect	

Source: Adapted from R. Ornstein (1977), *The Psychology of Consciousness.*

From this type of reasoning, some educators concluded that schools create a left-brain environment at the expense of many right-brain children. These educators argued that school activities emphasize and reward linear, verbal, and cause-and-effect learning and ignore or penalize the spatially oriented or intuitive thinker. This led educators such as Barbara Vitale (1982) to argue for more right-brain activities in schools. But while no one argues with the need for more creative activities in the classroom, the precise hemispheric division of functions is still unclear.

In general, the left-brain/right-brain controversy was a simplistic attempt to subdivide complex thought processes; it contributed more myth than fact to knowledge about how children learn. Today most educators take a whole-brain view. Learners may prefer a particular way of processing information (visual or spatial, for example), but as tasks become more complex, the left and right sides of the brain interact. The whole brain is involved both in solving a mathematical problem and in writing a poem (Yellin, 1983b).

The position taken in this text therefore is that both the left and right hemispheres of the brain play distinctive and interactive roles in all learning situations. Listening, speaking, reading, writing, viewing, and visual representing all affect the thought processes of the individual. Furthermore, oral language activities, such as discussing and explaining, enhance critical or higher-level thinking regardless of the task. In one study involving 300 schools in 21 different states, students were given specific instruction in higher-order thinking skills (HOTS). Each day, for 35 minutes, these students were encouraged to talk to one another about their own thought processes: how they solved problems, how they reasoned. Talking about thinking in this way helps people to develop *metacognition*, awareness of thought processes. At the end of the project, standardized tests revealed that students enrolled in the HOTS program improved in reading and mathematics skills as a result of the specific attempts to link language and thought (Pogrow, 1990).

Vignette *in the classroom*

Mrs. Brown is preparing a reading skill lesson. In years past, she has chosen this lesson from the teacher's manual accompanying her basal reader. It showed her how to set a purpose for reading, suggested questions for her to ask the children to test their comprehension, and gave her suggestions for follow-up activities. This approach was satisfactory for Mrs. Brown, but she was concerned that her students were passively awaiting her directions. Then the reading specialist in her school suggested that she read an article by Garner in *The Reading Teacher* (1984). This made her start thinking of reading as a problem-solving process, one that should call for more active participation by her students.

Now Mrs. Brown begins her reading lesson by having her students browse through the book or selection they will read; she calls this *sampling*. Through sampling, the students get a feel for the work they will read. Next Mrs. Brown asks them to read the first line or paragraph of the story and discuss what they think is going to happen later. This is the *prediction* step in reading. Then the students read further to check some of their predictions. This is the *confirming* step. Finally the children pause before completing the selection and discuss how they think the story ends. This is the *anticipating* step.

Students are allowed to work through these various steps in small groups or individually, moving at their own pace. Reading as problem solving allows students to utilize their own experiences and refer to other books they have read. Predicting as part of reading comes naturally to Mrs. Brown's students, mainly because it is fun. Mrs. Brown believes it makes them better problem solvers in general because it causes them to think rather than be dependent on her for answers and direction. Many teachers (like Mrs. Brown) are reading professional journals to find new ideas to help them in their teaching.

Language Acquisition

Many teachers, particularly in the upper elementary and middle school grades, focus their efforts on teaching a specific content subject, such as science or geography. They assume that their students already possess the necessary skills to learn these subjects. However, to be really effective, teachers need to know where students have come from and what they can do in a particular subject area. This is especially true in the language arts, for the various communication abilities build on one another over time.

The two areas of study that address language backgrounds of students are language acquisition and language development. *Language acquisition* is the way in which newborn infants begin the process of acquiring language. *Language development* includes the various factors that influence and shape the growth of language prior to and during school. All teachers need some knowledge of the theories of language acquisition to understand the language development of school-age children.

LANGUAGE ACQUISITION THEORIES

Three theories of language acquisition—behaviorist, innatist, and pragmatic—represent the major contrasting views among linguists today. Teachers familiar with these language acquisition theories can work more effectively in developing the oral language abilities of their students.

The Behaviorist Theory

The **Behaviorist Theory** that B. F. Skinner argued in his book *Verbal Behavior* (1957) states that language is like any other physical behavior: It can be controlled and shaped by altering the environment in which an organism lives. The behaviorist argument dominated scholarship in the 1950s because of the immense popularity of Skinner. Learning experiments using stimulus–response conditioning techniques to teach pigeons, mice, and rats how to manipulate mazes and obtain food flourished. It was a next logical step for Skinner to propose that the same stimulus–response conditioning could explain how human infants acquire language.

According to Skinner, an infant's brain is blank at the moment of birth. Immediately afterward, forces in the environment begin to imprint themselves on the child's brain. Most important of all, the parents' language provides the stimulus that starts the conditioning chain reaction in motion. Later, at that wondrous moment when the child responds by saying "Mama" or "Dada," the acquisition process begins in earnest. Mommy and Daddy support the child's efforts (response) by repeating the words, by smiling, and by hugging the child for appropriate language use (the rewards). In effect, the parents create a controlled environment for langua ge, in which they reward and respond positively to the child's appropriate imitation of their language.

The notion that language is acquired through imitation, rewards, and reinforcement is a powerful one that makes good common sense. A child raised in a home in which only Chinese is spoken naturally grows up speaking Chinese; a Chinese infant raised in a home in which the parents speak only French probably speaks French. However, linguists have long had a problem with the Behaviorist Theory. Menyuk (1988) has noted that assuming that language acquisition is mere imitation is also assuming that the young child has enormous powers of memorization. Yet to memorize all the possible language structures and variations within those structures is virtually impossible. Stoodt (1988) has also noted that young children acquire language in their early years at an extremely rapid rate, much too quickly to allow for constant reinforcement by parents (as the behaviorists have argued). Finally, linguists and parents alike have noted literally hundreds of examples of young children producing language that they almost surely did not hear any adult produce: "Grandpa, higher the swing, my feet are dragging." "I'm puttin' on my two pantses." "We breaked the toy." "I digged in the sandbox." Clearly something more than mere imitation is operating in the language acquisition process.

The Innatist Theory

In contrast to the behaviorist view, the **Innatist** (or Nativistic) **Theory** asserts that language acquisition in young children is a creative process that is more than mere imitation. Innatists such as Noam Chomsky (1974) and David McNeil (1970) have further argued that language, or the ability to acquire language, is innate to all human beings: The brain is not blank at birth, as the behaviorists claim, but rather is biologically programmed to learn language. Chomsky has gone so far as to argue for the existence in the brain of a language acquisition device (LAD), which is activated by a language environment to begin the acquisition process.

The evidence to support the innatist position comes from a number of sources. First, as noted previously, young children produce words and sentences that sound strange and often humorous to adults—language that is obviously not mere imitation. For example, in studies at Harvard University, young children were tape-recorded using terms such as *sheeps, deers, peoples, firemans, pantses, digged,* and *ringed.* Linguists call these terms *overgeneralizations* because the child overapplies a common rule, such as adding *-s* to make words plural or *-ed* to indicate past action. Figure 4.10 provides some examples of common childhood overgeneralizations. Earlier theories dismissed these as mere language errors, but the innatists have argued that they provide proof that language is creative. Innatists view young children as little linguists, testing hypotheses and creating new language forms.

Figure 4.10

Overgeneralizations in child language.

Nouns:	peoples, sheeps, fishes (no plural forms); mans, snowmans, mouses, knifes, tooths, feets (irregular plural form); pantses, sockses (double plural)
Adjectives:	greens, pinks
Verbs:	comed, drinked, goed, waked up, runned

A second argument of the innatists centers on the fact that only humans possess language. Without formal instruction, the average infant acquires language automatically. Chomsky has argued that this is because only the human brain is predisposed to acquire language. Animals are intelligent, but intelligence is not the necessary requirement for language; innate capacity is. Witness the fact that even severely retarded children acquire language. How could this be possible unless all humans are predisposed for language?

A third argument to support the innatist position comes from linguists such as Courtney Cazden who has studied the grammatical development of children. Cazden showed that despite attempts to get children to imitate adult language structures, children's oral production often remains uniquely creative. For example, a child asked to repeat the sentence "Give me the ball" produced "Give ball." When told to produce the sentence "Here's mommy's dirty socks," the child said, "Mommy sock" (Cazden, 1972). Earlier research by Jean Berko Gleason (1967) found similar results: A child who was asked "Did you say your teacher held the rabbits?" replied "Yes, she holded the baby rabbits." If language acquisition were strictly imitation, such common errors would not occur.

A fourth argument advanced by the innatists is the existence of *language universals* (Lenneberg, 1967). These are characteristics of language present in all languages throughout the world, regardless of the environment. For instance, all languages contain semantic, syntactic, and phonological features. All languages contain terms for describing people, places, things, and actions. These universals make it possible for a speaker of one language to learn other languages. If language were dependent only upon the immediate environment and upon rewards and reinforcement, such universals would be superfluous and foreign language learning next to impossible.

The Pragmatic Theory

Some theorists and many teachers feel that the true nature of language acquisition lies somewhere midway between the behaviorist and the innatist positions. These people believe that language is indeed unique to the human species and that therefore it must be innate, but they also argue that it needs to be triggered by an appropriate language environment (Norton, 1989). This position is known as the **Pragmatic** (or Sociocultural) **Theory** because of its emphasis upon the environment and social controls. Pragmatists believe that language is learned through parent–child interaction and the controlling nature of language through requesting, receiving, commanding, and so on (McCormick & Schiefelbusch, 1984).

The Pragmatic Theory represents the middle position in the debate over language acquisition, and it reflects the work of Michael Halliday described earlier in this chapter. Recall Halliday's seven functions of language and their importance for meeting the child's needs in the real world. Language is indeed highly practical. The interaction between infants and their parents also demonstrates the social nature of language learning. Mothers constantly adjust their language to carry on dialogues with their children (Wells, 1981). Infants, in turn, struggle with their truncated baby talk to converse with their parents. In short, language acquisition appears to be both highly functional and social.

Occasionally the functional and social aspects of language take a bizarre twist for which Behaviorist Theory cannot account. Innatists and pragmatists argue that such unusual language occurrences are difficult to explain but nevertheless proof of the inborn nature of language. The case of twins Grace and Virginia Kennedy is one such example (Wilwerth, 1979). In 1977, at the age of seven, they were taken from a school for the mentally retarded and brought to the San Diego Children's Hospital for examination. Their language sounded like this:

"Pinit, putahtraletungay."
"Nis, Poto?"
"Liba Cabingoat, it."
"Ya."

The twins spoke an original language, referred to by linguists as *idioglossia*. Idioglossia is extremely rare, but it does occur occasionally and always in twins. Grace and Virginia could talk to and understand each other, but neither their parents nor the linguists, speech pathologists, and psychologists who observed them could understand or explain this phenomenon. For hours the two girls would play and converse, oblivious to the grown-ups observing and tape-recording their mysterious tongue. Eventually, after much intensive remedial language therapy, the twins were taught to speak a halting form of English, but their strange original speech continues to puzzle scientists.

Brain Research Theory

The latest information on language acquisition, both first and second languages, comes from the field of brain research, or neurobiology. We know that at birth the newborn infant's brain is already a complex maze of neurons and electrical impulses, like the circuit wiring in a computer. Each connection from neuron to neuron, triggered by an environmental stimulus, means another piece of learning is taking place. By adulthood, the brain has 100 trillion connections (Begley, 1996).

Researcher Patricia Kuhl of the University of Washington has mapped the brains of infants in terms of how neurons respond to heard phonemes in the child's environment. At a much earlier age than previously recognized, infant brains are responding to language. By age 1, infant brains distinguish sounds in their environment as significant or not significant in terms of their own language. The more often a particular phoneme is heard, the more connections made in the auditory cortex of the brain. From sounds, the infant's brain moves toward words, already programmed by the initial electrical connections. At the same time, the brain is continually filtering out other phonemes and words that differ from the established language pattern. That, according to Kuhl, is why after age 10 it is so difficult to acquire a second language with the proficiency of a native speaker (Begley, 1996).

Further evidence for the early development of the brain and its impact on later learning goes beyond language acquisition. For example, at the University of California at Irvine, researchers are examining higher-order thinking and spatial reasoning in terms of early neuron electrical activity. They discovered that preschoolers who were taught to play the piano and given singing lessons were later found to have increased abilities to work mazes, draw geometric figures, and copy intricate patterns using two-color blocks. There seemed to be a connection between the brain's activity involving music and mathematical tasks (Begley, 1996).

Other researchers at Rutgers University and the University of California at San Francisco have studied language-based learning disabilities in children, namely, reading problems. Their theory is that reading problems in school-age children stem from earlier auditory distinction problems, the ability to hear the difference between /b/ and /d/, for example. In the auditory cortex of the brain, neurons respond to such differences in micro-seconds. Among learning-disabled children, the neuron response is 10 times as long as that of normal children. The researchers are working on developing computer-produced sounds that can be used to drill such children in the areas in which they are lacking (Hancock, 1996).

STAGES OF LANGUAGE ACQUISITION

Although it is not absolutely clear how language is acquired, there is agreement on the stages of language acquisition. Roger Brown of Harvard University is among the most well-known scholars in the field of early-childhood language acquisition. Brown and his colleagues conducted a classic longitudinal study of three children, nicknamed Adam, Eve, and Sarah. Tape recorders were placed in the homes of these children; their language was recorded and then analyzed. The methods used by Brown and his colleagues have since become the model for language acquisition research (Brown, 1974; Cazden, 1972). Further studies have confirmed the existence of the following four stages of language acquisition.

Stage 1: Babbling (birth to 12 months). Newborn infants emit a variety of undifferentiated sounds, almost as if they are testing the language spectrum. This form of vocal play is labeled *babbling*. To adults, older siblings, or other language users present, the undifferentiated sounds may eventually become recognizable as phonemes in a particular language. In English, these early significant sounds include both consonants and vowels ("ma ma"). Researcher Patricia Kuhl has measured the electrical impulses of neurons in babies and found that by age 6 months infants have already established "auditory maps" for their own language; by 12 months, the maps are complete (Begley, 1996).

But if the infant is capable of producing a great variety of sounds, why doesn't this variety persist into childhood language? The answer lies in the important role of adults. At some point, the infant begins to reproduce only those sounds to which the adult responds. Donoghue (1990) has called this process "rewarding selective responses." Since only certain sounds or meaningful words receive responses, meaningless language eventually drops off.

Stage 2: Holophrase (12 to 18 months).

Around the end of the first year, the child may utter a single recognizable word, called a *holophrase*. In English, common first words are *Mama, Daddy, cookie, bye, no,* and *yes.* However, the most significant aspect of such speech is the fact that the child is using this single word to represent an entire sentence. "Mama" may mean "Mama, please pick me up." "Dada" may mean "I want my Daddy now." Holophrases are generally nouns, verbs, or adjectives. Since the child cannot express the entire sentence, the meaning of the holophrase is conveyed by volume, intonation, facial expression, bodily gesture, and the specific situation. Parents can thus interpret the meaning of the single word and carry on a conversation with the child.

Stage 3: Pivot–open (18 to 24 months).

Pivot–open refers to the two-word stage of language acquisition. Like the holophrase, the two words uttered by the child represent an entire sentence in baby talk. The pivot word is derived from a limited grammatical class, such as the personal pronouns *my, your,* and *me.* The open word is usually a noun, an almost infinite class of words. Combining the two words results in simple sentences such as "My ball" and "Your cookie." Again, remember that the child is probably trying to say, "Where is my ball?" or "I want your cookie." The meaning of the complete sentence must be inferred from the situational context and the child's facial and body language.

Stage 4: Telegraphic (24 to 40 months).

The use of three or more words in the child's language to represent adult speech patterns begins in the telegraphic stage. Unlike adult speech, which is generally complete both semantically and syntactically, the telegraphic speech of children retains appropriate semantic elements but omits terms that serve a grammatical function only, terms that linguists call *functors*. Functors include prepositions, conjunctions, and articles. The child in the telegraphic stage of language acquisition might use sentences such as "Me feet cold, Mommy," or "Doggie go home." Like a telegram, the child's speech is missing certain words but retains the most important meaning-bearing terms. Also, as with the earlier stages, meaning is still highly dependent upon context and intonation. During the telegraphic stage, word order becomes important; thus begins the development of syntax (Bloom, 1991).

The telegraphic stage provides important evidence that children can recognize that the purpose of language is to communicate meaning. It also provides evidence that even very young children test hypotheses and revise their speech based on the feedback they get from parents. Though such language contains obvious grammatical errors and still sounds like baby talk, the telegraphic stage clearly leads toward the development of adult-sounding speech.

Factors Leading to Adult Language

Over time and with practice, a child's language grows and develops. By age 4, many children have a speaking vocabulary of 1,000 words or more and can create an infinite number of sentences. Kantrowitz and Wingert (1985) have noted that these early years of social and language growth are perhaps the most important in a person's life, and they go a long way toward explaining later academic success or failure.

Four factors in particular help explain how the child's language progresses during this period until it becomes similar to the language patterns of adults. These factors are reduction, expansion, extension, and environment.

Reduction is what the child does to the parents' language. When the child tries to reproduce what an adult has said, the result is often a reduced version of the adult sentence. For example, Father might say to Adam, "Goodbye, Adam. I'm going to work now." Adam might repeat the sentence as "Going work now." Although the sentence itself is reduced, the important meaning is retained. Even at a very early age, the child thus recognizes which are the meaning-bearing words.

Expansion refers to the common phenomenon recorded by Roger Brown and others in which parents almost automatically supply missing words in a child's speech patterns. For example, Adam might say, "My cookie gone." His mother would expand the sentence by saying, "Oh, your cookie is gone. Would you like another?" By adding the function word *is*, she expands the child's sentence and unconsciously demonstrates the role of grammar. Expansion is thus one way of stretching the child's speech and modeling standard grammatical sentences.

Extension goes a step further than expansion. In this process, the parent expands the child's sentence by adding function words but also extends the dialogue by adding new information. For example, little Eve might tug at her mother's apron and say, "Mommy, dindin good?" Her mother might reply, "Yes, dear, dinner is almost ready. We're having potatoes and chicken. You like that, don't you?" Note that this parent is not intentionally trying to teach a specific language pattern; rather, the language learning occurs naturally. What would you predict about a child's language growth if his or her parents continually responded with baby talk because they thought it was cute?

When taken together, expansion and extension go a long way toward explaining how children's language develops. They serve to support and encourage language in the young child. As discussed earlier, the verbal interactions between parent and child provide the scaffolding, or support network, that the child needs to grow as a language user. Thus in a very natural manner, scaffolding leads the child forward, encouraging language use and development.

Although some linguists have argued that the most significant unit of language is the word, language acquisition studies suggest that it is a still larger unit. The linguist David McNeil (1970) has argued that ultimately the acquisition of language comes down to the development of sentences. Conversations take place by employing sentences; meaning is conveyed through sentences. According to McNeil, when children struggle to reproduce or create their own sentences, they are engaged in hypothesis testing of the language based on their innate sense of the sentence. Thus McNeil, like Chomsky, subscribes to the belief in innate language abilities. McNeil's view about the centrality of the sentence for language development is particularly ironic considering that primary-grade instruction often focuses on the sound and word levels, as in phonics lessons.

The *environment* influences the way in which speech develops. All physically normal children acquire language automatically as long as their environment includes language. The ideal language environment is nonetheless difficult to define. Research studies conducted with young children have concluded that certain aspects of the environment are positive reinforcers of language while others are not (Lindfors, 1987). *Positive* environmental reinforcers of language include the following:

- The number of parent–child trips into the community
- The number of adults present around children
- Parental acceptance of the child's communication efforts
- Parental response to meaning rather than correct form

Negative environmental factors include the following:

- Few exposures to community language experiences, such as visits to the grocery store or department store
- Greater amount of time spent with other children than with adult language users
- Greater amount of time spent watching television than engaging in conversations
- Parental focus on form rather than meaning during conversation

Language acquisition is an ongoing process. However, educators generally use the term *acquisition* in relationship to the child from ages 1 through 6. This is not to say that the language acquisition process is complete by age 6; some English grammatical structures are not fully acquired until age 10 or 11. Some phonetic combinations, such as the triblend /thr/, are not even developed until the end of the primary grades. Figure 4.11 summarizes aspects of early language and cognitive development.

Figure 4.11   *Summary of early language and cognitive development.*

INFANTS AND TODDLERS
A. Importance of trust
B. Exploring and experimenting
C. Gross motor skills developed through crawling and walking
D. Fine motor skills developed through picking up objects
E. Egocentric; no sharing or waiting
F. Repetitious babbling (leads to speaking)

18-MONTH- TO 3-YEAR-OLDS
A. Major language development
B. Large muscle development (jungle gyms)
C. Lengthened attention span; carry on conversations
D. Vocabulary expands; listen to stories
E. Play with another child or small groups

3-YEAR-OLDS
A. Doing things for themselves
B. Competing with older siblings

4-YEAR-OLDS
A. Small motor skills developing (cutting, painting)
B. Scribbling; listening to others read

5-YEAR-OLDS
A. Improved memory; recognize words
B. Fine motor skills improving (write own names)

6-YEAR-OLDS
A. Interact with peers
B. Comparing to others
C. Speech developed; firsthand experiences
D. Learning by doing

7-YEAR-OLDS
A. Think and solve problems in their heads
B. Reliance on real objects to direct thinking
C. Lengthened attention span

Source: Adapted from B. Kantrowitz & P. Wingert (1985), "How Kids Learn." From *Newsweek*, 4/17/89, © Newsweek Inc. All rights reserved. Reprinted by permission.

Is There a Critical Period for Language Acquisition?

All normal children acquire language; however, the rate of acquisition and degree of facility with language vary considerably from child to child. In some cases, children even enter school without sufficient language skills to begin reading and writing. This has caused scholars in the field to ask, If a child has never been exposed to language, is there a critical period, an age beyond which language acquisition will not occur?

Obviously this is a difficult area to investigate because all children are exposed to language of some sort. However, there are some documented cases of young children raised in nonhuman speech environments. The classic case is that of the Wild Boy of Aveyron. In 1798, a young boy was found wandering around the forests of Aveyron, France. When first discovered, he crawled on all fours and growled like a wolf. He had no language or normal human traits other than his physical appearance. The government ordered that the boy be taken to an institution for deaf-mutes in Paris to be examined more carefully. There the boy came under the care of Dr. Jean Itard. Itard named the boy Victor and kept careful notes on his behavior and development (Lane, 1976).

In 1801, Dr. Itard brought Victor into his own home. There he proceeded to teach him to eat at a table, to dress himself, and to learn other formalities of socialized behavior. He also attempted to teach Victor to speak. His attempts for the most part met with frustration. Victor learned a few words but never really acquired speech. Itard concluded that the acquisition of language takes place in the first few years of life if stimulated by the presence of language. In Victor's case, there had been no early language stimulation. Had he passed the critical period for language acquisition? Itard never found out, for Victor died soon afterward. (The movie *The Wild Child* dramatizes the events of this real-life experiment in language.)

In 1970, another so-called wild child was discovered in California. A young girl was discovered by a social welfare worker. The child was partially crippled, malnourished, and filthy. She could not speak, and she constantly salivated and spat. Obviously she had been severely abused. "Genie," as she is called in the literature to protect her true identity, was taken by police to the Los Angeles Children's Hospital for what would become years of rehabilitation and special training. There she was studied and befriended by Susan Curtiss, a graduate student in psycholinguistics at UCLA. Over time, Curtiss eventually uncovered the facts behind Genie's early years and wrote a book about her life (Pines, 1981).

Genie's mother was partially blind and her father mentally ill at the time of her birth. As an infant, Genie was placed on a potty chair and restrained by a harness during the day. At night she was put into a straightjacket, placed in a wire-mesh crib, and isolated in an attic room. She was fed but never spoken to; if she cried, she was beaten. Eventually she stopped making any sounds at all. She remained in this condition until she was found and placed in the care of the Los Angeles Children's Hospital. Her estimated age was 13.

Genie was tested, studied, and worked with for years; her progress was videotaped. Curtiss focused her efforts on teaching Genie language. In listening tests, Genie's left ear functioned with 100 percent accuracy, but she had little consistent hearing in her right ear. Tests done on Genie's brain waves also suggested that the right hemisphere of her brain was functioning better than the left. Her tested IQ increased from 38 to 74 over a period of six years. However, on tests of auditory memory (a left-brain function), she still performed like a 3-year-old at the age of nearly 20.

Genie's unusual case raised anew the question of a critical period for language acquisition. Curtiss concluded in the affirmative. She hypothesized that normal hemispheric brain specialization is triggered by language acquisition. Because Genie had not been exposed to language, the left hemisphere of her brain began to atrophy. This meant she became overly dependent on the right side of her brain for all tasks. For example, Genie did learn to communicate by gesture, primarily by pointing. She also acquired some words that she could string in simple telegraphic fashion. However, she never acquired the grammatical principles that, according to Chomsky, underlie language use and are innate to all humans.

The story of Genie has a bizarre ending. Soon after Genie entered the hospital, her father committed suicide. Later, in 1978, her mother regained legal guardianship over Genie. Almost immediately she filed a suit against Curtiss and the Children's Hospital, claiming that her privacy and that of her daughter had been violated by all the publicity surrounding Genie. The treatment and research on Genie came to a sudden halt (Pines, 1981).

The issues of language acquisition and the critical period are still not resolved. Genie's display of nonverbal intelligence, despite her severe linguistic limitations, also raised new questions regarding the relationship between thought and language.

In the 1990s, the most important research done in the area of language acquisition and the existence of a critical period comes from the area of neurobiology, or brain research. We now know for certain that the nine months when the child is developing in the mother's uterine environment and the first year of life outside the womb are among the most crucial periods for the individual's later linguistic and intellectual development (Begley, 1996, 1997). Apparently there are "windows of opportunity" when the brain is literally creating itself neuron by neuron, connection by connection. Those "windows" are open for only a short time and then close forever. The proper environment, the proper stimulus at the right moment means that extraordinary learning takes place; conversely, if that opportunity is missed, the language stimulus is not present and crucial learning may be lost for good. The latest research in the area of language learning, done by Patricia Kuhl of the University of Washington, suggests that the auditory mapping of the brain through heard language in the child's environment is nearly complete by age one (Begley, 1996).

Language Development in the Classroom

Once children enter school, their oral and written language continue to develop in great spurts. Thus the elementary school years are known as the period of language development.

Language development, particularly during the early years of schooling, is probably the most important foundation upon which all other academic subjects rest. Educators have long known that it is easier to provide a strong language development program early in school than to provide remediation of difficulties in speaking, reading, and writing in the middle grades. The creation of a positive language environment in the classroom—one that allows for oral language and literacy skill development—is therefore the primary job of the elementary-grade teacher (Kantrowitz & Wingert, 1985).

In the past, most classrooms separated instruction of the various communication arts: Writing was taught separately from reading, and oral language lessons were kept separate from literacy. Today it is acknowledged that all the communication areas are closely linked. For example, speaking involves meaningful words and sentences, not isolated sounds, writing utilizes sentences and paragraphs, not words in isolation. Recall McNeil's assertion that the key unit of meaning in any language is the sentence. Even young children interacting in social situations naturally converse in sentences.

The area of reading offers another example of how oral language and real-world experiences provide the child with the natural context to begin the literacy acquisition process. When children first come to school, many of them can recognize in print and use in conversation certain familiar words, typically signs common in their community: *Stop, McDonald's, Wheaties.* Later they can identify signs around their school (*Boy's Room, Principal's Office*) and labels placed in primary classrooms (*desk, chalkboard, closet, art supplies, reading corner*). "What's this word?" is a common expression of kindergartners and first-graders as they encounter print on a more regular basis each day.

Research into how language abilities develop now connects oral language to literacy acquisition. This new research has important implications, particularly for children who come from economically disadvantaged homes and lack prior exposure to many of the language skills expected of them in school. Roser, Hoffman, and Farest (1990) have described a program for at-risk Hispanic children in the Brownsville, Texas, area. The goal of the program was to develop language and literacy skills simultaneously by bringing 1,000 children's literature books into kindergarten, first-grade, and second-grade classrooms. The books were organized into units. Every day the teacher would read aloud to the children and share the books in unique ways. For example, with the book *Bread and Jam for Frances*, the children ate bread and jam while they shared about the story. Language charts were used to record the children's ideas about the books and organize them to show comparisons and connections. From talking about books and keeping charts, the next logical step for the children was writing about the books. Their writings were first kept in journals and later polished into stories for other children to read. Finally, to help develop fluency in reading, predictable Big Books were used. The children listened to their teacher model the story, responded to it, mapped its major features through their charts, and eventually reread it with expression to the rest of the group.

Using observational data, teachers' own reports, and standardized achievement tests such as the California Test of Basic Skills, Roser and her colleagues concluded (1990):

> Our results indicate that a literature-based program can be implemented successfully in schools that serve at-risk students. Further, there is every indication that these students respond to such a program in the same positive ways as any student would—with enthusiasm for books, with willingness to share ideas and with growth in language and literacy. (p. 559)

Research into language development has also revealed that children grow and learn at different rates. Classroom teachers therefore should not try to make every student fit the same curriculum; rather, the curriculum should fit the child. For example, some children are already readers when they come to kindergarten while other children do not become readers until third grade. Instead of forcing the same program on all students, teachers should design activities and create learning environments to meet each individual child's needs. This is known as a *developmentally appropriate curriculum* (Kantrowitz & Wingert, 1985).

The developmentally appropriate curriculum also implies a natural melding of oral language, reading, and writing activities. The divisions schools sometimes make between the language arts subskills, such as by using separate periods for reading and writing and discouraging spoken lan-

Education means capacity for further education.

JOHN DEWEY

guage in class, are artificial and contrary to the way in which children learn to communicate.

Finally, experienced teachers recognize that language development also affects a child's self-esteem. David Elkind's (1988) research has shown that children use speech as one way to judge their abilities in school. On the playground, at recess, and in cooperative classroom settings, children's ability to communicate clearly to others is the key to being socially accepted. Children who feel insecure about their ability to communicate verbally often withdraw from social situations and may later resist other language-related tasks such as reading and writing. Poor performance in school is usually the result, particularly for young adolescents from low socioeconomic backgrounds, who often use antisocial behavior to mask their feelings of social inadequacy. An excellent description of this group can be found in Jay MacLeod's book *Ain't No Makin' It* (1987).

Give a man a fish and you feed him for a day. Teach a man to fish and you feed him for a lifetime.

CHINESE PROVERB

Halliday and Language Development

One way to conceptualize the role of language development is to refer again to the work of the British linguist Michael Halliday. According to Halliday (1982), language development includes three interrelated aspects:

1. *Learning language.* Children interact with adults and other children to construct their own language system using the symbols and functions of oral speech. The same process occurs in learning written language through modeling, experimentation, and trial and error, with the focus on meaning.

2. *Learning through language.* Children use language in school and in their communities to learn about the world and to acquire new knowledge and information. Through speaking, reading, and writing in content-area subjects, they discover that language is a tool to enhance thinking and understanding.

3. *Learning about language.* As they use language, children become aware of its nature and the various forms it can assume. They appreciate language jokes, puns, riddles, and advertisements that utilize plays on words. They recognize irregular spellings in advertisements that are used to catch a customer's attention, as in *Kountry Kitchen*. They use the language of grammar (nouns, verbs, subjects, clauses, and so on) to talk about their writing with other writers.

Halliday stressed that these three aspects of language development occur simultaneously and often subconsciously. They occur most naturally when children participate in a classroom social environment in which language is used in positive and meaningful ways.

It should be clear by now that children's language develops greatly during the early school years. By the end of this period, the phonological system is nearly complete. Syntactic development continues through exposure to reading and practice in writing. Morphological development, particularly vocabulary in content areas, also expands greatly during this period. However, in every classroom there are some children who experience difficulties using language. This may be because these youngsters come from homes in which English is not spoken, in which adults believe children should be seen and not heard, or in which there is little printed material. These students can be recognized by their inability to express themselves verbally and by the concomitant problems they encounter in learning to read and write.

Summary

Many of the major issues in the field of linguistics have implications for the language arts classroom. Teachers must have some working definition of language. Knowing something about the history of the English language can also give students a greater appreciation for how language has changed over time and is continually changing.

The work of Vygotsky, Bruner, and Piaget has also had an impact on classroom practices in the language arts, particularly in pointing out the significance of oral language development and social interaction. Similarly the Behaviorist, Innatist, and Pragmatist Theories of language acquisition are important for teachers to remember. Knowledge of these theories, as well as an understanding of language development and the issues surrounding nonstandard English, should also influence instructional practices.

With Children activities

PICTURE WRITING

The letters on a page are symbolic representations to which people have assigned meaning. Other languages use different symbols; for example, the Egyptians used pictures to present words and ideas. Create your own language combining pictures and letters to spell out secret messages; for example, a picture of an eye could stand for the pronoun *I*.

MAPPING LANGUAGE

Identify some common English words that have been derived from other languages, such as *patio, rodeo, pretzel,* and *boulevard.* Then draw a map of Europe and identify the countries from which these words came. Have your students work in groups to come up with as many foreign word borrowings and their countries of origin as possible.

LANGUAGE RECORDINGS

Discuss with your students the various language differences or dialects that people use. Then tape-record the speech of the children. Have them analyze their own speech. Tape-record speech samples from students and teachers in other classes. How many different dialects do you notice?

LANGUAGE DEVELOPMENT

With permission from parents and/or teachers, go to day care centers, preschools, and kindergarten classrooms and record the children's speech as they play with you and with their peers: 1-year-old, 18-month-old, 2-year-old, 3-year-old, 4-year-old, 5-year-old, and a kindergarten class. Take note of how language develops. Also note how they use language as described by Halliday.

technology *Software Evaluation*

Just as teachers must understand the uniqueness of the English language, they also need to be knowledgeable about some of the generic factors that earmark high-quality software, such as written documentation or instruction, adequate graphics and print, and a certain amount of user-friendliness. Teachers also need to be very clear about what they want the software to accomplish for their students and how well particular software complements their views about reading and writing. If teachers are emphasizing an integrated or balanced approach to reading and writing, it is likely they will concentrate more on word processing and computer tools than on drill-and-practice software, which is more appropriate for a separate skills orientation to the language arts. In other words, you need to set your goals first; then you need to search for high-quality software to facilitate meeting those goals.

One way of initiating the search for software is to review articles about and critiques of software in computer magazines, educational computing magazines and journals, and specific software directories. You may want to consult some of the following resources:

EDUCATIONAL COMPUTING MAGAZINES AND JOURNALS

Classroom Computer Learning

Computers in Schools

Electronic Learning

Teaching and Computers

Computers and Education

Computing Teacher

Education Computer News

SOFTWARE DIRECTORIES

Microcomputers in the Classroom: A Compendium of Courseware Reviews
Pro-Ed, 5341 Industrial Oaks Boulevard, Austin, TX 78735

Software Evaluation Exchange Dissemination (SEED)
200 Park Offices/Suite 204, Research Triangle Park, NC 27709

Only the Best
Education News Service, P.O. Box 1789, Carmichael, CA 95609

TESS: The Educational Software Selector
Epie Institute and Teacher's College Press, Box 839, Water Mill, NY 11976

MAGAZINES AND JOURNALS

Instructor

Language Arts

Learning

The Reading Teacher

However, a teacher should not rely on someone else's review to decide if a piece of software is appropriate for his or her students. To make a software evaluation uniform and efficient, teachers may want to use the form found in Figure 4.12.

Figure 4.12

Software evaluation form.

Name of program _____

Publisher _____

Copyright _____ Cost _____

Computer and memory required _____

Grade level(s) _____

Type of computer program (check as many as are applicable):

_____ Drill-and-practice   _____ Test development

_____ Tutorial   _____ Programming

_____ Simulation   _____ Mangement

_____ Information processing or retrieval   _____ Creativity

_____ Problem solving   _____ Gradebook

_____ Teacher utility   _____ Game format (graphics, music)

      Other _____

Program analysis

1. Is the content of the program accurate as well as relevant to language learning?

   _____

2. Are the program's stated objectives compatible with your curriculum objectives?

   _____

3. Does the program reflect the current research on language learning?

   _____

4. Is the program skills-oriented?

   _____

5. Does the program involve extended reading and writing?

   _____

6. Will the program be motivational for your students?

   _____

7. Does the program make provisions for special-needs students in your class?

   _____

8. Does the program have adequate documentation?

   _____

9. Does the program have features that will make it easy for you and your students to use?

   Appropriate difficulty level _____

   Proper print size _____

   Appropriate graphics _____

(continued)

Figure 4.12

Continued.

Effective feedback _____

User control of the pace of the program _____

Ability to save _____

Ability to self-correct any mistakes _____

Help commands _____

Teacher utility package _____

Management options _____

10. Are there guides for both the teacher and the students?

_____

11. Is this computer program the best way to achieve the desired learning?

_____

12. Is the program cost-effective for your classroom program?

_____

Source: Based on questions raised by E. Balajthy (1986), *Microcomputers in Reading and Language Arts.*

websites   *E-learning*

www.slanguage.com
This site gives the various dialects for the regions of the United States.

www.exploratorium.org/memory/index.html
This site permits one to explore a museum. Click on Memory at the Exploratorium in San Francisco. One can play games that expand the brain.

www.newhorizons.org
This site hosts a compendium of full-text articles and resources, including articles about brain research.

www.cnbc.cmu.edu/other/homepages.html
This site links to many centers, research groups, laboratories, and institutes studying how the brain works.

www.lanl.gov/worldview/
This site not only has many science and math games but has tons of brain games.

www.musica.uci.edu/index.html
This site helps answer questions like these: What effect does music have on learning? Should I play Mozart to my unborn baby? How does music affect emotion?

Related Readings

Brandt, R. (1997). On using knowledge about our brain: A conversation with Bob Sylwester. *Educational Leadership, 54*(6), 16–19.

> This article explains how magnetic resonance imaging gives mankind the ability to see inside the human brain. It discusses which part of the brain is used for various functions.

Dixon-Krauss, L. (ed.) (1996). *Vygotsky in the classroom: Mediated literacy instruction and assessment.* White Plains, NY: Longman Publishers.

> This book, written by various researchers, gives a biographical sketch of Vygotsky and explains how his theory of learning applies to Western literacy instruction. Chapter 6 explains how children use language to learn.

Schunk, D. (1996). Cognitive learning and complex processes. In D. Schunk, *Learning theories: An educational perspective.* Upper Saddle River, NJ: Prentice-Hall.

> This chapter explains the concept of learning based on constructivism. It also explains metacognition and how it affects the child's learning.

Trelease, J. (1995). *The read-aloud handbook* (3rd ed.). New York: Penguin Books.

> Trelease explains the importance of reading aloud to young children. He posits that a child's vocabulary is enhanced by a caregiver reading to children and talking about books. He provides lists of books that are good for each age.

References

Alexander, H. (1969). *The story of our language.* Garden City, NY: Doubleday.

Asimov, I. (1968). *Words from history.* Boston: Houghton Mifflin.

Begley, S. (1997, August 11). Wombs with a view: For the IQ it's not just genes but prenatal life, too. *Newsweek,* p. 61.

Begley, S. (1996, February 19). Your child's brain. *Newsweek,* pp. 55–58.

Bloom, L. (1991). *Language development from two to three.* New York: Cambridge University Press.

Bromley, D. (1988). *Language arts: Exploring connections.* Boston: Allyn & Bacon.

Brown, R. (1974). *A first language: The early stages.* Cambridge, MA: Harvard University Press.

Bruner, J. S. (1961). *A study of thinking.* New York: J. Wiley and Sons.

Bruner, J. S. (1962). *On knowing.* Cambridge, MA: Harvard University Press.

Bruner, J. S. (1978). The role of dialogue in language acquisition. In A. Sinclair, R. J. Jarvella, & W. M. Levelt (eds.), *The child's conception of language.* New York: Springer-Verlag Publishers.

Bruner, J. S. (1987). *Making sense: The child's construction of the world.* London: Metheun Publishing Company.

Calkins, L. (1983). *Lessons from a child: On the teaching and learning of writing.* Portsmouth, NH: Heinemann.

Carroll, J. B. (1964). *Language and thought.* Upper Saddle River, NJ: Prentice Hall.

Cazden, C. (1972). *Child language and education.* New York: Holt, Rinehart and Winston.

Chomsky, N. (1974). *Aspects of the theory of syntax.* Cambridge, MA: Harvard University Press.

DeHaven, E. (1983). *Teaching and learning the language arts.* Boston: Little, Brown and Co.

Donoghue, M. (1990). *The child and the English language arts* (5th ed.). Dubuque, IA: William C. Brown Co.

Elkind, D. (1988). *The hurried child: Growing up too fast too soon.* Reading, MA: Addison-Wesley.

Flower, L., & Hayes, J. (1980). The cognition of discovery: Defining a rhetorical problem. *College, Composition, and Communication, 31*(1), 21–32.

Fulwiler, T. (1987). *Teaching with writing.* Portsmouth, NH: Boynton/Cook Publisher.

Furth, H. (1970). *Piaget for teachers.* Englewood Cliffs, NJ: Prentice-Hall.

Garner, W. (1984). Reading is a problem solving process: Psycholinguistic strategies. *The Reading Teacher, 38*(1), 36–39.

Gleason, J. B. (1967). Do children imitate? *Paper presented at the International Conference on Oral Education of the Deaf,* Lexington School for the Deaf. New York, June 1967.

Goodman, Y., & Burke, C. (1988). Reading: Language and psycholinguistic bases. In P. Lamb & R. Arnold (eds.), *Reading foundations and instructional strategies in place.* Katonah, NY: Richard Owens.

Halliday, M. (1975). *Learning how to mean: Explorations in the development of language.* London: Edward Arnold Publishers.

Halliday, M. (1976). *System and function in language.* London: Oxford University Press.

Halliday, M. (1977). *Explorations in the functions of language.* New York: Elsevier North-Holland.

Halliday, M. (1978). *Language as a social semiotic: The social interpretation of language and meaning.* Baltimore: University Park Press.

Halliday, M. (1982). Three aspects of children's language development: Learning language, learning through language, learning about language. In Y. Goodman, N. Haussler, & D. Strickland (eds.), *Oral and written language development research: Impact on the schools.* Urbana, IL: National Council of Teachers of English.

Hancock, L. (1996, February 19). Why do schools flunk biology? *Newsweek,* pp. 58–61.

Hennings, D. (1989). *Communication in action: Teaching the language arts.* Boston: Houghton Mifflin.

Kantrowitz, B., & Wingert, P. (1985, April 17). How kids learn. *Newsweek,* pp. 50–57.

Laminack, L. (1990). Possibilities, Daddy, I think it says possibilities: A father's journal of the emergence of literacy. *Reading Teacher, 43*(8), 536–540.

Lane, H. (1976). *The wild boy of Aveyron.* New York: The Century Co.

Lass, R. (1984). *Phonology: An introduction to basic concepts.* New York: Cambridge University Press.

Lee, D., & Rubin, J. (1979). *Children and language.* Belmont, CA: Wadsworth Publishing Co.

Lenneberg, E. (1967). *Biological foundations of language.* New York: John Wiley and Sons.

Lindfors, J. (1985). Understanding the development of language structure. In A. Jaggar & M. T. Smith-Burke (eds.), *Observing the language learner.* Newark, DE: International Reading Association.

Lindfors, J. (1987). *Children's language and learning.* Englewood Cliffs, NJ: Prentice Hall.

MacLeod, J. (1987). *Ain't no makin' it.* Boulder, CO: Westview Press.

Malmstrom, J. (1977). *Understanding language.* New York: St. Martin's Press.

McCormick, L., & Schiefelbusch, R. L. (1984). *Early language intervention.* Columbus, OH: Charles E. Merrill.

McNeil, D. (1970). *The acquisition of language.* New York: Harper and Row.

Menyuk, P. (1988). *Language development: Knowledge and use.* Glenview, IL: Scott Foresman.

Meyers, L., & Hoffman, R. (1979). *Roots of modern English* (2nd ed.). Boston: Little, Brown.

Miller, I. (1985). *Semantics and syntax: Parallels and connections.* New York: Cambridge University Press.

Morris, W., & Morris, M. (1967). *Dictionary of word and phrase origins.* New York: Harper & Row.

Norton, D. (1989). *The effective teaching of language arts.* Columbus, OH: Merrill Publishing Co.

Ornstein, R. (1977). *The psychology of consciousness.* New York: Harcourt Brace Jovanovich.

Pearson, P. D., & Johnson, D. D. (1985). *Teaching reading comprehension.* New York: Holt, Rinehart and Winston.

Piaget, J. (1952). *The origin of intelligence in children.* New York: International Universities Press.

Piaget, J. (1959). *The language and thought of the child* (A. Gabain, trans.). London: Routledge and Kegan Paul, Ltd.

Piaget, J. (1964). *The psychology of intelligence.* Boston: Routledge and Kegan Paul, Ltd.

Piaget, J. (1965). *The language and thought of the child.* New York: Meridian Books.

Piaget, J. (1967). Language and thought from the genetic point of view. In D. Elkind (ed.), *Six psychological studies* (A. Tenzer, trans.). New York: Random House.

Pines, M. (1981, September). The civilizing of Genie. *Psychology Today,* pp. 28–34.

Pinnell, G. (1985). Ways to look at the functions of children's language. In A. Jaggar & M. T. Smith-Burke (eds.), *Observing the language learner.* Newark, DE: International Reading Association.

Pizer, V. (1976). *Ink, ark, and all that: How American places got their names.* New York: G. P. Putnam's Sons.

Pogrow, S. (1990). Challenging at-risk students: Findings from the HOTS program. *Phi Delta Kappan, 71*(5), 389–397.

Richmond, P. (1970). *An introduction to Piaget.* New York: Basic Books.

Roser, N., Hoffman, P., & Farest, T. (1990). Language, literature, and at-risk children. *The Reading Teacher, 43*(8), 554–559.

Sarafino, E., & Armstrong, J. (1986). *Child and adolescent development* (2nd ed.). St. Paul, MN: West Publishing Co.

Skinner, B. (1957). *Verbal behavior.* Englewood Cliffs, NJ: Prentice-Hall.

Smith, F. (1977). The uses of language. *Language Arts, 54,* 638–644.

Smith, F. (1988). *Understanding reading* (4th ed.). Hillsdale, NJ: Lawrence Erlbaum Associates.

Stoodt, B. (1988). *Teaching language arts.* New York: Harper & Row.

Tierney, R. (1990). Redefining reading comprehension. *Educational Leadership, 47*(6), 37–42.

Tough, J. (1984). How young children develop and use language. In D. Fontana (ed.), *The education of the young child.* Oxford: Basil Blackwell Publishers.

Vinacke, W. E. (1974). *The psychology of thinking* (2nd ed.). New York: McGraw-Hill Book Co.

Vitale, B. (1982). *Unicorns are real: A right-brained approach to learning.* Rolling Hills Estates, CA: Jalmar Press.

Vygotsky, L. (1962). *Thought and language* (E. Hanfmann & G. Vaka, eds. and trans.). Cambridge, MA: MIT Press.

Wardhaugh, R. (1972). The study of language. In R. Hodges & E. Rudorf (eds.), *Language and learning to read.* Boston: Houghton Mifflin Co.

Wells, G. (ed.) (1981). *Learning through interaction: The study of language development.* London: Cambridge University Press.

Wilwerth, J. (1979, December 19). Ginny and Gracie go to school: Kennedy twins. *Time,* p. 119.

Yellin, D. (1983a). Learning to spell. *Daily Oklahoman and Oklahoma City Times: The living textbook.* Oklahoma City, OK: *The Daily Oklahoman.*

Yellin, D. (1983b). Left brain, right brain, super brain: The holistic mode. *Reading World,* 23(1), 36–43.

Listening
and Speaking

5

IN THIS CHAPTER

overview

This chapter discusses the major components of listening and speaking, as well as specific teaching strategies and activities used in the classroom.

As you read the section on listening, note the importance of this area to the other language arts, particularly reading. Reflect also on the importance of creating the proper listening environment in the classroom. The Classroom Vignettes show you how teachers actually integrate listening into all the other language arts areas.

Speaking skills in the classroom have not been given the emphasis they deserve. As you read this section, think about the importance of speaking and how it relates to the other language arts, particularly writing. Note too the importance of creating a good oral language environment in the classroom and the great variety of speech and dramatic activities you can do with students.

Finally, keep in mind the connections between listening and speaking, reading, writing, and other subject areas.

Developing Listening Skills

This discussion begins with listening because listening comes first: It is the first skill exercised by the infant. The child hears and begins to understand language before he or she can speak, read, or write. Thus listening is really the starting point for all the other communication skills.

LISTENING DEFINED

Most people tend to take listening for granted because it is something everyone does unconsciously. Yet despite its universal nature, listening is often misunderstood. For example, many teachers make the assumption that a child who hears well is a good listener and therefore does not require instruction in listening. This is a false assumption because hearing and listening are not the same. Hearing is a physical act that involves the reception of sound waves through minute vibrations in the outer, middle, and inner portions of the ear. **Listening,** on the other hand, is a mental process; it involves the active conversion of sound waves into meaningful information by the brain.

This definition of listening should be examined in a bit more detail. As a mental process, listening depends more on the brain than on the ear. A person must have good hearing to initiate the listening process, but unless the brain is actively engaged, the sounds heard remain mere sounds. Bauman (1987) has suggested that listening involves the brain in a search for meaning amid all the sounds that the ear picks up. How many college students have sat through an hour-long lecture and left the room without understanding a thing? They heard the words, but they were not listening.

The other major point to remember is that listening cannot be separated from speaking. Listeners and speakers are interdependent: They rely on each other for the creation and exchange of information, or what Temple and Gillet (1989) have called *meaningful messages.* Listening and speaking are also the twin pillars of language that lead children toward literacy.

BACKGROUND RESEARCH IN LISTENING

More than 70 years ago, P. T. Rankin (1926) measured the amount of time people spent each day using various communication skills. He found that 10 percent of the time is spent writing, 15 percent reading, 25 percent speaking, and 50 percent listening, as shown in Figure 5.1. Thus half of all daily communication is done through listening.

Miriam Wilt (1950) conducted a similar study of children's communication behaviors in school. She found that the average student spent approximately 60 percent of the total time in school listening. Twenty-five years later, Devine (1978) found similar results and concluded that listening was the single skill most often used by children in school.

To place the importance of listening in another context, Sara Lundsteen (1979), a leading authority on listening, made the following comparison: It takes about a year for a person to write a book and a month to read a book, but in a single day a person listens to a book's worth of words.

Figure 5.1

Average time spent on communication activities.

LISTENING AS PROCESS

Many researchers have described the steps that a person goes through from the time sounds are heard in the environment to the conversion of those sounds into meaningful information by the brain (Lundsteen, 1989; Wolvin & Coakley, 1985). Freshour and Bartholomew (1989) reviewed the earlier literature on listening and came up with the following six steps in the listening process: receiving, attending, understanding, analyzing, evaluating, and reacting.

1. Receiving. The listening process begins when a person receives sounds from the environment. This is basically the act of hearing. Picture a group of first-graders listening to the teacher read Beatrix Potter's classic, *The Tale of Peter Rabbit.* They receive the words of the story, but they also hear other sounds: the sounds of a car horn in the street, the banging of a classroom door, children laughing in the halls, chairs scraping as their owners fidget.

2. Attending. As the story of Peter's adventures continues, the children begin to pick up on certain details, such as the names of the other rabbits and the description of the farmer's garden. The students now choose from the many sounds in their environment and attend to the voice of their teacher. They try to focus their attention on the story. But from time to time, they still become distracted by the other sounds of the environment. Attending is an ongoing process that must be checked by the teacher periodically. Eventually, however, attending means self-monitoring, paying careful attention to the task at hand.

3. Understanding. The purpose of listening is to understand the message heard. Pictures or mental images of the activities of the little rabbits, Mr. Mac Gregor's garden, Peter's escape, and so on should all be forming in the minds of the listeners. The words should be shaping themselves into thought. Understanding occurs gradually as the brain receives more and more information. As understanding increases, it becomes easier for the listener to attend, to focus, to block out extraneous noises. But attention does continue to wander, even in older students, which is why people must constantly monitor their listening if they want to understand. Understanding requires self-discipline.

4. Analyzing. Meaningful listening requires thinking about what is heard. Analysis is an aspect of understanding that involves raising questions about the validity of the information received. The first-graders in this classroom are familiar with Peter Rabbit. They know what is supposed to happen next and are already predicting the sequence in their minds. If their teacher changes a scene or misreads a sentence, they recognize it because the alteration does not fit their analysis and expectations.

5. Evaluating. As the teacher reads aloud, she is communicating a message, in this case, the events of a particular story. The student listeners either accept or reject that message. If they are interested in the story, have focused their attention on it, and are not easily distracted, they can evaluate the actions of the characters and cheer for Peter's escape or question whether going into the garden without permission was the right thing to do. Evaluative understanding demands concentrated involvement.

6. Reacting. True understanding only comes when the listener reacts or responds to the message in some way. Emotional response, such as clapping at the end of a happy story or booing the entrance of the villain (the Big Bad

Wolf in *Little Red Riding Hood*), is one type of reaction. Engaging in a discussion about the story after it has been read is another. Doing a creative follow-up activity, such as writing a sequel to the story or making a drawing featuring Peter Rabbit and his family, is still another way of reacting to content heard. Harvey and colleagues (1996) have noted that reacting can also include physical activity, such as role-playing a story heard. In each of these cases, the children must be able to remember the details of the story in order to react to it; thus memory is also a crucial part of the understanding process.

CREATING A POSITIVE ENVIRONMENT FOR LISTENING

Teachers want their students to be active, responsive listeners but often are not sure how to accomplish this objective. Lundsteen (1989) has suggested that they begin by creating an *emotional environment*, or positive climate, in which children see a purpose for and feel comfortable with exercising their listening skills. The Classroom Vignette that follows illustrates how one teacher changed her approach to listening.

The teacher in this Classroom Vignette is engaging in reflective teaching. She has taken time out to stop and think about her own performance in the classroom. She has analyzed the problem areas and even asked help of a colleague. She has formulated a plan to check her own teaching behavior, a form of teacher self-monitoring. In so doing, she has begun to model for her students the practices of a good listener.

IN & BEYOND THE CLASSROOM

Using Linda's list in Figure 5.2, observe a classroom teacher's listening behaviors. Add other listening behaviors as you see them. Does the teacher create a good classroom climate for listening? If so, how? Is there evidence that the teacher's listening behaviors carry over to the students' listening behaviors?

Figure 5.2

Linda's listening list.

	Yes	No
Did I listen to my students today?	___	___
Did I interrupt student talk?	___	___
Did I dominate class discussions?	___	___
Do I look at the children when they speak?	___	___
Do I listen to all children, those with special needs and others?	___	___
Do I remember what they've told me?	___	___
Do I think about (reflect on) what the students say?	___	___
Do I face my body to the child who's speaking?	___	___
Do I show by my facial expression that I am listening?	___	___

TYPES OF LISTENING

Children listen for a variety of purposes and in a variety of situations. Teachers who recognize this try to identify the different types or kinds of listening activities that go on during the school day. Winn (1988) has contended that when teachers can categorize the three different types of listening, they can better integrate listening instruction within the entire curriculum rather than confining it exclusively to the language arts. The first type is *social listening*, which generally occurs in relaxed classroom settings, at lunch, or during recess. This type of listening is used to further social relationships

Vignette *in the classroom*

Linda Paul has been teaching in the same school for five years, the last three years in second grade. Her students like her, her colleagues respect her, and she receives favorable ratings from her principal. But Linda is dissatisfied with her performance. Too often she comes home frustrated and disappointed.

"There's something wrong with my teaching," she tells a colleague one day over coffee in the teachers' lounge. "I know it, but I can't put my finger on the problem. Maybe I'm just burned out after five years."

"No way, Linda. You're one of our best teachers. I think you're being too hard on yourself. But if you like, I'll observe in your class this week. I've got a break period on Wednesday afternoon."

Wednesday arrives. Linda is a bit nervous, but once she starts her lesson, she forgets about her colleague sitting quietly in the back. The lesson goes well. Linda introduces a story and then reads part of it aloud to the class. She leads the class in a brief discussion and then helps them to get started in the follow-up activities. Linda is satisfied that the lesson was a success. After school, she waits outside the building to catch up with her friend.

"Linda, that was a great lesson," says the colleague, "but I think I know what the problem is that you couldn't quite identify."

"Go ahead; I'm waiting."

"Well, it's just that you don't listen to the kids."

"I what?"

"You don't listen to them. You talk to them, you direct them, you guide them, but you rarely listen to what they have to say. Or else you listen for a brief while and then cut them off because there's something more important you must do."

"Maybe you're right. I think what gets me most frustrated is when I'm reading or speaking to the children and they aren't listening to me. Perhaps I've taught them not to listen. You've really given me something to think about."

Linda is actually more upset than she appears. She tells her husband what happened, what her friend observed. They talk late into the evening, and Linda is unable to sleep. Instead she gets up, fixes herself some hot cocoa, and sits down at the kitchen table to ponder the issue of listening. An hour later, she has created a self-checking listening list, shown in Figure 5.2.

rather than to acquire information. A second common type of listening in school is *following directions*. This type is particularly important in content areas, such as math, science, and social studies, in which teachers often begin their lessons with directions that must be understood for the rest of the lesson to succeed. And finally there is *listening for pleasure*, such as listening either to the teacher reading a story aloud or to the music teacher playing a record.

Bromley (1988) has classified listening as informational, critical, and appreciative. *Informational listening* includes listening to store facts, remember ideas, and discover relationships. *Critical listening* involves analyzing, interpreting, and judging information. *Appreciative listening* is similar to listening for pleasure and includes listening to music, literature, poetry, and story telling. Figure 5.3 summarizes the different types of listening.

IN & BEYOND THE CLASSROOM

Using the chart in Figure 5.3, collect data on a single class during one school day. Categorize the different kinds of listening you observe. Identify subjects, activities, and times when listening is used most often. Do any patterns emerge?

Figure 5.3	Social listening	Listening before school, at lunch, during recess, during breaks from formal schoolwork
Types of listening.	Listening for directions	Listening to begin a lesson in math, science, or social studies
	Informational listening	Listening to remember facts, ideas, and relationships
	Critical listening	Interpreting information heard and making judgments
	Appreciative listening	Listening for pleasure to music, poetry, and literature

INTEGRATING LISTENING INTO THE CURRICULUM

A good listening program is integrated throughout the curriculum, and understanding the relationships between listening and reading, speaking, and writing is a good place to start that integration.

Listening and Reading

Recall that listening and reading are dual aspects of the receptive process, the way in which people receive information. Data received through listening or reading must be converted by the brain into meaningful information. Thus both listening and reading are active, cognitive processes because both involve thinking in the search for meaning (Pearson & Fielding, 1982; Reinking & Schreiner, 1985).

Constructing meaning from sounds (listening) or print (reading) requires that the listener or reader be familiar with language. For example, not knowing the meaning of the term *parallelogram* places the geometry student at a severe disadvantage in solving word problems. An inability to remember larger units of meaning, such as phrases, sentences, and paragraphs (either orally or in writing), further handicaps the student. Lundsteen (1979) demonstrated this fact with the following example. A student hears or reads a sign proclaiming *We are in support of striking Afghan hemp workers* and is confused. Do the creators of the sign support people refusing to work, or do they favor hitting these workers for poor performance? If the student cannot recall the context of the sentence, he or she is lost.

When comparing listening and reading, teachers remark that poor listening abilities often anticipate problems in reading. For example, children who cannot comprehend a sentence that is read to them will likely also fail to comprehend it when they read it silently. Lundsteen (1989) has even argued that remedial readers are also remedial listeners and that both receptive areas need to be addressed.

Listening and Speaking

The most obvious way in which listening and speaking are related is that they both share what Lundsteen has called a *common code.* The same sounds or phonemes used by the speaker are heard by the listener, and both must convert those sounds into meaningful units or words in order to communicate. Occasionally students may mishear similar-sounding words, such as "cup" for "cut" or "pen" for "pin." The latter example may also be a matter of dialect, since some dialects consider *pen* and *pin* to be homonyms. Speakers of nonstandard English who omit the final consonant sounds /t/, /d/, /r/, and /l/ may further confuse the listener by pronouncing the words "fat," "fad," "far," and "fall" all like "fa" (Lundsteen, 1979). The ability to hear fine distinctions among similar but not identical words is known as **auditory discrimination** and is often taught as a readiness skill in kindergarten and the primary grades.

Most children develop a listening/speaking vocabulary that exceeds their reading/writing vocabulary. This is only natural. Every day students hear and use words and expressions that they may not recognize easily when they read or be able to recall when they write. The common vocabulary of listening and speaking must later be transferred to the realm of print. This process is described later in the chapter.

Listening and Writing

Listening is part of the receptive process; writing is part of the productive process. Thus at first glance, it appears that the two are not closely related. But Lundsteen (1979) has noted that listening and writing are associated and actually support one another. For example, young writers often have difficulty recalling ideas and words they wish to use in writing. They then engage in **internal listening,** a process similar to speaking to themselves, to stimulate thought and memory. Some children even mouth the words they hear inside their heads before putting them down on paper. Even adults often listen to an inner voice to aid comprehension, especially when trying to write or read a particularly difficult passage. Finally, professional writers often read their own writing aloud, just to hear if it sounds the way they imagined it would.

Lundsteen (1979) referred to the research of Cooper, who in 1965 found that deaf children often have difficulty writing compositions. Unable to hear words, these children have difficulty producing them in written form because they are unable to rely on the inner ear that hearing youngsters automatically employ when writing.

Teaching Listening in the Classroom

Researchers are divided over whether or not listening should be taught as a separate skills lesson or as part of integrated content lessons (Devine, 1978; Pearson & Fielding, 1982; Watson & Young, 1986). This text takes the position that listening instruction should be an integral part of content areas and should always be related to speaking, reading, and writing. This does not exclude direct instruction in listening skills but places such instruction in proper perspective: Listening is always done for a purpose, not just for the sake of listening.

Before considering specific teaching strategies related to listening, keep in mind some general guidelines. First, as with all lessons, you should have a specific purpose as you begin instruction, and that purpose should be communicated clearly to the class. The purpose or aim can be stated verbally or written on the chalkboard. For example, a teacher who reads a story aloud or plays a recording of a children's book might give the following mini-lesson: "Today I want you to listen carefully as you hear about the adventures of three characters. See if you can detect clues as to who the hero of the story will be. Later we will discuss and write our own hero stories."

In addition to setting a purpose for listening, keep the following five tips in mind:

1. Model good listening habits yourself: Listen to your students; maintain eye contact with the speaker; nod or show some facial expression to indicate you understand what the student is saying.
2. Before speaking, make sure you have everyone's attention. Stop speaking if you think the students are not listening attentively.

3. Try not to repeat a child's response in class. Instead encourage students to listen to each other and to paraphrase what others have said.

4. During lengthy listening periods, encourage children to take written notes to help them remember what a speaker said.

5. Be aware of how the physical arrangement of your room affects listening comprehension. Are chairs arranged so that students speak face-to-face, or are children constantly turning their heads to see the speaker?

Good listening lessons can be taught with a variety of materials. Teachers may tape-record educational programs from the television and then play those tapes in class for students to listen to. A radio can be brought to class when there are special programs of interest for children, such as those regularly featured on National Public Radio. Commercial listening tapes can also be purchased that direct students to listen for specific skill areas such as identifying main characters, inferring details, and drawing conclusions. But most teachers see listening lessons as an ideal vehicle to bring children's literature into the classroom on a regular basis. Particularly for young children, listening to an exciting story read aloud by the teacher is an excellent way to acquire the skills that are needed when reading on your own (Brent & Anderson, 1993).

THREE APPROACHES TO TEACHING LISTENING

Whole-Group Approach

Occasionally the teacher can call the entire class together to teach a specific skill, such as listening for descriptive details. In one classroom, the teacher used the record of *Little House on the Prairie* as told by Julie Harris (available from Pathways of Sound, Cambridge, MA). She first led a discussion of what students already knew about the book. After the class members listened to the record, they discussed the details they remembered. A list was made on the chalkboard; discussion followed. Then each child wrote what she or he remembered from the story. As the teacher observed the students, she noticed which ones needed more practice in recalling descriptive details. Often such a mini-lesson has to be repeated for individual students following the whole-group presentation.

Laura Ingalls Wilder, the author of *Little House on the Prairie*, wrote a number of books based on her life and travels, such as *Little House in the Big Woods*. The teacher followed up this lesson by reading additional books by Wilder. Chapter books like the *Little House* series lend themselves to great listening skills lessons as well as animated discussions that can be sustained over a number of weeks.

Small-Group Approach

Small-group lessons are similar to whole-class lessons except that there are only three to five children in the group. The students are selected on the basis of a common skill need noted by the teacher during earlier lessons. It makes no sense to group children at the beginning of the year and keep them in the same groups all year long. As with the whole-class lesson, a specific purpose should be stated at the outset. For example, if a small group of fifth-graders did not understand the difference between the advertising propaganda techniques of name calling and card stacking (see Figure 5.4), the teacher could prerecord some radio advertisements that use the two techniques, have the small group critically listen to them, and then discuss as a small group which technique was used in each advertisement. Skill lesson repetition is important but should not be overdone. A teacher can tell when the students' attention has waned.

Learning Centers Approach

Many primary-grade teachers employ listening centers as a way for students to practice their listening skills. Any corner of a room can be set aside as the center. It should contain a table, some chairs, a tape recorder, a jackbox, headsets, and a record player. There might also be skill sheets on which students can write their responses to specific comprehension questions. Usually the listening tape is set up with pauses every few minutes during which the students can record their answers. The primary advantage of the listening learning center is that it gives children a chance to practice a skill while freeing the teacher to work with other students in the room.

Teachers of young children often create their own listening tapes to teach new skills based on books with which the students are familiar. For example, tape-recording excerpts from *Strega Nona* by Tomie dePaola and *Where the Wild Things Are* by Maurice Sendak allowed one teacher to reinforce attention to certain phonemic sounds and sound combinations. The children were directed to carefully listen to the story and write down, using their invented spelling, words that contained the identified sounds.

LISTENING SKILLS: IS THERE A FIXED SEQUENCE?

With listening, as with reading, educators have paid great attention to identifying and teaching a fixed sequence of skills, partly in response to the pressures of standardized tests. This is unfortunate, for tests mainly label children into gross categories and rarely provide teachers with instructional goals (Markle, 1973).

Various classifications, or taxonomies, have been used to create this fixed sequence of skills. Benjamin Bloom's *Taxonomy of Educational Objectives* (1956) is still among the most popular. A **taxonomy** arranges skills in a sequence that suggests a hierarchy, beginning with the easiest and moving toward the most difficult or complex. In the past, particularly in reading instruction, such sequencing of skills was the hallmark of instruction. Today many teachers are skeptical of any single, fixed sequence of skills to be used with all children. However, if used judiciously, a skills list can at least give a teacher, particularly a beginning teacher, a point at which to begin instruction.

Listening skills include recalling specific details, following directions, and drawing conclusions. Critical or higher-level listening skills involve analysis, evaluation, and judgment. These skills include listening to distinguish the relevant from the irrelevant, fact from fantasy, and fact from opinion; listening to detect author bias and prejudice; and listening to identify propaganda techniques. Generally, critical listening and reading skills are taught to older children, but Wright and Laminack (1982) found that even first-graders can exercise critical thinking skills. Today more and more standardized tests are evaluating these types of skills.

BEYOND THE CLASSROOM

Select one of the propaganda techniques and see how many examples of it you can find in a single day. Use newspapers, magazines, radio, television, lectures, and conversations. How might you teach this technique to elementary or middle school students? Record your ideas in your journal and try them out in a classroom.

One application of critical listening skills for children in their daily environment involves the propaganda techniques used to sell products and politicians. A generation of students has been raised on television commercials, unaware of the manipulation involved in advertising. Because advertising techniques involve the subtle use of words, phrases, and sentences out of context, classroom teachers should discuss such propaganda techniques as a regular part of the language arts curriculum. Figure 5.4 describes some common propaganda techniques.

Figure 5.4   *Some advertising propaganda techniques.*

Name calling	The use of derogatory labels to denounce, put down, or condemn a person or product. The purpose is to make the listener or reader pull back from the negative image created rather than evaluate the merits of the person or product. Words such as *pinko, commie,* and *cheat* are used in this manner.
Card stacking	Telling one side of the story or presenting only half-truths on an issue. The only information presented paints a favorable picture while omitting unfavorable points. For example, a TV commercial for a popular cereal talks about the vitamins and minerals it contains to give you energy and strong bones. Omitted are the amounts of sugar, preservatives, and food coloring, which weaken muscle tone, and rot teeth.
Plain folks	Approach used by many politicians to curry favor, approval, and support by portraying themselves as ordinary people; the "good old boy" approach. Such commercials often feature politicians with their shirtsleeves rolled up, wearing hardhats, picking crops, and, of course, kissing babies. One former president portrayed himself as an ordinary peanut farmer from Georgia; another had his picture taken chopping wood for the family fire.
Glittering generalities	The use of vague, general, but attractive expressions to paint a positive picture of a person or product without giving specific details or facts. For example, politician Smith begins his speech by introducing his lovely wife, Beth (president of the Ladies' Club), and his handsome son, Tom (captain of the football team); he then proceeds to describe his own activities as a Boy Scout leader, church deacon, and so on. All this is impressive but may have little to do with the office for which he is running.
Testimonial	A direct assertion by a well-known personality regarding the favorable characteristics of a product or an organization. Movie stars and athletes are used particularly because of their appeal to young people. The power of the technique lies not in what is being sold but in who is doing the selling. Bill Cosby tells kids to get their mothers to buy pudding; Michael Jordan sells sneakers.
Transfer	Similar to testimonial technique but more subtle. A man or woman, usually attractive, is shown using a particular product; then all sorts of positive things happen to that person, generally revolving around the opposite sex. Beer and perfume commercials often use this approach.
Bandwagon	Approach that emphasizes going along with the crowd or being a part of the group; the herd mentality. The appeal is to sameness and conformity, through such expressions as "Everyone who's anyone . . . "

LISTENING ACTIVITIES

It has been argued that many classroom teachers do not stress listening skills or feel comfortable teaching listening. Often such teachers assume that listening skills develop automatically over time. Still others believe that it is sufficient for students to engage in listening practice activities. But research has demonstrated that some systematic instruction is necessary for improvement in listening skills (Hoskisson & Tompkins, 1987; Wolvin & Coakley, 1985). Furthermore, the teaching of listening should not be confined solely to language arts classes. Listening lessons should also be integrated into other content areas, such as math, science, and social studies (Funk & Funk, 1989; Lundsteen, 1989). The following activities are applicable in any content area.

Listening/Reading Transfer Lesson

Several researchers have reported on the close relationship between listening and reading. Devine (1982) and Pearson and Fielding (1982) have shown that the skills used in listening parallel those used in reading comprehension. Sticht and James (1984) found 10 different studies showing that direct instruction in listening comprehension transfers to and improves reading comprehension.

Cunningham (1975) developed an activity to instruct students in listening and reading comprehension within a single lesson. Teachers have modified it into the listening/reading transfer lesson. It contains three basic elements: the use of children's literature as the listening/reading stimulus; active response from children at the listening level and then at the reading level; and finally students' explanations of their responses to demonstrate their understanding of the skill. In the following Classroom Vignette, the teacher has selected sequencing as the skill area to be taught.

The listening/reading transfer lesson can be used with any of the skill areas and can include a variety of activities to test the students' understanding of a concept. Listening and reading to identify sequence of events is just one example of a skill lesson. This format works equally well for teaching about finding main ideas, inferring specific details, drawing conclusions, and so on. Manipulating sentence strips is one possible activity; others include matching appropriate titles to selections, drawing pictures, and using dramatic acting. Regardless of the skill you choose to teach, the activity you employ, and the books you use, the steps in the listening/reading transfer lesson remain basically the same: You read aloud while children listen; the students complete the skill activity; and the children read silently and complete another skill activity.

Teacher Questioning for Listening Development

The primary way to teach listening comprehension skills is through questioning. Asking questions after children listen to a recording or hear a passage read to them is a traditional practice. However, the mere asking of questions does not mean that instruction is taking place. In fact, questioning students often resembles assessment, an oral test that students resent. In order to make questioning in the classroom part of the instructional process and not just another means of evaluation, teachers need to know something about the nature of questions.

There are different ways of classifying questions, most of them derived from the taxonomies referred to earlier. But questioning lists, like skill lists, can become lengthy and burdensome. The following hierarchy is intentionally short and simple. It contains four different types of questions: literal, inferential, evaluative, and applied.

Vignette in the classroom

It's Monday morning in Mrs. Whitebear's second-grade classroom. The students have gathered around her, talking to one another and waiting for the lesson to begin. This morning Mrs. Whitebear has prepared a mini-lesson about sequence of events and is using the listening/reading transfer lesson technique to teach it.

"John, I've brought some pictures this morning, and I wonder if you can help me arrange them on the ledge of the chalkboard," she says. The three pictures show a little boy waking up, getting dressed, and eating breakfast. John has no trouble arranging the pictures in the proper sequence.

"That's great, John. Tell the group how you knew where to place each picture."

"Well, it was easy," says John. "See, here he's still sleeping, or he just woke up. Then here he's putting on his jeans. And here's where he's eating breakfast with his mom and dad."

"Could we say that this happened first?" Mrs. Whitebear points to the picture of the boy in bed. John nods and the rest of the group agrees. "And this happened next?" Again the class agrees. "And this happened last. They're in order now, aren't they?

"Who would like to arrange the next series of pictures? This time, they are about a girl playing baseball," says Mrs. Whitebear. Mary volunteers, takes the pictures, and places them in order. Mrs. Whitebear has one last set of six pictures showing a man preparing dinner for his family. The children have no trouble discovering the correct sequence.

"I've brought two books today," Mrs. Whitebear tells her class. "One I'm going to read to you; the other you will read yourself. The first book is *Where the Wild Things Are,* which some of you already know. Listen carefully as I read the story. Try to remember the order of the adventures that happen to Max because after I'm finished reading, I will ask you to put these sentence strips from the story in the correct order."

The children listen carefully to the adventures of Max. Then in small groups, they are given large sentence strips in jumbled order, which they have to read and rearrange. Mrs. Whitebear encourages the students to talk and help one another read and arrange the sentence strips. When they are finished, one group is called up to the front with each child carrying a sentence strip. They arrange themselves in order, read their sentences, and explain the reasons for their arrangement.

"Now, boys and girls, I have another story for you, only this time you have to read it for yourselves. When you are done reading, get into your groups and see if you can arrange this new set of sentence strips just as we did before. Remember, as you read, try to keep the events in order. Remember what happened first, second, third." She hands out copies of *Alexander and the Terrible, Horrible, No Good, Very Bad Day* by Judith Viorst. She has selected this particular book because it follows Alexander's daily routine, and she believes the students will be successful in the sequencing of the strips.

Literal question. Calls for a response directly found in the material heard or read. This is also called *on-the-line reading* because the answer to the literal question is in the book. Taffy Raphael (1982) called this type the *right there question* because the answer is "right there" in the book. Probably because it is the easiest type of question to ask and answer, most teachers tend to overuse it. Basal reader manuals have also been heavily weighted toward questions focusing on factual information directly stated in the text.

Inferential question. Asks a question whose answer must be inferred from the facts given in a story or lecture. The answer is not directly stated and instead must be discovered by examining the literal information. Raphael (1982) called this *think and search.* Inferential questions are considered more difficult than literal questions because they require the student to use and analyze previous information. Often teachers expect students to respond to questions immediately; Gambrell (1983) found that teachers wait about one second for a child to respond. Giving a child an extra few moments to think before responding usually results in a longer and more thoughtful response. This is known as *wait time* or *think time.* As a teacher, you should train yourself to give students this time and avoid the tendency to call on another student if the first student does not respond quickly enough. Research has also shown that most teachers allow less wait time for remedial students than for brighter students (Bromley, 1988). So take time to wait while students think before answering.

Evaluative question. Asks the student to make a judgment about the material heard or read. It is not enough to know what happened in a story or even why it happened. Now the students must also assess the significance of the material in light of their own life experiences. Raphael (1982) called this *on my own.* For instance, a character in a story borrows a friend's bicycle in an emergency without asking permission. It is easy to tell what the character did and why he or she did it, but was this action right? Was it justifiable under the circumstances? Each student must judge this individually by evaluating the information, applying previous knowledge about related situations, and supporting his or her answer.

Applied question. Asks the student to apply the information heard or read to a totally different situation. In most taxonomies, the applied level is the highest level. Students must first remember the literal facts and then infer additional details and make judgments. Finally, they must recall personal experiences and see a connection between what they have experienced and what they have heard or read. Raphael called this *writer and me questions.* This final step, making the cognitive connection between two separate experiences, is what makes the applied question so difficult for many students. For example, after a month-long social studies unit on early explorers and discoverers, a fifth-grade teacher asked his students to write an essay showing the similarities and differences between exploration and discovery in the fifteenth and sixteenth centuries and space exploration in the twentieth century.

To help you better understand the importance of questioning as a teaching strategy, keep the following in mind. Your primary goal as a teacher, regardless of the content you are teaching, is to make children think. Any question that requires a single-word response ("What do you call a word that names a person, place, or thing?"), a yes-or-no answer ("In *The Yearling*, was Jody right in keeping his pet fawn in the yard?"), or only one correct answer ("Who was the first president of the United States?") does not promote in-depth thinking. Such limiting questions are called *closed questions.* They focus on single correct answers, usually at the literal level. A better type of question is the *open question,* which usually has more than one right answer and requires more thinking and support to justify the answer. A closed question may also be opened up through the addition of "Why or why not?"

Asking questions at the various levels is a key part of any teacher's repertoire. In addition, students should be encouraged to ask questions of the teacher and their peers. An activity that involves back-and-forth questioning between teacher and student or among students over common material heard or read is known as *reciprocal questioning*. Students' ability to ask questions is also one of the best indications of their understanding of material heard or read (Cohen, 1983).

Shoop (1986) used the idea of student questioning to create InQuest, an activity that combines listening, reading, and student questioning within a spontaneous dramatic presentation. First the teacher reads a story aloud (fictional biographies work well). As they listen, the students try to think of questions to ask the characters in the story. At a particularly crucial point, the teacher pauses in her reading and asks for two sets of volunteers. One group becomes the characters in the story; the other group consists of investigative news reporters who question the characters. In this role-playing setting, the mini-drama unfolds. The reporters ask and the characters answer questions about things that have already happened in the story and events or actions that may happen. Figure 5.5 is a list of fictional biographies that can be used with the InQuest activity.

Figure 5.5

Fictional biographies.

Avi. (1989). *The Man Who Was Poe.* New York: Orchard Books.

Bourne, M. (1983). *Uncle George Washington and Harriet's Guitar.* New York: Putnam.

Brenner, B. (1977). *On the Frontier with Mr. Audubon.* New York: Putnam.

Bulla, C. (1954). *Squanto: Friend of the Pilgrims.* New York: Thomas Y. Crowell.

Cooper, F. (1996). *Mandela.* New York: Philonel Books.

Fritz, J. (1969). *George Washington's Breakfast.* New York: Coward, McCann.

Fritz, J. (1974). *Why Don't You Get a Horse, Sam Adams?* New York: Coward, McCann.

Fritz, J. (1995). *You Want Women to Vote, Lizzie Stanton?* New York: G. P. Putnam's Sons.

Jakes, J. (1986). *Susanna of the Alamo: A True Story.* San Diego: Harcourt Brace Jovanovich.

Kellogg, S. (1988). *Johnny Appleseed.* New York: Morrow Publisher.

Krull, K. (1996). *Wilma Unlimited: How Wilma Rudolph Became the World's Fastest Woman.* New York: Harcourt Brace Jovanovich.

McGovern, A. (1975). *The Secret Soldier: The Story of Deborah Sampson.* New York: Four Winds.

Miers, E. (1968). *That Lincoln Boy.* New York: World Publishing Co.

Pinkney, A. (1994). *Dear Benjamin Banneker.* New York: Gulliver Books.

Pinkney, A. (1996). *Bill Pickett: Rodeo Ridin' Cowboy.* New York: Gulliver Books.

Sabuda, R. (1994). *Tutankhamen's Gift.* New York: Atheneum Press.

Stanley, D. (1993). *Charles Dickens: The Man Who Had Great Expectations.* New York: Morrow Junior Books.

Stanley, D. (1994). *Cleopatra.* New York: Morrow Junior Books.

Stanley, D. (1996). *Leonardo da Vinci.* New York: Morrow Junior Books.

Stanley, F. (1991). *The Last Princess: The Story of Princess Kaiulani of Hawaii.* New York: Four Winds Press.

Yep, L. (1982). *The Mark Twain Murders.* New York: Four Winds Press.

Structured Listening Activity

The structured listening activity (SLA) is an example of the direct, systematic approach to listening recommended by Devine (1982), Pearson and Fielding (1982), and others. It includes concept building, purpose setting, reading or telling, questioning, and recitation (Choate & Rakes, 1987). The following Classroom Vignette exemplifies a structured listening activity.

Vignette in the classroom

At the front of Mrs. Lopez's classroom is a large map of Canada. During the previous days, her class has studied the map and brainstormed what they know about Canada. The students made lists of cities and discovered that Canada is divided into large provinces. They listed geographic features such as mountains, rivers, and bays. They also saw a film about animal life in Canada. Then the teacher began reading aloud from E. B. White's *The Trumpet of the Swan.* The story begins with young Sam Beaver and his father on a camping trip in the north woods of Canada. One day Sam discovers a secret pond hidden beyond the swamp. There a pair of swans have chosen to make their nest.

Now Mrs. Lopez picks up the story again. "Today, class, I want you to listen carefully as I read the further adventures of Sam Beaver. If you're good listeners, you might learn some interesting facts about birds." She begins reading: "In the spring of the year, nest-building is uppermost in a bird's mind: it is the most important thing there is. If she picks a good place, she stands a good chance of hatching her eggs and rearing her young. If she picks a poor place, she may fail to raise a family. The female swan knew this; she knew the decision she was making was extremely important. . . . "

From time to time, the teacher pauses to ask the children a question to keep their attention focused: "What season of the year is it?" (literal). "Why do you think birds and other animals give birth in the spring?" (inferential). "Do you think Sam is doing the right thing by spying on the swans while they build their nest?" (evaluative). "What other things do you think Sam might do on his camping trip? Think of trips you've taken with your family" (applied). "What do you think a *marsh* is?" (vocabulary).

The lesson continues with the teacher reading and the students listening. When Mrs. Lopez stops reading, the children get into small groups and begin writing the facts they have learned. On their tables are dictionaries and other science and social studies reference books. Afterward, some of the groups decide to illustrate what they have heard so far. Other students are at the map trying to find the exact location that E. B. White may have used for this story.

Think Aloud Strategy

The think aloud strategy was originally developed to help students improve their reading comprehension (Davey, 1983). Its purpose is to demonstrate how to think through a problem or comprehension task. Such mental processes are often mysterious to children because they take place inside people's heads and cannot be viewed. They can be verbalized, however, which is the essence of a think aloud strategy. The teacher literally thinks aloud while speaking to the class about the passage she or he is reading. This process involves five steps:

1. Read aloud to the class from a story, pausing at important places.
2. When you pause, make predictions about what you think is going to happen next and why.
3. Describe the visual image that you are creating in your mind from having read the words in the story. Explain that you keep this mental picture in your head as you read.
4. Reading further, bring your own past experiences and knowledge to the story. Tell the class such things as "Oh, this reminds me of when I was . . ." or "I remember reading another story like this about . . ."
5. Occasionally stop and tell the class, "I'm puzzled. I don't quite understand this part of the story. Did I miss something earlier in the story? Or perhaps it will be clearer later." Verbalizing about comprehension difficulties is an important part of the think aloud strategy. It conveys to children that even adults can be puzzled. It also teaches children a common strategy that adults use: When puzzled or confused, don't stop listening or reading because often the author clarifies something later in the book or on the tape.

Education is a kind of continuing dialogue, and a dialogue assumes different points of view.

ROBERT HUTCHINS

If you teach listening or reading comprehension using the think aloud strategy early, your students can practice it throughout the school year. Making predictions and holding a mental image while listening or reading are among the best things students can do to improve their comprehension abilities. Predicting and creating mental images are also used in many other strategies, such as the directed listening thinking strategy, which is similar to Stauffer's (1975) directed reading–thinking activity (described in Chapter 6).

Stoodt (1988) has recommended the use of story schemata or maps for teaching listening skills. See Chapter 7 for a complete discussion.

LISTENING ASSESSMENT

The listening ability of students can be evaluated in a number of ways. Many standardized tests, such as the Durrell Listening-Reading Series or the Stanford Achievement Tests, have a listening subtest. Generally the test requires the teacher or some other examiner to read aloud from printed material. The students listen and then answer multiple-choice literal, inferential, and applied comprehension questions related to the material. There are also vocabulary questions related to specific terms mentioned in the sentence or paragraph.

IN & BEYOND THE CLASSROOM

Observe a classroom teacher. What examples of indirect and direct listening instruction do you see? Describe a strategy or an activity that relates to listening. What other opportunities exist in the classroom to relate listening skills to reading, writing, and speaking?

As an alternative to standardized reading tests, some teachers use informal reading inventories (described in Chapter 6). These tests are administered by one teacher to one student and allow for more accurate assessment. The *Classroom Reading Inventory* by N. Silvaroli (1996) is one popular example of an easy-to-use assessment instrument. This inventory is designed to assess independent, instructional, and frustration reading levels of elementary and middle school students. To determine whether the student can comprehend material at a higher level by listening than by reading, the *Classroom Reading Inventory* includes graded paragraphs as a listening assessment. The teacher reads the passage aloud and then asks the student questions. If the student answers correctly, the teacher reads the passage at the next level of difficulty. This continues until the student cannot answer the questions correctly. The listening capacity level of an individual student is determined in this way (Devine, 1982; Silvaroli, 1990).

Developing Speaking Skills

Speaking skills, like listening skills, are often neglected in the classroom or assumed to be an area that does not require instruction or facilitation. Some teachers believe that because children can talk, they can automatically communicate their thoughts. Research has shown this not to be the case (Holbrook, 1983). In order to communicate effectively through speaking, children must exhibit fluency, clarity, and an awareness of audience. Such verbal communication skills are learned through practice and observation of an effective speaker, such as the teacher.

In addition to the fact that most teachers do not place a high priority on oral language instruction, many teachers feel ill-prepared to teach specific speaking activities (Lange, 1981). The result is that students pass through their elementary years without instruction in or opportunity to practice oral communication skills. Later, in secondary school and beyond, these same students discover that their lack of oral language abilities severely handicaps them in school, community, and job-related tasks (Pigford, 1988).

To further understand the importance of speaking activities in the classroom, consider the following: Children with good oral language skills tend to learn to read more easily and to become better readers than other students. This was one of the conclusions reached by Walter Loban (1963) in his classic longitudinal study of children over a six-year period. Similarly Cox (1984) reviewed the literature on the relationship between reading and oral language and concluded that speaking helps to develop knowledge of word meanings, word parts, and syntax, which are important cues in learning to read.

In addition to reading, writing ability is enhanced through oral language activities. Stoodt (1988) noted that children with strong, effective speaking skills later become good writers. This is because the same language elements used in speaking are found in writing: For every oral construction, there is a written counterpart. Donald Graves (1989), a leading authority on children's writing, also stressed the significant role of oral language, particularly as it is used in the primary school grades, in preparing for or rehearsing written activities. And in her observations of young writers at the Mast Way School in New Hampshire, Jane Hansen (1987) found that children use oral language to learn about their subject, to rehearse aloud what they want to say in their writing, and to develop their ideas through oral conferencing. In short, Hansen concluded that encouraging classroom talk among students has a positive influence on "children's writing, reading and attitude toward learning (p. 190)."

It is generally believed that speech facilitates thought, particularly the higher-level thinking required in problem-solving situations. Vygotsky (1962) argued that talking is one way children come to know things. Harvey and colleagues (1996) found that talk in the classroom facilitates higher-level thinking and thus improves learning of subject matter. Psycholinguist Frank

Smith has contended that when children talk to themselves (inner speech), they are actually facilitating their own thought processes (Smith, 1982). These researchers have recommended that teachers utilize more small-group activities that permit children to speak to one another as a natural part of the learning process in school.

Finally, the teacher plays a key role—either positive or negative—in the oral language development of students. As far back as 1970, Flanders noted that most classrooms are dominated by teacher talk; nearly two-thirds of the talk in these classrooms is done by the teacher. Berry (1985) and Watson and Young (1986) found similar results from their observation of classrooms. The message is clear: Teachers talk too much in class and don't listen enough to their students. At least one study has shown that when classroom discussions are student-led rather than teacher-directed, more students tend to participate and the quality of divergent thinking is increased (Wilcox, 1976).

CREATING A POSITIVE ENVIRONMENT FOR SPEAKING SKILLS

For the teacher, the key to encouraging speaking skills in the classroom is creating the proper environment. In a good oral language environment, children feel relaxed, social interaction with peers is encouraged, and cognitive growth occurs (Gallas et al., 1996). To create a positive oral language environment, set some goals for your speaking skills program. One teacher stated four overall goals for her fourth-grade classroom:

1. To speak clearly with proper pronunciation and enunciation in order to communicate with others
2. To speak expressively with feeling and emotion and avoid the monotone
3. To speak effectively in different situations: with individuals, small groups, and the whole class
4. To utilize speaking in all the communication arts and content areas to further learning

To meet these goals, the teacher organized her instructional program around three requisite criteria: a positive, receptive teacher attitude; a variety of available materials; and a physical environment conducive to language use (Kear & Yellin, 1978; Yellin, 1983).

Develop a Positive, Receptive Teacher Attitude

Teachers must demonstrate by their behaviors that language use is important, that children should speak in class, and that what they have to say is valuable. Examine the Classroom Vignette that follows and identify the many ways this teacher demonstrates a positive, receptive attitude toward language.

Make a Variety of Materials Available

Although it is possible to conduct a language arts program without any materials other than a good teacher and a chalkboard, having the proper materials available motivates students and makes teaching easier. This is true for oral language development as well as the other communication arts. Figure 5.6 shows a minimum list of materials necessary to begin an effective speaking skills program.

Vignette *in the classroom*

It's 8:15 A.M. in the second-grade classroom of Mrs. Majors. She is at her desk preparing for the day, which doesn't officially start for another 15 minutes, but already a few students are in the room.

"Hi, Charlie. How was soccer practice yesterday?" she asks one of them.

"It was great, Mrs. Majors. I scored a goal—my first one. And tomorrow we play the Ramblers."

"That's neat. I hope your team wins, Charlie."

"Mrs. Majors, look what I brought," says a girl holding up a jar with a spider inside.

"Wow! Where did you get that spider? It's a beauty."

"I—I mean we, me and my brother—caught it in the garden, with a jar."

More of the students have entered the classroom. Many of them stop by Mrs. Majors's desk to chat with her, to share something, or just to say hi. Whenever a child comes to her, Mrs. Majors puts aside her attendance book or bus forms or whatever she's working on. There will be other times during the day—a few minutes here, a few minutes there—to work on these forms, but when her students speak, Mrs. Majors listens.

Jasmine and her best friend, Aretha, have gone to the bulletin board and are stapling up word cards they brought from home. The bulletin board is entitled "New Words We've Learned." Everyone gets to add a new word each week. The board is already half-full, and the students have suggested they should make it larger because they're learning so many new words.

Later in the day, several children talk about a rocket launch they recently saw on TV. Jack says the rocket is called a capsule, but the other students are not sure. "Why, Jack," Mrs. Majors says, "that's a great word. Let's add it to our list." Jack beams as Mrs. Majors prints the word on a card and gives it to him to place on the board. Any time a child uses an unusual word, phrase, or sentence, either orally or in writing, Mrs. Majors calls attention to it and praises the student's originality. Words are valuable in this classroom.

In addition to the bulletin board, there are mobiles hanging from the ceiling containing small cards with spelling words for the students to study. There is also a student-made chart of synonyms, antonyms, and homonyms the children have learned. Yet another chart details the history of some common place-names in the community.

Figure 5.6   *Materials for stimulating oral language.*

MATERIALS	USE
Variety of reading matter (paperbacks, magazines, newspapers)	For generating discussion
Tape recordings of favorite books	For poorer readers needing to participate in literature discussions
Teacher-made language arts games	For practicing specific vocabulary words, sentence structures
Pictures, photographs, filmstrips	For stimulating discussion and providing new ideas

(continued)

Figure 5.6 *Continued.*

Raw materials (clay, wood, cloth, and so on)	For using task-centered language while creating projects in small groups
Live plants or animals	For handling, naming, and talking about plants students are growing or animals they are raising
"Real-world" objects (walkie-talkie, eggbeater, pots, stethoscope)	Great for stimulating imaginary play leading to drama
Tape recorder and blank tapes	For reading stories and practicing language use
Puppets and puppet stage	Particularly valuable for encouraging shy children to speak in front of groups and for stimulating play writing

Figure 5.7

Sources for tapes, records, filmstrips, and films.

Encyclopaedia Britannica Educational Corporation, 425 Michigan Avenue, Chicago, IL 60601

Films Incorporated, 5547 N. Ravenswood Avenue, Chicago, IL 60640

Houghton Mifflin Co., Boston, MA 02107

McGraw-Hill Book Co., 330 W. 42nd Street, New York, NY 10020

Reader's Digest, Educational Division, Pleasantville, NY 10570

Troll Associates: Instructional Materials, 100 Corporate Drive, Mahwah, NJ 07430

Sunburst Communications, 39 Washington Avenue, P.O. Box 40, Pleasantville, NY 10570-3498

Educational Activities, Inc., P.O. Box 392, Freeport, NY 11520

Center for Humanities, Communications Park, Box 100, Mount Kisco, NY 10549

Bullfrog Films (environmental), P.O. Box 149, Oley, PA 19547

BFA Educational Media, 468 Park Avenue South, New York, NY 10016

Coronet: The Multimedia Co., 108 Wilmot Road, Deerfield, IL 60015

Generally these materials can be obtained quite easily. Some of them can be gathered by the teacher; others can be borrowed from the school library, the media center, or a public library. Parents can be solicited by letter to donate their usable discards; local businesspeople can be asked to donate cartons, packing material, and scrap cloth or metal. (A thank-you letter from the class is always appreciated by a donor.) Figure 5.7 lists additional sources for those who wish to incorporate various media into their classrooms.

Organize a Physical Environment Conducive to Language Use

The physical arrangement of a classroom that is most conducive to oral language development is organized around learning centers or small-group settings. A center can be a table, a workbench, or just a designated corner of the room. Each center should contain appropriate materials and poster-size instructions for using the center. Key words in the instructions can be highlighted or underlined for easier reading. Centers should be flexible and changed often enough to meet the needs of the students. Through learning centers or small-group activities, each child has the opportunity to participate, to interact with peers in a social learning situation, and to use oral language.

Traditionally classrooms have been whole-group–oriented: The teacher is the primary lecturer or questioner, and only a few students have a chance to respond. While whole-class activities may be beneficial in some circumstances, they limit, by their very nature and structure, the amount and freedom of language use by children. Small groups encourage more students to participate, while large groups inevitably become listening situations in which only one person (usually the teacher) has the chance to speak (Kear & Yellin, 1978). Thus to best encourage the development of speaking skills in young people, a classroom arranged around small groups is always superior to a large-group arrangement.

Small groups can be formed in many ways and are a valuable vehicle not only for enhancing academic learning but also for improving children's social skills. Moffett and Wagner (1991) have suggested five ways in which teachers can organize students into small groups:

1. *Self-selection.* Allow children to form their own groups by peer preference.
2. *Mixed ability.* Create groups of students with varying skill abilities in different areas to cooperate on a single project. This means selecting good readers as well as poor readers, children with artistic talents and those with organizational skills, and so on.
3. *Short-term.* Groups can be self-selected or teacher-created for short-term projects, such as making and maintaining a weekly class bulletin board. Once the goal has been achieved or the project completed, the group disbands.
4. *Long-term.* Some projects (such as social studies reports and dramatizations) require the formation of long-term groups that work together on a single project for weeks or even months.
5. *Random grouping.* For brief activities, one way to ensure a heterogeneous mixing of students is through random grouping. For example, have children call off the numbers 1 through 5. Then all the 1s form a group, the 2s another, and so on.

A teacher's ability to organize children into effective learning groups is one of the keys to a successful classroom. One thing for teachers to remember is to change groups throughout the day for different activities. David and Roger Johnson, in their text *Learning Together and Alone: Cooperative, Competitive and Individualistic Learning* (1987), have made a strong research-based case for using cooperative groups in the classroom. Hauchildt and McMahon (1996) found that small discussion groups changed resistant learners into enthusiastic learners when they were given a voice in the learning process. Spiegel (1996) found that when teachers trusted their students during small-group discussion, the students began to have "constructive transactions with the text" (p. 337). Ferguson and Young (1996) found small discussion groups useful with second-language learners as they acquired English. In short, research evidence supports the use of small groups to enhance academic success in reluctant learners, second-language learners, and all learners in general.

SPEAKING SKILLS: STRATEGIES AND ACTIVITIES

Once you have practiced forming groups, arranged your room, and acquired some materials, you are ready to begin instruction in speaking skills. Most oral language instruction takes place indirectly; that is, the teacher creates the positive climate and the motivational activity, and the students do the rest (Gallas et al., 1996). Creating the climate is accomplished through strategies that the teacher explains to the children. Within each strategy are many activities through which the students practice their oral expression (Yellin, 1983).

Conversation/Discussion

The conversation/discussion strategy simply seeks to engage children in talk with other children in a relaxed atmosphere. The classroom is the primary place where a child interacts socially with his or her peers; as such, it is the ideal environment in which to prepare each individual to enter the larger society. Socialization skills as well as language are enhanced when students engage in the conversation/discussion strategy.

Although conversation and discussion are presented as a single strategy, there are some significant differences between them. Conversation is infor-

IN & BEYOND THE CLASSROOM

In an elementary classroom, gather some children around you in a circle. Explain the guidelines for the conversation strategy and then join the circle as a member. To get the group started, suggest topics such as pets, favorite TV programs, weekend or vacation activities, and favorite sports or hobbies. Remember that once the talk starts, the children do not have to stick to the initial topic. Conversations are intentionally free and open-ended.

mal, general talk, while discussion is more formal, topic-centered talk (Gallas et al., 1996). The former is often spontaneous and relatively unstructured, while the latter focuses on a specific topic or purpose. Conversation and discussion are alike, however, in that they build on the student's home-learned experiences and serve to give practice in pronunciation, fluency, expression, and vocabulary. In addition, because it is nonthreatening, conversation/discussion helps young children build confidence to express themselves orally.

To begin, develop some guidelines for conducting conversation or discussion. Guidelines are most effective when developed cooperatively between teacher and students. One classroom came up with the following four basic rules, which they displayed on a poster:

1. Speak loud enough to be heard in your group but not so loud as to disturb others.
2. Only one person speaks at a time.
3. While one person is speaking, the other members of the group must actively listen to the speaker.
4. No one insults or offends any other member of the group.

A *conversation* is a verbal exchange of diverse ideas; wandering from one topic to another is acceptable as long as a thread of continuity is maintained from one speaker to the next. Conversation flourishes in an atmosphere in which children feel free to speak. Stoodt (1988) has described one second-grade teacher who has three different "talking times" each week. During these times, several students get in a circle and talk about whatever interests them. This is the "inner circle." Sitting around them in the "outer circle" are the rest of the students, who listen and observe. During the next talking time, the groups switch roles as talkers and observers. In this way, the students have the chance both to observe and to practice the skills of speaking in a group.

In the discussion strategy, sticking to the point is essential. The goal of a *discussion* is to reach a conclusion or solve a problem. Moffett and Wagner (1991) have referred to discussion as *task* or *topic talk*. According to them:

> Small group discussion should be a staple, significant classroom process given the same kind of importance and commitment afforded reading or writing activities. It is through discussing that learners face the challenge of defining, clarifying, qualifying, elaborating, analyzing, and ordering experiences, concepts, opinions, or ideas, thereby developing their thinking and verbalizing skills for reading and writing. (p. 85)

Before beginning a discussion, the topic should be clearly defined and understood by all. Usually it is stated in the form of a question such as, Should children have to do chores in order to earn an allowance? Other questions suitable for small discussion groups may arise from children's reading, particularly if they are organized into literature groups in which several children are reading the same book. Often students want to discuss the motives behind a character's actions in a particular story. After reading a book together, each member of the group can write down what she or he thinks lies behind the actions of a particular character. Then they can share and discuss their views with the group.

Additional sources for discussion topics include school events or experiences (How can the cafeteria food be improved?), current events (What can kids do to prevent crimes from occurring in the neighborhood?), and personal problems (How can a youngster learn to get along with a stepparent?). The last of these categories is particularly good for stimulating discussion among young people because all children have problems: problems with schoolwork, parents, siblings, and peers; concerns about their physical appearance; feelings of inadequacy in athletics or in relationships with the opposite sex. One way to initiate this kind of discussion experience is to have the students write their problems in the form of a letter addressed to a confidant. In Stillwater, Oklahoma, 12-year-old Shabana Kazi began her own school newspaper column, modeled on "Dear Abby" but aimed strictly at children her own age and younger. A classroom version of "Dear Shabana" can easily be set up, with different students taking turns answering the letters from their peers. The best letters then form the topic for small-group discussions during the week. Figure 5.8 shows an example of Shabana's column.

Dear Shabana

Figure 5.8

Sample "Dear Shabana" column.

DEAR SHABANA: I'm having a problem on the bus. I like to ride the bus because I have a lot of friends on the bus. But there's this one big high school kid who always makes sure he sits behind me. Then when I'm beginning to enjoy the ride, and am having a chit-chat with my friends, he hits me on the brain. And he does it every day, too. The next time he hits me on the brain, I'm going to punch him on the heart. He gets on my nerves. If I go tell the bus driver on him, he'll probably start laughing at me for being a tattle-tale and a chicken. Should I punch that kid on the heart? — Bullied

DEAR BULLIED: I know what it must be like to have a kid like that on your bus. He probably gives you the shivers. But never fear. I have an idea for you. When you get on the bus with your friends, don't let them sit in the same seat you are in. Have one of your friends sit behind you, another one in front of you and one beside you and so on. That way you will be surrounded by your friends and there will be no room for that high school kid. He will have to sit far away from you. That will keep him from hitting your brain and it will keep you from wanting to punch him on the heart. This should solve the problem.

DEAR SHABANA: I have a problem. I have bad handwriting. All summer, I've been trying my best to improve my handwriting. But I just can't. I can't help it. Nobody likes my handwriting except my little brother who is fascinated with cursive. My older sister says my writing is sloppy. My mom and dad say I need to improve very badly on it. My teacher last year even said it was illegible—I don't want to give my new teachers a bad impression. What should I do?
P.S. help me soon! — Illegible

DEAR ILLEGIBLE: When you are ready to give up, please remember that nothing is impossible. To improve your handwriting, you must take it slow and easy. In the beginning, you must do each letter slowly and carefully. Once that gets easy for you, try doing them a little bit faster. In no time, your writing will have improved immensely. You will feel proud of yourself. It may take time to improve your writing, but you can do it if you try.

Dear Shabana
P.O. Box 967
Stillwater, OK 74076

Source: Stillwater News Press. Reprinted with permission of Shabana Kazi and the *Stillwater News Press.*

A variation of the discussion strategy was developed by NASA as part of its space education program for upper elementary and middle school students. In this exercise, students are given a survival-type situation to discuss and a form to complete. The form lists various objects important to the survival of the group. The students discuss each item and then try to reach some sort of consensus regarding its importance to their imaginary situation. As they move down the list of objects, the number system changes and consensus becomes more difficult to reach, but the quality of the discussion improves greatly. Figure 5.9 offers a sample situation for this activity.

Figure 5.9	SPACE TRIP TO THE MOON

Sample NASA survival activity.

Instructions: You are a member of a space crew originally scheduled to rendezvous with the mother ship on the lighted surface of the moon. Because of mechanical difficulties, however, your ship was forced to land at a spot some 200 miles from the rendezvous point. During the landing, much of the ship and the equipment aboard were damaged; since survival depends on reaching the mother ship, the most critical items still available must be chosen for the 200-mile trip. Below are listed the 15 items intact and undamaged after landing. Your task is to rank them in order of their importance in allowing your crew to reach the rendezvous point. Place the number 1 by the most important item, the number 2 by the second most important, and so on through number 15, the least important.

____ Box of matches	____ Five gallons of water
____ Food concentrate	____ One case of dehydrated milk
____ 50 feet of nylon rope	____ Two 100-pound tanks of oxygen
____ Parachute silk	____ Map of the stars as seen from the moon
____ Portable heating unit	____ Signal flares
____ Two 45-caliber pistols	____ First-aid kit containing injection needles
____ Life raft	____ Solar-powered FM receiver-transmitter
____ Magnetic compass	

A more formal approach to discussion is through a **panel discussion;** generally panel members prepare themselves as experts on a particular topic and present various views or aspects of a topic too large for a single child to handle (Bromley, 1988). The other key difference between the panel discussion and other discussion groups is that the panel members address their remarks to an audience. The concept of audience is important because effective speakers always keep their audience in mind: They talk to the audience and adjust their tone and delivery to appeal to the audience. This is true of writers as well as speakers. Moffett and Wagner (1991) have contended that the benefits of having an audience include the fact that "the participants in the discussion have the advantage of feedback on their ideas from the other panelists and feedback on the quality of their interaction from the audience." Teachers who employ unit activities and group projects often use panel discussions to conclude or summarize a unit.

For older students, the debate is another fun activity (Bromley, 1988). A **debate** focuses on a question or issue that involves conflicting views or opposing sides and follows specific rules that must be taught beforehand to the children (Neff & Lengel, 1990). Both sides or teams prepare themselves by researching the issue, rehearsing their arguments, and deciding on their debate strategy. Often the teacher serves as moderator, keeping time and directing the back-and-forth presentations. As with panel discussions, the rest of the students serve as the audience in a debate and can actually vote at the end for the team they think presented the most effective arguments.

For both panel discussions and debates, students should keep in mind the following five guidelines (Pinnell, 1984):

1. Research your topic thoroughly using the library and community resources.
2. Remember to support your opinions with facts.
3. Organize your thoughts before you speak and stick to the topic.
4. Use notecards to recall important points but don't read to the audience.
5. Listen carefully to others and react to their remarks.

Making a poster to display these guidelines in the room prevents the teacher from having to repeat them in class.

Transactional Literature Discussions

Dugan (1997) describes transactional literature discussions (TLD) as an integrated talking, reading, and writing strategy. The TLD is a process that encourages students to discuss their ideas, listen to other opinions, and reflect on what they learned. Following are the six steps with a brief description:

1. *Getting ready.* This step includes skimming a number of books to see which one the group would like to read and discuss. Once the book is selected, the group members skim through pictures of picture books or skim chapter titles of chapter books and make oral predictions about the story. They spend time analyzing each other's predictions and test the reasons for each prediction.
2. *Reading and stopping to think aloud.* The teacher models what he or she is thinking as the group reads in order for students to learn how to think about the text as they read.
3. *Written response.* Time is given to students to write short responses to the reading on Post-its. These are self-selected responses, not responses to a set of teacher-directed questions.
4. *Discussion.* Students spend 15 to 30 minutes discussing their responses using the RQL2 strategy (Respond about likes or dislikes; Question aspects of the story they did not understand; Listen to classmates; Link story to one's life).
5. *Write.* Based on the discussion, students are given time to write in their journals.
6. Review. As a group, the students review what they learned about human nature, about things in nature, about themselves, or about any concepts in the reading.

Brainstorming

One of the best ways to generate a number of ideas in a short amount of time is through the brainstorming strategy. **Brainstorming** helps to stretch a student's imagination, encourages group cooperation, and leads to creative thinking through spontaneous contributions by all group members. James Moffett, an early advocate of the brainstorming strategy as a regular class-

IN & BEYOND THE CLASSROOM

During your classroom observation experience, gather a few children and teach them about the debate or panel discussion format. Brainstorm some topics the students are interested in, and help them prepare a short debate or panel discussion. Observe the students and note changes you might make the next time you use this strategy.

room activity, argued that it not only stimulates oral discussion but also is an excellent source for gathering ideas for writing (Moffett & Wagner, 1991). Key principles of brainstorming include the following:

- Select a problem or topic and react to it quickly.
- Designate one person in the group as the recorder of ideas.
- Accept and record all ideas or suggestions.
- Build on other people's ideas.
- Do not criticize anyone else's ideas.
- Initially, quantity of ideas is more important than quality.

Many teachers are familiar with brainstorming but do not utilize it effectively or frequently enough. If you plan to make the brainstorming strategy part of your teaching practices, there are some procedures you should follow. First, begin with a whole-class brainstorming session during which each student records his or her own ideas. Provide a problem question as a stimulus and a time limit to eliminate frivolous ideas and daydreaming. When time is called, let each student share his or her list. Next, open up the brainstorming session to everyone. You can record the ideas for the whole class at the chalkboard, modeling the role of the recorder. Finally, you may begin to evaluate some of the ideas in terms of their effectiveness in leading the class to a solution of the initial problem.

One fifth-grade teacher gave her class the following assignment: "While on a trip, your car breaks down and you are stuck for the day on a desolate country road. In the backseat, you find some old magazines. What are all the possible uses of a magazine you can think of?" The teacher then passed out copies of real magazines to the class. Figure 5.10 is part of the list this class brainstormed.

The brainstorming strategy can also be used to help students expand their vocabularies, particularly for writing. The teacher begins by presenting a common word, such as *walk*. The class is then asked to think of other, more descriptive words that could replace this one. One group that did this exercise came up with the following list: *stroll, glide, stumble, amble, shuffle, stomp, strut*. The teacher suggested that this group make a poster entitled "Walking Words" to display for the rest of the class. To reinforce the meaning of these terms, the teacher asked for volunteer students to briefly pantomime each of them. Other groups later came up with their own posters listing "Funny Words" (*laugh, giggle, hilarious*) and "Soft Words" (*cuddly, fuzzy, tender*).

The brainstorming strategy can be further extended by turning the list of brainstormed terms or ideas into schematic clusters. Webs or clusters have the advantage of showing relationships or connections among ideas rather than merely listing the ideas. Figure 5.11 shows the cluster diagram that emerged from a fifth-grade class discussion of prejudice after listening to their teacher read Florence Heide's *Sound of Sunshine, Sound of Rain*, which is about a blind African-American boy.

Figure 5.10

Sample brainstorming list.

Problem: What can you do with a magazine?

Read it	Fold it into a sun hat
Look at pictures	Make a megaphone
Clip out coupons	Use it for toilet paper
Use it as flyswatter	Arrange the pages
Make paper airplanes	into the letters SOS
Burn it for fuel	

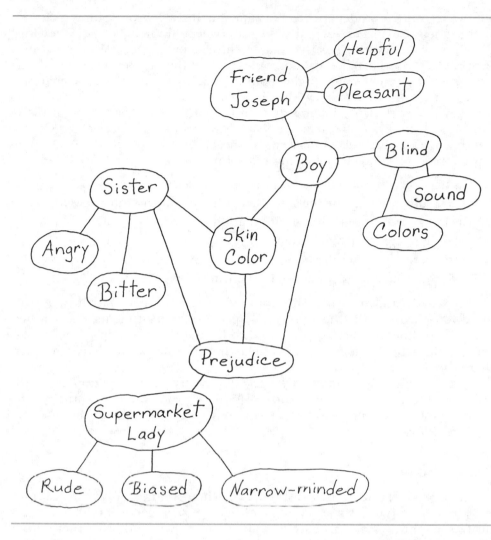

Figure 5.11

Sample schematic cluster:
Sound of Sunshine,
Sound of Rain.

Interviewing

Most information that is gathered by students for school projects comes from traditional resources: a dictionary, the encyclopedia, other library reference sources. Students need to learn that another way of gathering information is through *interviewing* (Moffett & Wagner, 1991), or asking someone for information or opinions. For example, when a student has been to the library in search of information regarding the proper soil, water, and sunlight conditions for growing a particular plant and is still not clear about what to do, it is time to ask for expert advice. Finding a specialist (a botanist, the owner of a nursery, an expert gardener) to interview would be a valuable shortcut to acquiring technical information. This is why knowing how to use the interview strategy as a research tool is so important.

Donald Graves (1989) has argued that the interview strategy is "one of the cornerstones of information gathering throughout a child's career as a learner" (p. 20). He recommends teaching young children about interviewing by having them poll their fellow classmates for information. In this simple

IN & BEYOND THE CLASSROOM

Lead a group of students in a brainstorming session on any topic of their choice. You serve as the recorder. Remember to accept all responses and encourage children to build on one another's ideas. When you are finished, reflect on what you can do with the information you have brainstormed (for example, record it as a cluster diagram).

polling technique, students choose a different interview or polling question to ask their classmates each day. Questions could include the following: Which is your favorite meal—breakfast, lunch, or dinner? Which is your favorite sport—baseball, football, or basketball? Which is your favorite color— red, green, or yellow? When the polling process is completed, a chart or graph can be prepared to show the class data.

Many older students are already familiar with the mechanics of an interview from having watched television stars such as Rosie O'Donnell or Oprah Winfrey, who utilize guest interviews as the basis of their shows. Good interviewers keep in mind the following six points:

1. Gather background information on the subject.
2. Learn something about the interviewee (person being interviewed).
3. Decide ahead of time on the information desired.
4. Formulate appropriate questions.
5. Anticipate follow-up questions based on responses of the interviewee.
6. Determine how to begin and end the interview politely.

Eventually students will want to interview actual experts rather than continue role-playing with their peers. For primary-grade students, the teacher might invite these experts to come to the classroom, while upper elementary and middle school students can conduct their interviews in the community after school.

Interviewing is an important strategy for gathering information and conducting research on many topics. However, you must eventually tie interviewing to real projects so that children see a relevance to the research they are doing.

Group Projects

A great deal of classroom talk is stimulated when children engage in real projects in small-group settings. When children get together to build, make, or create something, they naturally talk about it as they work; this **incidental talk** associated with a particular task is actually the foundation for all other talk experiences. To facilitate such talk in class, the teacher needs to assess students' interests and then decide with them on some projects that can be done in class. The key is that the task must be a real one if real language is to be generated (Moffett & Wagner, 1991). In addition, small-group projects involve reading, library research, note taking, organizing information, writing an outline, listening, and, of course, speaking.

Eliot Wigginton, a high school English teacher from Rabun's Gap, Georgia, used the notions of group projects and interviewing to create a unique method for teaching communication skills. As mentioned in Chapter 2, Wigginton had his students identify people in the community and surrounding areas who possessed unusual skills and talents. For example, there were men and women who had lived in the community for many years and still knew the old skills of moonshining, quilt making, hog dressing, log-cabin building, soap making, and faith healing. The students in Wigginton's class visited these people, interviewed them, taped the interviews, and then took the tapes to class. There, in small groups, the students transcribed the tapes and rewrote them as magazine articles. Other members of the groups helped with the organization, editing, and proofreading of the

> **IN & BEYOND THE CLASSROOM**
>
> With a small group of students, brainstorm a subject for a group project. Decide on what you will do and how you will do it. Then identify someone in the community to interview in relationship to the project. Help the students to arrange and conduct the interview. Evaluate what you learned as a teacher from this experience.

articles. In this way, Wigginton's class learned the traditional English grammar, punctuation, capitalization, and spelling skills in a very nontraditional manner. The simple magazine each class produced eventually became the basis for the *Foxfire* series of best-selling books, researched and written entirely by ordinary high school students (Wigginton, 1980). To learn more about the *Foxfire* experience, read Eliot Wigginton's book *Sometimes a Shining Moment* (1986).

Today many language arts teachers, inspired by Eliot Wigginton's success, have copied the *Foxfire* model. One middle school English teacher in Pawnee, Oklahoma, used this approach with his students, all members of the Pawnee Indian tribe. The students interviewed their parents and grandparents about the history and culture of the Pawnee tribe. They transcribed these interviews, illustrated the text with their own artwork, and produced a small booklet. Figure 5.12 shows an example of one student's finished product.

The Classroom Vignette on the following page shows how one teacher utilizes the group projects strategy.

Intellectual Kits

An **intellectual kit** is a collection of real materials or objects organized around a single category or sharing a common attribute, such as objects related to a farm or a collection of buttons. The purpose of the intellectual kits strategy is to encourage students' use of language to describe, categorize, and brainstorm uses of the objects and to role-play with the kit. Marie Clay was one of the early educators to suggest the use of real objects (as opposed to abstract or imaginary ones) to generate language and thought in young children. Preschool and primary-grade teachers use the kits to help children define similarities and differences among objects. Eventually this leads to the development of the skills of comparing, contrasting, and classifying (Inhelder & Piaget, 1964).

The teacher first prepares a kit suitable for the age level and interests of the children. Then the students are free to discover what the objects all have in common and to determine various ways of categorizing or dividing the objects, such as by size, color, shape, texture, or function. Through the manipulation of concrete objects, the children learn to label objects; to describe their attributes in relation to other objects; and to compare, group, and predict. The teacher's role is to build on students' responses, model new vocabulary terms when appropriate, and relate the materials in the kit to other learning situations and subjects. Finally, the children are encouraged to think of additional uses for the objects in the kit.

In Tucson, Arizona, the Tucson Early Education Model (TEEM) utilizes intellectual kits extensively to develop young children's language, thinking, and social skills. Teachers in the TEEM program develop their own kits from ordinary materials found around the home: beauty aids, bottles, boxes, brushes, clothing, combs, containers, fabric, footwear, gloves, hats, jars, jewelry, magazines, measuring devices, nails, rocks, seeds, shells, shoes, socks, soft

Figure 5.12

Sample transcribed interview.

THE DEERLADY

as told to

JEFF GOODFOX

by

Lawrence Goodfox, Jr.

Usually the Deerlady is seen at a pow-wow. One time several years ago at one of the pow-wows up north, the young people were dancing the Forty-nine Dance. This was after the evening program, and it was dark. As they were dancing, they began to smell a musty smell like an animal among them.

As they danced, one of the young people looked down and the person dancing next to him had hoofs! He looked at the face and it was a beautiful Indian girl—but from the side of the Indian girl's head there were horns coming out. She had skin like a deer.

This scared the young people so bad that they all ran. Someone turned the lights on to see the deerlady running toward the river. After this they never could find her.

The deerlady has been seen at other pow-wows during the night show.

Source: Reprinted with permission of Jeff Goodfox.

Vignette *in the classroom*

Mr. McGuffee's fourth-grade classroom is buzzing with excitement this morning. Today is the day the students meet in small groups to begin planning their group projects.

"OK, class," says Mr. McGuffee, "you all know what to do in your groups, so I'm going to give you 15 minutes to brainstorm about the projects that you'll be working on for the next two weeks. If there are no questions, go to work."

One of the groups has decided to make a small motor. In science class, they learned about magnets; now they want to apply this knowledge to a motor. They've already contacted the electricity shop teacher at the high school and arranged for a meeting after school.

"David and I will go to the library and check out some books on electricity, magnets, and stuff about motors," says Randy.

"I'll see if there are any filmstrips on motors or electricity we can use," says Margie.

"My dad has a whole garage full of stuff like wire, switches, and wood blocks," says Philip.

Another group has decided to build kites. Working in pairs, they are going to build three kites with different designs and materials and then see which one flies the best. Some of the members of the group have already gone to the library and found books and filmstrips about kites. They are all going to interview the owner of a hobby shop in town, who has said he can give them some tips on building their kites.

"Me and Delores are going to build a box kite," says Felicia. "We'll use sticks for the frame and butcher-block paper."

"We're using balsa wood for our frame," says Mike. "It's lighter and works better. We're also getting cellophane instead of paper."

"Don't forget to attach a cloth tail," says Ann. "This book I read said that kites fly better with a tail."

The group agrees that they will also make practice kites and then meet with Mr. Barker, the hobby shop owner, to get his suggestions for improving them before the final test.

---

objects, tools, and vegetables. One teacher designed an intellectual shape kit around the concept of *round*. She began with a dictionary definition of the word *round* and had the children add their own definitions ("it rolls," "it forms a circle"). Next she showed the children the objects in her kit: washers, corks, coins, balls, a rolling pin, an embroidery hoop, a spool, a ring, a coaster, checkers, pencils, hair rollers, a hatbox, buttons, wheels, an orange, cups, dishes, and bottle tops. She asked the children, "How is this object round? Is it round in the same way this object is?" "Which is more round—an orange or an egg?" From there, the children took over and began discussing and grouping the objects. Later in the period, they went on a "round walk" in the room, collecting more round objects for their kit. Other extension activities included listening to the teacher read *Round as a Pancake* and *Moon Man* by Tomi Ungerer, making round collage designs at the art center, and learning circle games and dances.

Some teachers like to introduce an intellectual kit by reading a book. Mrs. Murphy, a first-grade teacher, read *There Are Rocks in My Socks (Said the*

IN & BEYOND THE CLASSROOM

Create an intellectual kit and bring it into an elementary classroom. Observe as the children categorize and manipulate the objects. Record your observations in your journal. What kinds of language learning experiences did you observe? How could you extend these experiences into reading or writing?

Ox) by Pat Thomas. After the children had enjoyed the book and talked about it, Mrs. Murphy brought out a large box containing . . . socks, of course! There were long red Christmas stockings, little baby socks, athletic socks, women's nylons, wool socks, cotton socks, tennis booties, leg warmers, and so on. The children categorized the socks by size, color, material, and use. Then they talked about the different people who might wear these socks. Later the teacher brought markers, yarn, buttons, glue, needles, and thread and showed the children how to construct hand puppets out of socks.

Figure 5.13 outlines some guidelines for using intellectual kits.

BEFORE THE ACTIVITY

1. Decide on the type of kit
2. List the different objects to include
3. List your objectives
4. List the new vocabulary to be learned
5. Prepare questions to ask

DURING THE ACTIVITY

You:
1. Model language patterns
2. Use labels
3. Ask questions
4. Listen to children
5. Observe children
6. Evaluate

Children:
1. Manipulate objects
2. Label objects
3. Categorize objects
4. Ask questions
5. Role-play
6. Discuss with peers

Figure 5.13

Instructions for using an intellectual kit.

Dialogue Improvisation and Patterned Conversation

Ferguson and Young (1996) explain how they use dialogue improvisation and patterned conversation with second-language learners to provide these students with opportunities to use English in a safe, meaningful way. Both activities permit the students to use prior experiences as they learn the structure of the English language; both are also good to use for all learners.

In **dialogue improvisation,** students (with the teacher's help) create new dialogue for the characters in a familiar story as they act out a part of the story. For example, after reading *Annie and the Wild Animals* (Brett, 1985), the teacher passes out various animal puppets, such as a crocodile, giraffe, monkey, and raccoon, to the students. The teacher begins the improvisation by acting like Annie, who wants a new pet after losing Taffy, her cat. The teacher puts out cornflakes on a plate on the floor and begins to wonder aloud about who will come to eat the food. The children in turn come to the plate and respond to Annie's question, "Will you make a good pet?" The children respond by explaining why they would not be a good pet. The dialogue is patterned after Brett's phrase: "I wouldn't be a good pet because . . . " This type of improvisation gives students an opportunity to pattern the English phrase while adding their own reason for not being a good pet. Other books that Ferguson and Young suggest using for dialogue improvisation are *Pigs' Picnic* (Kasza, 1988), *"You Look Ridiculous," Said the Rhinoceros to*

Good teaching is one-fourth preparation and three-fourths theater.

GAIL GODWIN

the Hippopotamus (Waber, 1966), *A Bag Full of Pups* (Gackenbac, 1981), and *I Wish I Were a Butterfly* (Howe, 1987).

In **patterned conversation,** the teacher chooses literature with predictable texts such as *I Went Walking* (Williams, 1989); after numerous readings, the students, again with the use of puppets or props, become one of the characters. The students read the statement "I went walking," followed by the teacher asking, "What did you see?" followed by the child's response, "I saw a . . . "

Other books to use for patterned conversation are *Hattie and the Fox* (Mem Fox, 1986), *Who Is Tapping at My Window?* (Demming, 1988), and *Polar Bear, Polar Bear, What Do You Hear?* (Martin, 1991).

Show-and-Tell/Sharing

Show-and-tell is one of the oldest and most popular oral language activities used in the primary grades. Generally it consists of a brief talk by a student describing a favorite object brought from home. Moffett and Wagner (1991) called this *topic talk* since the topic for the child's monologue depends on the object brought from home. Roth (1986) has contended that the focus of this activity is on content and meaning and that it should be a regular part of the daily routine in an elementary school.

Although show-and-tell is a familiar and widely used activity in the primary grades, it is not a particularly effective oral language activity as currently practiced. This is because show-and-tell traditionally involves one child at a time getting up in front of the rest of the class. The rest of the students are expected to listen attentively. Try to picture this scene: Juan stands in front of the room holding up a toy robot he received for his birthday. He looks down and mumbles about his toy and who gave it to him. The children in the front can see the object, but they are also examining their show-and-tell objects in anticipation of their turns. Children farther back can neither hear Juan nor see the object clearly. They soon lose interest, fidget in their seats, and begin talking to their neighbors.

To make show-and-tell a truly meaningful oral language activity, divide the students into small groups. Then set aside time a few mornings a week for show-and-tell. To teach the strategy to young children, bring something from your own home that is meaningful to you. Show it to a small group of children and talk about it. Allow the children to handle the object and to ask you questions about it. In this way, they learn how to conduct the small-group show-and-tell activity in which everyone gets a chance to talk and share about his or her object. Small groups are also less intimidating to young children, particularly to those who are shy about getting up in front of a large group to speak.

Ewards (1996) suggests that another way to make show-and-tell a truly meaningful oral language activity is to ask parents to help their child prepare for show-and-tell. Ewards also suggests that the topic be based on an experience or a small item found on a nature hike instead of an expensive toy or object belonging to the child.

From the teacher's point of view, show-and-tell is an excellent opportunity for young children to use language to describe, to explain, and to elaborate. For the students, it is a chance to talk about favorite things from home and to connect home and family experiences with school learning. As the children become more and more familiar with show-and-tell, their presentations improve and their talks are more organized.

This common form of the activity is considered "free choice" show-and-tell since the children can bring any object of their choice from home to talk about. Another use of show-and-tell involves "structured choices." The teacher may wish to relate the show-and-tell period to other school activities. For example, one primary-grade teacher created a science unit about various animals, domestic and wild, found in North America. For show-and-tell, he asked each student to bring an object from home that represented an animal she or he had or would like to have as a pet. The next day the children brought in dog bones, rubber toys, catnip, a leash, photographs of pets, pictures cut out of magazines, a tuft of fur, a carved antler bone pendant, and so on. The same teacher asked his students to bring in objects from home to represent the various geometric shapes they were study-ing in math class: square, rectangle, circle, and triangle. Another teacher asked her class to bring in objects that represented their par-ents' occupations. Students brought such things as a Bible, a stethoscope, a calculator, a chef's hat, farm tools, and file cards. Any unit in any content area can lead to a fun and interesting show-and-tell activity.

For older students (grades 4–8), the show-and-tell strategy is altered slightly and called *sharing* (Kear & Yellin, 1978). The pri-mary difference is that in sharing, the object talked about must be a part of a demonstra-tion. The student brings in an object and demonstrates its use while also providing a verbal explanation of the activity. In one seventh-grade language arts classroom, for example, a boy brought in a deck of cards, a box, and a scarf and demon-strated some magic tricks. A girl brought in her violin and demonstrated the fingering and bowing technique used in playing the instrument. Another boy set up a chess set and demonstrated the opening moves in chess; another student demonstrated a stitch in her needlepoint display. Sharing is more sophisticated than show-and-tell and requires the students to plan and prac-tice before performing for the group. But like show and tell, it is essentially an exercise in clear communication and it begins with the teacher sharing (demonstrating) something from his or her background and experiences.

DRAMA AND ORAL LANGUAGE DEVELOPMENT

Television has made us a nation of spectators. Children view it from infancy and surveys reveal that they spend more hours in front of the screen each week than they spend in school. The current craze for video games has intensified this situation; therefore, it is more important than ever that we make opportunities available for children to experience par-ticipation in the arts. Creative drama is an ideal form for this participation, with its inclusion of the physical, mental, emotional, and social abilities of the participant. (p. 11)

Nellie McCaslin (1996) thus has summed up the thoughts of many child-hood educators about the importance of drama in the language arts curriculum. Drama is included in this section on oral language development because it truly is one of the great oral communication forms. Morgan and Saxton (1988) argued that dramatic presentations are also one of the best ways to develop children's oral communication skills. But drama is much more than oral communication, for through drama children learn about life, experience the emotions of characters they are portraying, and learn a greater appreciation of literature (Cottrell, 1987).

Drama can take many forms in the classroom, from the simple dress-up play of preschoolers to full-blown theatrical productions with costumes, scenery, and memorized scripts. Whatever the form, the objectives of drama in the classroom, according to McCaslin (1996), remain the same:

- To encourage creative and aesthetic development
- To improve children's abilities to think critically
- To create an environment in which social and cooperative skills flourish
- To improve the general communication skills of students
- To enhance the individual child's knowledge of self

Dramatic Play in the Primary Grades

Probably the first dramatics activity that young children encounter in school is the make-believe center, where children have a chance to dress up in simple costumes, play with blocks and toys, and use their imaginations to create simple stories. In kindergarten and first grade, such centers are among the most popular and sought after by children. With simple props and actions, students imitate the world around them and create strange and wonderful characters to amuse their friends. Some dramatic play activities may become very complex, involve many children, and last nearly the entire period, while other play dramas may span only a few minutes (McCaslin, 1996).

Creating a center to facilitate dramatic play is relatively simple: a few old hats, scarves, simple makeup, a toy car, a stuffed doll, and some cardboard boxes and away you go. With very little prompting, young children join with a few friends and create imaginative dress-up plays. A more formal approach to dramatic or dress-up play utilizes prop-kits. *Prop kits* are play centers focused on a single theme and similar to the intellectual kits described earlier.

Observing young children involved in dramatic play is an important part of a teacher's learning experience. Children's play is not mere play; it is serious. Through dress-up and dramatic play, students learn to take on other roles and to imitate important figures in their lives, such as mommy and daddy. According to noted child psychologist Bruno Bettelheim (1976), it is also a primary way in which young children learn to control their environment and deal with common situations and problems. Through observing children involved in dramatic play, you will soon realize why Virginia Koste, in her book *Dramatic Play in Childhood* (1988), called it "a rehearsal for life."

Movement or Warm-Up Exercises

Professional actors and actresses know the importance of "warming up" before a performance; it's similar to the stretching that an athlete does before going on the playing field. Young children should be introduced to simple warm-up or movement exercises to get them ready for more complicated aspects of drama. The Classroom Vignette that follows offers a few examples of how different teachers use warm-up or movement exercises.

Pantomime

The next step up from movement exercises is pantomime. **Pantomime** is defined by McCaslin (1990) as "the art of conveying ideas without words" (p. 73) and incorporates the gestures and expressions from movement exercises but is more intricate and longer than warm-up exercises. Pantomime is also more like theatre acting in the sense that an entire story can be told through the movements of the characters. Props and simple costumes can also be used, but no speaking is allowed. The most famous pantomimists, or *mimes* (such as the Frenchman Marcel Marceau), work alone on a bare stage. However, in introducing young children to the art of pantomime, it is best to start with small-group skits.

Vignette in the classroom

Teacher 1:

As part of a language arts unit on drama, the teacher has explained and demonstrated the notion of free movement to music. The desks and tables have been moved back against the walls of the room to create an open space in the center. "Now, children," says Mrs. Chang, "when I start the tape, I want you to move about the room using your arms, legs, and bodies to show how the music makes you feel." The tape begins with some slow classical music selections, moves into lively folk-dance tunes, and ends with some somber march music.

Teacher 2:

"Good morning, boys and girls," says Mrs. Bird-song. "Let's begin this beautiful day by singing our 'Good Morning Song.'" As the teacher and children sing the song together, they move their arms and bodies to imitate the little bird in the song.

Way up in the sky
  (stretch way up on your tiptoes)
The little birds fly
  (move your hands like you're flying)
While down in the nest
  (crouch down on the ground)
The little birds rest.
  (fold your head in your arms)
With a wing on the left
  (raise your left elbow)
And a wing on the right
  (raise your right elbow)
The little birds sleep all through the night.
  (rest your head)
The bright sun comes up
  (look up with your eyes wide open)
The dew falls away
  (flutter your fingers)
"Good morning, good morning,"
  (raise your arms to the sun)
The little birds say.
  (turn to your partner and shake his or her hand)

Teacher 3:

"OK, everyone," begins Mr. Johnson, "let's get real quiet and form a big circle. Shhh. Close your eyes. Listen carefully and you can hear it beginning to rain." The teacher rubs his hands together gently and the students imitate him. They rub harder. Then the teacher begins to snap his fingers—first one, then the other. The students do the same (it's raining harder now). The teacher slaps his legs. The students slap their legs, faster and faster (the rain is coming down very hard now). They stomp their feet (you can hear the thunder). Then the movements are repeated in reverse order as the rain gradually slows down and finally stops.

Teacher 4:

"Class, let's go on a bear hunt," says Ms. Aliota (slaps her legs to imitate walking). The children repeat her actions and chant, "Let's go on a bear hunt." As the teacher leads the hunt, the students repeat what she says and imitate her actions.

"I see a wheat field" (places her hand above her eyes and moves her head back and forth). "Can't go over it. Can't go under it. Let's go through it" (moves her arms through the field).

"I see a fence" (repeats looking gesture). "Can't go around it. Can't go under it. Let's go over it" (hands and arms climbing).

"I see a lake. Can't go over it. Can't go around it. Let's swim across it" (arms swimming).

"I see a tree. Can't go over it. Can't go under it. Let's climb up it" (wraps her arms around the tree and climbs, leg over leg; when she gets to the top of the tree, she looks for bears).

"I see a cave. Can't go over it. Can't go under it. Let's go in" (tiptoes in slowly). "I see two eyes" (touches her eyes). "I see two ears" (touches her ears). "I see a nose" (touches her nose). "I see a mouth" (touches her mouth). "IT'S A BEAR! RUN FOR IT!" (She repeats the actions in reverse order very quickly.)

One way to get older students involved with pantomime activities is to teach them the game Charades. In Charades, a famous person's name, a title of a book, movie, or song, or a well-known quotation is acted out using hand, body, and facial expressions. To play Charades, (1) establish common cues or signals, (2) show the number of words being acted out by holding up the same number of fingers, and (3) show the number of syllables in a word by placing the same number of fingers against your inner wrist. While one person acts out the charade, the rest of the group guesses.

In preparing for their skit, the members of each group plan and talk among themselves. They choose parts; decide on the movements they will use to convey their story; and make simple props, signs, or costumes, if necessary. This aspect of the preparation involves verbal communication. But once the group gets onstage (the front of the class), no talking is allowed; this is the real challenge of pantomime. Figure 5.14 contains some simple group pantomime skits that can be adapted for various grade levels.

Another kind of group pantomime skit can be based on a familiar story that the class has heard or read. Some favorite stories that can be easily adapted to pantomime skits include *The Three Bears* by Paul Galdone, *Where the Wild Things Are* by Maurice Sendak, *Strega Nona* by Tomie dePaola, *The Three Billy Goats Gruff* by Paul Galdone, *Charlotte's Web* by E. B. White, and *Homer Price and the Doughnut Machine* by Robert McCloskey.

Figure 5.14

Pantomime suggestions.

1. Wake Up: Waking up in the morning, washing up, getting dressed. Mom calls you to breakfast. Dad's already having his coffee. Uh oh, Dad's late for work and you're late for school. Hurry up and grab your books.

2. Play Ball: What a great day for a game! You're with your friends, the sun is shining, everyone has the gloves, bats, and balls. The game starts, but then . . .

3. Dinnertime: It's your turn to fix dinner for the whole family. What will you fix? Will they like it?

4. Dentist/Patient: What a toothache! Lean back. Relax. This won't hurt a bit. Let me out of here!

5. Go Fly a Kite: It's a windy day, just right for you and a friend to go kite flying. Careful, don't let it go too high. Watch out for those trees. Careful!

6. Homework Excuses: What? Forgot your homework again? Tell me about it, but remember—no words.

7. First Dance: Your shoes hurt. Your shirt/blouse won't stay buttoned. The music is too fast/slow. You really don't know how but . . .

8. First Date: You're nervous. The car won't start. You have to walk. You forgot the tickets to the concert. But . . . it turns out OK.

9. Job Interview: The first questions are easy. Your resume is in order. But then your stomach begins to rumble. (You should have had your breakfast!)

10. Plane Ride: Buckle yourself in. Here comes the flight attendant. Here comes lunch. Careful, don't spill anything. Uh oh, your neighbor needs to get out.

Choral Speaking

When considering the use of choral speaking with your class, you need to decide which form of the activity is most appropriate. There are several types of **choral speaking** from which to choose:

1. *Antiphonal or dialogue.* Poems with two parts or a question-and-answer format are appropriate for this type of speaking activity. Often the deep voices take one part while the light voices take the other; this usually translates into a dialogue between a group of boys and a group of girls. Some poems for which this approach is effective are "Who Has Seen the Wind?" by Christina Rossetti and the American folk song "Buffalo Gals."

2. *Line-a-group or line-a-child.* In this approach, individuals or small groups read one line of the poem at a time. They work to keep in harmony and tempo. Some appropriate poems are "The Sun Is Stuck" by Myra Cohn Livingston, "Let's Marry! Said the Cherry" by N. M. Bodecker, and "The ABC Bunny" by Wanda Gag.

3. *Refrain.* Narrative poems with a chorus are good candidates for refrain. A teacher or student can recite the story, with the other children in the class joining in on the chorus. Examples of poems with refrains are "The Green Grass Growing All Around" and "The Old Woman and the Pig."

4. *Unison.* Although unison speaking appears simple, it really requires skill for the students to keep together. Since everyone speaks every line, the rhythm and timing have to be perfect. Almost every poem is appropriate for unison speaking. Some particularly good poems are "My Name" by Lee Bennett Hopkins, "Dreams" by Langston Hughes, and "Mr. Skinner" by Bodecker.

5. *Cumulative speaking.* In cumulative speaking, one speaker begins with other speakers, one by one, joining the first speaker. This type of speaking helps the student who may be nervous or shy in front of classmates to gain confidence by speaking with others. Stories such as *I Know an Old Lady Who Swallowed a Fly*, retold by Nadine Bernard Westcott, and *Shoes from Grandpa* by Mem Fox can be used for cumulative speaking. Following is an example of the first part of *Shoes from Grandpa* to illustrate how this book can be used for cumulative speaking:

Grandpa:	My, Jessie, how you've grown! You'll need a new pair of shoes this winter, and I'll buy them.
Dad:	I'll buy you some socks from the local shops,
Grandpa & Dad:	to go with the shoes from Grandpa.
Mom:	I'll buy you a skirt that won't show the dirt,
Grandpa, Dad, & Mom:	to go with the socks from the local shops, to go with the shoes from Grandpa.

You may want to start choral speaking by just repeating some favorite poems to the children and having them join in with you. With longer poems, you may want the students to have copies of the text for reference. One pitfall you need to guard against is allowing this activity to become merely a test of oral fluency. The true goal is to help children understand the meaning of poems and to interpret that meaning through oral expression. For more information about using poems and stories for choral speaking and choral reading, check Tashjian's (1974) *With a Deep Sea Smile* and Pennock's (1984) "Choral Reading of Poetry Improves Reading Fluency."

Storytelling

Storytelling is one of the oldest forms of entertainment. Long before there was television, long before there was radio, families sat around the dinner table or gathered in front of the fireplace and told stories: funny stories about simpletons getting into trouble; scary stories with ghosts and goblins; legends and tales from faraway countries; and classic family stories that everyone knew by heart but wanted to hear again and again. Today the art of storytelling has been revitalized in the United States. Professional storytellers are appearing at festivals, in concerts, and in elementary and secondary classrooms to share their art form. In Oklahoma, for example, Lynn Moroney has revived many of the Native American stories, such as the star legends, coyote tales, and sky lore. In Portland, Oregon, Susan Strauss takes her tales of witches, queens, and goddesses into the classroom for students of all ages. In Pennsylvania, Linda Kumbaya Goss is the official storyteller of Philadelphia, where she tells African and African-American tales. Dave Kristy of Pittsburgh, Pennsylvania, uses his fiddle, banjo, and guitar to tell tall tales and regional stories of Appalachia. (For a complete listing of storytellers in your state, contact the National Association of Professional Storytellers, P.O. Box 309, Jonesborough, TN 37659.)

Teaching children to tell stories to their classmates is one of the most effective ways to develop speaking skills in young children. Trousdale (1990) has recounted how one teacher used storytelling to develop the oral communication abilities of a child. Piazza (1999) has also noted that storytelling in the classroom develops students' listening skills, improves their reading comprehension, and stimulates their interest in writing stories.

To teach storytelling to young children, it is not necessary to be a great storyteller. It is helpful, however, if you can demonstrate to children some of the characteristics of an effective storyteller. A good storyteller should do the following things (Trelease, 1995):

- Select a story that he or she really enjoys and that is appropriate for the audience.
- Be thoroughly familiar with the story; memorize only key phrases, not the entire story.
- Be imaginative and include gestures and facial expressions to convey meaning.
- Speak with expression, feeling, and emotion.
- Look directly at the audience; gaze about so that everyone feels involved in the story.

After you have demonstrated storytelling techniques, divide your class into small groups and have students practice telling stories to one another. Storytelling is an art form that develops only through practice. When ready, the children can share their stories with the entire class. Here are some activities to involve your students in the art of storytelling.

Talk boxes. Provide the group with three boxes containing 5 × 8 index cards. The cards in the first box contain brief descriptions of characters (a nurse, a football player, a train conductor). Those in the next box contain brief plot descriptions ("You are on a trip and have lost your luggage"), and those in the third box contain descriptions of settings (a busy street in downtown Chicago, a lonely forest in Vermont, a sunny beach in Florida). Each child in the group chooses one card from each box. They should study their cards for a few minutes and then make up a story that incorporates the character, plot, and setting listed (Kear & Yellin, 1978).

Story boxes. Teachers collect plenty of miscellaneous objects in their closets; here's an opportunity to use them. Into a box or large bag, put a variety of unusual objects (clothing, pictures, mementos from trips, old toys). Each child closes her or his eyes, reaches into the box or bag, and pulls out one object. After the children examine the object and think about it for a while, they should each make up a story that includes the object in some manner. Have them take turns telling their stories to the rest of the group (Kear & Yellin, 1978).

Wordless books. A wordless book tells a story through pictures only. Unlike easy-to-read books or picture storybooks, wordless books contain no print at all. While turning the pages slowly, the "reader" adds the narration and dialogue to create a complete story with beginning, middle, and end. Once children see the wordless book strategy modeled by the teacher, they quickly pick up on it and begin telling stories themselves. Karen D'Angelo (1979) found that wordless books make great inspirational sources for young writers. McGee and Tompkins (1983) also found that wordless books are useful in teaching reading. Students can first dictate a story based on a wordless book. After the teacher has recorded the story, the children can read it back to one another. Even older students enjoy creating and reading their own stories based on wordless books. Figure 5.15 lists some wordless books for use in the classroom.

Liar's goblet. Most children have heard of the lumberjack Paul Bunyan and his blue ox, Babe. They say that with one swipe of his ax Paul could cut down an entire tree, and that in less than an hour he could clear an entire forest. When Babe pulled the logs through the forest, entire valleys were formed.

Similarly, many children recognize the name of Pecos Bill, the cowboy. When just a baby, Pecos Bill became lost in the desert and was adopted and raised by coyotes. As an infant, he ate bear steaks and buffalo meat. As a man, he once lassoed a cyclone and rode it until it quit its howling ways.

The stories of Paul Bunyan and Pecos Bill are examples of tall tales. Children love to expand on and embellish their own adventures. The liar's goblet activity builds on the idea of the tall tale and on children's enjoyment of exaggeration. It can be taught in the form of a game. First you need a goblet (a cup, glass, or mug will do). One person in the group takes the liar's goblet and makes up a short but exaggerated tall tale. The next person in the group takes the goblet and says, "That's nothing; why I remember . . . " Each student tries to top the previous story; each story, though different, grows more exaggerated. Norma Livo (1986) has suggested having a liar's goblet contest, in which a panel of student judges votes to determine the most outlandish story. Figure 5.16 lists examples of tall-tale books.

Serial stories. This storytelling activity is also based on a game that many children are already familiar with. One person, usually the teacher or designated group leader, begins a story. At any point, the person stops and the next person in the group continues the story. Farnsworth (1981) referred to these continuous stories as *chain stories*. A variation on this activity utilizes a ball of yarn. When the first storyteller stops, he or she tosses the yarn to any other person in the group, who must then continue the story. The ball of yarn is tossed back and forth, making a web design. Finally, one person tosses the ball of yarn back to the person who originally began the story; this is the signal that the story is about to end. The final storyteller concludes by saying, "And that's the end of this yarn."

Figure 5.15

Wordless books.

The Lady and the Strawberry Snatcher (M. Bang, 1980)

Just in Passing (S. Bonners, 1989)

The Snowman (R. Briggs, 1978)

The Patchwork Farmer (C. Brown, 1989)

Do You Want to Be My Friend? (E. Carle, 1971)

In the Pond (E. Cristini, 1984)

Good Dog, Carl (A. Day, 1985)

Carl's Afternoon in the Park (A. Day, 1991)

Paddy's Pay-Day (A. Day, 1989)

The Yellow Umbrella (H. Drescher, 1987)

Paddy Under Water (J. S. Goodall, 1984)

Amanda and the Mysterious Carpet (F. Krahn, 1985)

The Swan (V. Mayo, 1994)

On Top (M. MacGregor, 1988)

The Gift (J. Prater, 1985)

Mouse Around (P. Schories, 1991)

Where's My Monkey? (D. Schubert, not dated)

Junglewalk (N. Tafuri, 1988)

Follow Me (N. Tafuri, 1990)

Free Fall (D. Wiesner, 1988)

Tuesday (D. Wiesner, 1991)

The Grey Lady and the Strawberry Snatcher (M. Bang, 1996)

Zoom (I. Banyai, 1995)

ReZoom (I. Banyai, 1995)

Figure 5.16

Tall-tale books.

John Tabor's Ride (E. C. Day, 1989)

Pecos Bill (S. Kellogg, 1986)

John Henry: An American Legend (E. J. Keats, 1965)

Paul Bunyan (S. Kellogg, 1984)

Johnny Appleseed (S. Kellogg, 1988)

Mike Fink (S. Kellogg, 1992)

Sally and Thunder and Whirlwind (S. Kellogg, 1996)

I Was Born Ten Thousand Years Ago (S. Kellogg, 1996)

The Song of Paul Bunyan and Tony Beaver (E. Rees, 1964)

Windwagon Smith (E. Rees, 1966)

Tall Tales of America (I. Shapiro, 1958)

Heroes in American Folklore (I. Shapiro, 1962)

American Tall Tale Animals (A. Stoutenburg, 1968)

Chalk or draw-along stories. In this activity, the storyteller begins the tale by drawing a circle or line on the board. As the story continues, the storyteller adds more details to the drawing. Eventually, when the story is completed, there is a finished drawing on the chalkboard. To teach this activity, draw and tell the entire story to a small group of children. When the students have learned the story and the picture drawing, they can tell it to another group of children who have not heard it yet. Figure 5.17 shows a chalk story version of "The Circus" as told by Rene Wojnoski, who teaches kindergarten in Ponca City, Oklahoma, and tells stories to her students as a regular part of her instruction.

New versions and new endings. Yet another storytelling activity involves changing elements in the story plot and/or altering the endings of familiar stories. It works particularly well with folktales and fairy tales. To start this activity, read a number of different versions of the same story to your students. For example, use a few different versions of *The Three Little Pigs.*

For a real change of pace, read to your class *The True Story of the Three Little Pigs* by A. Wolf (as told to Jon Scieszka). The story begins, "I'm the Wolf. Alexander T.

Figure 5.17

Sample chalk story: "The Circus."

Let's go to a circus. Here is the circus ring inside the tent.

We'll need some seats for the audience.

Inside the big ring are two small rings for the performing seals and dogs.

Another small ring in the center contains a cage where the lions perform.

Look! There's the high wire and net for the trapeze artists.

At the end of the tent is a big cage for the elephants. But who's that funny-looking man running all around?

Wolf. You can call me Al. I don't know how this whole Big Bad Wolf thing got started, but it's all wrong." Al Wolf then proceeds to explain how a great misunderstanding occurred between him and the three little pigs all because of a sneeze and a cup of sugar. This story is also a great vehicle for discussing point of view with the children. Explain that when a story is told from the point of view of a different character, it is quite different.

Puppetry and Storytelling

Like storytelling, puppets and masks have traditionally been associated with oral dramatic presentations. Linderman and Linderman (1984) have described the fascinating role puppets have played throughout civilization. For example, puppets have been found buried in ancient Egyptian tombs. In twelfth-century China, they were used to entertain the emperors. In sixteenth-century Japan, puppetry evolved into a complex theatrical world: Puppets were large figures (a few feet in height) and carved from wood, and it took a master puppeteer and a number of apprentices to operate a single puppet. Today in China, Japan, and Thailand, puppetry is an art form enjoyed equally by adults and children. Katherine Paterson's Newbery Medal–winning book *The Master Puppeteer* is an excellent story to read aloud to children to get them ready for their puppet-making activities.

As with so many other activities, creating the proper environment is the essential ingredient to a successful puppetry experience. Begin by creating a simple puppet stage in one corner of your classroom. This can be easily done by draping an ordinary table with an old tablecloth or with decorated butcher-block paper. Another way to create a stage is to cut out the bottom of a large cardboard box, cover the box with colorful paper, and make a simple cloth curtain to hang over the front. Once your puppet stage is in order, the students naturally gravitate toward it.

The next step is to gather some simple materials for creating easy-to-make puppets. Linderman and Linderman (1984) have suggested the following list of materials: cardboard tubing, boxes, paper cups, paper plates, egg cartons, gift wrapping, various colored and textured cloth, tongue depressors, pipe cleaners, wooden dowels, old gloves, feathers, string, ribbons, cellophane, socks, tissue paper, paper bags, sticks, plastic foam cups, cardboard, construction paper, scissors, tape, paste, glue, washable markers or paints, crayons, buttons, thread, yarn, and felt. Piazza (1999) also suggests matchboxes, whisk brooms, and floor mops. Literally any scrap material can be used in the construction of puppets. There are several different kinds of puppets that young students can make.

Sock puppets. Begin by having each child bring an old sock from home. Demonstrate that by placing your hand inside the sock—your fingers in the toe, your thumb in the heel—you can make the puppet come alive simply by opening and closing your hand. Next add some cloth, felt, buttons, beads, yarn, and so on to make the eyes, mouth, nose, and ears. Additional cloth or felt can be used to construct clothing for the puppet to extend over the puppeteer's arm.

Finger puppets. The simplest way to make a finger puppet is with an old glove. On each finger, draw, color, or paint facial features of different characters. You can add tiny bits of yarn, sequins, or buttons. Each finger should contain a face with a different expression or look. In this way, you have large groups of tiny character puppets who can talk back and forth. You can even create a puppet family on one hand.

Paper-bag puppets. Paper-bag puppets are another easy and inexpensive way to introduce children to puppetry. Depending on the size of the paper bag used, you can create all types of puppets. Large paper (*never plastic*) bags, for example, can be placed over children's heads and worn as full masks. Holes for the eyes, nose, and mouth can be cut and the bags decorated with crayon, magic marker, felt, cloth scraps, and bits of string. Ears, hair, even hats made from colored construction paper can be added onto the bag with glue, paste, or tape. Smaller paper bags lend themselves to hand puppets.

Stick-and-ball puppets. With a wooden dowel, tongue depressor, or bent coat hanger plus a plastic foam ball or old tennis ball, you can teach children to construct stick-and-ball puppets. First cover the ball with felt or cloth and draw in the facial features. Then decorate with string, small buttons, and so on. Next insert the stick to support the head. (With the tennis ball, you have to cut a small hole to insert the stick.) Finally, cover the stick with a loose cloth, decorated to form a distinctive costume for your puppet. Insert your hand beneath the cloth and grasp the stick. Your puppet is ready.

Shadow puppets. Shadow puppets are particularly popular in Asian countries. To create a shadow puppet, you will use stiff cardboard or oak tag. Cut your puppet shape from the flat pattern in profile because only this outline is seen by the audience. Intricate facial features are not necessary; the unique characteristics of the puppet come from the cut outline. Next, attach the cutout to a stick to be held by the student puppeteer. The unique effect created by the shadow puppet depends on the special stage that you create by stretching a sheet of translucent cloth tightly in a frame. Stand behind the frame and place a bright light behind the shadow puppet and the screen. The audience sees a dark silhouette or shadow against the light screen. Bring out other shadow puppets to create a captivating form of entertainment.

Improvisation

After children understand how bodily and facial gestures can suggest emotions and even tell a story, the next step is to add spoken dialogue. Using such freeform dialogue along with pantomimed gestures to tell a story is known as **improvisation**. This improvisation is different from dialogue improvisation, which was discussed earlier in this chapter. This type of improvisation does not have any structure to the dialogue; dialogue improvisation does. In improvisation, the dialogue of the various characters is improvised by the actors as the story unfolds; however, an improvisation is not totally unplanned. Generally the story is known in advance, and the actors alter the dialogue as they see fit. In improvisation, unlike theatre acting, a script does not have to be memorized. However, simple props, costumes, and even scenery can be used, and students enjoy creating these in class.

One recommended way to lead into improvisation is through the use of children's literature (McCaslin, 1996). First, identify some stories familiar to the class. If you are reading aloud to the students on a regular basis and giving children free time during the school day to read books of their own choice, this should not be a problem. Let the class divide into groups with each group selecting a favorite story. Figure 5.18 lists books that can be easily improvised in dramatic presentations.

As with puppetry, improvisations based on children's literature books eventually lead children to want to write and create their own improvisational plays. McCaslin (1996) has noted that improvisational drama often lends itself to dealing with real problems that affect students in their daily lives.

Atnold, T. (1987). *No Jumping on the Bed.* New York: Dial.
Freeman, D. (1968). *Corduroy.* New York: Viking.
Galdone, P. (1973). *The Little Red Hen.* New York: Seabury Press.
Galdone, P. (1975). *The Gingerbread Boy.* New York: Houghton Mifflin.
Galdone, P. (1984). *The Three Pigs.* New York: Clarion.
Howe, J. (1988). *Rip Van Winkle.* Boston: Little, Brown.
Hyman, T. (1983). *Little Red Riding Hood.* New York: Holiday House.
Jungman, A. (1989). *The Day Teddy Wanted Grandpa to Notice Him.* New York: Barron's.
Kamerman, S. (ed.) (1987). *Plays from Favorite Folk Tales.* Boston: Plays, Inc.
Piper, W. (1980). *The Little Engine That Could.* New York: Grosset and Dunlap.
Scieszka, J. (1989). *The True Story of the Three Little Pigs.* New York: Viking Kestrel.
Sendak, M. (1963). *Where the Wild Things Are.* New York: Harper & Row.

Figure 5.18

Books for improvisation.

Reader's Theatre or Story Theatre

Another form of dramatic presentation that increases children's comprehension of literature as well as develops oral language and pantomime abilities is reader's theatre, sometimes called story theatre (Forsythe, 1995; Martinez, Roser, & Strecker, 1998/1999). **Reader's theatre** has been defined by Laughlin and Latrobe (1990) as "a presentation by two or more participants who read from scripts and interpret a literary work in such a way that the audience imaginatively senses characterization, setting and action (p. 3)." Vocal intonation, facial expressions, and pantomime gestures can also be used to enhance the quality of the presentation. A narrator is often used to direct the various reader-actors on and off the stage and to communicate scene changes to the audience. Occasionally simple props and costumes are used to further suggest characters and setting.

Typically reader's theatre utilizes the literature of folktales such as *Arrow to the Sun: A Pueblo Indian Tale* by Gerald McDermott, fairy tales, plays written especially for children, and short prose selections. However, McCaslin (1996) found that professional reader's theatre productions also utilize historical works such as *Feast of Thanksgiving: The First American Holiday* by June Behrens, biographies, letters, news, articles, and even comic strips. Using literature that was not originally intended to be dramatized often requires that students write additional scenes, characters, and dialogue to ensure the audience follows the story. Figure 5.19 lists sources for reader's theatre, and Figure 5.20 lists books to use for reader's theatre. Figure 5.21 is an example of simply taking a story such as *Wind Says Good Night* by Katy Rydell, which has repetitive text, and writing it for reader's theatre.

Cheathem, V. (1977). *Skits and Spoofs for Young Actors.* Boston: Plays, Inc.
Durell, D. (1957). *Thirty Plays for Classroom Reading.* Boston: Plays, Inc.
Kamerman, S. (ed) (1987). *Patriotic and Historical Plays for Young People.* Boston: Plays, Inc.
Kamerman, S. (ed.) (1987). *Plays of Black Americans.* Boston: Plays, Inc.
Laughlin, M., & Latrobe, K. (1990). *Reader's Theatre for Children: Scripts and Script Development.* Englewood, CO: Litran's Unlimited.
Scott, L. (1961). *Fairy Tale Plays in Rhymes.* Los Angeles: F. A. Owen Publishing Co.
Sloyer, S. (1982). *Reader's Theatre: Story Dramatization in the Classroom.* Urbana, IL: NCTE.

Figure 5.19

Sources for reader's theatre.

Figure 5.20

Cumulative books to use in reader's theatre.

A Most Unusual Lunch (Robert Benders, 1994)

Shoes from Grandpa (Mem Fox, 1989)

Jack's Garden (Henry Cole, 1995)

Good-Night Owl! (Pat Hutchins, 1972)

The Old Woman Who Lived in a Vinegar Bottle (Margaret MacDonald, 1995)

The Bag I'm Taking to Grandma's (Shirley Neitze, 1995)

Too Much Noise (Ann McGovern, 1967)

"Not Now!" Said the Cow (Joanne Oppenheim, 1989)

Wind Says Good Night (Katy Rydell, 1994)

The Little Old Lady Who Was Not Afraid of Anything (Linda Williams, 1986)

The Napping House (Audrey Wood, 1984)

"Stop, Stop, You Big Old Bull!" (Harriet Zieffer, 1995)

Figure 5.21

Sample of reader's theatre.

Wind Says Good Night

by Katy Rydell

Nar #1:	It was late at night. All little children were in their beds, fast asleep. All except one. The night wind brushed against a window.
Wind:	Shh-h-h. Go to sleep. (Whispering)
Child:	I cannot fall asleep because outside, on the branch of a tree, Mockingbird is singing.
Wind:	Mockingbird, will you stop singing so the child can go to sleep?
Nar #2:	But Mockingbird loved to sing. Music spilled from deep in his throat, as he sang of green woods, bright flowers, and warm summer nights.
Mockingbird:	No! I can't stop singing until Cricket stops playing.
Nar #3:	From the tall grass by the back steps came the cheerful ring of Cricket's tune.
Wind:	Cricket, will you stop playing so Mockingbird will stop singing so the child can go to sleep?
Nar #4:	But Cricket didn't want to stop playing. His toes were tapping, his coattails flapping, as the melody flowed from his fiddle string.

Source: Adapted from *Wind Says Good Night* by Katy Rydell. Text copyright © 1994 by Katy Rydell. Reprinted by permission of Houghton Mifflin Co. All rights reserved.

Theatre Acting

Theatre acting includes all of the previously described oral language activities: movement exercises, pantomime, improvisation, speaking with feeling and expression, discussion and interpretation of scripts, and rehearsing. It also includes what for some children is the most difficult aspect of acting: the memorization of a script. Because of this requirement and the additional pressures that it places on young children, it is recommended that theatre acting come after students are already familiar with the other forms of oral expression. However, even very young children can be taught the rudiments of play acting.

Too often teachers are required by school administrators to have their class perform a play (the traditional Thanksgiving or Christmas auditorium performance) without any prior preparation in oral communication or acting. This is a mistake. Theatre acting should be part of the learning process that leads children to a greater appreciation of literature, builds confidence in oral communication abilities, and enhances social growth, including cooperative learning skills. Children's drama authority Nellie McCaslin (1996) has argued correctly that theatre acting is a vital part of the aesthetic education of children, which too often is missing or minimized in elementary curriculums.

To introduce theater acting in the elementary classroom, Dorothy Heathcote (1983) has recommended that teachers begin with discussion. Talk about the work to be performed. Encourage the children to make suggestions and decisions about the characters, the setting, the staging, and so on. Then improvise the play or story until everyone has a sense of the action, the movement of characters, and the overall theme of the play or story. Don't be afraid to revise lines, to change parts, or to recast characters. Depending on the nature of the work selected, older students may wish to do library research about the subject matter of the play or the specific time period depicted. Figure 5.22 suggests sources for theatre acting in the elementary grades.

Theatre acting represents the culmination of a dramatics unit. It brings together and integrates listening, speaking, reading, and writing skills like no other single activity. It gives students a heightened awareness of the power of literature to evoke emotions from an audience. It engages youngsters in critical thinking and discussion. However, choosing to do a full-scale play production in your class means a commitment of time and energy. You cannot squeeze it between spelling tests, ditto worksheets, and basal reader lessons. The sacrifices you make, however, are more than made up for by the excitement, enthusiasm, and genuine learning that take place when students discover their talents as actors.

Education is not filling a pail, but the lighting of a fire.
WILLIAM BUTLER YEATS

Figure 5.22

Plays for theatre acting.

Burack, S. (1970). *One Hundred Plays for Children.* Boston: Plays, Inc.

Burack, S. (1990). *Plays: The Drama Magazine for Young People.* Boston: Plays, Inc.

Hugher, T. (1974). *The Tiger's Bones and Other Plays for Children.* New York: Viking Press.

Murray, F. (1984). *Mystery Plays for Young Actors.* Boston: Plays, Inc.

SPEAKING ASSESSMENT

When a teacher wishes to assess the students' speaking abilities using a specific assignment, she should discuss with students from the beginning which areas will be assessed. This allows students to work on those skills while they prepare their assignment. It is then crucial that the teacher assess those specific skills during the assignment. At the beginning of the year, a teacher may want to emphasize only adequate coverage of content or volume and eye contact, in which case the rubric should include only those areas. However, toward the end of the year, the teacher may also require visual aids. In this case, it is important that she also assess the speaker's use of the visual aids. Figure 5.23 is an example of a rubric a teacher used for research presentations that were given toward the end of the year. Take note that on this rubric each aspect of the presentation is of equal importance. However, the rubric used for storytelling (Figure 5.24) is scored differently: the emphasis is on voice inflection, with each aspect of voice inflection given different value.

When a teacher uses a rubric, a student can see the specific strengths and weaknesses of his or her presentation. It is important, too, that a teacher (1) write general comments to encourage the student and (2) discuss the rubric with the student.

Figure 5.23

Rubric used for assessment of specific skills.

PRESENTATION OF RESEARCH

Name _____ Topic _____

Total Score _____ Grading Period 1 2 3 4

SUPERIOR = 5   EXCELLENT = 4   FAIR = 3   ADEQUATE = 2   WEAK = 1

CONTENT

_____ Clarity of purpose   _____ Supporting details

_____ Introduction   _____ Conclusion

_____ Main points   _____ Interesting

PRESENTATION

_____ Rate   _____ Standard English

_____ Volume   _____ Eye contact

VISUAL AIDS

_____ Neatly prepared   _____ Manipulation

_____ Appropriate size   _____ Support topic

GENERAL COMMENTS:

Vocabulary Development

In an integrated approach to the language arts, vocabulary development is a natural byproduct of listening and speaking. Jim Trelease (1995) in *The Read-Aloud Handbook* explains that reading aloud to children of all ages (from birth through middle school) is the most effective way to help a child enlarge his or her vocabulary. Evans (1992) found that reading to seventh-graders each day was not only a pleasant experience but also a great way to increase the average/low-average seventh-graders' vocabulary and reading ability. There is debate among researchers, however, as to whether or not direct instruction is necessary for learning specific vocabulary terms. For example, Blachowicz (1987) found that many teachers rely on basal reader manuals as the primary way to teach new vocabulary associated with the stories children read. Johnson and Pearson (1984) have argued for direct vocabulary instruction using semantic mapping techniques to help students relate new terms to their prior knowledge. Jiganti and Tindall (1986), however, have argued for a more inter-active approach such as dramatic acting to help children remember new words encountered in their reading.

The position of this textbook is that vocabulary knowledge develops in the normal course of engaging young children in listening, speaking, reading, and writing activities. However, at times teachers should use mini-lessons to

STORYTELLING CRITIQUE

Figure 5.24

Student _____

Story Title _____

	Score
APPROPRIATE MATERIAL (15 POINTS)	
Length (2 of 15)	_____
Engaging (5 of 15)	_____
Age appropriate (3 of 15)	_____
Interesting (5 of 15)	_____
FACIAL EXPRESSION (13 POINTS)	_____
VOICE INFLECTION (50 POINTS)	
Pleasing tone (5 of 50)	_____
Variety of pitch (10 of 50)	_____
Clear diction (10 of 50)	_____
Change for dialogue (10 of 50)	_____
Appropriate dialect (5 of 50)	_____
Variety of rate (10 of 50)	_____
APPROPRIATE BODY MOVEMENT (12 POINTS)	_____
SPECIAL EFFECTS/PROPS (10 POINTS)	_____
TOTAL SCORE	═══════

GENERAL COMMENTS:

---

teach vocabulary directly. In these cases, the following guidelines should be kept in mind (Rupley et al., 1998/1999):

- Always try to relate new vocabulary terms to students' prior knowledge and background.

- Focus on elaborating children's use of new terms rather than merely having them memorize definitions.

- Utilize activities that demand active student involvement in vocabulary learning, such as vocabulary games, dramatics, or writing activities, rather than passive fill-in-the-blank exercises.

- Help students develop strategies for acquiring new vocabulary independently, such as constructing concept wheels, semantic word maps, webs, and semantic feature analysis graphs.

- Build a conceptual base for the new vocabulary word.

VOCABULARY MINI-LESSONS

The following activities lend themselves to mini-lessons that reinforce specific aspects of vocabulary development.

Synonyms

Synonyms are words that have the same or almost the same meaning, such as *gigantic* and *enormous*. Knowledge of synonyms makes speech and writing more varied and interesting. Often young children rely on the same tired words over and over again because they lack synonym knowledge. Some synonym lessons can be tied to teaching students to use a dictionary or thesaurus. Other activities include having small groups brainstorm lists of synonym alternatives for commonly used words such as *said* or *talk*. These lists can later be displayed around the room as posters for easy reference when writing or reading. See Figure 5.25.

Antonyms

Antonyms are words that have opposite meanings, such as *hot/cold* and *fat/slender*. Teach a few common pairs of antonyms; then get students into small groups to brainstorm pairs of antonyms. Encourage them to use their

Figure 5.25

Synonym chart.

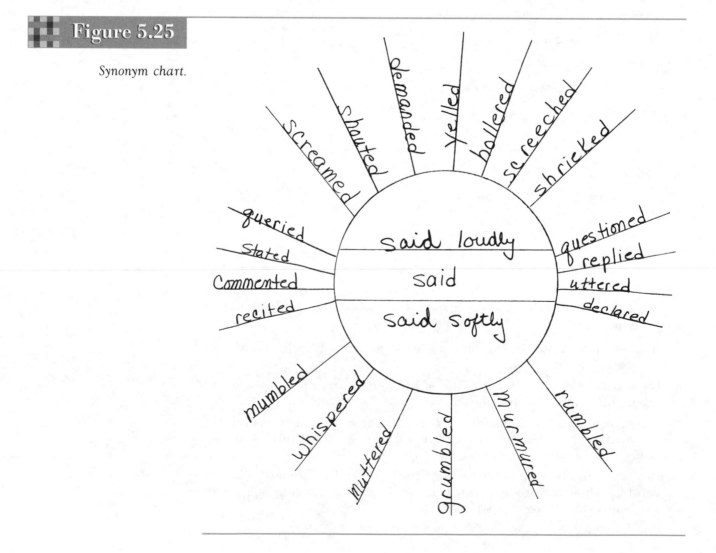

dictionaries to find new words and their opposites. Charts of the antonym pairs can be made to reinforce vocabulary learning.

Homonyms

Homonyms are words that sound alike but are spelled differently and have different meanings. Homonyms are often confused by children and appear as errors in their writing. Identify common homonym errors by analyzing students' writing. For example, *to/too/two, there/their/they're, which/witch, wood/would, deer/dear,* and *bear/bare* are often misused in children's writing. Review the spelling and meanings of these common homonyms with your class, but remember they will only be learned as students use them in their writing over time. The isolated mini-lesson is only a first step toward vocabulary development.

Multiple Meanings

Common words sometimes take on new meanings depending on the context. For example, many words can be used both as a noun (a playing *card*) and a verb (to *card* wool). The key to teaching multiple meanings of words is to focus on the contexts of sentences. Contextual clues are the most powerful of the reading strategies for determining meanings of commonly used words. In how many different contexts can you use the ordinary word *run*? (Clue: You can *run* around the block and get a *run* in your stocking.)

Neologisms

Neologisms are new words that have entered the language through extensive usage or as labels for new discoveries, inventions, products, fashions, and so on. Children need to understand that words are created by people and that language is constantly changing. Identifying new words that have entered the English language is one way of demonstrating language change over time. For example, find a dictionary from around 1945 and compare it to a dictionary printed in the 1990s. Note how many new words have been created in that 50-year period. Words associated with space exploration, computers, discoveries in chemistry and physics, new fashion designs, and inventions are all neologisms. Some examples are *astronaut, laser, microwave, silicon, carcinogen, arthroscope,* and *bell-bottoms.*

Portmanteaus

A *portmanteau* is a new word formed by combining two existing words and omitting some of their letters. Lewis Carroll, the author of *Alice in Wonderland,* provided many early portmanteaus, such as "*chuckle + snort = chortle.*" A common portmanteau students might recognize is the word *smog,* which weather forecasters used to describe certain very cloudy days made up of *smoke* and *fog.* A type of *motor hotel* is referred to as a *motel;* a light meal that comes after *breakfast* and before *lunch* is called *brunch.* See how many other portmanteaus the children can think of. The students may even wish to create their own portmanteaus. For example, one fourth-grade boy created a comic book character that was part *man* and part *bear* and called him *Bearan.*

Acronyms

An *acronym* is a word formed from the initials of an organization. This is a shortened way of saying something; over time, through wide usage, such acronyms have become accepted as actual words. For example, the military uses many acronyms. Children might recognize the word *M.A.S.H.* (from the TV show) as standing for Mobile Army Surgical Hospital. A soldier who is absent without leave is *AWOL*. The North Atlantic Treaty Organization is referred to as *NATO*. Many other groups and organizations employ acronyms: *NOW* stands for the National Organization for Women; *AIM* stands for the American Indian Movement. Brainstorm together additional acronyms.

Euphemisms

A *euphemism* literally is a "more pleasant sounding" word used instead of a term with negative connotations. Some euphemisms originate from social pressures of groups offended by certain inaccurate or inadequate terms. For example, the term *Native American* can be used instead of *Indian* since Christopher Columbus applied the later term in the mistaken belief that he had landed in India. Recently the term *sanitation engineer* has replaced *garbage collector* although the job remains the same. Other euphemisms are created to hide the true meaning of terms. The military refers to *defoliation programs* rather than *chemical warfare*. Other common euphemisms are *senior citizen*, *retirement village*, and *the dearly departed*.

IN & BEYOND THE CLASSROOM

Select one of the vocabulary activities mentioned and teach it to a small group of students. Record your impressions in your journal. Were all the students involved? What unexpected learning took place? What follow-up activities can you do with these vocabulary lessons?

Regionalisms

Regionalisms are expressions associated with particular geographic regions of the country. As such, they are closely related to dialects, the unique pronunciation characteristics of specific areas in the United States. Lessons on identifying regional expressions integrate nicely with geography lessons. For example, in the Northeast, people carry their groceries in a *bag*; in the Midwest, people use a *sack*. In the deep South, you may hear the term *poke*. All three terms refer to the same object. Similarly, depending on the region in which you happen to live or travel, you may hear different terms all referring to the same food: *pancakes, flapjacks, griddle cakes, johnny cakes, a stack*. How many different terms can you think of for a large seat generally found in a living room?

Summary

Listening and speaking skills are two of the important foundation blocks for literacy instruction. Students' listening abilities can be developed through listening centers, listening/reading transfer lessons, and critical listening activities, such as recognizing propaganda devices. Since students spend the majority of their time listening, it is important that their skills in this area be developed and related to the other language arts.

Speaking skills develop through the creation of a positive learning environment in the classroom and through practicing speaking in a variety of settings and activities. There are many oral language activities that teachers can use to engage their students: conversation, show-and-tell, and storytelling are but a few. Dramatic play, improvisation, and reader's theatre further develop speaking and acting abilities in a cooperative group setting. Theatre acting, which culminates in the performance of a play before a live audience, brings together all the communication skills in an exciting learning experience for teachers, children, and parents.

Vocabulary mini-lessons can also be taught to reinforce students' knowledge of synonyms, antonyms, homonyms, and other vocabulary constructs.

However, such lessons are most effective when they originate from children's questions or appear in the reading and writing activities that the students have selected.

activities *With Children*

The following activities can be presented in a game format and are helpful in developing the vocabulary and general speaking skills of young children. Work with a small group of students and explain or model the game. Then let them play the game while you observe how they use language and learn new vocabulary terms.

GOING ON A PICNIC

The teacher begins by saying, "We are going on a picnic and Ann is bringing apples." Each child then has to think of an object to bring that begins with the same initial sound as his or her own name. Later they can think of objects that begin with the same sound as a friend's name. Once the students understand the pattern, the game begins, with each child introducing as many children as possible using the pattern "We are going on a picnic . . . " A more challenging version of the game for older students includes the insertion of a descriptive adjective with the same initial sound before the noun. For example, "We are going on a picnic and Donald is bringing delicious doughnuts."

SALES PITCH

Explain to your class what a sales pitch is. Then have groups of students select a product and try to sell it to their classmates. Do this in small groups so that every child will have a chance to speak. This will give you a chance to observe children using their oral language skills.

IN YOUR OWN VOICE

First teach children how to give a brief talk on a topic of their choice. Then have them tape-record their voice. Teach them to analyze their own speech. Is it clear? Too fast? Interesting? Tape the speech a second time and have students try to improve from the first effort.

CATEGORIES

The teacher names a category (such as "vehicles") and then continues naming members of the category (car, bus, train, and so on). At any point, another person may say "Category" and start over with a new category (such as "vegetables"). This game is played to a rhythm as follows: clap, clap, snap, snap, [category/example] (clap, clap, snap, snap, *vehicles*; clap, clap, snap, snap, *car*; clap, clap, snap, snap, *bus*; and so on).

ALPHABET GAME

Tell what you see inside or outside the classroom beginning with the letter *a*. The next person repeats your sentence and adds an object beginning with the letter *b*. The third person repeats the two previous sentences and adds an object beginning with the letter *c*, and so on. For example, "I see an apple, a box, and a crayon." Encourage the children to use complete sentences.

GEOGRAPHY TRAIN

This game combines knowledge of geographic place-names, spelling, and vocabulary. The first person names a country, a city, a state, or some other place. The next person uses the last letter of the place-name to begin the next term. The game continues until someone cannot think of a name beginning with the last letter of the previous word. For example, "Ethiopia, Alaska, Arkansas, Switzerland, Denver, . . . "

NOUN TRAIN

This game is played using the same rules as Geography Train except that any nouns can be used, for example, "Book, kitchen, napkin, noodle . . . " Another variation on this would be a Verb Train.

CONTEXT CHALLENGE

This game emphasizes careful listening skills and particularly context clues. The teacher writes a challenge word on the board, one the students probably don't know, and then reads aloud a passage containing that word. The children can only use the context clues heard in the passage to determine the unknown word.

ORAL/AURAL MATH

One child dictates a simple addition, subtraction, multiplication, or division problem. The next student solves the problem aloud without using paper or pencil. Later, these oral word problems can combine addition, subtraction, multiplication, and other steps.

ORAL CLOZE

The Cloze technique (discussed in Chapters 9 and 10) involves omitting words from a passage in a reading exercise. The reader must then fill in the blank with an accurate word or phrase. Oral Cloze utilizes the same skill but is done strictly at the listening and speaking levels. This exercise requires careful attention and listening.

ORIGAMI

Origami is the Japanese art of paper folding. Teaching children simple paper-folding designs is a good way to teach following directions. Many Japanese children learn origami as a regular part of their school curriculum. Origami requires patience, precision, and careful observation and listening. To get started, check out some books from the library, such as Isao Honda's *How to Make Origami: The Japanese Art of Paper Folding* (1959) or F. Tembo's *Paper: Folded, Cut and Sculpted* (1974).

HOMONYM HOP

First think of as many homonym pairs as possible. Next come up with a silly definition for the word formed by the combination of each pair. See if your friends can guess the homonyms from your definition, for example: "A naked grizzly is a *bare bear*." "An unemployed rock star is an *idle idol*." "An ordinary jet is a *plain plane*."

technology The Video Camera

The video camera, now available in many schools, is a useful tool to promote speaking skills and to integrate the language arts with the entire curriculum. One activity that can be done by the entire class is to plan and produce a newscast.

Following are a few of the activities that take place as the students plan and rehearse for the production:

- They research (read) for information.
- They write the news pieces.
- They practice speaking and listening skills as they interview people for the newscast. The video camera can also be used in the interviews.
- The student who does the weather may need to review weather terms and geographic locations.
- Students who read the news will need to be sure about the correct pronunciations of places and people's names.
- Students who produce the advertisement spots will have a chance to write and sing jingles and then act out the advertisements.
- As the students polish for the final production, they will listen, view, and self-critique their contributions to the newscast.

Another way to use the video camera in the classroom is to have groups of children practice and tape reader's theatre, puppet shows, and skits. The students should be encouraged to view the presentation, work on fluency, and later show it to other classes and parents. As you can see, the video camera is a great tool to use as children become fluent speakers.

websites E-learning

www.enigmagraphics.com/stories/index.htm
This site provides links to online stories and professional storytellers.

www.3.ns.sympatico.ca/onstage/puppets/activity/index.html
This site explains how to make puppets.

www.yo.rim.or.jp/~tomte/maps-e.htm
This site contains information about Japanese puppetry. It is in Japanese and English.

ww.itdc.sbcss.k12.ca.us/curriculum/puppetry.html
This site shows puppets from around the world and informs students how to create their own puppets.

www.videomaker.com
This site is an outstanding magazine (print and electronic) for people interested in video production.

www.kidtools.com/

This site reviews purchasing information for numerous software titles for K–12.

www.csun.edu/~vceed009/languagearts.html

This site has many resources for language arts teachers, including those for speaking and listening skills.

Related Readings

Cottrell, J. (1987). *Creative drama in the classroom grades 4–6: Teacher's resource book for theatre arts.* Lincolnwood, IL: National Textbook Company.

> This book explains how to include creative drama as an educational tool. She explains how to do sidecoaching, role playing, pantomime, reader's theatre, puppetry, and improvisation with literature as well as other subjects such as social studies and science. Included are scripts that are ready to be used in the classroom.

Forsythe, S. (1995). It worked! Reader's theatre in second grade. *The Reading Teacher, 49*(3), 264–269.

> This article explains how to successfully use reader's theatre in the classroom. It includes a list of books to use for reader's theatre.

Martinez, M., Roser, N., & Strecker, S. (1998/1999). "I never thought I could be a star": A reader's theatre ticket to fluency. *The Reading Teacher, 52*(4), 326–334.

McCaslin, N. (1996). *Creative drama in the classroom and beyond* (6th ed.). New York: Longman.

> This book is a great starting point for teachers who have no experience in any of the creative dramatic activities. Included are scripts to be used in the various activities.

Trelease, J. (1995). *The read-aloud handbook* (3rd ed.). New York: Penguin Books.

> Trelease offers a theory for reading aloud to students of all ages. He explains what makes a book a great read-aloud book and gives lists for all ages.

References

Bauman, M. L. (1987). Listening, repetition and meaning. *Language Arts, 64*(1), 54–60.

Berry, K. (1985). Talking to learn subject matter/learning subject matter talk. *Language Arts, 62*(1), 34–42.

Bettelheim, B. (1976). *The uses of enchantment: The meaning and importance of fairy tales.* New York: Random House.

Blachowicz, C. (1987). Vocabulary instruction: What goes on in the classroom. *The Reading Teacher, 41*(2), 132–137.

Bloom, B. (ed.) (1956). *Taxonomy of educational objectives, the classification of educational goals, handbook I: Cognitive domain.* New York: David McKay.

Brent, R., & Anderson, P. (1993). Developing children's classroom listening strategies. *The Reading Teacher, 47,* 122–126.

Bromley, K. (1988). *Language arts: Exploring connections.* Boston: Allyn & Bacon.

Choate, J., & Rakes, T. (1987). The structured listening activity: A model for improving listening comprehension. *The Reading Teacher, 41*(2), 194–200.

Cohen, R. (1983). Self-generated questions as an aid to reading comprehension. *The Reading Teacher, 36,* 770–775.

Cottrell, J. (1987). *Creative drama in the classroom grades 4–6: Teacher's resource book for the theatre arts.* Lincolnwood, IL: National Textbook Company.

Cox, C. (1984). Oral language development and its relationship to reading. In R. A. Thompson & L. L. Smith (eds.), *Reading Research Review.* Minneapolis: Burgess Publisher.

Cunningham, P. (1975). Transferring comprehension from listening to reading. *The Reading Teacher, 29*(2), 169–172.

D'Angelo, K. (1979). Wordless picturebooks: Also for the writer. *Language Arts, 56*(7), 813–814, 835.

Davey, B. (1983). Think aloud: Modeling the cognitive processes of reading comprehension. *Journal of Reading, 27*(1), 44–47.

Devine, T. (1978). Listening: What do we know over fifty years of research and theorizing? *Journal of Reading, 21,* 296–304.

Devine, T. (1982). *Listening skills schoolwide: Activities and progress.* Urbana, IL: NCTE.

Dugan, J. (1997). Transactional literature discussions: Engaging students in the appreciation and understanding of literature. *The Reading Teacher, 51*(2), 86–96.

Evans, K. (1992). Reading aloud: A bridge to independence. *The New Advocate, 5*(1), 47–57.

Ewards, P. (1996). Creating sharing time conversation: Parents and teachers work together. *Language Arts, 73*(1), 344–349.

Farnsworth, K. (1981). Storytelling in the classroom: Not an impossible dream. *Language Arts, 58*(2), 162–167.

Ferguson, P., & Young, T. (1996). Literature talk: Dialogue improvisations and patterned conversations with second language learners. *Language Arts, 73*(8), 597–600.

Flanders, N. (1970). *Analyzing teaching behavior.* Reading, MA: Addison-Wesley.

Forsythe, S. (1995). It worked! Reader's theatre in second grade. *Language Arts, 49*(3), 264–265.

Freshour, F., & Bartholomew, P. (1989). Let's start improving our own listening. *Florida Reading Quarterly, 25*(4), 28–30.

Funk, H., & Funk, G. (1989). Guidelines for developing listening skills. *The Reading Teacher, 42*(9), 660–663.

Gallas, K., Anton-Oldenburg, M., Ballenger, C., Beseler, C., Griffin, S., Pappenheimer, R., & Swaim, J. (1996). Talking the talk and walking the walk: Researching oral language in the classroom. *Language Arts, 73*(8), 608–617.

Gambrell, L. (1983). The occurrence of think-time during reading comprehension instruction. *Journal of Educational Research, 77*(3), 77–80.

Graves, D. (1989). *Investigate nonfiction.* Portsmouth, NH: Heinemann.

Hansen, J. (1987). *When writers read.* Portsmouth, NH: Heinemann.

Harvey, S., Mcauliffe, S., Benson, L., Cameron, W., Kempton, S., Lusche, P., Miller, D., Schroeder, J., & Weaver, J. (1996). Teacher-researchers study process of synthesizing in six primary classrooms. *Language Arts, 73*(8), 564–586.

Hauchildt, P., & McMahon, S. (1996). Reconceptualizing "resistant" learners and rethinking instruction: Risking a trip to the swamp. *Language Arts, 73*(8), 576–596.

Holbrook, H. (1983). ERIC/RCS report: Oral language: A neglected language art? *Language Arts, 60*(2), 255–258.

Hoskisson, K., & Tompkins, G. (1987). *Language arts: Content and teaching strategies.* Columbus, OH: Merrill Publishing Co.

Inhelder, B., & Piaget, J. (1964). *The early growth of logic in the child.* New York: Norton and Co.

Jiganti, M., & Tindall, M. (1986). An interactive approach to teaching vocabulary. *The Reading Teacher, 39*(5), 444–448.

Johnson, D., & Johnson, R. (1987). *Learning together and alone: Cooperative, competitive and individualistic learning* (2nd ed.). Englewood Cliffs, NJ: Prentice Hall.

Johnson, D., & Pearson, P. (1984). *Teaching reading vocabulary* (2nd ed.). New York: Holt, Rinehart & Winston.

Kear, D., & Yellin, D. (1978, October). Oral language strategies for vocabulary development. Paper presented at SWIRA meeting, Little Rock, AR.

Koste, V. (1988). *Dramatic play in childhood.* Lanham, MD: University Press of America.

Lange, B. (1981). ERIC/RCS Report: Directing classroom communication. *Language Arts, 58,* 729–733.

Laughlin, M., & Latrobe, K. (1990). *Reader's theatre for children: Scripts and script development.* Englewood, CO: Litran's Unlimited.

Linderman, E., & Linderman, M. (1984). *Arts and crafts for the classroom* (2nd ed.). New York: Macmillan.

Livo, N. J. (1986). *Storytelling: Process and practice.* Littleton, CO: Libraries Unlimited.

Loban, W. (1963). *The language of elementary school children.* Champaign, IL: National Council of Teachers of English. Reading Research Report #1.

Lundsteen, S. (1979). *Listening: Its impact at all levels on reading and the other language arts.* Urbana, IL: NCTE.

Lundsteen, S. (1989). *Language arts: A problem-solving approach.* New York: Harper & Row.

Markle, S. (1973). Some thoughts on task analysis and objectives in educational psychology. *Educational Psychologist, 10,* 29.

Martinez, M., Roser, N., & Strecker, S. (1998/1999). "I never thought I could be a star": A reader's theatre ticket to fluency. *The Reading Teacher, 52*(4), 326–334.

McCaslin, N. (1990). *Creative drama in the classroom* (5th ed.). New York: Longman.

McCaslin, N. (1996). *Creative drama in the classroom* (6th ed.). New York: Longman.

McGee, L., & Tompkins, G. (1983). Wordless picture books for older readers, too. *Journal of Reading, 27*(4), 120–123.

Moffett, J., & Wagner, B. (1991). *Student-centered language arts* (4th ed.). Boston: Houghton Mifflin.

Morgan, N., & Saxon, J. (1988). Enriching language through drama. *Language Arts, 65*(1), 34–50.

Neff, R., & Lengel, A. (1990). That's debatable. *Teaching, 20*(6), 34–35.

Pearson, P. D., & Fielding, L. (1982). Research update: Listening comprehension. *Language Arts, 59*(6), 617–629.

Piazza, C. (1999). *Multiple forms of literacy: Teaching literacy and the other arts.* Upper Saddle River, NJ: Merrill.

Pigford, A. (1988). Teachers, let students talk. *Academic Therapy, 24*(2), 193–197.

Pinnell, G. (1984). Communication in small group settings. *Theory into Practice, 23*(3), 246–254.

Polette, N. (1986). *Reader's theatre from fairy tales, fantasy and myth.* St. Louis, MO: Book Lures.

Rankin, P. T. (1926). The measurement of the ability to understand spoken language. Unpublished doctoral dissertation, University of Michigan.

Raphael, T. (1982). Teaching questioning–answer strategies for children. *The Reading Teacher, 36*(2), 186–191.

Reinking, D., & Schreiner, R. (1985). The effects of computer-mediated text on measures of reading comprehension and reading behaviors. *Reading Research Quarterly, 20*(5), 536–552.

Roth, R. (1986). Practical use of language in school. *Language Arts, 63*(2), 134–142.

Rupley, W., Logan, J., & Nichols, W. (1998/1999). Vocabulary instruction in a balanced reading program. *The Reading Teacher, 52*(4), 336–346.

Scieszka, J. (1989). *The true story of the three little pigs.* New York: Viking.

Shoop, M. (1986). InQuest: A listening and reading comprehension strategy. *The Reading Teacher, 39*(7), 370–374.

Silvaroli, N. (1990). *Classroom reading inventory* (6th ed.). Dubuque, IA: Wm. C. Brown Publishers.

Smith, F. (1982). The unspeakable habit. *Language Arts, 59*(6), 550–554.

Spiegel, D. (1996). The role of trust in reader-response groups. *Language Arts, 73*(5), 332–339.

Stauffer, R. (1975). *Directing the reading–thinking process.* New York: Harper & Row.

Sticht, T., & James, J. (1984). Listening and reading. In P. D. Pearson (ed.), *Handbook of reading research.* White Plains, NY: Longman.

Stoodt, B. (1988). *Teaching language arts.* New York: Harper & Row.

Strother, D. (1987). Practical applications of research on listening. *Phi Delta Kappan, 68,* 625–628.

Temple, C., & Gillet, J. (1989). *Language arts: Learning processes and teaching practices* (2nd ed.). Glenview, IL: Scott Foresman & Co.

Trelease, J. (1995). *The read-aloud handbook* (3rd ed.). New York: Penguin Books.

Trousdale, A. (1990). Interactive storytelling: Scaffolding children's early narratives. *Language Arts, 67*(2), 164–173.

Vygotsky, L. (1962). *Thought and language.* Cambridge, MA: MIT Press.

Watson, K., & Young, B. (1986). Discourse for learning in the classroom. *Language Arts, 63*(2), 126–133.

Wigginton, E. (ed.) (1980). *Foxfire.* Garden City, NY: Doubleday and Co.

Wigginton, E. (1986). *Sometimes a shining moment.* Garden City, NY: Doubleday.

Wilcox, M. (1976). When children discuss: A study of learning in small groups. *Elementary School Journal, 76,* 302–309.

Wilt, M. (1950). A study of teacher awareness of listening as a factor in elementary education. *Journal of Educational Research, 43,* 626–636.

Winn, D. (1988). Develop listening skills as part of the curriculum. *The Reading Teacher, 42*(2), 144–148.

Wolvin, A., & Coakley, C. (1985). *Listening* (2nd ed.). Dubuque, IA: Wm. C. Brown Publishers.

Wright, J., & Laminack, L. (1982). First graders can be critical listeners and readers. *Language Arts, 59*(2), 133–136.

Yellin, D. (1983). *Integrating elementary language arts.* Dubuque, IA: Eddie Bowers Publishing Co.

Language and Literacy: The Reading Factor

6

IN THIS CHAPTER

Reading and writing are closely intertwined aspects of literacy. Chapter 6 and the chapters on writing acknowledge this important relationship and recognize the need to explore both factors simultaneously. The basic approach in this text is to focus on the integration of these processes; implicit in every statement is the idea that reading and writing are inseparable. However, in this chapter the emphasis is on the role that reading plays in language development and learning, while Chapters 8 and 9 concentrate on the role of writing.

In exploring reading, you will learn about currently accepted definitions and models of the reading process, significant reading research, and the competencies that children need to become successful readers. You will also examine major approaches to reading instruction: the basal reader, the literature-based, the language experience, and the balanced approaches. You will learn about holistic approaches to evaluation and some informal diagnostic strategies. Finally, you will look at some of the continuing developments in reading, including Reading Recovery, Success for All, and the Accelerated Reader programs.

As you read through the chapter, you should develop a heightened awareness of the psychological complexity of the reading process and the many critical issues associated with reading and writing instruction. This chapter is merely your first step toward understanding the factors crucial in the acquisition of literacy. Throughout your teaching career, you will be adding to and modifying the basic knowledge you gain from this chapter.

Language and Literacy

Literacy is one of the most important accomplishments of any society: it is the hallmark of civilization. However, coming up with an exact description of literacy can be difficult, and over the years the definition has changed. At one time, a person who could write and read his or her own name was considered literate. In more recent years, an individual's literacy level has been gauged by the highest school grade she or he has completed—a standard that is not always accurate. Currently, literacy is seen by many in terms of an individual's ability to function well in the workplace. This definition has grown out of the national concern about having people read and write well enough to create an effective workforce.

However, literacy really is much more than this. As Benjamin DeMott (1990) has written, literacy—reading and writing—is what helps people to understand each other, to connect with each other, and to know the truth for themselves. Literacy empowers people; it gives them the ability to acquire information for themselves. It makes them independent learners who are able to connect with and communicate with whomever they choose.

The mirror processes of reading and writing are also inseparable. Reading requires the written word; any writing requires a reader. The writer and the reader need each other; each is incomplete without the other. Therefore, it is essential that each individual develop both processes of literacy.

Of course, the reading aspect of literacy has its own special type of magic. A reader can unlock the code of those little black squiggles on paper and can make sense of someone else's words. A reader can visit other places and times, can give free rein to his or her imagination, and can create a special world of personal knowledge.

On the more practical, daily level, reading is needed in order to follow the directions for baking a cake, putting together a bicycle, completing a job application, or giving someone the proper dose of medicine. It helps people to find their way in strange cities by allowing them to follow a road map and read street signs. It also helps people read the labels and buy the right products in the stores. Without reading, an individual is lost and helpless in a literate world. It is disturbing that in recent years the United States, compared to other countries, has had a greater concentration of adults at the lowest levels of literacy on prose, document, and quantitative materials (Organization for Economic Co-operation and Development and Statistics Canada, 1998).

Apparently, the number of people in the United States not truly engaged in reading may be growing. The National Assessment of Educational Progress (NAEP, 1996) found that between 1992 and 1994 there were declines in average reading proficiency in certain groups across the nation. Our society can't afford to let any more of its members be uninvolved with reading; the teaching profession needs to help all people love to read.

BEYOND THE CLASSROOM

In the last several years, there have been many community efforts throughout the United States to combat the problem of illiteracy (for example, Literacy Volunteers of America). Find out what people in your community are doing to promote literacy for adults as well as children. You might even give some thought to volunteering time to help them.

Reading Defined

Reading, like literacy, has often been difficult to define. Many people have their own ideas about the process, ideas based on their experiences both in and out of school. An activity completed by one group of college-level methods students has illustrated this point (Blake, 1986). Each semester the incoming students conducted a small survey to find out how individuals define reading. The students interviewed people of different ages and backgrounds and received some surprisingly varied responses.

Children interviewed in this survey often defined reading as completing a workbook, sounding out letters, or reciting the alphabet. A certain number believed that reading was listening to a storybook or figuring out a story for themselves. The ideas of these young readers echoed the research of Johns and Ellis (1976), who found that children's views of reading generally reflect how they learn to read in school. Students also indicated that they saw reading as something that girls did more than boys (McKenna, 1997), and older students frequently reported negative attitudes about reading, which research links to poor reading ability in the upper grades (McKenna, Kear, & Ellsworth, 1995). Adults also gave some interesting responses, many of which were related to the ways in which they used reading in their schooling and work. However, most of their answers focused on reading as an attempt to comprehend information.

Research has now shown that real reading takes place only when meaning and understanding are present. Over the years, educators have definitely moved beyond the notion that reading is "a precise process" that involves "exact, detailed, sequential perception and identification of letters, words, spelling patterns and larger language units" (Goodman, 1967, p. 126). Beginning with Goodman's work, which viewed reading as a type of "psycholinguistic guessing game" (p. 127), an interaction between thought and language, specialists began to see that reading is much more than the exact perception of simple parts of language.

Later researchers have demonstrated that reading is actually a constructive process of obtaining meaning from text (Anderson, Hiebert, Scott, & Wilkinson, 1985). Good readers use their prior life experiences and their knowledge about books and language to help themselves construct meaning from the written page. They also try to monitor themselves as they read to see if what they are reading actually makes sense. In other words, reading is a very individual process in which what the reader already knows greatly affects what he or she learns from a text.

For example, consider what happens when you read the following sentence:

> As the storm approached, the people in the town stored provisions to make sure that they would survive.

Depending on what part of the world you are from, the storm might mean a snowstorm, a blizzard, a hurricane, a tornado, a monsoon, or a typhoon. Your ideas about provisions might vary from canned tuna and potato chips to dried meat or sacks of rice. Survival might mean "How do we get through a week without electricity?" or "Where can we get brush and wood to make a fire to keep us warm?" Your prior life experiences and the context of the reading situation affect your interpretation of the words in the sentence (Nagy & Scott, 1990).

In reading these words, you are also making use of your knowledge of both oral and written language. After years of speaking and listening, you don't have any trouble associating the letters with the sounds and figuring out the words. You also have some idea about the right intonation to use as you say the sentence. Your previous experiences with writing, grammar, and punctuation enable you to spot the subject and verb of the sentence without any trouble and to decide where the sentence begins and ends. In reading the sentence, your mind interacts with the text (writing) to construct meaning. The reading is not done in isolation; it is integrated with your prior knowledge and all the language arts, especially writing.

To acquire the habit of reading is to construct for yourself a refuge from almost all the miseries of life.

Somerset Maugham

MODELS OF READING

This view of reading as an active, constructive process is the result of theories and research models of the reading process. To date, documented models of reading include the bottom-up model, the top-down model, and the interactive model (Weaver, 1994).

Bottom-Up Model

The **bottom-up model of reading** has its origins in theories and approaches that emphasize precise identification, or *decoding*, of the individual parts of language; it follows a sequential or serial path that begins with an understanding of the sounds of language and their corresponding letters and moves word by word through sentences, paragraphs, and larger selections of text (LaBerge & Samuels, 1985). Through the perception and discrimination of these unique elements, the reader obtains meaning. Essentially, says this model, the language of the text holds the key to meaning. It is a common-sense approach (Weaver, 1994).

Since decoding, or "cracking the written code of the text," is of prime importance in this model, emphasis is placed on mastering the subskills of reading—those concerned with comprehension (such as identifying the main idea and details, following directions, making inferences, and predicting outcomes) as well as those that reflect the rules of language related to letters and sounds (such as phonics, structural analysis, spelling patterns, and syllabication). Proponents of the bottom-up approach believe that when readers have learned the various subskills well enough, reading becomes an automatic process of obtaining meaning from the text.

Although a body of research does support the belief that reading contains a hierarchy of subskills, there are some concerns about this approach to teaching reading. First, it is difficult to get reading specialists to agree on which subskills should definitely be learned by all readers (Burns, Roe, & Ross, 1996). Some suggested lists emphasize certain skills at the expense of others. Also, many reading educators are convinced that meaning lies not within the text but in the reader's mind and in the reader's ability to integrate that knowledge with learned strategies for decoding language.

Top-Down Model

Emphasis on the critical role that the reader's mind plays in comprehension is the cornerstone of the **top-down model of reading,** in which understanding, the key objective, takes place through the use of information in the mind rather than through the text itself.

As discussed in Chapter 4, research in psycholinguistics (Goodman, 1967, 1976) has shown that in processing language a person makes use of three cue systems:

1. *Graphophonic.* The relationship between the sounds of oral language and the letters in the text

2. *Semantic.* The actual meaning of the words and the context in which they are used

3. *Syntactic.* Grammar; the rules that govern the organization of the language

According to the top-down model, the reader uses these cue systems to make predictions or educated guesses about the meaning of what she or he is reading. What the reader expects or anticipates has a profound effect on how he or she actually perceives the textual material.

Suppose you are reading a passage about dolphins and come across a phrase that you read as *the silvery dolphins*, a description that you frequently associate with the mammals. However, further reading shows that the passage is referring to dolphins caught in an oil slick and that your interpretation of the phrase doesn't really make sense. Upon rereading the phrase, you see that it actually says *the slimy dolphins*. You have tested your original hypothesis for the meaning of the phrase and found that it doesn't work, that there is a mismatch (a *miscue*, in psycholinguistic terminology) between what you perceived and what is actually in the text. You looked for an overall meaning first; when you realized that your first attempt at understanding did not make sense, you then consulted the individual units of language for clarification. This process of attempting to grasp meaning first has caused proponents of the top-down model to view reading as a holistic experience rather than a series of language subskills.

In accordance with the top-down view, children should be given opportunities to use their minds in reading. They should have experiences with meaningful stories, literature, and **big books** rather than concentrating on specific language models or rules. However, this emphasis gives some educators cause for concern. They believe that in addition to meaningful experiences, many children truly need to learn specific strategies for processing language. In light of the success of the Reading Recovery program for at-risk first-grade students (an approach discussed later in this chapter), these concerns must be taken seriously.

Interactive Model

The **interactive model of reading** is an attempt to reconcile top-down and bottom-up processing; reading is viewed as a continual interaction between reader and text in which the reader brings meaning to and derives meaning from the page. In this construction of knowledge, the reader attempts to achieve understanding by using prior knowledge stored in mental units of information called *schemata* (Rumelhart, 1980) as well as specific learned strategies for decoding the language of the text.

Reading is thus a highly individualized and personal activity because each person's schemata and ability to use them are unique. How a person interprets a text depends a great deal on the schemata he or she has developed and how effectively they are used. Therefore, it is possible for two individuals to come to some very different conclusions about the same passage.

Many reading specialists agree with the theory behind the interactive model. However, there have been some questions raised concerning the specific ways in which the model functions. Are both forms of processing equally important, and do all readers use the processes simultaneously? So far, research has indicated that readers in the stage of emerging literacy may concentrate more on decoding the specific elements in the text than on recalling information in the mind; more mature, efficient readers appear to do the opposite. As more knowledge is gained through research, reading educators may have to modify these views. However, the essential point is that both top-down and bottom-up processing are essential components of reading comprehension. Reading educators need to recognize this when planning instruction for children.

Figure 6.1 offers a visual representation of how these models work. Although each model has its merits, the interactive view provides the most comprehensive and effective description of the reading process, especially when combined with a personal, *transactional relationship* to the world around us (Rosenblatt, 1978). In such a system, each student is part of a dynamic construction of meaning when engaging with text—a process in which cultural, social, and environmental factors influence his or her unique interpretation of the words on the page (Rosenblatt, 1994). While reading continues to be seen as a holistic construction of knowledge, it also requires specific strategies for understanding textual language. Many approaches for engaging with text are encouraged: experiences with real books and literature, use of specific strategies to facilitate understanding of text, development of story structure, use of questioning strategies, experiences with differing language patterns—basically the use of any technique for making reading an active, constructive undertaking.

> ### BEYOND THE CLASSROOM
>
> Interview three or four people about their definitions of the reading process. Be sure to include children of varying ages as well as adults in your sample. Make notes about their responses in your journal, and reflect on how their ideas relate to those presented in this chapter.

Figure 6.1

Three models of reading.

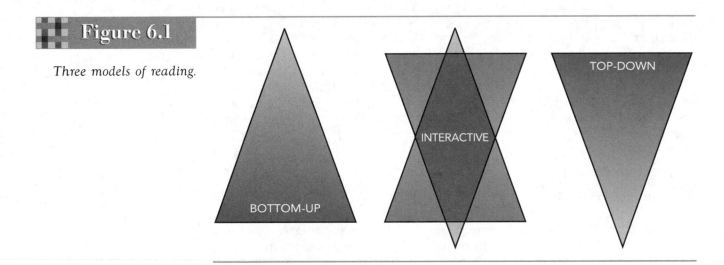

Reading Research

Over the years, much research has been conducted about the many complex factors involved in reading. Prominent research topics have included cognitive functioning, schema theory, metacognition, the proper role of phonics, characteristics of successful readers, and the effects of particular strategies to enhance reading comprehension. As a result, reports have emerged describing everything from students' achievement on national reading assessments to how students monitor their own cognitive processes. These research results constitute a significant body of knowledge concerning issues with a direct impact on learning to read and the type of instruction needed to facilitate this process.

Reading research is valuable to teachers in that it allows them to make a difference in the real world. In general, the research most helpful to educators is that which has provided information about how readers function, the impact of text upon comprehension, and the effects of classroom instruction. Therefore, for the purposes of this chapter, the research data from reading studies are presented in three categories, focusing on the reader, the text, and reading instruction.

THE READER

A child does not become a reader in a vacuum. She or he comes from a home and a family; as discussed in Chapter 2, the home environment is one of the greatest influences on how well any reader functions. Just as parents support and help a child in taking his or her few steps, they also provide the child's first encounters with the essentials of reading and writing. It is only natural that children look to their primary caregivers and protectors for role models and for encouragement in these important components of the communication process.

According to *Becoming a Nation of Readers* (Anderson, Hiebert, Scott, & Wilkinson, 1985), parents who expose their children to a wide variety of experiences—such as trips to stores, parks, zoos, and museums—and who then communicate carefully with the children about these experiences tend to produce more successful readers. Parents can also increase children's chances for reading success by using daily read-aloud sessions to show children that adults truly enjoy and value reading (Wigfield & Asher, 1984). Reading aloud to children has been shown to be the most important activity for fostering reading success (Anderson, Hiebert, Scott, & Wilkinson, 1985). In addition, the act of reading aloud together, each reader taking a turn, has the added benefit of evolving into a lifelong habit of successful social interaction (Martin, 1993).

The importance of the home in supporting reading and writing does not decrease once a child enters school. Parents should support classroom literacy instruction by attending school meetings and being well informed about school programs. It has been suggested that greater involvement and empowerment of parents results in more successful readers (Rasinski, 1989). In the *National Assessment of Educational Progress* (NAEP, 1996), students who indicated that they had received home support in the form of home reading materials and parental interest in their schoolwork were more proficient readers. These were the same children who read often, visited libraries, watched only a small amount of TV, and completed homework assignments.

From the child's experiences at home and at school, he or she develops a body of background knowledge that can be assessed and used in reading comprehension. This information that the reader already possesses is called *prior knowledge*. Readers use such knowledge to help them make sense of what they are reading, much as you did when reading the brief references to the storm and the dolphins. Of course the idea of the importance of prior knowledge in constructing meaning can be traced back to the work of Goodman (1967, 1976) and Smith (1982) on psycholinguistics. Recall that in the psycholinguistic system, the reader's expectations—related to the graphophonic, semantic, and syntactic cues in the text—are the driving factor in obtaining meaning from the text. These expectations arise from the reader's store of background knowledge, which in turn has been built on that individual's previous experiences.

Prior knowledge has proved to be a better predictor of recall from reading than verbal intelligence, word recognition, overall reading ability, or vocabulary knowledge (Anderson & Pearson, 1984). Such knowledge, said Tierney, "guides the reader through the text and allows him or her to suggest scenarios, make predictions, identify and empathize with characters, and relate to events or settings and their interplay" (1990, p. 38). Readers use background knowledge and expectations to construct meanings; they consciously access information that relates to what they are preparing to read or are actually reading. Use of prior knowledge makes engaging with text an extremely purposeful activity (Graves, Juel, & Graves, 1998).

Prior knowledge is also organized into schemata, which according to the interactive model play an important role in the development of reading skills. These schemata, "the building blocks of cognition" (Rumelhart, 1980, p. 33), are acquired through experiences: They are the generic theories individuals form about the world and the way it runs. Through the years, schemata shape people's expectations of what will or should happen, and they are necessary in processing any new information learned.

By drawing upon the "grocery-shopping schemata" that they already had in their heads, the children in the Classroom Vignette that follows are better able to comprehend the story. They have the ability to access a huge store of knowledge about shopping through their rich, internalized networks of schemata (Graves, Juel, & Graves, 1998). However, imagine what the case would have been had Mrs. Blackmon asked the same question of a child who had never seen a supermarket. How might this child have reacted to a story involving grocery shopping? Since meaning is constructed by comparing prior knowledge with new information (Bransford & Johnson, 1973), the child's lack of a particular schema—in this case, for grocery shopping—would have greatly limited his or her ability to obtain meaning from the story. The same would be true for any child who had not had opportunities to develop a storehouse of particular schemata.

Another area of research into cognitive functioning that has had a tremendous impact on reading instruction is that of metacognition. Ann Brown (1982) has defined **metacognition** as people's awareness of their own activities when they are reading, solving problems, and studying, as well as being an active learner capable of monitoring these processes. Basically, metacognition is what a child knows about his or her own thinking and how the child is able to monitor that thinking. It is what enables a child to become a strategic reader, capable of deciding when comprehension is or is not occurring and what to do when things don't make sense. Such readers are able to use their prior knowledge, identify purposes for reading, make predictions, focus on the content, reread any confusing parts, visualize the images in the text, and summarize information (Paris, Lipson, & Wixson, 1983).

An adage for metacognition might be "Reader, Know Thyself." Children who employ metacognition know both their strengths and their weaknesses as readers. One child might know that she or he is quite good at reading a passage and answering some simple questions about it but not so good at reading the same passage and writing an alternative ending for it. The child (or maybe the teacher) might then realize that it would be wise to spend some time practicing brainstorming and predicting strategies as well as rehearsing and drafting summaries. Realizing what you need to do is as important as realizing what you already do. Currently, metacognition is considered to be so important to the reading process that a study on how readers use it within reading strategies is being considered by the NAEP (NAGB, 1992–1998).

One activity for developing metacognitive knowledge that has received much attention is *reciprocal teaching* (Palincsar & Brown, 1986). In this approach, the teacher and students take turns at teaching. Initially the teacher models the needed behaviors and strategies, such as previewing, predicting, summarizing, and questioning. Then the process is gradually transferred to the students. Reciprocal teaching has been shown to be not only interactive but also a very effective and direct way of using teacher

Vignette *in the classroom*

Mrs. Blackmon, a second-grade teacher, plans to have some of the students in her class read a story involving grocery shopping. In order to find out about their schemata and to prepare them for the reading experience, she says to them, "Tell me what you know abut grocery shopping." The children's answers are random at first, but then it becomes apparent that the children have very individual interpretations of generally similar concepts. After some discussion, Mrs. Blackmon helps the students categorize their ideas.

GROCERY SHOPPING

Goal: To get the groceries and go home.

People Involved: You, your mother and/or father, other shoppers, the store people or clerks, the cash register person, the bagger.

Objects: Cart, shelves, aisles, place for meats and frozen food, different kinds of food, stuff to clean the house, flowers, things to drink, bags (plastic and paper), cash register, money.

Sequence of Events: Get to the store (walk, bicycle, car), get a cart, check your list, get what you need, get in line at register, pay, get your bags, put them in the car (if you have one), go home, unpack.

modeling to promote student understanding. According to Carter (1997), the use of reciprocal teaching has the ability to raise students' achievement scores after only one year of implementation. Now that is something worth trying.

To be successful, today's reader must be an active participant in reading, a participant equipped with knowledge of the world, knowledge of self as a reader, and knowledge of the strategies needed for successful reading.

THE TEXT

Obviously, the text is no longer the only determinant of successful reading comprehension; instead it has become what Pearson has termed a "blueprint for meaning" (1985, p. 726); a reader constructs his or her own interpretation or meaning from it (Collins, Brown, & Larkin, 1980). It is a basic guide or suggestion for meaning rather than the meaning itself. As mentioned earlier, it is quite possible for two readers to develop entirely different interpretations as they work their way through the same passage or text. The meaning is created through a multitude of interactions: the reader, the text, the classroom influences, and the environment (Ruddell & Unrau, 1994).

However, some aspects of the text still have an important impact on reading. It is easier for students to read texts for which they have prior knowledge and schemata; it is also easier for them to read materials with plenty of illustrations and less print on the page. Everyone has seen a poor reader go to the library and only look for thin books with lots of pictures and very little print.

Because textual difficulty affects children's comprehension, it is very important for teachers and schools to choose texts of appropriate difficulty levels. Many schools thus use **readability formulas,** which gauge the difficulty of a text by averaging the number of syllables and number of sentences for three 100-word passages and then assigning the text an approximate grade level (see Chapter 10 for a complete description of this process). However, there is controversy about the use of these formulas because they don't tell whether books have literary quality, interest for children, clear and accurate writing, or logical organization—factors that contribute to textual difficulty (Anderson, Hiebert, Scott, & Wilkinson, 1985).

It is very important that stories for early readers be well organized and have a definite structure. Typical story structure (discussed in Chapter 8) includes a setting, characters, a theme, a plot related to the goals of the characters, and an orderly sequence that makes sense to the reader. Through listening to well-formed stories, young children develop a sense of this story structure, which later helps them to comprehend stories in print. The closer a story fits the structure, the easier it is for young readers to comprehend it (Anderson, Hiebert, Scott, & Wilkinson, 1985).

Books that have a repeating verse or sentence pattern are ideal for beginning readers (McMackin, 1993). Such books can have repetitive language patterns, story patterns, or familiar sequences of numbers, days of the week, or months (Huck, Hepler, & Hickman, 1993). The repetition provides a reliable and consistent verbal scaffolding or support for the child (Bruner, 1973), thus freeing him or her to focus on other parts of the text. Alphabet books, counting books, cumulative tales, and books with predictable plots can all help young children become confident, joyful readers and writers (Saccardi, 1996). Their very predictability allows children to attend to meaning, syntax, graphophonics, and the overall context or direction of the story. Experiences with such books help emergent readers develop positive feelings about the reading process as well as increased vocabulary knowledge and practice in using context to construct meaning.

The transition from the stories of early reading to nonfiction or expository text has often been difficult for young readers. Since this type of text generally has less organization than stories, the reader has less to use as a guide in the construction of meaning. Research has indicated that when expository materials are clearly written and possess a logical organization, students tend to understand much more (Herman, 1984). Therefore, it is crucial that expository texts be more than just lists of facts; these books need to be especially well-organized texts containing adequate explanations, appropriate concepts, and accurate facts, all of which better enable children to understand them (Anderson, Hiebert, Scott, & Wilkinson, 1985).

Because text has an impact on reading, you, as a future teacher, need to make sure that you have many print resources in the classroom—more than just the school textbooks or basal readers. You need to use books that are accurate, interesting, clearly written, and organized in such a way that they can be easily understood by students. The books you use for reading instruction should contain variety and be real literacy events (Goodman, 1986). They should be worth reading.

THE INSTRUCTION

In the 1970s, Dolores Durkin (1978–1979) conducted research about comprehension instruction in elementary schools. The results of her work were actually quite disturbing: she and her colleagues found that essentially no reading comprehension instruction was taking place and that most class efforts were spent on either assessment or the development of simple word-recognition strategies. Fortunately, much research has since concentrated on defining the type of instruction needed to promote reading comprehension. The successful strategies that have emerged from that research can and should make a difference in every classroom (Tierney, Readence, & Dishner, 1995).

> *The elementary school must assume as its sublime and most solemn responsibility the task of teaching every child how to read. Any school that does not accomplish this has failed.*
>
> JACQUES BARZUM

Phonics

If reading is viewed as the construction of meaning, all aspects of reading instruction should be seen as ways to facilitate comprehension, including the teaching of phonics. The real value of phonics, and the subsequent knowledge of letters and sounds, is that it allows readers to automatically process print, freeing them to think about what the language is saying and to construct meaning from the text (Adams, 1990).

Research has shown that it is no longer a question of whether phonics instruction is needed but of how to implement it in order to promote successful reading. The key issue is one of helping children develop awareness of phonological relationships in a meaningful context, such as those found in literature books. Children need to see that the end product of the use of phonics is the construction of meaning; teachers must help students realize this fact in their period of emergent literacy. To help young children acquire literacy, remember that teachers must facilitate each reader's individual progress of particular skills (Strickland & Cullinan, 1990). Phonics is discussed in more detail later in this chapter.

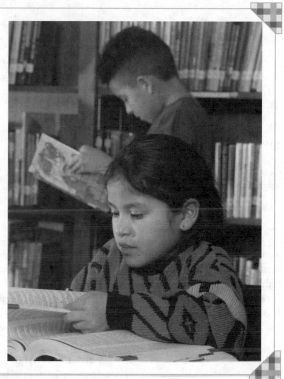

Other Means Toward Comprehension

Research has identified some specific comprehension competencies that students need to acquire: using prior knowledge, creating and answering questions, making predictions, evaluating what is important, summarizing, interpreting graphic information, visualizing and imaging, and monitoring understanding (Pearson, Roehler, Dole, & Duffy, 1992). Because certain children may have difficulty developing these abilities, teachers often need to use direct instruction in explaining thinking, problem-solving, and metacognitive processes. Such tactics may include the think aloud strategy as well as modeling and several types of questioning.

Think alouds. The think aloud strategy, which was mentioned in Chapter 5 in relation to listening, is a type of direct instruction that can aid children with reading comprehension (Davey, 1983). In using *think alouds*, the teacher reads a passage that might pose some comprehension problems; when confusion arises, the teacher shows students what to do to resolve it: make a prediction of what might happen; describe how to visualize or picture what has been read; make connections through analogies; clarify confusing points by talking about them; or use self-help strategies such as rereading, asking questions, or trying to change the way the story is viewed (Monahan & Hinson, 1988).

Modeling. Of course, a basic method of direct instruction is *modeling*, specifically teacher modeling of the reading behaviors children need. However, modeling alone won't work; it is important to provide a means of gradually turning over responsibility to students. Gordon (1985) has proposed a method that can be used in the modeling and transfer of any technique to students. First, the teacher asks questions about the technique, answers those questions, finds evidence for using the technique, and provides a line of reasoning. Through a series of practice sessions, students assume responsibility for each of the steps until they take ownership and become independent learners. Figure 6.2 illustrates Gordon's method.

Figure 6.2

Gordon's method for modeling strategies.

STAGES	ASKS QUESTIONS	ANSWERS QUESTIONS	FINDS EVIDENCE	LINE OF REASONING
I. Modeling	T	T	T	T
II. Guided Practice	T	T	S	S
III. Guided Practice	T	S	T	S
IV. Practice/Application	T	S	S	S
V. Student Control	S	S	S	S

T: Teacher
S: Student

Source: From Gordon, C. (1988). Modeling teaching strategies. *New Directions in Reading Instruction.* Copyright © 1988 by the International Reading Association. (Originally published in *Journal of Reading, 28,* Feb. 1985.) Reprinted with permission of Christine Gordon and the International Reading Association. All rights reserved.

Some teachers like to bring a book that they've read to class and to talk about it in the following manner:

When I first picked up this book and looked at the title, I asked myself, "Is this something that interests me?" Since I knew that [subject of book] are something that I love, I felt that I would probably enjoy the book.

Then I started to look at the cover, the headings of the chapters [if any], and the illustrations. I tried to figure out what I would find out from the book and even made a list of predictions or possibilities in my head. In this particular book, I really liked the illustrations because they went along well with the text. I also liked the way that the headings of each chapter gave me an idea of what was going to happen. So I decided that I definitely did want to read this book.

As I read the book, I helped my comprehension by always noting what was happening, the time and location, and who or what was involved. I did this so I would be sure to remember the important parts. Sometimes I would put a bookmark in a section that I really found interesting.

After I finished the book, I summarized it for myself and tried to figure out what it was really about. Then I tried to remember some similar books and to decide how the books were the same or different. Finally, I settled on why I [liked/disliked] the book and why I [would/would not] recommend it to my friends.

Questioning. One important outgrowth of much of the current research is that it has really changed the way teachers look at questions and questioning strategies. Questions are no longer the "who, what, when, where, why, and how" of literal information. Research has demonstrated that one of the most important aspects of questioning is the relationship between the question and the location of its answer, and that it is empowering to help students understand where to search for answers to questions (Raphael, 1984, 1986).

Raphael has outlined the four basic question–answer relationships (QAR), which were explained in Chapter 5.

1. *Right there questions.* Questions whose answers are easily found right in the text. "Who locked Rapunzel in the tower?" would be an example of this type of question.

2. *Search and find questions.* Questions whose answers can be found in the text but may require some searching. A typical question might be "List the things that Goldilocks did in the story."

3. *Author and me questions.* A special category of questions in which the reader must use his or her own background as well as the information in the text. "What do you think would have happened if Rapunzel had not had long hair?" would be such a question.

4. *On my own questions.* Questions that can be answered from background knowledge stored in the reader's head. "What do you think about people who use the belongings of others without asking permission first?" is an example of such a question.

Children who understand these relationships comprehend more and have higher levels of achievement (Raphael, 1986).

In recent years, another way of viewing the use of questions with texts has emerged: *Questioning the Author (QtA)* (Beck, McKeown, Hamilton, & Kucan, 1997). This QtA strategy is based on the idea of students constructing meaning as they proceed through a text. QtA supports immediate construction of meaning through discussion; students actively formulate their ideas while reading. The approach can be used with either expository, informational texts or narrative stories and involves the teacher interacting with the students as they try to build understanding of a text they are reading for the first time. The focus of QtA in the classroom is the use of queries that are posed by the teacher. The following list is a sample of different types of queries (Beck, McKeown, Hamilton, & Kucan, 1997, p. 45):

INITIATING QUERIES

- What is the author trying to say here?
- What is the author's message?
- What is the author talking about?

FOLLOW-UP QUERIES

- What does the author mean here?
- Did the author explain this clearly?
- Does this make sense with what the author told us before?
- How does this connect with what the author told us before?
- Does the author tell us why?
- Why do you think the author tells us this now?

NARRATIVE QUERIES

- How do things look for this character now?
- How has the author let you know that something has changed?
- How has the author settled this for us?
- Given what the author has already told us about this character, what do you think he's up to?

Source: Excerpt from Beck, I. L., McKeown, M. G., Hamilton, R. L., & Kucan, L. (1997), *Questioning the Author: An Approach for Enhancing Student Engagement with Text.* Reprinted with permission of Isabel L. Beck and the International Reading Association. All rights reserved.

While queries are an important aspect of this process, the benefits of constructivism in creating meaning lie in the ensuing discussion and interaction among the students and the teacher.

Connecting Reading and Writing

In the past decades, educators have come to realize more and more that reading is intricately tied to all the language arts, especially writing. One of the most exciting changes in reading instruction is the practice of combining reading with writing instruction (Tierney, 1990). This results in a more integrated, holistic approach to helping students become literate.

Writing is a good partner to reading because it helps children add to and clarify meaning for themselves—to make a book and the language of the book their own (Jensen & Roser, 1990). Both reading and writing are forms of communication; both are active thinking processes that get at meaning. Observations of language development in classes have shown that "in order to write, writers read. In order to learn from reading or respond to reading, readers often write" (Jensen & Roser, 1990, p. 11). Often, using writing to summarize information or restate what the author has said in a more concise format (Burns, Roe, & Ross, 1996) is what helps students truly get at the heart of what they've read. Therefore, it seems natural to make no real distinction between reading and writing in the classroom.

Students who see the connection between reading and writing actually are more perceptive about both processes. Having class opportunities to write helps students to learn reading and writing in meaningful ways. Allowing children to use process writing—to write and read letters and lists, to keep and share journals—helps them to see the problems and complexities of each process from both sides. They see reading as an author would; they see writing from the reader's point of view. In the end, they arrive at a clearer notion of what they need to do to make each process work for them. Combining class writing and reading instruction also serves as a meaningful way of helping students acquire the mechanics—grammar, punctuation, spelling—of writing (Anderson, Hiebert, Scott, & Wilkinson, 1985).

Teachers now appreciate that reading is an active, constructive process; writing is also an active way to construct meaning. It is important to implement these research findings and thereby empower children.

What Makes a Successful Reader? Competencies to Support Reading

In order to become successful, effective, and efficient readers, children need to acquire a number of *competencies*, mastery over certain types of reading behavior. Although there isn't always a rigid order in how these competencies should be acquired, the process is not random either. Children need to develop particular competencies during the period of emergent literacy, others while they are acquiring word recognition and vocabulary strategies, and still others as they continue to build comprehension.

EMERGENT LITERACY COMPETENCIES

Learning to read is not something that happens overnight for children. Nor does it occur in the same specific sequence of events and accomplishments for each child. However, in the years between birth and age eight, certain conditions are needed to support children's literacy development, specifically an environment that is both print-rich and language-rich (IRA & NAEYC, 1998). As an example of the powerful impact print in the environment can have on young children, Goodman (1989) has cited the fact that when children first come to school, many of them only print in capital letters. They do this because in their interaction with their environments, they have seen primarily capital letters on street signs, billboards, and advertisements.

As discussed earlier in this text, a print-rich environment begins with the home and with parents who not only read to their children but also talk to them and provide them with a wide variety of experiences. Teachers need to recognize the home–school connection in fostering literacy. They need to get and keep parents involved in informal, supportive activities and then build on that naturalistic learning in the classroom.

In the acquisition of literacy, cognitive development is certainly important. However, equally important is each child's knowledge about the "purpose and process of language" (Weir, 1989, p. 458). Because literacy and language learning have strong social and psychological bases (Teale & Sulzby, 1989), it makes sense to think of acquiring literacy as a type of "apprenticeship" (Wells, 1990, p. 15) in which children learn about language functions through meaningful activities guided by more competent language users (Rogoff, 1990; Tharp & Gallimore, 1989). In such an approach, the teacher is seen as a facilitator and model rather than an instructor.

Citing the work of a large number of researchers—including Clay (1979, 1991), K. Goodman (1980), Y. Goodman (1980), Lomax and McGee (1987), and Stein and Glenn (1979)—Searfoss and Readence (2000) have outlined competencies basic to the emerging literacy of the young child:

1. *Awareness of print.* Sensitivity to print in the environment, such as ads, signs, and billboards; the informational print of maps, recipes, and directions; job-related reading of parents; and fun reading of comics and pictures.

2. *Concepts about book print.* Ideas about what the print in books looks like and how it differs from other types of print.

3. *Story sense.* Ability to recognize the structure of a story; to develop the schemata for story structure; and to internalize the story elements of setting, characters, theme, plot, and resolution.

4. *Oral language development.* Communication competencies built on the development evident when the child enters school; developed in connection with beginning reading and writing since acquiring literacy is an interdependent process in which all the language skills support each other.

5. *Emergent writing.* Recognizing that scribbles, anything written down, needs to mean something and contain a message.

Children's emerging literacy can best be accommodated in classrooms in which reading and writing reflect the reading of the real world (White, Vaughn, & Rorie, 1986). In such environments, print dominates daily activities. Children and teachers are involved in book experiences in which they share books, read and tell stories, scribble and write about stories and experiences (often with invented spellings), and discuss the varied aspects of all that is happening in the class. Most of all, reading aloud to children is the single most important activity to build literacy in such classrooms (Bus, Van Izendoorn, & Pellegrini, 1995).

It is through literature-based activities that children learn how to handle a book, to differentiate the front cover from the back, to recognize the title page and author credits. Even more important, youngsters learn about the *directionality* of print: They see that it moves from left to right on the page and from the beginning to the middle to the end of a book. They begin to see the structural sequence in this progression. From their earliest experiences with books, children also move beyond their basic concepts about language and print to a visual and sound awareness of letters. They develop an alphabetic principle and an initial understanding of the pattern of the relationship between letters and sounds (Adams, 1990). Through rhyming and word games, they become linguistically aware of language sounds, which leads to phonemic awareness (IRA & NAEYC, 1998). Eventually, they become able to discriminate among letters, words, and sentences.

One final (and perhaps most important) competency that emerging readers and writers exhibit is a sincere interest and delight in books. They come to recognize that books are not only informative but fun and that people need to interact with them on a daily basis.

WORD RECOGNITION AND VOCABULARY DEVELOPMENT COMPETENCIES

In order to become automatic, efficient readers who can construct meaning from text, youngsters need to decode printed symbols into meaning very rapidly. They need to become competent in word recognition strategies that enable them to be fast and accurate readers. As with emerging literacy, the competencies related to word recognition and vocabulary development do not always develop in a rigidly specific order. In fact, it now appears to be most beneficial for teachers to help students develop the competencies as needed to construct meaning from text.

Although different reading situations demand different word competencies, they generally all work together to facilitate understanding of the text. Four fundamental areas in which readers need to develop competencies are the following:

1. *Sight vocabulary.* A store of words that the child recognizes on sight, which makes the reading process rapid and automatic and facilitates comprehension. Without a store of sight words, children must struggle to analyze print, a tactic that slows them down and can impede comprehension. Sight-word knowledge can be developed in conjunction with meaningful activities in the classroom.

2. *Phonics.* The structured relationship between phonemes (sounds) and graphemes (letters). For example, some facsimile of the sound "buh" is normally associated with the letter *b*. Because phonics is a way to get at meaning quickly, it is an area that receives much attention in the primary grades. In fact, Durkin (1988) reported that in kindergarten classes the most apparent type of reading instruction was phonics. Teachers do need to heed the advice of *Becoming a Nation of Readers* (Anderson, Hiebert, Scott, & Wilkinson, 1985)—it recommends that phonics be started early, worked on intensely, and concluded by the end of second grade. However, while the teaching of phonics is an important aspect of beginning reading instruction (IRA, 1997), it is wise to remember that phonics is only one factor, or cue system, in helping children construct meaning from text. Figure 6.3 lists the basic components of phonics.

Figure 6.3

Components of phonics.

Consonants include all letters other than *a, e, i, o,* and *u.* Consonants may be consistent (stand for a single sound) or inconsistent (stand for more than one sound, depending on the influence of adjacent vowels). Some inconsistent consonants include *c, g,* and *s.*

Consonant blends occur when two or three adjacent consonants are combined in a word but each consonant retains some of its original sound. For instance, in the word *play* the sounds of /p/ and /l/ are heard in the *pl* blend.

Consonant digraphs occur when two adjacent consonants are combined to form a single new sound. The most common digraphs are *ch, th, wh, sh,* and *ng,* as in the words *church, thin, when, ship,* and *ring.*

Vowels include the letters *a, e, i, o,* and *u,* each of which represents both a long and a short sound. The letters *y* and *w* may also exhibit vowel characteristics.

Long vowels	Short vowels
cake	cat
Pete	pet
rice	pit
rope	rot
mute	nut

Vowel digraphs occur when two adjacent vowels represent a single sound. Usually one of the vowels is sounded. Note the sound that you hear in the vowel digraphs in the following words: *boat, heat, pain.*

Diphthongs occur when two adjacent vowels are blended together to produce a single new sound. The most common are *ou* as in *about, oi* as in *toil, oy* as in *coy,* and *ow* as in *howl.*

3. *Structural analysis.* The ability to use meaningful word parts to decode an unknown word. By knowing the meaning of specific parts of the word, a child can figure out the meaning of the complete word. For example, the child who knows that the prefix *un-* generally means "not" or "to undo" has a head start in unlocking the meaning of words such as *unhappy*, *unfriendly*, and *untie*. Common elements inherent in structural analysis are illustrated in Figure 6.4.

Figure 6.4

Elements of structural analysis.

A **prefix** is a group of letters that when attached to the front of a root word modifies the meaning of that word.

Prefix	Meaning	Word
un-	not, undo	unhappy
bi-	two	bicycle
pre-	before	prepay
sub-	under	submarine

A **suffix** is a group of letters that when attached to the end of a root word also alters the meaning of that word.

Suffix	Meaning	Word
-less	without	penniless
-ous	full of	famous
-able	capable of being	acceptable

An **inflectional ending** is a letter or group of letters that when added to the end of a root word changes number, case, or gender (nouns); tense or person (verbs); or degree (adjectives). Some samples are *toys, witches* (nouns); *walks, walking, walked* (verbs); *older, oldest* (adjectives); and *Mary's* (possessive).

A **contraction** occurs when two words are combined into one word and some of the letters are omitted. The omitted letters are indicated by an apostrophe. Examples: *wasn't, what's I'll, they're, I'd, I'm, we've.*

A **compound** is a new word formed when two existing words are joined together. The pronunciation of the original words is usually retained in the new word, but the meaning of the compound may be altered in the process of combining. Examples: *workbook, cowboy, baseball, postcard, doghouse.*

4. *Context clues.* The surrounding textual cues that a reader uses to decode an unknown word. For example, in the following sentence a child would figure out the unknown word *wagged* by using known words and prior knowledge about dogs: *The happy dog wagged his tail.* The child would scrutinize the context of the print on the page to unlock the word's meaning by focusing on the way it is used. In general, proficiency in the use of context clues is tied to vocabulary development, which is initiated through the oral activities of Chapter 5 and refined as children engage in their own reading and writing.

While there is not total agreement on a particular sequence of instruction to develop word recognition competencies, it is widely acknowledged that embedding phonological awareness activities into a meaningful language arts program can greatly assist students in developing into successful readers and writers (Ericson & Juliebo, 1998). Word recognition and decoding strategies should be done in ways that actively involve each child working with words. Such instruction can be accomplished through chants, nursery rhymes, literature, poetry, storytelling, drama, writing, and alphabet songs and books. Cunningham and Hall (1997, 1998) recommend the use of a word wall with words categorized according to initial letter and sound as well as the creation of tongue twisters (Cleo the clown cleaned the closet). When children have become proficient in the basics of word recognition strategies, much of their continued vocabulary development can and should be related to the content areas in which the words most frequently occur.

COMPREHENSION COMPETENCIES

Reading comprehension is one specialized aspect of general language comprehension. As children use oral language to communicate with others through meaningful speech and perceptive listening, they employ comprehension strategies. When teachers question students in class, encourage discussions, and promote activities involving listening, they facilitate development of these strategies. All that remains is to encourage children to apply the same type of strategies to printed materials.

As with the other language arts, students learn to read by practicing their reading strategies with real books. When teachers provide children with the opportunity to read real texts, to use their prior knowledge, and to make predictions and judgments about what they are reading, they are handing their students the keys to reading comprehension.

It is generally recognized that there are several types, or levels, of comprehension for which students need to develop competencies: literal and interpretive as well as the higher levels of critical and creative comprehension (Burns, Roe, & Ross, 1996). However, these levels do not operate in isolation from one another. In successful reading, they most often operate together to help the reader obtain thorough understanding of the text.

Literal Comprehension

Literal comprehension involves getting meaning straight from the text; usually, the information is directly and plainly stated on the page. Students who are competent in this type of comprehension are able to get information from pictures, to find main ideas and details in text, to identify the sequence of events, and to comprehend the vocabulary used in the selection. Literal comprehension is generally considered the most easily achieved level of comprehension and includes the who, what, when, where, why, and how information.

Interpretive Comprehension

Interpretive comprehension involves obtaining meaning implied by statements in the text. The reader has to search for information, think about it, and interpret it. For example, a teacher might say to students, "Explain the differences between Cinderella and her sisters." In order to do this, the students have to review some information in the text and think about it before they can come up with an answer. It's a lot like reading between the lines.

A reader proficient in interpretive comprehension is able to detect theme and author's purpose; infer cause-and-effect relationships; predict events, outcomes, and results; make comparisons; and draw conclusions. Once children achieve this level, they are able to put information in their own words through paraphrasing and summarizing the main idea. The overall pattern of inferential processes activated during reading may have an impact on how much text is actually remembered (van den Broek, Risden, Fletcher, & Thurlow, 1996).

Vignette in the classroom

In her class, Mrs. Oliwa is reading a series of fairy tales with her young students. Among the tales included in the series is "Jack and the Beanstalk." Because giants play such an important role in this and many other tales, both teacher and children want to make sure that everyone can recognize the word *giant* automatically. To help **individual** children internalize the word, the teacher conducts several **individual** sessions using the five-step teaching plan for sight vocabulary advocated by Johnson and Pearson (1984):

1. *Seeing.* The teacher writes the word *giant* on the chalkboard. Then she says, "A *giant* is much, much bigger than an ordinary person. The *giant* in 'Jack and the Beanstalk' was 10 times larger than Jack." She also shows each child several illustrations of giants from various tales.

2. *Discussing.* The teacher encourages each student to tell what he or she knows about giants. Mrs. Oliwa adds her own observations and tries to clarify any misunderstandings that the children express.

3. *Using.* Then each child uses the word *giant* in a sentence or sometimes two sentences.

4. *Defining.* Because *giant* is a concrete word with pictures to go with it, and because the children have heard many stories about giants, most of the students don't have too much trouble defining it.

5. *Writing.* As a final step, each child writes the word on a word card and adds it to **individual** word banks. Many children also illustrate their cards.

Critical Comprehension

The third level of comprehension is known as *critical comprehension*, which occurs when the reader is able to integrate her or his own thinking with the information from the text. That is, the reader moves beyond the information mentioned on the page to make judgements about the content and the style of the text.

Individuals who comprehend at this level are able to differentiate among fact, fantasy, and opinion. They not only know what is relevant or irrelevant but can provide evidence to support their views. They respond emotionally to what they are reading. In addition, competent readers are able to visualize information from the text, to form mental pictures of what they have read. This ability often enables them to respond creatively through art, music, drama, and writing.

Creative Comprehension

The readers then move on to *creative comprehension* as the authors and communicators of new information. For example, a teacher can stop at the climax of a story and ask the students to write an ending. Or a teacher can finish reading a story or book and ask the students to provide ideas for a sequel.

How and when teachers should work with students to develop these competencies depend a great deal on the type of classroom, the demands of the activities in which the children are engaged, and the needs of the individual pupils. However, when it is necessary to help and support students in becoming strategic readers, there are many techniques that teachers can use. Some have already been mentioned, such as direct explanation lessons, modeling, think alouds, questioning, the question–answer relationships, questioning the author, and summarizing information.

Questioning is probably the most frequently used method for helping students develop proficiency in comprehension. Some questions are directed at the literal level, while others requiring more thought relate to the inferential and evaluative levels. Knowing where to find the answers to particular questions reduces the confusion that some students feel when faced with different types of questions. It certainly helps to know that literal questions can be answered directly from the text, inferential questions require a bit more searching, and evaluative questions require thought from each individual.

Of course there are many other strategies that teachers can use to help their students become competent readers: anticipation guides, story grammars and maps, semantic maps, dialogue journals and letters, and techniques to develop self-questioning. These and other comprehension strategies are discussed in Chapter 10.

> **BEYOND THE CLASSROOM**
>
> Interview several teachers in your practicum school or reading educators at your college, and in your journal summarize their thoughts on what makes a successful reader. You can then reflect on how these views compare and contrast with the information in this chapter.

Major Approaches to Reading Instruction

Reading books contains two different delights, both definable as learning. One is the pleasure of apprehending the unexpected: when one meets a new author who has a new vision of the world. The other is the pleasure of deepening one's knowledge of a special field.

GILBERT HIGHET

There are many ways to approach reading instruction, none of which is considered the only solution to the problem of making sure every child becomes literate. How you approach reading instruction is based partly on your own philosophy of reading and partly on the philosophy of the school district in which you teach. You can be sure that as you grow as a teacher, not only your views but also those of the school district will change. Therefore, it is very important for you to be receptive to a variety of ideas about teaching reading and for you to consider them carefully before deciding which ones really make sense to you and deserve a place in your classroom.

This chapter presents major aspects of several approaches to reading and writing: the basal reader approach, which over the years and in many different forms has been the predominant teaching method in many schools in the United States; the more child-centered literature-based approach, which involves thematic units and the content areas; the language experience approach, which uses children's experiences and language; and the eclectic balanced approach, which is currently being used. It is important to remember that there is no magic formula for teaching reading and that each approach has its own merits.

As you read through this section of the chapter, try to keep the different models of reading (described earlier) in mind. See which of the approaches most closely reflects the theories behind each particular model. By doing this, you will be able to formulate your own reading philosophy more clearly and to make more careful decisions about which overall approach and specific strategies you would prefer to use in your own classroom.

BASAL READER APPROACH

The basic idea behind the use of the **basal reader approach** is that a student must master a series of competencies or discrete skills as he or she progresses through reading. Reflecting the ideas of the bottom-up model, these published reading series have evolved over time; they tend to help students move from the part to the whole by prescribing the acquisition of skills and competencies in a systematic order and fashion (Mickelson, 1989). For many years, basal readers have been the most widely used reading program in American schools. Some or all aspects of the approach are still used in a great number of elementary classrooms.

Basal Reader Materials

The major component in the basal reader approach is the collection of materials that are used for teaching reading in the elementary grades. In general, these materials include the following:

- A series of graded children's readers, which generally range from K–8. The books are carefully graded between and within each grade level and get progressively more difficult through the use of controlled vocabularies. Only a certain number of new words are introduced per story; each story builds on the vocabulary of the previous one. Along with vocabulary development, each story tries to build word recognition and comprehension competencies.
- In addition to the children's readers, there are accompanying workbooks with ready-made activities for developing phonics, word recognition, and comprehension competencies and skills.
- A teacher's manual for each series contains detailed lesson plans for instruction in vocabulary, word recognition, and comprehension. These lesson plans follow a formula known as the directed reading activity (DRA), which is discussed in the following section.
- Supplementary materials, such as duplicating masters, cassette tapes, filmstrips, tests, computer software, and video programs, accompany each series. Over the years, the tests associated with basal readers have continued their importance as a way of determining whether or not students have mastered particular competencies or skills.

Traditional vs. Literature-Based Basal Series

Not all basal reader programs are the same. Some of the more traditional basal series that are still in use focus specifically on reading instruction that has sequenced, isolated skills work. They have very carefully controlled vocabulary instruction and are primarily teacher-centered. In addition, some may emphasize a single method, such as a linguistics (emphasizing the oral aspects of language and reading) or an intensive phonics approach (stressing the isolated sounds). Overall, traditional basals tend not to promote the integration of the language arts (Burns, Roe, & Ross, 1996). However, beginning with the 1990s fewer and fewer publishers have been producing traditional basal reading series (Hoffman et al., 1994).

What has emerged is a trend toward including more literature in the basal readers as well as suggestions for activities that will promote integration among the language arts that can be extended to other areas of the curriculum. Some basals are promoted as literature-based reading series (e.g., *Treasury of Literature*, Harcourt Brace & Company, 1995). This type of series includes actual literature selections (often unchanged) that are organized into units reflecting an underlying theme. Activities are suggested that help the students use strategies to decode words and unlock deeper comprehension. Ideas are provided for incorporating subject areas such as science, math, music, and art into the lessons associated with the particular theme. Magazines, trade books, and journals are often included to promote comprehension-extending activities. Recent research indicates that these new basals are having a positive effect on students and are helping them to be more independent as readers (Hoffman et al., 1998).

Directed Reading Activity

The major instructional strategy associated with basal readers is the **directed reading activity (DRA),** which is a special session for the specific purpose of teaching reading; separate sessions related to a single story or lesson often are spread out over a series of days.

Traditionally, a typical directed reading activity has included the following five steps (adapted from Tierney, Readence, & Dishner, 1995):

1. *Readiness.* Involves discussing previous experiences and activating prior knowledge to develop a conceptual background for the material. This also includes getting students interested in and excited about the reading material. During this readiness phase, the teacher introduces new vocabulary and reviews any strategies that might be needed in the lesson. The last step of the phase is to establish a purpose for reading—something that can be accomplished by either the teacher or the students. Teachers generally set purposes through questioning, while students can do it by predicting what the material may be about.

2. *Directed silent reading.* Is a type of guided reading in which the students silently read the story as the teacher guides them with appropriate questions and comments.

3. *Comprehension check and discussion.* Generally begins with the teacher asking the students comprehension questions and can evolve into a discussion, a debate, or even a dramatization with a bit of oral rereading.

4. *Oral rereading.* Consists of the students rereading selected passages of the text. This may be done as part of the discussion. It is important that the oral rereading have a purpose and not degenerate into a session in which students simply take turns reading selected passages aloud.

5. *Follow-up activities.* Are designed to extend knowledge. These may take the form of specialized strategy lessons on vocabulary or comprehension. The activities may also involve workbooks and skill sheets to build and strengthen specific competencies, or they may be projects related to the arts and the other content areas.

Basal Reader Controversy

There has been and probably will continue to be criticism or controversy about the use of all types of basal readers. Most of this is related to the perception that in the underlying basal philosophy, reading tends to go from smaller to larger units of understanding and can be accomplished through a sequence of skills or competencies learned in some type of order.

However, basal readers have been a tradition in reading instruction and will probably continue to have some impact on American education. The National Council of Teachers of English has recommended using basals flexibly or finding alternatives and supplements to them. Teachers are encouraged to be more involved with decision making and not to use information in the basal reader teacher's manual blindly. Teachers need to remember the importance of their role in the classroom reading situation.

If you do decide to use basal readers, you need to do it with intelligence and wisdom. You need to make sure that you have enough information about reading so that you become a knowledgeable professional who can make decisions about what is and what is not appropriate instruction for your students. If you find that some aspect of the basal program fits the needs of your classroom instruction, then you should use it. It is not the basal readers but your own philosophy and teaching sensitivity that will determine the quality of reading instruction in your class (Reutzel, 1989).

Basal Reader Supplements

There are many ways to supplement the activities of the basal program. Some activities that have worked well for teachers we know are the following:

- *Keeping a journal.* This activity allows children to reflect on what they have read and to unite the reading and writing processes. Particularly effective are dialogue journals, which enable a student to share ideas confidentially with a teacher or peer. The children begin to see that they have achieved something of value in their reading when they share it with others. The letters that appear in the Classroom Vignette on more holistic approaches are an example of the format a dialogue journal might take.

- *Sustained silent reading (SSR).* SSR gives children the opportunity to choose their own reading materials, to practice real reading with real books, and to become independent daily readers. One benefit of SSR is that students see their own teachers reading with them and conclude that daily reading is an important adult activity, something to which they should aspire. Also, having the freedom to choose their own books helps children develop literary tastes and preferences. (See Chapter 7 for further discussion.)

- *Sharing books.* This activity can provide students with the opportunity to read aloud or to orally express their ideas about a particular book they have been reading. They are able to unite speaking and listening with reading and writing. The activity also helps children see themselves as real readers. Ford (1989–1990) cites a study (Mundi, 1989) in which intermediate students advertised themselves as readers, and primary teachers rented them for oral reading sessions. The program eventually became known as Rent-a-Reader.

- *Directed reading–thinking activity (DRTA).* The DRTA is an alternative that may be used instead of the DRA with certain selections from the basal reader. In fact, it may be used with any selection of informational text. Stauffer (1969) outlined the format for the DRTA in two basic phases: The first promotes thinking and predicting; the second builds competencies or reading skills. In the first phase, the readers predict what they will learn, read to prove their predictions, and then evaluate and revise their original ideas. They continue this procedure with each segment of text until the selection is completed. The second phase of the activity varies according to the needs of the students. The teacher might use the opportunity to conduct a strategy lesson related to word knowledge, using context clues or monitoring metacognition. (See Chapter 10 for further discussion.)

Not wanting to reread a good book is like saying, "Paris? I've already been there."

FAYE MOSKOWITZ

IN & BEYOND THE CLASSROOM

Try to view a class in which the teacher uses the basal reader approach. Note the materials that are used and how the directed reading activity is conducted. Inquire about any strategies or techniques that the teacher uses to supplement the basals. You will probably want to include a summary of this observation in your journal.

Use of the above strategies helps broaden the basal reader approach and allows it to encompass a variety of language activities that integrate the language arts. These strategies provide a more holistic perspective to the approach in that they give the reader some purposeful and thought-provoking activities that incorporate the type of reading the student will encounter in real life. As with all new techniques, you will need to model these strategies for your students.

LITERATURE-BASED APPROACH

Over the years, there have been many changes in literacy education; one change that has had a tremendous impact on how schools approach the teaching of reading has been the advent of whole language. While whole language is difficult to define, Watson's succinct words tackle the complexities quite well: "Whole language is a perspective on education that is supported by beliefs about learners and learning, teachers and teaching, language and curriculum" (1989, p. 133). Thus stated, *whole language* crystallizes as a philosophical view about literacy education that says reading and writing progress from recognizing the whole of language to an understanding of the specific parts (Reutzel & Hollingsworth, 1988). Teachers subscribing to such a holistic viewpoint know how important it is to help young children understand about books and the purposes of reading and writing and believe that the best way to do this is to surround students with print, to read and tell stories to them, to encourage children to write and read their own stories, and to promote social and collaborative learning, using a **literature-based approach.** By involving students in learning choices and decisions, these teachers hope to develop each child's "ownership" of reading and writing. Their ultimate goal is to produce readers who are thoughtful and accomplished rather than merely skilled.

Guidelines for a Literature-Based Approach

For many teachers, a holistic view of literacy has evolved into using literature and children's responses to literature as the starting place for reading and writing instruction. These activities, most often associated with the interactive model of reading, can and do play a central, unifying role in the language arts curriculum (Strickland, 1987). However, for such a program to be successful, several important guidelines need to be followed. Many teachers have found the following suggestions helpful (Smith, 1988):

- Students need to have access to a wide variety of trade (story) books that they can choose for reading.
- Class time should be set aside for sustained silent reading (SSR) so that students can read in class. Giving the children this class time for individual reading is crucial because some of them do not read outside of school.
- Reading aloud by the teacher needs to be a daily event. This activity introduces books to children and shows them that the teacher really values reading.
- Students and teachers should share their ideas, likes, and dislikes about books with each other. Book sharing will increase students' curiosity about books.
- Children need to be encouraged to respond to books in a variety of ways, including retelling, art, drama, and cooking.
- Reading and writing activities related to books should be integrated. Writing activities must have a real purpose.
- Books can and should become integrated into other subject areas within the curriculum.

Some of these activities and ways of obtaining books are discussed in Chapter 7.

Strategies Used in the Literature-Based Approach

One way of helping you better understand how literature-based reading works in the classroom is to share aspects of various teachers' methods of implementing this approach.

Many teachers have always used some literature in their classrooms. It then becomes easy for them to expand what they do to a *whole-class reading* of a core text in which each student has a personal copy of the book (Zarillo, 1989); there may be both oral and silent reading followed by student responses in the format of retellings, creative dramatics, art projects, and individual writing activities. Other teachers, rather than using a core book, tend to focus on children's *individualized reading*, which is guided by students' self-selection of books, self-pacing, independent work, and sharing of what has been read (Bagford, 1985). This way of implementing literature-based instruction follows the principles of whole language outlined in Chapter 1. Teachers keep track of children's progress through conferences and develop strategy and skills lessons as needed (Bagford, 1985).

Teachers can also foster participation in *literature response groups* or *literature circles* (Short & Kauffman, 1995; Short & Klassen, 1993) in which there must be a sense of community in the classroom to support the intense and high-level talk that goes on among the students. Characteristics of such classrooms include the use of multiple texts with multiple copies, whole-group and small-group discussions, response journals, and literature logs (Strickland et al., 1989).

However, a significant number of teachers decide to use *themes* and *thematic units* as a way of organizing books and book experiences for the children and integrating them with other aspects of the curriculum. Such an integrated program is more structured, with more emphasis on content and skills development. For example, if a primary class decided to explore themes related to animals, typical units might be: Pets and Their Families, Wildlife Is Wonderful, Jungle Animals Far Away, and Fairy Tale Animals of Long Ago. Such a classroom would start the day with a read-aloud session, a serial reading of a book that the children enjoy and that reflects the theme of the current unit. As a response to the session, the teacher may use a writing activity, such as the dialogue letters featured in the Classroom Vignette, or class discussions about the book. These discussions can take a variety of forms. During one period, a teacher might want to stimulate further thinking about what has been read by asking particular comprehension questions and encouraging the students to summarize the information or make predictions about what might

happen next in the story. On some of these occasions, the teacher might realize that many of her students are having difficulty recognizing cause–effect relationships or drawing conclusions and take the opportunity to model a strategy lesson in which she or he demonstrates how to figure out relationships and draw conclusions about stories.

Other times a class might progress from talking about the read-aloud book to sharing information about individual books they are reading. In the sharing time, the children might retell parts of the stories they've read, explain why they chose certain books, describe what they like or dislike about any book, and even exchange books with one another. If the students are studying about cats, some stories they might mention are *Sam, Bangs, and Moonshine, Millions of Cats, The Owl and the Pussycat, A Cat's Tale, Cat and Canary,* or *Socks and The Tenth Good Thing about Barney.* Book sharing is particularly important because it encourages children to keep trying out new books.

Sustained silent reading would be another daily occurrence. Students select their own books and join their teacher in reading silently for 20 to 30 minutes. Everyone reads, and interruptions are not tolerated. SSR is important because it

Figure 6.5

Language experience chart.

WHY WE LIKE CATS

Mrs. Jackson likes cats because they purr.

Sonia likes cats because they like to play.

Ramona likes cats because they stretch and roll over.

Demont likes cats because they jump and climb.

Nicholas likes cats because they catch mice and bugs.

Sammie likes cats because they snuggle up to you.

Cassie likes cats because they are furry and warm.

Alex likes cats because they are curious and smart.

We all like cats because they are our friends and playmates.

helps children gain self-direction and independence in selecting and reading books. Often the books selected for SSR will reflect the current theme in the classroom. (See Chapter 7 on children's literature for further discussion.)

In some classrooms, children refine their language competencies through the language charts (of the language experience approach covered in the next section) and book-making activities. For example, the class featured in the Classroom Vignette created the Why We Like Cats chart that is pictured in Figure 6.5.

Several children in the Classroom Vignette have enjoyed reading the chart both silently and aloud. Sometimes Mrs. Jackson has caught one or two students standing in front of it and repeating the lines to themselves. Mrs. Jackson encourages their using charts because she believes that it helps children appreciate the pattern and structure of language. She has used this chart to help some of the students understand the use of independent and dependent clauses (and cause–effect relationships) in reading and writing.

Throughout the day, children in integrated literature programs continue to engage in language activities that enhance both language and content learning. During project time students rotate through a variety of centers that have been established. One group might be working at an arts center to get ready for a storytelling production, while others would be at the writing center either completing required log entries to keep track of books they are reading or writing ads for books they have finished. Sometimes students get the opportunity to write letters to a favorite author. If the room has a listening, language, and literature center, class members would have the opportunity to listen to book tapes. Many teachers find that it really helps some of the less capable readers to hear the tape as they follow along in the book. Very often, these students will tape themselves retelling a story they have just completed.

Projects are also a major part of the science and community centers that are established in many classrooms. These centers provide students with the opportunity to integrate language with other content areas and to gather information from actual observations, experiments, encyclopedias, databases, and nonfiction books. One class known to the authors was writing a report containing facts about local South Carolina fish and the fishing industry. Their teacher arranged a class visit from several marine biologists. The students spent several days of center time researching information about fish and developing a set of questions to ask the biologists. Eventually, they published a book containing much data about local fish.

Each day a teacher in a literature class needs to check on the progress of each child. She or he may decide to use center time to conference with individual students and to check on the proficiency of their language learning. Usually a conference doesn't last more than seven minutes and generally includes the following five steps:

1. Story sharing and discussion by the child
2. Comprehension questions that help the teacher determine the child's ability to think about the story
3. Child's oral reading of a story passage
4. Suggestions for activities to build language competencies, project work, and future book selection

5. Conference summary in which the teacher checks the child's log entries to assess how much reading is actually being done and notes the child's specific competencies and needs

Although literature-based classrooms are active and noisy, no one would call them disorganized. In fact, many teachers find they must take time to carefully structure and sequence the experiences for their classes; however, the children's success and continued enjoyment of reading make it all worthwhile.

Vignette in the classroom

This morning Mrs. Jackson has already started her daily read-aloud session with the class. She is doing a serial reading of the book *Bunnicula,* which is the rather lively story of the Monroe family and its pets—Harold the dog, Chester the cat, and a new pet rabbit whom Chester suspects of being a vampire. Through Harold's eyes, the children are learning about Chester's hysterical accusations and Harold's own valiant attempts to calm him. Many of the children are commenting about the two animal friends in their letters to Mrs. Jackson, who decided to incorporate letter-writing activities after reading research (Smith, 1982; Strickland, 1987) that pointed out the benefits of purposeful communication between teachers and students. Following are two letters representing a typical exchange in this classroom:

Dear Mrs. Jackson,

This book is neat. I really love mysteries. This is one. But I'm worried about Chester. He was acting crazy in the part read this morning. Where he used the towel and dressed up like a vampire and bit Harold on the neck. That's weird. You think

Chester is right about Bunnicula? I can't wait to find out.

Your Student,

Alice

Dear Alice,

I am very pleased that you are enjoying the book so much. One of my goals is to help the class see that reading is really fun for you to do.

Mysteries are my favorite stories, too. If you really like this book, you might want to read the sequel *The Celery Stalks at Midnight* during SSR time.

You know I think you are right to worry about Chester. Even though cats can do some pretty unusual things, Chester's behavior seems to surprise everyone. I guess we'll have to see what he does tomorrow.

Mrs. Jackson

LANGUAGE EXPERIENCE APPROACH

The **language experience approach (LEA)** is one that uses the child's own language and experiences in developing literacy. Language experience, which also reflects the top-down model, is not new; however, in recent years it has gained support through research related to emergent literacy, invented spelling, and impact of children's early writing on the acquisition of literacy (Tierney, Readence, & Dishner, 1995). While a number of people are associated with the language experience approach (Ashton-Warner, 1958, 1963; Stauffer, 1970), the words of Roach Van Allen (1973) appear to express the basic LEA philosophy best (1973, p. 158):

> What I can think about, I can talk about.
> What I can say, I can write—or someone can write for me.
> What I can write, I can read.
> I can read what I write, and what other people can write for me to read.

In the implementation of this approach, recommended for students of varying ages and abilities, there are a number of ways for a classroom to evolve. Within the class, there may be whole-class activities, group activities, or individual activities. To present a concise and comprehensible sample of how LEA works, we have adapted Stauffer's (1970) recommendations from Tierney, Readence, and Dishner (1995).

Strategies Used in the Language Experience Approach

Although a teacher may use many other types of literacy and hands-on experiences with his or her students, the following three activities—dictated experience stories, word banks, and creative writing—represent the basics of LEA.

Dictated experience stories. Whole-class–dictated stories are a way for students to become familiar with the LEA procedure and to begin to see reading as similar to talking. Every story must be generated by a stimulus in experience, which can be an event or a concrete object. Having the experience (e.g., making popcorn) or interacting with the object (e.g., creating pinwheels and going outside to test them) should generate a good bit of talk among the students. When the teacher feels they are ready, the students can begin dictating their ideas about what has transpired. The teacher will then record them on lined chart paper. Once the story is completed, the teacher will read it aloud first; then the teacher and the students will read it together. All during this time, the teacher will be pointing to each word as it is read. Art activities or the identification of known words may be used to bring closure to this initial session.

On the second day, the teacher may divide the class into groups and start by having them follow along as the story is read again. Then both teacher and students read in unison, while the teacher points to the words. Later selected children may read the whole story or just small portions of it. At this point, the children begin to name and locate words they recognize. Words that are known are underlined. A final step on the second day is to reread the dictated story, emphasizing the identification of underlined words. Any underlined word that is missed gets its underlining crossed over to show that it is not yet known.

On the third day, the teacher reproduces the story and distributes it to the students, who read it over and underline known words. The stories are kept in both class and individual portfolios. In addition to being done with a whole class, dictated stories may be created by small groups within the class or by individuals.

Word banks. Each student generates a word bank from the dictated stories. This bank only includes words that are recognized consistently and underlined in the story. These known words are written or typed on small cards (i.e., an index card) and filed in an alphabetic system. They become a dictionary resource for categorization activities, decoding activities, or the actual writing of stories.

Creative writing. Children begin creative writing with sentences constructed from the word banks. They can even start by laying out the word cards and then writing in words not in the bank. Students should be encouraged to write about anything they wish. Word processing can aid this process and encourage children to create their own books, which then become the reading materials for the class.

Teacher variations on this approach make it quite flexible and compatible with either basal readers or literature-based strategies. Rarely is LEA used in isolation. However, because of its merits of using the students' own language and experiences, it is recommended not only for very young and emergent readers (Collins & Shaeffer, 1997) but also for older students in the upper grades who are moving into content-area instruction (Burns, Roe, & Ross, 1996). At this level, they can keep logs of what they have read, describe projects they have completed, or document results of scientific inquiry activities. This approach is also beneficial for modeling the basic framework and construction of stories and helping students to evolve as authors.

BALANCED APPROACH

Over the years, there has been much debate about the merits of skills-based versus more holistic instruction. One solution has been the emergence of whole-part-whole instruction, which provides a **balanced approach** to literacy (Strickland, 1998) and appears to combine aspects of all the models of reading. Such a framework would generally involve the initial use of whole texts, either a book or a language experience chart, to promote the development of comprehension. This might then be followed by a specific skills or strategy activity (such as locating the *ch* sound in words) that would help students work toward developing phonemic awareness. Then students would have the opportunity to engage with whole texts again to apply what they have learned (Strickland, 1998).

In one sense, a balanced program is one that focuses on reading and writing for meaning while recognizing that systematic instruction to meet the needs of individual learners is essential. It is also a program in which the teacher is knowledgeable about the competencies and literacy strategies that his or her students need to develop and is able to document progress through the use of running records and analysis of writings and invented spellings (Strickland, 1998). It tends to be even more structured and separate skills–based than an integrated approach to literacy.

Strategies Used in the Balanced Approach

Classrooms that practice balanced reading instruction appear to use a variety of strategies: reading and writing workshops, rereading for comprehension and fluency, reading aloud, buddy reading, reading responses, journal writing, guided reading, and a daily message for practicing skills and strategies (Fowler, 1998). Often the *daily message*, which provides the important news of the school day, is a major vehicle for teaching phonics and other decoding skills. For example, the *ch* sound might first be noted in the message's comments about the first *chilly* weather of the fall. References to that *ch* sound might then be made during the teacher-directed or guided reading time, journal time, reading response, or book-sharing time (Fowler, 1998). By applying this new awareness to meaningful texts and activities, the students are able to make this knowledge their own.

One component of a literacy program based on the balanced approach that deserves more attention is guided reading. Although it is but one component of a balanced literacy program, guided reading is its core, for this is where teachers show children how to read and support their growth as readers (Fountas & Pinnell, 1996). Generally, in **guided reading** a teacher works with a small group of children and helps them learn how to use specific reading strategies independently; while doing this, the teacher must constantly observe the students and assess how well they are learning each strategy and its applications. It also requires that the teacher know quite well the specific needs of the children and the processes involved in reading. Fountas and Pinnell have identified the essential components of guided reading (1996, p. 4):

- A teacher works with a small group.
- Children in the group are similar in their reading development and are able to read about the same level of text.
- Teachers introduce the stories and assist students' reading in ways that help to develop independent reading strategies.
- Each child reads the whole text.
- The goal is for students to read independently and silently.
- The emphasis is on reading increasingly challenging books over time.
- Children are grouped and regrouped in a dynamic process that involves ongoing observation and assessment.

Because literature books, carefully grouped according to developmental difficulty, provide the texts for guided reading lessons, the newly learned strategies can readily be applied to the other balanced literacy reading components: reading aloud, shared reading, and independent reading. In turn, the literature can support as well as be a model and stimulus for the framework's writing components: shared writing, interactive writing, guided writing/writing workshop, and independent writing (Fountas & Pinnell, 1996).

Overall, the emergence of a balanced approach to literacy bodes well for reading instruction and for our children. The balanced literacy framework appears to have formed an eclectic approach (combining aspects of different approaches) from what the research has shown actually works in reading and writing instruction. More and more frequently, the way educators are implementing this approach is both systematic and organized.

The Classroom Vignette that follows illustrates a teacher's literacy strategy using newspaper articles.

HOW SUCCESSFUL ARE THE APPROACHES?

Research can be found to support all the approaches and to show that they can and do work. Basal readers have been a tradition in American classrooms; many people have learned to read with them and have learned to like reading. Tunnell and Jacobs (1989) cited an earlier report by Thompson (1971), who examined studies comparing the success of basal readers with that of individualized literature-based reading (one of our holistic approaches). Thompson found that of the 40 studies he reviewed, 15 were tied (the results

Vignette in the classroom

To help her students keep abreast of current events, Ms. Irwin has been having her class read articles in local newspapers. They are exploring the differing viewpoints about the U.S. troops returning from Operation Desert Storm in the Middle East. Today the class's assignment is to read "Air Base Ready for Flood of GIs" from *The News and Courier* in Charleston, South Carolina.

1. *Preparation.* Prior to actually reading the article, Ms. Irwin activates her students' prior knowledge about the information by asking them to tell her what they know about the troops and their homecoming from the war in the Persian Gulf. She organizes the children's responses on a chart similar to the one pictured in Figure 6.5 (seen earlier). She also asks the children to predict what they will learn in the news story and to use these predictions to guide their reading. Finally, she reminds them to read the story carefully so that they remember as much about it as they can. In this way she really helps them set a purpose for their reading.

2. *Reading.* Students read the material silently and indicate when they are finished.

3. *Recalling the facts.* The children recall as much information as they can about the article. Each remembered idea is recorded exactly as the child states it, even if it is not totally accurate. To assist with the recording process, Ms. Irwin has several student volunteers help write the recalls on the board. Right now the idea is to get the information down.

4. *Rereading to make corrections and additions.* After all the information is recorded, Ms. Irwin directs the class to reread the passages for any corrections or additional information. She indicates this by getting students to examine the ideas on the board to check for any mistakes or gaps in information. Then, with the help of the students, she corrects the inaccuracies and adds the new ideas that they find.

5. *Organizing the information.* The children and Ms. Irwin decide that the best way to organize the information from this article is to draw a timeline and to list the facts in chronological order to reflect the pattern of the text.

6. *Applying the information.* Ms. Irwin tries to get the students to see the relevance of this new information to their own lives. She asks them what impact this war and homecoming have on their own lives and on their views of their country.

7. *Testing.* As a way of gaining closure on the information, Ms. Irwin gives the class a brief short-answer quiz about the article. They then discuss the results as a way of seeing how well the strategy has worked for them. The children are encouraged to present their own ideas about the strategy and how they think it has helped them. Because this strategy is quite demanding, Ms. Irwin uses it no more than once a week.

of each approach were about equal), 24 studies favored the individualized literature approach, and 1 supported the basal system.

Tunnell and Jacobs (1989) have also cited a number of later studies reviewing the results of literature-based reading. Research by Eldredge and Butterfield (1986) compared the basal approach to five other reading methods, two of which contained a literature component. The overall results favored using literature combined with a series of strategy lessons on decoding, a method that sounds very much like the balanced approach to literacy.

There may not be a real answer to the question of which is the most successful approach for teaching children how to read. Perhaps the solution lies with teachers who have knowledge about reading, a commitment to their students, and the insight and courage to make educationally sound decisions about instruction. As a teacher, you hold the key to helping your students unlock the code of literacy. You, combined with appropriate materials and strategies, make the difference.

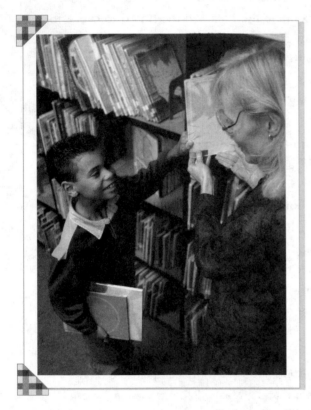

Assessing Reading

No matter which method you choose for your classroom reading instruction, you will want to keep track of the progress your students are making. Evaluation is integral to the whole process of instruction. Every time you implement a strategy or an activity in your classroom, you should be keeping an eye on how it is working and how the children are responding to it.

STANDARDIZED TESTS

In public schools, there has been a tendency to confine reading evaluation to the separate assessment periods associated with *standardized tests*, commercially available tests that measure a child's level of achievement. Some tests also give more specific information by diagnosing a child's individual reading strengths and weaknesses.

Achievement tests provide information about how well a child is functioning in selected aspects of reading. The two basic types of achievement tests are norm-referenced tests and criterion-referenced tests. *Norm-referenced tests* are used to compare each child's achievement level to national *norms*, or standards of performance. These norms are established by giving the tests to large groups of children around the United States and then using the normal distribution of the children's test scores to come up with a standard of achievement. Generally, these tests are used to record and compare the progress of groups of children as well as that of individuals. Comparing an individual child's score to this national standard provides information about how well the child is performing in comparison to others in similar conditions. Information from these tests is usually reported in percentiles and stanines.

On the other hand, *criterion-referenced tests* compare the child's achievement level not to that of other children but to a certain standard that has been set for demonstrating mastery of a specific type of learning. A criterion-referenced test might be used to demonstrate that a child has achieved a satisfactory level of competency in the ability to comprehend the overall idea of a story. Such testing only provides information about a particular child's progress in developing needed competencies; it does not compare that child to other students in any way.

A *diagnostic test* can be used to demonstrate where a child's reading strengths and weaknesses lie by identifying which competencies a child does or does not have. Diagnostic tests usually have specific criteria for determining levels of competency. The results of this type of test are often used to plan instruction and remediation.

However, while standardized tests provide general information about the success of reading instruction, they do not yield all the information teachers need to know about students' progress (Anderson, Hiebert, Scott, & Wilkinson, 1985). For example, they do not always measure a child's unique reading competencies or weaknesses, how well a student understands and differentiates between stories and expository text, or even a child's attitudes toward reading. Nor do these tests reflect the collaboration and interaction that are so often a part of real life assessment (Wineburg, 1997). *Becoming a Nation of Readers* (Anderson, Hiebert, Scott, & Wilkinson, 1985) has cautioned that, at best, standardized tests are a partial assessment that should be combined with observation of children's reading proficiency and habits as well as a review of children's responses to reading and interactions with others.

INFORMAL READING INVENTORIES

Another way for teachers to get more information about children's reading progress is to use an **informal reading inventory** (IRI), an informal evaluation technique designed to help diagnose a child's reading strengths or weaknesses through the oral reading of a series of graded word lists or sentences and text selections. The word lists or sentences are designed to give the teacher an idea of the child's approximate grade level of reading; the selections of text and accompanying comprehension questions help the teacher to determine which strategies the child uses to decode information and how much of the information the student actually comprehends. Informal reading inventories can be bought commercially. Well-known commercially prepared IRIs include the following:

- Bader, L. (1998). *Bader Reading and Language Inventory* (3rd ed.). Columbus, OH: Merrill.
- Flynt, S. and Cooter, R. B. (1999). *Flynt–Cooter Reading Inventory for the Classroom* (3rd ed.). Columbus, OH: Merrill.
- Johns, J. (1997). *Basic Reading Inventory—Preprimer to Grade Eight* (7th ed.). Dubuque, IA: Kendall/Hunt.
- Roe, B. (1999). *Burns/Roe Informal Reading Inventory* (5th ed.). Boston: Houghton Mifflin.
- Silvaroli, N. (1996). *Classroom Reading Inventory* (8th ed.). Madison, WI: Brown & Benchmark.

Through the use of an IRI, a teacher can assess each child's independent, instructional, and frustration levels of reading. The teacher can also determine a student's potential for reading by analyzing the child's ability to comprehend a passage that has been read aloud. The four levels of reading comprehension are:

1. *Independent level.* Indicates the grade level of materials a child can read on his or her own. This level is determined by the child's ability to recognize 99 percent of the words in the word list and to answer 95 percent of the reading comprehension questions correctly.
2. *Instructional level.* Signifies the level of materials that should be used for reading instruction. At this level, the child can recognize 95 percent of the words and answer 75 percent of the passage comprehension questions.

3. *Frustration level.* Occurs when a child begins to encounter great difficulty in reading and doesn't really comprehend much of what is happening. At this point, the child is able to answer less than 50 percent of the comprehension questions and to recognize less than 90 percent of the words from the word list. The child should not be required to read materials at the frustration level.

4. *Listening level.* Helps to determine a child's potential for reading. A child's ability to answer 75 percent of the questions about a passage that has been read aloud by the teacher is considered adequate in designating this level.

RUNNING RECORDS

An informal technique that is similar to an IRI and gaining in popularity is the running record. It has been advocated by Clay (1979, 1985, 1991) as a way of indicating how well a child is processing text. In a **running record,** the child reads a selection from a book or books with which he or she is quite familiar while both the teacher and the student are looking at the same text; as the child reads, the teacher codes the behaviors on a separate piece of paper while maintaining a position of neutrality. Checks are given for correct words; miscues that occur are noted with as much accuracy as possible. Types of miscues that are noted are substitutions, multiple attempts at a word, omissions and insertions, and the need to provide a word for the child. Self-corrections, which are a vital component of the record, are not considered errors.

In addition to quantitatively analyzing the records, a teacher also needs to look at them qualitatively. The teacher needs to note whether or not a student is using letter/sound cues, syntactic cues, or semantic cues when trying to comprehend the meaning of the text. Then the teacher can use the information from the running record to make informed and continuing decisions about future instruction. Running records are an important part of the guided reading component of a balanced literacy program (Fountas & Pinnell, 1996).

OTHER INFORMAL ASSESSMENT TECHNIQUES

Like standardized tests, IRIs and running records provide only a sampling of what a child is able to do in reading, a sampling that can easily be affected by a child's anxiety or response to distractions during the test period. These inventories too must be supplemented with other types of data, such as the teacher's own knowledge of the student's ability and information about the child's daily progress. Informal assessment, which can be conducted on a daily basis, includes observation; the use of conferences, checklists, and rubrics; and the examination of students' portfolios (their written responses to reading). These techniques embody the ideas of observation, interaction, and analysis put forth by Goodman (1989).

Observation

Observation can take place during all types of reading activities. For example, you might note that during silent reading, one child is always pointing to the individual words. This might give you a clue that the student is having some difficulty with word recognition and fluency, something you might want to question the child about later. Your goal is to document language development in a variety of literacy situations.

There are several ways you can keep track of your observations. You may simply want to jot your ideas down in a small notebook. However, it may be more efficient to keep more formal anecdotal records, which you can use for sharing information with administrators and parents. This type of record allows you to monitor both the entire class and individual children; it helps you to know where progress is occurring and where changes need to be made. A typical format of an anecdotal record can be seen in Figure 6.6.

Figure 6.6 *Anecdotal record form.*

Date	Student	Activity	Comments

Summary

Conferences and Checklists

Conferences are a way of interacting with students that allows you to learn specific information about individuals and to clarify any confusion you may have about a particular child's progress. Conferences can take a variety of forms. Although it may be informal, the conference has a specific structure. An excellent example is the one outlined in the Strategies Used in the Literature-Based Approach section of this chapter. The teacher in this example knows what to look for and uses questions and comments to get that information. She is also able to give future direction to the activities of each student. Frequently she uses checklists, such as the one in Figure 6.7, to document specific information.

Figure 6.7

Conference checklist.

READING CONFERENCE RECORD

Student's name _____ Date _____

Title _____

Type of material _____

	EXCELLENT	GOOD	OK	NEEDS HELP
WORD RECOGNITION				
Decoding				
Use of context clues				
Use of structural clues				
Use of dictionary				
Conceptual connections				
COMPREHENSION				
Main idea				
Supporting details				
Relationships				
(Cause/effect)				
(Compare/contrast)				
Description of characters				
Sequence of events				

LITERARY CONNECTIONS

Retelling summary: _____

Child's opinion of the material: _____

Further responses: _____

Suggestions for future reading: _____

Summary of the conference: _____

Rubrics

Rubrics provide specific criteria for evaluating student performance at differing proficiency levels. Students receive specific credit for minimal work, average work, or high-quality work. Some areas have developed state-wide standards and train teachers in how to be consistent in their scoring (Garcia & Verville, 1994).

Rubrics are very helpful in that they give students information about what is really expected of them. Figure 6.8 is an example of what a teacher might use for a reading rubric.

Portfolio Assessment: Analysis of Children's Responses

Yet another way of assessing progress is to review and analyze children's written responses to reading, usually kept in writing *portfolios*. Among other things, these responses might include a journal, a written summary of a story, several

ACTIVITY	CONSISTENT	INCONSISTENT
Reads and understands all independent books.	_____	_____
Completes daily and monthly reading.	_____	_____
Completes literature response log on time.	_____	_____
Has log that contains high-quality entries.	_____	_____
Contributes thoughtful comments to literature circles.	_____	_____
Listens and responds to peer comments in literature circles.	_____	_____
Completes all assignments on time.	_____	_____
Has work that shows effort and attempts to achieve quality.	_____	_____

Figure 6.8

A sample reading rubric.

POINT CREDIT SYSTEM

A—consistent for all areas (7 of 8)

B—consistent for most areas (6 of 8)

C—consistent for many areas (5 of 8)

D—consistent for some areas (4 of 8)

F—consistent in a few areas (3 of 8)

Source: Slightly adapted by permission of Regie Routman: *Invitations: Changing as Teachers and Learners K–12* (Heinemann, a division of Reed Elsevier, Inc., Portsmouth, NH, 1994).

drafts of a poem, a letter to a character in a story, a description of a character accompanied by a portrait, a completely new ending for a story, and some self-appraisal forms. Many educators advocate using portfolio models or checklists as a means of selecting what should go into each child's folder (Vizyak, 1997).

Teachers and students can work together to keep portfolios of selected writing projects. This not only provides information for the teacher but also encourages the students to engage in self-monitoring, an activity that empowers students by allowing them to take some responsibility for their own progress (Rief, 1990). In reviewing the various writings of the children, teachers can begin to make judgments not only about the students' reading comprehension but also about the increased sophistication of their written work. More specific information on how to maintain and evaluate children's writing portfolios as well as how to conduct individual conferences specifically related to evaluating writing can be found in Chapter 8.

Reaching At-Risk Readers

As with all areas of education, reading and writing are constantly being influenced by new developments. Today some encouraging breakthroughs are occurring in various areas of instruction for at-risk students. Following is a brief synopsis of three programs: Reading Recovery, Success for All, and the Accelerated Reader. While none of these provides *the* answer for reading education, they do provide *some* answers, even though many educators may be hesitant to provide unconditional endorsement for those answers.

READING RECOVERY PROGRAM

Reading Recovery is a short-term, early-intervention program that seeks to prevent reading failure rather than treat it through remediation. The target audience for the program is at-risk first-graders, who traditionally would fail to learn to read by the end of the year. The idea is to reach these children before they experience failure, to help them develop strategies that will make them readers rather than nonreaders.

The program was developed in New Zealand by Marie Clay (1979). Through her work with children, Clay had become convinced that children can and do develop concepts about letters and print, about reading and writing, and about how they all work together. When this happens, children can take charge of their own reading. These successful readers learn a system of behaviors that continues to operate on its own and allows them to be independent learners. Clay saw Reading Recovery as a way to help all children develop these specific reading strategies and to become independent readers who are involved with real books.

The at-risk first-graders chosen for the program receive specialized one-on-one instruction for 30 minutes each day. Pinnell (1988) described the typical cycle of instruction as one in which the child first reads short, predictable stories and then writes stories. During this time, there is discussion and interaction with the teacher in an "intimate process" (Pinnell, Fried, & Estice, 1990, p. 283) that builds an attentive relationship while providing needed instruction and insights. At the end of the lesson, the child is introduced to a more difficult book that he or she is expected to reread the following day. When the student has developed enough strategies to read on her or his own, the intervention ends. The child is then able to function without assistance in the regular classroom.

The original research and several follow-up studies in New Zealand by Clay (1985) appear to demonstrate the effectiveness of Reading Recovery. Children who have completed the program have returned to the regular classroom and have not needed further assistance. Studies in Ohio (Pinnell, 1988; Pinnell, DeFord, & Lyons, 1988) have also indicated that Reading Recovery is an effective program for first-graders in the United States who may be in danger of failing to learn to read. The program, which is based on the importance of helping children make connections between reading and writing (Pinnell, 1988), provides hope for children, parents, and especially reading teachers who have had to deal with the frustration of reading failure despite the use of myriad materials and countless hours of instruction. However, many districts have begun to rethink the cost of the program; with a one-teacher-to-one-student format, Reading Recovery can add considerable expense to a district's instructional budget (Collins & Stevens, 1997). Some school districts are scaling back and looking for other options, such as having a Reading Recovery teacher spend half of the school day in a classroom and the other half of the day in a Reading Recovery room (Collins & Stevens, 1997).

SUCCESS FOR ALL PROGRAM

Success for All is a program that targets early instruction for at-risk and low-achieving learners using a unique, comprehensive reading strategy. It has been used in schools that serve inner-city populations in high-poverty neighborhoods (Slavin, Madden, Dolan, & Wasik, 1996). While Success for All can be a vehicle for comprehensive school reform, its basic core is the innovative reading curriculum, which demands a school schedule allowing a 90-minute reading period. During this time, students are regrouped (from regular classes) into ability-level reading groups of no more than 20 students. During each 90-

minute period, there is intensive whole-group instruction, which focuses on language skills as well as reading and writing activities with whatever basal reader a particular school is using. Students work in cooperative groups as they develop strategies for understanding a story. Students also read trade books and share information on a weekly basis. As students progress, a systematic writing program is introduced, usually implemented in the second year of school (Tierney, Readence, & Dishner, 1995).

If students are not successful in the structured reading groups, they are then tutored by qualified teachers in one-on-one situations. These tutors support what the regular reading group is doing, identify reading problems, and work with the teachers to make instructional decisions about the children. Generally, systematic assessments are done every eight weeks to support the quality of the program.

One key to the success of the program is the teacher who acts as the program facilitator at each school site (Madden, Livingston, & Cummings, 1995). This person coordinates the all-important staff development for the teachers, works with them to solve problems, handles scheduling, and facilitates getting support for the families. The facilitator also organizes intensive classroom follow-up for the teachers.

The evaluations of Success for All indicate that its method can be replicated and that systemic school change can take place that gives each child an opportunity to succeed in school (Slavin et al., 1997). While the program is not a magic wand for reading problems, it most certainly is a comprehensive approach that combines early intervention, small class size, regrouping, tutoring, cooperative learning, and family support with a balanced variety of workable reading practices. The combination definitely does work (Ross, Smith, Madden, & Slavin, 1997).

ACCELERATED READER PROGRAM

Technology, both in and out of education, continues to be a fast-developing area. However, teachers need to be cautious about the ways they use it; they need to avoid falling into the habit of using computers or other electronic equipment for its own sake. Whatever is used in the classroom must satisfy a particular need, fulfill a specific purpose, or convey some aspect of instruction that might not be possible through other means. Technology is a tool or an aid, not an end in itself.

For teachers who want systematic formal assessment of books students have read, there is the **Accelerated Reader program,** a computerized reading management system for K–12 that manages and tracks literature-based reading. It has computerized tests for over 14,000 books that are found in most school libraries. After students read self-selected trade books, they take a quiz on the computer. The student selects the title and takes the short-answer quiz; the computer immediately reports the points the student earns. The points are based on the length of the book, the book's reading level, and the number of correct responses. Peek (1998) believes the program motivates students because they receive their results immediately and can track the number of total points they earn. The program also gives the teacher the student's grade-equivalent score, national percentile rank, and instructional level. The computer provides a letter with all this information, which can be shared with the student's parent or caregiver.

BEYOND THE CLASSROOM

Depending on your particular interests, you may want to continue investigating one of the programs presented in this section. You can begin by reading any article related to the topic in the Related Readings. Then, if sample classrooms are available, you might want to visit one and keep a record of your thoughts about the specific program and your observations concerning the way in which it functions.

With this program, there is no social interaction or discussion about each book with others. Also, the program does not encourage any writing extensions or creative responses. However, as a technology tool, the Accelerated Reading program works by helping the teacher manage the record keeping of the books read by all the students.

Summary

In today's society, reading and writing are not only essential aspects of literacy, they are also crucial for adequate daily functioning. Because reading is now viewed as an interaction between the mind of the reader and the print in the text, it is more important than ever for teachers to help children become independent readers, adept at constructing meaning from print for themselves. Your role as a teacher is to help your students by making use of the results of reading research on readers, text, and necessary instructional strategies. You should help students to take advantage of their prior knowledge, to link the known with the unknown, and to develop reading competencies as needed. Your goal is to create effective and efficient readers who have a repertoire of strategies at their command.

No matter which major approach you use for reading instruction, you will want to expose your students to actual books representing all types of meaningful text. You will want them to be able to monitor their own reading through prediction, summarization, thoughtful reflection, and self-questioning. They can respond to their reading through journals, logs, letters, and various other writing activities.

Throughout your career as a teacher, it will be important for you to reflect carefully on what you are doing and what types of reading materials and strategies you are using. You will need to remain knowledgeable about continuing developments in the field so that you can make decisions about which ideas to implement in your classroom. Most of all, you will want to be sure that what you do mirrors your philosophy and knowledge about reading. Only by practicing a method that you truly believe in will you ever be able to help someone else to learn to read.

With Children *activities*

BECOME A CHARACTER

Sometimes children develop a strong feeling for certain characters in a story they've read. You can expand and broaden this sensitivity by having the students compose a short sequel to the story—one in which they actually become the characters in question and behave in ways they deem appropriate. Younger children may want to dictate their ideas to the teacher or onto an audiocassette.

BOOK SHARING

Children really enjoy sharing books they have read. Also, many children can improve their oral fluency by preparing and reading stories aloud to others, especially to younger children. The older child gets the needed practice, and the younger child acquires a good reading role model.

BOOK ADS

Children can practice writing and reading summaries by composing ads for stories they wish to "sell" to their classmates. Each ad should include a two- to three-sentence summary highlighting the major points of the story. Both sellers and buyers learn the finer points of summarization.

CONTEXT CLOZE

Prepare several short reading selections in which you have systematically deleted words not readily recognized by your students. As the children try to understand the text, they will use selected cues from the words surrounding the deletions to help themselves. The purpose of the activity is to highlight the importance of using context to construct meaning. To provide feedback for the students, you may want to include the deleted words on the back of the selections. (See Chapters 9 and 10 for more information on cloze.)

REAL PRINT

Have the students bring boxes, bags, labels, and ads from home. They can then work in pairs and small groups to identify words and common names that they readily recognize. The correctly identified words can be written on cards and added to each child's individual sight-word bank. Children can later group known words in their banks according to sounds (beginning, middle, ending) or match up the word cards with the original words in the advertising.

technology CD-ROMs and Children's Literature

CD-ROMs are another way to introduce children to good literature. The CD-ROMs permit the students to interact with the story. The following list is great for prereaders, emergent readers, and reluctant readers because the text is highlighted as the story is read. At the end of each page, the reader has an opportunity to click on the various objects on the screen, and the objects tell more of the story. The newest CD-ROMs will even permit the reader to write responses to various parts in the story. Some tested titles are *Green Eggs and Ham* (with three learning games); *The Treehouse; Shelia Rae, the Brave; Stellaluna; Little Monster at School; Just Grandma and Me; Ruff's Bond;* and *Harry and the Haunted House.* All are available by contacting:

Broderbund
500 Redwood Boulevard
Novato, CA 94948-6121
Telephone: 415-382-4400

Other companies that have interactive CD-ROMs for elementary students include the following:

Houghton Mifflin
95 Madison Avenue
New York, NY 10016
http://www.dk.com

Learning Company
6493 Kaiser Drive
Fremont, CA 94555

Mecc
6160 Summit Drive N.
Minneapolis, MN 55430-4003

EDMARK
P.O. Box 97021
Redmond, WA 98073-9721

Home Page and Digital Cameras

One way to personalize your home page is to include photographs of you, subjects that interest you, or objects you are attempting to explain. There are two ways to include photographs. One method is to take any favorite picture that was taken with your regular camera and scan it onto your home page; the one extra piece of equipment you will need is a scanner.

The second way to include pictures is to use a digital camera, which records the image directly onto computer chips. Instead of film, digital cameras have either a removable memory card or a regular old floppy disk. Besides the digital camera, one needs a connection cable and transfer software, which are usually included with the camera.

Some advantages of the digital camera are that you do not have to pay for film processing and you may use software to edit and touch up pictures. Most digital cameras come with Adobe PhotoDeluxe, which is an image-editing program that is quite easy to use. Some disadvantages of the digital camera are that it is quite expensive (but the price is lowering as more companies are making them) and the computer needs a lot of memory (usually 100 MB is recommended).

A good introduction to the use of the digital camera is Julie Adair King's book *Digital Photography for Dummies* (published in 1997 by IDG Books Worldwide, in Foster City, CA).

E-learning

www.cbcbooks.org/

This site contains information about Children's Book Week and links to many children's book publishers.

gpn.unl.edu/rainbow

This site describes books featured on the PBS show, with recommended activities.

www.honors.unr.edu/~fenimore/en297/bohannon/sidewalk.html

Shel Silverstein shares his expertise and ability in drawing his illustrations and writing his poems.

www.reading.org

This is the site of the International Reading Association.

www.cochran.com/theodore

This site permits readers to interactively read *Theodore's Surprise Friend.* Children can choose different story endings.

www.harcourtschool.com

This site by Harcourt Brace has activities designed to be done by individuals or in cooperative groups.

www.eduplace.com/rdg/index.html

This is Houghton Mifflin's educational site of reading and language arts.

Related Readings

Baenen, N., Bernholc, A., Dulaney, C., & Banks, K. (1997). Reading Recovery: Long-term progress after three cohorts. *Journal of Education for Students Placed at Risk, 2*(2), 161–181.

Cunningham, P., Hall, D., & Defee, M. (1998). Nonability-grouped, multilevel instruction: Eight years later. *The Reading Teacher, 52*(8), 652–664.

Dudley-Marling, C., & Murphy, S. (1997). A political critique of remedial reading programs: The example of Reading Recovery. *The Reading Teacher, 50*(6), 460–468.

Fashola, O., & Slavin, R. (1997). Promising programs for elementary and middle schools: Evidence of effectiveness and replicability. *Journal of Education for Students Placed at Risk, 2*(3), 251–307.

Fountas, I., C., & Pinnell, G. S. (1996). *Guided reading.* Portsmouth, NH: Heinemann.

Hiebert, E. H., & Fisher, C. W. (1990). Whole language: Three themes for the future. *Educational Leadership, 47*(6), 62–64.

Pinnell, G. S., Fried, M. D., & Estice, R. M. (1990). Reading Recovery: Learning how to make a difference. *The Reading Teacher, 43*(4), 282–295.

Ross, S. M., Smith, L. J., & Casey, J. P. (1997). Preventing early school failure: Impacts of Success for All on standardized test outcomes, minority group performance, and school effectiveness. *Journal of Education for Students Placed at Risk, 2*(1), 29–53.

References

Adams, M. J. (1990). *Beginnning to read: Thinking and learning about print.* Cambridge, MA: MIT Press.

Anderson, R. C., Hiebert, E. H., Scott, J. A., & Wilkinson, I. (1985). *Becoming a nation of readers: The report of the Commission on Reading.* Washington, DC: National Institute of Education, The National Academy of Education.

Anderson, R. C., & Pearson, P. D. (1984). A schema-theoretic view of basals. In P. D. Pearson (ed.), *Handbook of reading research.* New York: Longman.

Ashton-Warner, S. (1958). *Spinster.* New York: Simon & Schuster.

Ashton-Warner, S. (1963). *Teacher.* New York: Simon & Schuster.

Bader, L. (1998). *Bader reading and language inventory* (3rd ed.). New Jersey: Merrill.

Baenen, N., Bernholc, A., Dulaney, C., & Banks, K. (1997). Reading Recovery: Long-term progress after three cohorts. *Journal of Education for Students Placed at Risk, 2*(2), 161–181.

Bagford, J. (1985). What ever happened to individualized reading? *The Reading Teacher, 39*(2), 190–193.

Beck, I. L., McKeown, M. G., Hamilton, R. L., & Kucan, L. (1997). *Questioning the author: An approach for enhancing student engagement with text.* Newark, DE: International Reading Association.

Blake, M. E. (1986). *Young readers' attitudes.* Unpublished manuscript.

Bransford, J. D., & Johnson, M. K. (1973). Considerations of some problems of comprehension. In W. G. Chase (ed.), *Visual information processing.* New York: Academic Press.

Brown, A. L. (1982). Learning how to learn from reading. In J. A. Langer & M. T. Smith-Burke (eds.), *Reader meets author/bridging the gap.* Newark, DE: International Reading Association.

Bruner, J. (1973). Organization of early skilled action. *Child Development, 44,* 1–11.

Burns, P. C., Roe, B. D., & Ross, E. P. (1996). *Teaching reading in today's elementary schools* (6th ed.). Boston: Houghton Mifflin Company.

Bus, A., Van Izendoorn, M., & Pellegrini, A. (1995). Joint book reading makes for success in learning to read: A meta-analysis on intergenerational transmission of literacy. *Review of Educational Research, 65,* 1–21.

Caldwell, J. (1985). A new look at the old Informal Reading Inventory. *The Reading Teacher, 39*(3), 168–173.

Carter, C. (1997). Why reciprocal teaching? *Educational Leadership, 54*(6), 64–68.

Clay, M. M. (1979). *Reading: The patterning of complex behavior.* Exeter, NH: Heinemann.

Clay, M. M. (1985). *The early detection of reading difficulties* (3rd ed.). Portsmouth, NH: Heinemann.

Clay, M. (1991). *Becoming literate: The construction of inner control.* Portsmouth, NH: Heinemann.

Collins, A., Brown, J. S., & Larkin, K. M. (1980). Inferences in text understanding. In R. Spiro, B. Bruce, & W. Brewer (eds.), *Theoretical issues in reading comprehension*. Hillsdale, NJ: Erlbaum.

Collins, J. D., & Stevens, L. M. (1997). Does Reading Recovery really work? *American School Board Journal*, 184(6), 38–39.

Collins, N. L. D., & Shaeffer, M. B. (1997). Look, listen, and learn to read. *Young Children*, 52(5), 65–68.

Cunningham, P., & Hall, D. (1997). *Month-by-month phonics for first grade*. Greensboro, NC: Carson-Dellosa Publishing Company.

Cunningham, P., & Hall, D. (1998). *Month-by-month phonics for upper grades*. Greensboro, NC: Carson-Dellosa Publishing Company.

Cunningham, P., Hall, D., & Defee, M. (1991). Nonability-grouped, multilevel instruction: A year in a first grade classroom. *The Reading Teacher*, 44, 566–571.

Cunningham, P., Hall, D., & Defee, M. (1998). Nonability-grouped, multilevel instruction: Eight years later. *The Reading Teacher*, 52(8), 652–664.

Davey, B. (1983). Think-aloud—Modeling the cognitive processes of reading comprehension. *Journal of Reading*, 27(1), 44–47.

DeMott, B. (1990). Why we read and write. *Educational Leadership*, 47(6), 6.

Dudley-Marling, C., & Murphy, S. (1997). A political critique of remedial reading programs: The example of Reading Recovery. *The Reading Teacher*, 50(6), 460–468.

Durkin, D. (1978–1979). What classroom observations reveal about reading comprehension instruction. *Reading Research Quarterly*, 14(4), 481–532.

Durkin, D. (1988). *A classroom observation study of reading instruction in kindergarten*. Champaign, IL: Center for the Study of Reading. Technical Report No. 422.

Eldredge, J. L., & Butterfield, D. (1986). Alternatives to traditional reading instruction. *The Reading Teacher*, 40(1), 32–37.

Ericson, L., & Juliebo, M. F. (1998). *The phonological awareness handbook for kindergarten and primary teachers*. Newark, DE: International Reading Association.

Farr, R. C., & Strickland, D. S. (1995). *Treasury of literature*. New York: Harcourt Brace & Company.

Fashola, O., & Slavin, R. (1997). Promising programs for elementary and middle schools: Evidence of effectiveness and replicability. *Journal of Education for Students Placed at Risk*, 2(3), 251–307.

Ford, M. P. (1989–1990). Maximizing literacy opportunities through cross-age groupings. *Reading Today*, 7(3), 14.

Fountas, I. C., & Pinnell, G. S. (1996). *Guided Reading*. Portsmouth, NH: Heinemann.

Fowler, D. (1998). Balanced reading instruction in practice. *Educational Leadership*, 55(6), 11–13.

Garcia, M., & Verville, K. (1994). Redesigning teaching and learning: The Arizona student assessment program. In S. Valencia, E. Hiebert, & P. Afflerbach (eds.), *Authentic reading assessment: Practices and possibilities*. Newark, DE: International Reading Association.

Goodman, K. S. (1967). Reading: A psycholinguistic guessing game. *Journal of the Reading Specialist*, 6(8), 126–135.

Goodman, K. S. (1976). Behind the eye: What happens in reading. In H. Singer & R. Ruddell (eds.), *Theoretical models and processes of reading* (2nd ed.). Newark, DE: International Reading Association.

Goodman, K. S. (1980). Viewpoints . . . from a researcher. *Language Arts*, 57(8), 846–847.

Goodman, K. S. (1986). Basal readers: A call for action. *Language Arts*, 63(4), 358–363.

Goodman, Y. M. (1980, January). *The roots of literacy*. Paper presented at the Annual Claremont Reading Conference, Claremont, CA.

Goodman, Y. M. (1989). Roots of the whole-language movement. *The Elementary School Journal*, 90(2), 113–127.

Gordon, C. (1985). Modeling inference awareness across the curriculum. *Journal of Reading*, 28(5), 444–447.

Graves, M. F., Juel, C., & Graves, B. B. (1998). *Teaching reading in the 21st century*. Boston: Allyn & Bacon.

Herman, P. A. (1984, December). *Incidental learning of word meanings from expository texts that systematically vary text features*. Paper presented at the National Reading Conference, St. Petersburg, FL.

Hiebert, E. H., & Fisher, C. W. (1990). Whole language: Three themes for the future. *Educational Leadership*, 47(6), 62–64.

Hoffman, J. V., McCarthey, S. J., Abbott, J., Christian, C., Corman, L., Curry, K., Dressman, M., Elliott, B., Matherne, D., & Stahle, D. (1994). So what's new in the new basals? A focus on first grade. *Journal of Reading Behavior*, 26, 47–74.

Hoffman, J. V., McCarthey, S. J., Elliott, B., Bayles, D. L., Price, D. P., Ferree, A., & Abbott, J. A. (1998). The literature-based basals in first-grade classrooms: Savior, Satan, or same-old, same-old? *Reading Research Quarterly*, 33(2), 168–197.

Huck, C., Hepler, S., & Hickman, J. (1993). *Children's literature in the elementary school* (5th ed.). New York: Harcourt Brace Jovanovich.

International Reading Association. (1997). The role of phonics in reading instruction: A position statement of the International Reading Association. *Indiana Reading Journal*, 29(3), 23–26.

International Reading Association & National Association for the Education of Young Children. (1998, July). Learning to read and write: Developmentally appropriate practices for young children. *Young Children*, 30–46.

Jensen, J. M., & Roser, N. L. (1990). Are there really 3 R's? *Educational Leadership*, 47(6), 7–12.

Johns, J. (1997). *Basic reading inventory—preprimer to grade eight* (7th ed.). Dubuque, IA: Kendall/Hunt Publishing Company.

Johns, J, & Ellis, D. (1976). Reading: Children tell it like it is. *Reading World*, 16, 115–128.

Johnson, D. D., & Pearson, P. D. (1984). *Teaching reading vocabulary* (2nd ed.). New York: Holt, Rinehart & Winston.

LaBerge, D., & Samuels, S. J. (1985). Toward a theory of automatic information processing in reading. In H. Singer & R. Ruddell (eds), *Theoretical models and processes of reading*. Newark, DE: International Reading Association.

Lomax, R. G., & McGee, L. M. (1987). Young children's concepts about print and reading. *Reading Research Quarterly, 22*(2), 237–256.

Madden, N., Livingston, M., & Cummings, N. (1995). *Facilitator's manual for success for all/roots and wings*. Baltimore: Johns Hopkins University, Center for Research on the Education of Students Placed at Risk.

Martin, P. (1993). Capture silk: Reading aloud together. *English Journal, 82*(8), 16–24.

McKenna, E. (1997). *Gender differences in reading attitudes*. Unpublished master's thesis, Kean College of New Jersey, ED 407653.

McKenna, M., Kear, D., & Ellsworth, R. (1995). Children's attitudes toward reading: A national survey. *Reading Research Quarterly, 30*(4), 934–956.

McMackin, M. C. (1993). The parent's role in literacy development. *Childhood Education, 69*(3), 142–145.

Mickelson, N. (1989). Point/counterpoint: The value of basal readers. *Reading Today, 7*(1), 18.

Monahan, J., & Hinson, B. (eds.) (1988). *New directions in reading instruction*. Newark, DE: International Reading Association.

Mundi, S. (1989). Rent-a-Reader. *Learning, 17*(5), 70.

Nagy, W. E., & Scott, J. A. (1990). Word schemas: Expectations about the form and meaning of words. *Cognition and Instruction, 7,* 105–127.

National Assessment of Educational Progress. (1996, March). *NAEP 1994 reading report card: Findings from the national assessment of educational progress.* <http://www.nces.ed.gov/NAEP/y25flk/rrcexec.shtml> (1998, July 15).

National Assessment Governing Board (1992–1998). *Reading framework for the National Assessment of Educational Progress: 1992–1998.* Washington, DC: National Assessment Governing Board.

Organization for Economic Co-operation and Development and Statistics Canada (1998, July 13). *Literacy, economy, and society: Results of the first international adult literacy survey, 1995.* <http://nces.ed.gov/pubsearch /index.html> (1998, July 15).

Palincsar, A. S., & Brown, A. L. (1986). Interactive teaching to promote independent learning from text. *The Reading Teacher, 39*(8), 771–777.

Paris, S. G., Lipson, M. Y., & Wixson, K. K. (1983). Becoming a strategic reader. *Contemporary Educational Psychology, 8*(3), 293–316.

Pearson, P. D. (1985). Changing the face of reading comprehension instruction. *The Reading Teacher, 38*(8), 724–738.

Pearson, P. D., Roehler, L. R., Dole, J. A., & Duffy, G. G. (1992). Developing expertise in reading comprehension. In S. J. Samuels & A. E. Farstrup (eds.), *What research has to say about reading instruction* (2nd ed.). Newark, DE: International Reading Association.

Peek, D. (1998). *Report portfolio: The Accelerated Reader.* Wisconsin Rapids: Advantage Systems.

Pinnell, G. S. (1988). *Success of children at risk in a program that combines writing and reading.* Champaign, IL: Center for the Study of Reading. Technical Report No. 417.

Pinnell, G. S., DeFord, D. E., & Lyons, C. A. (1988). *Reading Recovery: Early intervention for at-risk first graders.* Arlington, VA: Educational Research Service.

Pinnell, G. S., Fried, M. D., & Estice, R. M. (1990). Reading Recovery: Learning how to make a difference. *The Reading Teacher, 43*(4), 282–295.

Raphael, T. E. (1984). Teaching learners about sources of information for answering comprehension questions. *Journal of Reading, 27*(4), 303–311.

Raphael, T. E. (1986). Teaching question–answer relationships, revisited. *The Reading Teacher, 39*(5), 516–522.

Rasinski, T. V. (1989). Reading and the empowerment of parents. *The Reading Teacher, 43*(3), 226–231.

Reutzel, D. R (1989). Point/counterpoint: The value of basal readers. *Reading Today, 7*(1), 18.

Reutzel, D. R., & Hollingsworth, P. M. (1988). Whole language and the practitioner. *Academic Therapy, 23*(4), 405–415.

Rief, L. (1990). Finding the value in evaluation: Self-assessment in a middle school classroom. *Educational Leadership, 47*(6), 24–29.

Roe, B. (1999). *Burns/Roe informal reading inventory* (5th ed.). Boston: Houghton Mifflin.

Rogoff, B. (1990). *Apprenticeship in thinking: Cognitive development in social context.* New York: Oxford University Press.

Rosenblatt, L. M. (1978). *The reader, the text, the poem: The transactional theory of literary work.* Carbondale: Southern Illinois University Press.

Rosenblatt, L. M. (1994) The transactional theory of reading and writing. In R. B. Ruddell, M. R. Ruddell, & H. Singer (eds.), *Theoretical models and processes of reading* (4th ed.). Newark, DE: International Reading Association.

Ross, S. M., Smith, L. J., & Casey, J. P. (1997). Preventing early school failure: Impacts of Success for All on standardized test outcomes, minority group performance, and school effectiveness. *Journal of Education for Students Placed at Risk, 2*(1), 29–53.

Ross, S. M., Smith, L. J., Madden, N. A., & Slavin, R. E. (1997). Improving the academic success of disadvantaged children: An examination of Success for All. *Psychology in the Schools, 34*(2), 171–180.

Routman, R. (1991). *Invitations.* Portsmouth, NH: Heinemann.

Ruddell, R., & Unrau, N. J. (1994). Reading as a meaning-construction process: The reader, the text, and the teacher. In R. B. Ruddell, M. R. Ruddell, & H. Singer (eds.), *Theoretical models and processes of reading* (4th ed.). Newark, DE: International Reading Association.

Rumelhart, D. E. (1980). Schemata: The building blocks of cognition. In R. Spiro, B. Bruce, & W. Brewer (eds.), *Theoretical issues in reading comprehension.* Hillsdale, NJ: Erlbaum.

Saccardi, M. C. (1996). Predictable books: Gateways to a lifetime of reading (teaching reading). *The Reading Teacher*, 49(7), 588–590.

Searfoss, L. W., & Readence, J. E. (2000). *Helping children learn to read* (4th ed.). Englewood Cliffs, NJ: Prentice Hall.

Short, K., & Kauffman, G. (1995). "So what do I do?" The role of the teacher in literature circles. In N. Roser & M. Martinez (eds.), *Book talk and beyond*. Newark, DE: International Reading Association.

Short, K., & Klassen, C. (1993). Literature circles: Hearing children's voices. In B. Cullinan (ed.), *Children's voices: Talk in the classroom*. Newark, DE: International Reading Association.

Sigmon, C. M. (1997). *Implementing the 4Blocks Literacy Model*. Greensboro, NC: Carson-Dellosa Publishing Company.

Silvaroli, N. (1996). *Classroom reading inventory* (8th ed.). Madison: Brown & Benchmark.

Slavin, R., Madden, N., Dolan, L., & Wasik, B. (1996). *Every child every school: Success for All*. Thousand Oaks, CA: Corwin Press.

Slavin, R., Madden, N., Dolan, L., Wasik, B., Ross, S., Smith, L., & Dianda, M. (1997) Success for All: A summary of research. *Journal of Education for Students Placed at Risk*, 1(1), 41–76.

Smith, F. (1982). *Understanding reading* (3rd ed.). New York: Holt, Rinehart & Winston.

Smith, P. (1988). A fresh start with a reception class. In J. Hancock & S. Hill (eds.), *Literature-based reading programs at work*. Portsmouth, NH: Heinemann.

Stauffer, R. G. (1969). *Directing reading maturity as a cognitive process*. New York: Harper & Row.

Stauffer, R. G. (1970). *The language-experience approach to the teaching of reading*. New York: Harper & Row.

Stein, N. L., & Glenn, C. G. (1979). An analysis of story comprehension in elementary school children. In R. O. Freedle (ed.), *New directions in discourse processing* (Vol. 2). Norwood, NJ: Ablex.

Strickland, D. (1987). Literature: Key element in the language and reading program. In B. E. Cullinan (ed.), *Children's literature in the reading program* (pp. 68–76). Newark, DE: International Reading Association.

Strickland, D. (1998). What's basic in beginning reading? Finding common ground. *Educational Leadership*, 55(6), 6–10.

Strickland, D., & Cullinan, B. (1990) The Afterword. In M. Adams (ed.), *Beginning to read: Thinking and learning about print*, pp. 425–433. Cambridge, MA: MIT Press.

Strickland, D., Dillon, R., Funkhouser, L., Glick, M., & Rogers, C. (1989). Research currents: Classroom dialogue during literature response groups. *Language Arts*, 66(5), 192–205.

Teale, W., & Sulzby, E. (1989). Emergent literacy: New perspectives. In D. S. Strickland & L. M. Morrow (eds.), *Emerging literacy: Young children learn to read and write*. Newark, DE: International Reading Association.

Tharp, R. G., & Gallimore, R (1989). *Rousing minds to life: Teaching, learning, and schooling in social context*. New York: Cambridge University Press.

Thompson, R. A. (1971). *Summarizing research pertaining to individualized reading*. ERIC Document Reproduction Service, No. ED 065 836.

Tierney, R. J. (1990). Redefining reading comprehension. *Educational Leadership*, 47(6), 37–42.

Tierney, R. J., Readence, J. E., & Dishner, E. K. (1995). *Reading strategies and practices: A compendium* (4th ed.). Boston: Allyn & Bacon.

Tunnell, M. O., & Jacobs, J. S. (1989). Using "real" books: Research findings on literature-based reading instruction. *The Reading Teacher*, 42(7), 470–477.

Van Allen, R. (1973). The Language Experience Approach. In R. Karlin (ed.), *Perspectives on elementary reading: Principles and strategies of teaching*. New York: Harcourt Brace Jovanovich.

van den Broek, P., Risden, K., Fletcher, C., & Thurlow, R. (1996). A "landscape" view of reading: Fluctuating patterns of activation and the construction of a stable memory representation. In B. K. Britton & A. C. Graesser (eds.), *Models of understanding text*. Mahwah, NJ: Lawrence Erlbaum Associates Publishers.

Vizyak, L. (1997). Using a literacy portfolio in first grade. In R. B. Wiener & J. H. Cohen (eds.), *Literacy portfolios: Using assessment to guide instruction*. Columbus, OH: Merrill.

Watson, D. J. (1989). Defining and describing whole language. *The Elementary School Journal*, 90(2), 129–141.

Weaver, C. (1994). *Reading process and practice: From sociolinguistics to whole language* (2nd ed.). Portsmouth, NH: Heinemann.

Weir, B. (1989). A research base for prekindergarten literacy programs. *The Reading Teacher*, 42(6), 456–460.

Wells, G. (1990). Creating the conditions to encourage literate thinking. *Educational Leadership*, 47(6), 13–17.

White, J. H., Vaughn, J. L., & Rorie, I. L. (1986). Picture of a classroom where reading is for real. *The Reading Teacher*, 40(1), 84–86.

Wigfield, A., & Asher, S. R. (1984). Social and motivational influences on reading. In P. D. Pearson, R. Barr, M. L. Kamil, & P. Mosenthal (eds.), *Handbook of research on reading* (pp. 423–452). New York: Longman.

Wineburg, S. (1997). T. S. Eliot, collaboration and the quandaries of assessment in a rapidly changing world. *Kappan*, 79(1), 59–65.

Yellin, D., & Blake, M. (1994). *Integrating the language arts: A holistic approach*. New York: Harper Collins Publishers.

Zarillo, J. (1989). Teachers' interpretations of literature-based reading. *The Reading Teacher*, 43(1), 22–28.

Children's Literature: The Cornerstone of a Language Arts Program

7

IN THIS CHAPTER

overview

Chapter 7 provides an overview of the many different types of children's books and emphasizes the major role that literature plays in an integrated language arts program. In addition to finding out about good books for children, sources of information about them, and ways of evaluating them, you will explore techniques for sharing books with children and for facilitating students' varied responses to literature.

This chapter lists many examples of current books—some of them well known, others not so well known. There are short bibliographies and lists of teacher resources directly within the text to help you organize this information and make use of it readily in your work. The Appendix to this chapter also contains bibliographies of children's books that have won awards.

When you have finished this chapter and tried a few appropriate Beyond the Classroom activities, you should begin to understand why children's books form the basic content of the language arts program.

Children's Literature: The Cornerstone

Well-written children's literature exemplifies the very best of a language and culture. Through meaningful stories, children's books enable children to internalize various aspects of the culture that they are struggling to understand. Books allow children to journey to the past, explore the present, fantasize about what might be, and enjoy the legacy of folktales and fairy tales that illustrate the human condition. Child psychologist Bruno Bettelheim (1976) has claimed that literature is the best way for children to understand their cultural heritage and to develop views and values that give meaning to life. Good literature offers children a whole new world of experiences and feelings—ways of growing and becoming to last a lifetime.

Children's literature not only provides children with perspectives on life but also motivates children to become truly involved with language. When kindergartners hear Bill Martin's *Brown Bear, Brown Bear, What Do You See?* they often begin chiming in when the teacher starts each question-and-answer segment. They pick up the pattern of the refrain, play with it, and make it their own. Children do this because the language and the book are important to them. They realize that the book demands their response. Older students also have ways of responding to good literature.

CHILDREN'S LITERATURE DEFINED

Exactly what is children's literature? It is basically any material written primarily for children "that children continue to read and enjoy" (Huck, Hepler, & Hickman, 1993, p. 6). Today the range of children's literature extends from books, magazines, and comics through the media of records, films, videos, and computer adaptations of popular stories. Authors and artists involved in producing children's literature use language and images appropriate for children to convey important ideas and themes. In describing writing children's books, Peggy Parish, author of *Amelia Bedelia* (Thompson, 1984), has stated, "First you have to know what is of interest to children. . . . You have to make every word count. Also, in order to capture and hold a child's attention, there has to be a certain rhythm and flow in a story which complements its essential simplicity" (p. 25). Writing for children, a specialized form of communication, is no easy task.

Among the types of children's books currently available are picture books, poetry books, folktales and fairy tales, realistic fiction, historical fiction, fantasy, biography, and increasingly important information books. Concern with the merits of these books, and the search for proper methods of evaluating them, has led to the establishment of children's literature as a serious, respectable discipline that explores factors distinguishing high-quality children's books from those more commonly and derisively termed *kiddie lit*.

In addition, the term *KidLit* has been used (Rasmussen, 1989) "to describe both the good and the bad and the enjoyable and the dull of what's available for children today" (p. 9). Although not every book written for children is a classic, many books that fall short of this goal are entertaining, reasonably good, and very popular with children. The International Reading Association's *Children's Choices*, an annual catalog of books that children choose as their favorites, is testimony to the fact that children have some very definite ideas—and not always the same ideas that scholars have—about the books that they read.

Books abound in today's society. Some are great; some are not so great. As a teacher, you can help students acquire the ability to decide for themselves whether a book is great, reasonably good, or better left alone. The Classroom Vignette shows how one teacher uses children's literature in her classroom.

Vignette in the classroom

One year Ms. Carton decides to use the book *Sarah, Plain and Tall* by Patricia MacLachlan to introduce her fifth-graders to aspects of pioneer life on the prairie. She feels that this is a good way to make the period come alive for the children, to make them see that history is not just facts and events; it is populated with real people who laughed and cried as they lived their everyday lives. When the students finish their first reading of the book, many of them offer initial personal opinions.

John: I really like this book because it has a happy ending, and I love happy endings.

Marie: For me the saddest part of the book was the beginning, when the mother dies. I'm glad Sarah came to help them.

LaToya: I really got to know the people in this story. Now I understand a little of what it was like to live then.

Nilda: I liked the father. It was good for him to get another mother for the children.

Ms. Carton continues this line of thought with the following questions:

- Why is it important for Sarah to like Caleb and Anna and Papa?
- How does Sarah improve everyone's life? How does the family improve Sarah's life?
- How did you feel when Sarah finally decides to stay with the family?
- Which person is most like you—Sarah, Anna, Caleb, or Papa?
- What other books have you read about life on the prairie? How do they compare to *Sarah, Plain and Tall*?
- Have you read any other books by Patricia MacLachlan? What did you think about them?

As a conclusion to the project, Ms. Carton asks each student to explore and write about the message of the story in a daily writing journal. In this way, each child is able to give a unique interpretation to the story. Such activities help children to see the value of a piece of literature—its language, sense of story, moral, characters, and particular style.

CHILDREN'S BOOK CATEGORIES

As you begin to think about children's literature in the classroom, you should explore some of the various types of books available. This section provides brief descriptions of the major children's book genres along with several of the better examples of each type of book. Later, when you use these books with students, you can help them understand what is important about each book and how each story develops. You will thus contribute to their improved comprehension of the stories and increased knowledge of story structure.

Picture Books

Picture books allow children to comprehend a story through pictures alone or through pictures combined with text. Although picture books are generally considered appropriate for preschoolers or primary-age children, there are pictures in every type of book, even those intended for adults. These illustrations may be black-and-white or color drawings, woodcuts or other types of prints, watercolors, paintings, collages, or photographs, among others.

BEYOND THE CLASSROOM

Survey one or two of the teachers in your practicum school. Find out their definitions of the term *children's literature* and how they use it in the classroom. Ask them what techniques they use to help children recognize good books; record responses in your notebook. As you read through this chapter, give some thought to your own plans for using children's literature in the classroom.

In a successful picture book, the illustrations complement the text, add to it, and make it more expressive of the ideas the author is trying to communicate. Some examples of particularly successful picture books are the following:

- Carle, E. (1972). *The Very Hungry Caterpillar*. New York: Philomel Books. Much of the international popularity of this book lies in the colorful, bright collages that portray the eating adventures of the caterpillar.

- Cendrars, B. (1982). *Shadow* (M. Brown, trans. and illus.). New York: Charles Scribner's Sons. This book combines collages, woodblock prints, and paintings to give a true and vibrant description of the energy that is part of the African culture in the book.

- Hodges, M. (1984). *Saint George and the Dragon* (T. S. Hyman, illus.). Boston: Little, Brown and Company. Richly detailed and romantic paintings convey the subtleties of this ancient British tale. Even the borders in the book are filled with flowers indigenous to the area.

- Polacco, P. (1994). *Pink and Say*. New York: Philomel Books. This picture book embraces the meeting of two young boys during the Civil War through the burst of color and energetic movement in the illustrations.

- Yolen, J. (1987). *Owl Moon* (J. Schoenherr, illus.). New York: Philomel Books. Schoenherr's soft but precise and clear watercolors convey the pristine winter environment needed for owling. Figure 7.1 is an illustration from this work.

Figure 7.1   *Illustration from Owl Moon.*

For one minute,
three minutes,
maybe even a hundred minutes,
we stared at one another.

Source: From *Owl Moon* by Jane Yolen, illustrated by John Schoenherr, text copyright © 1987 by Jane Yolen, illustration copyright © 1988 by John Schoenherr. Used by permission of Philomel Books, a division of Penguin Putnam Inc.

Some subcategories of picture books that have evolved include wordless books and predictable pattern books. Each of these categories provides the teacher with special opportunities to meet the language needs of emerging readers and to encourage these young readers to make reading a lifelong habit.

In **wordless books,** pictures alone tell the story. Even young nonreaders can create a story from the illustrations. Such books give children the opportunity to use knowledge about story structure gained from listening to stories to create a story of their own. These books help children to develop inference skills since the entire story develops from whatever the child can "read" in the pictures. Some of the best examples of wordless books are John Goodall's series about a naughty pig, beginning with *The Adventures of Paddy Pork*; Martha Alexander's *Bobo's Dream*, a story about a plucky dachshund; Eric Carle's *Do You Want to Be My Friend?*; and any of Mercer Mayer's works, especially *A Boy, a Dog, and a Frog*. For a more detailed list of wordless picture books, see the bibliography in Jim Trelease's (1995) *The New Read-Aloud Handbook*.

Predictable **pattern books** are picture books that contain repetitive language and enable the young reader to predict which words are coming next. Even if children cannot read the words, they can often join in and follow the pattern. These books are another way of involving children with language learning. *Brown Bear, Brown Bear, What Do You See?* and other works by Bill Martin, Jr., are some of the best examples of this genre. Many other books, such as *The Teeny Tiny Woman* by Margot Zemach, *Chicken Soup with Rice* by Maurice Sendak, and *I Can't Said the Ant* by Polly Cameron, are also available. A selected bibliography of predictable pattern books can be found in *Readers and Writers with a Difference* by Rhodes and Dudley-Marling (1996).

Folklore

Folklore, or traditional literature, has its origins in the oral storytelling of primitive peoples; these tales were used for purposes of instruction and entertainment and were passed down from generation to generation. Often there are similar stories in different cultures: A Chinese version of "Little Red Riding Hood," *Lon Po Po*, won the Caldecott Medal in 1990. Among the different types of folklore are folktales and fairy tales, legends, myths, epics, and fables.

Folktales and **fairy tales** (tales with fairies and other supernatural beings) are among the most important types of children's literature available; one vital characteristic of such stories is the central character's struggle and ultimate victory over hardships. Bettelheim (1976) claimed that this story element teaches children that while life is not without unhappy situations, perseverance can lead to triumph. Other noteworthy story elements of folktales and fairy tales are characters that symbolize either only good or only evil; a long-ago, faraway setting; and a strong plot with much action culminating in the resolution of the original problem or conflict. Some of the tales that have been collected, recorded, and handed down to the present generation are "The Story of the Three Bears," "Cinderella," "Hansel and Gretel," "Rumpelstiltskin," "Beauty and the Beast," "Snow White," and "The Frog Prince."

A **legend** is a tale believed to have some historical basis, although it may not be possible to verify the truth of the story. Many legends originated in the United States—some based on true events, others on tall tales (the stories needed to illustrate the greatness of the new country). Examples of legendary characters still popular with children are Paul Bunyan and Pecos Bill. Some real individuals who have assumed legendary status are Davy Crockett, Johnny Appleseed, and even George Washington.

Myths are folktales that use the supernatural and the spiritual aspects of gods and goddesses to explain the unknown to people. They are a civilization's way of trying to make sense of what is happening around and within it. Generally, a myth attempts to explain the origin of a natural phenomenon, a custom, or a particular type of behavior. A wonderful example of a collection of myths is *In the Beginning* (1988), compiled by Virginia Hamilton and illustrated by Barry Moser. This book catalogs creation myths from around the world and, like most myths, is suitable for older readers.

Epics are tales of heroism describing the adventures of exemplary individuals. The oldest examples of this form are *The Illiad* and *The Odyssey*, which were written by the Greek poet Homer to celebrate the adventures of Odysseus as he battled through the Trojan War and spent years making his way home. Some of the more familiar epics describe the exploits of Robin Hood, King Arthur, Beowulf, Roland, Gilgamesh, and Finn McCool.

The **fable** is a brief story with a strong moral; they often involve animal characters that exemplify a single trait, such as industriousness or flattery. Fables offer many pithy sayings and simple lessons. Who does not remember the fox and the lesson of "sour grapes" or the race of the tortoise and the hare in which slow perseverance wins out over flashy speed? Although Aesop's collection is the best known, fables have also been handed down from India, Arabia, and France.

Modern Fantasy

Fantasy is that which is not real. Well-written fantasy can ignite children's imagination and provide them with a significant avenue for enjoying literature. An author who writes fantasy can be considered the modern equivalent of the traditional storyteller.

Fantasy ranges from the enchanting tales of Hans Christian Andersen to the magical animal tales of E. B. White and the science fiction of Madeleine L'Engle. Some well-loved examples of the fantasy genre are Michael Bond's *A Bear Called Paddington*, Margery Williams's *The Velveteen Rabbit*, the tales of Beatrix Potter, Rudyard Kipling's *Just So Stories*, and Maurice Sendak's classic *Where the Wild Things Are*. Some tales of enchantment for older readers are Natalie Babbitt's *Tuck Everlasting*, Lloyd Alexander's *Prydain Chronicles*, and J. R. R. Tolkien's *The Hobbit*, and the *Harry Potter* series by J. K. Rowland.

Realistic Fiction

Realistic fiction portrays life as it is. One of the goals of such fiction is to help children better understand the sometimes-harsh facts of life. Sutherland and Livingston (1984) have claimed that "when books portray characters who have fears or problems similar to those of the reader, they can help point the way to adjustment or solution, and they can ease the child reader's mind by showing that he or she is not alone in being afraid or resentful or discriminated against" (p. 547). "Realistic fiction can also illuminate experiences that children have not had" and "may become one way of experiencing a world we do not know" (Huck, Hepler, & Hickman, 1993, p. 197). Therefore, today's realistic fiction addresses not only the positive aspects of life but also its myriad problems and hardships. Authors such as Judy Blume, Cynthia Voigt, Betsy Byars, Paula Fox, Richard Peck, and Katherine Paterson are articulate spokespeople in outlining some of the very real situations young people face today.

In addition to problematic situations, adventures, animals, and mysteries form the basis of many realistic fiction stories. Typical adventure tales include *Julie of the Wolves* by Jean George, *Island of the Blue Dolphins* by Scott O'Dell, *A Rumor of Otters* by Deborah Savage, and *The Cay* by Theodore Taylor. Stories involving animals continue to be favorites; some of the best are *The Black*

Stallion by Walter Farley, *Where the Red Fern Grows* by Wilson Rawls, and *A Time to Fly Free* by Stephanie Tolan. Mysteries arouse the sleuth in children and sharpen their investigative abilities. *The House of Dies Drear* by Virginia Hamilton and *The Callender Papers* by Cynthia Voigt are challenging tales for advanced readers. For younger readers, the mystery cases of Encyclopedia Brown remain favorites.

Historical Fiction

Through **historical fiction,** students can get a realistic view of the past; based on careful research, these stories provide authentic settings, descriptions of events, and examples of people's behavior in a given time period. Such books make the past come alive for children and help them realize that there are real flesh-and-blood people behind historical facts. Nearly every period of history is represented in historical fiction. Young readers can learn about colonial times from Lobel's *On the Day Peter Stuyvesant Sailed into Town,* Turkle's *Thy Friend, Obadiah,* and Rappaport's *The Boston Coffee Party,* while their older counterparts can experience this period through Gary Paulsen's *Mr. Tucket.*

James and Christopher Collier's *My Brother Sam is Dead* gives students some perspectives on the Revolutionary War; Paula Fox's *The Slave Dancer* provides insights about slavery; and Irene Hunt's *Across Five Aprils* depicts some of the conflicts of the Civil War. Pioneer life is accurately recorded in MacLachlan's *Sarah, Plain and Tall;* even the cover, shown in Figure 7.2, faithfully depicts the period. More recent history is represented by Moskin's *I Am Rosemarie,* which describes life during the Holocaust. Other available historical fiction books include Maxine Schur's *Circlemaker,* Karen Cushman's *Midwife's Apprentice,* and Ellen White's *Road Home.*

Biographies

Biographies (and **autobiographies**) depict the lives of noteworthy men and women from all races and walks of life. As such, biographies provide children with role models as well as information about real places and times. Like historical fiction, biographies can make facts come alive for children; the best examples of this genre are carefully researched and objective in their portrayal of their subjects.

Younger readers enjoy Cynthia Rylant's *When I Was Young in the Mountains* as well as Clyde Bulla's *Lincoln's Birthday.* More advanced readers are drawn to the entertaining works of Jean Fritz, such as *Where Do You Think You're Going, Christopher Columbus?* They also enjoy reading *The First Woman Doctor* by Rachel Baker (the story of Elizabeth Blackwell), *Freedom Train: The Story of Harriet Tubman* by Dorothy Sterling, the Newbery Medal–winning *Lincoln: A Photobiography* by Russell Freedman and *We Flew Over the Bridge: The Memoirs of Faith Ringgold* by Faith Ringgold.

Information Books

Information books provide students with information and explain a variety of concepts. The topics of information books range from recipes to computers. In this Information Age, such books are assuming a particular importance for readers of all ages and levels.

Information books often provide young readers with their first experiences with nonfiction text. Usually the earliest information books that children come in contact with are alphabet books and counting books. Some of the perennial favorites in the former category are *Brian Wildsmith's*

Figure 7.2

Cover illustration from Sarah, Plain and Tall.

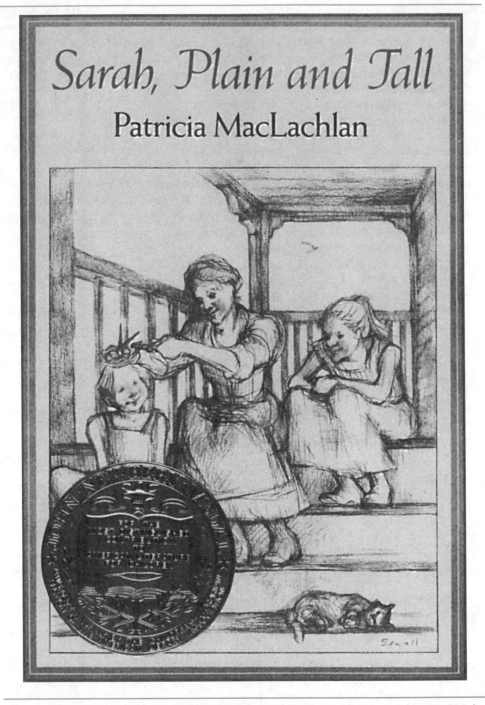

Source: Jacket art copyright © 1985 by Marcia Sewall. Jacket copyright © 1985 by HarperCollins Publishers, Inc. Used by permission of HarperCollins Publishers.

ABC, Ed Emberly's ABC, and Maurice Sendak's *Alligators All Around.* Favorite books about numbers include *Anno's Counting Book* and Sendak's *One Was Johnny.* Other information books that appeal to young readers are Peter Spier's *People* as well as *The Cloud Book, The Kids' Cat Book, The Popcorn Book,* and *The Quicksand Book,* all by noted author/illustrator Tomie dePaola.

For older readers, information books are essential sources of data in many content areas; they also provide the information necessary for nurturing each child's unique personal interests. Teachers should pay special attention to selecting books whose information is both current and accurate. Some content area books meeting these criteria are *The Sea World Book of Whales* by Eve Bunting, *The Flight of the Pterosaurs* by Keith Moseley, *The Story of the Statue of Liberty* by Ib Penick, *Black Holes* by Heather Couper and Nigel Henbest, and *A Lift-the-Flap Book: Inside the Body* by Giuliano Fornari. Books that have personal value for readers include Cole's *Working Kids on Working* and Benedict's *Safe, Strong, and Streetwise*, a needed book about keeping safe in today's world. In addition, there are many how-to books that students enjoy.

Poetry

Poetry has a special place in the classroom for the sheer enjoyment that it provides. Through poetry, writers express their innermost ideas and feelings about every possible subject; poets use concise and rhythmical language to create images that appeal to both the hearts and the heads of youngsters. Because poetry really exploits the musical qualities of language, it demands to be read aloud. In the elementary school, there should be little emphasis on the analysis of poetry; it should be experienced for itself.

One of the best authors to use when introducing poetry to students is Shel Silverstein. His *Where the Sidewalk Ends* and *A Light in the Attic* are favorites with students of all ages for the humorous images they provide. Other humorous poetry books are *If I Were in Charge of the World and Other Worries* by Judith Viorst and *You Be Good and I'll Be Night: Jump-on-the-Bed Poems* by Eve Merriam. Older children enjoy two Newbery Medal–winning books: Willard's *A Visit to William Blake's Inn* and Fleischman's *Joyful Noise: Poems for Two Voices*. Other poets whose work children love are Mary O'Neill, Jack Prelutsky, Myra Cohn Livingston, and Lee Bennett Hopkins.

When looking for individual poems to share with your class, check the following anthologies:

- Brown, M. (1993). *Under the Sun and the Moon and Other Poems*. New York: Hyperion Books for Children.
- Crump, F. (1990). *Mother Goose Nursery Rhymes*. Nashville, TN: Winston-Derek Publishers.
- Dyer, J. (1996). *Animal Crackers: Collection of Pictures, Poems, and Lullabies for the Very Young*. Boston: Little, Brown and Company.
- Phillips, L. (1995). *Random House Treasury of Best Loved Poems*. New York: Random House.
- Prelutsky, J. (1996). *Monday's Troll*. New York: Greenwillow Books.
- Schertle, A. (1995). *Advice for Frogs and Other Poems*. New York: Lothrop, Lee, and Shepard Books.
- Sword, E. (1995). *A Child's Anthology of Poetry*. Hopewell, NJ: Ecco Press.

Series Books

While series books do not have a reputation as fine children's literature, they are included here because of the fascination they have long had for young readers. Series books, being highly patterned, may provide a clear insight into the rules of reading for many new and transitional readers. Series detective stories allow immature readers to use strategies and make sense of what they are reading. The clues in the series detective stories help develop strategies for reading by providing a prime opportunity for the reader to notice details and then make appropriate choices and predictions. The reader can be caught and entranced by "the excitement of the detective

What is important—what lasts—in another language is not what is said but what is written. For the essence of an age, we look to its poetry and its prose, not its talk shows.

PETER BRODIE

when the clues are discovered" (Ross, 1995, p. 230). As a result, the established formula detective series by the Stratemeyer Syndicate (*Nancy Drew, The Hardy Boys,* and *The Bobbsey Twins*) are doing well. Publishers not only are bringing out updated versions of these series but also are publishing a variety of other successful books, including R. L. Stine's *Goosebumps* series and J. K. Rowling's *Harry Potter* books.

However, what is the attraction of series books for older children and young adolescents? According to Moran and Steinfirst (1985), their appeal is based on several characteristics. First of all, they demand little analysis and are easy to read, something for which the less capable, older reader is grateful. Because the plots are predictable (the good and righteous always win in the end), these books really promote comprehension: The reader always has an idea of what's coming. They also provide a respite from more intense realistic fiction while supplying young readers with competent heroes and heroines. However, when closely questioned, middle school readers appear to like more difficult, recommended literature as well as the easier series books (Greenlee, Monson, & Taylor, 1996).

So this is not a recommendation to use series books in place of fine literature, but you might consider them as a starting place for reluctant older readers or even nonreaders. When you convince such students to try series books, you open the door to helping them improve both as readers and as judges of good literature; such improvement is impossible if they do not read at all.

BEYOND THE CLASSROOM

Begin to be your own judge of children's literature by reading some of the books mentioned in this section. Keep notes about each book in your notebook or in a file of index cards. List the book's title, author, publisher, and date of publication. You will probably also want to include a story summary, an estimate of the appropriate reading level, and possible classroom uses. After conferring with your practicum teacher, you might want to try reading one of the books to your class.

Choosing Materials for the Classroom

Because literature plays such an important role in a successful language arts program, teachers need to be knowledgeable about obtaining appropriate materials that their students actually want to read. This section provides a brief overview of resources and guidelines to aid you as you begin selecting books for your classroom. It is particularly important for you to listen to your students and allow their ideas and interests to guide you in choosing classroom materials. You should also consider obtaining books to meet a variety of special needs, ranging from combating racism and sexism to helping students become more sensitive to the elderly and the disabled.

RESOURCES

After reading the preceding section, the first two questions that probably come to mind are, Where do I find all these wonderful books? and How do I know if they are appropriate for my students and our class goals? Fortunately there are a number of resources available to help you find quality books and magazines and to give you some guidance about appropriate classroom uses for them.

Before looking too far, you should first consult the librarians at your school and at your branch of the public library. They have a wealth of information about many different types of books and magazines that you can use in your classroom. You may want to consult anthologies of literature, directories of special books, publisher's catalogs, and biographical dictionaries listing authors and illustrators of children's books. One excellent example of a biographical dictionary is Barbara Rollock's (1988) *Black Authors and Illustrators of Children's Books*. In addition to these general references, there are other sources available to professional educators.

PROFESSIONAL ORGANIZATIONS

The following professional organizations publish journals that may also be helpful to you in selecting books for the classroom:

- American Library Association (ALA), 50 East Huron Street, Chicago, IL 60611
- The Children's Book Council (CBC), 568 Broadway, Suite 404, New York, NY 10012
- International Reading Association (IRA), 800 Barksdale Road, P.O. Box 8139, Newark, DE 19714-8139
- National Council of Teachers of English (NCTE), 1111 Kenyon Road, Urbana, IL 61801

PROFESSIONAL PUBLICATIONS

- *Bulletin of the Center for Children's Books*, published by the University of Chicago Graduate Library School, The University of Illinois Press, 13255 Oak Street, Champaign, IL 61820.
- *The Horn Book*, published by Horn Book, 11 Beacon Street, Suite 11, Boston, MA 02108.
- *The Lion and the Unicorn*, published by Johns Hopkins Press, 2715 N. Charles Street, Baltimore, MD 21218.
- *The New Advocate*, published by Christopher Gordon Publishers, 1502 Providence Highway, Suite 12, Norwood, MA 02062.
- *Teaching and Learning Literature with Children and Young Adults*, published by Holistic Education Press, Brandon, VT 05733.

CURRENT BIBLIOGRAPHIES

- Allen, M. (1996). *100 Years of Children's Books in America: Decade by Decade.* New York: Facts on File.
- *Children's Books in Print* (annual). New York: Bowker.
- Khorana, M. (1994). *Africa in Literature for Children and Young Adults: An Annotated Bibliography of English Language Books.* Westport, CT: Greenwood Press.
- Lima, C. (1993). *A to Zoo: Subject Access to Children's Picture Books.* New York: Bowker.
- Marantz, S. (1995). *Art of Children's Picture Books: A Selective Reference Guide.* New York: Garland Publishing.

ANNUAL BOOKLISTS

- "Children's Choices" published in *The Reading Teacher* by the IRA.
- "Notable Children's Trade Books in the Field of Social Studies" compiled by the National Council for the Social Studies and the CBC.
- "Outstanding Science Trade Books for Children" compiled by the National Science Teachers Association and the CBC.
- "Teacher's Choices" published in *The Reading Teacher* by the IRA.
- "Young Adult Choices" published in *The Journal of Adolescent and Adult Literacy* by the IRA.

PARENT RESOURCES

- Kaywell, J. (1993). *Adolescents at Risk: A Guide to Fiction for Young Adults, Parents, and Professionals.* Westport, CT: Greenwood Press.
- Lindskoog, J. (1989). *How to Grow a Young Reader: A Parent's Guide to Books for Kids.* Wheaton, IL: Harold Shaw Publishers.
- Lipson, E. (1991). *The New York Times Parent's Guide to the Best Books for Children.* New York: Random House.
- Trelease, J. (1995). *The New Read-Aloud Handbook* (2nd ed.). New York: Philomel Books.

GUIDELINES FOR JUDGING BOOKS

Using resources to locate recommended books is only the first step in acquiring appropriate materials for the classroom. You also want to be sure that the books you choose and help children choose for themselves combine high quality with the ability to meet particular needs within the classroom. Books that have won the Caldecott Medal (for illustration), the Newbery Medal (for literature), or other awards are certainly high-quality books (see the Appendix to this chapter for listings of these books). However, to be sure that a book meets your own criteria for excellence in the classroom, you need to examine it yourself. You likewise need to encourage your students to examine books and to make their own decisions about the merits and qualities of each book.

When evaluating a book, you may find it helpful to think about the guidelines listed in Figure 7.3. You should also model the evaluation process for your students so that they have a framework of specific criteria to use in judging books on their own.

If you or your students are trying to evaluate an informational or nonfiction book rather than a narrative, be sure that it meets the following two criteria:

Figure 7.3

Guidelines for evaluating literature.

1. **Prereading Information**

   What kind of book is this?

   What can my students predict about this story from the cover and title? From the illustrations? From the chapter titles? From the print size?

   How can I use this book in class?

2. **Story Line**

   Does the book tell a good story?

   What happens and how does it end?

3. **Setting**

   Where and when does the story take place?

   In view of the story line, does the setting make sense?

4. **Theme**

   What is the underlying idea of the story?

   Is this theme something my students can understand?

5. **Characters**

   Who are the characters?

   Are the characters appealing, consistent in their behavior, and free of stereotypes?

(continued)

Figure 7.3

Continued.

6. **Style and Format**

What is special about the way the author writes?

Is it easy to understand what the author is trying to say?

Do the pictures, colors, and cover fit the story?

Does the cover reflect what is within?

7. **Reactions**

How does this story make me feel?

What does the author do in parts of the story to cause these feelings?

Is this book as good as other books written by the same author? As good as other books on the same topic?

8. **Evaluation**

Why did I like or dislike this book?

What did this book help me to understand?

Would I recommend this book to my students? Why?

1. Facts and information in the text should be both current and accurate.
2. Clear, objective writing should reflect the logical organization of the text.

CUES FROM CHILDREN

Resources and guidelines are helpful in choosing books for the classroom; however, the most important information comes from children themselves. The students' interests and abilities help to determine what materials are appropriate for them.

Children have definite ideas about what they do and do not like to read, and their ideas about what constitutes a good book are not always in agreement with those of adults. One of the reasons that the IRA publishes "Children's Choices" is to make sure that children's voices are heard and that teachers heed what children have to say.

Research by Abrahamson (1980) analyzing the types of books children choose to read has shown that younger readers really enjoy fantasy, folktales, and realistic fiction. They want a story with a strong, sequential plot in which the main character faces and solves a problem. Humorous stories are popular, as are stories about children, animals, and families. Young children want the illustrations to complement the story.

Older readers like a variety of books (Sebesta, Calder, & Cleland, 1981). Their interests range from realistic fiction to informational books. They enjoy books with action, mystery, and suspense. They also want to read books that realistically depict the issues or problems they are currently facing (IRA, 1996) that allow them to escape problems through fantasy and science fiction. Sports stories also are of interest to both boys and girls (Feeley, 1982).

When trying to figure out which books appeal to your students, you need to get information about their special interests. Questioning them about the following areas should prove helpful:

- *General interests.* Leisure-time activities; favorite TV shows; hobbies; interests in games or sports; membership in clubs or groups; pets; favorite movies or videos

■ *Literary interests.* Current books children are reading; favorite topics; books they own; books they'd like to own; involvement with the library; comic books preferred; magazines; next book on their agenda

BEYOND THE CLASSROOM

Choose a literature book recommended either in this chapter or by another teacher, and use the guidelines in Figure 7.3 to evaluate it for yourself. Then evaluate an informational book according to the criteria presented in the text. Comment in your notebook about the benefits for both teachers and students of evaluating books.

Once a reading range is established within a class, the teacher needs to make sure that a wide variety of interesting books within that range is available. The teacher needs to guide students to materials that will provide successful experiences for both the gifted and the less capable readers. Although many children can choose books for themselves, individual conferences may be helpful for others.

Another way in which teachers can help to accommodate the varying interests and reading ability levels within a class is to use some of the excellent children's magazines that are available. The magazines are professionally packaged and include a variety of literary genres, writing styles, and reading levels. In your own class, you may want to include some of the magazines listed below:

■ *Children's Literature.* 7513 Shadywood Road, Bethesda, MD 20817-2065. Literary magazine that features well-known authors and illustrators.
■ *Cricket.* Open Court Publishing Company, 315 Fifth Street, P.O. Box 300, Peru, IL 61354. Features interesting stories for children.
■ *Ebony, Jr.* 820 S. Michigan Avenue, Chicago, IL 60605. Grades 1–12. Intended for African-American children.

BEYOND THE CLASSROOM

For more information about magazines, read "Magazines in the Classroom: Beyond Recreational Reading" by Olson, Gee, and Forester in the May 1989 issue of *The Journal of Reading,* or consult *Magazines for Kids and Teens,* by Donald Stoll. Note the variety of magazines available for children and see which ones are used in your practicum school.

■ *Highlights for Children.* P.O. Box 269, Columbus, OH 43272-0002. Preschool–grade 7. General information.
■ *National Geographic World.* 17th and M Streets NW, Washington, DC 20036. Grades 3–8. Social studies and general interest.
■ *Odyssey.* 1027 N. 7th Street, Milwaukee, WI 53233-1417. Grades 4–8. Astronomy and space science.
■ *Ranger Rick.* National Wildlife Federation, 8925 Leesburg Pike, Vienna, VA 22180. Grades 1–7. Wildlife.
■ *Spider.* Cans Publishing Company, 315 Fifth Street, Peru, IL 61354. Illustrated monthly publication for six- to nine-year-olds.

BOOKS TO MEET SPECIAL NEEDS

Choosing books to meet particular needs is an important part of any classroom literature program. Because today's society is complex and culturally diverse, it presents many situations that can cause confusion and misunderstandings in children. In addition, many students' personal lives involve problems and needs that can cause tension and frustration. Teachers can use books to help students understand themselves and others by sensitizing them to the variety of social issues in today's culture. While teachers may be hesitant about engaging in direct bibliotherapy and using books to promote mental health (Overstad, 1981), they can recommend books to promote social awareness and even *socioemotional growth* (Jalongo, 1983). Literature can become a way of meeting some of the special social needs of students living in a diverse culture.

MULTICULTURAL AWARENESS

At present, there is no doubt that the school population is multicultural, and respect for all ethnic groups is essential. Books that portray members of different cultural groups in a positive manner need to be part of every classroom.

To ensure that the books in your classroom adequately reflect today's social reality, you may want to consult some of the teacher resources listed below:

- Castro, R. (1997). *What Do I Read Next?: Multicultural Literature.* Detroit: Gale Research.
- DeMelendez, W., Ostertag, V., & Peck, J. (1997). *Teaching Young Children in Multicultural Classrooms: Issues, Concepts, and Strategies.* Albany, NY: Delmar Publishers.
- Hahn, J. (1996). "Literary Bridges: Linking Language Arts and Bilingual Education." *Primary Voices K–6,* 6(4), 31–34.
- Helbig, A., & Perkins, A. (1994). *This Land is Our Land: A Guide to Multicultural Literature for Children and Young Adults.* Westport, CT: Greenwood Press.
- Lind, B. (1996). *Multicultural Children's Literature: An Annotated Bibliography, Grades K–8.* Jefferson, NC: McFarland & Co.
- Rogers, T. (1997). *Reading Across Cultures: Teaching Literature in a Diverse Society.* New York: Teacher's College Press.

Typical of the children's books recommended to increase multicultural awareness are the following titles, with cultural emphasis in parentheses:

- Alexander, L. (1992). *The Fortune-Tellers.* New York: Dutton. (African)
- Ancona, P. (1993). *Pablo Remembers.* New York: Lothrop, Lee & Shepard Books. (Latino–Hispanic)
- Clifton, L. (1992). *Everett Anderson's Goodbye.* New York: Holt, Rinehart, & Winston. (African American)
- Climo, S. (1993). *The Korean Cinderella.* New York: HarperCollins. (Asian American)
- Cofer, J. (1995). *An Island Like You: Stories of the Barrio.* New York: Orchard Books. (Latino–Hispanic)
- Davis, D. (1992). *Behind Barbed Wire: The Imprisonment of Japanese Americans During World War Two.* New York: Dutton. (Asian American)
- Demi. (1990). *The Empty Pot.* New York: H. Holt. (Asian American)
- Garland, S. (1993). *Why Ducks Sleep on One Leg.* New York: Scholastic. (Asian American)
- Goldin, B. (1994). *Red Means Good Fortune: A Story of San Francisco's Chinatown.* New York: Viking Press. (Asian American)
- Gonzalez, L. (1994). *The Bossy Gallito: A Traditional Cuban Folktale.* New York: Scholastic. (Latino–Hispanic)
- Grimes, N. (1994). *Meet Danitra Brown.* New York: Lothrop, Lee & Shepard Books. (African American)
- Soto, G. (1990). *Baseball in April and Other Stories.* San Diego: Harcourt Brace Jovanovich. (Latino–Hispanic)
- Soto, G. (1995). *Chato's Kitchen.* New York: Putnam's. (Latino–Hispanic)
- Tompert, A. (1990). *Grandfather Tang's Story.* New York: Crown Publishers. (Asian American)

Books also can be used to sensitize children to other pressing social problems. Students' views of the elderly, the roles of women, and disabled individuals can be affected positively by the books they read. The following lists contain examples of books that can make a difference in how students see themselves and others:

THE ELDERLY

- Ackerman, K. (1988). *Song and Dance Man.* Illustrated by Stephen Gammell. New York: Knopf.
- Aliki. (1979). *The Two of Them.* New York: Greenwillow Books.
- Bauer, M. (1995). *When I Go Camping with Grandma.* Mahwah, NJ: Bridgewater Books.
- Crews, D. (1991). *Bigmama's.* New York: Greenwillow Books.
- dePaola, T. (1973). *Nana Upstairs and Nana Downstairs.* New York: Penguin.
- dePaola, T. (1981). *Now One Foot, Now the Other.* New York: Penguin.
- Drucker, M. (1992). *Grandma's Latkes.* San Diego: Harcourt Brace Jovanovich.
- Rylant, C. (1982). *When I Was Young in the Mountains.* New York: Dutton.
- Williams, D. (1992). *Grandma Essie's Covered Wagon.* New York: Knopf.

WOMEN'S ROLES

- Avi. (1990). *The True Confessions of Charlotte Doyle.* New York: Orchard Books.
- Beatty, P. (1984). *Turn Homeward, Hannalee.* New York: W. Morrow.
- Creech, S. (1994). *Walk Two Moons.* New York: HarperCollins.
- Cushman, K. (1994). *Catherine, Called Birdy.* New York: Clarion Books.
- Cushman, K. (1995). *The Midwife's Apprentice.* New York: Clarion Books.
- Lindgren, A. (1983). *Ronia, the Robber's Daughter.* New York: Viking Press.
- McCaffrey, A. (1976). *Dragonsong.* New York: Atheneum.
- McCaffrey, A. (1977). *Dragonsinger.* New York: Atheneum.
- Voigt, C. (1982). *Dicey's Song.* New York: Atheneum.

THE DISABLED

- Behrman, C. (1992). *Fiddler to the World: The Inspiring Life of Itzhak Perlman.* White Hall, VA: Shoe Tree Press. (physical disabilities)
- Betancourt, J. (1993). *My Name is Brain-Brian.* New York: Scholastic. (learning disabilities)
- Butler, B. (1994). *Witch's Fire.* New York: Cobblehill Books. (physical disabilities)
- Duffy, J. (1992). *Uncle Shamus.* New York: Scribner Young Readers. (blindness)
- Gordon, M. (1991). *Jumpin' Johnny Get Back to Work! A Child's Guide to ADHD/Hyperactivity.* DeWitt, NY: GSI. (attention deficit disorder)
- Gould, M. (1991). *Golden Daffodils.* Newport Beach, CA: Allied Crafts. (cerebral palsy)
- Krementz, J. (1992). *How It Feels to Live with a Physical Disability.* New York: Simon & Schuster. (physical disabilities)
- Krisher, T. (1990). *Kathy's Hats: A Story of Hope.* Morton Grove, IL: Albert Whitman. (serious or life-threatening conditions)
- Metzger, L. (1993). *Barry's Sister.* New York: Puffin. (cerebral palsy)
- Osofsky, A. (1992). *My Buddy.* New York: Henry Holt & Company. (physical disabilities)
- Philbrick, W. (1993). *Freak the Mighty.* New York: Scholastic. (learning disabilities)

> *Books are the windows through which the souls look out.*
>
> HARRIET WARD BEECHER

- St. George, J. (1992). *Dear Dr. Bell—Your Friend, Helen Keller*. New York: Putnam. (deafness)
- Wood, J. (1992). *The Man Who Loved Clowns*. New York: Putnam. (Down Syndrome)

BEYOND THE CLASSROOM

Read four books that have been recommended to meet special needs. Add the entries to the literature list that you started at the beginning of this chapter.

Children also face personal problems and stressful situations. Making appropriate books available to them can help them to see how others handle similar problems and to develop their own coping strategies. For example, children who have had an experience with death might appreciate reading Judith Viorst's *The Tenth Good Thing About Barney*, which tells of a boy whose cat has died, or Carol Carrick's *The Accident*, in which a dog is lost. A child involved in a divorce could identify with *The Kids' Book of Divorce* by Rofes and be relieved to know that he or she is not alone in this situation. Other problem situations depicted in books range from sibling rivalry to sexual abuse. While individual bibliotherapy is not within your realm as a teacher, having books available that address these issues can make a child's adjustment easier.

Children's Literature and Language Learning

The major focus of any integrated language program is to involve children with real language, to provide classroom experiences in which the language used really means something to the children (Goodman, 1986). With the exception of their own oral language, there is no language more meaningful to children than the language of books. A good book tells a story, a story definitely worth reading. And in telling these stories, such books provide both oral and written language models that shape the children's own use of language.

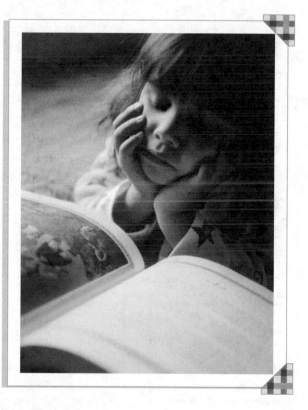

LANGUAGE MODELS

The language of books makes children aware of the many different ways in which they can use words to express their ideas. Children who have heard fairy tales use the traditional beginning "Once upon a time" in their own made-up tales. These words help children convey the idea of something that happened a long time ago. Without the model of the fairy tale, children might never learn how to convey this idea.

From books, children also learn that words express ideas. Books help children to expand their vocabularies as they develop a variety of concepts. For example, a book such as Tana Hoban's *Push-Pull, Empty-Full* helps youngsters learn about word opposites in a meaningful way. Eric Carle's books *The Very Hungry Caterpillar*, *The Grouchy Ladybug*, and *The Very Busy Spider* help children acquire proper scientific vocabulary in their ongoing study of scientific concepts.

Books also help children understand the intricacies of language. A book such as Mary Ann Hoberman's *A House Is a House to Me* introduces very young children to the figurative language of metaphors. Students learn that a rose is a house for a smell, a carton is a house for crackers, and a shell is a house for a snail. Other books handle figurative language humorously, such as Peggy Parish's *Amelia Bedelia* books and Fred Gwynne's *The King Who Rained* and *A Chocolate Moose for Dinner*. Still other books, including those of Dr. Seuss and Shel Silverstein, encourage children to actively play with language and zany ideas.

TEXT STRUCTURE

Another major advantage of using books is that they allow children to understand the structure of both *narrative* (stories) and *expository* (informational) text. Every story or narrative has a somewhat similar structure (Stein & Glenn, 1979). Figure 7.4 shows Cunningham and Foster's (1978) story grammar model, which succinctly describes the structure of stories.

Figure 7.4　　*Story grammar.*

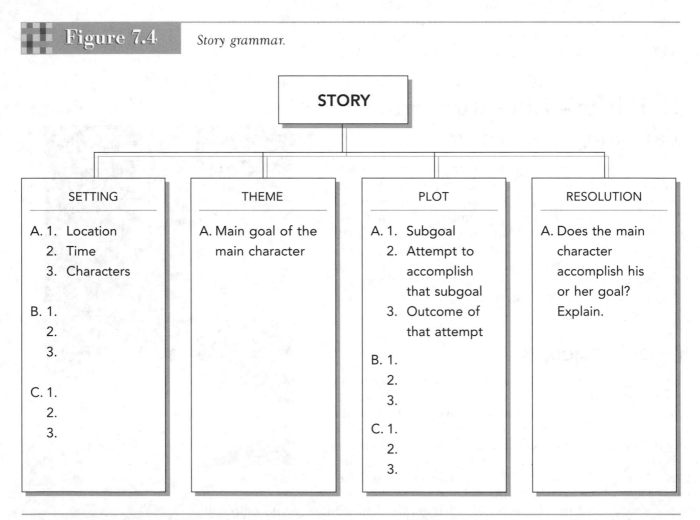

Source: Figure from Cunningham, James W. (1978, January). The ivory tower connection: A case study. *The Reading Teacher, 31* (4), 365–369. Reprinted with permission of James W. Cunningham and the International Reading Association. All rights reserved.

Children can only develop a sense of this story structure of schema by listening to stories or by reading stories themselves. After many book experiences, children begin to understand that stories have characters, a plot, a setting, and a theme. This understanding is particularly important because research (Marshall, 1983; Moore, 1995; Whaley, 1981) has shown that there is a relationship between children's awareness of these components and their ability to comprehend the story.

Informational or expository books don't necessarily share a single structure in the same way that narratives do. Actually, several studies (McGee & Richgels, 1985; Meyer & Freedle, 1979; Piccolo, 1987) have outlined five different patterns or text structures for such books: description, sequence, comparison/contrast, cause–effect, and problem/solution. Very often writers combine the text structures in their writing. The following excerpt from *Lincoln: A Photobiography* by Russell Freedman (1987) is an example of description:

> Lincoln was visibly nervous. He was wearing a new black suit and sporting a neatly clipped beard. He held a silk stovepipe hat in one hand, a gold-headed cane in the other. He put the cane in a corner, then looked around, trying to find a place for the hat. Stephen Douglas smiled and took the hat from him. (p. 68)

As is the case with narrative text, a student's knowledge of the structure or pattern of expository writing can affect comprehension (McGee & Richgels, 1985; Sinatra, 1991). With the variety of patterns utilized, it is not surprising that this type of writing provides more of a challenge for young readers than narrative stories. But by repeatedly exposing your students to informational nonfiction books and other expository writing, you can help them to be more sensitive to the language and text structures used in such books. Select nonfiction books for read-aloud sessions and include them in your science and social studies units. For example, a unit on Native Americans for students in the middle grades could be enhanced by some of the following informational books:

- Anderson, M. (1994). *The Nez Perce.* New York: Franklin Watts.
- Bleeker, S. (1982). *The Cherokee, Indians of the Mountains.* New York: Dodd, Mead & Co.
- D'Apice, R., & D'Apice, M. (1990). *The Algonquian.* Vero Beach, FL.: Rourke Publications.
- Johnston, J. (1983). *The Indians and the Strangers.* New York: Franklin Watts.
- Landaue, E. (1994). *The Hopi.* New York: Franklin Watts.
- Nabokov, P. (1982). *Native American Indians.* Chicago: Children's Press.

> ### BEYOND THE CLASSROOM
>
> Reflect on some of the statements that have been made about the benefits of using literature with children, and make notations in your notebook about your reactions to these ideas. You may also want to note your reaction to any particularly beneficial literature activities that you see used in your practicum classroom.

Involving Children with Books

In a school program promoting the development of language and reading abilities, one important goal is to make children want to read (Cullinan, 1987). Locating good stories worth telling and using them in the classroom definitely make students want to be involved with books. Good stories draw the reader in and ignite a special, personal response from each child (Kilpatrick, 1993). A great story, such as Sendak's *Where the Wild Things Are*, ignites as many reactions as there are children in the class. Some students identify with Max's defiance and punishment; others are thrilled and horrified by the "wild things." Still others focus on their relief when Max finally returns to his own room and the hot supper waiting for him.

ENVIRONMENT

However, teachers need to do more than merely locate good books and make them available for reading. They need to create an environment that draws children and books together and enables the students to grow and develop as readers. Setting aside special areas for quiet reading, establishing an accessible and well-stocked classroom library, and designing stimulating book displays and bulletin boards are all ways to promote successful book involvement. While there is no one set way to arrange a classroom, the floor plan in Figure 7.5 presents an arrangement that one teacher used successfully to establish a literature-oriented environment.

Figure 7.5   A *reading-friendly room arrangement.*

Book displays in the form of bulletin boards, dioramas, or easels are especially effective in featuring books associated with particular units of study in literature, science, social studies, and the other content areas. Successful displays can include book jackets or illustrations, book ads created by children, models of scenes from books, children's letters to the main character or author of a book, "wanted posters" for book characters, and journal entries from students who have particularly enjoyed a book. Book promotion initiates book involvement.

Other methods of book promotion are teacher modeling, book talks, reading aloud, the shared book experience, sustained silent reading, and storytelling.

MODELING

Successful literature-oriented teachers enjoy books and let their classes know it. They set aside time each day for reading aloud as well as for silent reading. They encourage their students to own and borrow books and make sure that classes have regular trips to the school library and media center. Such teachers can also guide students' thinking about books by providing a model of how to approach a book, proceed through it, and finally evaluate it.

BOOK TALKS

In a classroom, teachers are not the only ones who like to talk about books and share them with others. Among children, talking is a primary means of letting others know about special books and making recommendations for further reading. Book talks can take place anytime during the school day. They can occur in informal small groups during free time or as more formalized talks to an entire class. O'Halloran (1988) has noted that relatively informal book talks not only help children to get involved with books but also allow them to respond to books spontaneously in lieu of an assigned postreading activity.

Books are friends that never fail.

THOMAS CARLYLE

READING ALOUD

Everyone loves hearing a story, especially when the reader is excited and enthusiastic about it. Teachers who advocate and model reading aloud in their classrooms have found that this technique works with groups as diverse as preschoolers and university graduate students. There is just something about a good story that captures everybody's attention.

One of the most important aspects of reading aloud in the classroom is that it allows a teacher to promote books to students. It tells children that reading books is not just something to supplement the curriculum; it *is* the curriculum (Trelease, 1995). Students begin to realize that books are important, that they are the core of what goes on in the classroom and a primary means of getting information. They begin to see themselves following the lead of their teacher and reading books on their own.

When you start to use reading aloud in your classroom, you may want to keep in mind the following general procedures, adapted from the recommendations of Jim Trelease (1995):

- Examine and read a variety of children's books. In class, however, only share those books that you yourself enjoy—books that generate a great deal of enthusiasm.
- Practice reading a book outside of class and decide if you want to add to, shorten, or delete any particular parts.

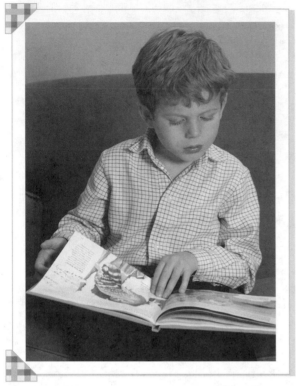

- Set aside a specific period each day for reading aloud. Children like routine and knowing that they can count on this activity each day.
- Make sure that you provide variety in the materials you read. Intersperse informational books with stories. Sometimes use a filmstrip and audiocassette of a book for the read-aloud session.
- When reading a book to the class, make sure that everyone can see you and the book.
- When you begin reading, help the students to get settled by asking them what they know or remember about a story. This helps them tune in to the session.
- Be sure to read slowly and clearly and to use expression in your voice. Make sure that the way you read reflects what is being said in the story.
- When possible, use props to add to the story and make it more visually appealing to the children. For example, if you were reading *Cranberry Thanksgiving,* you might want to bring in some cranberries to show the students.
- Allow time for children's questions and comments. Talking about the book helps students understand it and make it their own.
- Don't panic if things don't go smoothly the first time. Good read-aloud habits take practice.

SHARED BOOK EXPERIENCES

The shared reading of books is a literature approach to language learning suited for beginning readers. Based on the work of Holdaway (1991), this method is a classroom adaptation of the natural reading experiences that occur when a parent shares a book with a young child.

In the classroom, the teacher reads to groups of children and therefore uses oversized **Big Books** that allow everyone to see the pictures and text clearly. Before actually reading the Big Book, the teacher shows the title and illustrations and asks the students to predict what might happen in the story. Then she or he reads aloud while pointing to the words in the text. After the first reading, the whole group joins in reading the words in unison. This process continues until the children are familiar enough with the book to read it on their own. Cullinan (1987) has recommended that regular-size copies of the books also be available for individual reading.

Because children pick up rhymes and repetitive chants easily, predictable books are highly recommended for this activity. When a teacher is reading Galdone's *The Three Billy Goats Gruff,* it is natural for the children to chime in with the "Trip-Trap, Trip-Trap" of the goats crossing the bridge. The same thing occurs with the refrain of "Not I" that is repeated by the cat, the dog, the mouse, and the other animals in response to the hen's query in *The Little Red Hen* by Galdone. For teachers interested in using predictable books, Saccardi (1996) has recommended using three different types of texts: those with repeated cumulative events, those that invite drama, and those that lead to writing.

Obtaining the Big Books necessary for the shared book experience has sometimes been a problem. Some books are now available in this format from Scholastic (Hoberman's *A House Is a House to Me,* Sendak's *Chicken Soup with*

Rice, Brown's *Goodnight, Moon*, and many others) and the Wright Group (Wright Story Box Program). But many young readers enjoy helping teachers make their own Big Books and thus using a hands-on approach to literature.

SUSTAINED SILENT READING

Sustained silent reading (SSR)—sometimes known as uninterrupted sustained silent reading (USSR), drop everything and read (DEAR), or go read a book (GRAB)—should be an important aspect of any literature-oriented program. SSR involves setting aside classroom time for the students and the teacher to read books. It gives students the opportunity to practice their reading competencies with literature of their own choice.

Over the years, many researchers (Berglund & Johns, 1983; Hunt, 1970; McCracken, 1971) have suggested guidelines for implementing SSR. A key issue in the success of the strategy is modeling, for the teacher's own reading shows students that reading is important. In addition, the following five class rules are helpful in promoting successful SSR sessions (Blake, 1979):

1. Everyone reads.
2. Everyone makes his or her own reading choice. It can be anything—a comic book, a cereal box, a magazine, or *War and Peace*.
3. No one can interrupt once SSR begins. If someone does, everyone stops.
4. Students don't have to report on what they are reading, but if they want to, that's OK.
5. The SSR period is held at the same time every day.

SSR is really an excellent opportunity to let children practice their reading and become better readers. It can also be a major factor in awakening students to the joys of independent reading.

STORYTELLING

Storytelling was described in Chapter 5 as one method of stimulating children's vocabulary development and helping them master the sentence patterns of oral language. However, as a means of promoting interaction between the teller and the listener, storytelling also provides a way of sharing books with children and exposing them to the rich language models of literature (Strickland & Morrow, 1990). Imagine the delight of the child who hears, imitates, and even dramatizes the giant's refrain in "Jack and the Beanstalk": "Fee. Fie. Foe. Fum. I smell the blood of an Englishman." Equally important is the comfort found by the second-grader who is able to ease the pain over the loss of a poodle by recalling that the dog was frisky and smart and funny and clean; it was also snuggly and beautiful, and only once did it bite the cat's tail. In all, the child can list 10 good things about the little dog—a pattern internalized after listening repeatedly to the story *The Tenth Good Thing About Barney*, in which a boy fondly remembers his dead cat. How wonderful and satisfying it is for such a child to be able to reach into his or her storehouse of literature and find just the right words to express ideas and feelings.

Storytelling promotes the reading of literature. When a teacher tells a particular tale to children, he or she is issuing an invitation for them to read the book, to become better acquainted with the characters, and to establish their own personal understanding of the events. Through such storytelling efforts, the teacher gives the children a clear message: I think this is such a great story that I went to the trouble of learning it and preparing it so that you could know about it and enjoy it the way I do.

IN & BEYOND THE CLASSROOM

Select a story that you really like. After reading it aloud to students, jot down your ideas about the pluses and minuses of reading stories to children. Then prepare and *tell* the same story to a class. In your notebook, write a comparison of the advantages and disadvantages of both approaches to sharing stories, and use this exercise to help you with future decisions about the use of the techniques in your classroom.

Storytelling does have some important benefits that are absent in reading aloud. In storytelling, there is greater interaction and eye contact between the teller and the audience because the book is no longer a barrier between them. The teller can also improvise with the story and make it a richer experience for the audience. Finally, the variety of props that can be used in telling a story motivates children to use a similar collection of items in their own telling and retelling of the tale.

As a beginning storyteller, you may find it valuable to read about a storytelling experience of one of the authors in the Classroom Vignette that follows.

Although flannel boards and puppetry are two of the more popular methods for enhancing storytelling, other methods are also effective. Transparencies, slides, filmstrips, films, and videos are sometimes used by teachers to tell stories and by students to retell them to each other. The medium used often depends on the size of the group to whom the story is being told, the aspect of the story that is being emphasized, and the overall language competencies that the students are trying to master.

Vignette in the classroom

When I was trying to convey the importance of storytelling to my undergraduates, I decided that the only thing that would work would be an actual demonstration with a small group of children. I arranged for my students to observe me telling a story to a small group of five-year-olds in the kindergarten class associated with the college.

Because I wanted to ensure a measure of success, I chose to use a story from a book that I had previously read aloud to numerous kindergartners, first-graders, and second-graders. However, there were several other reasons that influenced my selection of *Pretzel* by Margaret Rey. First of all, the story is about two dachshunds—my favorite breed of dog. I also like the overall theme of the story, which is the importance of valuing each individual's unique traits. In addition, the story has a limited number of characters (two main characters) and a series of well-defined events.

Some professional storytellers feel that stories are not enhanced by props and should be told without them. I, an amateur storyteller, do not subscribe to that philosophy. I believe that the right prop can really enhance a story and help to focus the storyteller. Therefore, I began to explore which type of prop I might want to use.

Because I wanted to show the contrast between Pretzel's unusual length and the size of other dachshunds, and because the story has a limited number of characters and objects, I decided to use a flannel board. I made that choice based on data from *Storyteller,* in which Ross (1996) recommended using flannel boards to illustrate stories involving a comparison of sizes, folktales, scientific tales explaining phenomena, and accumulative tales such as *I Know an Old Lady Who Swallowed a Fly.*

I made my flannel board by covering a portable cork bulletin board with a large piece of tan felt. For the figures in the story, I chose brightly colored pieces of felt and enhanced facial features and decorations with magic markers.

Once the props were completed, I began preparing *Pretzel* for the kindergartners. As recommended by many authorities (Ross, 1996), I

(continued)

did not memorize the story. Instead I read it over many times to get a sequence of the events, and I developed a general timeline in my mind of what happened first, what happened second, and so on. I also tried to develop the personality and voice for Pretzel—who was proud, dignified, and helpful—and the traits of Greta, the other dachshund in the story—who was selfish, stuck-up, and spoiled. Once I began telling the story to myself, I began to use particular story phrases such as the following:

One morning in May five little dachshunds were born.

Pretzel suddenly started growing—and growing—and growing.

"I don't care for long dogs," said Greta.

Other than developing the haughty sniff associated with Greta, I didn't add any gestures to the story. However, I did decide to start the story by telling the children a little about my dachshund and allowing them to share some information about their pets. I also decided to let the close of the story be informal by giving the children some time to express their feelings about the story or to handle the felt props. Most of all, I practiced the story on tape, in the mirror, and in front of friends until they knew it almost as well as I did.

The actual telling went smoothly. With some help from the class's regular teacher, I set the board on a chair and gathered the small group of children around it. As planned, we spent a few minutes talking about my dachshund and the children's experiences with dogs and other pets. Then I launched into my rendition of *Pretzel*. I found that the practice really helped, and I was able to portray Pretzel and Greta in exactly the right light. The children really loved the characters and the story, and we spent several minutes at the end of the story handling the props and telling what we liked best about the tale.

The best part of the experience came after the actual storytelling. Because the children enjoyed handling the props so much, the teacher asked me to leave them in the classroom—a request I was glad to honor. She later told me that the children used the flannel figures frequently in attempts to retell the story and that she was reading the book to them to assist their comprehension of the story.

Also, the experience convinced my students that storytelling is not just a frill—something extra to do on a dreary afternoon. They began to understand that books and storytelling form a core component of a language development program.

Children's Responses to Literature

Through experiences with good literature, children develop a greater comprehension of story structure, gain more control over language, increase their oral fluency, develop the habit of reading daily, and experience emotional reactions. They become mature and sophisticated readers. This section explores activities to facilitate those responses: discussions, strategies for retelling, book publishing, creative drama and choral speaking activities, and oral and written methods for sharing books. All the activities help children to see how vitally important books are in every aspect of life.

DISCUSSIONS

Talk is a vital force for learning in the classroom. Modeling and book talks have already been discussed as ways in which to interest and involve children in literature. *Discussions* allow children to express personal responses informally, without preparation. Even if a child really dislikes a book, she or he should have a right to say so and to hear others' reactions to their feelings.

Discussions can be large-group or small-group activities, either guided by a teacher or controlled by the students. In one study (Strickland et al., 1990), several teacher/researchers studied literature response groups in which the children took control of the questioning and discussion. In such groups, talk proved to be an empowering force in learning.

Very often discussions can follow retellings or book talks and begin with personal responses. Students can then explore questions about the literary elements of characterization, setting, plot, and theme. They can also make predictions about books and compare books that they have read individually. The Classroom Vignette at the beginning of this chapter, discussing the use of *Sarah, Plain and Tall*, provides one example of a focused book discussion.

RETELLING ACTIVITIES

Retelling the story line of a book is a way for a child to reconstruct the story's meaning. The child is able to respond to literature by creating his or her similar version of the tale. According to Morrow (1985), retelling stories is a strategy that can improve oral language fluency, sense of story, and overall comprehension. Retelling strategies can include storytelling; the use of story structures, guides, and maps; the creation of books; and various forms of creative drama (described in detail in Chapter 5).

Storytelling

Storytelling comes naturally to children (Hamilton & Weiss, 1993). They are continually telling their teachers and peers the daily stories of their personal lives. From these stories, it is an easy progression to creating and telling the story lines of wordless picture books, such as *Bobo's Dream*.

Children can make effective use of all the props available to teachers: puppets, flannel boards, chalk stories, transparencies, slides, and self-created filmstrips. One type of story that works particularly well for children is the object story, in which the student uses an object or objects from the story to aid the retelling. At Christmastime one year, a sixth-grader decided to tell a modified version of Van Allsburg's *The Polar Express* to a group of primary children. Her props were a small train model and a reindeer sleigh bell, which helped to prompt her memory of the events in the story. The whole project turned out to be a successful activity that not only delighted the young children (who were able to jingle the bell) but also enhanced the sixth-grader's self-esteem and self-confidence as a speaker.

Story Grammars, Charts, and Maps

Helping children understand story structure and develop a story schema increases recall, comprehension, and ability to make predictions based on text (Mandler & Johnson, 1977). Research by Morrow (1985) has shown that this is especially true for young children. After children have experienced an emotional response to a book, it is important for the teacher to go back and help them understand why they enjoyed it by looking at the elements that are part of the story structure.

A **story grammar** (Cunningham & Foster, 1978; Mandler & Johnson, 1977) builds an outline of the major elements of a story and unites those elements into a readily comprehensible and usually typical structure (Smith & Bean, 1983). Figure 7.6 shows a sample story grammar of "Goldilocks and the Three Bears."

Figure 7.6 *Sample story grammar: "Goldilocks and the Three Bears."*

CLIMAX

The three bears return. They realize that someone has been in the house and confront Goldilocks in the baby bear's bed.

EVENT

Goldilocks wants to take a nap. After trying all the beds, she falls asleep on the small bear's bed.

EVENT

Goldilocks tries all three chairs. She decides on the small bear's chair and breaks it.

EVENT

Goldilocks tries all three bowls of porridge and eats the small bear's portion.

PROBLEM

While the bears are away, a little girl named Goldilocks comes by and decides to explore what is not hers.

SETTING

The three bears live in a house in the woods.

RESOLUTION

Goldilocks jumps from the bed and out the nearest window. The bears never see her again. They do not miss her.

Source: Adapted from L. Galda (1987), "Teaching Higher Order Reading Skills with Literature."

Character perspective charts (Shanahan & Shanahan, 1997) are another way of helping children respond to literature; based on the above research related to story grammars, a **character perspective chart (CPC)** appears to help children develop a more complete and well-rounded appreciation for stories and the viewpoints of all the characters therein. Such charts are especially good for stories where specific characters may be in conflict, such as Nyasha and Manyara of *Mufaro's Beautiful Daughters.* One fourth-grade teacher initiated a class discussion of that book by using the CPC illustrated in Figure 7.7. Such a chart is most helpful in organizing an in-depth analysis of different points of view in a story.

Story maps also build upon story structure and can be used along with questions to guide youngsters through a re-creation of a story. Some story

Figure 7.7   *Sample character perspective chart.*

CHARACTER PERSPECTIVE CHART: *MUFARO'S BEAUTIFUL DAUGHTERS*

Main character: Who is the main character?

Nyasha

Setting: Where and when does the story take place?

A village and city in Africa.

Problem: What is the main character's problem?

Dealing with her sister's (Manyara) bad temper.

Goal: What is the main character's goal? What does the character want?

To be good and kind and do the right thing.

Attempt: What does the main character do to solve the problem or get the goal?

Continues to be considerate and kind to every living creature.

Outcome: What happened as a result of the attempt?

The king recognizes her goodness; she becomes queen.

Reaction: How does the main character feel about the outcome?

Happy.

Theme: What point did the author want to make?

Kindness and goodness are rewarded.

Main character: Who is the main character?

Manyara

Setting: Where and when does the story take place?

A village and city in Africa.

Problem: What is the main character's problem?

Showing her sister's (Nyasha) kindness to be a weakness/concealing her bad temper.

Goal: What is the main character's goal? What does the character want?

To marry the king and be queen.

Attempt: What does the main character do to solve the problem or get the goal?

Secretly leaves early for the city to be the first to meet the king.

Outcome: What happened as a result of the attempt?

The king recognizes her faults; she becomes a servant in the king's household.

Reaction: How does the main character feel about the outcome?

Appears to be upset.

Theme: What point did the author want to make?

Selfishness is its own undoing.

Source: Adapted from Shanahan & Shanahan (1997), "Character Perspective Charting: Helping Children to Develop a More Complete Conception of Story." *The Reading Teacher, 50*(8), 668–677. Copyright by the International Reading Association. All rights reserved.

maps follow a sequential story line (Beck & McKeown, 1981) while others depict circular tales (Jett-Simpson, 1981).

To teach the use of story maps, begin with a very simple story, which in turn has a simple map drawing. After hearing a number of these stories, the children begin to internalize the structure of stories; this means they have created a mental schema they can apply to later stories heard or read. This mental schema allows youngsters to predict events and outcomes in new stories based on stories they have heard or read. To further aid the creation of the mental schema, story maps show the children what the story pattern looks like. Eventually the students can create their own story maps to help them remember and predict details in a story heard or read. The Classroom Vignette that follows illustrates the use of narrative story maps to aid listening and reading comprehension.

Vignette in the classroom

Mr. Funk's fourth-grade class has been listening to and reading various types of stories, including folktales. Today he is going to teach the students about the use of story maps to remember the structure of a folktale.

"I've brought another story today that I think you are going to enjoy," he says. "I want you to listen carefully as I read just the title and opening paragraph of the story. Then I want you to help me draw a kind of map of the story, or of what parts you think the story might contain." He begins reading the story "Clever Gretchen."

"Once upon a time there lived a lord who had a daughter named Gretchen, who was as clever as she was good, and pretty besides. Rich merchants and noblemen came from all over the country to ask her hand in marriage, but her father would have none of them. 'The man who marries my daughter,' said he, 'must be the best huntsman in the world.'" Mr. Funk stops reading at this point.

"What kind of a story do you call this?" he asks.

"A folktale," says Ramon.

"How do you know?" asks Mr. Funk.

"Because it begins with 'Once upon a time.'"

"Good for you," says Mr. Funk. "You remembered other stories we've heard that began the same way. Ok, using your previous knowledge of folktales, let's draw a map using some boxes and arrows to show the structure of this story, or at least what we think the structure will be. Afterward we'll read the rest of the story to check our ideas."

On the chalkboard Mr. Funk has pasted a large piece of butcher paper that he can write on with a magic marker. "What are the elements you might expect to encounter in this story just from having heard the first paragraph?" he asks.

"Well, there's a setting and some characters," says Bobby. "We already know there's Gretchen and the rich lord."

"There's also a problem," says Lindsay. "They've got to find the best huntsman in the world if Gretchen wants to get married. Otherwise she'll be an old spinster."

Mr. Funk writes the ideas on the paper in a list and then leads the students to create a story map outline.

As the discussion continues, they begin to fill in the map, guessing at the other aspects of the story. Then they listen to the rest of the story. Some of their guesses are correct; others are not and need to be revised. Figure 7.8 shows the revised narrative story map the class produced.

Constructing a **story map** is simply a matter of helping your children sequence in an illustration the events in a story. For example, suppose you have just finished Yorinks's *Hey, Al* with your class and you say to them, "Tell me what happened in this story." However, instead of just listing all the events on the chalkboard, you draw a circle and tell the children that they have to put the story events in the correct order around the circle. The completed diagram would look something like the one in Figure 7.9.

BOOK PUBLISHING

Children can use story knowledge to write and illustrate their own books. These stories may take the form of Big Books for younger children or individual books for older ones. (The mechanical aspects of book publishing are discussed in Chapter 8.)

Figure 7.8

Sample story map: "Clever Gretchen."

In a preschool class, a teacher had done repeated readings of John Langstaff's *Over in the Meadow*. After the children were completely familiar with the rhyme and the rhythm, they wanted to compose their own additions to the tale. However, the students decided they wanted to use pets in a backyard instead of wild animals in a meadow for their version, and they broke into small groups to compose separate verses, such as the following:

> Over in our backyard in the grass and the sun
> Lived an old mother cat and her little kitty one.
> "Purr," said the mother;
> "I purr," said the one;
> So she purred and was glad in the grass and the sun.

> Over in the backyard where a big bush grew
> Lived an old mother hound dog and her little puppies two.
> "Bark," said the mother;
> "We bark," said the two;
> So they barked and were glad where the big bush grew.

Book publishing not only allows youngsters to respond to literature, it also ignites their continuing interest in reading new books, books that have inspired writing by their peers.

Figure 7.9

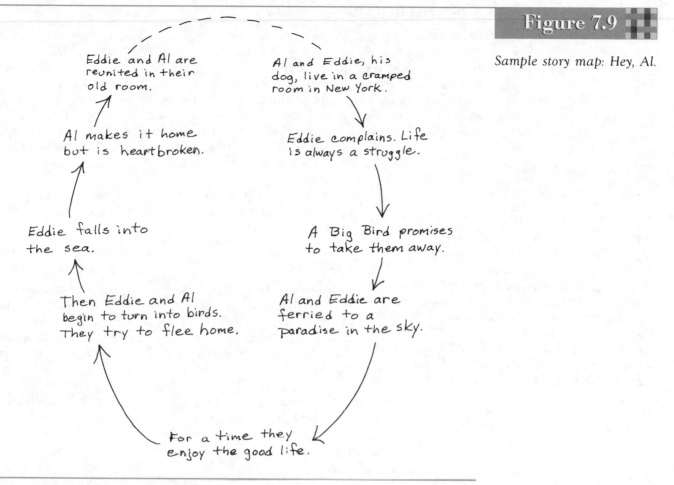

Sample story map: Hey, Al.

Source: Adapted from L. Galda (1987), "Teaching Higher Order Reading Skills with Literature."

CREATIVE DRAMA

Another way in which students can respond to literature is through the various activities of creative drama, such as pantomime, improvisation, or reader's theatre, all of which were discussed in Chapter 5. One additional aspect of creative drama is choral speaking. *Choral speaking* involves the oral reading of poetry or prose. It allows students to become active participants in interpreting and expressing the meaning of a familiar poem or story; it enables them to increase their oral reading proficiency within the security of a whole-group situation. Through choral speaking, children learn how to play with the language of literature and its grammatical structures and how to make it come alive through the clarity and quality of their voices.

You may want to start choral speaking by just repeating some favorite poems to the children and having them join in with you. With longer poems, you may want the students to have copies of the text for reference. One pitfall you need to guard against is allowing this activity to become merely a test of oral fluency. The true goal is to help children understand the meaning of poems and to interpret that meaning through oral expression. For more information about using poems and stories for choral speaking and choral reading, check Tashjian's (1974) *With a Deep Sea Smile* and Pennock's (1984) "Choral Reading of Poetry Improves Reading Fluency."

SHARING BOOKS

Book talks and bulletin boards have been mentioned previously as motivators for reading. While these activities definitely do interest children in reading books, they are primarily ways for readers to respond to literature. Just as a picture on a bulletin board shows the world what a child thinks about a book, a book talk enables a child to give his or her personal reaction to a story and to retell it in a very personal way. Some teachers extend this activity by encouraging students to write letters to a classmate who has completed a book talk. Figure 7.10 shows the letters that one teacher and two students wrote in response to a book talk.

Some other ways to encourage students to share stories with you and with each other are covered in the following paragraphs.

Journals

Journals can be as simple as having the students keep a brief record of what they are reading and how they feel about it. This type of activity gives clues as to what and how much children are reading. You may wish to introduce journal writing to your class by using books in which this type of writing plays a role. Two books to consider are *But I'll Be Back Again: An Album* by Cynthia Rylant and *Diary of an Early American Boy, Noah Blake, 1805* by Eric Sloane. (Also see Chapter 8.)

Letters

Writing letters provides students with an audience and gives them a real purpose or reason for expressing their feelings in response to a book. Some children may want to write to their teachers; others may want to write to the author of the book. One sixth-grade class wrote to Ursula LeGuin, the author of the Earthsea books (Rollin, 1985). Still others may want to write to the characters in the book and tell them just what they think of them. One book that many teachers like to use to encourage letter writing is Beverly Cleary's *Dear Mr. Henshaw*, which chronicles the correspondence between an author and a young fan.

Bumper Stickers

Creating bumper stickers is one interesting way for children to summarize and express their thoughts. You can obtain blank bumper stickers from many local printing companies. Have the students print their sayings on the stickers with indelible markers, as in Figure 7.11.

Wanted Posters

Students can demonstrate their understanding of a character in a story by designing a wanted poster describing the character's outstanding traits. A sample poster is pictured in Figure 7.12.

Figure 7.10

Sample letters in response to a book talk.

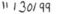

11-30-99

Dear Corey,

I'm glad I finally got to hear your book. You've had it here for a long time and I was curious about it. You did a very nice job reading it. I know everyone has the "gimmies" every now and then just like the bears. Thanks for reading!

Love,
Mrs. Neal

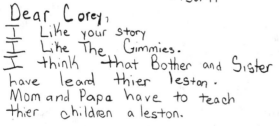

11 / 30 / 99

Dear Corey,
I Like your story
I Like The Gimmies.
I think that Bother and Sister have leard thier leston.
Mom and Papa have to teach thier children a leston.

love,
Tawana

Dear Cory,
I liked your story.
It was funny.
Thank you for reading to us.
You can read good.
Hope you can read agin.
PLEASE read to us agin

Meredith

Book Ads

Children can describe the outstanding attributes of a book by composing a newspaper ad in which they try to sell the book to their classmates. The ads can then be placed on a bulletin board along with student-created book jackets and removed as each new "buyer" decides to read a particular book. The success of an ad depends on whether or not another student chooses to read a book because of it.

Mobiles, Collages, and Models

Making physical models of a story can help art-oriented students express themselves. For example, a child might make a mobile of all the characters and important artifacts in "Hansel and Gretel." The completed project would include the forest, the bread crumbs, the gingerbread house, Hansel's cage, and the oven, as well as the characters of the mother, the father, the children, and the witch. A collage might include an unusual arrangement of drawings from the story as well as some pieces of important objects mentioned in it. A child who chooses to do a model of a scene from "Hansel and Gretel" might show a miniature version of the interior of the cottage or the witch's gingerbread house.

Figure 7.11

Sample bumper sticker.

BEYOND THE CLASSROOM

Think of five other ways in which children can share books. Include them in your notebook with brief descriptions and predictions of how you think they might work in your classroom.

Figure 7.12

Sample wanted poster.

WANTED! DEAD OR ALIVE

Winnie the Pooh

Winnie the Pooh is a small bear of little brain who likes to eat honey. He is known to associate with Christopher Robin, Piglet, Eeyore, Kanga, Roo, Tigger, Rabbit, and Owl. Was last seen hanging out at the House at Pooh Corner. Any information leading to his whereabouts will be rewarded with a $500.00 reward and a small pot of honey.

Summary

Literature is the central component of language learning. Good books give children reasons to read and provide them with strong language models, which in turn help children to formulate and express their reactions. Your knowledge of the different types of books and magazines available for classroom use will help you in selecting appropriate materials for your class.

However, the best method of choosing books is to listen to the needs and wants of your own students. They and their peers are more than willing to give you plenty of ideas about which books to stock in the reading center.

As a teacher, you play a crucial role in involving students with literature. Children imitate adults, so by letting your students see that you read on a daily basis and that you truly enjoy books, you are encouraging them to see reading literature as a desirable, "adult" activity. When you couple your modeling with storytelling, reading aloud, and sustained silent reading, you have the basic ingredients to initiate a successful literature-based language program.

Encourage your students to be creative and to respond to literature in a variety of ways. Although discussion is a commonly used technique in classrooms, help your students to see that journal writing, retelling stories, using story maps, developing book talks, writing ads for books, and creating murals are equally valid ways of responding to books. Most of all, help children to see how reading literature can be an enjoyable daily habit.

With Children *activities*

AUTHOR EXPERTS

Encourage your students to read several books by the same author and to make notes about similarities in the books. Then help them gather some factual information about the author's life and work. When the research is completed, the students can construct a bulletin board display highlighting particular books and important facts about the author's life. The "expert" students can also host a discussion in which they answer other students' questions about the author.

BOOK MURALS

Students can respond to books with particularly intriguing illustrations by creating a class mural (painting on a wall or bulletin board) of a favorite scene. This technique also works very well with informational books, especially those about nature. One first-grade class did a terrific job with a prehistoric mural about dinosaurs.

BOOK WORMS

Help keep track of how many books your students are reading by creating a "book worm." Decorate a face for your worm and attach it to a high spot on a wall. Then cut out the first round segment of the worm and write down the title, author, and location of a book that you have just read. Write your own name at the bottom of the segment and attach it next to the face. Tell your students to do the same every time they complete a book. Before you know it, your book worm will stretch around the room.

CHARACTER PARADE

Set aside a time for students to dress up as a favorite character in a book. After each student has given three hints about the identity of her or his character, classmates have to guess. The student who successfully guesses the identity of the character becomes the next one to present.

CIGAR-BOX STORIES

Each child in the class should glue a small piece of felt to the inside of a cigar box. Have felt available so that children can make characters and objects from favorite stories they have read. Students can store figures from the different stories in manila envelopes. Whenever a child wants to retell or review a story, the cigar box can be used as a personal flannel board.

CLASS BOOK FILE

Encourage your students to create a file box of children's books for class use. Each time a child finishes a book, he or she should complete an index card listing the title, author, and location of the book. Also ask the student to include a brief opinion of the book and a signature. When other children are looking for something to read, they can consult the cards in the file for suggestions.

PERSONAL CHRONICLES

You can help children understand how simple storytelling is by encouraging them to share the stories of their daily lives. You may want to set aside a brief period every day for a few students to share stories of something that happened at home, on the way to school, or at the playground. Some children may even want to record their stories.

technology   *Videos*

The Internet and CD-ROMs are sources of great information about authors and stories, and many great videos are also available about authors. For example, one Trumpet Club series of videos takes the viewer into the authors' writing studio. While the children "visit" the studios, the authors give some background information about their childhood, explain how they became interested in writing and illustrating, and often tell where they get the inspiration for the books and illustrations. If a school cannot afford to have an author visit the school, the videos are wonderful, inexpensive ways for the students to meet the authors. Two delightful videos available from Trumpet Club are *Marc Brown: Creator of Arthur*, and *Mem Fox*.

Today many companies make videos based on children's literature. Raymond Briggs's *The Snowman*, released by SVS, Inc., is beautifully done as a wordless video. The music is relaxing, and the scenes spark the imagination as the viewer watches the adventure of the snowman and the little boy. Delta Education's many wonderful videos on current children's literature include the titles *Chicken Sunday* and *Thunder Cake* by Patricia Polacco, *Mrs. Piggle Wiggle* by Betty MacDonald, *Ralph the Mouse* by Beverly Cleary, and *Frog and Toad* by Arnold Lobel. For a free catalog, write to:

Delta Education
P.O. Box 3000
Nashua, NH 03061-3000

E-learning websites

www.kn.pacbell.com/wired/bluewebn
If you enter SUBJECT and ENGLISH then READING, you will be connected to many authors of children's literature. All authors give details about their books; many include their e-mail address.

www.pbs.org/rogers
This site includes activities for children and a book list of stories that correlate with the Mr. *Rogers* TV program's themes. Lyrics for the songs from the show are also included.

www.acm.org/crossroads
This site, written by students and for students, includes book reviews and is available in Spanish.

www.scils.rutgers.edu/special/kay/kayhp2.html
This site includes great lists of multicultural books by the many different groups represented in the United States. It also lists materials for connecting literature to learning across the curriculum.

www.kidsvista.com/index.htm
This site links children with other sites relating to literature, science, social studies, games, the arts, and many other topics.

www.ucalgary.ca/~dkbrown/index.html
This site has children's literature discussion groups, book reviews, and resources for parents and teachers.

www.enigmagraphic.com/stories/index.htm
This site has online stories and specializes in storytelling.

gopher://lib.nmsu.edu:70/11/.subjects/Education/.childlit
This site gives information about authors and book awards; it also has online texts.

www.users.interport.net/~fairrosa/
This site gives lists of children's literature, background information, and other resources.

www.carolhurst.com/
This site gives book reviews, has activities to use with the books, and also lists the books according to themes.

funnelweb.utcc.utk.edu/~estes/estes2.html
This is another site that lists books according to themes.

ipl.org/youth/AskAuthor/
This site gives biographical information about authors and has interviews with well-known authors and illustrators.

gpn.unl.edu/rainbow/
This site gives lists and describes the books that are on the "Reading Rainbow" show.

www.mrtc.org/~twright/animals/english/alphabet.html
This site has each letter of the alphabet represented as an animal with a clickable image, which leads to facts about the animal. Although this site is

simple for first readers, the humuhumunukunukapau and xuprocar will wake up any scholar who may think the alphabet is boring.

www.publishersweekly.com/bsl/currentChildrens.asp

This site has the publishers' weekly children's best-seller lists.

www.yahoo.com/Arts/Humanities/Literature/Genres/ Children_s/Authors/

This site has information about children's authors.

www.ctw.org/sesame/printplay/letters/

This site has the alphabet according to Sesame Street. There is a printable page to color for each letter, and accompanying collections of the same for numbers and shapes.

www.janbrett.com

This is Jan Brett's home page, which contains interactive activities for kids to read and draw.

www.nene.ac.uk/lrs/subjects/Education/children.html

One can use this site to find poetry, folktales and fairy tales, reviews, and authors. It gives great background information.

www.ucs.mun.ca/~sherry/bunting.htm

This is the home page of Eve Bunting, author of *Smokey Night*. It includes fun activities.

www.acs.ucalgary.ca/~dkbrown/authors.html

This is considered the children's literature Web guide, with tons of authors. Many e-mail addresses are included.

www.aaronshep.com/rt/

This site has Aaron Shephard's reader's theatre scripts.

darsie.ucdavis.edu/tales/

This is an archive of folktales from around the world.

www.isomedia.com/homes/jmele/joe.html

This site has multicultural book reviews.

www.cs.cmu.edu/books.html

Over 6,000 books are accessible online at this site.

www.ipl.org/reading/books/index.html

Over 7,000 books are accessible online here.

www.ala.org/

This is the American Library Association's home page.

www.ala.org/alsc.caldecott.html

This site lists the Caldecott award and honor books, with information about each.

www.ala.org/alsc/newbery.html

This site lists the Newbery award and honor books, with information about each.

Related Readings

Barry, A. (1998). Hispanic representation in literature for children and young adults. *Journal of Adolescent and Adult Literacy, 41*(8), 630–637.

Beck, I., McKeown, M., Hamilton, R., & Kucan, L. (1997). *Questioning the author: An approach for enhancing student engagement with text.* Newark, DE: International Reading Association.

Cullinan, B. (1992). *Invitation to read: More children's literature in the reading program.* Newark, DE: International Reading Association.

Hendershot, J., & Peck, J. (1998). The view from Saturday: A conversation with E. L. Konigsburg, winner of the 1997 Newbery Medal. *The Reading Teacher, 51*(8), 676–680.

Routman, R. (1991). *Invitations: Changing as teachers and learners K–12.* Portsmouth, NH: Heinemann.

Watson-Ellam, L. (1991). *Start with a story: Literature and learning in your classroom.* Portsmouth, NH: Heinemann.

References

Abrahamson, R. F. (1980). A plot structure analysis of children's favorite picture books. *The Reading Teacher, 34*(2), 167–170.

Allen, M. (1996). *100 years of children's books in America: Decade by decade.* Facts on File.

Beck, I., & McKeown, M. G. (1981). Developing questions that promote comprehension: The story map. *Language Arts, 58*(8), 913–918.

Berglund, R., & Johns, J. (1983). A primer on uninterrupted sustained silent reading. *The Reading Teacher, 36*(6), 534–539.

Bettelheim, B. (1976). *The uses of enchantment.* New York: Knopf.

Blake, M. (1979, September). SSR revisited. *Teacher,* 95–98.

Castro, R. (1997). *What do I read next?: Multicultural literature.* Detroit: Gale Research.

Children's books in print. (Annual). New York: Bowker.

Cullinan, B. (1987). Inviting readers to literature. In B. Cullinan (ed.), *Children's literature in the reading program.* Newark, DE: International Reading Association.

Cunningham, J., & Foster, E. O. (1978). The ivory tower connection: A case study. *The Reading Teacher, 31*(4), 365–369.

DeMelendez, W., Ostertag, V., & Peck, J. (1997). *Teaching young children in multicultural classrooms: Issues, concepts, and strategies.* Albany, NY: Delmar Publishers.

Feeley, J. (1982). Content interests and media preferences of middle graders: Differences in a decade. *Reading World, 22*(1), 11–16.

Galda, L. (1987). Teaching higher order reading skills with literature: Intermediate grades. In B. E. Cullinan (ed.), *Children's literature in the reading program.* Newark, DE: International Reading Association.

Goodman, K. (1986). *What's whole in whole language.* Portsmouth, NH: Heinemann.

Greenlee, A., Monson, D., & Taylor, B. (1996). The lure of series books: Does it affect appreciation for recommended literature? *The Reading Teacher, 50*(3), 216–225.

Hahn, J. (1996). Literary bridges: Linking language arts and bilingual education. *Primary Voices K–6, 4*(3), 31–34.

Hamilton, M., & Weiss, M. (1993). Children as storytellers: Teaching the basic tools. *School Library Journal, 39*(4), 30–33.

Helbig, A., & Perkins, A. (1994). *This land is our land: A guide to multicultural literature for children and young adults.* Westport, CT: Greenwood Press.

Hickman, J. (1984). Research currents: Researching children's responses to literature. *Language Arts, 61*(3), 278–284.

Holdaway, D. (1991). Shared book experience: Teaching reading using favorite books. In C. Kamii, E. Ferreiro, F. Siegrist, H. Sinclair, B. Cuttings, J. Milligan, M. Manning, G. Manning, B. Lewis, R. Long, & B. Engle (eds.), *Early literacy: A constructivist foundation for whole language.* Washington, DC: National Education Association.

Huck, C., Hepler, S., & Hickman, J. (1993). *Children's literature in the elementary school* (5th ed.). New York: Harcourt Brace Jovanovich.

Hunt, L. C. (1970). The effect of self-selection, interest, and motivation upon independent, instructional, and frustration levels. *The Reading Teacher, 24*(2), 146–154.

International Reading Association (1996). Young adults' choices for 1996. *Journal of Adolescent & Adult Literacy, 40*(3), 201–208.

Jalongo, M. R. (1983). Bibliotherapy: Literature to promote socioemotional growth. *The Reading Teacher, 36*(8), 796–803.

Jett-Simpson, M. (1981). Writing stories using model structures: The circle story. *Language Arts*, 58(3), 293–300.

Kaywell, J. (1993). *Adolescents at risk: A guide to fiction for young adults, parents, and professionals*. Westport, CT: Greenwood Press.

Khorana, M. (1994). *Africa in literature for children and young adults: An annotated bibliography of English language books*. Westport, CT: Greenwood Press.

Kilpatrick, W. (1993). The moral power of good stories and a selection of great books for children and teens. *American Educator: The Professional Journal of the American Federation for Teachers*, 17(2), 24–35.

Lamme, L. L. (1987). Children's literature: The natural way to learn to read. In B. E. Cullinan (ed.), *Children's literature in the reading program*. Newark, DE: International Reading Association.

Lima, C. (1993). *A to zoo: Subject access to children's picture books* (3rd ed.). New York: Bowker.

Lind, B. (1997). *Multicultural children's literature: An annotated bibliography, grades K–8*. Jefferson, NC: McFarland & Co.

Lindskoog, J. (1989). *How to grow a young reader: A parent's guide to books for kids*. Wheaton, IL: Harold Shaw Publishers.

Lipson, E. (1991). *The New York Times parent's guide to the best books for children*. New York: Random House.

Mandler, J. M., & Johnson, N. S. (1977). Remembrance of things parsed: Story structure and recall. *Cognitive Psychology*, 9(1), 111–151.

Marantz, S. (1995). *The art of children's picture books: A selective reference guide*. New York: Garland Publishing.

Marshall, N. (1983). Using story grammar to assess reading comprehension. *The Reading Teacher*, 36(7), 616–619.

McCracken, R. (1971). Initiating sustained silent reading. *Journal of Reading*, 14(8), 521–524, 582–583.

McGee, L., & Richgels, D. J. (1985). Teaching expository text structure to elementary students. *The Reading Teacher*, 38(8), 739–748.

Meyer, B., & Freedle, R. (1979). *The effects of different discourse types on recall*. Princeton, NJ: Educational Testing Service.

Miles, S. (1991). *Adoption literature for children and young adults: An annotated bibliography*. Westport, CT: Greenwood Press.

Moore, S. (1995). Focus on research: Questions for research into reading-writing relationships and text structure knowledge. *Language Arts*, 72(8), 598–606.

Moran, B., & Steinfirst, S. (1985). Why Johnny (and Jane) read whodunits in series. *School Library Journal*, 31(7), 113–117.

Morrow, L. M. (1985). Reading and retelling stories: Strategies for emergent readers. *The Reading Teacher*, 38(9), 870–875.

Norton, D. E. (1990). Teaching multicultural literature in the reading curriculum. *The Reading Teacher*, 44(1), 28–40.

O'Halloran, S. (1988). An experienced teacher tells how. In J. Hancock & S. Hill (eds.), *Literature-based reading programs at work*. Portsmouth, NH: Heinemann.

Olson, M., Gee, I., & Forester, N. (1989). Magazines in the classroom: Beyond recreational reading. *The Journal of Reading*, 32(8), 708–713.

Overstad, B. (1981). *Bibliotherapy: Books to help young children*. St Paul, MN: Toys 'n Things Press.

Pennock, C. (1984). Choral reading of poetry improves reading fluency. *Highway One*, 7(3), 21–22.

Piccolo, J. A. (1987). Expository text structure: Teaching and learning strategies. *The Reading Teacher*, 40(9), 838–847.

Rasmussen, M. (1989, May/June). Kidlit or kiddy lit derisive or not? *Martha's Kidlit Newsletter*, p. 9.

Reutzel, D. R. (1985). Story maps improve comprehension. *The Reading Teacher*, 38(4), 400–404.

Rhodes, L., & Dudley-Marling, C. (1996). *Readers and writers with a difference* (2nd ed.). Portsmouth, NH: Heinemann.

Rogers, T. (1997). *Reading across cultures: Teaching literature in a diverse society*. New York: Teacher's College Press.

Rollin, L. W. (1985). Exploring Earthsea: A sixth grade literature project. *Children's Literature in Education*, 16(4), 195–202.

Rollock, B. (1988). *Black authors and illustrators of children's books*. New York: Garland.

Ross, C. (1995). If they read Nancy Drew, so what?: Series book readers talk back. *Library and Information Science Research*, 17(3), 201–236.

Ross, R. (1996). *Storyteller*. Little Rock, AR: August House Publishers.

Saccardi, M. (1996). Predictable books: Gateways to a lifetime of reading. *The Reading Teacher*, 49(7), 588–591.

Sebesta, S., Calder, J., & Cleland, L. N. (1981). Story structure in children's book choices. Paper presented at the Conference on Language Arts in the Elementary School. Portland.

Shanahan, T., & Shanahan, S. (1997). Character perspective charting: Helping children to develop a more complete conception of story. *The Reading Teacher*, 50(8), 668–677.

Sinatra, R. (1991). Integrating whole language with the learning of text structure. *Journal of Reading*, 34(6), 424–433.

Smith, M., & Bean, T. W. (1983). Four strategies that develop children's story comprehension and writing. *The Reading Teacher*, 37(3), 295–301.

Stein, N. L., & Glenn, C. G. (1979). An analysis of story comprehension in elementary schoolchildren. In R. O. Freedle (ed.), *New directions in discourse processing*. Norwood, NJ: Ablex.

Stoll, D. R. (ed.) (1997). *Magazines for kids and teens* (2nd ed.). Glassboro, NJ, & Newark, DE: Educational Press Association of America & International Reading Association.

Strickland, D. (1987). Literature: Key element in the language and reading program. In B. E. Cullinan (ed.), *Children's literature in the reading program*. Newark, DE: International Reading Association.

Strickland, D. S., Dillon, R. M., Funkhouser, L., Glick, M., & Rogers, C. (1990). Research currents: Classroom dialogue during literature response groups. *Language Arts*, 66(2), 192–200.

Strickland, D. S., & Morrow, L. M. (1990). Family literacy: Sharing good books (emerging readers and writers). *The Reading Teacher*, 43(7), 518–519.

Sutherland, Z., & Livingston, M. C. (1984). *The Scott Foresman anthology of children's literature*. Glenview, IL: Scott, Foresman & Company.

Tashjian, V. A. (1974). *With a deep sea smile*. Boston: Little, Brown & Company.

Thompson, B. (1984, December 23). Children's books need careful review. *The News & Courier*, Charleston, SC.

Trelease, J. (1995). *The new read-aloud handbook* (2nd ed.). New York: Penguin Books.

Whaley, J. (1981). Grammars and reading instruction. *Language Arts*, 34(7), 762–765.

CHILDREN'S LITERATURE

Ackerman, K. (1988). *Song and dance man*. (Stephen Gammell, illus.). New York: Knopf.

Alexander, L. (1964–1968). *Prydain chronicles*. New York: Holt, Rinehart & Winston.

Alexander, L. (1992). *The fortune-tellers*. New York: Dutton.

Alexander, M. (1970). *Bobo's dream*. New York: Dial Press.

Aliki. (1979). *The two of them*. New York: Greenwillow.

Ancona, P. (1993). *Pablo remembers*. New York: Lothrop, Lee & Shepard Books.

Anderson, M. (1994). *The Nez Perce*. New York: Franklin Watts.

Anno, M. (1977). *Anno's counting book*. New York: Crowell.

Avi. (1990). *The true confessions of Charlotte Doyle*. New York: Orchard Books.

Babbitt, N. (1975). *Tuck everlasting*. New York: Farrar, Straus, and Giroux.

Baker, R. (1987). *The first woman doctor*. New York: Scholastic.

Bauer, M. (1995). *When I go camping with Grandma*. Mahwah, NJ: Bridgewater Books.

Beatty, P. (1984). *Turn homeward, Hannalee*. New York: W. Morrow.

Behrman, C. (1992). *Fiddler to the world: The inspiring life of Itzhak Perlman*. White Hall, VA: Shoe Tree Press.

Benedict, H. (1986). *Safe, strong, and streetwise*. Boston: Atlantic.

Betancourt, J. (1993). *My name is brain-Brian*. New York: Scholastic.

Bleeker, S. (1982). *The Cherokee: Indians of the mountains*. New York: Dodd, Mead & Co.

Bond, M. (1960). *A bear called Paddington*. Boston: Houghton Mifflin.

Brown, M. W. (1947). *Goodnight, moon*. New York: Harper & Row.

Brown, M. W. (1993). *Under the sun and moon and other poems*. New York: Hyperion Books for Children.

Bulla, C. (1966). *Lincoln's birthday*. New York: Crowell.

Bunting, E. (1988). *The sea world book of whales*. New York: HBJ's Children's Books.

Butler, B. (1994). *Witch's fire*. New York: Cobblehill Books.

Cameron, P. (1961). *I can't said the ant*. New York: Coward, McCann, and Geoghegan.

Carle, E. (1971). *Do you want to be my friend?* New York: Crowell.

Carle, E. (1972). *The very hungry caterpillar*. New York: Philomel Books.

Carle, E. (1977). *The grouchy ladybug*. New York: Crowell.

Carle, E. (1985). *The very busy spider*. New York: Philomel.

Carrick, C. (1976). *The accident*. New York: Seabury Press.

Cendrars, B. (1982). *Shadow*. Translated from the French and illustrated by Marcia Brown. New York: Charles Scribner's Sons.

Cleary, B. (1983). *Dear Mr. Henshaw*. New York: William Morrow and Company.

Clifton, L. (1992). *Everett Anderson's goodbye*. New York: Holt, Rinehart, & Winston.

Climo, S. (1993). *The Korean Cinderella*. New York: Harper-Collins.

Cofer, J. (1995). *An island like you: Stories of the barrio*. New York: Orchard Books.

Cole, S. *Working kids on working*. New York: Lothrop, Lee & Shepard.

Collier, J., & Collier, C. (1974). *My brother Sam is dead*. New York: Macmillan.

Couper, H., & Henbest, N. (1996). *Black holes*. New York: Doring Kindersley.

Creech, S. (1994). *Walk two moons*. New York: Harper-Collins.

Crews, D. (1991). *Bigmama's*. New York: Greenwillow Books.

Crump, F. (1990). *Mother Goose nursery rhymes*. Nashville, TN: Winston-Derek Publishers.

Cushman, K. (1994). *Catherine, called Birdy*. New York: Clarion Books.

Cushman, K. (1995). *The midwife's apprentice*. New York: Clarion Books.

D'Aspice, R., & D'Aspice, M. (1990). *The Algonquian*. Vero Beach, FL: Rourke.

Davis, D. (1992). *Behind barbed wire: The imprisonment of Japanese Americans during world war two*. New York: Dutton.

Demi. (1990). *The empty pot*. New York: H. Holt.

dePaola, T. (1973). *Nana upstairs and Nana downstairs*. New York: Penguin.

dePaola, T. (1975). *The cloud book*. New York: Holiday House.

dePaola, T. (1977). *The quicksand book.* New York: Holiday House.

dePaola, T. (1978). *The popcorn book.* New York: Holiday House.

dePaola, T. (1979). *The kids' cat book.* New York: Holiday House.

dePaola, T. (1981). *Now one foot, now the other.* New York: Penguin.

Dixon, F. (1927–). *The Hardy Boys series.* New York: Simon & Schuster.

Drucker, M. (1992). *Grandma's latkes.* San Diego: Harcourt Brace Jovanovich.

Duffy, J. (1992). *Uncle Shamus.* New York: Scribner Young Readers.

Dyer, J. (1996). *Animal crackers: A collection of pictures, poems, and lullabies for the very young.* Boston: Little, Brown & Company.

Emberly, E. (1978). *Ed Emberly's abc.* Boston: Little, Brown & Company.

Farley, W. (1944). *The black stallion.* New York: Random House.

Fleischman, P. (1988). *Joyful noise: Poems for two voices.* New York: Harper & Row.

Forbes, E. (1943). *Johnny Tremain.* Boston: Houghton Mifflin.

Fornari, G. (1996). *A lift-the-flap book: Inside the body.* New York: Dorling Kindersley.

Fox, P. (1973). *The slave dancer.* New York: Bradbury.

Freedman, R. (1987). *Lincoln: A photobiography.* New York: Clarion Books.

Fritz, J. (1981). *Where do you think you're going, Christopher Columbus?* New York: Coward-McCann.

Gackenbach, D. (1977). *Harry and the terrible whatzit.* New York: Clarion.

Gag, W. (1938). *Millions of cats.* New York: Coward.

Galdone, P. (1973). *The little red hen.* New York: Scholastic Press.

Galdone, P. (1973). *The three billy goats gruff.* New York: Seabury Press.

Garland, S. (1993). *Why ducks sleep on one leg.* New York: Scholastic.

George, J. (1972). *Julie of the wolves.* New York: Harper & Row.

Goldin, B. (1994). *Red means good fortune: A story of San Francisco's Chinatown.* New York: Viking Press.

Gonzalez, L. (1994). *The bossy gallito: A traditional Cuban folktale.* New York: Scholastic.

Goodall, J. (1968). *The adventures of Paddy Pork.* New York: Harcourt Brace Jovanovich.

Gordon, M. (1991). *Jumpin' Johnny get back to work! A child's guide to ADHD/hyperactivity.* DeWitt, NY: GSI.

Gould, M. (1991). *Golden daffodils.* Newport Beach, CA: Allied Crafts.

Greenaway, K. (1978). *Kate Greenaway's Mother Goose.* New York: Gramercy Publishing Company.

Grimes, N. (1994). *Meet Danitra Brown.* New York: Lothrop, Lee & Shepard Books.

Gwynne, F. (1970). *The king who rained.* New York: The Young Reader's Press.

Gwynne, F. (1987). *A chocolate moose for dinner.* Englewood Cliffs, NJ: Prentice-Hall.

Hamilton, V. (1968). *The house of Dies Drear.* New York: Macmillan.

Hamilton, V. (1988). *In the beginning.* (B. Moser, illus.). New York: Harcourt.

Hoban, T. (1972). *Push-pull, empty-full.* New York: Macmillan.

Hoberman, M. (1978). *A house is a house to me.* New York: Penguin USA.

Hodges, M. (1984). *Saint George and the dragon.* (T. S. Hyman, illus.). Boston: Little, Brown & Company.

Hope, L. (1904–). *The Bobbsey Twins series.* New York: Grosset & Dunlap, Simon & Schuster.

Howe, D., & Howe, J. (1979). *Bunnicula.* New York: Atheneum.

Hunt. I. (1964). *Across five Aprils.* New York: Follett.

Johnston, J. (1983). *The Indians and the strangers.* New York: Watts.

Keene, C. (1930–) *Nancy Drew series.* New York: Grosset & Dunlap, Simon & Schuster.

Kipling, R. (1932). *Just so stories.* New York: Scott, Foresman and Company.

Kraus, R. (1970). *Whose mouse are you?* New York: Macmillan.

Krementz, J. (1992). *How it feels to live with a physical disability.* New York: Simon & Schuster.

Krisher, T. (1990). *Kathy's hats: A story of hope.* Morton Grove, IL: Albert Whitman.

Landaue, E. (1994). *The Hopi.* New York: Franklin Watts.

Langstaff, J. (1957). *Over in the meadow.* New York: Harcourt Brace Jovanovich.

LeGuin, U. (1968–1972). *The Earthsea trilogy.* New York: Parnassus, Atheneum.

Lindgren, A. (1983). *Ronia, the robber's daughter.* New York: Viking Press.

Lobel, A. (1971). *On the day Peter Stuyvesant sailed into town.* New York: Harper & Row.

MacLachlan, P. (1985). *Sarah, plain and tall.* New York: Harper & Row.

Martin, B., Jr. (1983). *Brown bear, brown bear, what do you see?* New York: Henry Holt & Company.

Mayer, M. (1967). *A boy, a dog, and a frog.* New York: Dial Press.

Mayer, M. (1976). *There's a nightmare in my closet.* New York: Dial Press.

McCaffrey, A. (1978). *Dragonsinger.* New York: Atheneum.

McCaffrey, A. (1986). *Dragonsong.* Toronto, NY: Bantam Books.

Merriam, E. (1988). *You be good and I'll be the night: Jump-on-the-bed poems.* New York: Morrow.

Metzger, L. (1993). *Barry's sister.* New York: Puffin.

Moseley, K. (1986). *The flight of the pterosaurs.* New York: Smithsonian Institution.

Moskin, M. (1972). *I am Rosemarie*. New York: Dell Publishing.

Nabokov, P. (1982). *Native American Indians*. Chicago: Children's Press.

O'Dell, S. (1960). *Island of the blue dolphins*. Boston: Houghton Mifflin.

O'Neill, M. (1961). *Hailstones and halibut bones: Adventures in color*. New York: Doubleday.

Osofsky, A. (1992). *My buddy*. New York: Henry Holt & Company.

Parish, P. (1963). *Amelia Bedelia*. New York: Harper & Row.

Paterson, K. (1990). *The tale of the Mandarin ducks*. (L. Dillon & D. Dillon, illus.). New York: Lodestar/Dutton.

Paulsen, G. (1994). *Mr. Tucket*. New York: Delacorte.

Penick, I. (1986). *The story of the statue of liberty*. New York: Holt, Rinehart, & Winston.

Philbrick, W. (1993). *Freak the mighty*. New York: Scholastic.

Phillips, L. (1995). *Random House treasury of best loved poems*. New York: Greenwillow Books.

Polacco, P. (1990). *Babushka's doll*. New York: Simon & Schuster.

Polacco, P. (1994). *Pink and Say*. New York: Philomel Books.

Prelutsky, J. (1996). *Monday's troll*. New York: Greenwillow Books.

Rappaport, D. (1988). *The Boston coffee party*. New York: Harper.

Rawls, W. (1961). *Where the red fern grows*. New York: Doubleday.

Rey, M. (1944). *Pretzel*. New York: Harper & Row.

Ringgold, F. (1995). *We flew over the bridge: The memoirs of Faith Ringgold*. Boston: Little Brown.

Rofes. (1981). *The kids' book of divorce*. Lexington, MA: Lewis.

Rylant, C. (1982). *When I was young in the mountains*. New York: Dutton.

Rylant, C. (1988). *But I'll be back again: An album*. New York: Orchard.

Savage, D. (1986). *A rumor of otters*. Boston: Houghton Mifflin.

Schertle, A. (1995). *Advice for frogs and other poems*. New York: Lothrop, Lee, & Shepard Books.

Schur, M. (1994). *Circlemaker*. New York: Dial.

Sendak, M. (1962). *Alligators all around*. New York: Harper & Row.

Sendak, M. (1962). *Chicken soup with rice*. New York: Scholastic Press.

Sendak, M. (1962). *One was Johnny*. New York: Harper & Row.

Sendak, M. (1963). *Where the wild things are*. New York: Harper & Row.

Silverstein, S. (1974). *Where the sidewalk ends*. New York: Harper & Row.

Silverstein, S. (1981). *A light in the attic*. New York: Harper & Row.

Sloane, E. (1977). *Diary of an early American boy, Noah Blake, 1805*. New York: Ballantine.

Soto, G. (1990). *Baseball in April and other stories*. San Diego: Harcourt Brace Jovanovich.

Soto, G. (1995). *Chato's kitchen*. New York: Putnam's.

Spier, P. (1988). *People*. New York: Doubleday.

Steptoe, J. (1987). *Mufaro's beautiful daughters*. New York: Lothrop, Lee & Shepard.

Sterling, D. (1987). *Freedom train: The story of Harriet Tubman*. New York: Scholastic.

Stine, R. L. (1984–). *The Goosebumps series*. New York: Scholastic.

St. George, J. (1992). *Dear Dr. Bell—your friend, Helen Keller*. New York: Putnam.

Sword, E. (1995). *A child's anthology of poetry*. Hopewell, NJ: Ecco Press.

Taylor, T. (1969). *The cay*. New York: Doubleday.

Tolan, S. (1983). *A time to fly free*. New York: Scribner.

Tolkien, J. R. R. (1938). *The hobbit*. Boston: Houghton Mifflin.

Tompert, A. (1990). *Grandfather Tang's story*. New York: Crown Publishers.

Turkle, B. (1969). *Thy friend, Obadiah*. New York: Viking.

Van Allsburg, C. (1985). *The polar express*. Boston: Houghton Mifflin.

Van Haeringen, A. (1989). *A cat's tale*. New York: Oxford University Press.

Viorst, J. (1971). *The tenth good thing about Barney*. New York: Macmillan.

Viorst, J. (1981). *If I were in charge of the world and other worries*. New York: Atheneum.

Voigt, C. (1982). *Dicey's song*. New York: Atheneum.

Voigt, C. (1983). *The Callender papers*. New York: Fawcett Juniper.

Westcott, N. (1980). *I know an old lady who swallowed a fly*. Boston: Little, Brown & Company.

White, E. (1995). *Road home*. New York: Scholastic.

Wildsmith, B. (1963). *Brian Wildsmith's abc*. New York: Watts.

Willard, N. (1981). *A visit to William Blake's inn: Poems for innocent and experienced travelers*. New York: Harcourt Brace Jovanovich.

Williams, D. (1992). *Grandma Essie's covered wagon*. New York: Knopf.

Williams, M. (1975). *The velveteen rabbit*. New York: Avon.

Wood, J. (1992). *The man who loved clowns*. New York: Putnam.

Yolen, J. (1987). *Owl moon*. (John Schoenherr, illus.). New York: Philomel Books.

Yorinks, A. (1986). *Hey, Al*. New York: Farrar, Straus & Giroux.

Zemach, M. (1976). *The teeny tiny woman*. New York: Scholastic Press.

Appendix: Awards for Children's Books

NEWBERY MEDAL

Each year the Newbery Medal is awarded to the most distinguished literature book for children.

1999 *Holes*, Louis Sachar (Frances Foster/Farrar, Straus & Giroux)

1998 *Out of the Dust*, Karen Hesse (Scholastic)

1997 *The View From Saturday*, E. L. Konigsburg (Atheneum Books for Young Readers)

1996 *The Midwife's Apprentice*, Karen Cushman (Clarion Books)

1995 *Walk Two Moons*, Sharon Creech (HarperCollins)

1994 *The Giver*, Lois Lowry (Houghton Mifflin)

1993 *Missing May*, Cynthia Rylant (Orchard Books)

1992 *Shiloh*, Phyllis Naylor (Atheneum)

1991 *Maniac McGee*, Jerry Spinelli (Little, Brown & Company)

1990 *Number the Stars*, Lois Lowry (Houghton Mifflin)

1989 *Joyful Noise: Poems for Two Voices*, Paul Fleischman (Harper & Row)

1988 *Lincoln: A Photobiography*, Russell Freedman (Clarion Books)

1987 *The Whipping Boy*, Sid Fleischman (Greenwillow)

1986 *Sarah, Plain and Tall*, Patricia MacLachlan (Harper & Row)

1985 *The Hero and the Crown*, Robin McKinley (Greenwillow)

1984 *Dear Mr. Henshaw*, Beverly Cleary (William Morrow)

1972 *Mrs. Frisby and the Rats of NIMH*, Robert C. O'Brien (Atheneum)

1971 *Summer of the Swans*, Betsy Byars (Viking Press)

1970 *Sounder*, William H. Armstrong (Harper & Row)

1969 *The High King*, Lloyd Alexander (Holt, Rinehart & Winston)

1968 *From the Mixed-up Files of Mrs. Basil E. Frankweiler*, E. L. Konisburg (Atheneum)

1967 *Up a Road Slowly*, Irene Hunt (Follett)

1966 *I, Juan de Pareja*, Elizabeth Borton de Trevino (Farrar, Straus & Giroux)

1965 *Shadow of a Bull*, Maia Wojciechowska (Atheneum)

1964 *It's Like This, Cat*, Emily Neville (Harper & Row)

1963 *A Wrinkle in Time*, Madeleine L'Engle (Farrar, Straus & Giroux)

1962 *The Bronze Bow*, Elizabeth George Speare (Houghton Mifflin)

1961 *Island of the Blue Dolphins*, Scott O'Dell (Houghton Mifflin)

1960 *Onion John*, Joseph Krumgold (Crowell)

1959 *The Witch of Blackbird Pond*, Elizabeth George Speare (Houghton Mifflin)

1958 *Rifles for Watie*, Harold Keith (Crowell)

1957 *Miracles on Maple Hill*, Virginia Sorensen (Harcourt Brace Jovanovich)

1956 *Carry on, Mr. Bowditch*, Jean Lee Latham (Houghton Mifflin)

1955 *The Wheel on the School*, Meindert Dejong (Harper & Row)

1954 *. . . And Now Miguel*, Joseph Krumgold (Crowell)

1953 *Secret of the Andes*, Ann Nolan Clark (Viking Press)

1952 *Ginger Pye*, Eleanor Estes (Harcourt Brace Jovanovich)

1951 *Amos Fortune, Free Man*, Elizabeth Yates (Dutton)

1950 *The Door in the Wall*, Marguerite de Angeli (Doubleday)

1949 *King of the Wind*, Marguerite Henry (Rand McNally)

1948 *The Twenty-One Balloons*, William Pene du Bois (Viking Press)

1947 *Miss Hickory*, Carolyn Bailey (Viking Press)

1946 *Strawberry Girl*, Lois Lenski (Lippincott)

1945 *Rabbit Hill*, Robert Lawson (Viking Press)

1944 *Johnny Tremain*, Esther Forbes (Houghton Mifflin)

1943 *Adam of the Road*, Elizabeth Gray (Viking Press)

1942 *The Matchlock Gun*, Walter Edmonds (Dodd)

1941 *Call It Courage*, Armstrong Sperry (Macmillan)

1940 *Daniel Boone*, James Daugherty (Viking Press)

1939 *Thimble Summer*, Elizabeth Enright (Rinehart)

1938 *The White Stag*, Kate Seredy (Viking Press)

1937 *Roller Skates*, Ruth Sawyer (Viking Press)

1936 *Caddie Woodlawn*, Carol Brink (Macmillan)

1935 *Dobry*, Monica Shannon (Viking Press)

1934 *Invincible Louisa*, Cornelia Meigs (Little Brown)

1933 *Young Fu of the Upper Yangtze*, Elizabeth Lewis (Winston)

1932 *Waterless Mountain*, Laura Armer (Longmans)

1931 *The Cat Who Went to Heaven*, Elizabeth Coatsworth (Macmillan)

1930 *Hitty, Her First Hundred Years*, Rachel Field (Macmillan)

1929 *The Trumpeter of Krakow*, Eric P. Kelly (Macmillan)

1928 *Gay Neck: The Story of a Pigeon*, Dhan Mukerji (Dutton)

1927 *Smoky, the Cowhorse*, Will James (Scribner)

1926 *Shen of the Sea*, Arthur Chrisman (Dutton)

1925 *Tales from Silver Lands*, Charles Finger (Doubleday)

1924 *The Dark Frigate*, Charles Hawes (Atlantic/Little Brown)

1923 *The Voyages of Doctor Doolittle*, Hugh Lofting (Lippincott)

1922 *The Story of Mankind*, Hendrik Van Loon (Liveright)

CALDECOTT MEDAL

Each year the Caldecott Medal is awarded to the most distinguished children's picture book.

1999 *Snowflake Bentley*, Mary Azarian (Houghton Mifflin)

1998 *Rapunzel*, Paul O. Zelinsky (Dutton's Children's Books)

1997 *Golem*, David Wisniewski (Clarion Books)

1996 *Officer Buckle and Gloria*, Peggy Rathmann (G. P. Putnam)

1995 *Smokey Night*, David Diaz (Harcourt Brace)

1994 *Grandfather's Journey*, Allen Say (Houghton Mifflin Company)

1993 *Mirette on the High Wire*, Emily Arnold McCully (G. P. Putnam)

1992 *Tuesday*, David Wiesner (Clarion)

1991 *Black and White*, David Macaulay (Houghton Mifflin)

1990 *Lon Po Po*, adapted and illustrated by Ed Young (Philomel Books)

1989 *Song and Dance Man*, Karen Ackerman, illustrated by Stephen Gammel (Knopf)

1988 *Owl Moon*, Jane Yolen, illustrated by John Schoenherr (Philomel Books)

1987 *Hey, Al*, Arthur Yorinks, illustrated by Richard Egielski (Farrar, Straus & Giroux)

1986 *The Polar Express*, Chris Van Allsburg (Houghton Mifflin)

1985 *Saint George and the Dragon*, retold by Margaret Hodges, illustrated by Trina Schart Hyman (Little, Brown)

1984 *The Glorious Flight: Across the Channel with Louis Bleriot*, Alice and Martin Povensen (Viking Press)

1983 *Shadow*, Blaise Cendrars, translated and illustrated by Marcia Brown (Scribner's)

1982 *Jumanji*, Chris Van Allsburg (Houghton Mifflin)

1981 *Fables*, Arnold Lobel (Harper & Row)

1980 *Ox-Cart Man*, Donald Hall, illustrated by Barbara Cooney (Viking Press)

1979 *The Girl Who Loved Wild Horses*, Paul Goble (Bradbury)

1978 *Noah's Ark*, Peter Spier (Doubleday)

1977 *Ashanti to Zulu*, Margaret Musgrove, illustrated by Leo and Diane Dillon (Dial Press)

1976 *Why Mosquitoes Buzz in People's Ears*, retold by Verna Aardema, illustrated by Leo and Diane Dillon (Dial Press)

1975 *Arrow to the Sun*, adapted and illustrated by Gerald McDermott (Viking Press)

1974 *Duffy and the Devil*, retold by Harve Zemach, illustrated by Margot Zemach (Farrar, Straus & Giroux)

1973 *The Funny Little Woman*, Lafcadio Hearn, retold by Arlene Mosel, illustrated by Blair Lent (Dutton)

1972 *One Fine Day*, Nonny Hogrogian (Macmillan)

1971 *A Story A Story*, Gail E. Haley (Atheneum)

1970 *Sylvester and the Magic Pebble*, William Steig (Windmill Books)

1969 *The Fool of the World and the Flying Ship*, retold by Arthur Ransome, illustrated by Uri Shulevitz (Farrar, Straus & Giroux)

1968 *Drummer Hoff*, adapted by Barbara Emberley, illustrated by Ed Emberley (Prentice-Hall)

1967 *Sam, Bangs and Moonshine*, Evaline Ness (Holt, Rinehart & Winston)

1966 *Always Room for One More*, Sorche Nic Leodhas, illustrated by Nonny Hogrogian (Holt, Rinehart & Winston)

1965 *May I Bring a Friend?* Beatrice Schenk de Regniers, illustrated by Beni Montresor (Atheneum)

1964 *Where the Wild Things Are*, Maurice Sendak (Harper & Row)

1963 *The Snowy Day*, Ezra Jack Keats (Viking Press)

1962 *Once a Mouse*, Marcia Brown (Scribner's)

1961 *Baboushka and the Three Kings*, Ruth Robbins, illustrated by Nicholas Sidjakov (Parnassus)

1960 *Nine Days to Christmas*, Marie Hall Ets and Aurora Labastida (Viking Press)

1959 *Chanticleer and the Fox*, adapted and illustrated by Barbara Cooney (Crowell)

1958 *Time of Wonder*, Robert McCloskey (Viking Press)

1957 *A Tree Is Nice*, Janice Udry, illustrated by Marc Simont (Harper & Row)

1956 *Frog Went A-Courtin'*, retold by John Langstaff, illustrated by Feodor Rojankovsky (Harcourt Brace Jovanovich)

1955 *Cinderella*, illustrated and retold by Marcia Brown (Scribner's)

1954 *Madeline's Rescue*, Ludwig Bemelmans (Viking Press)

1953 *The Biggest Bear*, Lynd Ward (Houghton Mifflin)

1952 *Finders Keepers*, Will Lipkind, illustrated by Nicolas Mordvinoff (Harcourt Brace Jovanovich)

1951 *The Egg Tree*, Katherine Milhous (Scribner's)

1950 *Song of the Swallows*, Leo Politi (Scribner's)

1949 *The Big Snow*, Berta and Elmer Hader (Macmillan)

1948 *White Snow, Bright Snow*, Alvin Tresselt, illustrated by Roger Duvoisin (Lothrop)

1947 *The Little Island*, Golden MacDonald, illustrated by Leonard Weisgard (Doubleday)

1946 *The Rooster Crows*, Maude and Miska Petersham (Macmillan)

1945 *Prayer for a Child*, Rachel Field, illustrated by Elizabeth Orton Jones (Macmillan)

1944 *Many Moons*, James Thurber, illustrated by Louis Slobodkin (Harcourt Brace Jovanovich)

1943 *The Little House*, Virginia Lee Burton (Houghton Mifflin)

1942 *Make Way for Ducklings*, Robert McCloskey (Viking Press)

1941 *They Were Strong and Good*, Robert Lawson (Viking Press)

1940 *Abraham Lincoln*, Ingri and Edgar Parin d'Aulaire (Doubleday)

1939 *Mei Li*, Thomas Handforth (Doubleday)

1938   *Animals of the Bible*, Helen Dean Fish, illustrated by Dorothy P. Lathrop (Lippincott)

CORETTA SCOTT KING AWARD

This award is presented annually at the American Library Association Convention to honor children's books by, for, and/or about African Americans. It was established in memory of Dr. Martin Luther King, Jr., and in honor of Coretta Scott King, his wife. The text award began in 1970, and the illustration award was added in 1979.

1999   Text: *Heaven*, Angela Johnson (Simon & Schuster)

Illustration: *I See the Rhythm*, T. Igus (author) M. Wood (illus.) (Children's Book Press)

1998   Text: *Forged By Fire*, Sharon M. Draper (Atheneum)

Illustration: *In Daddy's Arms I Am Tall: African Americans Celebrating Fathers*, Javaka Steptoe (Lee & Low)

1997   Text: *Slam!* Walter Dean Myers (Scholastic Press)

Illustration: *Minty: A Story of Young Harriet Tubman*, Jerry Pinkney (Dial Books for Young Readers)

1996   Text: *Her Stories*, Virginia Hamilton (Blue Sky Press)

Illustration: *The Middle Passage: White Ships Black Cargo*, Tom Feelings (Dial Books)

1995   Text: *Christmas in the Big House, Christmas in the Quarters*, Patricia and Frederick McKissack (Scholastic)

Illustration: *The Creation*, James Ransome (Holiday House)

1994   Text: *Toning the Sweep*, Angela Johnson (Orchard Books)

Illustration: *Soul Looks Back in Wonder*, Tom Feelings (Dial Books)

1992   Text: *Now Is Your Time! The African-American Struggle for Freedom*, Walter Dean Myers (HarperCollins); *Night on Neighborhood Street*, Eloise Greenfield, illustrated by Jan Spivey Gilchrist (Dial)

Illustration: *Tar Beach*, illustrated by Faith Ringgold (Crown); *Night on Neighborhood Street*, Eloise Greenfield, illustrated by Jan Spivey Gilchrist (Dial); *All Night, All Day: A Child's First Book of African-American Spirituals*, selected and illustrated by Ashley Bryan (Atheneum)

1991   Text: *Road to Memphis*, Mildred D. Taylor (Dial); *Black Dance in America*, James Haskins (Crowell)

Illustration: *Aida*, as told by Leontyne Price, illustrated by Diane and Leo Dillon (Harcourt)

1990   Text: *A Long Hard Journey*, Patricia and Frederick McKissack (Walker and Co.)

Illustration: *Nathaniel Talking*, Eloise Greenfield, illustrated by Jan Spivey Gilchrist (Writers and Readers Publishing)

1989   Text: *Fallen Angels*, Walter Dean Myers (Scholastic)

Illustration: *Mirandy and Brother Wind*, Patricia McKissack, illustrated by Jerry Pinkney (Knopf)

1988   Text: *The Friendship*, Mildred D. Taylor, illustrated by Max Ginsburg (Dial)

Illustration: *Mufaro's Beautiful Daughters*, John Steptoe (Lothrop)

1987   Text: *Justin and the Best Biscuits in the World*, Mildred Pitts Walter (Lothrop)

Illustration: *Half a Moon and One Whole Star*, Crescent Dragon Wagon, illustrated by Jerry Pinkney (Macmillan)

1986   Text: *The People Could Fly: American Black Folktales*, Virginia Hamilton, illustrated by Leo and Diane Dillon (Knopf)

Illustration: *The Patchwork Quilt*, Valerie Flournoy, illustrated by Jerry Pinkney (Dial)

1985   Text: *Motown and Didi*, Walter Dean Myers (Viking)

Illustration: No award given

1984   Text: *Everett Anderson's Goodbye*, Lucille Clifton, illustrated by Ann Grifalconi (Holt)

Illustration: *My Mama Needs Me*, Mildred Pitts Walter, illustrated by Pat Cummings (Lothrop, Lee & Shepard)

1983   Text: *Sweet Whispers, Brother Rush*, Virginia Hamilton (Philomel)

Illustration: *Black Child*, Peter Mugabane (Knopf)

1982   Text: *Let the Circle Be Unbroken*, Mildred D. Taylor (Dial)

Illustration: *Mother Crocodile = Maman-Caiman*, Birago Diop, translated and adapted by Rosa Guy, illustrated by John Steptoe (Delacorte)

1981   Text: *This Life*, Sidney Poitier (Knopf)

Illustration: *Beat the Story-Drum, Pum-Pum*, Ashley Bryan (Atheneum)

1980   Text: *The Young Landlords*, Walter Dean Myers (Viking)

Illustration: *Corn Rows*, Camile Yarbrough, illustrated by Carole Byard (Coward)

1979   Text: *Escape to Freedom: A Play About Young Frederick Douglass*, Ossie Davis (Viking)

Illustration: *Something on My Mind*, Nikki Grimes, illustrated by Tom Feelings (Dial)

1978   *African Dream*, Eloise Greenfield, illustrated by Carole Byard (Day)

1977   *The Story of Stevie Wonder*, James Haskins, illustrated with photos (Lothrop)

1976   *Duey's Tale*, Pearl Bailey, photos by Arnold Skolnick and Gary Azon (Harcourt)

1975   *The Legend of Africania*, Dorothy Robinson, illustrated by Herbert Temple (Johnson)

1974   *Ray Charles*, Sharon Bell Mathis, illustrated by George Ford (Crowell)

1973   *I Never Had It Made*, Jackie Robinson as told to Alfred Duckett, illustrated with photos (Putnam)

1972   *Seventeen Black Artists*, Elton Clay Fax, illustrated with photos (Dods)

1971   *Black Troubadour: Langston Hughes*, Charlemae Rollins, illustrated with photos (Rand)

1970   *Martin Luther King, Jr.: Man of Peace*, Lillie Patterson, illustrated by Victory Mays (Garrard)

The Process of Writing 8

IN THIS CHAPTER

overview

Today many teachers are emphasizing real writing activities in their classrooms. While reading instruction once dominated the primary- and elementary-grade classrooms, writing is now viewed as an equal partner with reading; the two are often taught together. This chapter reviews the different approaches to teaching writing, with a focus on the process approach.

The process approach has been widely used in classrooms in New Zealand and Australia for the past 30 years. However, not until the 1980s did it become popular in classrooms in the United States. Chapter 8 describes in detail a three-stage process writing model: prewriting, writing, and postwriting. Within each of these three stages, you will examine typical activities that aid in the writing process.

To further help you understand the importance of writing within a language arts program, this chapter introduces a number of different types of writing, including various journals, letters, stories, reports, and poetry. As you study them, think about how real writing activities reinforce various skill areas of writing, which will be discussed in specific detail in Chapter 9.

Brief History of Writing Instruction

Prior to the beginning of the twentieth century, the teaching of writing was either ignored, minimized, or focused entirely on skill drills. Classroom teachers were most concerned that their students master the mechanics of writing such as handwriting, spelling, punctuation, and capitalization. Consequently, instruction focused on having children copy passages from the board, take dictation, and memorize rules. There was very little actual creative writing done in class.

Early attempts at reforming the curriculum in America's schools, such as *The Committee of Ten Report* in 1894 and *The Hosic Report* of 1917, suggested that children be encouraged to write about their own life experiences, but few teachers actually followed this advice (Burrows, 1976).

Up until 1960, the English language arts curriculum emphasized reading instruction at the expense of writing activities. What writing was done was characterized by a rigid reliance on teacher-assigned topics, grammar drills, and rule memorization.

Beginning in the 1960s, a new view began to emerge that linked thought to language to writing. Essentially this view argued that mental processes were enhanced through the use of language, both spoken and written. Vygotsky proclaimed that "thought is born through words." Just as a child's speech is an extension of the child's actions, so too a child's writing is an extension of thought (Vygotsky, 1962, 1978). The American linguist James Moffett took a similar view. Moffett's theory of language, described in *Teaching the Universe of Discourse* (1968), focused on "the inner workings behind the talking, reading and writing." Mental thoughts, he argued, move through oral and visual representations. The work of Vygotsky, Moffett, and others caused teachers in the 1960s to consider the relationship among thought, speech, and writing.

In the 1970s, James Britton (1973, 1978, 1986) built on the work of Vygotsky and Moffett. His research, done with secondary students in England, led him to conclude that knowledge is a process, not a storehouse of facts. He urged teachers to focus on the process of students' thinking as it related to writing instruction instead of stressing isolated skills. Writing authority Donald Murray, of the University of New Hampshire, similarly urged his students to view writing as an act of discovery, a way of finding what they have to say (Murray, 1978).

Researchers in the 1970s were also changing the way they approached writing. Previously writing research had focused on gathering large samples of writing, counting errors, and then categorizing those errors; such research influenced teachers' instructional focus on error remediation. The newer approach studied smaller groups of students in the actual act of writing. Janet Emig (1971) observed a group of twelfth-graders while they wrote; later she interviewed them about their writing. She found that writing is unique to the individual and does not follow a fixed formula; nor do students rely on memorized rules. This was contrary to the popularly held belief that rule memorization, particularly in grammar instruction, leads to improved writing. Donald Graves (1973) took a similar case study approach to describe the writing processes used by 7-year-olds. He too noted the uniqueness of the writing act and the importance of the classroom environment for encouraging writing. Skills and drills alone, he concluded, do not make a writer.

Other research studies of students' writing were critical of the writing performance of students and the instructional practices of teachers. James Britton and a team of researchers analyzed thousands of essays by British high school students and found that the type of writing assignments influenced the development of a writer's skills. The Britton team found that school writing assignments focused almost exclusively on communicating factual information rather than on exploring personal feelings and thoughts or solving problems (Britton, 1973, 1978, 1986).

In the United States, Arthur Applebee conducted a similar large-scale analysis of students' writing. He found that the predominant mode of writing in American secondary schools involved fill-in-the-blank or short-answer exercises. He called this *mechanical writing* (Applebee, 1981). Next he studied the writing samples of 55,000 students in grades 4, 8, and 11 and found that most students in all grades—regardless of economic status—were "unable to write adequately except in response to the simplest of tasks" (1986). Something was still drastically wrong with writing instruction in the schools.

Traditional Approaches to Teaching Writing

If you have been taught to write in a particular manner throughout 12 years of schooling, that method has had an influence on the way you write and your attitudes toward writing. Talk with your parents; you will probably discover that they were taught to write by the same method you were. When certain practices go unchallenged, they become accepted. Parents and students begin to think of them as immutable; teachers consider them sacred. Even when research in writing contradicted these classroom practices, they remained unchanged.

What are these traditional practices in writing? There are many, but three stand out: assigned topics, the one-shot approach, and skills as writing.

ASSIGNED TOPICS

For many teachers, creative writing consists primarily of assigning topics to students: "What I did for my summer holiday"; "If I had a dog"; "My scariest Halloween"; "The products of Brazil." Creative writing books still contain these story topics or starter sentences. There is nothing intrinsically wrong with such topics except that students might not want to write about summer vacation, dogs, Halloween, or Brazil. This is particularly true if the teacher assigns a single topic to an entire class of 25 or more students. There is absolutely no way that a teacher could expect every one of those students to be excited about the same topic. In other words, assigning topics ignores the principle of motivation, which is the key to a successful lesson.

ONE-SHOT APPROACH

Related to teacher-assigned topics is the one-shot approach to writing: A teacher assigns a topic in class and the students write on that topic in a single sitting (perhaps they are allowed to finish it at home). Each student then turns in the composition, report, or story; the teacher grades and returns it. For years, this was the way writing was taught by many teachers. However, this is clearly not teaching; this is testing. Giving a student one chance to produce a creative, original work in a limited amount of time is a test. It does not teach children anything about where writers get their ideas, how they begin stories and poems, how they organize and develop characters, how they revise and edit, and so on. The one-shot approach at its best gives students practice in producing something from scratch. At its worst, it is a painful, often humiliating experience, particularly for the student who fears writing and cannot produce the required piece in the given amount of time.

SKILLS AS WRITING

The third most common type of the traditional approaches is the definition of writing in terms of the skills involved in writing. There are skill worksheets, skill workbooks, skill software packages, and so on. Basically all skill activities are alike in that they dissect the writing act into little pieces: nouns, verbs, adjectives; rules for spelling, rules for capitalizing, rules for punctuating. This dissection often results in the separation of instruction into 10 minutes of spelling, then 15 minutes of handwriting, 15 minutes of grammar, and so on. Donald Graves (1990) called this approach the "cha-cha-cha curriculum."

Defining writing in terms of skills is misleading for another reason: In writing, the sum of the parts does not equal the whole. That is, mastery of all the skills of writing (usually determined by some sort of standardized test) does not make one a writer. You may be a good speller but not be able to write an interesting, coherent sentence. You may know how to identify the adverbs in a sentence but not be able to string sentences together into a logical paragraph. You may be able to list the uses of periods, commas, and quotation marks but still not be able to write realistic dialogue within a story. In short, these skills are the tools used in writing, but they do not *equal* good writing.

Although the three traditional approaches to teaching writing still persist in many classrooms, a new approach has also taken hold. All the research in the 1960s and 1970s that suggested students really need to write in order to learn to write came together in 1974 when the federal government funded a grant to support the Bay Area Writing Project at the University of California at Berkeley. Founded by James Gray, the Bay Area Writing Project introduced elementary and secondary schoolteachers to the workshop approach to teaching writing. Teachers using this workshop method go through a series of stages in writing, such as drafting, revising, and editing; this came to be known as the process approach.

Teachers who completed the Bay Area summer writing workshops went back to their school districts across the United States and taught this process approach to their colleagues in staff development meetings; another unique aspect of the Bay Area Writing Project was its focus on teachers teaching teachers. The program was so successful that it eventually became the National Writing Project, which now funds workshops for teachers in every state of the union, who in turn disseminate the ideas of process writing (Goldberg, 1989).

The success of the process approach to writing can be seen in the results of the 1992 National Assessment of Educational Progress (NAEP). Over 30,000 students in grades 4, 8, and 12 were asked to respond to various writing tasks. Preceding the task, students were given a blank sheet of paper and encouraged to do prewriting. Data were also gathered on students, teachers, and administrators regarding instructional practices in their schools. The overall results showed that "students whose teachers encouraged certain aspects of process writing averaged higher performance on the NAEP writing assessment" (NAEP Facts, 1996, p. 1).

A Process Approach Model

A **process approach** to writing involves a series of stages that leads a writer from the discovery of an idea through a number of revisions, culminating in the production of an original work. In the course of the process, writers may spend many hours thinking about writing; talking to other writers; listening to other writers; reading books, magazines, and newspapers; making doodles, notes, and outlines; writing, revising, stopping in disgust or frustration, and then starting again. All this is part of the process; this is how writers write.

There is no magic formula to be memorized. There is, however, a general process that can be taught to students as a series of stages that will help them on their way to becoming writers.

James Britton (1978), Janet Emig (1971), L. Flower and R. Hayes (1994), Donald Graves (1994), Nancie Atwell (1998), Lucy Calkins (1994), and others have described models of process writing consisting of three main stages: prewriting, writing, and postwriting, all of which act and react with each other in a recursive manner. Figure 8.1 shows the three stages, their related steps, and the interactive nature of the process.

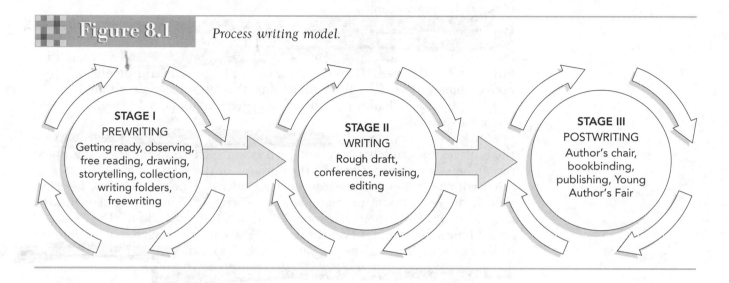

Figure 8.1   *Process writing model.*

STAGE I
PREWRITING
Getting ready, observing, free reading, drawing, storytelling, collection, writing folders, freewriting

STAGE II
WRITING
Rough draft, conferences, revising, editing

STAGE III
POSTWRITING
Author's chair, bookbinding, publishing, Young Author's Fair

STAGE ONE: PREWRITING

The process approach does not begin with writing. It begins with thinking about writing: What do I want to write about? What are the things that interest me? What do I care about? These are the thoughts that preoccupy writers, child and adult alike. Donald Graves has called this the *rehearsal stage* of writing (1994). This is the time when writers plan and organize their thoughts. It is the first essential stage in the writing process. In fact, Donald Murray (1985) has contended that it is the most important stage. It is also the most ignored stage.

The *prewriting stage* consists of a number of steps that teachers may use to support and motivate students during this portion of the writing process.

Getting Ready

Getting students ready to write involves providing them with three things: time to write, space to write, and the materials for writing. A set time should be designated each day as writing time. It can be the first thing in the morning, a period before lunch, or the last period of the day. Teacher and students should decide together when the best time for writing is, based on the school schedule.

Finding just the right place to write is next. For some children, it is a favorable corner of the room or a specially designated writing table; others prefer to write at their own desks. Some students like to crawl under the teacher's large desk and work. In some schools, students can even take their chairs out into the hallway or work in a special section of the library.

The materials for writing include paper (lined and unlined), pencils, pens, felt-tip markers, writing folders, notebooks, crayons, scissors, scotch tape, and paste. For most writers, getting ready to write means going through a mini-ritual of arranging pencils, pens, papers, and so on. Additional materials might include a classroom library for doing research work, reference books such as dictionaries and encyclopedias, computer/word processing access, and picture files for stimulating the imagination.

Observing

"I can't think of anything to write about, Teacher." This is a complaint heard all too frequently in the elementary grades. Students think that ideas should come to them automatically; they don't realize that sometimes writers need to seek out fresh ideas when their creative wells are dry. One way to do this is through observation.

Observation for the purpose of stimulating writing can be very simple or involve considerable time and planning. For example, one day you might take children on a brief field trip around the school grounds. Have them carefully observe the trees, flowers, plants, and playground equipment. Do they notice something interesting? Something they just took for granted in the past? Why is that chattering squirrel burying nuts beside the large oak tree? There's a story idea!

On another day, take them on a field trip inside the school building. Are there places the students have not been before? The nurse's office, the cafeteria kitchen, and the area behind the curtains of the school auditorium are all filled with potential writing subjects for students. One teacher took her class to visit the boiler room in their elementary school. There they spoke with the custodian. Back in their classroom, their teacher read aloud *The Planet of Junior Brown* by Virginia Hamilton, a story about a young boy who actually hides out and lives in the basement of his school. Afterward the children decided to write a mystery story set in their own school.

Free Reading

Charlotte Huck (1987), an authority on children's literature, has said that reading a variety of books leads children to experiment with different literary forms in their own writing. For example, second-graders who read Judith Viorst's *Alexander and the Terrible, Horrible, No Good, Very Bad Day* wanted to write about their own terrible days. Reading Jean George's *My Side of the Mountain* inspired one fourth-grade boy to keep a journal on his next camping trip. Marguerite de Angeli's Newbery Medal–winner, *The Door in the Wall*, sent a group of girls to the library to research more about fourteenth-century England in order to write their own adventure novel. Scott O'Dell's *Sing Down the Moon* caused a group of Native American students in Oklahoma to write to Navaho students in Arizona. And reading Shel Silverstein's humorous verse has encouraged many a child to try writing poetry.

Thus a writing program should also include free time each day for students to read and to talk about books (Atwell, 1998). The two cannot be separated nor taught as distinct entities. Rather than talking about the reading program or writing time, Jerry Harste (1990) has argued for a *literacy curriculum*, in which students are invited to read and write throughout the day as a natural part of the learning process—as natural as listening and speaking.

Drawing

For many children, drawing is the best way to get ready to write. Children often have a vague idea of what they want to say but don't know where to begin. So they draw doodles, scribbles, cartoons, or illustrations from stories they have read. As children draw, they are discovering the stories in their head. Drawing for many students is a form of rehearsing; this is even true of older youngsters.

In her book *In the Middle* (1998), Atwell has written about one student named Jeff. Jeff was older than the rest of the class—already 16—but barely reading at the primary level. He'd been retained in earlier grades and was thought to be learning-disabled. While the other students in Atwell's class did various prewriting activities, Jeff sat alone, mumbling to himself and drawing. Each day in class while the others wrote, Jeff drew. One day, as Atwell prodded him to get busy and write in class, Jeff explained, "This is the way I do it, the way I write" (p. 8). For Jeff and many other students, drawing is the way to rehearse ideas before putting them into words.

Storytelling

Research has shown a natural link between hearing and telling stories and students' desire to write stories (King, 1989; Short, Harste, & Burke, 1996). From hearing, telling, and reading stories, children intuitively acquire the basic concepts of stories: Aspects of plot, setting, and character and a sense of sequential ordering of events are first tested at the oral level through storytelling. Later, these same storytellers want to write their stories to share with even more people. Like drawing, oral storytelling serves a rehearsal function prior to writing.

Collection

Two things make writing difficult for many youngsters: They feel they have nothing to say, and they don't know how to spell all the words they want to include in their stories. Both issues are real for children and must be addressed by teachers. Too often a potentially good writing lesson degenerates into a sea of waving hands and shouting voices: "Teacher, how do you spell . . . ?" One way to help students overcome these twin feelings of inadequacy is through collection. Collection is a type of brainstorming that helps children acquire the ideas, words, and information they will later use in their writing (Murray, 1990).

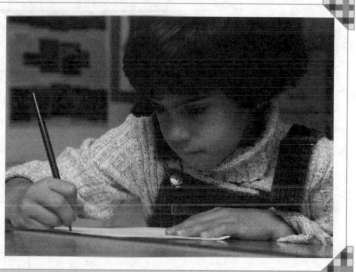

In this strategy, the teacher introduces a topic to the whole class. Better still, children volunteer topics they would like to write about, such as the NASA space shuttle, the upcoming World Series, or a mystery story set in Tahiti. The class selects one of the topics on which to do a collective brainstorming. Ideas and terms are called out. The teacher writes them on the board. This is done quickly, and everyone's suggestions are accepted. When finished, the class has a graphic representation of the ideas and also an accurate spelling of some of the words they may want to use in their writing. The next step is to transfer this list to a poster or file folder that can serve as a source of ideas and correct spellings in the days of writing to come. Once the collection strategy has been demonstrated, youngsters can do their own brainstorming in small groups or individually without the teacher's help.

Collection can also be done in ways other than mere listing. For example, brainstorming can take the form of an outline, a web diagram, or a cluster. *Outlining* begins with mental brainstorming but results in a written outline to help a writer sequence a series of events or points more clearly. It can be used with all types of writing but lends itself particularly well to report writing or persuasive essays. In using outlining, students learn to set up their ideas in a form like the one in Figure 8.2.

	GENERIC	EXAMPLE: TEXAS INDEPENDENCE

Figure 8.2

Outline format.

I. Main Idea
   1. Supporting detail
   2. Supporting detail
II. Main Idea
   1. Supporting detail
   2. Supporting detail
III. Main Idea
   1. Supporting detail
   2. Supporting detail

I. Political Issues
   1. Expansion of slavery
   2. Independence from Mexico
II. Economic Issues
   1. Trade with United States
   2. Expansion of cotton into Texas
III. Two Major Battles
   1. The Alamo
   2. San Jacinto

Webbing is a technique that extends mental brainstorming by placing the terms generated into a diagram that resembles a spider's web. Each term is connected to another by a strand of the web; the lines in a web diagram indicate the relationships among the various terms generated. Like outlining, webbing allows the student to see the entire picture along with the separate parts of the work to be created. Webbing is also referred to as *semantic mapping* (Johnson, Pittelman, & Heinlich, 1986). It is a valuable guide that can keep students on track, show them where they need to go, and maintain a coherent flow in their writing. Figure 8.3 shows a web created by a second-grade class.

Figure 8.3

Sample second-grade web: Animals.

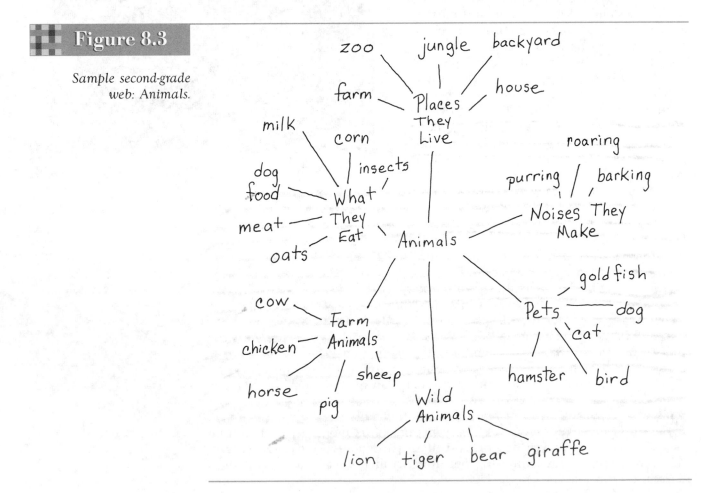

A cluster diagram is another variation of the outline; it is similar to the web diagram. To create a **cluster diagram,** students begin with a single word (the theme, subject, or key concept), write it in the center of the page, and circle it; as students think of related terms, they circle them and connect them with lines to the central term. The result is a diagram of lines and circles indicating a type of schema or outline the writer may follow. Rico (1983) developed the cluster diagram as a way to get students to picture what an entire piece of writing may look like before beginning to write. Tompkins (1990) has recommended clustering as a way to help elementary students recognize how one idea is associated with another and how all ideas in a written work relate to a main theme. Figure 8.4 shows a cluster diagram.

BEYOND THE CLASSROOM

Many students start writing or try to start before they are really ready to write. They have not done any preliminary activities such as the ones described here. Visit an elementary classroom and work with a small group of writers in search of topics. Teach them how to outline, web, or cluster. Then observe how the children use these techniques to organize their writing. What positive aspects do you note? What difficulties do the students encounter? Make an outline, web, or cluster to represent your own experience teaching these students.

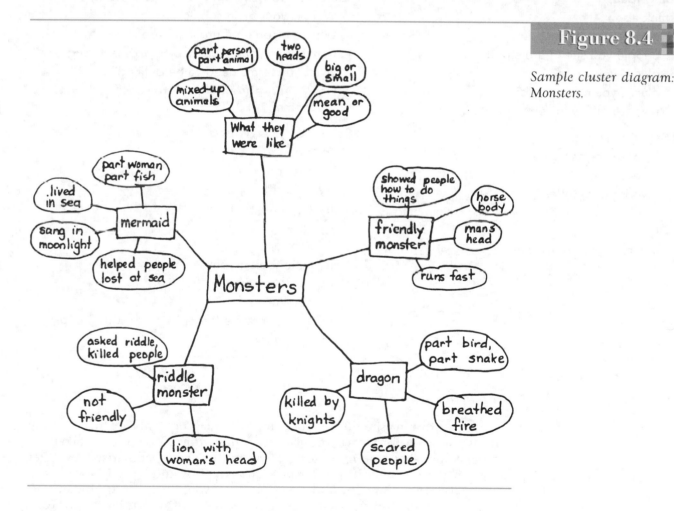

Figure 8.4

Sample cluster diagram: Monsters.

Writing Folders

The writing folder is highly personal; no two look exactly alike. A writing folder can be an ordinary file folder. Students write their names on their folders and decorate them. Each folder contains blank paper for drawing as well as lined paper for writing. Students use these folders daily for drawing,

The only way to teach them to write correctly is to have them write.

FANNY JACKSON COPPIN

doodling, and making lists of things to write about later. A student's folder may also contain outlines for stories, research notes for reports, character sketches, quotes, or snatches of dialogue. When kept on a regular basis, the folder becomes the source of ideas for later written works. The key is to use the folder regularly so that writing becomes a daily habit. (Writing folders are discussed in more detail later in this chapter.)

Nancie Atwell (1998) structures how her eighth-graders use their folders by stapling forms inside the folders. For example, one form is a list of ideas for writing that a student can refer to when the creative well runs dry. Another form lists the titles and dates of work that the student has finished and serves as a chronological record for the school year. Personal skill lists are kept on a form called "Things I can do." Figure 8.5 is an example of some different lists that can be included in folders to help students get ready to write.

Figure 8.5   *Ideas for folder lists.*

Finding Ideas

Think about:

    people you know

    people you see in the street

    places you've been

    places you'd like to visit

    favorite gifts you've received

Make lists about:

    favorite sports figures

    favorite movie stars

    favorite book titles

    favorite cartoon and comic book characters

    favorite colors

    favorite types of clothing

Questions to Ask Yourself Before Writing

    What is your main subject?

    What are some different subtopics?

    Can you compare your subject to something else?

    What key terms need to be defined?

    Do you move from general to specific, or the reverse?

Some Possible Writing Forms

    Try a poem

    Try a letter

    Try a short story

    Try a chapter in a novel

    Try an essay

    Try a report

    Try an autobiography

    Try a book review

    Try a folktale

    Try a collaborative (group) writing with friends

    Try a mystery story

Freewriting

A writing program should include time each day not only for free reading but also—obviously—for writing. The term *freewriting* has, however, taken on a special meaning among writers. It was coined and popularized by Peter Elbow in his books *Writing Without Teachers* (1973) and *Writing with Power* (1981). Elbow was searching for an activity that would help his freshman English composition students overcome their fear of writing. Freewriting as one of the prewriting activities in a process approach is now also widely used with elementary-grade students who fear the blank page (Frager et al., 1987). For anyone who has experienced "writer's block," **freewriting** is most useful and includes the following three steps:

1. Try to relax and clear your mind for a moment.

2. When the teacher gives the signal, start writing on anything you can think of but don't stop or pause.

3. Continue writing until the teacher gives the signal to stop (usually after about five minutes).

That's it: continuous writing for five minutes without pausing and without worrying about spelling or punctuation or sentence structure. Just let your thoughts flow onto the paper. At first this activity may seem strange to your students, especially if they have been raised on the notion that writing should look neat and mechanically correct on the first effort. Stress that this is an exercise to get them started in writing and that they should relax and enjoy it.

Elbow also described a variety of follow-up activities that can be used with the freewriting exercise. Students can reread their own freewriting material and search for words, phrases, sentences, or ideas they might later want to develop into a story, poem, or essay. Or they can read their freewriting to a friend, perhaps even to the whole class. Elbow suggested focusing freewriting from time to time on specific topics such as, How much allowance should a fourth-grader get and why? The rules are the same except that all the students now write on a single topic for 5 or 10 minutes. Remember that the idea is still to explore a topic rapidly without concern for the mechanics of writing.

The Classroom Vignette that follows shows one teacher leading her students into writing.

Vignette in the classroom

Mrs. Guen is settled into a big, overstuffed chair in one corner of the room. Around her on the floor sit 18 first-graders, listening and watching as she reads to them from Eric Carle's *The Very Hungry Caterpillar*. As she reads aloud, she shows the students the pictures of the caterpillar moving from page to page, gobbling everything up in sight and gradually changing into a butterfly. When she is finished reading, she asks, "What did this story make you think of?" Hands shoot up. She calls on Teri.

"Last week we found that caterpillar and put him in a jar."

"Yeah, and we also found a spider and some ants," chimes in Ramon.

"That's right, boys and girls. We went on a field trip and found all sorts of interesting insects right around our own school. Janey, what was your favorite insect?"

"The caterpillar, I guess," says Janey, looking around shyly.

"Mine was the icky worm we stepped on," says Jonathan, making the rest of the group laugh.

"OK now. Each one of you imagine your favorite insect, and let's pretend to move around the room like a butterfly, a caterpillar, a spider, or whatever you want."

Soon all the students are crawling, slithering, walking on all fours, flapping their arms. They giggle, laugh, bump into each other, and then collapse in a heap. Then their teacher gathers them together again; they brainstorm all the words they can think of about their insects. The teacher writes the list on the large pad attached to the easel.

"Now, boys and girls, take out your writing folders. There's extra paper and pencils at the writing center if you need them. You may want to draw a picture of what we've been talking about or start a story or perhaps write a poem about an insect."

Most children take a crayon or pencil and go off with best friends to draw. Some of the children go to their desks, hunch over their paper, and begin to write. A few clamor around the teacher, asking for more help to get started on a drawing or story.

STAGE TWO: WRITING

Writing is the second major stage in a process approach; there are four main steps in this stage: producing the rough draft, conferencing about the draft, revising the content and structure of the work, and finally editing to correct the mechanics of writing.

Producing the Rough Draft

All writers write from a *rough draft*. Children need to be taught this beginning in the first grade. Primary-grade teachers sometimes use the term *sloppy copy*, which the children can more easily understand. The children know this is their time to get their ideas down on paper, to begin to shape their stories, poems, pen pal letters, and so on. Intermediate teachers continue to reinforce the idea of the rough draft with their students. By middle school, it should be second nature to the student to work from rough drafts.

Teaching the concept of rough drafts is one way to help young writers achieve that final, polished product that looks like a real story or poem they might read in a book. Generally speaking, the more drafts a child writes, the better the final copy. Each successive draft, like chisel strokes on a piece of marble, refines the work just a little more. This is what Donald Murray meant when he described writing as a craft.

Youngsters who are not used to writing rough drafts need the teacher's assistance to keep them going. Explain to them that in a rough draft the writer's goal is to get ideas down on paper and complete the work, be it a poem, story, essay, newspaper article, or science report. Get them to focus on the content, not the mechanics; it is the latter that trips up most young writers (Sommers, 1994). Children get frustrated easily when they cannot spell a word, forget how to use capital letters, or make even the slightest error. Primary-grade students scrunch over their papers, biting their lips as they try to draw a *q* or *z*. The first error or smudge, wham! They ball up their papers, throw them away, and start again. It's no wonder that after 20 minutes of so-called writing time these students barely complete one sentence.

In mini-lesson lectures, provide students with the following tips for writing rough drafts:

- Write on one side of the page only; use the back for taking notes.
- Skip lines and leave wide margins for adding material later.
- Cross out rather than erase; you may want to reuse something later.
- Date and number your various drafts; keep a record of your progress.

Conferencing

At some point during the writing stage, children discover that they are writing for someone—a reader—this is the concept of **audience.** Awareness of audience is something that teachers work to develop in their student writers, but it takes time and practice. One way to help young writers achieve this sense of audience awareness is through conferencing. Donald Graves (1994), Lucy Calkins (1994), Nancie Atwell (1998), N. Sommers (1994), and Mary Heller (1990) have all stressed the importance of conferencing. Before studying the different types of conferences, keep in mind that the three main purposes of **conferencing** are to provide positive feedback and encouragement to the student, to answer any questions the student may have, and to discover any problem areas that may need to be retaught. It is primarily through conferencing—not through the awarding of grades—that students grow as writers.

Teacher–pupil conferences. Once a student has produced a rough draft, she or he is ready for a teacher–pupil conference. Most teacher–pupil conferences are brief and informal. Nancie Atwell (1998) likes to carry a small chair with her and sit next to her students while they read their rough drafts to her. As with all conferences, the first focus should be on the content of the piece, what the writer is trying to say. Later the teacher and pupil may talk about specific trouble spots in a work, such as how to punctuate dialogue in a story. The teacher should move about the room continually, meeting with students for brief chats and listening to them read aloud passages they are proud of or need help with.

Some teachers prefer to set up more formal conferences with their students (Heller, 1990). The teacher may call a child to his or her desk and ask the child to read the story aloud. Then the teacher and pupil can discuss the written work. If formal conferences are used, the children should know about them in advance. Set up a schedule and post it in the room. This gives students a chance to prepare for the conference and perhaps redo their rough drafts one more time. Donald Graves stressed in *A Fresh Look at Writing* (1994) that teachers should ask questions during the conference rather than make suggestions or give advice: Does your opening paragraph introduce the main character or describe the setting for your story? Have you repeated something that can be omitted? How can you make your dialogue sound more realistic? If your ending comes too soon, how can you keep the reader in suspense a bit longer? A teacher can always tell children how to improve their work; the skill in conferencing is to "nudge" writers toward discovering this for themselves.

Peer-to-peer conferences. Paralleling the teacher–pupil conference is the peer conference between two or more children. Peer conferences are important for a number of reasons. First, they relieve some of the pressure on teachers to meet with every student every day. With class sizes averaging 25 or more, it is physically impossible for the teacher to conference with every child each day. Second, feedback from other students is a powerful motivator. It is not necessary for peers to comment and critique every item in one another's papers, just to respond to them. Finally, peer-to-peer conferences reinforce the notion that the teacher is not the only audience willing and able to read what children have written (Calkins, 1991, 1994).

To help students develop some basic conferencing skills, you need to set some guidelines. Discuss with your class and demonstrate some of the kinds of questions they might ask one another during a conference: questions about the beginning, middle, or end of the work; questions about the characters, setting, or plot. They should focus on the content of the work. Is it clear what the writer is trying to say? If not, where is the problem? Avoid nit-picking about mechanical errors such as spelling, capitalization, and punctuation. Figure 8.6 lists some suggestions for peer conferences.

To reinforce what conferencing should and should not be like, one middle school teacher modeled the *fishbowl technique.* The teacher asks for a student volunteer to help act out a conference. Teacher and pupil sit facing each other with the rest of the class seated around them observing—like watching two fish in a fishbowl. The teacher and student then role-play two different conferences, a poor one and a good one. A poor conference has the teacher and pupil pointing out each other's errors: "You misspelled *hippopotamus* again, dummy." "Don't you

Figure 8.6

Suggestions for peer-to-peer conferences.

1. Bring question list and refer to it.
2. Read draft orally to partner.
3. No proofreading of mechanical errors at these sessions.
4. Rotate conferencing partners.
5. Ask questions rather than give suggestions.
6. Have option of conferencing only with teacher.

When I began to write, I found this was the best way to make sense out of my life.

JOHN CHEEVER

know *Virginia* begins with a capital?" "You forgot to indent your paragraph." Finding errors is easy, but it is certainly not helpful to a writer to hear about them constantly. A good conference is one that centers on the content of the piece being read. The reader shows a genuine interest in the work. "Hey, this is really neat about Dracula dying in the end. I'm not exactly sure how it happened. Can you tell me more?" After the children have observed the teacher and student in the fishbowl, the teacher asks for student volunteers to continue the role playing until satisfied that the entire class has at least some idea as to what should take place during a peer-to-peer conference.

The success of a conference is best measured by the quality of the discussion between the writer and reader. When both parties interact with each other in a positive and constructive manner, both benefit. The author gains a new perspective from the knowledge and insights of another person. Reading and discussing the writer's work allow the reader to see how the other person handled a topic that she or he might be writing on someday.

Revising and Editing

Revising and editing are the two final steps that a writer does during the writing stage. Classifying these steps can be a bit misleading, for writers actually revise and edit throughout the entire writing process, beginning with the prewriting stage (writers revise and edit in their heads) and continuing through the rough draft. But it is not until the end of the writing process, when a writer has a completed work in front of him or her, that the focus should be on revising and editing.

A second problem with revising and editing is that the two terms are often confused or used interchangeably. In one sense, revising and editing are the same: They both involve making changes to a rough draft as part of the process of crafting a piece of written work into final form. On the other hand, they are different in perspective: *Revising* involves looking at the entire work, whereas *editing* focuses on changes at the word and sentence level.

The term *revision* means "to resee" a work: to look at a piece of writing with new eyes (Murray, 1990). It also means to rethink and reflect on what you are trying to say (Fulwiler, 1987b). Is your writing clear? If not, perhaps you need to add something, possibly an example or additional details to support your argument. Does your writing flow smoothly from one idea or scene to another? If not, you may need to reorder your paragraphs, restructure a sentence or two, strengthen your opening, or beef up the middle. Have you chosen just the right words to make your point strong enough? Perhaps another word would do, one that is clearer, more specific, or more colorful. Changing, omitting, altering, and rearranging are what revision is about. Revision is the big picture.

Many writers consider revision the key to successful writing; Toby Fulwiler has called it "the operational core of the composing process" (1987b, p. 60). The writer may omit redundant material and add clarifying details or examples. A weak opening may need to be reworked. Perhaps the best lead sentence occurs in the third paragraph and needs to be moved to the beginning. Conclusions or endings may need to be altered to reflect earlier changes. And in some cases, revision means discarding what has been painstakingly written and starting again. Figure 8.7 summarizes some issues concerning revision.

Figure 8.7

Steps in revision.

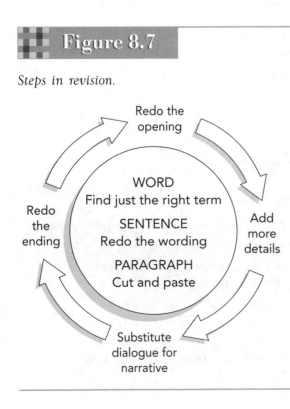

Redo the opening

Add more details

Substitute dialogue for narrative

Redo the ending

WORD
Find just the right term

SENTENCE
Redo the wording

PARAGRAPH
Cut and paste

The capacity to revise successfully is the mark of a mature writer. Young children therefore find revision difficult. Consequently, they focus on editorial changes, such as correcting spelling mistakes, rather than on redoing an entire sentence or discovering where a paragraph might be omitted. A first-grader may be satisfied with her or his rough draft and merely want to recopy it in neater handwriting. This is not true revision, but at least it establishes a pattern for building on later. Second- and third-graders learn to cut and paste, move sentences around, and change words. Still older students may go through three or four revisions, while also discussing their papers with a number of friends, before they feel satisfied that they have said exactly what they intended to say. Professional writers often rewrite an opening sentence in a short story, a line in a poem, or the final paragraph of a novel dozens of times over many months.

> *There is no good writing, only rewriting.*
> JAMES THURBER

There is no one correct way to revise. Some writers rework each sentence before moving on to the next. Others work rapidly, getting down the entire piece as quickly as possible and then going back to smooth and polish the work. Donald Murray (1990) has recommended "listening to the text" while reading it aloud. The key is in recognizing that interesting, clear, effective writing does not happen by accident; it is the result of much rewriting.

If revision means seeing the big picture, then editing requires using the fine lens. Both steps are necessary for clear, concise, effective writing; in this sense, editing can be taught as a part of the revision process. However, teachers often find that this encourages students to focus exclusively on making changes only at the word level (editing) and not at the sentence, paragraph, and organizational levels (revision). Therefore, editing should really be taught as a separate skill that comes after revising.

There are two substeps involved in editing: proofreading and correcting. *Proofreading* is a slow, word-by-word reading to identify errors. Reading slowly in search of misspelled words, incorrectly used punctuation marks, capital letter omissions, tense shifts, run-on sentences, sentence fragments, and so on is difficult for young children. Correcting the errors once they are found may be even more difficult. But editing can be made less painful if you use one or more of the following techniques:

1. Teach students to read their own work after they are finished.
2. Pair off students to read each other's papers.
3. Create editing circles in which groups of children are taught to skim or read one another's papers but only for a single type of error. For example, one child might read to identify possible spelling errors, another student would look for capitalization errors, a third child for punctuation errors, and so on.
4. You are the final editor, indicating possible changes by a pencil check mark and then returning the paper for the child to make the corrections. Take care not to give the student too many things to correct at once. Figure 8.8 shows examples of some common proofreading marks with which children should become familiar.

When editing skills are taught properly, students see them as part of the refining process. Editing is a final chance to clean up the rough spots in a work in order to communicate more clearly with a reader (Murray, 1990). Writers understand that misspelled words, incorrectly used punctuation, sentence fragments, and so on throw a reader off track. Too many errors may even cause the reader to begin focusing on the errors rather than the story. This is why editing is so important.

BEYOND THE CLASSROOM

Select a piece you or someone else has written. Reread it with an eye to revising and editing to make the piece clearer and more concise. Use the proofreading marks as shown in Figures 8.8 and 8.9.

Figure 8.8   *Some proofreading marks.*

Mark	Use	Example
$\wedge$	to insert (add) a letter, word, or sentence	*were* The boys $\wedge$ hungry.
$\P$	to begin or indent a paragraph	$\P$ Four horses left the corral. They headed across the fields and toward the mountains. Soon they were gone from sight.
e	to delete (take out) a letter, word, or sentence	We had to ~~the~~ leave the party at 8:00 P.M.
$/$	to change a capital letter to a lowercase letter	My Friend John left his bike in the street.
$\underline{\underline{}}$	to change a lowercase letter to a capital letter	They flew to charleston, South Carolina.
⬭ SP	to check the spelling of a word	He rode his (bicicle) to school. *SP*

Figure 8.9 shows a student's rough draft with some editing marks. Study it to see what changes the student should make next.

STAGE THREE: POSTWRITING

The final stage in a process approach is *postwriting*, bringing the work to completion in a form suitable for sharing with others. This may mean using a word processing program to create a professional-looking manuscript either to place on the class bulletin board or to submit to the school newspaper for possible publication. It can also mean reading the work aloud to the entire class or having still another conference with the teacher. And occasionally postwriting includes getting a written piece ready to submit for a grade.

In the traditional approach to teaching writing, a student always submitted a paper to the teacher to be graded. The teacher thus became the only audience for the child and the grade the sole reason for writing. It is no wonder that so many students hate writing and associate it with red marks and letter grades.

Sharing is a positive alternative to grades. The child who finishes a story, poem, or play wants to share it with as many others as possible. Popular ways of sharing written work include:

- Displaying the written piece on an author's bulletin board
- Performing the piece as reader's theatre with some friends
- Mailing letters to pen pals, businesses, or relatives
- Placing reports in the library for others to use

Figure 8.9

> *Where the Earth Ends*
>
> Where do does the earth end?
> Hi! I'm Amy and this stories story's
> about a girl named pamela who wents to no know
> where
> wear the earth ends but no one
> gives her the answer.
>   One day a girl named Pamela went
> outside. Her long soft black hair
> hanging in her face. Her Dad was
> looking at the sunset. " Dad where
> does the earth end? The earth ends
> where nobody goes." he said. She Pamela
> thought she needed a better anser.
> So she went and found her Mom
> sitting on the couch. She and asked
> "Mom where does the earth end? The
> earth has no end" her Mom said.
> But it must end," said Pamela. Then
> her Mom said strangely, I'll tell you
> the truth later."
>   End Part One

Sample rough draft with editing marks.

- Performing an original story or play with puppets

Following are some additional ways for sharing students' writings that teachers have found to be successful postwriting motivational activities.

Author's Chair

Many primary-grade teachers like to encourage children to be comfortable reading aloud from their own writing to the rest of the class. One way of doing this is by establishing a time for *author's chair* as a part of the regular writing program (Graves & Hansen, 1983).

Renee Rogers, a teacher in Red Rock, Oklahoma, uses author's chair with her first-graders as follows: A chair is placed prominently at the front of the room. At a certain time of the day, Mrs. Rogers calls the entire class together. Teacher and children alike sit comfortably on the carpet. She then asks for volunteers to read their work. Sometimes these are works in progress, but most often they are finished pieces. While the child is reading, the rest of the group listens politely. When the child is finished reading, Mrs. Rogers asks for comments from the group. The students know they are expected to say something positive about the work. Positive comments—not negative corrections—build self-confidence in young writers. The children can also ask questions of the author if they would like to know more about something. When the students' questions falter, Mrs. Rogers steps in. Not all children volunteer for author's chair immediately, but as the school year progresses, even the shyest child in Mrs. Rogers's class eventually wants to share something he or she has written.

Bookbinding

In the past, bookbinding in the classroom was considered an enrichment activity to be done once in a while (Purdy, 1973; Weiss, 1974). Today, bookbinding is an integral and popular part of the process approach to writing. It is also one of the most motivating ways to get students to read. Following are some of the many ways to help children bind their written stories into books that can be read by others for years to come (Rhoten & Yellin, 1993).

Staple bookbinding. Staple pages together with a cover. Use colored mystic tape to cover the staples and reinforce the book spine. Any type of cover may be used, but this technique does not work well with oversized books. A bookbinding learning center can also facilitate this process.

Ring bookbinding. Use a hole punch to make at least two holes along the back of the pages and the book cover. Insert the rings to form the binding for the book. Shower curtain rings, key rings, even chicken rings (for banding poultry) are excellent for ring bookbinding.

Stitched bookbinding. Using a hole punch, make holes along the left side of the book cover and pages. Using a blunt-end needle or special plastic needle, sew the pages together. Yarn, quilting thread, even dental floss or fishing line all work well.

Library bookbinding. This is the ultimate in bookbinding, and the result is something children will treasure for years. You will need contact paper, stiff cardboard, needle, thread, and glue or book tape. Since this process is a bit complicated for young children, it is an excellent opportunity to involve parent volunteers in your classroom. The steps are as follows:

1. First, decide on the size of your book and cut your contact paper larger than the book size.
2. Place two pieces of cardboard for the front and back covers on the contact paper, leaving a half-inch space between the covers and at least a one-inch border around the top, bottom, and sides.
3. Fold back the contact paper to cover the edges of the cardboard, taking care to miter the corners.
4. Cut paper for the book pages that is twice the width (you will be folding it in half) but the same height as the book size you want. Allow an extra sheet for title and end pages.
5. Using your needle and thread, sew the pages together down the middle. This is where the spine of the book will lie.
6. Place the sewn pages on top of the covers, aligning the sewn portion down the spine of the book.
7. Attach the end pages to the book covers using glue or book tape. Glue may also be used to reinforce the spine.

Publishing

For students conditioned to think of writing in terms of red marks and teacher grades, the notion of actually publishing their own writing for others to read may seem strange. Yet all across the country, student-published works are becoming more and more common. As described earlier in this text, Eliot

Wigginton's high school students produced original pieces, revised and edited them, and then published the best in a school magazine that was sold throughout the community. For these students, publication was a natural final step in the writing process (Wigginton, 1986).

In Boothbay Harbor, Maine, Nancie Atwell's eighth-graders similarly look forward to publishing their stories, articles, and poems in professional journals throughout the country. She calls this "going public" with students' work. It was Atwell, in her book *In the Middle* (1987), who really popularized the notion of publishing the works of student writers as a way of teaching them about various audiences. As Atwell has said, "A sense of audience—the knowledge that someone will read what they have written—is crucial to young writers" (p. 265).

Another opportunity for publishing children's writing is a nationwide contest sponsored by Landmark Editions (1420 Kansas Avenue, P.O. Box 4469, Kansas City, MO 64127), called the Written and Illustrated series. Divided into age groups, students submit their original manuscript stories and illustrations. Every national winner in each age category is then invited to Kansas City where they work with professional editors and artists to produce a hardcover professional-looking book of their work. Some of the book title winners and their child authors include Stacy Chobsky, *Who Owns the Sun* (1988); Lisa Gross, *The Half & Half Dog* (1988); and Elizabeth Haidle, *Elmer the Grump* (1989).

Kids Magazine and *Cricket* are two professional journals that publish children's writing. Bringing these to class and reading a sample article, story, or poem written by children will excite your students to want to submit their own work for publication. You will, of course, need to explain to them that national magazines such as these receive hundreds of submissions every month from children all over the country; therefore, getting a piece accepted for publication is quite difficult. If you do decide to submit students' writing to professional publications, make sure that you read the journal first to acquaint your students with the type of material it publishes, the style it prefers, and any other special requirements. All this information is usually contained in the front of the journal in a section labeled "Information for submitting manuscripts." Figure 8.10 lists some journals that publish student writing, which you may wish to explore with your students. Figure 8.11 lists some Web sites where students can post original writings.

Young Authors' Fair

One of the most exciting postwriting events a school can conduct for students is a Young Authors' Fair (Dowling, 1980; Hahn, 1983; Humphrey & Rodden, 1972). Such a fair is a celebration of writing, during which students of all ages and all grade levels submit their best writing in a bound book format. The books are displayed on tables in a large area such as the school cafeteria. Parents and special guests are invited to attend and browse around the book displays. Students have a chance to visit the fair during the school day to see their own books on display and read the books of their friends in other classes.

Figure 8.10

Professional publications for students' writing.

Boy's Life
1325 Walnut Hill Lane
Irving, TX 75602

Child Life
P.O. Box 567
Indianapolis, IN 46206

Ebony, Jr.
820 S. Michigan Avenue
Chicago, IL 60605

Jack and Jill
P.O. Box 567
Indianapolis, IN 46206

Scholastic Scope
50 W. 44th Street
New York, NY 10036

Cricket
1058 8th Street
La Salle, IL 61301

Highlights for Children
803 Church Street
Honesdale, PA 18431

Kids Magazine
P.O. Box 3041
Grand Central Station
New York, NY 10017

Stone Soup
P.O. Box 83
Santa Cruz, CA 95063

Anthology of Poetry by Young Americans
Anthology of Poetry, Inc.
P.O. Box 698
Asheboro, NC 27204-0698

www.realkids.com/
Features true adventure stories written by children ages 8–14.

www.acloserlook.com/9603acl/children_youth/realkidsrealadventures.html
Features a site for students to write reviews to stories that are posted by other students.

www.inkspot.com/
Features a site for young writers to have peer conferences on the Internet.

plaza.interport.netkids.space/
Permits students to share their writings with others.

www.en-garde.con/kidpub
Gives students an opportunity to publish their stories.

www.woodwind.com:80/cyberkids/
Features writing contests, with winning entries published in the electronic magazine at this same site.

www.kidpub.com
Publishes any type of writing at this site.

Organizing a Young Authors' Fair requires schoolwide cooperation. A parent–teacher organization can take a lead role in this project. Classroom teachers need to be reminded of the final date for submitting entries. Students select their best or favorite work to be displayed. Since the purpose of the fair is to provide an opportunity to recognize and praise young writers, no competitive awards are given; every child who contributes an original work in bound book form receives a certificate of participation. Figure 8.12 is an example of such a certificate.

Prewriting, writing, and postwriting—these are the three stages of the process approach to writing. Each stage in turn contains various steps or activities that teachers may wish to incorporate into their classroom instruction. When begun in the first grade and continued throughout the elementary years, the process approach helps children to gain confidence in themselves as writers and, most important, to enjoy writing as a form of communication.

IN & BEYOND THE CLASSROOM

Select one of the suggestions for postwriting activities, such as bookbinding. Then find an elementary classroom whose teacher will allow you to work with a small group of children. Teach the students this activity and record the experience in your journal.

Teaching with a Process Approach

Many authors, including Nancie Atwell (1998), Lucy Calkins (1991), Brian Cambourne (1988, 1995), Donald Graves (1991, 1994), Jane Hansen (1987), and Shelley Harwayne (1992), have described approaches to teaching that utilize a process writing model with a workshop approach to classroom organization. The diagrams on pages 320–321 summarize the key elements in teaching about process writing and organizing a writing workshop classroom.

Brian Cambourne (1988) describes eight conditions for process writing to take place. (See Chapter 1 for Cambourne's Learning Theory.) As discussed earlier, all eight (immersion, demonstration, expectation, response, employ-

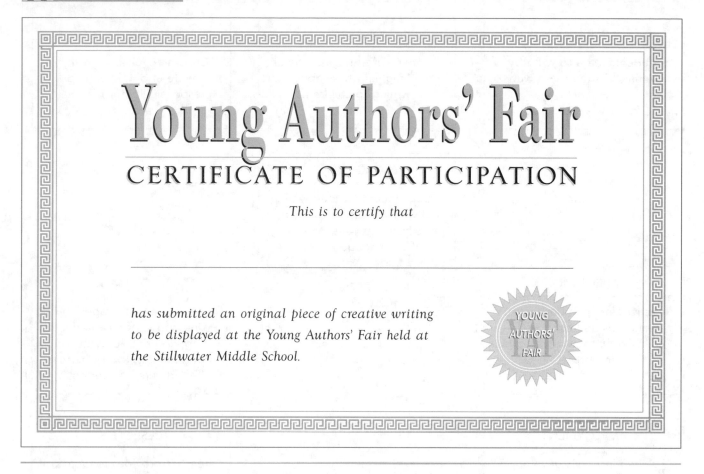

Figure 8.12   *Young Authors' Fair certificate.*

Young Authors' Fair

CERTIFICATE OF PARTICIPATION

This is to certify that

_____

has submitted an original piece of creative writing to be displayed at the Young Authors' Fair held at the Stillwater Middle School.

YOUNG AUTHORS' FAIR

ment, responsibility, approximation, and engagement) are interrelated; the first seven are dependent upon the final condition, student engagement. Immersion, demonstration, expectation, and response are led by the teacher. Employment, responsibility, and approximation are the conditions the child brings to the writing process (see Figure 8.13).

Atwell (1998) posits that the time set aside for the writing workshop needs to follow a set sequence of events in order for the students to have a sense of structure. The sequence of the five main events of the writing workshop are explained in Figure 8.14.

One of Cambourne's eight conditions that is necessary in process writing is responsibility. One way for students to learn responsibility is to edit their work. In order to make editing easy for the students, the teacher often posts checklists near an Editing Corner. The checklists are reminders for students to follow the standard English rules used for publishing. Figure 8.15 is a poster that reminds students to check their use of capitalization and punctuation.

Teachers who use the process approach to teach writing are making an offer to their students; they are saying, "Let's join together in a writing club to help each other as readers and writers." In preparing for this writing workshop approach to literacy, six key elements must interact: time, choice, response, structure, mini-lessons, and community (see Figure 8.16). Read the Classroom Vignette that follows to see how the process approach affects one student's writing process.

Figure 8.13   *Conditions required for process writing (based on Cambourne).*

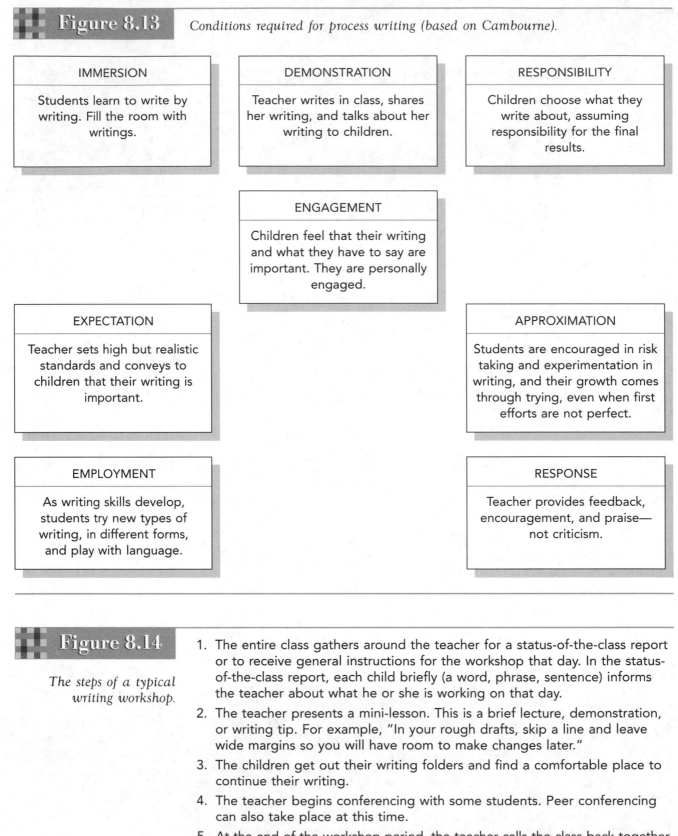

IMMERSION

Students learn to write by writing. Fill the room with writings.

DEMONSTRATION

Teacher writes in class, shares her writing, and talks about her writing to children.

RESPONSIBILITY

Children choose what they write about, assuming responsibility for the final results.

ENGAGEMENT

Children feel that their writing and what they have to say are important. They are personally engaged.

EXPECTATION

Teacher sets high but realistic standards and conveys to children that their writing is important.

APPROXIMATION

Students are encouraged in risk taking and experimentation in writing, and their growth comes through trying, even when first efforts are not perfect.

EMPLOYMENT

As writing skills develop, students try new types of writing, in different forms, and play with language.

RESPONSE

Teacher provides feedback, encouragement, and praise—not criticism.

Figure 8.14

The steps of a typical writing workshop.

1. The entire class gathers around the teacher for a status-of-the-class report or to receive general instructions for the workshop that day. In the status-of-the-class report, each child briefly (a word, phrase, sentence) informs the teacher about what he or she is working on that day.

2. The teacher presents a mini-lesson. This is a brief lecture, demonstration, or writing tip. For example, "In your rough drafts, skip a line and leave wide margins so you will have room to make changes later."

3. The children get out their writing folders and find a comfortable place to continue their writing.

4. The teacher begins conferencing with some students. Peer conferencing can also take place at this time.

5. At the end of the workshop period, the teacher calls the class back together. Writing problems may be discussed. Suggestions for workshop improvements are made. Volunteers share their work in progress in author's chair.

Did I . . .	Check if yes
use complete sentences?	_____
capitalize the first word in each sentence?	_____
end statements with periods?	_____
end question sentences with question marks?	_____
indent paragraphs?	_____
check for spelling errors?	_____
capitalize all proper nouns?	_____
use quotation marks to indicate dialogue?	_____

Figure 8.15

Editing checklist.

Figure 8.16   *Writing workshop elements (based on Hansen, Atwell, Graves).*

CHOICE

Children choose their topics, genres, materials, how to use their time; make choices about drafting, revising, editing, etc.

RESPONSE

Teachers listen to children; peer group responding; conferencing on a regular basis.

TIME

Writers need large blocks of uninterrupted time during the school day.

STRUCTURE

Establish a definite workshop routine:
Status of the class,
Mini-lesson,
Time to write,
Conferencing,
Group sharing.

MINI-LESSONS

Teacher demonstrates and explains in a brief lesson needed skills, concepts, and procedural matters to facilitate workshop independence.

COMMUNITY

Students share their knowledge and skills with others; collaborative writing; buddy teams for editing; cooperative group research and writing; author's chair.

Vignette *in the classroom*

One day Ms. Giacobbe is conferencing with Tommy, a first-grader, when she notices he has changed something in his writing. She asks him about it and he replies, "Easy. When I read it, it wasn't right. I left words out."

As Ms. Giacobbe observes Tommy at work over the school year, she notices him rereading what he has written more and more and then revising his work. For example, Tommy draws an arrow to show that a word is missing and needs to be inserted. When asked why he used the arrow, Tommy says he saw his teacher use it at the chalkboard one day. This 7-year-old is discovering for himself how reading and writing work together.

During other conferences with his teacher, Tommy makes still more revisions in his writing.

When asked to share his stories with other children during author's chair, the questions they raise cause him to make still more revisions. Ms. Giacobbe notices that other changes are occurring in Tommy's writing. After doing author's chair a few times, Tommy begins adding more details and trying to explain things more clearly. Obviously Tommy is anticipating the questions the other students might ask him the next time he does author's chair. Tommy has discovered the importance of audience.

For Tommy, writing and reading go hand in hand. The more he writes, the more he reads; the more he reads, the more he writes. As others (teachers and peers) comment on his writing, he is stimulated to write still more and with a greater awareness of his readers.

Types of Writing

All the recent research on writing has demonstrated that in order to improve as writers, students must write on a daily basis and—ideally—choose what they write about. Although choice is most important, teachers of writing also introduce children to different types of writing. This is not the same as assigning topics. Within each type of writing, students are still free to write on topics that interest them the most. However, exposing young writers to different types and styles of writing is one of the responsibilities of the teacher. Following is a summary of some of the different types of writing activities young people enjoy.

JOURNALS

Clutter is the disease of American writing. We are a society strangling in unnecessary words, circular constructions, pompous frills, and meaningless jargon.

WILLIAM ZINSSER

Writers keep journals; journals are the lifeblood of writing. Through journals, writers explore their thoughts, discover their topics, and try out new techniques. Encouraging primary-grade children to keep journals leads to more reading, increased vocabulary usage, and fluent writing. Thus, introducing students to journal writing is one of the first things a teacher should do (Fulwiler, 1987a; Short, Harste, & Burke, 1996; Tway, 1984).

Spiral-bound notebooks or small looseleaf-binder books make the best journals. Journals can also be made by stapling lined paper into an ordinary folder. The key is not what the journals look like but how they are used. Journals help to establish the writing habit. Toby Fulwiler put it this way: "I no longer trust to chance. . . . Journals work because I use them actively every day to write in, read from, and talk about" (1987b, p. 15).

Following are some different types of journals to consider using with your students.

Personal Journals (Diaries)

Many children are already familiar with this type of journal. A *diary* is a record of children's personal thoughts or a recounting of the daily events in their lives. Often it deals with the ordinary and the mundane, but it provides a nice record of events in the previous weeks, months, and years. Even very young children can be taught to keep personal journals on a regular basis. Hipple (1985) has described how kindergarten children benefit from journal writing that is a mixture of drawings, scribbles, and random letters. Manning, Manning, and Hughes (1987) found that first-graders became confident writers when they drew and wrote about things that were most personal to them.

One way in which teachers can lead their students into personal journal writing is by reading to them from children's books in which one or more characters keep a journal. Follow-up discussions on why people keep journals helps to motivate youngsters to keep journals themselves. Figure 8.17 lists some popular children's books in which diaries play an important role and the grade levels for which each book is appropriate.

Figure 8.17   *Children's books and journal writing.*

Ada, A. F. (1994). *Dear Peter Rabbit.* New York: Atheneum Books for Young Readers. (1–3)

Ada, A. F. (1998). *Yours Truly, Goldilocks.* New York: Atheneum Books for Young Readers. (1–3)

Adlier, D. A. (1985). *Eaton Stanley and the Mind Control Experiment.* New York: Dutton. (3–6)

Blos, J. (1979). *A Gathering of Days.* New York: Scribner. (4–6) (Newbery Medal)

Cleary, B. (1983). *Dear Mr. Henshaw.* New York: William Morrow. (3–6)

Cleary, B. (1984). *The Ramona Quimby Diary.* New York: William Morrow. (2–6)

Conrad, P. (1992). *Pedro's Journal: A Voyage with Christopher Columbus.* WA: Turtleback Publishers. (5+)

Denenberg, B. (1997). *So Far From Home: The Diary of Mary Driscoll, an Irish Mill Girl.* New York: Scholastic. (5+)

Denenberg, B. (1998). *The Journal of William Thomas Emerson: A Revolutionary War Patriot.* New York: Scholastic. (5+)

Fitzhugh, L. (1964). *Harriet the Spy.* New York: Harper & Row. (3–6)

Frank, A. (1952). *Anne Frank: The Diary of a Young Girl.* New York: Doubleday. (6+)

Garland, S. (1998). *A Line in the Sand: The Alamo Diary of Lucinda Lawrence.* New York: Scholastic. (5+)

Goffstein, M. B. A. (1984). *A Writer.* New York: Harper & Row. (4–6)

Hahn, M. D. (1983). *Daphne's Book.* New York: Clarion Books. (4–6)

Hesse, K. (1997). *Out of the Dust.* New York: Scholastic Press. (4–6) (Newbery Medal)

Hest, A. (1994). *The Private Notebooks of Katie Roberts, Age 11.* IL: Candlewick Press. (5+)

Hoban, L. (1976). *Arthur's Pen Pal.* New York: Harper & Row. (K–3)

Keats, E. J. (1968). *A Letter to Amy.* New York: Harper & Row. (K–3).

Lorbiecki, M. (1997). *My Palace of Leaves in Sarajevo.* New York: Dial Books. (6+)

Lowry, L. (1984). *Anastasia, Ask Your Analyst.* Boston: Houghton Mifflin. (3–6)

Mills, C. (1986). *The One and Only Cynthia Jane Thornton.* New York: Macmillan. (3–6)

Murphy, J. (1998). *West to the Land of Plenty: The Diary of Teresa Angelino Viscardi.* New York: Scholastic. (5+)

Reig, J. (1978). *Diary of the Boy King Tut-Amen.* New York: Scribner. (6+)

Sharmat, M. W. (1982). *Mysteriously Yours, Maggie Marmestein.* New York: Harper & Row. (3–6)

Taylor, E. J. (1986). *Rag Doll Press.* New York: Alfred Knopf. (K–3)

Taylor, J. (1992). *Letters to Children from Beatrix Potter.* New York: Frederick. (5+)

Woodruff, E. (1994). *Dear Levi: Letters from the Overland Trail.* New York: Alfred A. Knopf. (5+)

Dialogue Journals

A *dialogue journal* is a written conversation between two people, usually the teacher and a student (Gambrell, 1985; Shuy, 1987). It can be used in a variety of ways for a variety of purposes. For example, sometimes a child wishes to share something with the teacher, but there just isn't time in class or the child is too shy to speak up in front of others. So he or she writes a brief note to the teacher about any topic of his or her choosing. The teacher reads it and then writes back to the child. Sometimes the dialogue journal may be passed back and forth in this manner over many weeks.

Other times a dialogue journal is used by a student to ask questions related to the content in a subject area. "Mrs. Jones, I didn't understand what you meant by a *peninsula* today. I know it's some kind of geography shape, I think. Could you explain it again?" The teacher then writes a response to the child.

Teachers can also initiate a dialogue journal with their students about nonacademic matters. Staton (1980) found that dialogue journals are excellent for counseling children about personal problems. Often teachers don't have the time to talk with individual children about school or home difficulties that may be interfering with a child's academic work. So they write about it. Figure 8.18 is an example of the dialogue journal format.

Figure 8.18

Sample dialogue journal entries.

Dear Kevin,

In class today I noticed that you had trouble keeping your eyes open. You put your head on your desk and dozed off to sleep. I hope it was a good nap, but I'm concerned. Are you still watching the late show on TV? Perhaps you are staying up too late on school nights. Or is something else the matter?

Sincerely,
Mrs. Wanowski

Dear Mrs. Wanowski,

I don't know. I just don't feel well sometimes. I get headaches. So I close my eyes and it feels better. Did you see Monster from the Black Lagoon last night? It was real scary. I'll try not to fall asleep again.

Your Student,
Kevin

Dear Kevin,

No, I didn't see Monster from the Black Lagoon. But, I heard from some other people that it is really good. It started at 11:00 P.M. That means you didn't get to sleep until after 1:00 A.M. Maybe that's why you are getting headaches. I also noticed you rubbing your eyes a lot. When I was your age, my mother took me to have my eyes checked. The doctor recommended I wear glasses. At first I didn't like the idea, but then I got used to them. Let's talk about this after class.

Sincerely,
Mrs. Wanowski

Literary Response Journals

Many young people dislike literature because of the way it is taught: The teacher questions the class as a whole about facts in the book (who did what to whom and why). Teacher questions mean teacher control. Teacher questions also imply that there are specific correct answers that must be guessed or memorized. For many students, this kills the appeal of reading books.

But literature is meant to be enjoyed, to be experienced, to be savored in a highly personal manner. A literary response journal can help students to realize this. The *literary response journal* encourages youngsters to write their feelings and reactions to the books they have read (Barone & Lovell, 1990). Primary through secondary students can use literary response journals to enhance their pleasure and comprehension of books.

One way to introduce literary journals in the classroom is to organize students into small groups based on the book they have chosen to read. Each day in class, the group has time to read and talk about the book. Students may also use some of this time to write about the book. Or they may choose to do their journal writing at home. The key to writing a literary response journal is to focus on personal reactions to the book. James Britton (1973, 1978) has called this *expressive writing*, in which the primary audience is the person writing. Louise Rosenblatt (1989) has referred to this as reading literature *aesthetically*, in which the experience the reader has with the work is the most important factor.

J. D. Salinger's book *Catcher in the Rye* is about the experiences of an angry adolescent named Holden Caulfield. Holden attends a private boarding school, and he has few friends. He curses constantly and is generally portrayed in a negative manner. However, as the book progresses, Salinger leads the reader to experience some of the pain that Holden is experiencing. Following is an excerpt from the literary response journal of one girl who read this book in the class of Marion MacLean (1985). Notice how the writer personalizes her reaction to the main character:

> Holden seems to feel that his parents don't want him because he is always shipped from one boys school to another. And neither of the other children went to boarding school.
>
> He seems to be devistated by his brother's death. Not just devistated, but puzzled and angry at himself, the world, and life. Life most of all. And everyone in it. I think that's why he hates everyone he comes in contact with. It's just a way of letting that deep sadnes and anger out.
>
> Holden at the beginning of this book was a repulsive person who cussed about everything, but by the end of this book I cryed because I felt his pain so much! I wanted to reach out and help him.

Teachers such as Marion MacLean use literary response journals as an integral part of their literature lessons. They find that journal writing about literature encourages students to read aesthetically and to create their own meaning based on personal experiences. Students who keep literary response journals about the books they are reading not only gain an enhanced appreciation for literature but also find that writing stimulates discussions with other students who have read the same book and have had different reactions to it.

Reading Logs

Younger children not accustomed to keeping a literary journal can begin with a reading log. A *reading log* is a list of books a child has read during the school year plus comments about each book. Often this is done on a chapter-by-chapter basis. To guide children in writing in their logs, some teachers provide them with "thought questions." As with the literary response journal for older students, the thought questions are intended to get the young reader to respond to the book at an intellectual or emotional level rather than merely summarizing each chapter. Examples of thought questions include:

- Which character in the book might you select as a friend? Why?
- Which character do you dislike? Why?
- Have you ever had a problem similar to the one in this book?
- What in this story is familiar to you? A place? An object? An event?
- What puzzles or bothers you most about this story?
- Would you recommend this book to a friend? Why?
- Draw a picture that represents the main thing you remember about your book.

To help young children get started in keeping reading logs, provide them with a sample of the format, in addition to the thought questions. Figure 8.19 is an example of such a format.

Figure 8.19   *Reading log format.*

Title of Book	Author	Date Begun	Date Finished	Comments
The Class Trip (Sweet Valley Twins)	Francine Tripp	Feb. 18, 1999	March 23, 1999	I liked where they went on a trip and Jessica got lost.

Child's Name: _____

Writer's Journals

A *writer's journal* can be a separate journal or can be incorporated with other types of journal entries such as freewriting exercises, personal diary entries, even reading logs. The difference is that the writer's journal contains reflections on another piece of writing by the author of the journal: how it's going, where the problems lie, what changes need to be made, how much extra research needs to be done. Following is an example of a young girl writing in her journal about a poem she is trying to write. The poem is about saying good-bye to her best friend, who moved to a new home.

January 14—I'm trying to write a poem about Janey. She was my best friend and I still miss her. I remember how we used to roller skate everyday after school, round and round in our driveway, while we listened to the Beatles. I don't know if I should try and make every other line rhyme or what.

January 20—I've finished my poem, I think. It's longer than I imagined. I think I need to go back and take out some stuff. It sounds corny. But the part about skating to the Beatles is good. I can picture it like it was yesterday.

Learning Logs

Journal writing is a process of reflection, a form of thinking. Toby Fulwiler (1987a) noted that having students record what they have learned in particular subject areas is one way to help them understand difficult subject matter. Lucy Calkins (1994) has referred to these content journals as *learning logs.*

Too often, particularly in the upper grades, teachers pigeonhole writing as something done only in English class. However, many teachers of content areas such as math, science, social studies, art, and music are discovering the benefits of journal writing in their classrooms. They report that students actually learn and retain more information when they are asked to write about it. This is as true for describing a science experiment as it is for explaining the solution to a mathematics problem or relating how a particular piece of music makes the writer feel.

Fulwiler (1987b) has contended that learning logs can be used at different times and for different reasons. A biology teacher may ask his students to bring their learning logs along on a science field trip to record data. A history teacher might begin a lecture on the Civil War by asking his students to write down what they already know about Abraham Lincoln. A geometry teacher may stop the lesson with 10 minutes remaining and have her students write a summary of what they have learned during the period. Primary-grade teachers could ask their students at the end of the day to complete the sentence, "Today I learned . . . "

Simulated Journals

In the *simulated journal*, according to Tompkins, "students assume the role of another person and write from that person's viewpoint" (1990, p. 44). For example, a fifth-grade social studies class is studying about the early discoverers and explorers. From their textbook and additional biographies found at the library, the children have read about the lives of Columbus, Pizarro, Cortez, da Gama, Balboa, Magellan, Cabot, and Cabral. Their teacher asks them to select their favorite explorer and write a journal as if they were that person. These first-person simulations give students a chance to use their imaginations and at the same time incorporate what they have learned about historical figures. The same learning activity can be used to enhance other subject areas: Students can pretend they are Vincent van Gogh, Marie Curie, or Wolfgang Amadeus Mozart.

Journal Writing Tips

Whatever kind of journal writing you employ in your classroom, remember the following tips:

- You can collect and read students' journals, but do not grade them. Grading causes children to focus on mechanics rather than on their real thoughts about a subject.
- Journals are rarely rewritten; they are done as first drafts. So allow for misspellings and grammatical errors. Focus on the ideas and the feelings in the writing.
- Have students keep journals on a daily basis. Five or 10 minutes each day is usually all it takes to maintain a journal.
- Encourage children to reread their journal entries and use them as sources of ideas for later writing activities.
- Keep a journal yourself and write with the students in class. Practice what you preach.

STORIES

Children love to create stories. First they create them in their heads; then they want to tell these stories to their friends and family. Eventually they want to write them down. This natural desire to tell stories is what the teacher of fiction writing taps in young children.

All children have a story—indeed many stories—to tell: about the bully who picks on kids after school; about the boy who found a wallet on the school bus; about the day she broke her arm and had to go to the hospital; about the time his dog had six puppies out in the garage; about the strange old woman who lives down the block and chases kids from her yard with a broom; about leaving the old neighborhood to move to another state when Dad got transferred. This is the basis for fiction writing: Experiences, feelings, and beliefs are the source of all writing (Graves, 1989a). Unfortunately, many youngsters don't consider their own lives interesting enough to tell others about. Thus, one of the teacher's first tasks is to convince students that others are interested in what they have to say.

Writing one's own experiences in the form of a story is referred to as *narrative writing*. What makes a story a work of fiction rather than autobiography is that the author alters certain facts—changes the setting, embellishes the characters, or otherwise fictionalizes the events. But at the heart of a good story is an author's own experience. Patricia MacLachlan, a well-known children's author, wrote *Cassie Binegar* about a girl who liked to hide under the dining-room table and listen to the conversations of others. After she had written this book, MacLachlan's mother told her that she had done the same thing as a child (Courtney, 1985).

How do young children acquire the concept of story to apply to their own writing? First, they must hear stories told and be read to frequently (Applebee, 1978). Professional writers have noted that their earliest inspirations stemmed from hearing stories read to them by their parents (Courtney, 1985). Teachers reinforce story knowledge by reading aloud to their students daily. Second, children must begin to think of themselves as authors to acquire the concept of authorship (Lamme, 1989). Lamme has suggested four ways to do this:

1. Discuss with children that books are written by people called authors, not by some mysterious machine.
2. Reinforce this fact by doing author studies: reading several books by the same author; writing follow-up letters to the author.
3. Invite an author to speak to your school or school district. More and more schools are combining a visit by an author with their Young Authors' Fair program.
4. Make the author's chair activity a regular part of the reading/writing workshop so that children can experience firsthand how an author feels reading his or her work to a responsive audience.

In addition to these holistic strategies, more traditional or direct instructional strategies can be used to teach the basic elements of the narrative story structure. Teaching children to understand the various components of a story improves the quality of their writing. A direct instructional mini-lesson includes the following four steps:

1. Identify the specific skill/comprehension area to be taught based on your observations and discussions with children.
2. Select a children's book that exemplifies what you want to teach.
3. Discuss the skill within the context of the book. Do this with the entire class in a mini-lesson.

4. Then, using a modeling strategy, direct students to practice the skill in their writing. Figure 8.20 is an example of a first-grader modeling the plot of "The Little Red Hen."

Mini-Lesson: Beginning, Middle, and End

Basic to the concept of story are the notions of beginning, middle, and end. These are difficult concepts to grasp if the child has not heard many stories read aloud before coming to school. Typically very young children, who are egocentric and lack recognition of outside audience, start thoughts in the middle, assume their readers can read their minds, and end stories when they run out of paper.

To teach these concepts, select some highly predictable books that include three easily recognized parts. Pause after the beginning and ask the students what they think the story will be about. The beginning of a book usually introduces the main character(s), the problem to be resolved, and the setting. Next, read the middle portion of the book. Discuss with the children that the middle of the book further develops the characters along with the plot (the action in the story). Finally, read the last section of the book, in which the main character solves the problem and the theme (or message) of the story is revealed.

To help young children grasp the concepts of beginning, middle, and end, have them sketch out their stories first as three separate drawings. Drawing is an important aspect of developing a sense of structure and sequence for stories. Older students can draw cluster diagrams to help them structure stories in their minds. *Where the Wild Things Are* by Maurice Sendak and *Alexander and the Terrible, Horrible, No Good, Very Bad Day* by Judith Viorst are two easy-to-follow books for young children that lend themselves to teaching about beginning, middle, and end.

Figure 8.20

Sample story using modeling strategy and invented spelling.

Mini-Lesson: Plot (Conflict, Climax, and Resolution)

For many young children, what makes for a memorable book is what happens in the story, the action (Seuling, 1984); this is called the *plot*. In fiction, the plot begins with a conflict or problem to be solved. For example, in Jean George's *Julie of the Wolves*, the problem is literally one of how to survive in the wilderness; in Paula Fox's *The Slave Dancer*, a 13-year-old boy is kidnapped and taken to West Africa on a slave ship. Eventually the various events in a story build to a high point, or *climax*; then the action turns and the solution begins to unfold. In the end, there is *resolution*, or a solving of the problem.

To help children write better plots, some teachers use an exercise called the *five-minute plot*. First, set a timer for five minutes; everyone writes quickly, sketching out a plot for a story containing a character, a problem, and a solution. Afterward students compare their five-minute plots for the three main elements. This exercise can be practiced once a week until children become adept at outlining stories quickly.

Mini-Lesson: Setting (Place and Time)

The particular place in which a story is set—a large city, a small country town, the deep woods, an exotic tropical island—is not an accident. Authors choose their settings carefully and research them thoroughly. The time period of a story—past, present, future—is also significant. For example, Esther Forbes's story *Johnny Tremain* takes place around the time of the Revolutionary War. Mildred Taylor's *Roll of Thunder, Hear My Cry* is set in Mississippi in the 1930s; the discrimination felt by the African American family in this story is a reflection of the time and place in which they live. Elaine Konigsburg chose the Metropolitan Museum of Art as the setting for *From the Mixed-Up Files of Mrs. Basil E. Frankwiler*. Other classic children's books in which place and time are especially crucial to the story line are *Strawberry Girl* by Lois Lenski and the *Little House* series by Laura Ingalls Wilder.

Mini-Lesson: Character Development

Fiction books are centered around a conflict or problem to be resolved by a main character. Main characters are often introduced within the first paragraph of a book, which is called the *lead*. The lead sets the tone of the story (Graves, 1989a). Often characters are developed through their actions, the way they resolve their problems. Different types of conflicts or problems are possible. One type involves an individual in conflict with the larger society. In *Journey Home*, author Yochiko Uchida explores the issues of discrimination and prejudice faced by Japanese Americans during and after World War II. In this story, a young girl and her family return home to California after being unjustly placed in a concentration camp in Utah, only to find more injustices awaiting them. A different type of character conflict is revealed in books such as *Call It Courage* by Armstrong Sperry. In this book, the main character, Mafatu, must conquer his fear of the sea and prove himself worthy to be the son of a chief. In *Sam, Bangs and Moonshine* by Evaline Ness, a young girl's innocent lies eventually lead to tragedy, which in turn causes her to face the truth about herself. Finally, there are books in which the main character must face the problem of survival in a hostile natural environment. In *Island of the Blue Dolphins* by Scott O'Dell, young Karana survives alone on an island for 18 years. In two of Jean George's popular books, *Julie of the Wolves* and *My Side of the Mountain*, survival in the wild plays a central role in explaining the development of the main characters.

IN & BEYOND THE CLASSROOM

Select one of the mini-lessons on story structure and teach it to a small group of children using the books suggested or any others. After your reading and discussion, have the children do a group collaboration story of the story structure taught. Record your observations in your journal regarding students' attitudes and learning from this experience.

Mini-Lesson: Theme (Message)

Theme is often confused with plot. *Plot* is the action, what is happening in the story. However, the characters' actions usually have greater significance than is first apparent. Perhaps the main character learns a lesson, grows wiser, matures in some way, or struggles with forces of good and evil; these are the common *themes* of children's books. However, themes are rarely stated directly. Instead, theme must be inferred by the reader from the action in the story. In both *The Yearling* by Marjorie K. Rawlings and *A Day No Pigs Would Die* by Richard Peck, two young boys grow toward manhood by confronting death. Identifying the theme or themes of a book in small groups leads to higher-level discussions and more critical thinking than mere identification of what is happening in the story.

Mini-Lesson: Role of the Narrator

A story can be told in the third person, in which a narrator stands back from the action and relates a story, or the same story can be told in the first person, in which the narrator is the main character in the story, describing events as they occur. In the latter case, the *narrative distance* between the character and the reader is very small; the reader feels as though the events are actually happening to him or her. A story can also be told from the point of view of another character in the story. The importance of who is telling the story can be made clear to young children by reading to them Judy Blume's *The Pain and the Great One*, in which different characters recount the same story. In *The True Story of the Three Little Pigs*, a classic fairy tale is recounted from the wolf's point of view.

PLAYS

Chapter 5, covering speaking skills development, stressed the importance of placing children into small groups to tell stories. Often oral language activities, such as storytelling, improvisation, and reader's theatre, lead children to want to write their own plays.

One way to begin play or script writing is to have a group of students work cooperatively on a single play; this is known as **collaborative writing.** The elements of a play are the same as in fiction writing: plot, setting, character, and theme. The main noticeable difference in play writing is the emphasis placed on dialogue. Although dialogue can and often does play an important role in story writing, it plays a preeminent part in a play. The story line or plot is literally carried by what the characters say (McCaslin, 1996).

The key element in writing good dialogue is making it true to the character; that is, the words must fit the character's role. This is why authors use slang expressions, colloquial speech, and regional dialects to emphasize a character's traits. Young children may be confused at first by the unusual spellings that result from an author's attempt to approximate a dialect ("We be workin' mighty hard des deays"). Explain that this is an example not of poor spelling but rather of good dialogue, spoken by a real character.

Figure 8.21 shows some excerpts of a play written by a group of fifth-grade students using dialogue to carry the story line.

These students had read a number of plays; eventually they wanted to try their own hand at writing one. Then they wanted to act it out for their fellow classmates. This is the way a natural communication cycle works in the classroom: Children read and hear stories and plays read to them; they begin to tell stories to their friends; they get together as a group and write their own play; and finally they act it out for others to see, hear, and appreciate.

When children first attempt to write dialogue, they will use and misuse quotation marks and other punctuation associated with dialogue. This is only natural, as they are beginning writers. As they read and study models of dialogue written by professional authors, they become more familiar with the proper use of punctuation. As they practice writing dialogue, they eventually develop ease at handling the quotation marks, commas, and periods that once gave them so much trouble.

Figure 8.21

Sample play dialogue.

"Hello!" the woman shouted. "Is anyone there?"

"Ruthie?" Laura's voice asked from the darkness. "Is that you?"

"Yeah, it's me. Where are you? I can't see."

"Gimme a match. I'll turn on the light." Laura moved through the tunnel toward the light.

"Come on," the woman called again. "It's getting cold here."

"Hey, you're not Ruthie," Laura said and dropped her voice to a whisper, now afraid to move.

NONFICTION

Nonfiction writing (also known as *expository writing*) covers a broad range of writing genres; generally speaking, it is written to convey information, share discovered facts, recount a personal event meant to inform or entertain, describe a procedure or instructions for doing something (e.g., a recipe), explain a natural process in science, persuade a reader to believe something, or promote a particular point of view (Wray & Lewis, 1997).

For many elementary-grade students, nonfiction writing is difficult because they have had little experience with it. Unlike narrative writing, which sounds similar to our spoken language, informative writing sounds different from the way we normally speak. Compounding this difficulty is the manner in which it is taught. Many teachers merely assign topics ("Do a report on the African Sahara Desert.") without really explaining the steps involved in report research and writing. Wray and Lewis (1997) suggest the following four-step model to lead children into writing nonfiction, informative text:

1. *Demonstration.* The teacher models the steps of researching and writing nonfiction material to the entire class.
2. *Joint activity.* A group of students write a single collaborative piece of nonfiction.
3. *Supported writing.* The teacher provides guiding questions or an outline to assist an individual student.
4. *Independent writing.* The student researches and writes on his or her own, following a process approach and with assistance by the teacher as needed.

The following subareas of nonfiction writing are among the most commonly taught in the elementary and middle grades.

Autobiographies

An *autobiography* is the story of a person's life written by that person. Many famous people have written autobiographies intended for younger audiences. For example, the writer/illustrator Tomie de Paola told about his early life in *The Art Lesson.* Dorothy Hamill has shared with children what it's like to be a champion Olympic ice skater. Hundreds of children have been enthralled by Helen Keller's *The Story of My Life.* Reading any one of these stories or any other autobiography helps young writers to understand the nature of autobiographical writing. Even young children can be encouraged to tell about themselves.

Biography and Research Reports

A *biography* is a story written about a person's life by someone other than that person. For example, Barry Denenberg wrote *Stealing Home,* the story of Jackie Robinson, who broke the color barrier in professional baseball. Biographical writing leads youngsters into exploring the world of research. Research at the elementary-grade level is often misunderstood. Youngsters can do many types of research; the most common is library research. In researching to write a biography of George Washington, a student might:

- Look up "George Washington" in the encyclopedia.
- Examine the card catalog for books about George Washington.
- Use the *Dictionary of American Biographies* for a brief sketch of Washington.
- Do an Internet search on George Washington, using Yahoo.

The main difficulty in using any of these resources is that they are generally written at a level beyond the reading ability of a child. Thus children simply copy from books and turn in the work as their own because they know no better. Students must be taught how to paraphrase and how to cite a reference source. But these are skills that come much later, through extensive research report writing.

There are other ways to do research in addition to library research. Biographies can be written about living people, even people the children know. For example, a parent, a relative, a friend, a local police officer, a postal worker, or a storekeeper would make an excellent subject for a first biography. This kind of research requires children to gather data by conducting interviews (Graves, 1989b). Recall how Eliot Wigginton's students used the interview technique to gather firsthand information about people in their community, which they later wrote as informational articles in the *Foxfire* series.

Of course, research writing does not have to be confined to people. Any topic of interest to a child is suitable for a research report—from airplanes to zoos, from boats to penguins. Letting children choose their own topics to research and write on is crucial to maintaining enthusiasm in a project. Even young children can write research reports on topics that interest them. Their research may come from reading or being read to, from simple informational books, from viewing films or filmstrips, or, most likely, from their own experiences.

Susan Sowers reported on one first-grade classroom in which the students wrote *All About . . .* books. Then the teacher put the separate books together into one large class-collaboration book to share and be displayed in the room (Sowers, 1985). *All About . . .* books are not really research reports but rather lists of facts that young children have discovered about some subject. The emphasis is on sharing information. They are a first step in teaching young children how to write research reports. Figure 8.22 gives some examples of one first-grade class's *All About . . .* books. Note that the teacher has chosen to correct the children's original invented spelling for the final copy, which is sent home to parents. This is not necessary, but it is a teacher's choice.

Figure 8.22

Excerpts from All About . . . *books.*

All About My Cat

My cat is white and black.
My cat drinks milk.
My cat plays with a yarn ball.
My cat is named Checkers.
I really love my cat.

All About My Doll

My doll can speak.
She has a button that you push.
She has blond hair.
The hair is real.
I can dress my doll.
She walks and her arms move.

All About Snakes

I have a pet snake.
Snakes eat mice.
Snakes lose their skin.
Snakes feel smooth.
They are not slimy like people think.
Some snakes are poisonous.
Mine is not.

Vignette *in the classroom*

Quest: Interactive Writing

Mrs. Ally Sharp teaches sixth and seventh grades in the gifted and talented program at Stillwater Middle School in Stillwater, Oklahoma. For some time she has been using an idea in her program that successfully motivates these adolescents to get actively involved in their own individual projects and share the results with others; it's called Quest. Let's take a look at Mrs. Sharp's class to see how Quest works.

Today is fifth-grade visitation day, and for the sixth-graders, it is their time to shine. Fifth-grade

(continued)

Continued.

students will be "shadowing" their middle school buddies through part of the school day. In Mrs. Sharp's room, the walls, desks, and shelves are filled with various strange-looking projects: boxes of tiny plants, an intricately constructed miniature castle, a homemade guitar, a cellophane-wrapped plate of homemade cookies, various model planes and boats, and beautifully done paintings and crafts. The fifth-graders were puzzled. What was all this stuff? One young girl asked her sixth-grade buddy, "What do you do in here?" Before her buddy could respond, other sixth-graders crowded around, all anxious to tell her about Quest.

"You do whatever you want, but you can't have done it before."

"You have to try to be successful, too. I mean your project doesn't have to be a success, but you have to try hard and . . . "

"You have to learn something. Even if you don't learn how to do your project right the first time, you learn patience." A number of sixth-grade heads nodded in agreement.

To help the fifth-graders understand Quest even more, Mrs. Sharp had members of her class tell about their Quest experience. One student told about riding a unicycle. Another student described a home movie he had made; a third cooked dinner for his family for a week. Another student made bath salts. One boy described his efforts at building a paper clock. The whole class laughed as they remembered his description of all the experts he went to for help in reading and understanding the directions to this project.

In S. E. Hinton's book *The Outsiders*, Johnny, who is dying, says that "Sixteen years ain't long enough. I wouldn't mind it so much if there wasn't so much stuff I ain't done yet and so many things I ain't seen." Mrs. Sharp used this to get her stu-dents thinking about things they hadn't done but would like to do. Then they discussed how some of these might become ideas for individual class projects. Finally, the class decided on a criteria list that became the Quest Recipe, which each student must fill out after completing his or her Quest so that others can use it at a later time. Here is the recipe:

1. A title for the Quest
2. A list of necessary materials
3. An estimation of the time required
4. An explanation of what can be learned
5. A step-by-step guide to completing the Quest

Each year the Quest projects have changed slightly as each class modified them to meet their own needs and interests. The seventh-graders argued that the Quest presentation should include proof that you did something and that it worked, at least to a certain extent. Other classes suggested a timetable beginning with the first week, a week to change your mind if you wanted to, an update on your progress during the third week, and the presentation on the fourth week.

Today the Quest projects have expanded to include a community service component (such as working at the Humane Society or providing flowers to a nursing home) and a computer listserv where students from different classes e-mail one another with Quest ideas and suggestions for working together on larger projects. Everyone keeps a journal on their Quest projects: their successes, their failures, and (most importantly) what they learned. At the end of the school year, many of the students wanted to design Quest projects they could do over their summer vacation. These students see Quest as more than a school assignment; it's a learning challenge that is personally meaningful to them.

LETTERS

Letter writing, like report writing, is another example of *functional writing*, that is, writing that serves a practical purpose. Other examples of functional writing include outlining, note taking, writing directions, copying recipes, making shopping lists, planning for a vacation, and completing application forms.

In most elementary classrooms, letter writing is used almost exclusively to teach proper form without any concern for the content or purpose behind writing letters (Florio, 1979; Greene, 1983). This is a grave mistake. By overemphasizing form, teachers may inadvertently be making children more reluctant letter writers because they begin to believe that their ideas are not worthwhile (Yellin, 1988). The solution, therefore, is to create real situations and give students real reasons for writing letters. This is the only way to motivate lessons on letter writing.

The two most common types of letters taught are the friendly letter and the business letter. As the name suggests, the *friendly letter* is written to someone the student knows (parents, relatives, friends in other cities or states) or would like to know better (pen pals). *Business letters* are written to a store, a company, or even a public figure such as a state senator or representative to make requests, ask for information, lodge complaints, and so on.

As with any other writing form, the process writing steps should be followed. First, discuss why people write letters. Brainstorm some of the things students might wish to say in their letters. Have them write the rough draft and then revise and edit it. Perhaps they can share it with a friend in class before writing the final, clean copy. Remember, these letters are to be mailed. Writing pretend letters, even with primary-grade children, does not have the same motivating effect as the real thing.

Figures 8.23, 8.24, and 8.25 offer examples of and suggestions for these letter forms.

Figure 8.23   *Suggestions for writing letters.*

FRIENDLY LETTER

1. Write to a relative in another town whom you have not seen in a while.

2. Write to a friend you have not seen or heard from in a while.

3. Write to your parents, inviting them to come to the next special school event.

4. Write to a pen pal in another class, school, or state. Pen pal information can be found in such magazines as *Teacher, Learning,* and *Instructor* as well as by writing to Pen Pal Letter Exchange, 910 Fourth Street SE, Austin, MN 55912.

5. Write a thank-you letter following a field trip or presentation by a guest speaker.

6. Write a thank-you letter for gifts received for Christmas or a birthday.

BUSINESS LETTER

1. Write for information to the Chamber of Commerce of a state you are studying. The local American Automobile Association in your community can provide the address.

2. Write to a company regarding a product you have bought or wish to buy. These can be complaints, compliments, or requests. The address is contained on the box or package (usually in very fine print).

3. Write letters to the editors of newspapers regarding school and educational issues.

4. Write letters to your congressional representative or senator on issues of interest to young people.

Figure 8.24

Sample pen pal letter.

Dear Nancy,

I am Reading A Book cood it
Looked Like Spilt Milk
I Like tise Book. I mad
A Book cood the Day
it is A Good Book will you
Make me A Book
yes ☐   No ☐   will you
I will Make you A Book
if you Make me One
Ok, we plad. A gavm
cood rat's we Mad a
Class Book   we Mad A
game   Josi

Figure 8.25

Sample letters.

827 Cherry Lane
Tucson, AZ 85719
April 8, 19—

Dear Janice,
   My parents have been really
great this year. They put new
wallpaper in my room with
flowers and pretty colors.
They also promised me a new
bike if I do well on my
report card.
   Only two more weeks
till school is over. I can
hardly wait to visit you.
Please write and tell me
what to bring. I've got a
new bathing suit you'll love.
                    Love,
                    Patty

704 Holly Drive
Madison, WI
53593
May 2, 19—

Great Plains Mail Order Co.
1014 North Main Street
Omaha, NE 64371

Dear Sir:
   I ordered the three-
piece camping dish set
advertised in your
catalog. It arrived the
other day. One of the
detachable handles
is missing.
   Please send me
a new handle. Or
should I return the
whole set for a new
one? Either way, I
am waiting to hear
from you.
                    Sincerely,
                    Robert J. Glock

POETRY

Poetry is fun. Poetry is music. Poetry appeals to the emotions. Unfortunately, too many children are taught to dislike poetry—perhaps not intentionally, but they are taught to regard poetry as something so difficult, highbrow, or complex as to be beyond the gifts of ordinary people. Even adults are intimidated by poetry. Perhaps it goes back to that one terrible day in junior high when you were asked to recite in front of the whole class Edgar Allan Poe's "Annabel Lee." Or perhaps it was your freshman year in high school when the teacher called on you to explain what John Keats was really saying in his poem "Ode on a Grecian Urn." Or perhaps it was that assignment in some long-forgotten class to write a poem using the iambic pentameter form. Talk about pressure. Talk about fear. Talk about frustration.

One result of early negative experiences with poetry is that today teachers either gloss over it quickly in the curriculum or teach it without joy and enthusiasm. The purpose of this section is to correct the bad image that poetry has and to demonstrate that poetry really is fun. Children enjoy reading and writing poetry. It has a genuine place in an integrated language arts curriculum.

What Is Poetry?

Letting go
in order to hold on
I gradually understand
how poems are made.

Source: How Poems Are Made by Alice Walker.

Aristotle called poetry the most philosophic of writings, a chance to reflect on the really important things in life. Thomas Macaulay likened the poet to the artist: one paints with colors, the other with words. Poetry and art are alike in many ways. Robert Frost viewed poetry as metaphor, "saying one thing and meaning another." Coleridge, however, believed poetry was not about truth but about pleasure. Take your pick. There are probably as many definitions of poetry as there are poets (Norton, 1997). But memorizing a definition is not what poetry is about. Rather, it is about being sensitive to language, to a particular choice of words, to a specific arrangement of thoughts. A poem can make you laugh or cry. Poems are emotional; they evoke feelings. They are also difficult to fully explain. Sometimes you have to struggle with a poem a bit, to go beyond the surface words to a meaning that lies below.

One of the things that makes poetry difficult for young people is the terminology used in classroom textbooks. Terms such as *iambic pentameter*, *assonance*, and *metonymy* serve only to confuse. Having children analyze poems to search for figurative language or to identify a particular rhyme scheme only results in frustration. Such exercises also consume valuable time that could be better spent helping children enjoy a poem at their own level.

What role, then, does figurative language play? First, the technical terminology of poetry is for the teacher. In order to better understand how poets use language or how certain effects are achieved through words, some knowledge of technical terms is necessary. But it is not necessary to make memorization of these terms the content of your poetry lesson. Following are some common terms used in poetry and prose:

- *Simile.* A direct comparison using *like* or *as*. Poets use comparisons to explain feelings that cannot be easily explained. Christina Rossetti writes, "My heart is like a singing bird." And Wordsworth tells his reader, "I wandered lonely as a cloud."
- *Metaphor.* A comparison without using *like* or *as*. When the poet says, "My love is a rose," he is not saying that she has petals and a spiny stem but rather that she is so lovely that images of nature come to mind.
- *Alliteration.* A repetition of initial sounds in a series of words. Shakespeare writes of the "Merry maids of May." Tongue twisters, such as "Peter Piper picked a peck of pickled peppers," also use alliteration to play with language for sound effect.
- *Personification.* Giving human characteristics to inanimate objects. Joyce Kilmer describes "A tree who lifts its leafy arms to pray." Shakespeare talks about old age in terms of "Time's cruel hand."
- *Onomatopoeia.* Words written to represent a literal sound from nature— the "hiss" of a snake, the "buzz" of bees, the "grrrr" of a tiger. Cartoon language also employs onomatopoeia, as in "snap" (the tree limb in the wind) and "crack" (the sound of the bat as it meets the ball).
- *Hyperbole.* A gross exaggeration to convey strong emotions or evoke humor. An adult writes, "My heart is broken in two." A child writes, "I could eat a horse." Shel Silverstein has poor Cynthia (who would not take the garbage out) creating a trail of garbage across the entire United States.

Figure 8.26

Stages in a poetry unit.

1. Exposure
2. Sharing
3. Memorizing
4. Choral speaking
5. Copywriting
6. Illustrating
7. Writing poetry
   A. Free verse
   B. Acrostic
   C. Couplet
   D. Diamante
   E. Haiku
   F. Concrete (or visual)

- *Oxymoron.* A poetic device that creates surprise by placing two opposite or contradictory terms back to back. Here are some examples: slow rapids, jumbo shrimp, silent scream, sweet sorrow, definite maybe, exact estimate, and working vacation.

Teaching Poetry: An Alternative Approach

It is the authors' contention that the problem with teaching poetry to young children is this overemphasis on technical terminology and analysis, which can dominate many poetry lessons. Stressing definitions and analysis takes the life and fun out of poetry for young people. It makes poetry so complex as to deny its beauty to the young reader. However, alternative teaching procedures do exist for elementary teachers. These procedures not only teach children something about poetry but, more important, allow them to enjoy poetry.

Since poetry is not a usual part of the curriculum in many school districts, each teacher has to create his or her own syllabus. Poetry can be taught throughout the entire school year or incorporated into a unit that might last a few weeks. Figure 8.26 shows the stages in a poetry unit.

Exposure. The simplest way to introduce a poetry unit is by reading poetry aloud with your students—all types of poetry; this is known as *exposure.* As with any oral reading activity, you should first familiarize yourself thoroughly with a poem. Next, practice reading the poem aloud with enthusiasm and feeling. Finally, learn something about the poet to share with your students. In the book *Poetspeak: In Their Work, About Their Work* by Paul Janeczko (1983), various poets have described what it means to write a poem, how poetry is a reflection of their own lives, and how one poem can have many different meanings, depending on the reader.

During this first stage, all the children need do is listen and enjoy. They should not be tested over the poem or asked to do any sort of follow-up activity. The key is for the teacher to select a variety of poetry that holds their interest and appeals to their senses. Figure 8.27 is a bibliography of poetry sources suitable for the elementary grades.

If you really want to excite students with poetry as performance, bring professional entertainers to your school. Theatrical productions are stimulating as well as entertaining.

Figure 8.27

Sources for poetry.

Adoff, A. (1995). *Street Music: City Poems.* New York: HarperCollins.

Baylor, B. (1986). I'm in Charge of Celebration. New York: Charles Scribner.

Broderbund, P.O. Box 6144, Novato, CA 94948-9861. J. Prelutsky, *New Kid on the Block* (CD-ROM).

Bruchae, J. (1995). *The Earth Under Sky Bear's Feet.* New York: Philomel Books.

Bruchae, J. (1996). *Between Earth and Sky.* San Diego: Harcourt Brace.

Bruchae, J. (1996). *The Circle of Thanks.* Mahwah, NJ: Bridgewater Books.

dePaola, T. (comp.) (1988). *Tomie dePaola's Book of Poems.* New York: G. P. Putnam's Sons.

(continued)

Fleischman, P. (1985). *Joyful Noise: Poems for Two Voices.* New York: Harper & Row.

Glaser, I. J. (1995). *Dreams of Glory: Poems Starring Girls.* New York: Atheneum.

Hall, D. (ed.) (1985). *The Oxford Book of Children's Verse in America.* New York: Oxford.

Hopkins, L. (comp.) (1988). *Side by Side: Poems to Read Together.* New York: Trumpet Club.

Hughes, L. (1986). *The Dream Keeper and Other Poems.* New York: Alfred A. Knopf/Borzio Books.

Janeczko, P. B. (comp.) (1985). *Pocket Poems: Selected for a Journey.* New York: Bradbury.

Jones, H. (ed.) (1993). *The Trees Stand Shining: Poetry of the North American Indians.* New York: Dial Books.

Kennedy, X. J., & Kennedy, D. M. (eds.) (1982). *Knock at a Star: A Children's Introduction to Poetry.* Boston: Little, Brown.

Livingston, M. C. (sel.) (1991). *Lots of Limericks.* New York: McElderry Books.

Lobel, A. (1983). *The Book of Pigericks.* New York: Harper & Row Publishing.

Morrlson, L. (comp.) (1992). *At the Crack of the Bat.* New York: Hyperion Paperbacks for Children.

Opie, I. (ed.) (1996). *My Very First Mother Goose.* Cambridge, MA: Candlewick Press.

Prelutsky, J. (1990). *Something Big Has Been Here.* New York: Greenwillow Books.

Prelutsky, J. (1993). *A Nonny Mouse Writes Again!* New York: Knopf.

Prelutsky, J. (ed.) (1983). *The Random House Book of Poetry for Children.* New York: Random House.

Schenk de Regniers, B., Moore, E., White, M., & Carr, J. (comps.) (1988). *Sing a Song of Popcorn.* New York: Scholastic.

Seattle, C. (1991). *Brother Eagle, Sister Sky.* New York: Dial Books.

Silverstein, S. (1981). *Falling Up.* New York: Harper & Row.

Figure 8.27

Continued.

Sharing. The next stage in a poetry unit is sharing. Once children have heard a variety of poems read aloud by their teacher over the course of a few days, they want to share favorite poems of their own. Most children have a favorite poem they have heard a parent recite, read in a book, or learned in a previous class. The choice is up to the child. Not every student will bring a poem to share, but many will. Build on the enthusiasm of a few; the rest of the class will catch the poetry fever.

Sharing can be done as a whole-class activity, with one child reading aloud a favorite poem to the rest of the class. Even better, however, is to break the class into small groups. Arrange their chairs in circles so that everyone is facing one another. Then let each child in the group take a turn sharing a poem she or he has brought. Sharing in small groups simply allows more students the chance to read their favorite poems in a shorter amount of time.

As with the exposure stage, sharing should be nonthreatening. This is a time for children to enjoy reading and hearing poetry without worrying about what to do next with it. There is no need to test children on the poems they share or to include worksheets to evaluate skill knowledge. Sharing is about the affective domain of learning (Koch, 1970).

Memorizing. Memorization of poetry has taken a bad rap. This is unfortunate because there is nothing intrinsically wrong with having students memorize poetry. In fact, it is through memorization that a child really comes to know a poem at a variety of levels. Edmund Farrell (1989) has said that "memorizing poetry is a means of possessing the poem that can be attained in no other way: poetry must move from the head to the heart to the viscera." The key—as with any activity for children—is not to overdo it.

You might begin by memorizing a short poem yourself and presenting it to the class. Explain to your students how you prepared for this. Show them the poem on an overhead transparency and go over the lines that you wanted to stress, that you thought were most important. Also share with your students the lines that gave you the most trouble. Let them inside your head. By verbalizing aloud for students how to think through a problem or task, teachers can take some of the mystery away from basic problem-solving situations.

When the children are ready to try some memorization, let them select their own poems. Don't assign poems to be memorized; again, choice is important. Of course, many children simply look for the shortest poem they can find.

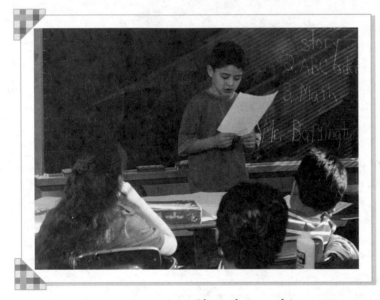

This is all right. Children have to begin somewhere, and short poems are certainly less intimidating to memorize than long ones.

Another way to help students with the memorization activity is to pair students up and have them work together in memorizing their separate poems. When it comes time for them to present their poems to the rest of the class, they can use the buddy system: One child stands before the class reciting a memorized poem while his or her buddy sits directly in front, with the actual poem serving as a prompter if the reciter should forget a line or two. Remember, the emphasis should be on enjoyment; memorization and recitation are for the fun of it. In the early stages of a poetry unit, you must cultivate the positive attitude in children that poetry can be fun.

Choral speaking. Another fun activity to do as part of a poetry unit is choral speaking. In *choral speaking,* all of the children in the class or in a small group take turns reading different parts of the same poem (Stewig, 1981). The emphasis is on the pleasurable sound effect that this creates. Reading poetry aloud to appreciate how it sounds is one of the real pleasures of poetry—a pleasure that is often denied youngsters when the focus is on analyzing the poem for deeper hidden meanings. As with any oral reading, choral speaking requires that the children practice the poem together for optimum effect.

As discussed in Chapter 5, there are a number of different types of choral speaking. The simplest is reading in *unison:* The entire class reads the same poem aloud together. The effect is a strong, clear sound that fills the room. In the *refrain* method, one child serves as lead reader. She or he reads the main part of the poem while the rest of the class joins the leader on the refrain or chorus. Turn taking involves dividing the entire class up into as many groups as there are lines or stanzas in the poem. The first group reads the first line/stanza, the second group the second line/stanza, and so on. This technique requires careful listening and accurate timing by all readers. Even more complicated but also immense fun is the *round.* In this choral speaking technique, one group begins by reading a long poem such as *The Charge of the Light Brigade.* When these students reach the second line or stanza, another group begins reading from the beginning of the poem while the first group continues reading. At the next stanza, a third group beings reading while the two previous groups continue their reading. Children enjoy the sound effects of the round and want to try it again.

Copywriting. Copying a favorite poem is a common activity for professional poets (Janeczko, 1983). It is through the act of copying that poets get a feel for rhyme, rhythm, line breaks, imagery, and language used by other poets. Oddly enough, teachers often consider copying a low-level activity. Nothing could be further from the truth. By encouraging students to identify favorite poems and copy them into their notebooks, you are helping them internalize some of the subtler differences between poetry and prose, which are difficult to explain in the abstract to young children but become demonstrably clear from a copying activity. Of course, as with memorization, take care not to overdo this activity, causing it to become so much busywork, like the endless worksheets that children suffer through daily.

Many students want to create their own poetry books of favorite poems. Having them copy different kinds of poems into their notebooks is among the best forms of preparation for writing original poems. Professional poets have done this for years; children can discover it for themselves. Another way to preserve and display favorite poems is to tack them to a bulletin board or hang them from a "poetree" (Hopkins, 1972).

Illustrating. A companion activity to copying poetry is illustrating. On the top half of a page, have students copy a favorite poem. They should leave room on the bottom half to draw an illustration. Many poets, such as Shel Silverstein, illustrate their own poems. At first children may copy these drawings, but eventually they want to select poems without illustrations and create their own. Drawing is a fun exercise and often leads children to want to write their own poems.

Writing poetry. The preceding activities are all part of a poetry unit that may lead children to want to write poetry. Writing poetry can be a fun and rewarding activity—or it can be frustrating and dull. The key is how the teacher presents it. If you keep the following guidelines in mind, teaching poetry can be one of the most exciting learning experiences your students encounter:

- Remember that not all poetry has to rhyme. In fact, writing rhyming poetry is quite difficult for young children with limited vocabularies.
- Show examples of the different types of poetry forms. Children need to see how poetry looks, how it differs visually from prose.
- Be flexible when teaching a fixed poetic form (such as the haiku); not all children will be able to come up with the exact number of syllables per line as is technically required. Proficiency comes with practice.
- Begin by writing a group poem on the board. The children contribute the lines and you record them. Don't be afraid to change lines. Revision is part of poetry writing, too.
- When the students write, you should write at your desk or at the chalkboard. Let your students see you thinking, composing, revising, and editing.

Types of Poetry

Poetry writing can be taught to any grade. First, show an example of the poetry type (e.g., acrostic) on the chalkboard, a poster, or an overhead. Poetry looks different and needs to be seen before children can write a particular form. Second, read the poem aloud and encourage students to read with you. Enjoy the sound of poetry. In some cases, point out the physical features of the poem, such as the number of lines, the syllables per line, or the rhyme

Figure 8.28

Sample free verse.

This is Just to Say	Dear Cat
by William Carlos Williams	by Lorraine Fedison
I have eaten	Please
the plums	for
that were in	give
the icebox	me
	for
and which you were	watching
probably	your
saving for breakfast	eyes
	gleam
Forgive me	in
they were delicious	the
so sweet	night.
and so cold	

Source: "This Is Just to Say" by William Carlos Williams, from *Collected Poems, 1909–1939, Vol. I*. Copyright © 1938 by New Directions Publishing Corporation. Reprinted by permission of New Directions Publishing Corporation.

Figure 8.29

Sample magnet poems.

Beautiful butterfly sparkle
with joy
get up and go
stop in wind.
—2nd grade

The color of dreams
sun, cloud, ocean, stars, moon
live in my heart
They are cool
joy and awesome
—3rd grade

(if any). Next, write a class collaboration of the poem by imitating the poem you have just read. Imitation writing, or patterning, is an important step for children's first attempts at poetry writing. Finally, turn your class loose to write and enjoy whatever poetic form pleases them. Following are some different types to consider.

Free verse is a modern form of poetry invented in the twentieth century; the lines do not rhyme, and it sounds more like prose writing but looks like poetry. Free verse poems can tell a story, paint a picture, or describe a person or a scene. Because the lines do not have to rhyme, free verse is generally easier for young children to write. In Figure 8.28, there is a free verse poem by William Carlos Williams; next to it is an imitated or patterned poem written by a sixth-grade girl from Brooklyn, New York.

Another variation on free verse is *magnet poetry*. A commercial magnet board can be purchased that contains hundreds of individual magnet words. The words can be easily moved around the board to form lines of poetry. Figure 8.29 shows examples of magnet poetry done by second- and third-grade children in Jenks, Oklahoma.

The **acrostic** is a simple poetic form in which a single word is written vertically on a page. Then each letter forms the initial letter of a word or line of poetry. Acrostics can have one word per line or be more elaborate. The examples in Figure 8.30 reveal the variety that even a simple form like the acrostic can take. Children may wish to select their own names or a friend's name to begin their first acrostic. Remember

Figure 8.30

Sample acrostic poems.

Moving	Dreaming	Sitting
Around	About	Always
Running	Visions	Mumbling
Yelling	Everyday	

When the snow falls
It makes
Nice patterns on
The sidewalk and
Everywhere children are
Running and laughing to be free

Aubree has an
Umbrella
Because it is
Raining
Everywhere
Everywhere

to write your acrostic on the chalkboard as the students are writing theirs.

A **couplet** is two lines of poetry. Couplets are the building blocks for longer poems. Figure 8.31 shows Christina Rossetti's poem "Wind," in which the second and fourth lines rhyme, as do the sixth and eighth. Using the patterning technique to introduce poetry writing, first write a class collaboration poem using different first lines. Everyone in the class can contribute lines beginning with the words, "Who has . . . " and "But when . . . " (For example, "Who has touched the sun?" "Who has heard the grass?" "Who has held the rain?")

The **diamante** is a seven-line poem written in the shape of a diamond (Tiedt, 1970). It follows some strict rules. First, select two subject nouns that are opposites—for example, night and day, boy and girl, child and adult. The first noun goes on the first line; the second goes on the last (seventh) line. On line two, write two adjectives that describe the first subject noun. On line three, write three participles or verbs ending in *ing* that tell about the first subject noun. On line four, write four nouns—the first two relating to the first subject noun, the last two relating to the second subject noun. (In other words, the focus of the poem shifts in the middle of line four.) On line five, write three participles related to the second subject. On line six, write two adjectives describing the second subject. Figure 8.32 shows some examples of the diamante poetry form.

The **haiku** is a Japanese form of poetry that is very popular both in the United States and in Japan. In fact, all Japanese schoolchildren learn to write haiku (Atwood, 1973). Many Japanese adults have made writing haiku their passion. Even the former emperor of Japan enjoyed spending hours each day composing haiku. But don't be fooled by its appearance: The haiku may look easy, but it is actually a very challenging poetic form because of its restrictions. It has only three lines and a total of 17 syllables. The syllables are arranged as follows: 5 in the first line, 7 in the second, and 5 in the third. Finally, the subject matter of haiku is always nature or the seasons. The best haiku present a single image that conveys a deep emotion. And all this is done in three short lines! Figure 8.33 presents two poems by students modeling famous Japanese haiku.

The **limerick** is a funny five-line verse that follows a specific rhyming pattern: *aabba*. That is, lines one and two rhyme, lines three and four rhyme, and line five rhymes with lines one and two. Edward Lear popularized the limerick in his *Book of Nonsense* published in England in 1846. Figure 8.34 is one of Edward Lear's own limericks.

In working with elementary students in the New York City area, Kenneth Koch also developed a number of simple poetry structures that permit even the most

Figure 8.31

Sample couplets.

Wind

by Christina Rossetti

Who has seen the wind?
  Neither I nor you:

But when the leaves hang trembling,
  The wind is passing through.

Who has seen the wind?
  Neither you nor I:

But when the leaves bow down their heads,
  The wind is passing by.

Figure 8.32

Sample diamante poems.

Form

Noun
Adjective   Adjective
Participle   Participle   Participle
Noun   Noun   Noun   Noun
Participle   Participle   Participle
Adjective   Adjective
Noun

Example

Elephant
Huge,   Leathery
Lumbering,   Charging,   Snorting
Jungle,   Beast,   House,   Rodent
Scampering,   Scratching,   Squeaking
Timid,   Meek
Mouse

Figure 8.33

Sample haiku.

The first day of spring
walking near the water, now,
one lovely egret.

In the winter snow
a silent mountain waiting
quiet but awake.

Figure 8.34

Sample limerick.

There was a young lady of Norway,
Who casually sat in a doorway;
When the door squeezed her flat,
She exclaimed, "What of that?"
This courageous young lady of Norway.

Figure 8.35

Sample student collaboration poems.

I wish Superman wore a red cape and lived in
  Disney Land.
I wish Beetle Bailey didn't wear a frown in
  Hollywood.
I wish Charlie Brown wore a blue suit to Tulsa
  and
I wish orange and yellow Garfield lived in Italy
  eating spaghetti.

I used to be a baby
But now I am a boy.
I used to love arithmetic
But now I play with toys.

inhibited child to feel comfortable writing poetry. These different forms and other suggestions for teaching poetry to children are contained in Koch's book *Wishes, Lies, and Dreams* (1970).

One of the simplest forms developed by Kenneth Koch is the "I wish" poem (Koch, 1970). As a whole class, begin the first line of a poem with the words "I wish . . ." Write this line on the chalkboard. Then ask other children in the class to contribute additional lines to the poem, each one beginning with the words "I wish." This is how a class collaboration poem is constructed. Later, individual students can compose their own "I wish" poems with as many lines as they want. Koch also suggests that for a greater sense of unity, writers should follow two rules:

1. Every line should contain a color, a comic strip character, and a city or country.
2. Every line should begin with the words "I wish."

Another simple form created by Koch is "I used to . . . But now I . . ." In this poetic structure, each child in the class contributes a couplet employing the opening words "I used to" on the first line and "But now I" on the second line. By combining many of these couplets through the collaboration process, a longer poem is created. Figure 8.35 shows student collaboration poems based on patterns developed by Koch.

Finally, **concrete** or **visual poetry** involves writing individual words or entire poems in shapes to represent the meaning of the words or poem. It is a form of word play that children enjoy, just for the fun of it. Sometimes poets incorporate concrete elements into a traditionally written poem for special emphasis or for aesthetic effect. Figure 8.36 gives examples of both ways of using concrete or visual poetry.

Figure 8.36

Sample concrete or visual poetry.

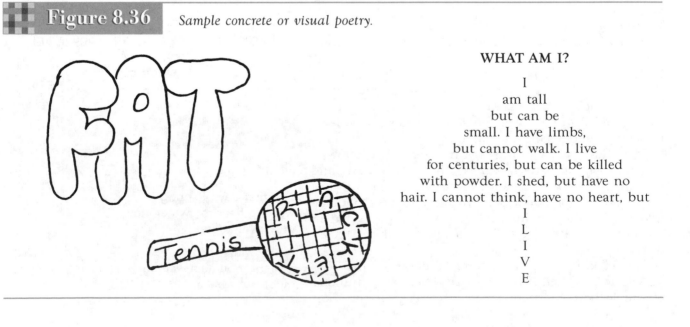

WHAT AM I?

I
am tall
but can be
small. I have limbs,
but cannot walk. I live
for centuries, but can be killed
with powder. I shed, but have no
hair. I cannot think, have no heart, but
I
L
I
V
E

Assessing Writing

Evaluation and assessment of student learning are undergoing great and significant changes. In the mid-1980s, standardized tests were criticized severely. Consequently, test critics and literacy researchers alike (Gomez, Grau, & Block, 1991) contended that assessment for the 1990s and beyond "should be modified to match more closely the tasks in which students engage in their classroom experience" (p. 620).

For many teachers, having to grade, assess, or evaluate the creative act of writing is particularly difficult. How do you distinguish an "A" paper from a "B"? What effect does an "F" have on a child's future writing? Should you give letter or number grades? Is an "85 percent" any more meaningful than a "B–"? For many teachers, evaluating writing means taking a red pen and correcting student errors. Goodman, Goodman, and Hood (1989); Smith (1988a); White (1985); and others have argued that grades and written corrections of any kind actually have a harmful effect on children's desire to write. Even teachers' narrative comments on papers may not be as helpful as some believe. Research has shown that students interpret teachers' written comments on their papers to mean that what is important is the correct appearance of the paper rather than what is said in a paper (Searle & Dillon, 1980).

Great writing evolves more from great encouragement than from great criticism.

JOHN MASEFIELD

Other assessment practices, particularly standardized tests, are now being questioned. Monroe (1991) has described them as a "narrow and confining view" of what learning and teaching are all about. Denny Taylor (1991) has argued that assessment should reflect the child's perspective and should be based on observing individual students at work. And Chittenden and Courtney (1989) have made it clear that evaluation techniques must reflect the emerging literacy skills and growth of children over time.

Clearly what is needed are more flexible alternatives to the traditional means of evaluating students' work in general and their writing in particular. This is especially true for teachers using a process approach to writing. Such alternatives exist, have been used successfully, and are gaining wider acceptance among teachers, parents, and administrators (Yellin, 1991). Following are some alternative methods of evaluating students' writing that stress positive, motivational results rather than punitive or critical assessments.

TEACHER–PUPIL CONFERENCES

One-on-one conferences between student and teacher about the content of a student's writing are by far the most effective way to evaluate student work. Conferences are supportive, helpful in identifying immediate strengths and weaknesses, and respectful toward the child as an author rather than as an object to be labeled. Conferences can be brief or lengthy, but the focus is always on discussing the content and purpose of the written work. Mechanics are only discussed in terms of how they affect the message that the writer is trying to communicate; a sloppy paper that can't be deciphered needs to be reworked regardless of how important the content may be.

TEACHER OBSERVATIONS

In an article entitled "Kidwatching: An Alternative to Testing," Yetta Goodman (1978) stressed the importance of teachers watching children in the classroom as a means of assessing their progress and needs. As discussed in Chapter 3 of this text, taking time to watch children is an important but often neglected role of the professional educator. Much can be learned by observing young writers at work: What activities do they engage in during the prewriting stage? Do they outline or diagram prior to writing a rough draft? Do they seek feedback from other students? What kinds of revisions do they make before coming to the teacher for help? Do they make some attempt at proofreading and editing? Without knowledge of the student's behaviors during writing, a teacher is at a loss as to how to help that student improve.

ANECDOTAL RECORDS

Along with observation, teachers need to keep anecdotal records of what students do during the writing process. These can be simple notes jotted in a looseleaf binder, one page per child. Later the notes on a single child can be developed into a brief narrative report to be shared with the child's parents. The focus should be on what the student is actually doing—strengths and weaknesses—not merely labeling, grouping, or grading the child.

STUDENT JOURNALS

By reading children's journals about the books they have read and the things they are writing, a teacher (and parent) can get an insider's view into what the student is doing and how he or she feels about reading and writing. Student journals are a good record of what actually takes place in the classroom. Unlike a single exam on one day, student journals give a more rounded picture of what a child has done throughout the year.

STUDENT SELF-EVALUATION

Students who keep journals on a regular basis eventually begin to evaluate their own writing. They recognize what they are good at (e.g., writing strong leads that capture the reader's attention) and what they still need to learn (e.g., how to develop a complex plot without giving away the ending too soon). Self-evaluation also applies to the mechanics of writing. Students who think of themselves as writers want to improve their handwriting, spelling, and usage skills, for they know that these can mar an otherwise interesting story. Jane Hansen (1987) has recommended that students keep a three-column chart as follows: "Skills I Learned," "Things I'm Working On," and "Things I Plan to Learn." You will find that students can be very honest in their assessment of their own work and don't need a standardized test score to tell them they need to watch out for run-on sentences.

PORTFOLIOS

The portfolio has become the most popular form of alternative assessment (Farr & Tone, 1998). It is now being used to assess reading achievement and writing development, as well as knowledge and skills learned in content areas (Frazier & Paulson, 1992; Gomez, Grau, & Block, 1991; Valencia, 1990). Portfolios are also one of the great motivating materials to encourage students, particularly low achievers, to take pride in their work.

A writing portfolio may appear to be only a collection of a student's writing; however, if used for assessment, it becomes a powerful tool for students to evaluate their own progress. Writing portfolios are used to encourage the student when he or she does not feel like any progress has been made, to integrate writing with thinking, to develop self-assessment, and to act as a springboard for student–teacher discussion when evaluating progress (Farr & Tone, 1998).

Writing portfolios represent students' work. The portfolio folders can be as simple as a file folder that has been decorated by the student. Some teachers prefer the pocket folder so papers don't easily fall out. Some teachers use three portfolios for each student so the writing process remains organized. One portfolio contains the published works that the student does throughout the year. These works are final copies of different genres that were edited and published in the classroom, put in the class or school newspaper, or sent to some individual. This portfolio is called the *Portfolio of Published Works.* The second portfolio for a child contains all the pieces that the student attempted, including all steps of the writing process—brainstorming, first drafts, revisions, and final copy. This portfolio is called the *Portfolio of All My Work.* The third portfolio contains only the composition on which the child is working; it is called the *Working Portfolio.* It is helpful to have each portfolio in a separate storage area that is easily accessible to the student.

In the Portfolio of Published Works, the teacher staples a form that records all published works. Figure 8.37 is an example of the "My Published Works" form. On this form, the student records all the work that he or she has published in some manner. It may be a letter of thanks sent to the principal or a poem written for a school newsletter.

Figure 8.37   *Portfolio form for student's published works.*

MY PUBLISHED WORKS

Name _____

DATE	TITLE	GENRE	AUDIENCE/PLACE OF PUBLICATION

In the Portfolio of All My Work, the teacher can staple a form that records all works with the student's comments. See Figure 8.38 for an example of the "All My Works" form. On this form, students record all the various types of compositions they have attempted. Not all these works need to be completed; however, they will have a record of everything they tried to write. The comments can be something like "I didn't finish it because I got stuck on it."

Figure 8.38   *Portfolio form for all student's works.*

ALL MY WORKS

Name _____

DATE STARTED	DATE ENDED	TITLE/GENRE	COMMENTS

In the Working Portfolio, the teacher staples a form that records skills the teacher taught the student during the editing stage, a conference, or a mini-lesson. Figure 8.39 has an example of the "Skills I Learned" form. On this form, the students make a record of things they learned during a mini-lesson, during a teacher–student conference, or from a classmate while reading the classmate's work.

Figure 8.39   *Portfolio form for skills student learned.*

SKILLS I LEARNED

Name _____   Grading Period   1   2   3   4

DATE	SKILLS	EXAMPLE

In the Working Portfolio, the teacher can also staple a form that records students' ideas for future works. Figure 8.40 is an example of "Bright Ideas for New Works" form. At times throughout the year, the students may read or hear something that gives them a great idea for a poem or story; however, they may be in the middle of another story and want to complete it before beginning a new piece.

If the three types of portfolios are used with useful evaluation and comment forms, the portfolios will become a "repository of a student's thought and expression" (Farr & Tone, 1998, p. 10).

In order for the portfolio to be used to integrate writing with thinking, there must be plenty of time for reflection after a student completes a work. Reflection and self-evaluation can be done if the student completes an evaluation form such as the one found in Figure 8.41. During a teacher–student

---

Figure 8.40   *Portfolio form for student's future writing ideas.*

BRIGHT IDEAS FOR NEW WORKS

Name _____

IDEA	GENRE	WHERE I GOT THE IDEA

conference, the teacher's "Quarterly Teacher–Student Evaluation" form (see Figure 8.42) and "Portfolio Assessment Rubric" (see Figure 8.43) can be discussed. At this time, the teacher may receive insight about the student's strengths and writing habits. If they are used properly, the forms can give encouragement to the student. These two forms should be stored by the teacher to be used for evaluation at the end of the grading period.

Figure 8.41   *Portfolio form for student's self-assessment.*

SELF-ASSESSMENT FORM

Name _____   Date _____

Name of work _____

1. I got my idea from _____

   _____

   _____

2. I got the background information from _____

   _____

   _____

3. The part that was hard to write was _____

   _____

   because _____

   _____

   _____

4. I especially liked this part _____

   _____

   because _____

   _____

   _____

5. I could improve it by _____

   _____

   _____

6. New vocabulary words I used _____

   _____

   _____

Teacher's Comments _____

   _____

   _____

Figure 8.42   *Teacher's quarterly evaluation form.*

QUARTERLY TEACHER–STUDENT EVALUATION

Name _____   Quarter   1   2   3   4

Date _____

1. What was your favorite piece of work this quarter? Explain why. _____

_____

_____

_____

2. What piece did you like the least? Explain why. _____

_____

_____

_____

3. Did you make good use of your time? Explain. _____

_____

_____

_____

4. What things did you learn about yourself as you were writing? _____

_____

_____

_____

5. Which type of new genre will you attempt next quarter? Why do you want to try it? ____

_____

_____

_____

6. What one thing would you like most to learn next quarter? _____

_____

_____

_____

Student's Signature _____

Teacher's Signature _____

Figure 8.43   *Teacher's portfolio assessment rubric.*

GOALS		Excellent 5	4	3	2	Poor 1
WRITING PROCESS	uses various prewriting strategies (brainstorming, webbing, illustrating, etc.)					
	writes a rough draft (ability to put thoughts on paper)					
	revises rough draft (checks details, sequence, clarity, etc.)					
	edits/proofreads (alone, with peers, or with teacher)					
	publishes or shares (final copy or oral reading to classmates or teacher)					
WRITING SKILLS	writes complete sentences					
	uses descriptive words in writing					
	uses correct format when writing paragraphs					
	uses correct format when writing letters					
USAGE	makes subjects and verbs agree					
MECHANICS	punctuates at the end of sentences					
	capitalizes the beginning of sentences					
	uses commas correctly					
	uses quotation marks correctly					
	capitalizes proper nouns in writing					

Teacher Comments:

Source: Reprinted with permission of the Mid-Del School District, Oklahoma.

If you would like to learn more about alternative methods for evaluating students' work, some good sources are *Portfolio Assessment: Getting Started* by Allan De Fina (1992); *Practical Assessments for Literature-Based Reading Classrooms* by Adele Fiderer (1995); *Alternative Assessment Techniques for Reading & Writing* by Wilma H. Miller (1995); *Assessment Is Instruction: Reading, Writing, Spelling, and Phonics for All Learners* by Susan Mandel Glazer (1998); *Classroom Based Assessment* by Bonnie Campbell Hill, Cynthia Ruptic, and Lisa Norwick (1998); *Creating Writers: Linking Assessment and Writing Instruction* by V. Spandel and R. Stiggins (1990); and *In Teachers' Hands: Investigating the Practice of Classroom Assessment* by R. Stiggins and N. Conklin (1992).

Summary

The process approach is one method of teaching writing as part of an integrated approach. In the prewriting phase, teachers try to help their students find ideas to write about by having them keep journals, brainstorm, and tell stories. In the writing phase, students produce rough drafts and then revise and edit those drafts. Teacher–pupil conferences play an important role in revising and editing. Finally, in the postwriting phase, students learn a variety of ways to share their works with others, including author's chair, bookbinding, and publishing.

Along with the process approach to teaching writing, there should be a great deal of writing going on in the classroom every day. There are a number of different types of writing suitable for children, including the writing of journals, letters, stories, reports, plays, and poetry. Whole units can be built around poetry writing.

Finally, alternative ways of assessing writing are becoming increasingly important. In addition to merely giving a grade to written work, teachers now use observations, anecdotal records, and portfolios. These are much more meaningful assessments of what children have actually written and learned about writing.

With Children activities

CLASS BULLETIN BOARD

With a group of students, put together a bulletin board of students' writings. Encourage parents and administrators to visit your room and examine the bulletin board. This is a first step toward getting away from grading every single paper a child writes.

YOUNG AUTHORS' FAIR

Ask each student to select his or her best written piece from the semester and bind it in a hardbound book form. Then arrange for a large display area, such as the gymnasium or auditorium, to display the children's bound books. Give every student who participates a certificate rather than awarding prizes to the best work.

CLASS MAGAZINE

With access to a typewriter and a copying machine, you can create your own class magazine. It doesn't have to be fancy, but it should convey to the students the notion of publication in a real journal. Then invite students to submit their best works (fiction, nonfiction, poetry, and so on). Form a student committee to select works for the magazine. Another committee can help with the proofreading, editing, and layout.

SONG WRITING

Play some popular rock, country and western, or rap music in class. Discuss the lyrics with your class. Then have children work in small groups to produce their own songs. They should revise and edit them the way they would any other piece of written work.

TEACHER WRITING

Keep your own journal for a few weeks; then bring it to class to share with your students. Discuss with them why you keep a journal. When students write stories, letters, or poems in class, you should write also. Share your writing with the children. Save your rough drafts and final copies to show development from one stage to another.

GREETING CARDS

Ask each student to bring in a commercial greeting card. Discuss the cards as a whole class: the artwork, design, message, poetry, humor, and so on. Then instruct each child to select a special occasion or person and design a greeting card with a message, saying, or original poem.

WRITING RECIPES

Bring in some food recipes and discuss them with the entire class. Then discuss other areas in which recipes can be used. Here is a child's "recipe for success": "First, take two cups of laughter and mix in a winning smile. Then sprinkle generously with determination. Next, add a cupful of organization. Spread it all over with intelligence. Bake until beautiful." Create other recipes for love, happiness, or good health.

PARENT INTERVIEWS

Have your students find out about their parents' childhoods by interviewing them. Were they shy? Popular? Good at sports? Did they have a favorite toy? TV program? Book? Song? What was their most embarrassing moment? Who were their friends? Where did they live? Have students transcribe this oral interview into an article or fictional short story.

DISPLACED CHARACTERS

Take any favorite character from literature. What would that person think, say, or do if she or he lived in the present? For example, take Huck Finn off the Mississippi River and place him in an inner-city classroom made up of children of various ethnic backgrounds. How would he react to the racial tensions today?

technology *E-mail and Collaborative Internet*

Teachers who use the integrated approach to the language arts want the students' writing to have purpose. One excellent way to ensure purpose of writing is to have students use the Internet for corresponding with others. There are many ways to incorporate the use of technology with the students' writing. For example, the students can use e-mail to write to their favorite authors. At the end of this chapter in the E-learning websites section, there are a number of sites that have authors who respond to their fans through the use of e-mail. Leu (1997) gives the following sites for other types of authentic writing:

1. Students can send questions concerning famous scientists, architects, astronauts, and other people to the following:
   - www.askanexpert.com/askanexpert/index.html
   - www.madsci.org

2. Students can acquire a pen pal from around the world by contacting one of the following sites:
   - www.hi.com/au/keypal1.asp
   - www.keypals.com/p/keypals.html
   - web66.coled.umn.edu/schools.html

3. If students desire to do collaborative projects with students in other classrooms around the world, they can visit one of the following:
   - www.keil.ukans.edu/~monarch/
     (This site is for those interested in the study of monarchs.)
   - www1minn.net:80/~schubert/NickNacks.html#anchor100100
     (This site explains how to develop a project.)
   - www.classroom.net/contact
     or
   - www.gsh.org/gsh/class/projsrch.html
     or
   - www.kidlink.org:80/KIDPROJ/
     (These last three sites permit teachers either to post a topic that interests their students or to check out the postings and respond to one of the requests.)

4. When students complete an original poem or story, they can now share it with the world by posting it on one of the following sites:
   - www.cyberkids.com/
   - www.kidpub.org/kidpub/

5. Finally, students can share reviews of their favorite books at the following:
   - i-site.on.ca/booknook.html

E-learning *websites*

www.learner.org.exhibits/literature/
This site helps with the techniques of writing a short story.

www.sfwa.org/writing/basics.html
This site discusses careless speech and well-written materials to help writers in understanding the challenge of writing.

db.cochran.com/li_showElems:theopage:thoe:4119:0.db
This site will permit you to find a pen pal in another country or state.

www.ncte.org
This is the site for the National Council of Teachers of English. It gives teaching ideas, conversation, public policy, publication information, and much more.

www.Kidpub.org/Kidpub/
This is a place for students to publish stories on the Net and to read stories written by other students.

www.Kids-space.org/
This site permits students to share their art, music, and writings with others.

Related Readings

Atwell, N. (1998). *In the middle: New understandings about writing, reading, and learning* (2nd ed.). Portsmouth, NH: Boynton/Cook Publishers.

> Atwell explains the how and the why of setting up the reading and writing workshop. She uses the workshops with middle school students; therefore, she gives some characteristics of middle school students and examples of their work. She writes as if she is talking to the reader.

Calkins, L. M. (1994). *The art of teaching writing* (2nd ed.). Portsmouth, NH: Heinemann.

> Calkins gives background on the characteristics of the different-aged students—from nursery school to adolescents. She clearly explains the structure of the writing workshop and how to encourage students to write in other areas of their lives.

Graves, D. (1994). *A fresh look at writing.* Portsmouth, NH: Heinemann.

> The chapters on helping children share their writing with others, helping them evaluate their own writing, and helping them learn conventions of writing are particularly helpful. He also explains how to begin using portfolios.

Farr, R., & Tone, F. (1994). *Portfolio and performance assessment: Helping students evaluate their progress as readers and writers* (2nd ed.). Fort Worth, TX: Harcourt Brace College Publishers.

> This is a great book for someone who has never used portfolios before. It explains how to set up portfolios so that they become meaningful tools of self-evaluation.

Fiderer, A. (1995). *Practical assessments: For literature-based reading classrooms.* New York: Scholastic Professional Books.

> The book has assessment forms that may be copied and used by the classroom teacher. Some are for the teacher to use, and others are for the student to use for self-assessment.

Smith, J., & Warwick, E. (1997). *How children learn to write.* Katonah, NY: Richard C. Owen Publishers.

> This book gives developmental information about children and writing. It explains Graves's process approach, Cambourne's model of literacy, and Flower and Hayes's model of learning.

References

Applebee, A. (1978). *The child's concept of story: Ages 2 to 17.* Chicago: University of Chicago Press.

Applebee, A. (1981). *Writing in the secondary school: English and content areas.* Urbana, IL: NCTE. NCTE Research Report No. 21.

Applebee, A., Langer, J., & Mullis, J. (1986). *The writing report card: Writing achievement in American schools.* Princeton, NJ: National Assessment of Educational Progress, Educational Testing Services.

Atwell, N. (1984). Writing and reading literature from the inside out. *Language Arts, 61*(3), 240–252.

Atwell, N. (1987). *In the middle.* Portsmouth, NH: Boynton/Cook Publishers.

Atwell, N. (1998). *In the middle: New understandings about writing, reading and learning* (2nd ed.). Portsmouth, NH: Heinemann.

Atwood, A. (1973). *My own rhythm: An approach to haiku.* New York: Scribner's.

Barone, D., & Lovell, J. (1990). Michael the show and tell magician: A journey through literature to self. *Language Arts, 67*(2), 134–143.

Brandt, R. (1997). On using knowledge about our brain: A conversation with Bob Sylwester. *Educational leadership, 54*(6), 16–19.

Britton, J. (1973). *The development of writing liabilities.* London: Macmillan.

Britton, J. (1978). The composing process and the functions of writing. In C. Cooper & L. Odell (eds.), *Research on composing: Points of departure*. Urbana, IL: NCTE.

Britton, J. (1986). *Language and learning*. New York: Penguin.

Burrows, A. (1976). Research then and now. In S. Lundsteen (ed.), *Help for the teacher of written composition: New directions in research*. Urbana, IL: ERIC Clearinghouse on Reading and Communication Skills.

Calkins, L. (1991). *Living between the lines*. Portsmouth, NH: Heinemann.

Calkins, L. (1994). *The art of teaching writing* (2nd ed.). Portsmouth, NH: Heinemann.

Cambourne, B. (1988). *The whole story: Natural learning and the acquisition of literacy in the classroom*. Jefferson City, MO: Scholastic.

Cambourne, B. (1995). Toward an educational relevant theory of literacy learning: Twenty years of inquiry. *Reading Teacher*, 49(3), 183–190.

Carbo, M. (1997). Reading styles times twenty. *Educational Leadership*, 54(6), 38–42.

Chafel, J. (1997). Children's views of poverty: A review of research and implications for teaching. *The Educational Forum*, 61(1), 360–371.

Chittenden, E., & Courtney, R. (1989). Assessment of young children's reading: Documentation as an alternative to testing. In D. S. Strickland & L. M. Morrow (eds.), *Emerging literacy: Young children learn to read and write*. Newark, DE: International Reading Association.

Clark, B. (1986). *Optimizing learning: The integrated educational model in the classroom*. Columbus, OH: Merrill.

Courtney, A. (1985). Profile: Patricia MacLachlan. *Language Arts*, 62(7), 783–787.

De Fina, A. A. (1992). *Portfolio assessment: Getting started*. New York: Scholastic.

Dowling, R. (1980). Ohio young authors. *Ohio Reading Teacher*, 27(2).

Dunn, R. (1996). *How to implement and supervise a learning styles program*. Alexandria, VA: ASCD.

Elbow, P. (1973). *Writing without teachers*. New York: Oxford University Press.

Elbow, P. (1981). *Writing with power*. New York: Oxford University Press.

Emig, J. (1971). *The composing processes of twelfth graders*. Champaign, IL: National Council of Teachers of English.

Farr, R., & Tone, B. (1998). *Portfolio and performance assessment: Helping students evaluate their progress as readers and writers* (2nd ed.). Fort Worth, TX: Harcourt Brace College Publishers.

Farrell, E. (1989, April). *Giving voice to poetry: Oral interpretation in the classroom*. Paper presented at the National Council of Teachers of English Meeting, Charleston, SC.

Fiderer, A. (1995). *Practical assessments for literature-based reading classrooms*. New York: Scholastic.

Florio, S. (1979). The problem of dead letters: Social perspectives on the teaching of writing. *Elementary School Journal*, 80(1), 1–7.

Flower, L., & Hayes, J. R. (1994). The cognition of discovery: Defining a rhetorical problem. In S. Perl (ed.), *Landmark essays on writing process*. Davis, CA: Heragoras Press.

Frager, A., Tway, E., Gandei, L., Hammond, T., Hordie, J., Mohler, P., & Whitt, J. (1987). The uses of free writing in the elementary school. *Oklahoma English Journal*, 2(1), 1–16.

Frazier, D., & Paulson, F. (1992). How portfolios motivate reluctant writers. *Educational Leadership*, 49(5), 62–65.

Fulwiler, T. (1987a). *The journal book*. Portsmouth, NH: Boynton/Cook Publishers.

Fulwiler, T. (1987b). *Teaching with writing*. Portsmouth, NH: Boynton/Cook Publishers.

Gambrell, L. (1985). Reading–writing interaction. *The Reading Teacher*, 38, 512–515.

Glazer, S. M. (1998). *Assessment is instruction: Reading, writing, spelling, and phonics for all learners*. Norwood, MA: Christopher-Gordon.

Goldberg, M. (1989). Portrait of James Gray. *Educational Leadership*, 47(3), 65–68.

Gomez, M., Grau, M. E., & Block, M. (1991). Reassessing portfolio assessment: Rhetoric and reality. *Language Arts*, 68, 620–628.

Goodman, K. S., Goodman, Y., Hood, W. J. (eds.) (1989). *The whole language evaluation book*. Portsmouth, NH: Heinemann.

Goodman, Y. (1978). Kidwatching: An alternative to testing. *National Elementary Principals' Journal*, 57, 41–45.

Graves, D. (1973). Children's writing: Research directions and hypothesis based upon an examination of the writing processes of seven-year-old children. *Dissertation Abstracts International*, 34, 6255A. Doctoral dissertation, University of New Hampshire.

Graves, D. (1978). We won't let them write. *Language Arts*, 55, 636.

Graves, D. (1989a). *Experiment with fiction*. Portsmouth, NH: Heinemann.

Graves, D. (1989b). *Investigate nonfiction*. Portsmouth, NH: Heinemann.

Graves, D. (1990, July 27). *The process writing model*. Paper presented at OKTAWL Conference, Norman, OK.

Graves, D. (1991). *Build a literate class*. Portsmouth, NH: Heinemann.

Graves, D. (1994). *A fresh look at writing*. Portsmouth, NH: Heinemann.

Graves, D., & Hansen, J. (1983). The author's chair. *Language Arts*, 60(2), 176–183.

Greene, J. (1983). *The nature and development of letter writing in Hispanic and Anglo children using a school-based postal system*. ERIC Document No. ED 234416.

Hahn, J. (1983, May). *Organization of a young authors' fair*. Paper presented at International Reading Association 28th Annual Convention, Anaheim, CA.

Hansen, J. (1987). *When writers read*. Portsmouth, NH: Heinemann Books.

Harste, J. (1990). Jerry Harste speaks on reading and writing. *The Reading Teacher*, 43(4), 316–318.

Harwayne, S. (1992). *Lasting impressions: Weaving literature into the writing workshop.* Portsmouth, NH: Heinemann.

Heller, M. (1990). *Reading–writing connections: From theory to practice.* New York: Longman.

Hill, B., Ruptic, C., & Norwick, L. (1998). *Classroom-based assessment.* Norwood, MA: Christopher-Gordon.

Hipple, M. (1985). Journal writing in kindergarten. *Language Arts, 62*(3), 255–261.

Hodgin, J., & Wooliscroft, C. (1997). Eric learns to read: Learning styles at work. *Educational Leadership, 54*(6), 43–45.

Hopkins, L. (1972). *Pass the poetry, please!* New York: Citation Press.

Huck, C. (1987). *Children's literature in the elementary school* (4th ed.). Fort Worth, TX: Harcourt Brace College Publishers.

Humphrey, J., & Rodden, S. (1972). Encouraging young authors. *The Reading Teacher, 25*(7), 643–651.

Janeczko, P. (1983). *Poetspeak: In their work, about their work.* New York: Bradbury Press.

Johnson, D., Pittelman, S., & Heinlich, J. (1986). Semantic mapping. *The Reading Teacher, 39*(8), 778–783.

Kehoe, B., & Mixon, V. (1997). *Children and the Internet.* Upper Saddle River, NJ: Prentice Hall.

Kennedy, X. J., & Kennedy, D. M. (1982). *Knock at a star: A child's introduction to poetry.* Boston: Little, Brown.

King, M. (1989). Speech to writing: Children's growth in writing potential. In J. Gason (ed.), *Reading and writing connections.* Boston: Allyn & Bacon.

Koch, K. (1970). *Wishes, lies, and dreams.* New York: Chelsea House Publishers.

Koch, K. (1973). *Rose, where did you get that red?: Teaching great poetry to children.* New York: Random House.

Lamme, L. (1989). Authorship: A key facet of whole language. *The Reading Teacher, 42,* 704–710.

Leu, D. J. (1997). Exploring literacy on the Internet: Caity's question: Literacy as deixis on the Internet. *The Reading Teacher, 51*(1), 62–67.

MacLean, M. (1985, April). *Writing to learn about literature.* Paper presented at National Council of Teachers of English, Houston, TX.

Manning, M., Manning, G., & Long, R. (1994). *Theme immersion inquiry-based curriculum in elementary and middle schools.* Portsmouth, NH: Heinemann.

Manning, M., Manning, P., & Hughes, D. (1987). Journals in first grade: What children write. *Reading Teacher, 41*(3), 311–315.

Manzano, R. (1992). *A different kind of classroom: Thinking with dimensions of learning.* Alexandria, VA: Association of Supervision and Curriculum Development.

McCarthy, B. (1997). A tale of four learners: 4Mat's learning styles. *Educational Leadership, 54*(6), 46–53.

McCaslin, N. (1996). *Creative dramatics in the classroom* (6th ed.). New York: D. McKay Co.

Miller, W. H. (1995). *Alternative assessment techniques for reading & writing.* West Nyack, NY: The Center for Applied Research in Education.

Moffett, J. (1968). *Teaching the universe of discourse.* Boston: Houghton Mifflin.

Monroe, D. (1991). Qualities of a school district culture that supports a dynamic process of assessment. In J. A. Roderick (ed.), *Context-responsive approaches to assessing children's language.* Urbana, IL: National Conference on Research in English.

Murray, D. (1978). Internal revision: A process of discovery. In C. Cooper & L. Odell (eds.), *Research on composing: Points of departure.* Urbana, IL: NCTE.

Murray, D. (1985). *A writer teaches reading* (2nd ed.). Boston: Houghton Mifflin.

Murray, D. (1990). *Write to learn* (3rd ed.). New York: Holt, Rinehart, & Winston.

NAEP Facts (1996). National Center for Education Statistics. Washington, DC: U. S. Department of Education, p. 1.

Norton, D. (1997). *The effective teaching of language arts* (5th ed.). Columbus, OH: Merrill.

Perrine, L. (1962). *Poetry: Theory and practice.* New York: Harcourt, Brace, Jovanovich.

Pool, C. (1997). Maximizing learning: A conversation with Renate Nummela Cain. *Educational Leadership, 54*(6), 11–15.

Purdy, S. (1973). *Books for you to make.* New York: J. B. Lippincott.

Rhoten, L., & Yellin, D. (1993). Bookbinding: Promoting authorship in emerging readers. In C. Collins (ed.), *Teaching the language arts.* Boston: Allyn & Bacon.

Rico, G. (1983). *Writing the natural way.* Los Angeles: Jeremy Tarcher.

Rosenblatt, L. (1989). Writing and reading: The transactional theory. In J. Mason (ed.), *Reading and writing connections.* Boston: Allyn & Bacon.

Routman, R. (1996). *Literacy at the crossroads: Crucial talk about reading, writing and other teaching dilemmas.* Portsmouth, NH: Heinemann.

Savage, J. (1998). *Teaching reading and writing: Combining skills, strategies and literacy* (2nd ed.). Boston: McGraw-Hill.

Searle, D., & Dillon, D. (1980). Responding to student writing: What is said or how it is said. *Language Arts, 57,* 773–781.

Seely, A. (1995). *Integrated thematic units.* Westminster, CA: Teacher Created Materials.

Seuling, B. (1984). *How to write a children's book and get it published.* New York: Charles Scribner's Sons.

Short, K., Harste, J., & Burke, C. (1996). *Creating classrooms for authors and inquires* (2nd ed.). Portsmouth, NH: Heinemann.

Shuy, R. (1987). Research currents: Dialogue as the heart of learning. *Language Arts, 64,* 890–897.

Slavin, R. (1996). Neverstreaming: Preventing learning disabilities. *Educational Leadership, 53*(5), 4–7.

Smith, F. (1988a). *Joining the literacy club.* Portsmouth, NH: Heinemann.

Smith, F. (1988b). *Understanding reading* (4th ed.). Hillsdale, NJ: Lawrence Erlbaum Associates.

Sommers, N. (1994). Revision strategies of student writers and experienced adult writers. In S. Perl (ed.), *Landmark essays on writing process*. Davis, CA: Heragoras Press.

Sowers, S. (1985). The story and the "all about" book. In J. Hansen, T. Newkirk, & D. Graves (eds.), *Breaking ground: Teachers relate reading and writing in the elementary school*. Portsmouth, NH: Heinemann.

Spandel, V., & Stiggins, R. (1990). *Creating writers: Linking assessment and writing instruction*. New York: Longman.

Staton, J. (1980). Writing and counseling: Using a dialogue journal. *Language Arts, 57*, 514–518.

Sternberg, R. (1997). What does it mean to be smart? *Educational Leadership, 54*(6). 20–25.

Stewig, J. (1981). Choral speaking: Who has the time? Why take the time? *Childhood Education, 57*, 25–29.

Stiggins, R., & Conklin, N. (1992). *In teachers' hands: Investigating the practice of classroom assessment*. New York: State University of New York Press.

Taylor, D. (1991). From the child's point of view: Alternate approaches to assessment. In J. A. Roderick (ed.), *Context-responsive approaches to assessing children's language*. Urbana, IL: National Conference on Research in English.

Tiedt, I. (1970). Exploring poetry patterns. *Elementary English*, 1083–1084.

Tompkins, G. (1990). *Teaching writing: Balancing process and product*. Columbus, OH: Merrill Publishing Company.

Tway, E. (1984). *Time for writing in the elementary school*. Urbana, IL: National Council of Teachers of English.

U.S. Department of Education (1996). National Assessment of Educational Progress. Office of Educational Research and Improvement. Washington, D.C.

Valencia, S. (1990). A portfolio approach to classroom reading assessment: The whys, whats, and hows. *The Reading Teacher, 43*, 338–340.

Vermette, P. (1998). *Making cooperative learning work*. Upper Saddle River, NJ: Merrill.

Vygotsky, L. (1962). *Thought and language*. Cambridge, MA: MIT Press.

Vygotsky, L. (1978). *Mind and society: The development of psychological processes*. Cambridge, MA: Harvard University Press.

Wang, M., Reynolds, M., & Walberg, H. (1995). Serving students at the margins. *Educational Leadership, 52*(4), 12–17.

Weiss, H. (1974). *How to make your own books*. New York: Thomas Y. Crowell.

White, E. M. (1985). *Teaching and assessing writing*. San Francisco: Jossey-Bass.

Wigginton, E. (1986). *Sometimes a shining moment: The Foxfire experience*. New York: Doubleday.

Wong, H., & Wong, R. (1991). *The first days of school: How to be an effective teacher*. Sunnyvale, CA: Harry K. Wong Publishers.

Wray, D., & Lewis, M. (1997). *Extending literacy: Children reading and writing non-fiction*. New York: Routledge.

Yellin, D. (1988). My pen pal goes to college: A functional approach to literacy learning. *The Writer's Slate, 4*(1), 1–8.

Yellin, D. (1991). Will evaluation kill whole language? *Kansas Journal of Reading, 7*, 49–54.

The Tools of Writing

9

IN THIS CHAPTER

overview

This chapter focuses on the skills or mechanics associated with writing. We refer to them as the tools of writing. The primary tools discussed here are handwriting, spelling, capitalization, punctuation, and grammar. Traditionally these skills or tools were taught in isolation from other literacy acts and relied heavily on textbook exercises and rule memorization. This method reflected the predominant view of learning based on behavioral psychology. Behavioral psychology emphasized memorization, drill, and much repetition of isolated skill activities.

The new approach to skills learning is based on cognitive psychology, which argues that children actively construct their own knowledge when involved in authentic tasks. Children, we now know, learn best when they can see a real personal purpose in what they are learning. Effective classroom teachers support constructivist learning by serving as resources who help children as needed, who conference often with students, and provide specific information in mini-lessons that minimize interruption of the process of writing.

A balanced approach recognizes that many school districts still require skills to be taught and tested separately from writing. Therefore, this chapter is also intended to give you the background information in each of the skill areas to prepare you for the real classroom situations you will face.

Handwriting, spelling, capitalization, punctuation, and grammar skills develop slowly, over time, and primarily through exposure to extensive reading and writing activities in all subject areas: science, social studies, literature, etc. Only when students see a real reason for writing and are aware of the audience for whom they are writing will these skills take on meaning.

The Beginnings: Reasons for Writing

To understand the importance of the tools of writing, recall the reasons for writing. Chapter 8 stated that all writing depends on experience. Children must have experienced something they want to write about, something they want to express in a more permanent form than speech, something they want to share with others. Experience, permanence, sharing—these are the foundation blocks of writing.

Children also need experience with the world of print. Specifically, they need to see and use the tools of writing. Charles Temple and his associates (Temple, Nathan, Burris, & Temple, 1988) summarized much of the research about how young children go about acquiring the tools of writing in the following sequence:

1. Many children begin writing by drawing.
2. At some point, the child calls his or her drawings writing.
3. Squiggles and scribbles that might be letters appear within the drawing, but only the child can "read" them.
4. By seeing print, children eventually begin to employ the distinctive features of letters and words in their writing, even though they do not yet recognize the relationship between sounds and symbols.

The linguist Noam Chomsky (1974) pointed out that there appears to be an innate capacity in children to use language for communication purposes. Research by Ferriero and Teberosky (1983) has shown that children also have an inborn need to communicate in a variety of ways, including print. Young children, for example, experiment with paints, chalk, clay, paper, and pencil long before they enter school. In this way, they begin to discover and reconstruct for themselves the nature of literacy.

In the preschool years, many children have experiences they wish to share verbally with others. This kind of informal talk should be encouraged by teachers. To make the child's speech record more permanent, a teacher may encourage a child to "write or draw me a picture of what you saw or did." Picture drawings accompanied by scribbled words build on what the child has already experimented with at home. Drawings and early scribbles at home or at school are thus the child's first acquaintance with the tools of written communication.

In school, teachers can build on this natural curiosity about reading and writing by using the child's own language to create stories through the **language experience approach (LEA)** (Stauffer, 1980; see Chapter 6 for discussion of LEA). Although often considered a beginning approach to reading instruction, LEA is also an excellent way to introduce young children to the tools of writing in the classroom. The steps in LEA are as follows:

1. The child dictates a story.
2. The teacher records the story.
3. The teacher reads the story back to the child.
4. The child reads the story back to the teacher.
5. The child traces or copies the story, with teacher assistance.

It is the last step that makes LEA a viable instructional approach in a writing program. Early in her career of researching the acquisition of literacy, New Zealand's Marie Clay (1975) noted that tracing and copying are strategies commonly used by preschoolers. Clay also noted that children later begin to generate their own writing by employing invented spellings, another strategy in the natural acquisition of writing. Tracing, copying, and inventing symbols provide a young child's first encounters with the tools of writing; thus they are a part of the language experience approach, which leads young children into the process of writing. Figure 9.1 gives some more teaching suggestions for using LEA as a beginning instructional approach to writing.

Figure 9.1

Suggestions for using the language experience approach.

- Vary the nature of the experiences used to inspire group charts (class dictates to teacher), key-word vocabulary (individual students' word banks), and individual stories. Use field trips, objects, films, and discussion.

- Try cutting an experience chart story into sentence strips. Later let each child manipulate the strips to reform the story; this is the notion of "composing."

- Type up a student's experience story with a primary typeface and make copies for the rest of the class. This is one way to share stories with a wider audience.

- In taking dictation, do not be concerned initially with whether a child's language is grammatically correct. At a later time, when the student is comfortable with the approach, changes in the story form can be made.

- Take dictation from children using a variety of means: chalk, pencil, pen, computer.

- Display experience charts and language-experience stories on bulletin boards around the room and in school hallways for others to read and enjoy.

Handwriting: An Individualistic Tool

Surprisingly, handwriting is still a major issue of discussion among elementary classroom teachers. We say surprisingly because the modern approach to writing focuses on the creative process of writing, not the mechanics of penmanship (Graves, 1994; Norton, 1997). Handwriting is nevertheless an important tool that all young children need to learn. Recall your own student days as a beginning writer learning to produce the letters of the alphabet for the first time as you read this section.

In the past—and to some extent today—handwriting instruction has occupied a preeminent place in the writing program (Ediger, 1979). In fact, in some schools it *was* the writing program. Traditionally it was called *penmanship*, and its goal was to create a form of writing that looked like a mirror image of the models shown in the workbook. Achieving this goal took hundreds of hours of practice stretched over weeks, months, and years. Formal penmanship lessons began in first grade and stretched into the intermediate grades. There were few challenges to this type of instruction because writing in these schools was defined as handwriting.

Today most educators take a new view toward handwriting instruction and its place in the language arts curriculum. Gone are the days when handwriting lessons focused on body posture, the position of the paper, how to hold the pencil, and achieving perfection. It is true that sitting up straight, securing the paper with one hand while writing with the other, and holding the pencil loosely between the thumb and two forefingers (rather than holding it like a spear) help to improve the appearance of writing (Lamme, 1979). However, authorities now agree that *beautiful* handwriting is not the goal; *legible* handwriting is (Norton, 1997; Stewig & Nordberg, 1995; Tompkins, 1998).

LEGIBILITY

Legibility is the single most important point about handwriting to be remembered (Farris, 1991; Hodges, 1991). *Legibility* means that a child's handwriting can be read by someone other than the writer. It doesn't have to be perfect; it may not look beautiful. But if the teacher can read the handwriting, it is acceptable. Like so many other aspects of learning, a child's handwriting improves over time as the child sees a need for it to improve. Constant drilling on letter formation or the use of handwriting lessons as punishment only reinforces negative attitudes in children toward handwriting in particular and writing in general. Bing (1988) found that when teachers stressed perfect handwriting, students became so worried about constructing the letters they lost sight of the purpose of writing, which is to convey thoughts and feelings.

Teachers may feel pressured to make their own handwriting and that of their students conform to the models shown in the workbooks of the particular handwriting program adopted by a school system. Study Figures 9.2 and 9.3, which show samples from two popular handwriting programs; Zaner-Bloser and D'Nealian. Note the similarities and differences between these two programs, but do not be intimidated by them. Remember that the goal of handwriting instruction is the legibility of students' writing, not some artificial standards of perfection.

Figure 9.2 *Zaner-Bloser handwriting model.*

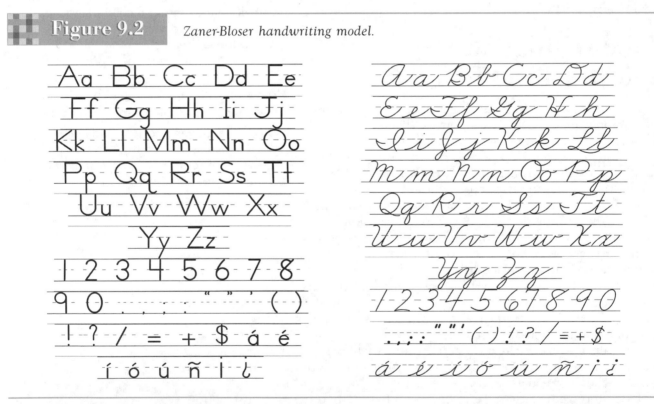

Source: From *Handwriting: A Way to Self-Expression,* © 1993, Zaner-Bloser, Inc., Columbus, Ohio. Used with permission from Zaner-Bloser, Inc.

The more recent innovation in handwriting styles, the D'Nealian method, is named after its inventor Donald Neal Thurber (1987). Like other handwriting types (e.g., Zaner-Bloser), the D'Nealian method introduces manuscript and cursive strokes through student workbooks (K–8) that encourage tracing, copying, and much practice of individual strokes and letters. What makes D'Nealian somewhat unique is that the manuscript letters are slightly slanted, like cursive letters, and the cursive letters do not contain some of the old-fashioned swirls and flourishes. In theory, this should make the transition from manuscript to cursive writing easier; indeed this is the reason Thurber developed his new writing style. According to classroom teachers who have used D'Nealian, however, this method is no better or no worse than any of the other commercial handwriting materials available. It is what the individual teacher does with the material that makes the difference.

What, then, constitutes legibility? In addition to whether or not handwriting can be read by someone other than the writer, legibility is characterized by four main elements: size, slant, spacing, and distinction.

There are letters of two *sizes* in the English alphabet: lowercase (small) and uppercase (capital) letters. Children need to be taught the difference and encouraged to use each type appropriately. The child who writes with all capital or all small letters eventually discovers that she or he is confusing the reader, particularly in the cases of sentence beginnings and proper nouns. However, even many adults occasionally use small and capital letters inappropriately, so the teacher should not make a major issue of this with the young child just beginning to write.

In some handwriting programs, a definite rule is also given for the *slant* of letters. For example, a program might advise that all cursive letters slant to the right at a 45-degree angle. This again is an artificial and unrealistic standard to put before children. *Consistency* of slant is what makes for legible handwriting. Some children have no slant in either their manuscript or cursive writing; it consists of straight up-and-down strokes. Other children slant their letters slightly to the right. Left-handed children may slant their letters to the left. As long as the slant is consistent within and between words, it should be acceptable—because it is legible.

There are two types of *spacing* that affect legibility: between letters and between words. A small, consistent amount of space should be left between letters even in cursive writing, in which the letters are joined with a sweep stroke representing the space. A slightly larger, but again consistent, space should be left between words. The key point is consistency. If a child uses inconsistent spacing between letters and words, the writing becomes more difficult to read and possibly illegible.

Distinction refers to the fact that certain letters in the English alphabet look alike. For example, in cursive writing, an *i* can be mistaken for an *e* if the writer omits the dot above. Similarly the letters *o*, *a*, and *u*, if not written carefully, can be confused. Clearly, letter distinction is as much an issue of spelling as it is of handwriting, for the two are related. Illegible handwriting looks like sloppy spelling, which only confuses and annoys a reader. Once the teacher identifies for the child which letters need to be written with more care, the student accomplishes the rest through practice in real writing activities. Having students write *aaaaaaooooouuuuu* dozens of times is not the solution.

Figure 9.4 illustrates the characteristics of legibility. If you keep these elements in mind, no individual writing program should intimidate you. Once you can read a child's handwriting, you can get on with the real teaching of writing: as a process in which students create stories, poems, reports, and so on. Leave the endless drills and artificial handwriting exercises to someone else.

Figure 9.3

D'Nealian handwriting model.

Source: D'Nealian® Handwriting Model from *D'Nealian® Handwriting Book 2* by Donald Neal Thurber. Copyright © 1999 by Addison-Wesley Educational Publishers, Inc.

Figure 9.4

Characteristics of legibility.

SIZE:

The boy and girl visited New York City.
THE BOY AND GIRL VISITED NEW YORK CITY.
the boy and girl visited new york city.

SLANT:

I love to eat vanilla ice cream.
/I/love/to/eat/vanilla/ice/cream./
\I\love\to\eat\vanilla\ice\cream.\
I love to eat vanilla ice cream.

SPACING:

space   s p a c e
He left his socks in the room.
H elef t hi ssoc ks int he r oo m.

DISTINCTION: ⌣ l ⌣ ⌣ l = about

Contrary to popular belief, handwriting is not a complex cognitive process. It is a psychomotor skill, requiring cognitive abilities that are developed over time through extensive practice. Practice is the key, and the kind of practice a child engages in determines the effectiveness of a handwriting program. This means that handwriting activities should be enjoyable as well as meaningful. They should provide the child with practice in the necessary letter, word, and sentence constructions. All of this means real writing activities as opposed to artificial drills.

Chapter 8 identified some of the many real writing experiences that young children can have, including writing pen pal letters, short stories, and research reports. These activities and many more are also the basis of developing sound handwriting skills. Thus handwriting skills are developed not in isolated lessons, but through extensive use of the process approach to writing.

READINESS SKILLS FOR HANDWRITING

Young children need some direct instruction in the formulation of letters. In the past, this meant whole-group and full-period lessons beginning in kindergarten and continuing throughout the elementary grades. However, not all kindergarten or first-grade children are ready for formal handwriting lessons. According to Lamme (1979), there are a number of prerequisites that should be met before direct instruction begins. These prerequisites are also referred to as the *readiness* skills of handwriting.

Small-Muscle Development

To hold a pencil properly requires development of the small muscles in the hand, fingers, and wrist. Very young children who have difficulty holding their pencils steady may need more practice with manipulative tasks such as assembling jigsaw puzzles and attaching snap beads. Molding with clay and papier-mâché also helps develop small-muscle strength. Small-muscle coordination is enhanced by such activities as zipping, buttoning, screwing caps on jars, and tying knots. Art activities such as painting, coloring, and drawing are also good readiness predictors, as is the ability to cut with small scissors.

Eye-Hand Coordination

Writing requires coordination between what the brain thinks, what the eye sees, and what the small muscles of the hand want to do. Manipulative play activities, such as block constructions, typing, sewing, weaving, and hammering nails into wood, all develop the eye–hand coordination necessary for fluency in writing. The ease (or difficulty) with which young children handle paper-and-pencil activities, such as dot-to-dot constructions and mazes, is also a good indicator of readiness for formal handwriting instruction.

Ability to Hold a Writing Tool

Normal-size pencils are difficult for young children to hold and manipulate easily. To prepare students for this writing task, provide them with a variety of utensils, such as bottles, strainers, various-size containers, sticks, toy shovels, and spades, to hold and manipulate. Simple gardening activities and cooking activities also give children practice in holding and manipulating various-size objects. When students wish to write, suggest that they begin with thick magic markers that require less pressure than crayons to produce a clear image on paper. Later, encourage them to use a variety of writing tools, such as felt-tip markers, thick pencils, crayons, and chalk, until they feel comfortable in their ability to hold and manipulate a normal-size pencil.

Letter and Word Perception

In addition to psychomotor skill, handwriting also requires visual perception. That is, children need to recognize and note the differences among similar-looking letters and words. In the past, teachers believed that drilling children on the alphabet was the way to achieve this. Today educators recognize that writing readiness parallels reading readiness. By reading aloud to children, allowing them to examine books, and immersing them in a print-rich environment, adults encourage children to naturally acquire a visual knowledge of certain letters and words. These experiences become the building blocks for beginning writing.

DIRECT INSTRUCTION IN HANDWRITING

Although the debate between the relative benefits of direct versus indirect skills instruction continues, in the area of handwriting the experts are in agreement: Some direct instruction in the early grades on letter formation, size, slant, and proper spacing between letter and words is needed (Hodges, 1991). In addition, children need to be given a specific purpose for why they are writing, help in controlling the pen and pencil to produce legible writing, and of course constant encouragement of their writing efforts.

Teachers introduce letter formation to their students as part of the preschool and primary-grade curriculum. Many schools also invest in elaborate kits and expensive computer software programs to teach handwriting.

However, research shows that the individual teacher's attitude toward handwriting has more influence on students' handwriting than any other factor (Manning & Manning, 1981). A teacher's positive attitude is the key to ensuring positive attitudes toward handwriting in children. Consequently, handwriting exercises should never be used as punishment.

Perhaps the best form of direct instruction that teachers can give their students is modeling of good handwriting practices (Temple, Nathan, Burris, & Temple, 1988). Modeling the strokes of the letters at the chalkboard or on an overhead projector is one way to instruct young children in handwriting. This can be further expanded by using the **VAK** (visual–auditory–kinesthetic) **technique:**

Visual. Let the children see you constructing letters and words on the chalkboard, at an overhead projector, or seated side by side with an individual student. To construct letters and words themselves, children must be able to visualize the strokes involved; to do this, they must see you demonstrating these strokes. To further assist this visual learning, have the letters of the alphabet displayed in the classroom at a child's eye level.

Auditory. Many children are auditory learners. This means that they learn best by hearing the instructions for letter formation. Even predominantly visual learners, however, benefit from auditory reinforcement as part of handwriting instruction. Describe the strokes as you demonstrate them visually. For example, say, "To make the capital B, I first put my pencil at the top of the line and slide it straight down to the bottom line. Next I make two humps. . . ." You can also verbalize about particular features of certain letters; for example, "Notice, children, that the tail of the g goes below the line."

Kinesthetic. The term *kinesthetic* refers to learning that is enhanced through physical movement of the body. Grace Fernald popularized this technique in 1943 as an approach to teaching remedial reading. She believed that children would learn to read words and remember them better if they wrote them. She advocated tracing and copying words as a learning reinforcement. Today kinesthetic activities that reinforce handwriting instruction include writing letters in sand, salt, and shaving cream and shaping letters with clay and yarn.

WHAT SHOULD BE TAUGHT IN HANDWRITING?

Knowing how to teach something is only part of the process; your next decision is what to teach. This is as true of handwriting instruction as it is of any other content area. Should you introduce 1 letter at a time until all 26 letters of the alphabet have been studied? And if so, in what order should they be introduced? Or can a few letters be introduced in a single lesson?

Recall from Chapter 8 that one of the primary considerations of any writing program is the element of time: How teachers and pupils use their time in class is crucial. The less time spent on formal, direct instruction in handwriting, the more time is available for real writing activities. Teaching a few letters in a single lesson saves time. One way to do this is to introduce letters based on the similarity of strokes involved in the production of those letters. Figure 9.5 suggests a possible sequence for introducing letters based on the strokes involved.

Figure

Possible groupings of letter strokes.

MANUSCRIPT

Lowercase

Counterclockwise circles: a, c, e, o

Counterclockwise circles, then straight lines: d, g, q

Straight lines: i, j, (k), l, t

Straight lines, then clockwise circles: b, p

Canes or humps: h, m, n, r, (f)

Diagonal lines: (k), v, w, x, y, z

Miscellaneous: (f), k, u, s

Uppercase

Straight lines: E, F, H, I, L, T

Circles: C, G, O, Q

Curved lines: B, D, J, P, R, S, U

Diagonal lines: A, K, M, N, V, W, X, Y, Z

CURSIVE

Lowercase—Beginning Strokes

Undercurve: b, e, f, h, i, j, k, l, p, r, s, t, u, w

Downcurve: a, c, d, g, o, q

Overcurve: m, n, v, x, y, z

Lowercase—Ending Strokes

Undercurve: a, c, d, e, f, h, i, k, l, m, n, p, q, r, s, t, u, x

Overcurve: g, j, y, z

Check-stroke: b, o, v, w

Lowercase—Size or Height

Minimum: a, c, e, g, i, j, m, n, o, q, r, s, u, v, w, x, y, z

Intermediate (or three-quarters): d, p, t

Full upper loop: b, f, h, k, l

Descending: f, g, j, p, q, y, z

Uppercase

Cane-stem: H, K, M, N, Q, U, V, W, X, Y, Z

Backward or direct oval: A, C, D, E, O

Forward or indirect oval: B, P, R

Double loop: I, L

Boats: F, G, S, T

Descending: J, Y, Z

Ideally, direct instruction in handwriting should be taught as mini-lessons. In using mini-lessons, the teacher might talk about a few letters, model them on the board, and then allow the students to practice the letter strokes using copying or various kinesthetic activities, but this entire process should only take a short while. Bing (1988) has recommended that no more than 15 minutes per day be spent on handwriting in isolation; the remainder of the period should be spent on real writing activities. For students who need additional practice in making their letters, kinesthetic activities should be set up at learner centers, where students can work at their own pace throughout the day practicing the particular skills they need. Additional practice in handwriting skills can be incorporated into functional activities in the classroom. Figure 9.6 suggests some activities for both primary and intermediate students who need additional practice in handwriting.

Figure 9.6 *Functional handwriting activities.*

PRIMARY GRADES

- Label lockers, chairs, tables, closets, centers, and so on.
- Make nameplates for books.
- Label paintings and other art projects.
- Sign dittoed letters sent home to parents.
- Sign own milk receipts.
- Write names to check attendance, lunch count, and so on.
- Write stories, poems, and simple plays.
- Write simple invitations and thank-you cards.
- Copy and write letters to parents about school events.

INTERMEDIATE GRADES

- Write labels, stories, poems, letters, plays, book reports, reports for social studies, invitations, letters of thanks, announcements, articles for school newspaper, and so on.
- Keep lists or records, diaries, and journals.
- Take notes in class; make outlines.
- Keep attendance reports and weather reports.
- Make plans for classroom activities.

CONTROVERSIAL ISSUES IN HANDWRITING INSTRUCTION

Although it is the contention of the authors that handwriting instruction should not play a predominant role in the language arts curriculum, there are nevertheless a number of important controversies surrounding the issue of handwriting that teachers should be aware of. Unfortunately, in the past these controversies have had the effect of focusing teachers' attention on handwriting, with the result that real reading and writing activities were sometimes excluded from the classroom. This section addresses some of these controversies briefly, but teachers should use their time in class judiciously and not get sidetracked by these issues.

Tracing vs. Copying

Grace Fernald (1943) popularized the use of tracing over letters as a reinforcement technique for learning to read. **Tracing,** as an activity that has young children writing over predrawn lines or dots that form the letters, is widely advocated in the early lessons of most handwriting workbooks. However, a few studies have contended that **copying,** an activity that has students reproducing on a blank piece of paper letters or a passage written from the blackboard or some other chart, is a more valuable activity (Askov & Greff, 1975; Hirsch & Niedermeyer, 1973). At least one study (Foerster, 1972) tried to prove that tracing was actually harmful to children because by forcing students to stay on the lines/dots, teachers were inhibiting the development of a natural handwriting stroke. Teachers seem to be divided on this issue.

The position of this text is that teachers should confine their handwriting instruction to mini-lessons and minimize the amount of time spent on drills in isolation in order to maximize writing time in the classroom. Thus, in this view, the tracing versus copying controversy is not an issue.

Reversals in Writing and Reading

Many teachers and even more parents are overly concerned by the reversals that students make in their writing and in their reading. Reading or writing *was* for *saw* or *b* for *d* is an example of a reversal. The thing to remember is that reversals occur commonly among young children in the beginning stages of reading and writing (Wilde, 1997). Feder and Weber (1986) found that most reversal problems disappear as children grow older and mature. Therefore reversals should not be seen as a major problem, let alone lead to teachers labeling students as dyslexic!

Instead, you should help children to recognize how these similar letters and words are shaped. Show them the direction of the strokes. Then let the students write without calling attention to the problem. Often by focusing a child's attention on a minor reversal problem, teachers blow the problem totally out of proportion. Soon the child is afraid to put pencil to paper for fear of making errors.

Left-Handed Writers

As with reversals, many of the problems associated with left-handed students can be teacher-created. By calling students' attention to the differences between right- and left-handers, teachers actually exaggerate the problem. Howell (1978), for example, contended that left-handed writers (about 10 percent of a class) are so unique that they require special instruction, separate from the rest of the class. Harrison (1981) suggested a number of ways to help the left-handed student, including slanting the paper in the opposite direction of the right-handed student and crooking the hand in a special way. A simpler solution is in order. Most teachers (and most students) are right-handed; therefore instructional examples should be from the right-handed point of view. With a little personal attention, left-handed children can adjust their letter strokes to make their writing legible. The main point left-handers need to remember is this: The English writing system goes from left to right. Therefore, right-handed children can be lazy and rest their hand on the page, sliding it along as they write. Not so for left-handed children: Since the pencil moves ahead of the hand, a left-hander must be taught to raise the wrist slightly so as not to drag his or her hand across the paper and smear the writing.

Cursive Writing

Today most children are taught to write by learning the manuscript stroke first, but for hundreds of years in Europe cursive writing was the only handwriting used or taught. In the United States, cursive writing was taught exclusively from colonial times until 1921 (Moore, 1986). In that year, Marjorie Wise introduced a new form of writing from England: manuscript print writing. Since 1921, handwriting instruction in this country has undergone a strange evolution. In kindergarten and first grade, children are introduced to the printed manuscript style. Around grade 3, they are asked to stop using manuscript writing and learn the cursive or continuous joined stroke (Hodges, 1991). Children are expected to use cursive writing in the remainder of the elementary grades and into middle schools. This creates a number of problems, particularly among boys.

A summary of handwriting research studies (Allred, 1977) found that males of all ages dislike handwriting more than females and believe they have very poor handwriting. For some boys, the inability to master cursive writing creates negative attitudes toward school in general and results in poor achievement. Furthermore, research showed that embarrassment over poor handwriting led to low self-esteem and disruptive behavior among boys in the classroom.

Sometime around junior high school, formal handwriting instruction drops out of the curriculum entirely, and students are told they can write in either manuscript or cursive, or even type (word process) their papers. The only requirement teachers have is that the students' work be legible. One result is that many students—particularly boys—revert back to manuscript writing because it is generally more legible. This raises the question, Why teach cursive writing at all?

Surveys have shown that many students, teachers, and parents believe that cursive writing is important because it is faster than manuscript strokes, it is necessary for a legal signature, and it is a more adult or grown-up style of writing (Moore, 1986). The research, however, does not support those beliefs (Peck, Askov, & Fairchild, 1980). Cursive is no faster than manuscript; if speed were the issue, teachers should be teaching students shorthand. Second, a printed signature is just as legal as a cursive one. Furthermore, many adults use manuscript as their primary writing style; others even mix the two strokes together. Finally, applications and forms usually must be printed or typed. In fact, there is no real reason for teaching cursive writing other than that it allows students to read other people's cursive writing and is a tradition in most schools. Teachers should thus minimize the amount of time spent on cursive writing: Introduce it in grade 3 as a special unit and then drop formal instruction, except for those students who require individual help. Teachers can much better use that valuable time for real reading and real writing in the classroom.

Figure 9.7 shows the handwriting differences in one second-grade class. Some of these students require much teacher assistance, some require a lit-

Figure 9.7

Second-grade handwriting samples.

tle, and others write nearly as well as many adults. Note also the handwriting samples of two fourth-grade students in Figure 9.8. Although both students are considered average in handwriting by their teacher, their handwriting is certainly legible—actually, it is quite excellent. Does it make sense to require such students to spend time in formal handwriting lessons for the next three years? Or could that time be better spent in other aspects of reading and writing?

A number of people have suggested alternatives to spending a large amount of time instructing young children first in manuscript and then in cursive. One approach combines handwriting instruction and drawing to teach calligraphy (D'Angelo, 1982). *Calligraphy* is the art of beautiful or elegant writing. Children are taught to use a variety of instruments to create a flowery script for decorating and illustrating. In the course of this fun activity, many youngsters find that their normal handwriting improves and becomes more legible. A unit in calligraphy might be just what is needed for students in the upper elementary grades who are frustrated by the rote drill and practice of too much handwriting instruction.

Spelling: Dealing with Demons

Unlike handwriting, in which there has been a decline in research interests, research in the area of spelling has actually increased in the past 25 years (Hodges, 1991). Researchers want to know how young children acquire their knowledge of traditional *orthography* (spelling patterns), how spelling acquisition relates to language acquisition, and how learning to spell is influenced by general reading and writing. Spelling has even been identified as a measure of overall school effectiveness (Moats, 1995).

For years there has been strong research evidence to support the notion that young children learn to spell best when they are encouraged to read and write extensively (Bissex, 1980; Buchanan, 1992; Gentry, 1987; Wilde, 1997). Through wide reading, children are exposed to many words visually; through writing, youngsters retrieve those words from memory and reproduce them using invented spelling. Over time, with practice in real reading and writing, children's spelling improves. And as Ronald Cramer (1978) has accurately noted, "The final test of good spellers is how well they spell words in compositions, not how well they spell words on tests or in spelling bees" (pp. 104–105).

Nevertheless, the most widespread spelling practices in schools today emphasize drill and repetitious practice exercises. Practice drills, it is argued, improve a child's memorization skills through visual, auditory, and motor activities, especially with the corpus of hard-to-remember words known as *demons*. This is true to some extent. However, rule-memorization drills and practice exercises to teach spelling have been sorely overused, to the extent that there is often little time left in a class period for any writing. Students also become quickly bored with the repetitious nature of such tasks (Buchanan, 1992; Gill & Scharer, 1996).

Figure 9.8

Fourth-grade handwriting samples.

As a teacher of spelling, you must make some important decisions regarding how to teach, what to teach, and how much time to devote to spelling. To make these decisions, you need to know something of the history of the English spelling system (as well as the relationship between spelling and word meanings) and the developmental stages of spelling that occur in children's writing.

HISTORICAL PRACTICES IN TEACHING ENGLISH SPELLING

Recall from Chapter 4 that the English language (both word meanings and spellings) has been influenced by many other languages. Words borrowed from French (*bouquet*), Spanish (*patio*), German (*pretzel*), Italian (*spaghetti*), and other languages make up a significant portion of the words children read and write. This is important to remember because it reflects the varied background and changing nature of American English spelling, which is more complex than mere rule memorization implies.

The current emphasis in spelling textbooks and workbooks on rote memorization of rules and word lists can be traced to the influence of Noah Webster (1758–1843) and his famous *Blue Book Speller*. Webster—a schoolteacher from Goshen, New York, who wrote a dictionary, a grammar book, and a reader in addition to the speller—was a fiery patriot who intended in his books to delineate what he felt were the read differences between American English and the language spoken in Great Britain. For nearly 100 years, Webster's speller and reader were the dominant textbooks in this country's classrooms.

This emphasis on rote memorization of word lists persisted into the twentieth century. In the 1920s, for example, students were given lists of words—sometimes as many as 50 per week—and taught to memorize and regurgitate them on the test at the end of the week. Those who were not successful were "retaught" the words with the switch or by writing them over and over again until their fingers ached.

Following the influence of Webster's *Blue Book Speller*, much of the early spelling research in the twentieth century focused on trying to answer the question, "What words should children learn to spell in each grade?" (Hodges, 1991). According to spelling authority Richard Hodges, 600 studies alone were done to answer this question prior to 1940. Various word lists, each one claiming to be the definitive list, filled America's classrooms. Along with the word lists was the assumption that having students memorize such lists was the best way to learn to spell.

Among the most famous of these spelling lists was the Basic 10,000 Words compiled by Ernest A. Horn in 1926. Horn's 10,000 words made up the spelling curriculum in many elementary classrooms. However, these were actually words that Horn selected because he thought children ought to know them; no consideration was given to whether children actually used them in their writing. In 1945, Henry Rinsland corrected this situation by constructing a new list of 3,000 spelling words based on their frequency of use by school-age children (Yellin, 1983). This list was considered to be a major improvement in spelling instruction because it was based on the principle of *social utility* (how useful the words were to children). However, Rinsland still advocated that spelling be taught through rote memorization. Figure 9.9 lists the 100 most frequently used words as identified by Rinsland.

In 1951, at Stanford University, a systematic analysis of the 3,000-word spelling list was begun. The prevailing belief among educators at the time was still that rote memorization was necessary because American English spelling, with its many foreign word borrowings, was highly erratic and therefore unpredictable. Only by memorizing each word as a separate entity could one learn to spell. Paul Hanna, a well-known linguist and head of the Stanford team, set out to challenge this belief. Hanna believed—and eventually

a	eat	in	our	there
all	for	is	out	they
am	girl	it	over	this
and	go	just	play	time
are	going	know	pretty	to
at	good	like	put	too
baby	got	little	red	tree
ball	had	look	run	two
be	has	made	said	up
big	have	make	saw	want
boy	he	man	school	was
but	her	me	see	we
can	here	mother	she	went
Christmas	him	my	so	what
come	his	name	some	when
did	home	not	take	will
do	house	now	that	with
dog	how	of	the	would
doll	I	on	them	you
down	I'm	one	then	your

Figure 9.9

Rinsland's 100 most frequently used words.

proved—that the English spelling system contains definite patterns based on a finite number of phoneme–grapheme relationships, which can be easily learned, understood, and applied by all students in their writing (Hanna, 1971). This was a major advancement in spelling instruction, but a more important discovery was yet to come.

DEVELOPMENTAL STAGES OF SPELLING

The newest approaches to spelling research have gone way beyond identifying lists of words to spell or rules to memorize. Instead, spelling research began to recognize the complex nature of English spelling as an interaction among "lexical, grammatical and semantic features of language" (Hodges, 1991, p. 776). Perhaps even more importantly was what researchers discovered about the nature of spelling as children mature.

In the 1970s through the 1990s, linguists who were observing young children writing at various ages concluded that children learn to spell in developmental stages (Beers & Beers, 1981; Buchanan, 1982; Chomsky, 1971; Gentry, 1984, 1987; Read, 1986). The significance of this discovery cannot be overstated. These and other researchers found that children learn to spell gradually, in stages, trying out and discovering (unconsciously) the rules of the English spelling system for themselves. Young children use temporary spellings for words in this process of discovery. As they grow older and have more contact with print through reading and writing, their spelling acquires the characteristics of standard spelling constructions. There are four major developmental stages of children's spelling.

Prephonetic stage. Preschoolers and primary-grade children invent their own ways of spelling words and writing sentences, ranging from random scribbles to actual letters in the *prephonetic stage*. Early invented spellings lack any relationship between sounds and symbols. Later invented spellings approximate consonant sounds but omit vowels entirely.

Phonetic stage. During grades 1 through 3, youngsters become more aware of the sound–symbol relationship of written language in the *phonetic stage.* In their writing, both consonant and vowel sounds are represented by actual letters of the alphabet. Vowels, however, are often still misused or omitted. The concept of words (as represented by larger spaces between groups of letters) develops. Though invented spellings are still used, the child's writing now more closely approximates standard English spelling.

Orthographic stage. The *orthographic stage* overlaps with the phonetic stage, depending on the individual child's development. In this stage, there is a more consistent use of vowels within syllables and an expansion of the correct use of consonants. The child's awareness of spelling patterns grows enormously. Problem areas still persist with double consonants, the schwa sound, contractions, and silent letters.

Morphemic/Syntactic stage. If children have been exposed to print and encouraged to write using their invented spellings during the primary grades, sometime around the upper elementary grades they should begin to acquire an understanding that the English spelling system is influenced by word meanings and word order as well as pronunciation; this is the *morphemic/syntactic stage.* Word meanings influence knowledge of spelling because similar words are spelled alike. For example, *family, familiar,* and *familiarity* and *manage, manager,* and *managerial* are related morphologically, and this relationship is reflected in their spelling. Similarly, understanding word parts and word order (*syntax*) helps students correctly spell words with prefixes and suffixes (*jumped, running,* and *remaking*). Knowledge of word meanings and grammar, along with phonetic understanding, thus helps the child become a more accurate speller. Figure 9.10 gives examples of writings from each of the developmental stages in spelling.

Figure 9.10

Examples of the developmental stages of spelling.

PREPHONETIC STAGE

= Daddy   = Baby   = Cat

PHONETIC STAGE

We tuk a trp
Thre boys wint swimn

ORTHOGRAPHIC STAGE

The ridder was siting on the hors.
I cant fite in the batel

MORPHEMIC/SYNTACTIC STAGE

The babies were sleeping happily under the tree.

Source: Adapted from C. Beers and J. Beers (1981), "Three Assumptions About Learning to Spell"; C. Read (1986), *Children's Creative Spelling;* J. R. Gentry (1987), *Spel . . . Is a Four-Letter Word.*

For a more in-depth look at spelling as a developmental process, two recommended books are J. R. Gentry's *Spel . . . Is a Four-Letter Word* (1987) and Charles Read's *Children's Creative Spelling* (1986). Read the Classroom Vignette that follows; it shows Brittany's spelling in the various stages.

Vignette *in the classroom*

Brittany has written over 40 books. She is 7 years old. Her mother, a teacher, has been saving all of her drawings, scribbles, and writings since she was an infant. A look at Brittany's progress as a writer exemplifies the developmental stages of spelling. The only difference is that Brittany has moved at a much faster pace than most children, perhaps because she was encouraged by her parents.

Brittany's first interest in print occurred when she was only a few months old. Books were among her favorite playthings, often winning out over toys. Her parents read to her every day. Two of her favorite books were *Animal Sounds* and *My Goodnight Book*. She also enjoyed sitting with books, examining them carefully page by page.

When Brittany was 2 years, 3 months old, her mother purchased some magnetic letters to place on the refrigerator. One day, without being instructed, Brittany took the letters down and began matching them to letters in her picture books. Within a few months, she was playing games with her parents, such as "What does ——— begin with?" Her parents continued reading to her, and her personal library continued to grow.

At age 3 1/2, amid her drawings and scribbles, Brittany began printing the letters of the alphabet. Her parents bought her an assortment of crayons, pens, markers, and paper as her interest in writing grew. During this time, her spoken vocabulary also expanded enormously. By age 4, she was constantly asking about the words on signs, billboards, cards, junk mail, and the Sunday comic strips. One month after her fifth birthday, she wrote her first word using invented spelling: BLREA (ballerina).

Early in her writing, Brittany began labeling her drawings and creating little books she could read to her parents. Figure 9.11 shows Brittany's early invented spellings and some of her drawings. The typed comments are her mother's.

When Brittany entered kindergarten, the teacher used various learning centers in the room. One of these was a writing center, where the children were encouraged to write using their invented spellings. There were crayons, pens, pencils, and colored paper available to the children. Brittany often chose to work at the writing center. Figure 9.12 is one of her earliest examples from school using invented spellings.

One day during Brittany's kindergarten class, an Oklahoma storyteller, Lynn Moroney, told the Native American story of "Baby Rattlesnake." Brittany was so inspired that she sat down the next day and wrote her own story. As with her previous books, Brittany drew the pictures first and then added the text. The story is fragmented; this is common among young writers, who often assume that their audience knows what they know and thus fail to fill in the missing pieces. Figure 9.13 shows Brittany's version of "Baby Rattlesnake."

Figure 9.11

Excerpt from BRITTANYS ANLBOK.

She drew and labeled a whole zoo of animals, each on its own sheet of paper:

HBPADAS (hippopotamus)

ALAFAT (elephant)

KAML (camel)

BALEGOT (billy goat)

LAPRD (leopard)

TAIGR (tiger)

BDRFLAIE (butterfly)

SWAND (swan)

BAR (bear)

ALGADR (alligator)

GRAF (giraffe)

I showed her how the papers could be arranged and stapled together with a front and back cover. A title was added, <u>BRITTANYS ANLBOK</u> (animal book), and so began Brittany's career as an author.

Source: Reprinted with permission of Diane and Brittany Moser.

Figure 9.12

Brittany's invented spellings.

HADDDLKAT	hey diddle diddle cat	TSESSHTAN	to see such fun
ATHAFATL	and the fiddle	THDASHRAN	the dish ran
KOGAMTOVR	cow jumped over	AWAWAAIS	away with a sp
THEMON	the moon	ON	oon
THADOGLAF	the dog laughed		

What can we as teachers and researchers learn from Brittany's writing? Clearly, Brittany is learning to spell and write in the course of her experimenting with language. Her growth is evident. The so-called errors that she makes are part of that growth. Teachers and parents will not be concerned by children's invented spelling when they recognize it as a natural part of children's writing development, just as overgeneralizations in children's early speech are a natural part of language development (Weaver, 1996).

If you would like to learn more about young children's early development in writing and spelling, read Lester Laminack's *Learning with Zachary* (1991), a year-by-year account of one child's growth in written language.

Figure 9.13

Brittany's THE STORE ABAT BABY RATLSNAK.

Source: Reprinted with permission of Diane and Brittany Moser.

Implications for Instructional Practices

The developmental stages of spelling suggest specific instructional practices for teachers to follow. Buchanan (1992) gives appropriate instructional strategies to use with students during each stage of development (see Figure 9.14). Clay (1993) and Joseph (1998/1999) found that word boxes are helpful with children who have difficulty hearing the sounds within a letter when they are writing a word. A **word box** is a rectangle divided into the number of letters that are in a word. For example, if the teacher is working with a child who is having a difficult time spelling *hot*, the teacher would divide a rectangle into three boxes (see Figure 9.15). At first, counters are used as a child hears the sound of each letter. For example, when the student recognizes the /h/ sound, the child moves a counter into the first box. As he or she recognizes the /o/ sound, the child puts a counter into the middle box; as he or she recognizes the /t/ sound, a counter is placed into the third box. Later magnetic letters replace the counters in order for the student to see the exact spelling of the word.

Figure 9.14

Appropriate classroom practices for each stage of development.

PREPHONETIC

1. Have a large variety of writing materials available.
2. Respond to students' writing in a positive manner.
3. Label objects in the room.
4. Put name of students on their completed papers.
5. If child asks, "How do you write ——— ?" write the word for them.
6. Display alphabet cards with pictures that begin with that letter.

PHONETIC

1. Point to words when reading charts and Big Books.
2. Frequently use the Language Experience Approach (LEA).
3. Write short poems on sentence strips, and have students arrange them in order.
4. Using sentence pockets, sentence strips, and 3 × 5 cards, have students match words on the card with words on the sentence strip.
5. Use uninterrupted sustained silent writing (USSW).
6. Play with magnetic letters and word families.
7. Use wall charts with words or phrases that are often used in writing (e.g., "Once upon a time . . . ").

ORTHOGRAPHIC

1. Make personalized dictionaries: When a student asks how to spell a word, put it in his or her dictionary; later ask the student to look it up in his or her dictionary.
2. Continue to use USSW.
3. Help students with developing strategies such as, "What do you do when you're stuck on a word?"
4. Play word games (Word Bingo, Scrabble).
5. Use word webs when studying a particular concept in science or social studies.

MORPHEMIC/SYNTACTIC

1. Work with roots, affixes, and inflections.
2. Play with compound words, portmanteaus, and acronyms.
3. Play a form of the TV show "Wheel of Fortune."
4. Work with correct spelling during an editing conference; let the student know a word is misspelled, but don't give the correct spelling. Give a strategy.
5. Do crossword puzzles.

Source: Adapted from Buchanan (1992), *Spelling for Whole Language Classrooms.* Winnipeg, Canada: Whole Language Consultants Ltd.

Figure 9.15

H	O	T

Word box.

In the middle and upper elementary grades, spelling typically becomes a more formalized part of the curriculum. Practice exercises are completed, tests are given over spelling lists from workbooks, and grades are awarded. This is unfortunate because it conveys the message that what is important is absolute accuracy in spelling. One result of this tendency is that creative writing lessons often degenerate into a sea of waving hands: "Teacher, how do you spell . . . ?" "Teacher, how do you spell . . . ?" Harp (1988) has argued that instead of using textbook spelling lists, children should be allowed to develop their own individualized spelling lists of words from their writing. In this way, a much more positive atmosphere toward spelling can be created.

An additional exercise for upper elementary children is to present spelling patterns inductively, as a problem-solving task. Children are presented with groups of related words and told to study them. In small cooperative groups, the students discuss the similarities and differences among the words. The groups also hypothesize about the possible spelling principles exemplified by each word. To test their hypotheses, they need to come up with other example words. In the Classroom Vignette that follows, the teacher is using the inductive approach to teach a mini-lesson on spelling.

Vignette in the classroom

In the past, Mrs. Jones has taught spelling to her fourth-grade students by presenting a list of words to them on Monday, having them do drill exercises during the rest of the week, and taking a retest on Friday for a spelling grade. This was mostly a copying routine with little thought or discussion. Now she uses a mini-lesson to encourage students to think and talk about their spelling words.

She begins by saying "I've written two groups of words on the board. Study them carefully. What do you notice about them that makes them alike? In your cooperative groups, talk about these simi-larities. Can you discover any rules about the sound of /f/ that will help you as spellers?" The teacher reveals the following two groups of words for the children to examine:

1. fun   foolish   free
   stiff   bluff   puff
2. rough   cough   tough
   photo   graph   telephone

The children study the words for a few minutes, then get into their groups. They talk and write and

(continued)

point to the words. Mrs. Jones walks about the room encouraging the discussion. Eventually some of the groups come up with the following rules:

RULE 1: The sound of /f/ at the beginning of words is often spelled *f*, while at the end of words it is spelled *ff*.

RULE 2: The sound of /f/ can also be represented by *gh* in the final position of words and *ph* in any position within a word.

"That's great," says Mrs. Jones. "Now let's test our rules by finding other words with the sound of /f/."

Figure 9.16 lists a number of high-utility spelling rules. These are traditional spelling rules taken from commercial texts. They may be taught as mini-lessons using the inductive approach rather than merely memorized by students. Remember, however, that too much time spent on any form of rule learning is time taken away from writing activities, in which the real learning takes place.

Figure 9.16 *High-utility spelling rules.*

RULE 1

When two vowels appear together in the same syllable, a single long vowel sound is often heard.

Examples: seizure, siege, loathsome, feasible, drainage, sleazy, leasable

RULE 2

The long vowel sound /e/ at the end of a word is often spelled -*y*.

Examples: dropsy, gypsy, stability, hegemony

RULE 3

In spelling the vowel digraphs *ie* and *ei*, the *i* usually comes before the *e* and you hear the long /e/ sound. However, after the letter *c* or when the digraph sounds like long /a/, then the *e* comes before the *i*.

Examples: believe, receive, neighbor, viewpoint, conceive, reign

Exceptions: weird, seize, science

RULE 4

When adding a suffix that begins with a vowel (-*ing*) to words ending in silent *e* (*bake, dance*), remember to drop the silent *e*. When adding a suffix beginning with a consonant, keep the *e*.

Examples: dance/dancing, value/valuable, fame/famous, elope/elopement, imagine/imaginary

RULE 5

Monosyllabic words ending in a single consonant preceded by a single vowel double the consonant when adding a suffix that begins with a vowel.

Examples: drum/drumming, stop/stopping, big/biggest, snub/snubbed, skim/skimmed

RULE 6

Words ending in -*y* and preceded by a consonant change the *y* to *i* before adding the suffix unless the suffix begins with *i*.

Examples: carry/carrier, carrying; study/studious, studying; fly/flies, flying; luxury/luxurious

RULE 7

Add the suffix -*able* to root words that end in silent *e* or to root words that take the prefix *un-* (*available, advisable*). Keep the *e* with soft *c* and *g* words (*manageable, serviceable*). Add the suffix -*ible* to root words that combine with -*ion* (*suggest/suggestion/suggestible*) and to words that without the suffix ending are not meaningful (*incredible, visible*).

Examples: admirable, confirmable, indescribable, immiscrible, accessible, perfectible

Source: Reprinted with permission of David Yellin and the *Daily Oklahoman*.

Figure 9.17 has some general information concerning letter sounds that may be helpful to you as a teacher. They may also be taught as mini-lessons to your students.

1. The *k* is silent when followed by *n* (know, knob).
2. When *gh* follows the vowel *i*, the *gh* is silent (might).
3. At the beginning of a word, the *w* is silent when followed by *r* (write).
4. At the end of words, the *b* is silent when it follows *m* (comb).
5. *C* sounds like /k/ when followed by *a, o,* or *u* (cat, cot, cut).
6. *C* sounds like /s/ when followed by *i, e,* or *y* (city, center, Cinderella).
7. *G* sound like /g/ when followed by *o, a,* and *u* (gone, game, gun).
8. *Ph* is /f/ (telephone, photograph).
9. *Q* is always followed by *u* and sounds like /kw/ (quick).

Figure 9.17

Generalizations about letter sounds.

Source: Adapted from *Phonics in Proper Perspective* (8th ed.) by Arthur W. Heilman, © 1989. Reprinted by permission of Prentice Hall, Inc. Upper Saddle River, NJ.

Figure 9.18 has some generalizations relating to syllabication. Again these are given to you, the teacher, in order for you to help your students.

1. Syllables are determined by vowel sounds (road = 2 vowels, but only 1 vowel sound; com-plete = 3 vowels, but only 2 vowel sounds; si-tu-a-tion = 5 vowels, but 4 vowel sounds).
2. When there are double consonants in the middle of words, the word is syllabicated between the two consonants (hid-den, gen-tle).
3. When there is one consonant in the middle of a word, the consonant goes with the second syllable if the preceding vowel is long (stu-dent, be-gan). If the preceding vowel is short, the consonant goes with the first syllable (mod-el, pan-el).
4. Digraphs and consonant blends remain together (teach-er, fa-ther).
5. The affixes form separate syllables (re-peat-ing, grate-ful).

Figure 9.18

Generalizations relating to syllabication.

Source: Adapted from *Phonics in Proper Perspective* (8th ed.) by Arthur W. Heilman, © 1989. Reprinted by permission of Prentice Hall, Inc. Upper Saddle River, NJ.

Zutell (1996) explains the directed spelling thinking activity (DSTA), which is patterned after the directed reading thinking activity. The DSTA is based on the belief that students need to be actively engaged when attempting to solve spelling problems. The DSTA, which is done as a class activity, uses the following eight steps:

1. The teacher gives a brief spelling test over words that have a related pattern (e.g., trade, brave, came, bake, which follow the VCe pattern).
2. The students offer predictions of the spelling of the new word.
3. The students give reasons for their spelling.
4. Students formulate evidence of the pattern.
5. Students brainstorm for other words that follow that pattern and add them to the list.

6. Students continue to add words that they find to the list.
7. The teacher reminds them of the pattern when they are struggling with a word that follows the pattern.
8. Students keep a personalized list of words they know, sorting them according to the patterns.

With the DSTA, students are discovering the pattern while working with the words instead of the teacher giving the spelling pattern and then the list of words for the students to memorize.

Spelling and the Proofreading Process

Finally, there is developmental research to support the direct instruction in proofreading skills for elementary and especially middle school, junior high, and high school writers (Riefer, 1987). *Proofreading* is the ability to read a text to discover errors that need to be corrected. In spelling, this means carefully reading what you have written to recognize words that just don't look or sound right. According to Wilde (1996), proofreading for spelling errors is best taught in conjunction with the editing stage of a process approach to writing. For young children, however, proofreading is a difficult skill that will take years to develop, but it is important enough for teachers to introduce it early. The simplest instructional approach is to ask children to reread what they have written, looking for any possible spelling errors (Riefer, 1987). Working with a friend could make this a fun activity, but it is the individual habit of proofreading that the teacher is really trying to develop.)

Using the Dictionary

Elementary-grade students need to be taught to use the dictionary. Adults know that when they do not know how to spell a word, they can either ask a friend or look it up in the dictionary. Even young children can use simple speller dictionaries. Elementary-grade students can be taught to use junior dictionaries or an electronic dictionary, which has made dictionary use fun for students. Large, unabridged dictionaries should be avoided because they contain too much extraneous material and too many abbreviations for children to use easily. And ease of use is the key to dictionary lessons. If a child cannot be taught how to find a word in the dictionary quickly, he or she will grow up with a distaste for using dictionaries.

Dictionary lessons should begin by reviewing the alphabet. When children know the position of each letter within the alphabet, they can turn to that portion of the dictionary on the first try. Start by dividing the dictionary into three parts: beginning (*a* through *h*), middle (*i* through *p*), and end (*q* through *z*). Ask students, "Which part of the dictionary would you turn to first to find the word *clarion*?" Next, teach children about the guide words found at the upper corners of the page. All the words on the page fall between these two guide words. This activity takes considerable practice, but it is well worth it if it helps students to feel comfortable using the dictionary as a tool in writing.

As students become comfortable using the dictionary as a learning resource on a regular basis, they note that spelling and vocabulary knowledge go hand in hand. Knowing how to spell a word without knowing what it means makes no sense. Such words will never be used in a child's writing.

Regular use of the dictionary as part of a writing program leads children to learn about prefixes, suffixes, and root words. Dictionaries also contain synonyms and antonyms of words. This knowledge, in turn, helps children to enlarge their vocabularies and improve their spelling. Further use of the dictionary leads older students into lessons about the origins of words. For example, most students are surprised to learn that many common English words were actually derived from foreign place-names: *baloney* comes from the Italian city of *Bologna*: *frankfurter* comes from *Frankfurt*, Germany; the *sardine* gets its name from the island of *Sardinia*; *tangerine* refers to the port city of *Tangiers*, Morocco; and even the common word *turkey* refers to the African guinea fowl that was imported to Europe from *Turkish* ports.

Spelling Logs

A companion to using the dictionary is teaching children to keep their own spelling logs (Zutell, 1996). **Spelling logs** are records of an individual child's misspellings on tests and from written work; next to the misspelling is the correct spelling. Students who study the spelling words they want to use in their writing are more likely to learn these words.

Spelling tests can even be generated from the words that children want to learn rather than from artificial lists in spelling books. By individualizing spelling in this manner, teachers can help each student to grow as a speller and a writer without comparison to other children and without overemphasizing spelling list memorization.

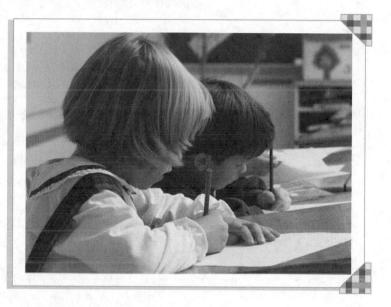

THREE PLANS FOR TEACHING SPELLING ON A WEEKLY BASIS

Again, it is the contention of the authors that spelling improves only through real writing activities done as part of a process writing approach. However, many schools still require their teachers to teach spelling in a systematic fashion on a weekly basis (Allred, 1977; Manning & Manning, 1981). Such schools may require that teachers test spelling weekly. For that reason, this chapter includes three fairly traditional plans for teaching and testing spelling on a weekly basis. Spelling authority Edmund Henderson (1985) has noted that formal weekly spelling plans are often tied to basal reader programs. The plans presented here are suitable for third grade and above, provided the students are well into the orthographic stage of spelling proficiency. You will want to modify them to suit your needs. Note that the key to preparing students for weekly tests in each plan is the variety of practice activities.

Plan 1: Pretest/Study/Retest

This first plan is a widely used approach to teaching spelling in the elementary grades (DiStefano & Haggerty, 1985). A *pretest* is given at the beginning of the week, usually on Monday. The teacher says each word, uses it in a sentence, and then repeats it. Students copy the words in their notebooks. Students may exchange papers or grade their own papers as the teacher calls off or writes the correct spellings on the board. Sometimes the teacher discusses specific features of words—silent letters, unusual endings—that might confuse children.

The *study* portion of this plan occurs during the middle days of the week. Each day, for about 15 minutes, students do various practice activities: writing the words five times each, writing the words in sentences, alphabetizing the words, looking up the words in the dictionary, completing a spelling crossword puzzle, and using the words in a short story or poem. The best activities, of course, are those that relate spelling and meaning in some purposeful content.

At the end of the week, a *retest* is given. Every elementary school child knows that this is the test that counts: It is for a grade that goes in the teacher's gradebook. Usually the teacher collects these papers, grades the tests, and returns them on Monday. Some teachers have experimented with allowing students to grade their own papers immediately after each test. Other teachers have formed student committees to help grade the tests. This practice is appropriate if you want your students to assume some of the responsibility for learning.

There are a number of major drawbacks to this first plan, despite its widespread popularity. First, too much time is often spent testing. Second, teachers assume that the students copy the words correctly at the beginning of the week and study this corrected list for the test on Friday. Don't assume! Teachers should move about the room and check that the children have indeed corrected their spelling errors accurately. Finally, many teachers tend to rely on a single practice activity, usually, "Write your words 10 times each." By varying the practice activities, teachers provide more quality study time for their students (Brown & Ellis, 1994; Moats, 1995).

Plan 2: Study/Test/Study

This plan differs from the first plan in organization. On Monday and Tuesday, children *study* their spelling words, which have been introduced with a ditto handout or on the chalkboard. Practice activities again should be varied and interesting: Have students use a spelling game such as hangman or concentration as well as student-created word-search puzzles. Have each student pair off with a buddy and devise study activities. Again, these activities should not exceed 15 minutes per day for optimum effect.

During the middle of the week—on Wednesday or Thursday—the *test* is given. This is a single test given for a grade. The teacher may grade the papers, or again students may be involved in their own grading. A criterion is set before the test, say, 90 percent. Any child who meets the criterion is excused from further study activities later in the week. This is the incentive to do well on the midweek test.

During the final day or two of the week, only those students who failed to meet the criterion *study* the spelling words. Again, it is important that the study activities be interesting ones that the students do not resent. If the group of children engaged in this study period is a small one, this is also an opportunity for the teacher to work with individual students who may need more help.

This plan has a few obvious advantages. Since there is only one test during the week, there is more time to study and more time to do practice exercises relevant to writing. The students who do well on the test can use the additional time at the end of the week for free reading and creative writing activities of their own choosing. A potential disadvantage is the negative attitudes of those students who do not do well on the midweek test and must do additional practice. But a teacher's positive attitude and rapport with students can offset this. If students perceive the additional practice exercises as punishment, something is wrong and needs to be changed (Brown & Ellis, 1994; Moats, 1995).

Plan 3: Self-Study

In this little-used approach, a test is given at the beginning of the week in the traditional manner (say the word, use it in a sentence, repeat the word). Immediately following the test, the children *self-correct* their papers. The teacher calls off the correct spelling *letter by letter* and displays the words visually on an overhead projector. This is to ensure that the students copy the correct spellings of the words they must study. As with the previous plan, the teacher should still walk about the room double-checking that some students haven't made careless errors in their correcting. Such errors are more common than most teachers realize.

The remainder of the week is spent doing a variety of practice exercises. Students can complete cloze exercises (discussed later in this chapter) using their spelling words, break into teams for spelling games, engage is classwide spelling bees, play spelling tic-tac-toe with a partner, and so on. Using spelling words in their written stories, reports, letters, and poems is still, of course, the best practice children can get.

Retesting for a grade does not take place at the end of the week. Instead, the following week, a new list of words is given and the practice exercises continue. About once every three or four weeks, there is one fairly long spelling test that all students must take. Such an approach has the advantage of minimizing the amount of time spent testing for grades and maximizing the study time. However, the one monthly test is a real challenge to most students' ability to study a large number of words. For this reason, this plan is recommended only for older students who are well into the morphemic/syntactic stage of spelling.

School systems that use weekly approaches to spelling instruction generally utilize spelling books or spelling lists to determine the words to be tested. Selecting children's spelling words from prescribed lists leaves much to be desired. If you must teach, test, and grade spelling on a weekly basis, some of the words should come from the children. Examining their writing will clue you in to the kinds of words that each student misspells most frequently; often children in the same grade have similar spelling-word difficulties. Another source of spelling words should be the other content-area subjects that the children are studying. Words taken from social studies, science, math, art, music, and so on help to reinforce learning in those content areas as well as to give students practice in spelling. Such functional spelling lists are superior to textbook lists, which often have little relevance to the spelling needs of a particular class and even less relevance to the individual student.

In summary, spelling is currently taught in most classrooms on a weekly basis. Formal spelling lists are still used in most schools, but teachers supplement these commercial lists with functional lists that students generate from their own writing or from other content areas like science, social studies, and math. See Figure 9.19 for some spelling tips to use when teaching spelling. Teachers of young children must continually remind themselves of the developmental nature of spelling and be more accepting of children's invented spelling efforts. At all grade levels, spelling is best taught within the stages of the writing process where learning to spell and edit is a natural part of learning to write (Gentry, 1987; Hodges, 1991; Wilde, 1996).

Figure 9.19

Spelling tips.

1. *Use daily free reading.* By encouraging regular reading, students are exposed to thousands of new words. Over time and with use in writing, these words become part of a student's spelling vocabulary.

2. *Use daily free writing.* Spelling develops through practice: the more practice, the better. Incorporating some free writing time each day reinforces weekly spelling skills lessons.

3. *Keep a personal speller dictionary.* From both their reading and writing, students are encouraged to write down the words they wish to learn in their own speller dictionary. The correct spelling of the word, along with a simple definition, is all that is needed.

4. *Use the dictionary.* Students need to be introduced to the dictionary as a resource tool early in their school years. Begin with simple primary-grade dictionaries and work up to the large unabridged dictionaries. Finding the spelling of an unfamiliar word requires predicting the spelling of the word and then using a trial-and-error approach. Dictionary usage is a habit that takes time to develop.

5. *Maintain a class word wall.* Many teachers cover one section of a class wall with butcher-block paper. Children are encouraged to write their favorite words or new and unusual words they have encountered in their reading on the wall. Throughout the year, the word wall list grows and remains for an easy reference.

6. *Use spelling games.* Practicing spelling is drudgery for some students. Effective teachers try to make this practice more fun by incorporating various spelling games such as word searches, crossword puzzles, spelling jumbles, spelling relay, or big words (see the *With Children* activities at the end of the chapter).

Grammar: Meaning, Not Memorizing

"None of the studies reviewed for the present report provides any support for teaching grammar as a means of improving composition skills. If schools insist upon teaching the identification of parts of speech, the parsing or diagramming of sentences, or other concepts of traditional grammar (as many still do) they cannot defend it as a means of improving the quality of writing" (Hillocks, 1986, p. 138).

Most of us speak or write conventionally without being able to specify the rules.

FRANK SMITH

If you were to walk into an elementary or middle school classroom and announce that you were going to teach a grammar lesson, the resulting reaction would be predictable: moans and groans and nasty looks. Grammar for most children is like foul-tasting medicine. Many teachers report that it is difficult to teach and burdensome for students to learn (Smith, 1986). Clearly there are problems with teaching grammar, particularly in the elementary grades.

In 1963, Braddock, Lloyd-Jones, and Schoer completed a report titled *Research in Written Composition.* After reviewing the research studies dealing with all aspects of written composition, they concluded that "the teaching of formal grammar has a negligible or, because it usually displaces some instruction and practice in actual composition, even a harmful effect on the improvement of writing" (pp. 37–38). In 1986, George Hillocks of the University of Chicago edited a similar review of the research on written composition and concluded—as had Braddock, Lloyd-Jones, and Schoer—that grammar instruction, particularly in the elementary grades, does more harm than good to the development of children's writing. The latest review of the research on grammar, done by Constance Weaver (1996), reaffirms the case against teaching formal grammar lessons in the elementary and middle school grades. Instead she finds that the best way for students to apply and learn grammatical concepts is through revising and editing their own writing. Other well-known English educators have recommended that at the very least formal grammar instruction be postponed until the high school years (Haley-James, 1981; Moffett & Wagner, 1983; Noguchi, 1991).

Despite this research evidence against teaching grammar in the elementary grades, the practice continues. Like cursive writing, it is a tradition that persists in the face of research to the contrary. For this reason, the following section addresses the whys, whats, and hows of grammar. But as long as grammar instruction is part of the elementary curriculum, teachers need to understand and teach it in proper perspective to the rest of the language arts curriculum.

GRAMMAR AND USAGE

Some textbooks use the terms *grammar* and *usage* interchangeably. This is more confusing than helpful, since there are distinctions between the two. *Grammar* provides the terminology and rules to describe the structure of a language, including words and sentences. How words are structured is known as *morphology*, while the way in which those words are arranged in sentences is called *syntax*. Grammar study includes both the word and sentence levels of language. Although people can be said to speak with proper grammar, more often *grammar* refers to written forms of language that do or do not conform to certain rules (Weaver, 1996).

Usage, on the other hand, is more concerned with the particular choice of words or language structures (phrases and sentences) used by an individual, generally at the oral level. Whereas grammar is structured by written rules, usage is influenced more by regional and situational factors. Some people talk about usage in terms of acceptable and unacceptable language, depending on the social situation. For example, the use of slang expressions, *ain't*, and double negatives may be appropriate among teenagers on the basketball court but inappropriate during a job interview. Some grammarians even equate usage with language etiquette (Newkirk, 1978). Earlier chapters described the issues surrounding standard and nonstandard speech; these are usage issues.

Clearly, then, part of the confusion for teachers and students alike is that most people have different conceptions of what grammar really is or is not (Weaver, 1996). Some would say that grammar equals the parts of speech, the major word elements of language. Others would argue that grammar is the larger units, the syntactic structures of our language, such as phrases, clauses, and different types of sentences. Your grandparents probably think of grammar in terms of correctness: using correct subject–verb agreement or avoiding double negatives. Your English composition professor probably discussed grammar under sentence style and effective syntactic options. Finally, there still persists among some the belief that studying formal grammar enhances mental discipline and social graces (Woods, 1986).

WHICH GRAMMAR SHOULD BE TAUGHT?

Added to the controversy over whether or not to even teach grammar in the elementary grades—most whole language advocates are against it—is the issue of which grammar to teach because there are many grammars. This section discusses three of those grammars (traditional, structural, transformational-generative) and identifies the strengths and weaknesses of each.

Traditional Grammar

Traditional grammar is the oldest of the grammars and also the one most frequently taught in schools in the United States. It is sometimes referred to as *prescriptive* grammar because it prescribes or lists the rules that govern language. Based on a model from Latin, which at one time was considered the perfect language, **traditional grammar** focuses on rules and definitions. Eighteenth-century grammarians, such as Joseph Priestley and Robert Lowth, recorded those rules and definitions and urged their memorization as part of the English curriculum for schoolchildren. The most well known of these rules and definitions concern the eight parts of speech. Indeed, the parts of speech are taught throughout the elementary grades and well into high school. This fact alone should give you some idea of the complexity associated with traditional grammar and why many educators believe it is inappropriate to teach traditional grammar at the elementary level. The following summary (Pixton, 1978) only scratches the surface of the information related to the parts of speech:

IN & BEYOND THE CLASSROOM

Observe a traditional grammar lesson being taught in the elementary grades. What specific lesson did you observe? What teaching procedure did the teacher use? How could you tell if the children had learned anything? How long did the lesson take? Was any real writing included in the grammar lesson? Suggest alternative ways of teaching the same grammar content.

---

1. *Nouns.* Names of persons, places, and things. Nouns also serve as subjects and as direct and indirect objects. They may be common (*university*) or proper (*Oklahoma State University*) and show possession (*the boy's coat*). Nouns are also either singular (*fox*) or plural (*foxes*).

2. *Pronouns.* A subclass of nouns that take the place of nouns. There are personal pronouns (*I, you, he, she, it, we, they*) and relative pronouns (*who, whose, whom, which, that*).

3. *Verbs.* Words that express action or state of being. Verbs can change form to indicate time, which is called *tense:* present (*takes*), past (*took*), future (*will take*). Linking verbs are forms of the verb *to be* (*is, are, was, were*).

4. *Adjectives.* Words that modify or describe nouns (the *large, green* tree). Adjectives can indicate comparisons, such as *pretty/prettier/prettiest.* The articles *a, an,* and *the* are sometimes considered a special group of adjectives that mark the presence of a noun.

5. *Adverbs.* Words that modify or describe verbs (Robin *frequently* jogs to work), adjectives (The horse was *extremely* hungry), or other adverbs (Betty left the room *very* angrily).

6. *Prepositions.* Words that show a relationship between the subject noun of a sentence and another noun or pronoun (called its *object*). Common prepositions are *under, over, on, into, by, for,* and *from.*

7. *Conjunctions.* Words that join or connect words, phrases, or clauses. Coordinating conjunctions, such as *and, but, for,* and *or,* join equal elements in a sentence (Amy *and* Harry are doctors).

8. *Interjections.* Exclamatory words that express strong feeling or emotion without serving any other grammatical function in a sentence (*Oh!*).

Structural Grammar

A second type of grammar, structural grammar, is also referred to as *descriptive grammar* because it describes language rather than prescribing rules. One of the first linguists to utilize the structural/descriptive approach was Edward Sapir in *Language: An Introduction to Speech* (1921). As the title of his book suggests, **structural grammar** views speech or oral language as being of primary importance. Other important structuralists and their works include

Leonard Bloomfield, *Language* (1933), and Charles Fries, *The Structure of Language* (1952).

The structuralists argued that a grammar for a particular language should effectively describe that language. It was the early structuralists who discovered that every language has a system for sounds (which they called *phonology*), a system for establishing word meanings (*morphology*), and a system for arranging words into larger meaningful units (*syntax*). Terms such as *phoneme, morpheme,* and *syntax* are commonly used in grammar books today to describe the nature of language and are one of the contributions of the structuralists.

Although some grammarians view structural grammar as a big improvement over traditional grammar, the two are similar in many ways. Structuralists still talk about the eight basic parts of speech, although they use different terminology. For example, *function* words are those parts of speech that serve grammatical functions only, such as articles and some conjunctions. Prepositions are referred to as *phrase markers.* As with traditional grammar, structural grammar is quite complex and difficult for elementary-grade children to learn beyond superficial memorization of technical terms and examples.

Another aspect of structural grammar that is readily visible in many elementary classrooms is the use of sentence patterns to teach English. Every language has certain common sentence patterns that are the building blocks of extended discourse; English is no exception. According to the structuralists, by learning the common patterns of English, students can find similar patterns in books to enhance their reading and utilize these patterns to improve their writing. Indeed, increasing complexity of language structures is one mark of a maturing writer. Figure 9.20 shows examples of seven common sentence patterns. Each pattern is represented by a pair of sentences: one constructed by a child, the other taken from a children's literature book. Such grammar activities do seem to be an improvement over rule memorization or sentence diagramming.

Pattern 1   Noun phrase–Verb

           Examples: The two girls danced.

                     The train started.

           (Bishop, B. (1979). *Ralph Rides Away.* New York: Doubleday and Co.)

Pattern 2   Noun phrase–Being verb–Prepositional phrase

           Examples: The ladies were at the circus.

                     The elephant was on the phone.

           (Reinach, J. (1980). *Wait! Wait! Wait!* New York: Weekly Reader Books/Euphrosyne.)

Pattern 3   Noun phrase–Action verb–Prepositional phrase

           Examples: The boy leaped into the pool.

                     Everyone stared at the goggles.

           (Keats, E. (1969). *Goggles.* Toronto: Macmillan.)

Pattern 4   Noun phrase–Helping verb with action verb–Prepositional phrase

           Examples: The children were reading from their book.

                     I am calling on the telephone.

           (Hoban, R. (1964). *A Baby Sister for Francis.* New York: Harper & Row.)

Figure 9.20

Common sentence patterns and their children's literature sources.

(continued)

Figure 9.20

Continued.

Pattern 5   Noun phrase–Verb–Object

          Examples: The boy kissed the girl.

                    Paul licked the spoon.

         (Brown, M. (1963). *Ice Cream for Breakfast.* New York: Franklin Watts.)

Pattern 6   Compound elements

          Examples: The boy walked to the store and bought some candy.

                    She cooked the meals and washed the dishes and made the beds.

         (Galdone, P. (1973). *The Little Red Hen.* New York: Seabury Press.)

Pattern 7   Complex sentences and compound-complex sentences

          Examples: She walked into the kitchen where she found a large carriage with a large doll lying in it.

                    The town where he lives is secluded, and I would like to live there, too.

         (Schlein, M. (1975). *The Girl That Would Rather Climb Trees.* New York: Harcourt Brace Jovanovich.)

In one sense, then, the structural approach to grammar—particularly its emphasis on sentence patterns—is an improvement over traditional grammar. It takes the focus away from individual words in isolation and places it on large, meaningful units. By discussing sentence patterns and having children actively create sentences, teachers are giving their students a more realistic taste of what writing is about and how grammar relates to writing.

Transformational-Generative Grammar

Transformational-generative grammar (TG grammar, for short) is the brainchild of the linguist Noam Chomsky; it is described in his seminal work *Syntactic Structures* (1957). **Transformational-generative (TG) grammar** is concerned with analyzing and describing the intuitive rules of language that all native speakers possess. It is this unconscious knowledge that allows children to produce grammatically correct sentences and recognize ungrammatical ones even at a very young age. More recently, Stephen Krashen (1991) showed that the same intuitive principles are at work in the acquisition of a second language.

There are a number of differences between TG grammar and the other grammars. First, TG grammar focuses on studying the meaning of real sentences rather than on memorizing rules, labeling isolated words, or imitating sentence patterns. Second, TG grammar identifies two distinct levels of language: surface structure and deep structure. *Surface structure* refers to the physical features of language: sounds and symbols. This is what the previous grammars focused on exclusively. TG grammar stresses the second and more important level, *deep structure*, which describes the underlying meaning of a sentence.

A few examples clarify the significant differences between the two levels. In the sentences *Felipe hit the ball* and *The ball was hit by Felipe*, the same deep structure meaning is evident even though the surface structures of the

BEYOND THE CLASSROOM

Examine some children's literature books and select passages from these books that represent the various patterns of the English language. Then use these to teach children to write their own sentences by modeling the pattern. Avoid using technical terminology. Notice how even young children can model various sentence patterns correctly without knowledge of grammatical terms.

sentences appear different. TG grammarians would say these sentences are basically the same; traditional grammarians would say they are different because the subjects of the sentences are different. Conversely, in the sentences *Juan is easy to please* and *Juan is eager to please*, the surface structures are almost exactly the same, but the deep structure meanings are very different. In reading and writing, underlying meaning—not surface appearance—is most important. By focusing on sentence meaning rather than appearance, TG grammarians anticipated holistic language arts practices that begin with meaningful texts to discover underlying principles.

The next group of sentence examples should clarify these differences even more. Examine the following sentences carefully:

Flying planes can be dangerous.

Visiting professors can be a bore.

If you were told to diagram or label these sentences, you might have difficulty because each of these single sentences contains at least two distinct meanings. Can you identify them? These are called *ambiguous* sentences. To fully understand which meaning was intended by the author, the reader needs to know the context in which they appeared.

Although by focusing on meaningful whole sentences TG grammar leads in the right direction, it is still too complex and esoteric for elementary-school children. Chomsky described a grammar to be discussed and debated at the graduate level in college, not taught in the fourth grade. However, other linguists and educators have devised activities based upon the concepts of TG grammar that can be appropriately taught in the upper elementary and middle schools. These include sentence transformations, word substitutions, sentence expansions, and sentence combining, some of which are discussed below.

APPROACHES TO TEACHING GRAMMAR

Traditional Approaches

Parsing. The main teaching approach to traditional grammar uses textbook and workbook exercises in which children underline and label the parts of speech, illustrated as follows, which is known as *parsing*:

      N.   V.   Prep.   Adj. N.
The boy walked near the big house.

Although parsing is now considered an old-fashioned activity, this is the way standardized tests still evaluate knowledge of grammar. Another traditional grammar exercise involves labeling the four kinds of sentences: declarative (statement), interrogative (question), imperative (command), and exclamatory (exclamation). Additional activities include identifying phrases and clauses and classifying sentences as simple, compound, complex, and so on. Such exercises are essentially passive; they give students practice in underlining and labeling but do not require them to create sentences or paragraphs.

Diagramming. Another activity associated with traditional grammar is diagramming sentences. Although also considered old-fashioned, it is still found in many textbooks and required in many upper elementary and middle school curriculums. A *sentence diagram* is a visual picture that identifies the parts of speech in a sentence. Instead of defining the parts of speech verbally, the sentence diagram does it visually. Figure 9.21 shows some sample sentence diagrams. Note that these are among the easiest of sentences to diagram. Diagramming compound and complex sentences is considerably more difficult.

Figure 9.21

Sample sentence diagrams.

1. Horses gallop.

2. Lizards eat flies and earthworms.

3. Lena was named to the team.

4. The girl plays piano beautifully.

Sentence diagramming is difficult to teach and frustrating for many children to learn. Most teachers resort to direct lecture presentations, and children memorize the sample patterns to pass the test. Above all, these activities take up large amounts of class time that could be much better spent in other ways. At one time, it was believed that diagramming sentences made students better writers; this was the justification for spending so much time on this activity. Research has shown this not to be the case (Braddock, Lloyd-Jones, & Schoer, 1963; Hillocks, 1986). The best that can be said about sentence diagramming instruction is that it makes children better sentence diagrammers. It does not make them better writers or speakers of the language.

Still another criticism of the way traditional or formal grammar is taught comes from Stephen Krashen (1993). Krashen argues, and many grammar authorities agree, that what passes for the teaching of grammar in most classrooms is merely the testing of assigned textbook exercises.

Finally, there is a strong argument made by Noguchi (1991) that by spending less time on traditional grammar lessons, both teacher and students will have more time to work on revising and editing issues, which are the real keys to improving students' writing skills. For Noguchi, less is more. We would agree. Less time spent on memorizing rules or diagramming sentences means more time available to focus on clarity and effectiveness in writing.

Nontraditional

Cloze technique. An alternative to emphasizing memorizing and diagramming is to teach the parts of speech using the cloze technique. Recall that the **cloze technique** was originally designed to assess reading comprehension by omitting every *n*th term from a passage and asking the student to provide the exact missing terms. Cloze has also proven to be a successful teaching technique (Marlow & Reese, 1992). For teaching the parts of speech, the teacher photocopies a passage from a basal reader or children's literature book and deletes the parts of speech she or he wishes to emphasize—verbs, for example. Students then have to provide the missing words or ones "close" enough in meaning to be acceptable. Using the cloze technique to teach grammar within the context of real sentences is a preferable activity to labeling and underlining. Figure 9.22 summarizes the steps of this technique.

Figure 9.23 is a sample of a cloze test.

Proofreading. As part of the process writing approach, children are taught to proofread and edit their own writing from rough copy to final copy (Tompkins, 1998). This activity also helps students to distinguish correct grammatical structures from nonsentences. In the process writing approach, although teachers do not stress grammatical terminology, the students are actually dealing with and learning about the eight basic parts of speech. Correcting written work so that the message comes across clearly to the reader involves a writer's intuitive understanding of and ability to use the rules of language to create meaningful sentences (Smith, 1986). Thus process writing actually helps children acquire traditional grammar knowledge, albeit at the unconscious level.

Figure 9.22

Steps of the cloze technique for teaching grammar.

Step 1 Present a sentence or paragraph with all the examples of a single part of speech omitted, such as verbs.

Step 2 Ask the students to brainstorm in small groups all the possible words that fit in the blanks.

Step 3 Ask students, "What do all these terms have in common?" Again the groups can discuss and brainstorm to come up with a generalization. This generalization may or may not fit the definition of a verb.

Step 4 Have the students generate their own sentences with verbs omitted and exchange these with friends.

Figure 9.23

A sample cloze test.

Directions: Read the two paragraphs. Fill in the missing blanks with verbs to make the sentences correct.

When Wilma Rudolph _____ four years old, she _____ an attack of double pneumonia and scarlet fever. She was _____ crippled, her left leg paralyzed. The doctors _____ that only with special treatment could she _____ to _____ back the use of her leg.

Every week Wilma's mother _____ her on the long round trip between Clarksville, Tennessee, and the clinic in Nashville. The entire family _____ the proper way to _____ Wilma's leg. By the time she _____ eight years old, Wilma _____ able to walk again with the help of a specially built shoe.

Corrected Version

When Wilma Rudolph _was_ four years old, she _had_ an attack of double pneumonia and scarlet fever. She was _left_ crippled, her left leg paralyzed. The doctors _said_ that only with special treatment could she _hope_ to _get_ back the use of her leg.

Every week Wilma's mother _took_ her on the long round trip between Clarksville, Tennessee, and the clinic in Nashville. The entire family _learned_ the proper way to _massage_ Wilma's leg. By the time she _was_ eight years old, Wilma _was_ able to walk again with the help of a specially built shoe.

Children's literature. Another alternative to the traditional approach to teaching the parts of speech and figures of speech is through children's literature (Yellin, 1986). Many teachers today try to integrate grammar instruction with a combined reading/writing program. Such an integrated grammar lesson might include the following steps or activities. First, the teacher would read aloud a selection from a particular children's literature book. The students would listen to the piece and then discuss it. The teacher would direct the students to attend to a particular aspect, such as descriptive language or comparisons. For example, in Wilson Rawls's *Summer of the Monkeys* (1976), the narrator says that when he was born, "I was as pink as a sunburnt huckleberry, and as lively as a young squirrel in a corn crib" (p. 10). The class would then provide their own descriptions and comparisons.

Ruth Heller has a collection of concept books that focus on the parts of speech. A teacher can do many activities with one of these books. For example, after reading and discussing Heller's *Many Luscious Lollipops: A Book about Adjectives*, a teacher can write down on the chalkboard all the adjectives that the students remember from the book. Then he or she can have the students use those adjectives to describe items in the classroom. Using the same book, the teacher could go through the book again and write on Post-it notes different adjectives that the students can use to describe the delightful illustrations. For a third activity, the teacher could have the students make their own book of adjectives by drawing pictures and using adjectives to describe their illustrations.

Using another book, the teacher could have the class substitute their own words in sentences selected from the book read. The substituted words would be directed at specific parts of speech, such as adjectives or adverbs.

The books found in Figure 9.24 lend themselves to lively discussions about parts of speech that can later be incorporated into mini-lessons based on students' writing needs.

Figure 9.24	*Animalia* (1986) by Graeme Base (alliteration)
	Some Smug Slug (1996) by Pamela Duncan Edwards (alliteration)
Books to use to reinforce grammar concepts.	*Four Famished Foxes and Fosdyke* (1995) by Pamela Duncan Edwards (alliteration)
	Elephants Aloft (1995) by Kathi Appelt (prepositions)
	Behind the Mask (1995) by Ruth Heller (prepositions)
	A Cashe of Jewels: And Other Collective Nouns (1987) by Ruth Heller
	Merry-Go-Round: A Book of Nouns (1990) by Ruth Heller
	Kites Sail High: A Book About Verbs (1988) by Ruth Heller
	Mine, All Mine: A Book About Pronouns (1997) by Ruth Heller
	Many Luscious Lollipops: A Book About Adjectives (1989) by Ruth Heller
	Up, Up and Away: A Book About Adverbs (1993) by Ruth Heller
	Fantastic! Wow! and Unreal: A Book About Interjections and Conjunctions (1998) by Ruth Heller
	A Chocolate Moose for Dinner (1976) by Fred Gwynne (homonyms)
	Word Wizard (1998) by Cathryn Falwell (play with words)
	Brown Bear, What Do You See? (1967) by Bill Martin (direct address)

Sentence transformations. According to TG grammar, the basis for all sentences is the *kernel sentence:* a simple, active, declarative sentence. Kernel sentences, in turn, can be changed or transformed into other surface structures. Native speakers of a language make these transformations unconsciously. However, by understanding how kernel sentences are transformed into more complex sentences, students can utilize this knowledge to improve their own writing. Study the following example of six transformations beginning from one kernel sentence: *The boy sells papers.*

1. *Negative.* The boy does not sell papers.

2. *Passive.* Papers are sold by the boy.

3. *Negative-passive.* Papers are not sold by the boy.

4. *Question.* Does the boy sell papers?

5. *Negative-question.* Doesn't the boy sell papers?

6. *Negative-passive-question.* Aren't the papers sold by the boy?

Try your own kernel sentence and make similar transformations. In working with young children, teach one transformation at a time, when you feel the children are ready to handle that new structure.

A mini-lesson on the formation of questions might involve a teacher instructing the class as follows.

I've noticed in your writing that some of you are beginning to use the question mark. Today I want to talk to you about how question sentences are written. On the chalkboard, I've written the sentence, *Anna plays jump rope after school.* Beneath it, I've change this sentence into the question sentence, *Does Anna play jump rope after school?* Notice that to make a question I used the word *does,* changed *plays* to *play,* and ended the sentence with a question mark. Here is another way to write a question sentence: *Will Anna play jump rope after school?* Who can come to the board and write still another question sentence?

A few students volunteer and come up to write their questions. "That's good," concludes the teacher. "Now everyone continue working on whatever you were writing. I'll come around if you need help."

Notice how the mini-lesson takes the form of a brief lecture supplemented by a few examples. The teacher could also have assigned a page in a workbook or textbook for additional practice. Instead, he directs the students to spend the rest of their time writing on their own. As he assists children in the course of the week, some of the students experiment with writing questions.

Word substitutions. Even very young children can learn to create new sentences when given an existing sentence. To begin a mini-lesson on this topic, a teacher might write a sentence on the chalkboard with one word underlined: *Maria likes to play.* She then draws a line through the underlined word and above it substitutes another word—*jump, run,* or a similar verb. Then she asks, "Children, does this word still make sense in the sentence? How does it change the sentence?" After a brief discussion, she directs the students to work in small groups and create their own sentences by changing the underlined word. Next she underlines two words in the sentence: *Maria likes to play.* Again the children work in small groups creating new sentences such as *Betty likes to study* and *He likes to swim.*

Notice that in this mini-lesson the teacher uses a cooperative learning discovery approach. The children working in small groups help one another to discover new ways of changing sentences. Substitution exercises such as this one give students practice in revision at the word level; writers often go back to change words in sentences to convey just the right meaning.

Sentence expansions. Young children begin by writing simple sentences and generally work up to writing longer, more involved sentences. The following exercise gives students practice in expanding their sentence repertoire. This is another example of a practice exercise that develops students' ability to revise their writing.

A mini-lesson on sentence expansion might begin with the teacher showing the children some short, simple sentences on the board: *The boy runs. The puppy barked.* Next the teacher explains that one way to develop sentences is

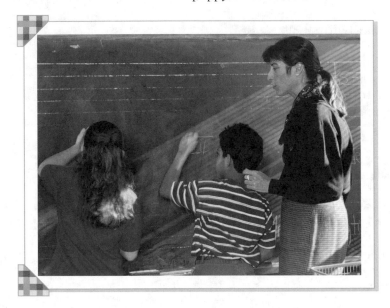

by adding adjectives, adverbs, articles, and so on to make them longer and more interesting: *The young boy runs to school. The happy puppy barked excitedly.*

The teacher puts another example on the board: *Trees sway.* This time she asks the students to work in small groups, adding a word (or words) to see how long they can make the sentence. After a few minutes, she asks one of the groups to come forward and write its expanded sentences on the board:

Trees sway.

Tall trees sway.

Tall trees sway lazily and softly.

Tall trees sway lazily and softly in the afternoon breeze.

Sentence combining. Sentence combining has a relatively long history (Christie, 1980; Cooper, 1973; Mellon, 1969; O'Hare, 1973; Strong, 1993). The purpose of sentence combining is to expand students' syntactic fluency in writing by getting them to create structures they might not ordinarily write. The principle behind this technique is similar to sentence expansion but requires a greater facility with written language structures. In doing sentence combining exercises, teachers need to remember that there is more than one correct way to combine sentences. The mini-lesson example uses a discovery-type format.

The teacher might start by writing two sentences on the board. Beneath them, he writes one more sentence that combines the information from the first two. Then he gives the rules for sentence combining as follows: (1) You may move words around and change punctuation, (2) you may also add or delete words, but (3) you must write only one sentence that still retains the meaning of the first two sentences. Following are some examples:

1. a. The wind was strong. The leaves fell to the ground.

   b. The leaves fell to the ground because the wind was strong.

2. a. Philip is my friend. Philip plays basketball. Philip likes to do chemistry experiments.

    b. My friend Philip plays basketball and likes to do chemistry experiments.

The largest body of research on writing and writing instruction concurs: Teaching grammar in isolation from authentic writing does not result in writing improvement (Amiran & Mann, 1982; Elley, Barham & Wyllie, 1976; Hillocks & Smith, 1991; McQuade, 1980; Neill, 1982; Rosen, 1987; Weaver, 1996). As with any other teaching approach, teachers need to compare the amount of time spent in class with the benefits to students.

The grammar activities described in the sections above appear to help students in some aspects of writing. However, they are still highly artificial, forcing students to work from someone else's examples. More simply put, letting students write their own sentences, paragraphs, and stories on topics they really care about is a much better reinforcement of the skills you are trying to teach. Letting students discuss their writing at length with fellow students and yourself is the best way to get them to revise and edit their own work. In the course of these genuine writing activities, grammatical growth and understanding take place naturally in an atmosphere that is positive and supportive.

The research arguments against the teaching of formal grammar in isolation from real reading and writing activities are formidable but complex. If you would like to read more about studies done on grammar methods and their effectiveness or lack thereof, we recommend Constance Weaver's book, *Teaching Grammar in Context* (1996), as a recent summary of the research in this area.

Punctuation and Capitalization: Two More Tools of Writing

The issues surrounding punctuation and capitalization are ones that are best dealt with in the middle steps of the process writing approach under proofreading and editing (Tompkins, 1998). As discussed in Chapter 8, the following is a possible five-step approach for teachers to take in this area:

1. In a mini-lesson, model for students how to proofread. Photocopy a student's composition and demonstrate proofreading on an overhead in front of the class. Read the composition aloud, letting your voice indicate pauses, stops, rising, and falling. Do this for punctuation and capitalization errors only. Leave spelling, handwriting, paragraphing, and other editing for later lessons. Trying to teach too much in one lesson is a common fault.

2. Then edit (make the changes) on the overhead copy for all the students to see. Use a grammar textbook to check any corrections if you need to; this shows students how reference books were intended to be used.

3. Next provide the class with sample paragraphs in which the punctuation and capitalization have been omitted. Allow students to work in pairs or small cooperative groups to correct these paragraphs.

4. Allow the rest of the period for students to write. As individual students complete their rough drafts, encourage them to use their proofreading

Teaching demands not just desirable personality attributes but specific skills. Skills are not ends in themselves, but they are necessary tools.

Jacob S. Kounin

and editing skills. Then have them get together with fellow students for a second proofreading/editing session.

5. Finally, conduct proofreading/editing conferences with individual students. Although conferences should focus on the content and ideas of the written work, this is also the ideal time for the teacher to assess a student's skill in handling punctuation and capitalization matters. Based on this evaluation, additional mini-lessons on specific areas can be designed for small groups of students or perhaps even the whole class if necessary.

PUNCTUATION

Punctuating sentences properly is difficult for young children, particularly for beginning writers who have not read much. As children move through the grades, if they have been allowed to read and write a great deal, their punctuation skills improve automatically (Atwell, 1998; Calkins, 1994). Why is this so?

There are two views regarding punctuation and how it should be taught. One view holds that punctuation is part of traditional grammar and can be taught by memorizing rules. A second view argues that punctuation is a reflection of spoken language—the pauses, stops, pitch, and stress that people give to language when they speak (Chafe, 1988). Most professional writers subscribe to the latter view, claiming that when they write, they also try to hear how the language sounds. Reading aloud, hearing the

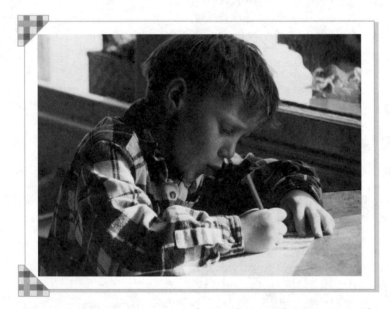

sounds of the words, and noting the amount of emphasis they wish to convey in a particular sentence determine how writers punctuate (Welty, 1983). Obviously, however, such writers are also familiar with the rules of punctuation and with what commas, periods, exclamation marks, and other marks tell a reader. Thus it appears that punctuation is a matter of both recognizing intonation units (by reading aloud or hearing your inner voice) and applying appropriate punctuation. There is also evidence to support the notion that, just as with spelling, young children invent their own punctuation marks and creative use of punctuation (Cordeiro, Giacobbe & Cazden, 1983). For example, young children will commonly put a period at the end of every line they write, despite the instructions from the teacher to put the period at the end of the sentence. For the beginning writer, a line of writing is a sentence. The more children read and write, the more they acquire what Chafe (1988) has called the "mental image of sound" necessary to convey meaning through punctuation.

Figures 9.25 and 9.26 summarize the uses of some of the common punctuation marks. These lists should serve as a reference for you in helping students and as a guide to the kinds of mini-lessons that might be taught; the latter, of course, should be determined by the needs of your students—based on their own writing, not the directives of a textbook.

A mini-lesson on the period or comma might look like this: After explaining one or more of the rules for using periods or commas, the teacher reads a brief paragraph taken from a children's literature book. When finished, she

Figure 9.25   *Rules for using periods and commas.*

PERIOD

Use a period . . .

1. at the end of a sentence making a statement
2. after abbreviations of titles when the name of the person follows
3. after abbreviations of days of the week and months of the year

Examples

1. The men drilled for oil.
2. Mrs. Baker, Dr. Jones, Capt. Ahab, Rev. Smith
3. Mon., Wed., Sun., Jan., Aug., Oct.

COMMA

Use a comma . . .

1. to separate the day from the year
2. to separate the names of a city and a state
3. after the greeting in a friendly letter
4. after the closing of a letter
5. to separate items in a list
6. between long independent clauses connected with *but, and, or, nor*
7. to set off parenthetical information
8. to separate the speaker from a quotation

Examples

1. Lindsay was born on May 4, 1982.
2. Bethany, OK 73008
3. Dear Pamela,
4. Yours truly,
5. Karen bought milk, bread, and cheese.
6. Aubree thought she would swim all day, but the rain changed her plan.
7. Pat Jones, our coach, led the team.
8. John said, "I'm leaving."

or he displays that same paragraph on an overhead transparency with the periods and comma omitted. Together, the teacher and students discuss how to punctuate the paragraph. When they are finished, they compare their work with the original paragraph. Next, another unpunctuated paragraph is given to small groups of students to punctuate. Again, the answers can be compared with the original work.

CAPITALIZATION

Like punctuation, capitalization is best taught in mini-lessons and only when students' writings indicate they are ready for such information. Memorizing rules in isolation from real writing makes little sense to the child. Instead, stress in your mini-lesson that when writers capitalize properly, they are helping their readers to identify proper nouns, to know when a sentence begins, and so on. This in turn helps the reader understand the message that the writer is trying to convey. Figure 9.27 lists a few basic capitalization rules for the elementary and middle school grades.

IN & BEYOND THE CLASSROOM

Select a paragraph from a favorite children's literature book. Retype that paragraph, omitting all capital letters and punctuation marks. Then teach a mini-lesson to a small group of students on some of the common rules of capitalization and punctuation. Give them your paragraph to correct and discuss.

DAILY ORAL LANGUAGE PROGRAM

Some classroom teachers have approached the teaching of writing skills using a unique variation on the mini-lesson. Each day the teacher would write two or three sentences on the board. These sentences contain either

Figure 9.26   *Rules for additional punctuation marks.*

Rules	Examples
1. Use a *question mark* after a sentence that asks a question.	1. What is the capital of Virginia?
2. Use an *exclamation mark* after a sentence that expresses strong feeling.	2. Help! My desk is on fire!

3. Use an *apostrophe* to . . .
  A. indicate a contraction
  B. show possession
	3.
	  A. cannot = can't
	  B. Mary's dress is lovely.

4. Use *quotation marks* . . .
  A. to set off a direct quotation
  B. for titles of articles
  C. for poem titles
  D. for song titles
	4.
	  A. Henry said, "Leave here at once!"
	  B. "The Day I Left Here"
	  C. "Casey at the Bat"
	  D. "The Star-Spangled Banner"

5. Use a *colon* . . .
  A. to indicate a following explanation or listing
  B. after the greeting in a business letter
	5.
	  A. They brought the following items to camp: sleeping bag, toothbrushes, and clothes.
	  B. To Whom It May Concern:

6. Use a *semicolon* to separate two closely related independent clauses.	6. Harold made the highest grades in school; he expects to win a scholarship.
7. Use a *hyphen* to divide a word at the end of a line (but only at a syllable junction).	7. He found himself disbelieving what the president had said.

Figure 9.27   *Rules for capitalization.*

Capitalize . . .	Examples
1. the first word in a sentence	1. Our school play is tomorrow.
2. the names of people	2. Margaret and Susan are sisters.
3. the pronoun *I*	3. Do you think I should go to the party?
4. the names of streets, cities, and states	4. We live on Mulberry Road in Sacramento, California.
5. the names of days, months, and holidays	5. On Thursday, December 25, we will celebrate Christmas.
6. the names of rivers, countries, and continents	6. The Amazon River flows through Brazil in South America.
7. the names of languages and nationalities	7. The French, Spanish, and British signed the treaty.
8. the sections of a country	8. They live in the Southwest.

errors of the type that the students had been making in their writing or difficult skill questions from standardized tests that the teacher had noted from previous classes. The children can volunteer the corrections orally, or they can work on the sentences at their seats. In a brief mini-lesson of 5 to 10 minutes, the teacher reviews with the whole class the corrections to be made.

In 1989, Vail and Papenfuss published a complete series of these sentences, along with mini-lessons, to aid the teacher. Known as the *daily oral language program*, this is another way that teachers can present skills knowledge in writing without taking much time away from the revising, editing, and publishing stages of process writing.

The Computer and Word Processing Programs: Another Tool for the Writer

In recent years, more and more computers have been appearing in elementary schools. In some cases, they are found in individual classrooms. In other schools, a special room has been designated as the computer room; it contains 20 or more machines. Students are sent to the computer room for instruction on a fixed schedule during the week.

Computers have become useful tools for the young writer; however, keyboarding can be an issue when using them. Although there is some disagreement about the exact role of rigorous keyboarding instruction, more schools are realizing the importance of students being proficient in keyboarding and publishers are providing programs to implement it. Among the programs that have been reviewed are the following: Microtype, Ultra-Key, Kid Desk, The Wonderful World of PAWS, Success with Typing, Superkey, Type of Learn, Typing Tutor III, and Keyboard Success.

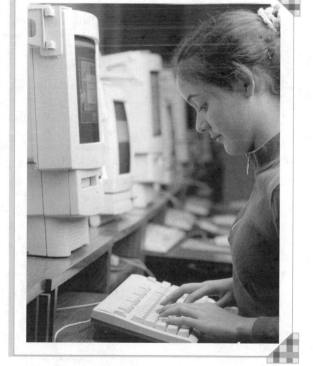

Many educators maintain that students do profit from possessing adequate keyboarding skills and knowledge about the major keys and functions of the word processing programs. It is helpful for the student to know about the *control key*, which can change the way many keys function; the *escape key*, which allows one to get out of a program; and the *return key*, which moves the cursor to the following line.

When working with keyboarding, teachers should remember to give students plenty of time to practice their keyboard competencies and to monitor each student's progress by providing appropriate feedback.

In any integrated language arts classroom, word processing programs should be an important feature. Although other types of information processors do have implications for classroom instruction, word processing programs have the potential to revolutionize both reading and writing instruction.

Word processing programs turn the computer into a "supertypewriter" that can be used to input, edit, format, and generally arrange text—as well as do graphics and illustration—on a page. Any word processing program combined with a printer enables the writer to outline, write, edit, revise, and print out anything he or she might want to express. The word processing programs carry the student through the entire writing process without the time-consuming mess and bother of traditional methods of editing and rewriting. One aspect of these programs that is especially helpful in the editing stage is the spell checker and grammar checker. These programs can also save paper when the editing is done on the computer.

Fortunately there are some word processing programs designed for the primary reader/writer. Among these are Bank Street Writer III and Magic Slate II, which both have picture icons to help children decide which function of the program they want to use. Write for Kids has picture icons plus the capability of reading back the child's story.

There are also many programs that support children's initial writing attempts by including graphics with text. Some examples are The Story Starter, The Story Maker, Story-Book Weaver Deluxe, Storybook Maker, Dazzle Draw, KoalaPad, The Print Shop Deluxe, SuperPrint, and Explore-a-Story. Claris Words is another word processing program that permits students to use the mouse to illustrate their stories and then to add color.

> **BEYOND THE CLASSROOM**
>
> Select one of the word processing programs listed here and use it. Then write a critical review of the program in terms of its usefulness with elementary-grade children.

Summary

To be an effective writer means to communicate clearly with an audience. This requires the effective use of the mechanics or tools of writing. In the past, so-called writing programs overemphasized the teaching of handwriting, spelling, grammar, capitalization, and punctuation to the extent that little actual writing ever took place in the classroom. This is changing with the emphasis on process writing.

Today the tools of writing are seen in a balanced perspective and taught as part of the process approach. Handwriting is taught in the early grades and emphasizes the legibility of a child's handwriting. In the area of spelling, invented spelling is recognized as a developmental part of children's writing growth. Punctuation and capitalization are taught through mini-lessons and the discovery approach when appropriate. Rote memorization and drills are minimized. The role of grammar instruction as isolated drill is also being reexamined in favor of more meaningful activities with direct application to real writing and reinforced through extensive reading. Finally, the potential of the computer, with word processing programs, is being integrated in elementary-school writing programs as another tool to aid the writer in the creative process of composing.

A final suggestion would also be in order. Although most classrooms rely on textbooks to teach grammar, punctuation, capitalization, etc., the textbooks are generally too complex and too confusing for easy understanding. We would instead recommend two handbooks, written expressly for young children to answer the questions they have about the mechanics of language. For grades 4 and 5, see *Writers Express: A Handbook for Young Writers, Thinkers, and Learners* (1995) by Kemper, Nathan, and Sebranek (published by Write Source, Burlington, WI). For grades 6 to 8, see *Write Source 2000: A Guide to Writing, Thinking, and Learning* (1995) (3rd ed.) by Sebranek, Meyer, and Kemper (also published by Write Source, Burlington, WI).

activities *With Children*

BIG WORD SPELLING

A word is given in jumbled alphabetical order, for example, aeefgiorrrrt. Using all the letters, what word can you come up with? Answer: refrigerator. Next draw three columns on your paper: Column one for 2-letter words, column two for 3-letter words, and column three for 4-letter words. Now list as many words as you can in each of the columns using the original letters. Finally, do this activity with a word of your own choosing and give it to a friend.

SPELLING RELAY

In small groups, students collaboratively spell words. One student begins by naming the first letter of a word. Each subsequent student adds a letter toward the creation of a real word. As each student adds a letter, the word that the next student is thinking of may change. Keep going until one student either is stuck or can only add a letter that will complete the word.

SENTENCE RELAY

Play this game in the same way as spelling relay, except have each person in the group add a word. The object is to build long sentences without completing a sentence. The game ends when a word is given that makes a complete sentence.

CHAIN SPELLING

This spelling game is played with the same rules as Geography Train (see the With Children activities section in Chapter 5). A student begins by spelling any word. The next person in the group must think of and spell a word that begins with the last letter of the word spelled by the first person. The game continues until someone cannot think of a word beginning with the last letter of the previously mentioned word.

HANDWRITING PICTURES

Using individual letters or groups of letters from the alphabet, create pictures. You can add eyes, legs, and so on to create stick figures or add other features to create houses, trucks, and trains.

JUMBLED SENTENCES

Select headlines or lead sentences from newspaper articles. Cut up the sentences into separate words. Give the separate word cards to a group of students to unscramble. Depending on which aspect of grammar or punctuation you want to emphasize, the jumbled sentence or headline could contain descriptive adjectives, prepositional phrases, semicolons, and so on.

CROSSWORD PUZZLES

Share some crossword puzzle examples with your class. Describe how they are created, with definitions, words running horizontally and vertically, and blank spaces darkened. In small groups, have the students create their own crossword puzzles using the week's spelling words.

TOUCH CENTER

Create a learning center around tactile activities for reinforcing handwriting and spelling. Use sand trays, shaving cream, glue and macaroni, strings, and clay. Young children can create the letters of the alphabet, while older students can practice writing difficult spelling words.

PUNCTUATE THIS!

Each child copies one paragraph from the book that is being read but omits the punctuation marks and capital letters. Have students exchange paragraphs around the group and correct one another's paragraphs. They can use the book model to check their work.

COMBINING SENTENCES

Books written for young children use many short sentences. Have your upper elementary and middle school students select a children's book written for primary-grade children. Then ask them to rewrite three or four sentences, combining them into one sentence. Remember, they may add and delete words as well as add new punctuation marks.

LABELS, LABELS

To help students practice their handwriting skills with a functional purpose, take a class "trip" around your room and identify all the things that need labels. For example, children can label their desks and lockers, various learning centers, supply closets, bulletin boards, and special file cabinets.

SPELLING PATTERNS

Teach children some simple English spelling patterns. Then have them look through their reading books for example words to fit the patterns. How many words of the same patterns can they find? Examples: C–V–C (*cat, hat, bad, sad, pig, dog, wig*); C–V–C+E (*save, game, bike, like, tone, dove, bone*); C–V–V–C (*rain, leaf, coat, need*).

CIRCUS SPELLING

Have students come to the circus. For each ride they want to go on, they have to get a ticket. To get a ticket, they have to spell the three words listed on the ticket. See who can collect the most tickets. Example words: *clown, popcorn, roller coaster*. Variations on the tickets can be used with County Fair, Sports Events, Travel Agents, and similar activities.

 Computer-Assisted Instruction and Collaborative Internet technology

Computer-assisted instruction (CAI) consists of drill-and-practice programs and tutorials that can be used to provide reinforcement and instruction in the individual language arts skills. Although some of these programs have been criticized as expensive "workbooks" that should not be overused or abused, they may have a place in your classroom as you seek to improve or reinforce particular competencies in your students. However, if you do use these programs, make sure they are related to meaningful classroom learning experiences.

If you desire to use CAI in your classroom, what should be some of your concerns? First of all, there should be a close match between the program and the goals and content of your language arts curriculum. The type and amount of reinforcement the program provides should be adequate and motivational; the program should be self-pacing for the students and easy to use. If these features are missing, the program will probably not meet the needs of your students.

Drill-and-practice programs can provide reinforcement for previously taught areas of language instruction. As such, they may enhance language, reading, and writing competencies in children. In a drill-and-practice program, a student is given a structured sequence of related tasks to be completed. Since practice is a key factor within these programs, the student is often given several chances to complete each task correctly and then given feedback on the correctness of the answers. Students should be rewarded for correct answers and given minimal discouragement for those that are incorrect. The *Sticky Bear Series, Reading Rabbit, Bailey's Book House,* and *Super Solvers Spellbound* are four programs that have worked well and provided acceptable reinforcement with early learners. *Cloze Plus* and *Cloze Test* are two programs that provide reinforcement in using context clues to figure out a word in a passage.

One way of ensuring that a CAI program focuses on the overall language needs of students is to determine whether the software has a teacher utility. Such a feature allows the teacher to customize instruction by using words that are currently part of the students' language, reading, writing, and researching activities. If a class is researching dinosaurs, a teacher might want to reinforce students' new vocabulary about dinosaurs with computer puzzles, word searches, cloze exercises, spelling checkups, or sight-word flashcards. To do this, the teacher might select programs such as *Crossword Magic, Wordsearch, Magic Spells,* and *E-Z Learner.* A teacher can use these programs as word banks for the new vocabulary words the students are acquiring.

websites   *E-learning*

webster.commnet.edu/HP/pages/darling/grammar.htm

This practical presentation teaches and reviews grammar. There are clever presentations of language pitfalls.

www.mrtc.org/~twright/animals/english/alphabet.htm

From antelope to zebra, each letter of the alphabet is represented by a clickable image, which leads to facts about the animal.

www.puzzlemaker.com/

This site permits you to create mazes, word searches, crosswords, and more for any lesson.

www.studyweb.com

This site is a collection of educational Web sites classified in different fields, including grammar and composition.

www.ipl.org/youth/AskAuthor/

This site connects you to home pages of young adult authors. You can dialogue with the authors through e-mail.

www.snowcrest.net/kidpower/authors.html

This site lists authors who are willing to visit your school.

www.grammarnow.com

This site is an e-mail site for proofreading any manuscript.

www.grammarlady.com

This site includes grammar rules and is a hotline for posting questions about composition.

www.wolinskyweb.com/word.htm

This site features resources of sites that have fun with words.

Related Readings

Buchanan, E. (1992). *Spelling for whole language classrooms.* Winnipeg, Canada: Whole Language Consultants Ltd.

> This book gives detailed descriptions of the spelling stages through which most children pass. It also gives strategies to use for each stage; many are in the form of games.

Cunningham, P. M. (1995). *Phonics they use: Words for reading and writing* (2nd ed.). New York: HarperCollins College Publishers.

> This book explains the main aspects of the sounds of words and gives a great number of strategies to use to facilitate children's becoming aware of the different sounds within words.

Goodman, K. (1993). *Phonics phacts: A common-sense look at the most controversial issue affecting today's classrooms!* Portsmouth, NH: Heinemann.

> Goodman explains why teaching phonics in isolation is not effective. In detail, he explains phonology, orthography, and phonics. He also gives some background on the politics of phonics.

Heilman, A. W. (1998). *Phonics in proper perspective* (8th ed.). Upper Saddle River, NJ: Merrill.

> Heilman explains the purpose and the limitations of phonics as well as the controversy over direct instruction of phonics. He does give some generalizations that teachers should know as they help young learners to read and write.

Strickland, D. S. (1998). *Teaching phonics today: A primer for educators.* Newark, DE: International Reading Association.

> A well-known educator/researcher gives some good guidelines to finding the balance between intensive phonics and the holistic approach. She gives practical strategies that support beginning readers and writers. She

has one chapter on communicating the phonics issue to parents and the community.

Wilde, S. (1997). *What's a schwa sound anyway? A holistic guide to phonetics, phonics, and spelling.* Portsmouth, NH: Heinemann.

This is an excellent resource book that gives some basic insights into linguistics that teachers should know as they work with students. The more teachers know, the more helpful they can become when students struggle with reading and writing.

References

Allred, R. (1977). *Spelling: The application of research findings.* Washington, DC: National Education Association.

Amiran, E., & Mann, J. (1982). *Written composition, grades K–12: Literature synthesis and report.* Portland, OR: Northwest Regional Educational Laboratory.

Askov, E., & Greff, F. (1975). Handwriting: Copying vs. tracing as the most effective type of practice. *Journal of Educational Research, 69,* 96–98.

Atwell, N. (1998). *In the middle* (2nd ed.). Portsmouth, NH: Boynton/Cook Publisher.

Beers, C., & Beers, J. (1981). Three assumptions abut learning to spell. *Language Arts, 58,* 573–580.

Bing, S. B. (1988). Handwriting: Remediate or circumvent. *Academic Therapy, 23,* 509–514.

Bissex, G. (1980). *GNYS at WRK: A child learns to write and read.* Cambridge, MA: Harvard University Press.

Bloomfield, L. (1933). *Language.* New York: Holt.

Braddock, R., Lloyd-Jones, R., & Schoer, L. (1963). *Research in written composition.* Champaign, IL: NCTE.

Brown, G., & Ellis, N. (eds.) (1994). *Handbook of spelling: Theory, process and intervention.* New York: John Wiley & Sons.

Buchanan, E. (1992). *Spelling for whole language classrooms.* Winnipeg, Canada: Whole Language Consultants Ltd.

Calkins, L. (1994). *The art of teaching writing* (2nd ed.). Portsmouth, NH: Heinemann.

Chafe, W. (1988). What good is punctuation? *The Quarterly of the National Writing Project, 10,* 8–11.

Chomsky, C. (1971). Write first, read later. *Childhood Education, 47,* 296–299.

Chomsky, N. (1957). *Syntactic structures.* The Hague: Mouton.

Chomsky, N. (1974). *Aspects of the theory of syntax.* Cambridge, MA: Harvard University Press.

Christie, J. (1980). Sentence combining practice. *Practical Applications of Research, PDK Newsletter, 2*(4).

Clay, M. (1975). *What did I write?* Portsmouth, NH: Heinemann.

Clay, M. (1993). *Reading recovery: A guidebook for teachers in training.* Portsmouth, NH: Heinemann.

Cooper, C. (1973). An outline for writing sentence-combination problems. *English Journal, 62*(1), 96–102, 108.

Cordeiro, P., Giacobbe, M., & Cazden, C. (1983). Apostrophes, quotation marks and periods: Learning punctuation in the first grade. *Language Arts, 60,* 323–332.

Cramer, R. (1978). *Children's writing and language growth.* Columbus, OH: Merrill Publishing Company.

D'Angelo, K. (1982). Developing legibility and uniqueness in handwriting with calligraphy. *Language Arts, 59,* 23–27.

DiStefano, P., & Haggerty, P. (1985). Teaching spelling at the elementary level: A realistic perspective. *The Reading Teacher, 38,* 373–377.

Dodd, A. (1988). Demons, dictionaries, and spelling strategies. *English Journal, 77,* 52–53.

Ediger, M. (1979). Good handwriting a must for students in our schools. *Reading Improvement, 16,* 112–113.

Elley, W. B., Barham, I. H., & Wyllie, M. (1976). The role of grammar in a secondary English curriculum. *Research in the Teaching of English, 10,* 5–21. Reprinted from *New Zealand Journal of Educational Studies,* May 1975, *10,* 26–42.

Farris, P. (1991). Views and other views: Handwriting instruction should not become extinct. *Language Arts, 68,* 312–314.

Feder, J., & Weber, C. (1986). Remedies for reversal. *Academic Therapy,* 87–90.

Fernald, G. (1943). *Remedial techniques in basic school subjects.* New York: McGraw-Hill.

Ferriero, E., & Teberosky, A. (1983). *Writing before schooling.* Portsmouth, NH: Heinemann.

Foerster, L. (1972). Teachers, don't let your first graders trace! *Elementary English, 79,* 431–433.

Francis, W. (1964). Revolution in grammar. In H. Allen (ed.), *Readings in applied linguistics.* New York: Appleton-Century-Crofts.

Fries, C. (1952). *The structure of language.* New York: Irvington.

Gentry, J. R. (1984). Developmental aspects of learning to spell. *Academic Therapy, 20*(1), 11–19.

Gentry, J. R. (1987). *Spel . . . is a four-letter word.* Portsmouth, NH: Heinemann.

Gill C. H., & Scharer, P. L. (1996). "Why do they get it on Friday and misspell it on Mondays?" Teachers inquiring about their students as spellers. *Language Arts,* 73(2), 89–109.

Graves, D. (1994). *A fresh look at writing.* Portsmouth, NH: Heinemann.

Haley-James, S. (ed.) (1981). *Perspectives on writing in grades 1–8.* Urbana, IL: National Council of Teachers of English.

Hanna, P. (1971). *Spelling: Structure and strategies.* Boston: Houghton Mifflin.

Harrison, S. (1981). Open letter from a left-handed teacher: Some sinistrial ideas on the teaching of handwriting. *Teaching Exceptional Children,* 13, 116–120.

Heilman, A. W. (1998). *Phonics in proper perspective* (8th ed.). Upper Saddle River, NJ: Merrill.

Henderson, E. (1985). *Teaching spelling.* Boston: Houghton Mifflin.

Hillocks, G. (1986). *Research on written composition.* Urbana, IL: ERIC Clearinghouse on Reading and Communication Skills.

Hillocks, G., & Smith, M. W. (1991). Grammar and usage. In J. Flood, J. M. Jensen, D. Lapp, & J. R. Squire (eds.), *Handbook of research on teaching the English language arts.* New York: Macmillan.

Hirsch, E., & Niedermeyer, F. (1973). The effects of tracing prompts and discrimination training on kindergarten handwriting performance. *Journal of Educational Research,* 67, 81–86.

Hodges, R. (1991). Smart spelling. *Instructor,* 100(7), 69–70.

Hodges, R. (1991). The conventions of writing. In J. Flood, J. M. Jensen, D. Lapp, & J. R. Squire (eds.), *Handbook of research on teaching the English language arts.* New York: Macmillan.

Howell, H. (1978). Write on, you sinistrials! *Language Arts,* 55, 852–856.

Joseph, L. (1998/1999). Word boxes help children with learning disabilities identify and spell words. *The Reading Teacher,* 52(4), 348–356.

Kemper, D., Nathan, R., & Sebranek, P. (1995). *Writers express: A handbook for young writers, thinkers, and learners.* Burlington, WI: Write Source.

Krashen, S. (1991). Bilingual education: A focus on current research. In *National Clearinghouse for Bilingual Education,* vol. 3. Washington, DC.

Krashen, S. (1993). *The power of reading: Insights from the research.* Englewood, CO: Libraries Unlimited.

Laminack, L. (1991). *Learning with Zachery.* Portsmouth, NH: Heinemann.

Lamme, L. (1979). Handwriting in an early childhood curriculum. *Young Children,* 20–27.

Lamme, L. (1989). Authorship: A key facet of whole language. *The Reading Teacher,* 704–710.

Manning, M., & Manning, G. (1981). *Improving spelling in the middle grades.* Washington, DC: National Education Association.

Marlow, L., & Reese, D. (1992). Strategies for using literature with at-risk readers. *Reading Improvement,* 29(2), 130–132.

McQuade, F. (1980). Examining a grammar course: The rational and the result. *English Journal,* 69, 26–30.

Mellon, J. (1969). *Transformational sentence combining: Method of enhancing the development of syntactic fluency in English composition.* Urbana, IL: NCTE. Research Report No. 10.

Moats, L. C. (1995). *Spelling: Development, disability and instruction.* Baltimore: York Press.

Moffett, J., & Wagner, B. (1983). *Student-centered language arts and reading, K–13* (3rd ed.). Boston: Houghton Mifflin.

Moore, S. (1986). Curse you, cursive writing. *Reading Research and Instruction,* 25(2), 139–141.

Neill, S. B. (1982). *Teaching writing: Problems and solutions.* Arlington, VA: American Association of School Administrators. ERIC Document 191 007.

Newkirk, T. (1978). Grammar instruction and writing: What we don't know. *English Journal,* 67, 48–54.

Noguchi, R. (1991). *Grammar and the teaching of writing: Limits and possibilities.* Urbana, IL: National Council of Teachers of English.

Norton, D. (1997). *The effective teaching of language arts* (5th ed.). Columbus, OH: Merrill.

O'Hare, F. (1973). *Sentence combining: Improving student writing without formal grammar instruction.* Urbana, IL: NCTE Research Report No. 15.

Parks, S., & Black, H. (1990). *Organizing thinking: Graphic organizers.* Pacific Grove, CA: Critical Thinking Press and Software.

Peck, M., Askov, E., & Fairchild, S. (1980). Another decade of research in handwriting: Progress and prospect in the 1970s. *Journal of Education Research,* 73, 283–298.

Pixton, W. (1978). *Some conventions of standard written English* (2nd ed.). Dubuque, IA: Kendall/Hunt Publishing Co.

Pooley, R. (1957). *Teaching English grammar.* New York: Appleton-Century-Crofts.

Read, C. (1986). *Children's creative spelling.* London: Routledge and Kegan Paul.

Rice, J. (1987). The futility of the spelling grind. *The Forum,* 23, 163–172, 409–419.

Riefer, D. (1987). Is backwards reading an effective proofreading strategy? ERIC Document ED 281 175.

Rosen, L. M. (1987). Developing corrections in student writing: Alternative to the error hunt. *English Journal,* 76(3), 62–69.

Sapir, E. (1921). *Language: An introduction to speech.* New York: Harcourt Brace Jovanovich.

Sebranek, P., Meyer, V., & Kemper, D. (1995). *Write source 2000: A guide to writing, thinking, and learning* (3rd ed.). Burlington, WI: Write Source.

Shurley, B., & Wetsell, R. K. (1989). *The Shurley method: English made easy.* Cabot, AR: Shurley Instructional Materials.

Shurley, B., & Wetsell, R. K. (1997). *Shurley method English made easy.* Cabot, AR: Shurley Instructional Materials. Information Packet Booklet.

Smith, M. (1986). Grammar and the manipulation of syntax. In G. Hillocks (ed.), *Research on written composition.* Urbana, IL: ERIC Clearinghouse of Reading and Communication Skills.

Stauffer, R. (1980). *The language experience approach to the teaching of reading.* New York: Harper & Row.

Stewig, J. W., & Nordberg, B. (1995). *Exploring language arts in the elementary school.* Belmont, CA: Wordsworth.

Strong, W. (1993). *Sentence combining: A composing book* (3rd ed.). New York: McGraw Hill.

Temple, C., Nathan, R., Burris, N., & Temple, F. (1988). *The beginnings of writing* (2nd ed.). Boston: Allyn & Bacon.

Thurber, D. (1987). *D'Nealian handwriting: Grades K–8.* Glenview, IL: Scott Foresman.

Tompkins, G. (1998). *Language arts: Content and teaching strategies.* Columbus, OH: Merrill.

Vail, N., & Papenfuss, J. (1989). *Daily oral language. Level 1–12.* Evanston, IL: McDougal, Littell.

Weaver, C. (1996). *Teaching grammar in context.* Portsmouth, NH: Boynton/Cook Publishers.

Welty, E. (1983). *One writer's beginnings.* New York: Warner Books.

Wilde, S. (1996). A speller's bill of rights. *Primary Voices K–6, 4*(1), 7–10.

Wilde, S. (1997). *What's a schwa sound anyway? A holistic guide to phonetics, phonics, and spelling.* Portsmouth, NH: Heinemann.

Williams, C. (1997). *An examination of the effects of Shurley English on the writing performance of fourth grade students.* Doctoral dissertation, Oklahoma State University, Stillwater, OK.

Woods, W. (1986). The evolution of nineteenth century grammar teaching. *Rhetoric Review, 5*(1), 4–20.

Yellin, D. (1983). Learning to spell, spelling to learn. *The Living Textbook: Daily Oklahoman and Oklahoman City Times.*

Yellin, D. (1986). Teaching grammar through children's literature. *The Florida Reading Quarterly, 22*(4), 10–13.

Zutell, J. (1996). The directed spelling thinking activity (DSTA): Providing an effective balance in word study instruction. *The Reading Teacher, 50*(2), 98–108.

Reading and Writing Across the Curriculum

10

IN THIS CHAPTER

overview

Because reading and writing are vital skills in today's society, it is important that children learn very early how to utilize them in processing information. Since every aspect of the elementary school curriculum provides the child with information, integrating reading and writing across the curriculum is a natural and effective way to achieve this goal. With such an approach, children are able to see that reading and writing (as well as speaking and listening) are needed and valuable ways of interacting with information from science, social studies, health, math, music, art, and any other subject area.

This chapter provides insights about the rationale and the approaches that can be used to foster such an integrated curriculum. Various strategies are presented, such as the directed reading–thinking activity, graphic organizers, semantic feature analysis, and semantic webbing, all of which can be used to assist students in obtaining and responding to information. Also, special emphasis is placed on utilizing techniques that will help your students to become strategic readers and writers—able to acquire information efficiently, monitor themselves, and become independent learners. Success in acquiring and reacting to information from text allows children to gain confidence in themselves as learners.

The final section of the chapter is devoted to thematic units that use reading and writing strategies to help students interact with content information. This approach provides ways of exploring and organizing information so that it is meaningful to learners; included are various assessment and other forms. The use of thematic units can integrate the curriculum so successfully that language activities can and do play a major role in all the content areas. Also included is a thematic unit on folktales.

Why Reading and Writing Across the Curriculum?

Over the years, there have been many different views about the role of reading and writing within the elementary classroom curriculum. The discrete view sees reading and writing as activities that should be done for their own sake. In this approach, reading and writing are often taught in separate periods of the school day, are seldom related to each other, and are rarely—if ever—integrated with the other content areas.

The whole language and the integrated approaches consider reading and writing as closely related ways of learning new information. Through experiences with reading and writing, children learn how to learn. They become literate and develop into independent self-educators who can acquire all types of content information.

Not only do reading and writing help people to learn, they are actually motivators for each other. In reading, people are trying to find information, locate ideas, and comprehend what the text really says. To accomplish this task, readers use prior knowledge and often make predictions about what they expect to learn. In writing a summary of material or including it for an entry in a reading/writing log, readers are able to clarify and even analyze the ideas they've gathered. And it is this analysis that may further motivate a person to reread and study the material or to seek out other information to enhance what was learned from the text. In other words, reading promotes writing, which in turn encourages further reading (Vacca, Vacca, & Groves, 1995). The processes build on each other as ways of obtaining meaning.

In an integrated approach, reading and writing become natural ways of making content come alive for students. Through these processes, students can take charge of their learning by interacting with textual material in a variety of ways. To get a better idea of how this happens, read the following Classroom Vignette, in which content and process learning are integrated.

Vignette *in the classroom*

Mrs. Castleberry's second-grade class has just embarked on a unit of study involving caterpillars and the ways in which they grow and change. The title for the thematic unit is "Caterpillars and Change—What Really Happens?" The basic information for much of the unit comes from science. However, reading, writing, literature, poetry, health, math, art, and social studies all play major roles in the project.

As a way of arousing the children's interest in the topic, Mrs. Castleberry reads *The Very Hungry Caterpillar* by Eric Carle to them. Not only are the students fascinated by Carle's lively and imaginative

(continued)

pictures, they are very interested in the variety of foods that the caterpillar ate. When they learn that the caterpillar got a stomachache from all its eating, several of the children exclaim, "I'd have one too if I ate all that stuff!" In the end, everyone is delighted that the caterpillar turned into a beautiful butterfly, an event that they celebrate by decorating colorful tissue-paper butterflies.

To prepare students for the information they will be encountering throughout the unit, Mrs. Castleberry also has students begin to fill in the Caterpillar Information Chart (pictured in Figure 10.1). It is an adaptation of an interactive learning chart that is sometimes used in the directed reading–thinking activity (Monahan & Hinson, 1988).

For the next few weeks, the entire class is involved in a series of caterpillar-related activities. In addition to engaging the help of the school librarian in locating simple entries about caterpillars from encyclopedias and dictionaries, students consult a variety of information books, including the following:

Hogner, D. (1964). *Moths.* New York: Thomas Y. Crowell Company.

Hunt, J., & Selsam, M. (1987). *A First Look at Caterpillars.* New York: Walker & Co.

McClung, R. (1949). *Sphinx: The Story of a Caterpillar.* New York: William Morrow & Co.

McClung, R. (1965). *Caterpillars and How They Live.* New York: William Morrow & Co.

Norsgaard, E. J. (1988). *How to Raise Butterflies.* New York: Dodd, Mead & Co.

Terry, T. (1988). *The Life Cycle of a Butterfly.* New York: The Bookwright Press.

Watts, B. (1986). *Butterfly and Caterpillar.* Morristown, NJ: Silver Burdett Co.

Watts, B. (1989). *Keeping Minibeasts: Caterpillars.* New York: Franklin Watts.

As a way of summarizing its findings, one group of children writes a book of information about caterpillars entitled *Caterpillars—Everything You Always Wanted to Know and Then Some.*

Many students also do firsthand research by observing a variety of caterpillars, cocoons, and chrysalides with a magnifying glass and recording data about their findings on a features chart (pictured in Figure 10.2). The class is a bit surprised to find such a variety of different caterpillars and to learn that some caterpillars turn into moths rather than butterflies.

Mrs. Castleberry finds that most of the class is very interested in learning what caterpillars eat. She has one group of students research the different food sources of caterpillars and report on them to the class. The group that undertakes this task finds that the diet of the caterpillars is primarily vegetarian, with an emphasis on green, leafy foods. The children feel that this is a very healthy diet and decide to apply this to their own lives by becoming more aware of healthy foods they should be eating. They enjoy this aspect of the unit so much that as a culminating activity for the project the class decides to have a Healthy Caterpillar Snack Party at school. They plan and write a menu and an invitation for the other second-grade class:

Please come to a Healthy Caterpillar Snack Party
Where: Room 213 in Longmeadow School
When: April 12, 10:30 A.M.
Given by: Mrs. Castleberry's class
Menu: Carrot sticks
            Celery sticks with peanut butter
            Radish curls
            Apple slices
            Pear halves
            Lettuce leaves with pineapple
            Apple juice
Door prizes will be 3-D paper caterpillars made by members of the class. R.S.V.P. by April 5.

Needless to say, the students in both second-grade classes have a great time and enjoy some very healthy snacks.

Figure 10.1

Caterpillar information chart.

Caterpillar Information Chart			
What We Know About Caterpillars	**What We Think About Caterpillars**	**What We'll Learn About Caterpillars**	**What We Learned About Caterpillars**
Caterpillars turn into butterflies. We like them.	Spring might be the best time to see them. Some live in a chrysalis.	We'll be able to find out if a caterpillar lives in a chrysalis or a cocoon.	We learned that there are many kinds of caterpillars. The ones that turn into butterflies live in a chrysalis. The ones that turn into moths live in a cocoon.

Figure 10.2

Caterpillar data collection chart.

Caterpillar Data							
Name	**Moth/ Butterfly**	**Hair**	**Spines**	**Pattern**	**Body**	**Horns**	**Tail**
Wooly Bear	Moth	Fine		Light, middle, and dark end	Curls, round	No	Curls, not forked

SUPPORTIVE RESEARCH

A great deal of the rationale for integrating reading and writing across the curriculum comes from research and published reports that have outlined what this country needs to do to become a "nation of readers." Research has indicated that the most logical place for developing reading, writing, and thinking competencies is in content areas such as social studies and science (Anderson, Hiebert, Scott, & Wilkinson, 1985).

Because reading materials in subject areas are much different from the narrative stories that many young readers are accustomed to reading, they can present a challenge to constructing meaning and achieving complete comprehension (Anderson, Hiebert, Scott, & Wilkinson, 1985). Instructional approaches that help prepare students for complex textual concepts and ideas, that show them how to use specific learning processes and strategies, and that outline ways for them to respond to varied textual resources can go a long way toward helping students comprehend needed information.

Reading and writing are tools for learning that allow students to clarify, refine, and apply their knowledge. Because reading and writing strategies are so vital to students in comprehending new information, researchers have coined the term **content literacy**—the ability to use reading and writing for the acquisition of new content (McKenna & Robinson, 1990). Content literacy includes general literacy skills, content-specific literacy skills (such as map reading), and some prior knowledge of content. Once students have acquired content literacy, the process of building new knowledge is greatly facilitated. Typical daily instruction allows such students to engage in the active construction of content knowledge through the use of reading activities (directed reading–thinking activity, graphic organizers) as well as writing strategies (dialogue journals, reading logs).

This approach to learning content gives children the opportunity to find things out and to think for themselves. William Bigelow's students (Bigelow, 1989) discovered this when they learned in their social studies class that textbooks had not told them the whole truth about Columbus's "discovery" of America. They found out that the real reason Columbus came to America had more to do with money and economics than with proving that the world was round. They were also amazed by the cruel way he treated the people who were already living in the Americas. These students found out that they should not necessarily trust authorities for all their information; they realized they needed to become active participants in their learning, to create their own meaning as they progressed (Bigelow, 1989).

BEYOND THE CLASSROOM

Interview two or three classroom teachers in your practicum school to find out how they integrate aspects of the language arts across the curriculum. Ask them for specific ideas related to units and activities they have developed. Then take notes on your findings in your journal and refer to them as you gather more information to use in your own classroom.

A PURPOSE FOR REAL READING AND WRITING

Goodman (1996) has stated that children should read "real language," material that is really worth reading. According to Goodman and many other educators, a child's experiences with text should be *literacy events*, in which the child reads materials that he or she needs and wants to read. These literacy events can involve reading a story, an informational text, or a combination of several different types of texts. The important thing is that the child have a self-imposed purpose for reading and writing—such as finding out about caterpillars and their characteristics, their eating habits, and the variety of ways in which they change. When children have such a purpose for acquiring information, they can then become active information seekers and can begin to develop an integrated knowledge base. This type of knowledge resembles the information obtained in the real world rather than the segmented bits of isolated information that are too often found in classrooms.

Integrating the reading and writing processes across the curriculum thus establishes a clear purpose for learning. The content of the curriculum provides students with a reason for acquiring information; the actual reading and writing makes the learning an active process in which the readers are involved with the material.

Through this content literacy process, children are able not only to acquire content information but also to improve their reading and writing competencies. Children do not learn to read and write in a vacuum; they learn to read and write by reading and writing about something (Tompkins, 1997). When reading and writing become tools for understanding, creating, and communicating information, children have the opportunity to practice, refine, and extend the literacy skills they already possess by engaging in something meaningful.

CONSTRUCTING CONTENT KNOWLEDGE

Active involvement in reading and writing about a topic leads to the construction of new knowledge and adds to each student's base of content information. In turn, this growing base of knowledge helps students to understand any new information they encounter. Actually, there is a cyclical pattern to the relationship between a student's base of content knowledge and the use of reading and writing activities as methods of acquiring further information (Vacca, Vacca, & Groves, 1995). The more background knowledge a student possesses, the easier it is for that person to implement reading and writing activities to integrate new content, thus increasing the base of knowledge and facilitating the continued use of reading and writing strategies. In effect, the more knowledge one has, the more one is able to acquire.

In such an approach to learning, both content and process goals are important. The *content goals* relate to the significant information in the text, while the *process goals* focus on what the student needs to do to acquire that knowledge. To attain both sets of goals, the emphasis prior to reading should be on activating each student's prior knowledge. During reading, teacher-modeled strategies should be used to actively involve students in learning. And after reading, students should work to organize and synthesize information for transfer to other learning situations (Tompkins, 1997).

Reading and writing across the curriculum helps children to maximize their acquisition of content knowledge. They are able to acquire significant chunks of information rather than fragmented, isolated bits. Learning is holistic and meaningful. Also, by building up a store of knowledge, the students enhance their ability to use reading and writing to process information and construct new knowledge. They become able to extend their knowledge and to add to their store of information whenever they wish (Tompkins, 1997). This integrated approach puts the students in charge of learning, which is really what education is all about.

Text Considerations

Because reading and responding to text form a significant part of any content curriculum, one of the first things you must consider when you are integrating the language arts across the curriculum is the impact of the different types of text upon your students. Books in the various content areas tend to be difficult for youngsters to comprehend. Factors that contribute to text difficulty include the organization and structure of the text, the number of concepts the text addresses, the readability of the text, the appropriateness of the text for the students and the purpose of the class, and the accuracy of the information in the text (Vacca, Vacca, & Groves, 1995). Textbooks in the various content areas also make use of the specialized vocabularies of those subjects, many of which can be confusing and difficult for students to acquire.

ORGANIZATIONAL PATTERNS

As described in earlier chapters, stories (or narrative text) have a particular structure that includes a setting, characters, a theme, a plot of actions or events (all of which are related to the goals of the characters), and a resolution. Moving into the different content areas involves a transition from structured narrative stories to informational, or expository, text. This type of text generally has not one but many structures, which can be especially confusing for young readers. Typical expository text can be organized according to cause–effect, comparison–contrast, enumeration, sequence, and problem–solution (Vacca & Vacca, 1998).

Cause–effect texts show the causal relationship between one set of ideas and facts and the resulting outcomes. This pattern or relationship points out that one item is unable to exist without the others. The following paragraph is typical of a cause–effect text:

> Hurricane Hugo hit the South Carolina coast with greater force than any storm in current history. As a result, homes, businesses, beaches, wetlands, and forests were completely destroyed. Damages were estimated in the billions of dollars.

The *comparison–contrast* pattern of text organization focuses on the similarities and differences that are evident in the topics of particular passages. For example:

> After the Civil War, many of the farmers who had lived in Vermont decided to move to the new lands of the West. In setting up their new lives and farms, these people continued with many of the familiar chores associated with farm life: clearing the land; setting up barns and fencing pastures; plowing, planting, and harvesting the fields, as well as caring for the livestock. However, there were some major differences between the western land and that of Vermont. The new land had few rocks and fertile soil—two benefits the hearty Vermonters could really appreciate.

In *enumeration*, or listing, the author describes important information about a particular topic. The author may focus on facts or on particular characteristics and features. The following would be a typical listing passage:

> Polar bears live in the very cold Arctic regions of Russia, Canada, Norway, and Greenland. Their black skin, which absorbs the sun, helps to keep them warm even though their fur is white. The polar bears' fur is actually very unique. The hairs are hollow, which helps collect the sun's rays and drives the heat right to their black skin. Another part of their body that keeps them from freezing is their four inches of fat. They have fur on every part of their body except their noses. They even have fur on their feet to keep them warm and to keep them from falling on the ice. Their favorite foods are seals, walruses, and fish.

Sequence involves putting ideas and topics into a particular time order. One way to recognize sequence is through its use of dates and time periods to help organize a passage. An example of this pattern might be:

In 1971, when Magdalena Estrada was six years old, she contracted a serious virus that left her right leg limp and lifeless. After two years of treatment, doctors in her native Guatemala felt that they could do no more for Magdalena. So, in 1984, several children's relief organizations arranged to bring Magdalena to the United States for further treatment and physical therapy. Within six months Magdalena was able to walk with only the help of a cane, and within a year she was able to walk on her own again.

One final organizational pattern of expository text is that of *problem-solution*. Such a pattern shows how a problem develops and then outlines the solutions to the problem. Take a look at the following example:

The increasing incidence of acquired immune deficiency syndrome (AIDS) has been a cause of great concern within the American population. To counteract this problem, many groups have lobbied for more government support for research regarding the treatment of AIDS victims. The resulting publicity from these efforts has caused a heightened awareness of the disease and its consequences. People have finally begun to recognize the value of education in stopping the spread of AIDS.

Researchers such as Meyer (1975) have long recognized these patterns but have described them with somewhat different terminology: covariance (cause–effect), adversative (comparison–contrast), attribution (enumeration), time order (sequence), and response (problem–solution). However, no matter which terminology is used, the fact remains that the complex patterns of organization in expository text make it more difficult for students to comprehend and respond to the essential information.

Therefore, it is crucial that expository materials used in the classroom be as clearly written and as well organized as possible. They should also be written at a level within the conceptual reach of the students who will be reading them. As a teacher, you will need to take a role in deciding whether or not the texts you use have these characteristics. One of the ways you can work toward this goal is by checking on the readability of the materials that you want to use with students.

READABILITY

How readily or easily a text can be read is called *readability* (Monahan & Hinson, 1988). Recently, the definition of readability has been expanded to encompass factors within the reader as well as aspects of the written text. The level of difficulty of the textual material quite definitely has an impact upon comprehension. How difficult a text is depends upon the length of the sentences, the complexity of the words and language, the writing style and purpose of the author, the organization of the content, and the layout or appearance of the material. In addition, each reader's prior knowledge of the content, purpose for reading, understanding of the vocabulary, and interests and attitudes have an effect on how well that person is able to understand what she or he is reading (Manzo & Manzo, 1997).

One way of helping to determine readability is with conventional **readability formulas,** which generally graph the average length of the sentences and the average number of syllables per word (word complexity) in a text. Among the accepted and used formulas are the Dale-Chall readability formula (Dale & Chall, 1948a, 1948b) and the Fry readability graph (Fry, 1977). Estimates of textual difficulty can be hand-calculated by following directions and then graphing the results, as illustrated in Figure 10.3. Readability can also be computed with specialized computer programs, which greatly ease the burden of this task for the teacher.

Figure 10.3   *Fry readability graph.*

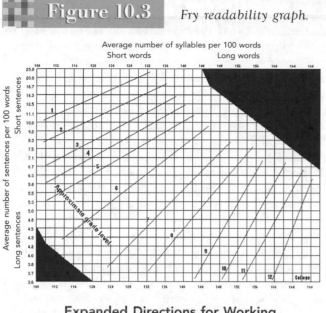

Average number of syllables per 100 words
Short words   Long words

Expanded Directions for Working Readability Graph

1. Randomly select three (3) sample passages and count out exactly 100 words each, beginning with the beginning of a sentence. Do count proper nouns, initializations, and numerals.

2. Count the number of sentences in the hundred words, estimating length of the fraction of the last sentence to the nearest one-tenth.

3. Count the total number of syllables in the 100-word passage. If you don't have a hand counter available, an easy way is to simply put a mark above every syllable over one in each word, then when you get to the end of the passage, count the number of marks and add 100. Small calculators can also be used as counters by pushing numeral 1, then push the + sign for each word or syllable when counting.

4. Enter graph with *average* sentence length and *average* number of syllables; plot dot where the two lines intersect. Area where dot is plotted will give you the approximate grade level.

5. If a great deal of variability is found in syllable count or sentence count, putting more samples into the average is desirable.

6. A word is defined as a group of symbols with a space on either side; thus, *Joe, IRA, 1945,* and & are each one word.

7. A syllable is defined as a phonetic syllable. Generally, there are as many syllables as vowel sounds. For example, *stopped* is one syllable and *wanted* is two syllables. When counting syllables for numerals and initializations, count one syllable for each symbol. For example, *1945* is four syllables, *IRA* is three syllables, and & is one syllable.

Note: This "extended graph" does not outmode or render the earlier (1968) version inoperative or inaccurate; it is an extension. (Reproduction permitted—no copyright)

Source: "Fry's Readability Graph: Clarifications, Validity, and Extension to Level 17," *Journal of Reading,* 21 (December, 1977), 249.

While readability formulas can be helpful in giving basic information about text difficulty, they are controversial because they don't tell the whole story about how readable or appropriate a text is for individual children. To really determine the suitability of texts for students, it is best to heed the recommendations outlined in *Becoming a Nation of Readers* (Anderson, Hiebert, Scott, & Wilkinson, 1985), which urges analysis of a variety of factors related to successful text comprehension.

TEXT/READER INTERACTION

In order to determine how suitable textual material is for particular children, it is wise to consider the interaction that should occur between the reader and the text. A teacher needs to examine the background knowledge or experience of the reader; the purpose of the material; its relevance, interest, and appropriateness; and the overall predictability of the material for the reader (Manzo & Manzo, 1997).

Some teachers may even want to make use of an interactive strategy such as cloze (Bormuth, 1968) to help determine how well a child can read and comprehend a particular selection (see the box on the next page).

To use cloze successfully:

1. Select a text passage somewhere between 100 and 500 words. This material should come from a prospective reading assignment that is not familiar to the students.

2. Leave the first and last sentences intact. Then randomly select a word in the second sentence to delete. Continue deleting every 5th word until 50 words have been removed. (Avoid deleting proper names.) For younger children or those who find reading difficult, consider deleting every tenth word.

3. Administer the test passage to the students by first explaining to them that they should do this activity individually, without assistance from any textbook. Students may take as long as they need to complete the passage filling in missing words as they read. (Consider giving students some prior experiences with cloze passages before you use this technique for assessment. That way students will be familiar with the procedure and will not experience initial confusion, which might invalidate the results of the procedure.)

4. When scoring the student passages, only count as correct the exact words deleted from the text. Accepting synonyms usually does not change a score radically and may interfere with the accuracy of the measurement.

5. Determine and record each student's cloze percentage score (number correct × 2). A score of 60 percent or above is an indication that the selection can be read independently by a student. A score between 40 and 60 percent implies that the selection can be used for instruction. However, you will need to supply the students who score in this range with some instruction or guidance. Any score below 40 percent suggests that the passage is too difficult for the student and may be a cause of frustration. It would probably be better to find another selection.

When Wilma Rudolph was four years old, she had an attack of double pneumonia and scarlet fever. She was left crippled, __1__ left leg paralyzed. The __2__ said that only with __3__ treatment could she hope __4__ get back the use __5__ her leg.

Every week Wilma's __6__ took her on the __7__ round trip between Clarksville, Tennessee, __8__ the clinic in Nashville. __9__ entire family learned the __10__ way to massage Wilma's __11__. By the time she __12__ eight years old, Wilma __13__ able to walk again __14__ the help of a __15__ built shoe.

However, being __16__ to walk wasn't enough __17__ Wilma. She became very __18__ in sports. When she __19__ high school, she decided __20__ try out for the __21__ team. Wilma made the __22__. By her sophomore year, __23__ had become the outstanding __24__. The track coach of Tennessee State University __25__ her play. He suggested __26__ she   should try out __27__ the track competition. She __28__ and was an unbeatable __29__ star throughout high school.

Wilma __30__ for a track competition __31__ the U.S. and the Soviet Union. __32__ illness struck. It took __33__ for her to regain __34__ health. She had to __35__ harder than ever to __36__. And qualify she did, __37__ while running she pulled __38__ thigh muscle. Another setback. __39__, a few months before __40__ was to enter the Olympics, __41__ had to have her __42__ out. Complications arose, and __43__ took weeks for her __44__ recover. All the time __45__ kept thinking hard about __46__ Olympics.

When the doctors __47__ said Wilma was well, __48__ began to make up __49__ lost time. She trained __50__ the other athletes rested, always keeping in mind the Olympic games. After days of hard training, Wilma qualified. And in the Summer Olympics of 1960, Wilma Rudolph ran away with three gold medals.

1. her	10. proper	19. entered	28. did	37. but	46. the
2. doctors	11. leg	20. to	29. track	38. a	47. finally
3. special	12. was	21. basketball	30. prepared	39. Then	48. she
4. to	13. was	22. team	31. between	40. she	49. for
5. of	14. with	23. she	32. Again	41. she	50. while
6. mother	15. specially	24. player	33. months	42. tonsils	
7. long	16. able	25. saw	34. her	43. it	
8. and	17. for	26. that	35. train	44. to	
9. The	18. interested	27. for	36. qualify	45. she	

Source: Text adapted from *Skill by Skill Organizing Information* by Sandra M. Brown and Sharon Levitt. Copyright © 1983, 1976 by Modern Curriculum Press.

Words are systematically deleted from a passage of text; the student is then required to predict the correct word for each deletion. This technique is effective because it provides some information about the individual's prior knowledge of that material and also indicates how predictable and cohesive the language of the material is for the child. In essence, cloze identifies a child's potential for comprehending selected materials.

Although the cloze procedure may not be something you want to use with every selection of text, it is one way of assessing children's potential for interaction with text. It can supplement your knowledge about the literary quality, cohesion, and teachability of particular texts.

> ### BEYOND THE CLASSROOM
>
> For more information about choosing suitable materials for children to read, check out "Consumer Beware! Selecting Materials for Whole Language Readers" by Ken and Yetta Goodman in *The Whole Language Catalog* (1991).

Helping Children Build Information

Reading and writing across the curriculum helps children to build their store of knowledge—a cognitive stockpile of information that can be used to facilitate comprehension of any future text.

Within an integrated curriculum, teachers basically need to be concerned with helping students to develop the following comprehension and communication competencies:

- Understanding and effectively using the specific vocabularies of the various subject areas
- Developing strategies to guide and facilitate individual comprehension
- Knowing how and when to implement such strategies
- Being able to use a variety of resources to reinforce and support comprehension
- Developing writing as a learning tool for comprehension and communication

In the following section, these various strategies and techniques are classified into two major groups: those that are most often used for concept understanding and those that guide and assist comprehension.

CONCEPT UNDERSTANDING

Successfully acquiring content information depends on the ability to understand a wide variety of concepts. And understanding these concepts is, in turn, dependent on being familiar with the specific or technical vocabulary of a particular subject area. Therefore, in order to obtain information from the curriculum, students need to have extensive word knowledge *and* be aware of the strategic links between specialized content vocabularies and their underlying concepts.

Teachers can assist students in their endeavors to obtain information by providing learning experiences that expose children to strategies that help them learn how to develop vocabulary knowledge independently. Then the students can continue to gather information on their own. Some of the strategies that teachers have used successfully to accomplish this are graphic organizers (or word maps), semantic mapping techniques (list–group–label), semantic feature analysis, and possible sentences.

Graphic Organizers

A **graphic organizer** provides a visual structure for new vocabulary and uses charts, timelines, etc., to organize the vocabulary and concepts of a particular topic (Parks & Black, 1990). A graphic organizer is really a framework for comprehension: It enables students to visualize the relationships among concepts in a text or passage and then to analyze how those concepts work together. Some of the different formats for graphic organizers include outlines, diagrams, timelines, flowcharts, hierarchic organizers, webs or mapping charts, and causal charts. See Figures 10.4 through 10.7 for examples.

Figure 10.4 *Timeline organizer.*

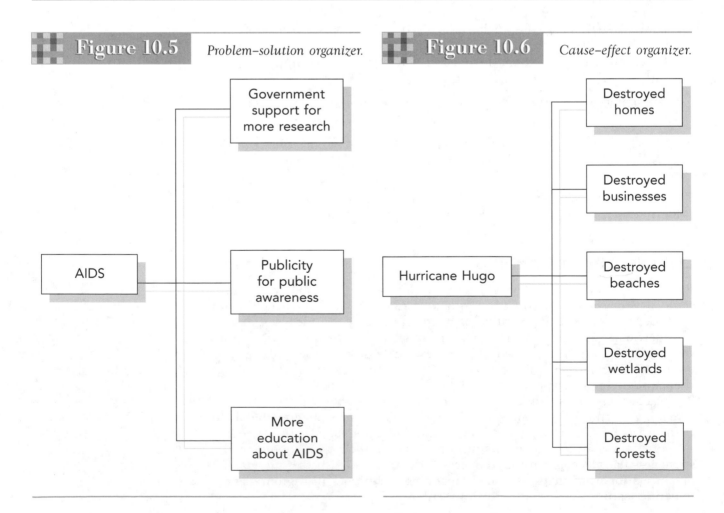

MAGDALENA ESTRADA

Magdalena was born	She got a virus and her leg went limp	Guatemala doctors could do no more for her	Went to the U.S. for help	She could walk again
1965	1971	1974	1984	1985

Figure 10.5 *Problem–solution organizer.*

AIDS → Government support for more research / Publicity for public awareness / More education about AIDS

Figure 10.6 *Cause-effect organizer.*

Hurricane Hugo → Destroyed homes / Destroyed businesses / Destroyed beaches / Destroyed wetlands / Destroyed forests

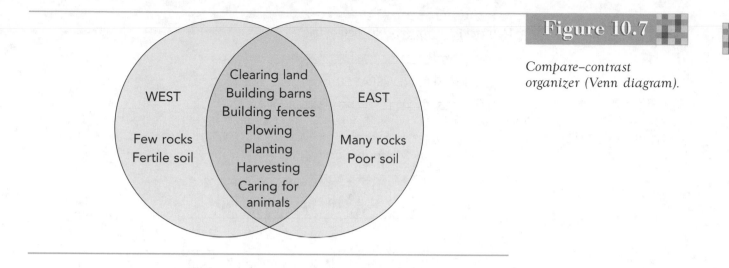

Figure 10.7

Compare–contrast organizer (Venn diagram).

It should be noted that graphic organizers have multiple uses. They can be developed by the teacher to introduce new vocabulary and concepts. To do this, a teacher should identify the key words in a lesson, arrange them in a diagram, and present it to the students (Moore, Readence, & Rickelman, 1988). Organizers can also be used for a comprehension check or review. In this approach, the teacher provides the children with copies of key vocabulary and allows them to work in small groups to construct their own diagrams. Of course, the teacher provides assistance and support (Parks & Black, 1990). In a review lesson, it may also be beneficial to give students a diagram that has been partially completed and then let them finish it on their own. The additional guidance of the diagram serves as a catalyst for the students' recollection of concept organization. Figures 10.8 and 10.9 show two approaches to using graphic organizers to build visual as well as verbal structures for specialized vocabulary.

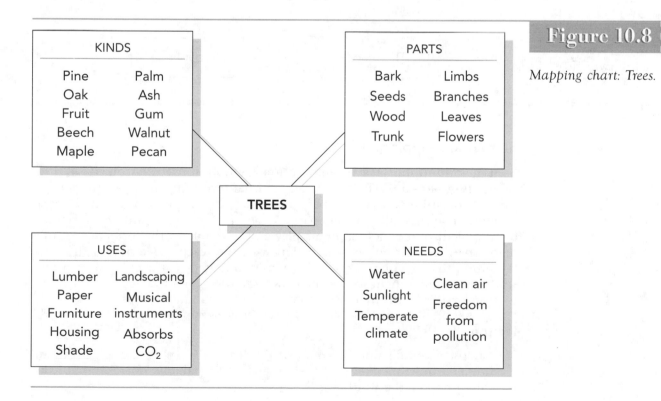

Figure 10.8

Mapping chart: Trees.

Figure 10.9   *Heirarchic organizer: The newspaper.*

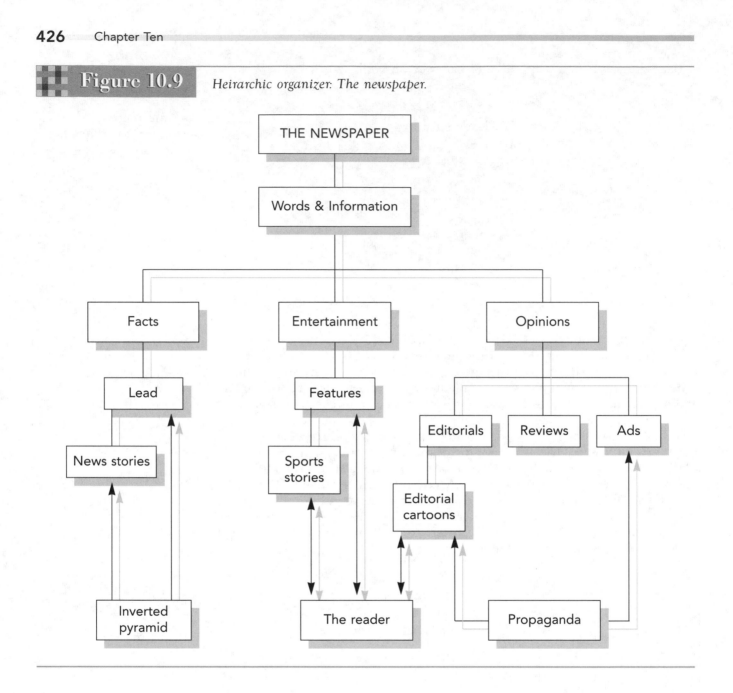

Semantic Mapping

Semantic mapping is a vocabulary strategy (Johnson & Pearson, 1984) also called *list–group–label* (Taba, 1967); as a visual technique, it helps students to expand, organize, and remember new concepts. Although the format of a semantic map is similar to the map version of a graphic organizer, the actual development of it is not. Students play an active role in the formation of the map. Their interaction and discussion with the teacher determines the configuration that the map takes. The key to this strategy is the empowerment of students: helping them to use their own knowledge and categorization skills to see new relationships among concepts and vocabulary terms.

These six steps are helpful in developing a semantic map (Johnson & Pearson, 1984):

1. Choose a central word from a text that the children are using. If you are doing a unit on different wildlife and their habitats, for example, you might choose the word *owls*.

2. List the word on a large piece of paper or on your chalkboard.

3. Encourage the children to list words related to the chosen topic on a separate piece of paper and to categorize them if they can.

4. Have students share their lists of words orally. Put words on the map in agreed-upon categories.

5. Be sure to have students label the categories on the map. It helps them with categorization.

6. Encourage the students to discuss the map with you and with one another. In this way, they begin to see the relationships among the terms.

A semantic map developed about owls might look like the one pictured in Figure 10.10.

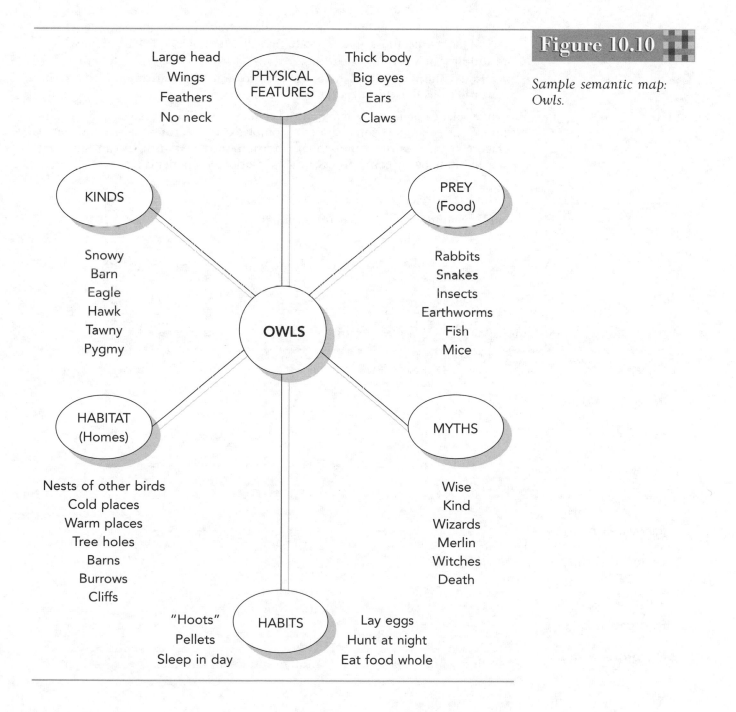

Figure 10.10

Sample semantic map: Owls.

Semantic Feature Analysis

A **semantic feature analysis** is a categorization activity that uses a matrix to illustrate the similarities and differences between related terms. It enables all types of students to activate their prior knowledge as a way of facilitating the acquisition of specific content vocabulary and concepts.

When preparing to use this strategy with your students, use these six steps as a guide (Johnson & Pearson, 1984):

1. Decide upon a category or topic, such as *sea habitats.*
2. List some terms in this category (*ocean, salt marsh, coral reef*) in a column on the left side of the page or chalkboard.
3. Help children to decide on some characteristics or features shared by the words (salt water, cold water, waves, plants, animals). List these across the top of the page or chalkboard.
4. Place a + in the appropriate box to indicate that an item in the category possesses a feature and a − to indicate that the item does not have the feature.
5. Add any new terms or features.
6. Discuss the matrix and help students to note the features shared by the words as well as the uniqueness of each word.

In a science project developed at the elementary school located on Sullivan's Island, South Carolina, some students completed the feature analysis illustrated in Figure 10.11. Because of the school's location on the Atlantic Ocean, studying water habitats has become an essential educational experience.

Figure 10.11   *Sample semantic feature analysis: Sea habitats.*

	Salt water	Deep water	Shore or shallow water	Rocks	Sandy or muddy bottom	Cold water	Warm water	Brackish water	Waves	Plants	Animals
Ocean	+	+	+	+	+	+	+	−	+	+	+
Rocky intertidal	+	−	+	+	?	+	+	−	+	+	+
Kelp forest	+	−	+	+	?	+	−	−	+	+	+
Estuary	−	−	+	−	+	+	+	+	−	+	+
Salt marsh	−	−	+	−	?	+	+	+	−	+	+
Sandy beach	+	−	+	−	+	+	+	−	+	+	+
Continental shelf	+	+	+	−	+	+	+	−	+	+	+
Coral reef	+	+	?	+	−	−	+	−	+	+	+
Sea grass bed	+	−	+	−	+	+	+	+	+	+	+
Mangrove swamp	+	−	+	?	+	−	+	+	?	+	+

Possible Sentences

Not all vocabulary techniques have to be visual illustrations. One successful strategy, called **possible sentences** (Moore & Moore, 1986), relies primarily on verbal predictions to enhance vocabulary and concept development. Teachers introduce their students to this procedure by presenting new vocabulary in conjunction with familiar words. The students use the words to make up sentences; then they read textual material to verify the correctness of their sentences. Using possible sentences involves the following five steps:

List important vocabulary terms. For the passages related to the sea habitat project mentioned previously, a teacher might start by listing and pronouncing the following terms with the children: *ocean, rocky intertidal, salt water, tides, seaweeds, kelp forest, waves, beach, estuary, sea grasses, mud,* and *brackish water.*

Formulate sentences. The students in the class are then asked to use two or more of the words from the list in a sentence. This sentence should contain information that students think will actually be in the text. Even if the "possible sentence" is not correct, the teacher records it. This process continues until all the words have been used at least once. Sentences produced from the list in the sea habitat project might include the following:

- A *kelp forest* has lots of *seaweeds* and *salt water.*
- *Tides* and *waves* have an effect on a *rocky intertidal.*
- In an *estuary,* the *mud* and *brackish water* provide a good home for young sea animals.
- *Sea grasses* limit the *ocean's* ability to erode the *beach.*

Check sentences. Children read the passages to see if their sentences are correct.

Evaluate sentences. After everyone has completed the reading, each sentence is evaluated. Some sentences may need to be omitted; others may need to be restated. For example, students may want to clarify the fourth sentence by stating that sea grasses actually protect the beach from being battered by the ocean's waves.

Generate new sentences. The last step is to generate new sentences and to check them for accuracy. Once these are confirmed, children should be encouraged to add them to their reading logs or journals.

This technique is especially good for arousing prior knowledge and encouraging interaction with the text through the use of predictions. It is a good activity to involve an entire class with a text.

BEYOND THE CLASSROOM

For more information on vocabulary development in the content areas, consult Chapter 9 of *Teaching Reading Vocabulary* by Johnson and Pearson (1984). In addition, you may want to record some activities that teachers in your practicum school use and even try your own hand at developing a vocabulary activity for the students in your practicum class.

COMPREHENSION ACROSS THE CURRICULUM

Although understanding the definitions and meanings of vocabulary words is definitely part of comprehension, true understanding comes from being able to interpret extended passages of text. To do this, children must be able to use what they already know as a way of understanding new information.

They must be able to access their prior knowledge and connect the unknown with the known. In this way, they are able to process information and construct new knowledge for themselves.

Strategies for Building on Prior Knowledge

It has often been stated that teachers are to build on prior knowledge. Guillaume (1998) offers the following five strategies to use when activating students' prior knowledge:

1. Inspect the pictures of the text to be read and discuss and/or predict what is happening in the pictures.
2. Provide any artifacts, posters, models, etc., of the topic to be studied and discuss them before beginning the study of the topic.
3. Provide music, art, or poems that relate to the topic and discuss them before the study.
4. "Factstorm" by giving students two to three minutes to jot down words or phrases that they think are associated with the topic.
5. Prepare a wall chart of K–W–L (What I *know*, What I *want* to learn, and What I *learned*) and fill it in with the students' information and questions. See Figure 10.12 for an example on polar bears.

Figure 10.12

Sample wall chart.

TOPIC: POLAR BEARS		
What I Know K	What I Want to Learn W	What I Learned L
They are white. They live in Arctic.	What do they eat? Are they mean?	They have fur on their feet to keep them from slipping on the ice.

There are many strategies available to help teachers facilitate the growth of comprehension in their students. This section presents some of these strategies in two groups: questioning strategies and guidance strategies.

As with all teaching, you must realize that you need to model the strategies, give students the opportunity to practice them, and provide feedback as the students attempt to make them their own. It might be a good idea to use the reciprocal teaching format described in Chapter 6 of this text for helping your students to internalize some of the techniques recommended.

Questioning Strategies

Questioning is probably the most frequently used technique for aiding comprehension. Through the use of questions and *questioning strategies*, teachers can help students achieve the various levels of comprehension and know where to locate specific types of information. Chapter 6 included a discussion on how to use knowledge of the *question–answer relationship (QAR)* as a way of guiding and simplifying the search for information. By helping students understand exactly where to look for information (on the page, in their own heads, or in both places), teachers enable them to have more control over their own learning.

ReQuest. ReQuest is another way in which teachers can use questioning as a means of empowering students by helping them learn how to ask their own questions. However, in order to do so, teachers need to follow the modeling guidelines set forth by Manzo (1968, 1969). The technique he developed incorporates reciprocal questioning and critical thinking in a one-on-one teaching situation.

A teacher prepares for **ReQuest** by making sure that the material used for developing the questions is appropriate for the student and lends itself to making predictions, selecting several points at which the student can pause and make some predictions, and initiating the session through the following nine steps (Manzo, 1968; Searfoss & Dishner, 1977):

1. Each participant receives a copy of the reading selection.
2. Both the teacher and the student read the first sentence(s) silently. Then the teacher closes the book and tells the child to ask the types of questions a teacher would ask and to ask them the way a teacher would ask them. The student asks as many questions as he or she sees fit.
3. The teacher responds to the questions, reinforces appropriate questions, and requests rephrasing of questions that are unclear.
4. The child finishes questioning and closes the book. Then the teacher takes over questioning the student. At this time, the teacher tries to model appropriate questioning behavior and to use a variety of question types.
5. The procedure is repeated with the second sentence. (With older students, a teacher may want to start reading a few sentences at a time rather than just one.)
6. This process continues until enough of the selection has been read (probably the first paragraph or so) for the student to make a prediction about what the rest of the selection is about.
7. The teacher then asks the student to justify the prediction. If the prediction is reasonable, the student continues with silent reading. If not, the exchange of questions continues and the student makes another prediction at a later point.
8. Now the teacher directs the student to read to the end of the selection in order to compare the prediction with what really did happen.
9. The teacher follows up with a discussion about the merits of the prediction and why it might be possible to have several logical and plausible conclusions to the same selection. It is best to avoid the idea of one right answer. The student might even be given the opportunity to write a new ending for the text.

Semantic webbing. Still another comprehension activity based on questioning is semantic webbing (Meinbach, Rothlein, & Fredricks, 1995; Parks & Black, 1990). **Semantic webbing** helps students develop a map of the information by organizing ideas and visually illustrating the relationship among concepts in the reading material. At the center of each web is the *core question.* Attached to the center are several web strands representing the chil-

BEYOND THE CLASSROOM

Try to extend your knowledge about semantic webbing by reading "Reading, Thinking, and Semantic Webbing" (Schwab & Coble, 1985) in *The Science Teacher.* This article illustrates how to use semantic webs in the content areas. After reading it, you may want to try developing a semantic web with some of the students in your practicum class.

dren's answers to the question. The strands, in turn, are supported by the strand supports, which generally consist of important facts and information from the story. The strand ties show the relationship of the strands to each other. Figure 10.13 shows a semantic web based on "The Three Little Pigs."

Figure 10.13

Sample semantic web: "The Three Little Pigs."

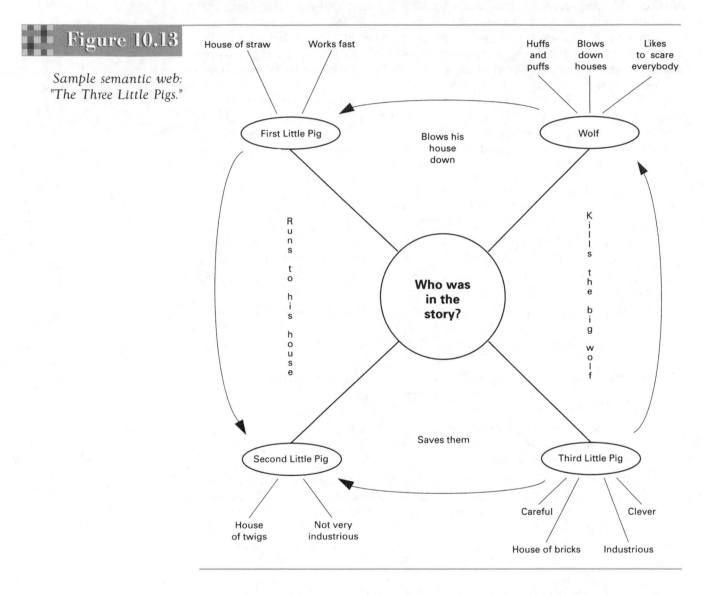

Such a web organizes the story so that the children can see certain relationships and gain a deeper understanding of what the material is about. How the web develops depends on the core question. If the question had been "What happened?" the web would have taken a different direction: The information would have been organized around the sequence of events in the story. The question and how it is stated assist the students in getting the information.

Guidance Strategies

Teaching is the art of assisting discovery.

MARK VAN DOREN

Guidance strategies empower students to become strategic readers, readers who have developed metacognition and are able to motivate and monitor themselves as they comprehend information. By providing assistance based on the needs of your students, you can help them to become independent, self-confident learners in all areas. (See Chapter 6 for more information on metacognition and strategic readers.)

In general, *guidance strategies* are used during the reading process as a way of arousing interest and focusing attention. They help children to activate prior knowledge, to monitor the comprehension process, and to provide needed follow-up during the postreading period. This section describes three strategies to help guide the reading process from beginning to end: the directed reading–thinking activity, the guided reading procedure, and reading guides.

Directed reading–thinking activity (DRTA). The DRTA was originally conceptualized by Stauffer (1969) as a process to help students set purposes for reading. As such, it is particularly suited for selections in the content areas.

During the **directed reading—thinking activity (DRTA),** the teacher helps the reader identify purposes for reading, guides the reader through the reading process, monitors the reader to determine any difficulties, helps the reader develop comprehension, and helps the reader develop particular skills as appropriate. Activities during the prereading, reading, and postreading stages are as follows:

- *Prereading.* Have students activate any prior knowledge by viewing the title, pictures, and headings of the material. Encourage students to make predictions about the selection based on their observations. Write their ideas on the board or a chart.
- *Reading.* Have students read to verify their predictions. Extend their thinking by encouraging them to verify their predictions, summarize what they've read, and predict what might happen next.
- *Postreading.* Discuss what the students have read and the accuracy of their predictions. Encourage the children to point out sections of the material that support or disprove their predictions. Allow the children to discuss the process and summarize what they have learned for themselves.

After the postreading session, you might want to go back and use this particular material for the development of specific student competencies, such as the use of context clues or summarization.

The DRTA has proved to be a very successful reading strategy—so much so that in recent years much attention has been focused on it. One modification has been the development of the chart pictured in Figure 10.14. This chart serves to activate and record each reader's prior knowledge about a topic as well as her or his predictions and summarization notes about the reading selection.

Figure 10.14 *DRTA adaptation chart.*

WHAT DO YOU . . .

Know You Know?	Think You Know?	Think You'll Learn?	Know You Learned?

Guided reading procedure (GRP). The guided reading procedure, as discussed in Chapter 6, is intended to provide practice in certain strategies needed to develop as an independent reader. The **guided reading procedure (GRP)** involves student collaboration, the use of self-questioning and self-correction techniques, and the organization of information. It is most appropriate for materials containing a multitude of facts needed for future reference.

Reading guides. Both the DRTA and GRP are designed to be used as group strategies. However, at times you may want to employ an activity that individual students can use independently. The **reading guide** consists of having individual students make decisions about a series of statements at the different levels of comprehension; the purpose of the strategy is to guide the student in comprehending a selection by showing him or her the relationship among the ideas. The statements in the guide also serve as initiators for student discussion of the material.

Figure 10.15 presents an example of a guide that a primary teacher used to help the children in her class understand that animals are adapted in special ways in order to survive in their habitats. She wanted them to organize their ideas about this concept by classifying the animals according to where they live.

Figure 10.15

Sample reading guide.

TOPIC: ANIMALS ARE ADAPTED TO LIVE IN DIFFERENT HABITATS.

Part I

As you read the text, check the statements that are true.

____ 1. *Adapted* means that an animal fits into its habitat.

____ 2. An animal that is adapted cannot get food and water.

____ 3. Deserts are hot and do not have much rain.

____ 4. The polar areas near the North and South Poles are cold most of the year.

____ 5. Polar bears live near the North Pole.

____ 6. Penguins live near the South Pole.

____ 7. Some of the biggest and fastest animals live in the grasslands.

____ 8. Rain forests are hot and wet.

____ 9. Whales live in the ocean.

____ 10. Whales breathe through fins.

Part II

Classify the animals listed according to where they live. Write each word under the proper heading.

blue whale	kangaroo rat	cattle	ptarmigan	jackrabbit
boa	rattlesnake	buffalo	shark	ermine
zebra	camel	sheep	tree frog	octopus
rhino	penguin	ocelot	seal	arctic tern
musk ox	polar bear	killer whale	walrus	parrot
arctic hare	giraffe	sea urchin	lizard	monkey

Deserts	Polar Areas	Grasslands	Rain Forests	Water

One specialized type of guide calls students' attention to the dominant textual pattern in the reading materials. By helping students to recognize and then use a major textual pattern to organize their ideas, you can encourage students to develop metacognitive knowledge about relationships in textual information.

Figures 10.16 and 10.17 show two pattern guides that have been used successfully with middle school students. Both guides were developed to facilitate the children's understanding about the Hohokam and the Anasazi Indians as part of a unit on Native Americans. One guide was developed to highlight the interaction of causes and effects on various aspects of tribe members' lives; the other compares the two groups on a variety of factors.

Figure 10.16   *Sample reading guide (cause–effect).*

THE HOHOKAM AND THE ANASAZI

Match the effects on the right with the causes on the left.

Causes

_____ 1. The Ice Age ended and the desert formed.

_____ 2. The Hohokam lined the irrigation canals with clay.

_____ 3. The Hohokam built and lived in pit houses.

_____ 4. The Anasazi planted crops near streams with plenty of rain.

_____ 5. The Anasazi took great care in building the pueblos.

_____ 6. The Anasazi could remove the ladders to the pueblos.

_____ 7. A great drought came.

Effects

A. Enemies could not get into the homes.

B. They were even better farmers than the Hohokam.

C. The Anasazi packed up and disappeared.

D. After thousands of years, the people learned to farm to survive.

E. The farmers were protected from the hot daytime sun and the sharp cold at night.

F. Many of the Anasazi pueblos are still standing.

G. The water took longer to soak into the ground.

Figure 10.17   *Sample reading guide (comparison–contrast).*

THE HOHOKAM AND THE ANASAZI

The Hohokam	In relationship to:	The Anasazi
	Geographic Location	
	Farming Techniques	
	Housing	
	Crafts	
	Fate	

Responding to Information: Writing to Learn

Previous chapters have described the writing process and stressed its importance in developing children's communication competencies. Chapters 8 and 9 also outlined specific methods for enhancing classroom writing as well as appropriate approaches to evaluation.

This section focuses on the benefits of using writing as a tool for learning throughout the curriculum. Because writing is part of the total communication process, it should be united as much as possible with the other language arts of reading, speaking, viewing, visual representing, and listening. Through writing, many students can get ready for reading and learning; then they can use writing to respond to what they have read and to link or summarize all the information they have acquired. For students, the curriculum can become a cycle of writing, reading, thinking, and then more writing to reflect upon and extend their thinking (Tompkins, 1997).

Writing is very much an individual process. It lets people clarify their own thoughts and helps them to understand themselves and to make their ideas understood by others. Therefore, classroom writing shouldn't be forced but should come as a natural part of learning (Tompkins, 1997).

It is important to allow students the same opportunities for self-expression and communication with others that they have in real life. With this concept in mind, the following section is organized around two broad ideas: writing for self—which includes freewriting as well as writing journals, diaries, and logs—and writing for others—which includes various types of letters, telecommunications activities, the use of language experience, paragraph frames, and book publishing. Many of these concepts have been introduced in earlier chapters but deserve further consideration in the context of writing across the curriculum.

BEYOND THE CLASSROOM

For more information on strategies to guide comprehension, read "Story Map Instruction: A Road Map for Reading Comprehension" (Davis & McPherson, 1989) in *The Reading Teacher*. It outlines several different ways of constructing comprehension maps for literature that can be integrated throughout the curriculum. Then you might want to try your hand at constructing a map and recording it in your journal.

WRITING FOR SELF

Writing for self encompasses the idea of **freewriting** (also called *quickwrites*) for personal expression (Elbow, 1973), a way of communicating your ideas to yourself, digging within yourself, and just saying what comes to mind about whatever you are involved in. This might mean writing a poem, a personal statement, a daily diary, or just a series of jottings. These ideas have been explored in Chapter 8, which chronicles the writing process. However, one type of personal writing particularly suited to the content areas is that of keeping a journal.

Journal writing actually allows writing to become a natural part of the classroom process. Students can use their journals as a way of reflecting on classroom situations or of keeping a record of science experiments, social studies research, or personal reactions to classroom presentations in art or music.

To be successful, journal writing should become part of the daily classroom routine, with a particular block of time (5–20 minutes, depending on your class) devoted to it in the same way that time is set aside for sustained silent reading. In this type of individual activity, children should have the freedom to write whatever they feel and think without having to worry about spelling, grammar, and mechanics.

Following are two journal entries written by children in Ms. Terri Neal's third-grade class showing how two different children responded to a classroom science presentation on snakes:

Today we had a visitor, her name was Karen she had snakes, there—names were Checkers. Because it's stomach looked like checkers. And the other snakes name was Tasha! I don't know why she named her that! We asked questions too! The class had fun! Some people got scared! I wish the snake would eat the rat! Checkers started to get out of the aquairam!

I like when the snake was chasing the mouse. And Tosha tried to whrap around the mouse and the mouse got away. I am glad that the snake did not get the mouse. If I was little I would not be scared, I got to hold Tosha and checkers.

Another way of referring to this type of journal is as a *learning log* (Vacca & Vacca, 1998). This name gives the student the idea that the entries are supposed to chronicle her or his learning. It is also a way for students to state problems and clarify certain aspects of learning in a risk-free atmosphere.

A specialized form of journal writing begins to cross the bridge between writing for self and writing for others. In a **dialogue journal,** students write their thoughts and messages to the teacher, who then responds to them in a supportive and nonevaluative manner. This type of journal, described in greater depth in Chapter 8, allows children to carry on a "conversation" in writing (Atwell, 1998). It also enables the teacher to provide a writing model for students. Some sample dialogue journal entries appear in Figure 10.18.

As with all personal classroom writing, when engaging in dialogue journals, you as the teacher must be careful to respect the privacy of students in addition to respecting the value of their thoughts.

WRITING FOR OTHERS

Writing for others involves communication and sharing of ideas. One of the easiest, most basic, and most widely used activities in writing for others is letter writing. Letters may be written in response to material being studied in class and may or may not be sent. Letters not intended to be sent (Vacca & Vacca, 1998) can be used to engage students in a role-play situation to expand their thinking about information they have acquired. For example, students who have been studying about the destruction of the rain forests might summarize their findings in an open letter to Brazilian ranchers and developers. In such a letter, the students might point out the need to save the forests for the welfare of the world as well as that of Brazil.

On the other hand, letters to be sent can engage the students in real-life communication with teachers, classmates, parents, and even authors of books being used by the class. Strickland (1987) has termed letters that catalog a continuing interaction between students and teachers about a particular topic or book *dialogue letters.* (See Chapter 8 for an actual classroom sample of dialogue letters.)

An extension of sending letters is the use of *telecommunications.* Students can become involved in school, district, and national computer networks.

Figure 10.18

Sample dialogue journal entries.

Feb. 28, 2000

I loved "James and the Giant Peach". The cariter I liked was the Cenepede. I wish that the anuts were nicer. I am Glad the James found a nice home even if it was a seed. I an glad that James have lots of friends.

Gadeer,

I agree. This story is great. However, I think that my favorite character is James.

Like you, I'm glad that he did find a home and has lots of friends.

If you like this type of fantasy writing, you will probably enjoy some of the other books that Roald Dahl has written. If you'd like, I'll get a list of titles together.

T. Johnson

They can exchange ideas, letters, jokes, and any other imaginable information through the use of computers and a modem. Several classes have even become involved in networks that allow them to have pen pals in other parts of the country and all over the world. When students send information to such faraway friends, they invariably take great pains to make sure that it is interesting and accurate in every way.

Another method of using writing to develop and extend knowledge is through *language experience*. The content areas generally provide a wealth of experiences for both primary- and middle-level students. They have experiments in science, problems to solve in math, simulations and role plays in social studies, projects in art, and performances in music and theatre. Completing a language-experience chart following one of these activities or events allows the children to think about and internalize the learning as well as to communicate it to others. Barrow, Kristo, and Andrew (1984) have recommended using science language experience with individuals and small groups who have investigated or manipulated science-related objects. This process includes four steps (Barrow & Andrew, 1981):

1. The teacher provides manipulatives for students to investigate. The teacher may post questions about the manipulatives to stimulate discussion.
2. Students dictate or write about their observations.
3. Children illustrate these stories as an additional interpretation of the experience. The teacher may direct younger students to draw what they see first, as a support for the subsequent writing.
4. Students share their experience stories and illustrations with teachers, peers, or parents.

Two examples of science language–experience stories appear in Figure 10.19.

Figure 10.19

Sample science language-experience stories.

Meal Worm

He is squshy and squirmy. He is sleppy. He has rough skin. They are slow and thin. They are little. He is scraney Kathryn

The meal worm

This worm lives in a forest. He is very happy. One day a boy got the worm and put him in a jar. The boy said this worm is little, soft and ticklish. The worm was happy from then on. Peter.

A further extension of using writing to learn in the primary grades involves the use of *paragraph frames* (Cudd & Roberts, 1989). These frames use a cloze procedure of sentence starters to help organize a child's paragraph into one of the common organizational patterns of content-area text. Frames can be organized to sequence, enumerate, react to reading, or compare and contrast. A sample paragraph frame is illustrated in Figure 10.20.

Source: From Cudd, E. T., & Roberts, L. L. (1989, February). Using Writing to Enhance Content Area Learning in the Primary Grades. *The Reading Teacher, 42*(6), 392–404. Reprinted with permission of Evelyn T. Cudd and the International Reading Association. All rights reserved.

Figure 10.20

Sample paragraph frame.

As always, book publishing, either individually or as a group, is another way for children to consolidate and internalize information for themselves as they communicate it to others. Book publishing can take a variety of forms. Many children create books by retelling stories they have read or that have been read to them. In the content areas, children can vary this approach by publishing books containing factual information. Yet another interesting approach to the mechanics of writing was demonstrated by one sixth-grade class that wrote its own grammar book and kept it as a resource in the classroom. (See Chapter 8 for a discussion of the mechanics of book publishing.) Read the Classroom Vignette that follows to see how some schools use reading and writing across the curriculum.

Vignette *in the classroom*

What do Avondale Elementary School (Birmingham, Alabama), Bertrun E. Glavin Elementary School (Winnipeg, Manitoba), Bel Pre Elementary School (Silver Spring, Maryland), Dunn Middle School (Danvers, Massachusetts), Delmar-Harvard School of Investigative Learning (University City, Missouri), Capshaw Elementary School (Cookeville, Tennessee), and Sheldon Elementary School (Sheldon, Vermont) have in common? These are some of the 1996/1997 winners of the Exemplary Reading Program Awards given by the International Reading Association. Another thing these schools all have in common is their integrated focus on using reading and writing throughout the curriculum.

At the Avondale Elementary School, children in grades 1 through 3 take a writing workshop twice a week. Older students can select a Writing Club as part of their extracurricular activities. The school also hosts children's book authors as well as professional storytellers and illustrators at a day-long workshop for parents and children.

In Winnipeg, Manitoba, the Bertrun E. Glavin Elementary School started a Home Reading Project in 1990. From a home–school partnership, the program has evolved into an integrated program that includes gifted and talented classes, multicultural activities, and conflict management programs. All children in the program check out books from the school library to bring home to read to their parents as part of the school curriculum.

The Bel Pre Elementary School hosts a monthly Books and Breakfast program for parents of Title 1 students. Professional educators demonstrate techniques parents can use with their children to support reading and writing at home. The program also encourages parents to volunteer at the school in various capacities.

In Danvers, Massachusetts, the Dunn Middle School launched a reading and study skills training program for all its sixth-grade teachers of math, science, social studies, and English. Teachers even got the school schedule changed to allow for a yearlong course for students titled Reading in the Content Area.

In University City, Missouri, the students at Delmar-Harvard School of Investigative Learning write, illustrate, and edit books about their families and community. Parent volunteers help with the typing and binding of the books.

The students of Capshaw Elementary School do sustained silent reading on a schoolwide basis every day. In every class, there is a specially designated area where read alouds and silent reading take place. Some rooms include reading tents, an elevated reading loft, or bathtubs filled with pillows. The principal has her own reading corner equipped with a comfortable rocker from which she reads aloud to small groups of children each day of the week.

The entire village of Sheldon, Vermont, is working to create a literate community. Grandparents, parents, and students are involved in various literacy activities. Local bookstores issue free coupons for books. Author and illustrator workshops go on throughout the school year. Children and adults alike take the Literacy Pledge to turn off the television and read.

Thematic Units: The Key to Integration

There are three types of thematic units: the intradisciplinary, the interdisciplinary, and the inquiry-based. Each uses a theme and is based on the philosophy of using authentic viewing, reading, and writing to learn more about the world in which students live. All three of these types emphasize the interrelatedness of the language arts; however, the planning of each is somewhat different. In the intradisciplinary unit, all the aspects of the language arts (reading, writing, speaking, listening, viewing, and visual representing) are integrated as the students study an author or a particular genre that the teacher selects. In the interdisciplinary unit, the teacher goes beyond literature and authors and selects a theme, such as the rain forest or ocean life, and integrates the theme in all content areas: math, social studies, art, literature, music, science, etc. In the inquiry-based unit, the teacher permits the students to select the topic, which might be gum and candy, and integrates that topic in all the content-area subjects. See Figure 10.21 for a quick glance at the similarities and differences among the three types of units. From the diagram, it is easy to see that the common thread of all three types of units is the interrelatedness of the language arts.

	Integration of Language Arts	Integration of Content Areas	Planner
Intradisciplinary	yes	no	teacher
Interdisciplinary	yes	yes	teacher
Inquiry-based	yes	yes	students

Figure 10.21

Relationship of the three approaches to integrated units.

INTRADISCIPLINARY UNIT

With the **intradisciplinary unit** approach, the teacher integrates the language arts while studying authors or a particular genre. The students read books of their choice that are appropriate for their reading level, they view different types of material, they listen to classmates' points of view in literature discussion circles, and they visually present their responses to the literature. The teacher selects the author or genre and plans appropriate activities for the unit. Specific skills are taught as the need arises during the actual unit.

For example, a first-grade teacher may choose to study Eric Carle, a favorite author of many first-graders. One week before the unit is to begin, the teacher announces the study and encourages students to browse through the books that she or he has placed on a table in the classroom. The teacher knows that most first-graders cannot read the texts, but they can view the pictures. On the Friday before the unit begins, the teacher takes a poll of the students' favorite Carle books. On Monday, the teacher begins to read to the students the book that received the most votes. While reading, the teacher has the students look at the pictures and predict what will happen. The teacher may decide not to finish the book when reaching the climax and have the students as a class dictate an ending while the teacher writes it on a large chart. Or the teacher may have each student draw his or her ending; then the teacher will write a caption under each student's picture. The students are encouraged to share their endings at the end of the work time. After this, the teacher reads the rest of the book in order for the students to compare their ending with Eric Carle's ending. On Tuesday, the teacher takes another Eric Carle book and does a different activity with it. Throughout the unit, the teacher has the students discuss and compare the unique artwork of the books and then teaches the children how to create collages from tissue paper, the technique that Carle uses. The teacher also gives some biographical information about Eric Carle. Throughout the unit, the language arts are integrated while students spend time viewing, reading, discussing, writing, and visually representing.

When teachers use the intradisciplinary unit approach with older students, the classroom may become a Reading/Writing Workshop. A teacher's goal for the school year may be to expose the students to the different genres. At the beginning of each new unit, the teacher would introduce the genre, such as historical fiction, by explaining that type of literature, introducing authors who write historical fiction, and providing large stacks of books of varying reading levels from various authors. Students would choose which books to read and choose how to respond to the literature. Some students who choose the same author would form literature circles to discuss the similarities and differences of the various books. If the author is living, students could e-mail the author or browse the author's Web page. During a historical fiction unit, another group of students who all read different books from a particular era, such as the Civil War, could combine the information they learned into a skit and perform it for the class.

As you can see, the language arts are totally integrated in the intradisciplinary unit approach: The students are listening to others, reading books of their choice, writing pieces that are authentic, viewing different types of materials, and visually presenting their responses to the literature. It is difficult to separate these language arts skills because they complement each other. The Class Vignette that follows is an example of the intradisciplinary unit approach in a fifth-grade classroom.

Vignette *in the classroom*

One fifth-grade teacher decided to do an author study on Beverly Cleary. The teacher collected many of Cleary's books and made them available to the students. Four students chose to read the same book, *Dear Mr. Henshaw* (1983). Since the story is told entirely through the letters and diary of a young boy, the students also became interested in letter writing.

One day the teacher joins the group. John wants to share with her a serious passage about divorce, a topic that is painfully real to him. The teacher encourages him to read it aloud so that the group can discuss it. However, Alex, another boy in the group, says that he thinks the book is actually pretty funny. Again, the teacher encourages him to read aloud to support this. After both students have read aloud from their chosen passages, the entire group wonders how a book can be funny and serious at the same time. Two students decide to write their own letters to the author, asking her some of the questions that are puzzling them. One student decides to write his own book, using letters to tell the story. The last student decides to make a diorama that depicts the book.

The students selected their own book to read. They met in literature discussion groups periodically to talk about the book and to share favorite passages. Choice of reading material, silent reading, discussion, and writing—these are the elements that make up the integrated approach. Note, too, that the book choice and related activities were student-initiated. The teacher chose the author and then served as a resource to help students, but she did not dictate exactly what students were to do.

INTERDISCIPLINARY UNIT

The interdisciplinary unit uses a somewhat different type of integrated approach. The **interdisciplinary unit** integrates the entire curriculum by using one unifying theme that includes many content areas, such as math, science, social studies, literature, music, and art. The interdisciplinary unit integrates more than the language arts. Reading, writing, listening, speaking, viewing, and visual representing are the means to gather information and to share information that is learned. This approach provides students the opportunity to understand concepts in a holistic fashion as they relate to the world. A broad conceptual theme, chosen by the teacher, is used to promote cognitive growth in the content areas. Large blocks of time are given to students to learn about many aspects within the overall theme.

Central to the success of the interdisciplinary unit is appropriate planning of the unit. Because the theme is the core of the unit and provides a structure for organizing activities, it is important for the teacher to spend some time thinking about which themes would be most appropriate for the class, would involve the greatest number of available resources, and would encourage students to be active learners. The themes that are eventually chosen should reflect the curriculum for that grade level and the overall objectives for that group of students. When developing the unit, the teacher must be sure that it contains the following information and guidelines (Seely, 1995):

- The title and theme must reflect the content of the unit that will interest the students as well as fit the required state curriculum.

- The major objectives of the unit and the concepts to be learned must reflect the required skills for that grade level.

- The resources to be used by the students and teacher may be classified as either reading materials or media resources. They can include Web sites; addresses (both e-mail and postal) of businesses, experts in the field, clubs, authors, etc.; and possible guest speakers.

- The projects and activities can be whole-group, small-group, or individual. They can also be Internet projects with students from other places.

- The methods for evaluating the unit, such as learning portfolios, anecdotal records, checklists, or informal testing, must be made known to the students before the unit begins.

One example of an interdisciplinary unit may be the history of the state in which the students are living. Some possible areas within this broad theme would be the history of the state, its natural resources, and exciting places to visit as well as great authors, famous people, and great inventors from that state. In order for the interdisciplinary approach to be successful, the areas studied and skills developed during the time the topic is studied must be relevant and authentic; they cannot be "tacked on." Lapp, Flood, and Farnan (1996) believe that "effective curriculum integration occurs when the content from one subject area is used to enhance or enrich the content of another" (p. 418).

Choice is given to the students. They get to choose which questions to answer, which resources to use to gather the information, and how to present their findings to the rest of the class. They may choose to write an informational book, write and perform a skit, make a diorama, draw a mural, make a computer presentation, write a script and videotape a presentation as a documentary, or use any other creative way. In this type of classroom, the necessary material is learned because the students share their findings with other students; however, all the students did not read the same chapter of one text nor did they listen to the teacher lecture on the information.

Figure 10.22 shows an interdisciplinary unit on Oklahoma, a required unit for fourth-graders in Oklahoma. Figure 10.23 is a list of possible integrated projects for the unit. Figure 10.24 has a list of books by Oklahoma authors. This unit can be modified to fit any state by changing authors, famous people, natural resources, etc.

Figure 10.22 *Interdisciplinary study of Oklahoma.*

MUSICIANS/ARTISTS

Woody Guthrie
Hanson Brothers
Garth Brooks
Reba McIntire
Greg Burns
Mike Wimmer
Brooks & Dunn
Vince Gill

AUTHORS

Helen Saller
Bill Wallace
Anna Myers
Dian Regan
Darleen Beard
Sherrin Watkins
Harold Keith
S. E. Hinton
Virginia Stroud

OTHER FAMOUS OKLAHOMANS

Wiley Post
Will Rogers
Geronimo
Shannon Lucid
Roy Rogers
Chuck Norris
Ron Howard
Gene Autry

SPORTS

Jim Thorpe
Shannon Miller
Gill Morgan
Brian Watts
Frank Wyatt Lewis

OKLAHOMA

SCIENCE/GEOGRAPHY

Crude oil
Tornadoes
Earthquakes
Space
Snakes
Bird migration
Caves
Grasslands
Rivers/Lakes
Rose rock
Earth formation

SOCIAL STUDIES

Indian territory
Trail of Tears
Land Run
Dust Bowl
Native tribes
Historical trails
Oil boom/bust

MATH

Figure the miles of famous trails
Graph oil prices (supply and demand)
Study sections of land while staking land in the Land Run

1. Using an Oklahoma state map, have students find the shortest distance between various towns, cities, and vacation spots.

2. Using an Oklahoma state map, trace Route 66 and have students find how many miles long the route is in Oklahoma. Have them research Route 66 to find out why and when it was an important route through Oklahoma.

3. Using an Oklahoma state map, have the students trace the Chisholm Trail and find out how many miles long it was. Have them research the trail to find out when and why it was so important.

4. Have students research the significance of the Trail of Tears; have them write and perform a play, based on their findings.

5. Interview an oil-field worker to find out how oil rigs are set up and how much oil they pump. Have students build a model of a rig that will pump oil (cooking oil).

6. Have students find out the price of oil per barrel for the last 40 years and use a bar graph to show their findings.

7. Research the Land Run and reenact it with the other fourth-graders, wearing costumes that fit the era. Have students build covered wagons.

8. Have groups of children find out why one of the people listed under "Other Famous Oklahomans" (see Figure 10.22) was famous. Have them make a class book of famous Oklahomans.

9. Have groups of students research living recording artists (Hanson Brothers, Garth Brooks, etc.) to determine how they became popular and what it takes to record a CD; have them trace one of the recording artist's world or national tours. Have groups of children compose a song and record it on tape to play to the class and/or parents.

10. Read some books written by an Oklahoma author (see Figure 10.22) and have the children invite one of them to their school to talk about their work.

11. Invite an Oklahoma artist (e.g., Greg Burns or Mike Wimmer) to your school to tell about his or her artwork. Have students draw or paint, using techniques similar to those the artist used.

12. Give small groups of students a Native American tribe to research. Using a video camera, have the students produce a TV special about their findings. Have them invite some members of various tribes to talk to the class about their customs and use the presentation as part of the video.

13. Read *Children of the Dust Bowl* by Jerry Stanley; then have some children write and perform a skit or play, based on this book and other sources.

14. Research Shannon Lucid's life to determine how she became an astronaut who was chosen for the spaceflight with the Russian spaceship.

15. Invite Shannon Miller to your class to talk about gymnastics and the Olympics.

16. Invite a TV weatherperson to come and explain tornadoes and how people can protect themselves during a tornado.

17. Have a small group research the types of snakes in Oklahoma and create an information brochure on the types of snakes.

18. Have students map bird migration to and from Oklahoma on a U.S. map.

19. Have a small group of students study the terrain of Oklahoma and create a model of the state's terrain.

20. Have a small group of students research the rock formation in which crude oil is found; have them create a model.

21. If your school is named after a famous Oklahoman (e.g., Wiley Post, Jim Thorpe), have the students find out why she or he was famous; then have students write a pamphlet to publish and share with parents during an open house.

Figure 10.23

Some integrated projects for an integrated unit on Oklahoma.

Figure 10.24 *Recommended books by Oklahoma authors (with possible extended studies).*

Darleen Bailey Beard

The Pumpkin Man from Piney Creek (1995). New York: Simon & Schuster Books. (pumpkin farming and honesty)

The Flimflam Man (1998). New York: Farrar Straus Giroux. (origins of town festivals and how people bamboozle one another in business)

Twister (1999). New York: Farrar Straus Giroux. (Oklahoma weather)

Sherrin Watkins

White Bead Ceremony (1994). Tulsa, OK: Council Oak Books. (customs of the Shawnee tribe; pronunciation key of Shawnee words included)

Ceremony of the Green Snake (1995). Tulsa, OK: Council Oak Books. (customs of the Shawnee tribe)

Harold Keith

Rifles for Watie (1957). New York: A Harper Keypoint Book. (Civil War and the Cherokee Indians, with their alphabet)

Anna Myers

Red-Dirt Jessie (1992). New York: Walker & Co. (death and dying and trust)

Rosie's Tiger (1994). New York: Walker & Co. (Korean War and Koreans attempting a life in the United States)

Graveyard Girl (1995). New York: Walker & Co. (yellow fever and the effects on society)

Spotting the Leopard (1996). New York: Walker & Co. (the Great Depression as well as zoo animals and their natural habitats)

The Keeping Room (1997). New York: Walker & Co. (Quakers)

Dian Curtis Regan

The Curse of the Trouble Dolls (1992). New York: Henry Holt & Co. (different customs)

The Thirteen Hours of Halloween (1993). Morton Grove, IL: Albert Whitman & Co. (origins of the many Halloween costumes)

Princess Nevermore (1995). New York: Scholastic. (royal protocol and the world of magic)

Dear Dr. Sillybear (1997). New York: Henry Holt & Co. (homonyms)

Virginia Stroud (author and illustrator)

Doesn't Fall Off His Horse (1994). New York: Dial Books. (how a Cherokee boy becomes a man and other ceremonies of the Cherokee tribe; also the type of art Stroud uses)

A Walk to the Great Mystery (1995). New York: Dial Books. (ways of the Cherokee medicine woman; also the type of art Stroud uses)

Bill Wallace

Beauty (1988). New York: A Minstrel Book. (how to care for horses)

A Dog Called Kitty (1988). New York: A Minstrel Book. (various types of dogs and how to care for them)

Christmas Spurs (1990). New York: A Minstrel Book. (Stetson cowboy hats and the cowboy's life)

The Final Freedom (1997). New York: A Minstrel Book. (Geronimo and Native Americans as well as the World Fairs)

Upchuck and the Rotten Willy (1998). New York: A Minstrel Book. (characteristics of pets)

Mike Wimmer (illustrator)

All the Places to Love by Patricia MacLachlan (1994). New York: HarperCollins Publishers. (oil painting)

Home Run by Robert Burleigh (1998). San Diego: Harcourt Brace. (oil painting and the world of Babe Ruth)

Other Sources

Children of the Dust Bowl by Jerry Stanley (1992). New York: A Trumpet Club Special Edition. (photographs of families and the account of their trek to California during the 1930s)

Oklahoma Adventure Guide, 8005 South I-35, Suite 205, Oklahoma City, OK 73149-2932. (set of three guides that feature highlights from the following three areas of Oklahoma: central, northeast, and northwest)

Oklahoma Today: Official Magazine of the State of Oklahoma. Oklahoma City, OK: Oklahoma Today. (features people, places, and events in Oklahoma; published seven times a year)

Out of the Dust by Karen Hesse (1997). (study of the Dust Bowl in Oklahoma and Newbery Award books)

Another example of a curriculum web developed around the interdisciplinary unit of beasts and monsters is found in Figure 10.25. The starting point for the unit was the book *The Beast of Monsieur Racine* by Tomi Ungerer.

Figure 10.25   *Sample curriculum web:* The Beast of Monsieur Racine.

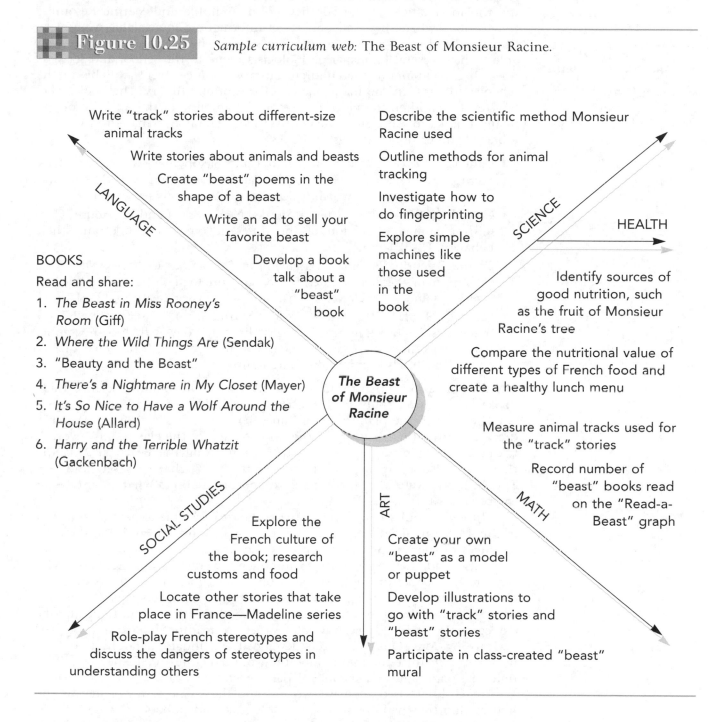

A third example of an interdisciplinary unit title, "Fish—Our Friendly Neighbors," was developed by some elementary-school teachers in South Carolina. The concepts that they wanted their students to understand were the following:

1. A wide variety of fish are available in local South Carolina waters.
2. All the fish have distinctive characteristics that are adapted to their needs and specific habitats.

3. Local fish are a natural resource that provides us with benefits.

With these ideas in mind, the teachers went about locating many resources available to themselves and their students. They started by contacting the local offices of the South Carolina Wildlife and Marine Resources Department, where they were able to get information on available pamphlets, films, and videos as well as appropriate sites for field trips. They were even able to have several local marine biologists come to the school and serve as research consultants to the children. Library resources were available at the school and through the main branch of the public library. The books were targeted for children in grades K–5. A small sampling of these books follows (many thanks to Amy Steinmueller, Assistant Librarian, Charleston County Library, who compiled the list of books):

- Carle, E. (1987). *A House for Hermit Crab.* Saxonville, MA: Picture Book Studio, Ltd. Tells of a hermit crab that has outgrown its old shell and moves into a new one, which it decorates with various sea creatures. (K–2)
- Cole, J. (1986). *Hungry, Hungry Sharks.* New York: Random House. Contains a simple discussion of the different types of sharks and their behavior. (1–3)
- Oxford Scientific Film. (1981). *Jellyfish and Other Sea Creatures.* New York: G. P. Putnam's Sons. Examines, in text and photographs, the physical characteristics and life cycles of jellyfish and related sea creatures. (2–4)
- Paige, D. (1981). *A Day in the Life of a Marine Biologist.* Mahwah, NJ: Troll Associates. Follows a marine biologist through a day at the oceanographic institute as she gathers samples, charts animal behavior, and works on her own research. Photographs. Reading Rainbow Series. (3–5)

The teachers also referred to the annual listing of "Outstanding Science Trade Books for Children," published in *Science and Children,* for additional books.

Then began the planning and implementation of activities for the children. The initial motivation for the unit in each of the classrooms involved taking students on a walk on a nature trail along the beach and having them compose a language-experience chart about what they saw and felt. The children were also encouraged to speculate about what might be in the ocean.

Through inquiry and research, the children were able to gain a great deal of information. They made use of the school library and its standard resources of dictionaries, encyclopedias, videodiscs, and computer programs. They also had the opportunity to interview several marine biologists, who came to the school during designated blocks of time. The students outlined questions for the biologists addressing the three major concepts of the unit prior to each visit. Other activities for getting information from trade and reference books included DRTA, GRP, a variety of reading guides, and journals or learning logs. One class even developed a standard data sheet to help record and organize the information they found. Figures 10.26 and 10.27 illustrate one blank and one completed data sheet.

The children used language, writing, and the arts as a way of sharing the information they had obtained. Some students made a booklet of "Fish Facts" from their data sheets. Other classes created a mural of an ocean full of fish, posters of fish, and want ads describing the characteristics of the fish. An alternative activity might have been a skit called "A Day in the Life of a Marine Biologist," about the marine biologists who had served as consultants at the school.

When it came time for evaluating the interdisciplinary unit, teachers felt that it was most appropriate to keep work portfolios of the inquiry and writing activities that the students completed. They also kept their own journals

As you teach, emphasize what interests you.

WILLIAM GLASSER, M.D.

SOUTH CAROLINA FISH   Name_____

Figure 10.26

Common fish name _____ Scientific name _____

Blank data sheet: Fish.

In what part of S.C. is it found?_____

Size range (How small or big is it?)_____

What does it look like? Describe it in words and draw a picture.
(color—patterns—fins—tail)

Drawing	Description

In which aquatic habitats can this fish be found? (Check them)

____ocean   ____sandy beach   ____river   ____continental shelf

____estuary   ____lake   ____salt marsh   ____coral reef

Describe the habitat of this fish. Where is it **most** likely found?_____

_____

_____

During which months of the year can you find this fish?_____

Is this a good fish to eat?_____

Tell an interesting fact about this fish_____

_____

_____

_____

Fisherman interviewed _____

Name of book used to check information _____

---

of the project, in which they included anecdotal records of the students' progress. Teachers also monitored the journals the children kept and made comments that helped to guide each student's work.

INQUIRY-BASED UNIT

The **inquiry-based unit** is much like the interdisciplinary unit; however, the students as a class brainstorm for broad topics that interest them and then vote as a class on which one to study. After they decide on the broad topic (i.e., space), they brainstorm the many different areas to study that are related to the broad topic, such as planets,

BEYOND THE CLASSROOM

You might want to try brainstorming a curriculum web—the initial step in planning a unit. Pick a topic or theme and use the web illustrated in Figure 10.28 as a guide. It might help to choose a selection of literature as the core for the unit. Then ask your practicum teacher to give you feedback on it; record the web and comments in your journal.

Figure 10.27

Completed data sheet: Fish.

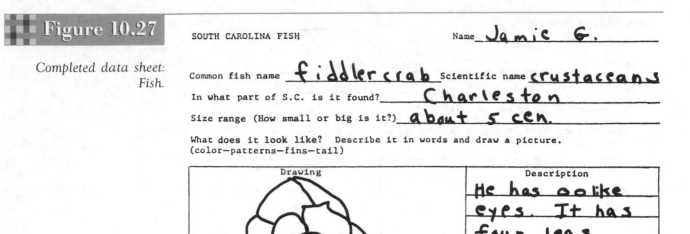

SOUTH CAROLINA FISH   Name _Jamie G._

Common fish name _fiddlercrab_ Scientific name _crustaceans_

In what part of S.C. is it found? _Charleston_

Size range (How small or big is it?) _about 5 cen._

What does it look like? Describe it in words and draw a picture.
(color—patterns—fins—tail)

Drawing	Description
	He has oo like eyes. It has four legs, no nose & one mouth

In which aquatic habitats can this fish be found? (Check them)

___ocean   ✓sandy beach   ___river   ___continental shelf

___estuary   ___lake   ✓salt marsh   ✓coral reef

Describe the habitat of this fish. Where is it most likely found? _Their habitat is on a beach. They're most likely found on the beach_

During which months of the year can you find this fish? _Summer_

Is this a good fish to eat? _no_

Tell an interesting fact about this fish _It is so small you could step on it and not even know it_

Fisherman interviewed _Mr. Harris & Bob Graham._

Name of book used to check information _Fiddler Crabs._

Kennedy Space Center, and astronauts. During this brainstorming session, it is important that the students, with guidance from the teacher, decide on questions that the individual students want to answer in order for there to be structure. The teacher needs to carefully guide students in making sure all the content areas are covered and that the study and activities are both well balanced and possible within the set amount of time given for the unit.

The following scenario is an example of the inquiry-based approach. After a discussion among the students of why gum chewing was "outlawed" in their new building, they decided that gum/candy would be a great topic to study. The teacher asked for suggestions on how to incorporate the various subjects, such as math, science, social studies, music, art, literature, and health. The teacher was confident that plenty of reading, writing, viewing, listening, and discussion would emerge from the study. After brainstorming, the students decided on the areas pictured in Figure 10.28.

Figure 10.28 *Web for inquiry-based unit on candy and gum.*

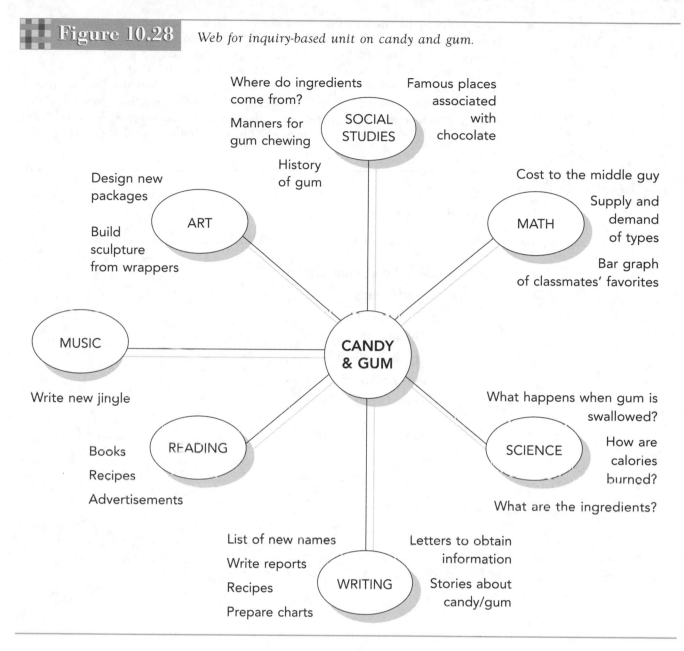

Researchers who promote the inquiry-based approach to language arts "surmise that learners will feel more of an investment in their studies if they peruse meaningful content through student-directed inquiry in small groups or individually" (Guthrie & McCann, 1997, p. 130).

ASSESSING THE INTEGRATED CURRICULUM

In all three integrated approaches using thematic units, the assessment must be different from teacher-made tests and worksheets with single right answers. The assessment must be authentic in nature and "based on what students actually do in a variety of context at different points throughout the instructional year" (Seely, 1995, p. 59). The assessment may include check-lists, anecdotal records, learning logs, dialogue journals, portfolios, teacher conferences, peer assessment, and self-assessment (Manning, Manning, & Long, 1994; Meinbach, Rothlein, & Fredricks, 1995). Since so much of the time is spent in the process, there must be assessment of how each student spent each day and how well the student worked cooperatively in small groups. See Figure 10.29 and Figure 10.30 for some alternative assessment forms. Figure 10.31 is a rubric for a writing assignment. Different elements of the writing assignment are given points; the points reflect the importance of that particular element as it pertains to the entire writing project. Other authors with assessment forms and ideas for evaluation are Atwell (1998), Fiderer (1998), Rickards and Cheek (1999), and Spandel and Stiggins (1990).

Figure 10.29

Cooperative learning self-assessment form.

Today's date _____

I worked with (names of group members) _____

Name of activity/project _____

Check if the statement fits you

_____ I talked quietly

_____ I shared materials

_____ I listened well to others

_____ I did not demand my own way

_____ I did my share of the work

_____ I cleaned up the area

Today I learned from (name of classmate) _____ the following:

_____

_____

_____

_____

_____

_____

Today I taught (name of classmate) _____ the following:

_____

_____

_____

_____

_____

_____

_____

Signature _____

_____

Student _____   Date _____

Project _____

	Superior	Good	Adequate	Needs Work
Creative				
Accurate information				
Well organized/attractive				
Indicates research				
Bibliography (correct amount of references)				
Bibliography format correct				
Clearly presented				
Participation in the group				

Additional comments

_____

_____

_____

_____

_____

_____

Discussed with student on this date _____

Student's signature _____

Figure 10.30

Teacher's evaluation form.

	Possible Points	You Earned
1. Separate cover sheet, name, date, title	5 pts.	_____
2. Typed, double-spaced, stapled, neat appearance	5 pts.	_____
3. Does your work say something important?	40 pts.	_____
4. Is it written in a clear and interesting manner?	30 pts.	_____
5. Did you proofread and edit for errors?	20 pts.	_____
TOTAL POINTS	100 pts.	_____

Figure 10.31

Rubric for writing assignment.

SAMPLE THEMATIC UNIT—FOLKTALES

Following is a thematic unit on folktales, developed by Jerita Whaley, a fourth-grade teacher at Westwood Elementary School in Stillwater, Oklahoma. Each student signed an individual contract (see Figure 10.32) indicating which activities he or she would do to meet the requirements for a specific grade; the teacher also signed each contract. The signatures showed that both pupil and teacher understood the terms of the contract. Also included are lists of the activities from which students could choose and an annotated bibliography.

From the Learning Skills Activities, it is easy to see that the teacher engaged the students in higher-level thinking skills. From the Literature Appreciation Activities, it is evident that there is an integration of literature, geography, history, language, music, drama, visual art, and poetry as the students engage in all areas of the language arts.

Figure 10.32 *Thematic unit on folktales, including a student contract, a list of possible activities, and an annotated bibliography.*

CONTRACT

Student _____   Date _____

Teacher _____

I, _____ , agree to read _____ folktales and finish the activities required in order to obtain a particular grade.

The grade I contract for is _____

A = Assignments from:
    Learning Skills . . . . Choice of 3 activities
    Literature Appreciation . . . . Choice of 3 activities
    Art/Music/Drama . . . . Choice of 2 activities

B = Assignments from:
    Learning Skills . . . . Choice of 2 activities
    Literature Appreciation . . . . Choice of 2 activities
    Art/Music/Drama . . . . Choice of 2 activities

C = Assignments from:
    Learning Skills . . . . Choice of 2 activities
    Literature Appreciation . . . . Choice of 1 activity
    Art/Music/Drama . . . . Choice of 1 activity

I, _____ , understand my responsibilities and will fulfill them to the best of my ability.

Date contract fulfilled _____

Student's signature _____

Instructor's signature _____

(continued)

Figure 10.32 *Continued.*

LEARNING SKILL ACTIVITIES

1. Choose your favorite folktale and write it as a sensational news story for the school paper. (Application)

2. After reading at least two versions of the same folktale, make a list of ways they are alike and ways they are different. (Compare & contrast/analysis)

3. Make a list of new words as you read each folktale. Choose a friend to help you make a crossword puzzle. (Vocabulary knowledge/synthesis)

4. Read the first two pages of a folktale with a friend. Each of you writes a prediction for the next event. Read the folktale, then compare your predictions with what happened next. Which do you like best? Why? (Prediction/evaluation)

5. Make a story web or map of one of the folktales you read. (Comprehension/analysis)

6. Rewrite one event in a folktale so that the ending is different. Rewrite the ending. (Analysis/prediction)

7. Invent a code system and send a message about a character in a folktale to one of your friends. (Synthesis)

8. Choose a folktale character and pretend that you have the power to bring that character to your house for an evening. Without telling your family the details about the character, how do you think they will react to the way your "friend" behaves? Write about your family's response. (Inference/analysis)

9. Memorize a poem from another country and share it with the class. (Knowledge)

10. Imagine a setting for a story. When the picture is clear in your mind, draw a picture of the setting. Write a description. (Synthesis)

11. Select a story to retell from another point of view. You could, for example, be the "bad guy" and justify your actions. (Evaluate)

LITERATURE APPRECIATION ACTIVITIES

1. Interview 20 people to determine their favorite folktales. Graph your findings.

2. Read folktales to five other people in school. You must make arrangements with teachers for the reading. Get signatures from each person you read to.

3. Draw a map of a country and list at least three folktales that have been popular in that country.

4. Write a report about your favorite folktale author, reteller, translator, editor, or illustrator. Share it with the class.

5. Make a list of the "bad guys" in at least 10 different folktales. Write a sentence about each, describing that person's rottenness.

6. Make a list of all the "good guys" mentioned in at least 10 different folktales. Try to think of one or two traits each one possesses that makes that person a "good guy."

7. Write your own folktale or version of a folktale. Get a friend to illustrate it for you.

8. Lead your literature group in a brainstorming activity and make a cluster diagram of the discussion. Possible topics might be giants, enchanted people, talking animals in folktales, ways magic is used, and so on.

9. Make a list of words or phrases used in making comparisons. Find at least 10 similes or metaphors, and identify the folktale you found them in.

10. Write a riddle about one of the characters in a fairy tale of your choice. See if a friend can guess the riddle.

11. Use a haiku to describe the setting from one folktale. Select the words to give a complete picture.

12. An acrostic poem begins each line with a letter from a person's name. Select a character, and write his or her name vertically on your paper. Each line should tell something about the character of your choice.

13. Write a poem or song expressing your response to events in a folktale.

ART/MUSIC/DRAMA ACTIVITIES

1. Make a tape of at least five folk songs for a class sing-along.

2. Choose an illustrated folk song book to practice, sing, and share with a small group.

3. Make a mobile to illustrate your favorite folktale.

4. Make an attractive book jacket for a folktale.

5. Design and draw a dragon or other monster suitable for a great folktale. Write a detailed description of the monster's unique physical qualities.

6. Find three or four other people who have read the same folktale and perform one or two episodes from the book.

7. Draw your four favorite castles, whether they come from your dreams or something you have seen.

8. Memorize a folktale for a storytelling session with a small group in kindergarten or first grade.

9. Illustrate a folktale for a friend, or draw four or more detailed illustrations for a folktale of your choice.

(continued)

Figure 10.32   *Continued.*

10. Practice calligraphy and write a "Hear Ye, Hear Ye" message that the town crier might proclaim about an important event in a fairy tale you like. Mount it on two dowel rods or pencils.

11. Study heraldry and design a shield to represent your family. Make it in felt for the bulletin board.

ANNOTATED BIBLIOGRAPHY

Ahlberg, J., & Ahlberg, A. (1986). *The jolly postman or other people's letter.* Boston: Little, Brown and Co. The postman makes deliveries, "Once upon a bicycle," to favorite fairy tale characters. This book can be a wonderful inspiration for all kinds of writing activities.

Andersen, H. C. (1986). The Emperor's new clothes. In W. F. Russell (ed.), *More classics to read aloud to your children.* New York: Crown Publishers. The Emperor's new clothes are the biggest hit ever until a child in the crowd tells the truth. If an innocent child cannot see the clothes, then the Emperor has none. (Denmark)

Arbuthnot, M. H. (1984). Clever Manka. In *The Arbuthnot anthology of children's literature.* Chicago: Scott Foresman & Co. Manka's cleverness is a threat to her new husband until he rediscovers his sense of humor. (Czechoslovakia)

Carrick, C. (1989). *Aladdin and the wonderful lamp* (D. Carrick, illus.). New York: Scholastic. This tale from Arabia is a less detailed version of the lamp than the version by Andrew Lang. (Arabia)

Ehrlich, A. (1981). *Hans Christian Andersen's "The wild swans"* (Susan Jeffers, illus.). New York: Dial Books. A courageous princess must face terrible hardships to free her 11 brothers from a wicked curse. Susan Jeffers's enchanting illustrations are vibrant with life and form a perfect backdrop for this incredible story, in which love again is triumphant. (Denmark)

Grimm, J., & Grimm, W. Snow White. In N. Lewis (ed.), *The twelve dancing princesses and other tales from Grimm* (L. Postma, illus.). New York: Dial Books. This version is a translation true to the original tale from the Brothers Grimm. The witchy stepmother gets it in the end. (Germany)

Hastings, S. (1985). *Sir Gawain and the loathly lady* (J. Wijngaard, illus.). New York: Lothrop, Lee & Shepard Books. King Arthur's life depends upon his answer to the question, What is it that women most desire? Beautiful illustrations depict how Arthur is saved by the loathly lady who gives him the answer in return for being allowed to marry one of his knights. (England)

Hodges, M. (1984). *Saint George and the dragon* (T. S. Hyman, illus.). Boston: Little, Brown & Co. This golden legend from Edmund Spencer's *The Faerie Queen* tells of George, the Red Cross Knight, and fair and faithful Una, who encourages him to slay the terrible dragon that has been terrorizing her father's kingdom. The illustrations by Hyman in this English tale are her best yet. (England)

Kaplan, I. (1967). Little Rosa and Long Leda. In *Fairy tales from Sweden* (C. Calder, illus.). Chicago: Follett Publishing Company. This version of the Cinderella–Snow White tale does not involve a glass slipper, but the stepmother is a real witch. Despite being changed into a goose by the stepmother's evil magic, kind Queen Rosa is saved by her husband, the King, and they all live happily ever after. (Sweden)

Louie, A. (1982). *Yeh-Shen* (E. Young, illus.). New York: Philomel Books. This tale dates from the T'ang dynasty (618–907 A.D.); the oldest version of the "Cinderella" tale is Italian, dating from 1634. Since the Yeh-Shen story predates that tale, Cinderella seems to have made her way from Asia to Europe. In this version, a young Chinese girl overcomes the wickedness of her stepsister and stepmother to become the bride of a prince. Instead of a fairy godmother, she has the help of a golden fish. (China)

Macaulay, D. (1977). *Castle.* Boston: Houghton Mifflin. This Caldecott Honor book and ALA notable traces the step-by-step planning and construction of a thirteenth-century castle and town, from the hiring of a skilled master engineer to the testing of the buildings' defenses when hundreds of Welsh soldiers attack. The incredible pen-and-ink illustrations show the castle and town, the tools the workers used in their labors, and the weapons the soldiers used to defend their castle and town.

MacMillan, C. (1967). The Indian Cinderella. In V. Haviland (ed.), *North American legends.* New York: Collins. The younger sister escapes her cruel older sisters when she wins the sometimes-invisible Strong Wind as her husband. (Northeast Woodland Indians)

Mobley, J. (1979). *Star husband* (A. Vojech, illus.). New York: Doubleday & Company. This sensitive story from the legends of the Great Plains Indians is a beautiful adaptation of a story told by the Old Ones. Full-color illustrations depict the stars as people and show a mortal girl who wishes for one beautiful star, which becomes her husband. This is a reassuring affirmation of the natural cycle of life, death, and rebirth. (Great Plains Indians)

(continued)

Figure 10.32 *Continued.*

Morris, W. (1987). *The magic leaf* (J. Chen, illus.). New York: Atheneum. Through vibrant watercolor illustrations, readers are introduced to a swordsman and scholar named Lee Foo. Because he reads so many books, Lee Foo thinks he is very clever. He solves his problems so foolishly in trying to appear clever that he gets into a great deal of trouble. When he returns home humbler and wiser, he finally realizes that he is no longer interested in clever plans. (China)

Myers, S. (1979). *The enchanted sticks* (D. Diamond, illus.). New York: Coward, McCann & Geoghegan. This Japanese tale is about an old man who conquers a robber chief with the help of enchanted sticks. The enchanted sticks have already kept the old man company, dancing, playing games, and spelling out messages. Later they lead him in rescuing a young maiden from the terrible robbers. The end of the story also offers a good opportunity for a math exploration. (Japan)

Newman, D. L. (1967). The tar baby. In V. Haviland (ed.), *North American legends*. New York: Collins. The lazy rabbit outwits the other animals even after he gets stuck in the tar baby. This is very much like an Uncle Remus tale. (West Virginia)

Pevear, R. (1987). *Our king has horns.* (R. Rayevsky, illus.). New York: Macmillan. A young barber is about to lose his life for revealing the king's terrible secret. This version of an old Georgian folktale about the persistent nature of truth is retold with wit and beautiful illustrations. (Russia)

Poranzinska, J. (1987). *The enchanted book: A tale from Krakow* (B. Smith, trans.; J. Brett, illus.). New York: Harcourt Brace Jovanovich. In this folklore from Poland, the miller's youngest daughter succeeds in outwitting an evil sorcerer. There is a common element of girls becoming enchanted birds with the German tale of Jorinda and Jorjingle. (Poland)

Robinson, A. (1979). Kelfala's secret something. In *Three African tales* (C. Byard, illus.). New York: G. P. Putnam's Sons. The jester is an important part of African culture, even today. This story from Kenya is told by the Kikuyu, who provide a view of their culture through this tale about a clown named Kelfala who falls in love with the beautiful Wambuna and tries to win her with his clever trick. (Kenya)

Rogasky, B. (1982). *Rapunzel* (T. S. Hyman, illus.). New York: Holiday House. This is a favorite version of this classic tale from the German Brothers Grimm about a girl raised by a witch in a tall tower. This version's happy ending includes the handsome prince and twins. The illustrations are incredibly beautiful and detailed. (Germany)

Rogasky, B. (1986). *The Water of Life* (T. S. Hyman, illus.). New York: Holiday House. This Brothers Grimm tale, by this author-illustrator team, is even more beautifully done than *Rapunzel*. It has all the classic elements of a great story. To cure his dying father, a prince searches for the Water of Life. He finds an enchanted castle, a magic sword, and a beautiful princess. Despite his brothers' treachery, goodness and love triumph. (Germany)

Seeger, P. (1986). *Abiyoyo* (M. Hays, illus.). New York: Macmillan. After a man and his son are ostracized from a town because the people are upset by their singing and magic tricks, they use their talents to make Abiyoyo, the terrible giant, disappear. The people then bring them back into the town and join in the song, Abiyoyo! (Africa)

Stewig, J. (1988). *The fisherman and his wife* (M. Tomes, illus.). New York: Holiday House. Stewig uses clear descriptive language in his version of this Brothers Grimm tale. He unveils a story of the satisfied fisherman, his demanding wife, and a magic fish. The wife's greediness brings riches, power, and glory to her while depleting the earth's resources. At last she gets what she deserves. This tale could lead children to ask, If we greedily devour the earth's resources, will we get what we deserve? This is a wonderful classic. (Germany)

Williams-Ellis, A. (1987). Baba Yaga. In *Tales from the enchanted world* (M. Kemp, illus.). Boston: Little, Brown & Co. A young girl's stepmother sends her to the witch's house on an errand. Her clever consideration and kindness to the witch's animals and servant help her escape from the terrible clutches of Baba Yaga. (Russia)

Summary

Using reading and writing in the content areas is a natural, almost commonsense way of allowing students to apply and extend what they know about language. Such an approach gives special meaning to reading and writing instruction because it encourages the students to use these processes in acquiring real and necessary information.

Using reading and writing in the content areas is also important not only in expanding language competencies but also in developing each student's content literacy—the cyclical ability both to use a store of background knowledge in comprehending new content information and to know what strategies to use to facilitate getting and applying that information. Students may then use the newly acquired knowledge to facilitate further comprehension.

Remember that the purpose of using reading and writing across the curriculum is to aid students in their ability to internalize knowledge—and to give children a real and meaningful reason for using reading and writing. By doing this, teachers can help children not only to appreciate language but to become proficient users of it in their daily lives.

With Children activities

CLASS CHOICE

Have the class vote on a favorite book and build a unit around it. Then brainstorm activities related to the book. Use a diagram with the six branches of reading, writing, listening, speaking, viewing, and visually representing. This diagram should get you started on planning a literature unit.

COMMUNITY COMMUNICATION

As part of a social studies unit on community and community service, children can correspond with individuals in local nursing homes or other institutions. The exchange of letters will give the students many opportunities for reading and writing. They may want to share events of their daily lives, important happenings, or original writings.

MAKE A MAP

After the students have had a number of experiences reading, drawing, and labeling maps, they may want to create a map depicting the location of a favorite story. For example, after reading *Owl Moon*, several children might want to draw a map showing the route that the little girl and her father took from the farm to the woods and back again.

LEARNING LOG

Encourage each student to keep a learning log in which he or she summarizes what learning has taken place each day. Periodically, you may want to make comments in their logs.

CLASS NEWSLETTERS

Let students assume the responsibility for writing a weekly or monthly newsletter home to parents. In it, they can summarize the progress of learning in the classroom and highlight special events. You may even want to do the newsletter on the computer with the help of software such as The Newsroom.

FACT BOOKS

In many areas of the curriculum, students can create their own books of facts. Whenever children study a particular topic, such as animal habitats, they can begin to collect particular facts that interest them. Then they can organize these facts into a book format and publish it for others to enjoy.

technology Simulation Games and Problem-Solving Programs

Simulations deserve a place in language arts instruction because they provide motivation for reading, researching, and writing. Simulations allow a particular situation or aspect of a content area to come alive for students and allow a child to experience something that would not be possible merely through text. Because many simulations involve text, they motivate students to read. Further, software programs, such as the *Oregon Trail II*, *Yukon Trail*, and *The Golden Spike*, require students to make decisions while playing them, thus encouraging higher-level thinking skills.

Computer programs may be categorized in various ways according to their problem-solving capabilities. These programs demand logical reasoning from those who play them. Some software programs that do involve problem solving and decision making are *The Puzzler*, *Ace Detective*, *Gizmos and Gadgets*, *Where in the World Is Carman Sandiego?*, and *Junior Detective: Carman Sandiego*. These text-based programs encourage users to try the predictions and evaluation strategies common to the psycholinguistic theory of reading in order to make decisions and solve problems. In *The Puzzler*, students view a story page by page. They are asked to figure out the answer to a question at the beginning of the story and are allowed to make a prediction about it after each page. As the story continues, some predictions or guesses are discounted while others gain credibility. In the end, there is no single correct answer to the initial question. Each student must support her or his interpretation through logic—a competency that reading teachers are continually trying to develop in their students.

Two CD-ROMs offering a wealth of information are *Leonardo, the Inventor* by Intelliquest and *David Macaulay: The Way Things Work* by Houghton Mifflin. Both of these include much reading, with interaction by the user.

websites   E-learning

www.si.edu.organiza/museums/nmah/notkid/ubh/00intro.htm
Here's a fun way to explore American history by looking at artifacts.

www.BiologyLessons.sdsu.edu/
This site includes lessons about molecules, cells, and population biology. The lessons have students predict, answer questions, collect data, and reflect.

www.kidvista.com/index.html

This site is for children. It will link them to sites relating to literature, the arts, science, social studies, games, sports, and many other areas.

educate.si.edu/

This site informs teachers about Smithsonian educational resources and provides approaches to integration of the various subjects.

www.hawastsoc.org/solar/

This site is a beautiful introduction to the solar system and includes science and history.

www.fi.edu/weather/nino/nino.html

This site explains El Niño in simple terms.

www.2010.atmost.vivc.edu/(GH)/guides/home.rxml

This site give teachers information about cloud formation and includes a variety of student projects in a variety of subjects. Online guides to meteorology include instructional resources curriculum.

www.althorp-house.co.uk/

This site takes you to the late Princess Diana's home.

st.pauls.london.anglican.org/home.htm

This site takes you to St. Paul's Cathedral where Princess Diana was married to Prince Charles.

www.ipl.org/ref/POTUS/

This site links to POTUS: Presidents of the United States. It includes texts, sound bites, photos, and film clips.

www.ipl.org/cgi-bin/reading/news.out.pl

This site contains numerous newspapers from the United States and around the world.

sln.fi.edu/

This Franklin Institute Science Museum site is great for teachers and students.

www.enc.org

This is the site of the Eisenhower National Clearinghouse for Math and Science. It has action ideas and lesson plans for all grades.

www.learner.org/exhibits/garbage/global.html

This site is about garbage and how to shrink landfills.

www.monticello.org/Day/A Day in the Life.html

This site, based on Jefferson's home, has information about all his talents.

www.corbis.com/jefferson/pres/pres_frame_p01.html

This site is about Thomas Jefferson and includes many of his quotes.

www.nortonsimon.org/index.html

This site has information about Michelangelo and his art in Florence, Italy.

www.cc.emory.edu/CARLOS/ODYSSEY/index.html

This is for younger students, to get them interested in ancient history.

kids.msfc.nasa.gov/

This site is designed for students to learn about space, astronauts, spacesuits, shuttles, and other planets.

scout.cs.wisc.edu/kids/archive/KIDS-970930.html

This site connects kids with Math Is Fun!

www.win4edu.com/minds-eye/fish/

Two classes are matched, based on grade (1–8) and language. One class writes a description of an imaginary habitat; the other class designs an insect/fish for the habitat.

www.kidsfood.org/

This site is designed for third- to fifth-graders to teach them about food and nutrition. A teacher's guide, which gives lesson plans and activities, is provided.

fyiowa.webpoint.com/fitness

This site answers questions about exercise, correct ways to do activities, and how to prevent injuries.

www.fi.edu/

This site gives information about city water and how it is produced. It explains how to conserve water.

www.igc.apc.org/green/resources.html

This site connects to the Franklin Institute and gives information about various waterways and other environmental topics.

www.envirolink.org/

This site is an environmental information service, which focuses on environmental, cultural, and exploration issues around the world.

volcano.und.nodak.edu/

This is a site designed for teachers and students who desire to learn more about volcanoes.

www.usgs.gov/

This site has U.S. maps and earth science data.

www.ngdc.noaa.gov/

This site is a data center for geophysics, climatology, and glaciology.

lwww.deepspace.ucsb.edu/rot.htm

This site offers students access to equipment and software used by research scientists (e.g., telescopes).

www.nasa.gov/

This is NASA's home page.

www.unige.ch/sciences/terre/esr/contents.htm

This site links to over 300 earth science resources and Web pages.

www.geolsoc.org.uk/gs3etfrm.htm

This site connects teachers to resources and other sites helpful to teaching earth science.

www.coreknowledge.org/

This site has lesson plans for all subjects on many themes for all grades.

pw2.netcom.com/~giardina/medieval.html

This site has information on medieval customs.

www.packer.edu/Acess/Faculty/History/Rosec/Rose.html

This site has information about the history of medieval times.

www.castles.org/
This site has information about specific castles and how they were built.

www.middleweb.com/CurrMiddleAge.html
This site has information about the Middle Ages and the customs of that time.

learner.org/exhibits/middleage/clothing.html
This site displays the costumes of the Middle Ages.

Related Readings

Chancer, J., & Rester-Zodrow, G. (1997). *Writing, art, and inquiry through focused nature study*. Portsmouth, NH: Heinemann.

> This book explains how one California class used the moon and its changing position as a topic for their inquiry study for 28 days. The children, with their parents, recorded in their journal the moon's position and any questions they had. Each day, they were given time to share their questions and find answers. The teacher included writing, reading, art, science, and music in the study.

Davenport, M. R., Jaeger, M., & Laurintzen, C. (1995). Negotiating curriculum. *The Reading Teacher* 49(1), 60–67.

> This article gives information on a thematic unit of the culture and geography of the Appalachian region of the United States.

Fennessey, S. (1995). Living history through drama and literature. *The Reading Teacher* 49(1), 16–19.

> The article explains how a thematic unit on Langston Hughes and the entire idea of racial prejudice came alive when the students used drama to interpret parts of history.

Fiderer, A. (1995). *Practical assessments for literature-based reading classrooms*. New York: Scholastic Professional Books.

> This book has ready-to-use forms for response evaluations, miscue records, self-evaluation checklists for literature responses, and home-reading records.

Manning, M., & Manning, G. (1994). *Theme immersion: Inquiry-based curriculum in elementary and middle schools*. Portsmouth, NH: Heinemann.

> The authors distinguish between thematic units led by teachers and theme immersion led by teachers and students, with opportunity for students' inquiry in areas that interest them. Appendix B is especially useful because it gives a list of literature books to use for a wide range of topics—apartheid to architecture to the Civil War.

Parks, S., & Black, H. (1990). *Organizing thinking: Graphic organizers*. Pacific Grove, CA: Critical Thinking Press & Software.

> This book has templates of graphic organizers, along with examples of how to use them for the different content areas.

Seely, A. E. (1995). *Integrated thematic units*. Westminster, CA: Teacher Created Materials.

> This book explains the difference between various types of thematic units. It include theories to support this type of teaching.

References

Anderson, R. C., Hiebert, E. H., Scott, J. A., & Wilkinson, I. (1985). *Becoming a nation of readers: The report of the Commission on Reading.* Washington, DC: National Institute of Education, the National Academy of Education.

Atwell, N. (1998). *In the middle* (2nd ed.). Portsmouth, NH: Heinemann.

Barrow, L. H., & Andrew, B. (1981, April). Activity-oriented science plus language experience approach = science language experience. Paper presented at the meeting of the National Science Teachers' Association, New York, NY.

Barrow, L. H., Kristo, J. V., & Andrew, B. (1984). Building bridges between science and reading. *The Reading Teacher, 38*(2), 188–192.

Bigelow, B. (1989). Discovering Columbus: Rereading the past. *Language Arts, 66*(6), 635–643.

Calkins, L. (1994). *The art of teaching writing.* Portsmouth, NH: Heinemann.

Cudd, E. T., & Roberts, L. (1989). Using writing to enhance content area learning in the primary grades. *The Reading Teacher, 42*(6), 392–404.

Dale, E., & Chall, J. S. (1948a). A formula for predicting readability. *Educational Research Bulletin, 27,* 11–20.

Dale, E. & Chall, J. S. (1948b). A formula for predicting readability. *Educational Research Bulletin, 28,* 37–54.

Davis, Z. T., & McPherson, M. D. (1989). Story map instruction: A road map for reading comprehension. *The Reading Teacher, 43*(3), 232–240.

Elbow, P. (1973). *Writing without teachers.* New York: Oxford University Press.

Fiderer, A. (1998). *Practical assessment for literature-based reading classrooms.* New York: Scholastic.

Fry, E. (1977). Fry's readability graph: Clarifications, validity, and extensions to level 17. *Journal of Reading, 21*(3), 242–252.

Goodman, K. (1996). *Ken Goodman on reading: A common-sense look at the nature of language and the science of reading.* Portsmouth, NH: Heinemann.

Guillaume, A. (1998). Learning with text in the primary grades. *The Reading Teacher, 51*(6), 476–486.

Guthrie, J. T., & McCann, A. D. (1997). Characteristics of classrooms that promote motivations and strategies for learning. In J. T. Guthrie & A. Wigfield (eds.), *Reading engagement: Motivating readers through integrated instruction.* Newark, DE: International Reading Association.

International Reading Association. (1997/1998, December/January). Ideas for administrators: Shining examples. *Reading Today, 15*(3), 10.

Johnson, D. D., & Pearson, P. D. (1984). *Teaching reading vocabulary* (2nd ed.). New York: Holt, Rinehart & Winston.

Lapp, D., Flood, J., & Farnan, N. (1996). *Content area reading and writing instructional strategies* (2nd ed.). Boston: Allyn & Bacon.

Manning, M., Manning, G., & Long, R. (1994). *Theme immersion inquiry-based curriculum in elementary and middle schools.* Portsmouth, NH: Heinemann.

Manzo, A. V. (1968). Improving reading comprehension through reciprocal questioning. Unpublished doctoral dissertation, Syracuse University.

Manzo, A. V. (1969). The ReQuest procedure. *Journal of Reading, 13*(3), 123–126.

Manzo, A., & Manzo, U. (1997). *Content area literacy: Interactive teaching for active learning* (2nd. ed.). Upper Saddle River, NJ: Merrill.

McKenna, M. C., & Robinson, R. D. (1990). Content literacy: A definition and implications. *Journal of Reading, 34*(3), 184–186.

Meinbach, A. M., Rothlein, L., & Fredricks, A. (1995). *The complete guide to thematic units: Creating the integrated curriculum.* Norwood, MA: Christopher-Gordon Publishers.

Meyer, B. J. F. (1975). *The organization of prose and its effect in memory.* Amsterdam: North-Holland.

Monahan, J., & Hinson, B. (eds.) (1988). *New directions in reading instruction.* Newark, DE: International Reading Association.

Moore, D. W., & Moore, S. A. (1986). Possible sentences. In E. K. Dishner, T. W. Bean, J. E. Readence, & D. W. Moore (eds.), *Reading in the content areas* (2nd ed.). Dubuque, IA: Kendall/Hunt.

Parks, S., & Black, H. (1990). *Organizing thinking: Graphic organizers.* Pacific Grove, CA: Critical Thinking Press & Software.

Rickards, D., & Cheek, E. (1999). *Designing rubrics for K–6 classroom assessment.* Norwood, MA: Christopher-Gordon Publishers.

Schwab, P. N., & Coble, C. R. (1985). Reading, thinking, and semantic webbing. *The Science Teacher, 52*(5), 68–71.

Searfoss, L. W., & Dishner, E. K. (1977). Improving comprehension through the ReQuest procedure. *Reading Education: A Journal for Australian Teachers, 2,* 22–25.

Seely, A. (1995). *Integrated thematic units.* Westminster, CA: Teacher Created Materials.

Spandel, V., & Stiggins, R. (1990). *Creating writers: Linking assessment and writing instruction.* New York: Longman.

Stauffer, R. (1969). *Directing reading maturity as a cognitive process.* New York: Harper & Row.

Strickland, D. (1987). Literature: Key element in the language and reading program. In B. E. Cullinan (ed.), *Children's literature in the reading program.* Newark, DE: International Reading Association.

Taba, H. (1967). *Teacher's handbook for elementary social studies.* Reading, MA: Addison-Wesley.

Tompkins, G. (1997). *Literacy for the 21st century: A balanced approach.* Upper Saddle River, NJ: Merrill.

Vacca, R. T., & Vacca, J. L. (1998). *Content area reading* (6th ed.). Glenview, IL: Scott, Foresman & Company.

Vacca, J., Vacca, R., & Groves, M. (1995). *Reading and learning to read* (3rd ed.). New York: HarperCollins College Publishers.

Working with a Diverse Population

11

IN THIS CHAPTER

overview

Elementary teachers working with classes of 20 to 40 students encounter children with a variety of intellectual, physical, and social needs. While students are expected to acquire specific knowledge bases and social skills, wise teachers provide classroom environments with a wide degree of tolerance for individual differences. Knowledgeable teachers also read beyond established norms to embrace the diversity found in such rooms and to accommodate special needs with respect and enthusiasm.

This chapter focuses on children from diverse backgrounds and special needs. Its emphasis is on sensitizing you to some of the needs of these children within regular education settings. Suggestions for modifying language arts instruction as presented in this chapter form a rich resource for teachers who provide instruction to children with diverse backgrounds and special needs.

Historically, special-needs children and children from diverse backgrounds were not given special attention in the regular classroom. Many special-needs children were found in rooms or schools away from the regular classroom. Children from diverse backgrounds were expected to "melt into" and become one of the students represented in the regular classroom. However, by the mid-1970s, a heightened awareness of civil rights resulted in public outcries that forced educators to listen to those children whose needs were special and whose backgrounds were different. In the 1980s, these students were *mainstreamed* into the regular classroom, which implied that for part of the regular school day these students were in a regular self-contained classroom. For most of the day, however, they were down the hall in a special education setting with a special education teacher. In the 1990s, inclusion emerged. In the *inclusive* classroom, students of all abilities and diverse backgrounds spend the majority of their time in the regular classroom with special education teachers by their side, or they go to a special education teacher in a special education room for a small period of time each day. Today there are many studies being done on the advantages and disadvantages of the inclusive classroom.

In this chapter, the following topics will be discussed: at-risk children, the diverse cultures in American schools, the Ebonics controversy, English as a second language, legislation and the disabled, and the talented and gifted. In each section, the special traits and needs of students will be addressed as well as some practical classroom strategies to use with these students.

Children with Special Needs

Today's classroom is characterized by diversity of all sorts. Teachers encounter students with varying intellectual, physical, linguistic, emotional, social, and cultural needs in the same classroom. The challenge for teachers is to embrace this diversity and strive to meet the individual needs of all students.

All students can learn.

CHRISTOPHER MORLEY

Among the many groups of children with special needs are those labeled at-risk. **At-risk children** often experience learning difficulties in school for a variety of personal, social, and family reasons (Maring & Furman, 1985). They may come from families living below the poverty line and experience drug and alcohol abuse. Or they may enter school without sufficient English skills to allow them to compete in the classroom with their peers. They may have mild learning disabilities that put them behind the often rapid pace of the classroom. Whatever the cause or causes, at-risk students are often the first to experience school failure and the first to drop out before acquiring the basic skills.

In many traditional classrooms, children encounter a narrowly defined environment with hard-and-fast expectations for achievement. Such expectations are based on a business-management mentality in which learning is measured primarily by test scores derived from standardized achievement tests. The quality of education is defined by how well children perform in reading, writing, and arithmetic in comparison to children with no disabling conditions who are from predominantly white, middle-class homes. How such a system has emerged in this highly developed society is a matter for sociological debate; the outcome, however, is about a 25 percent yearly school dropout rate (Institute for Educational Leadership, 1989).

Numerous studies have attempted to analyze the reasons why so many children and adolescents leave the school system before graduation. Lists of contributing factors include both student variables and school or organizational variables (Woman, Brunicks, & Thurlow, 1989). Student characteristics include low reading scores (Nadeau & Miramontes, 1988), low cognitive scores and low socioeconomic status (Lichtenstein, 1987), grade repetition (Garibaldi, 1992), and poor attendance and disruptive behavior (Wang, Reynolds, & Walberg, 1995).

Minority students may also find themselves in the at-risk category. This is particularly true for many African American, Native American, and Hispanic students who have lower academic achievement scores than their middle-class peers. Low academic achievement and low socioeconomic status are two of the major factors that cause students to drop out before graduation (Chall & Curtis, 1991; Rumberger & Larsen, 1998). In the past two decades, the minority populations in U.S. schools have increased enormously, especially in large urban areas such as New York, Chicago, Houston, Los Angeles, Dallas, Miami, and Washington, DC; this means the issue of at-risk minority students is one that almost all teachers will encounter.

While students with such characteristics appear to be front-runners for failure in traditional schools, some of the responsibility clearly belongs to the educational system itself. Apparently the system has difficulty adapting to students whose needs are not addressed in schools founded on a middle-income, normal learning-abilities model. The view that school characteristics contribute to the success or failure potential of students is shaking belief systems in the hallowed halls of many public schools. The question surreptitiously creeping out of the public schools woodwork is, "Are we talking about marginal students when in fact we ought to be talking about marginal teaching?" (Hahn, 1987).

The following is a list of books that prospective teachers and veteran teachers alike should read as they prepare themselves for working with diverse populations in the twenty-first century (all published by the National Educational Service in connection with Phi Delta Kappa of Bloomington, IN):

> ### BEYOND THE CLASSROOM
>
> Ask an administrator in your local school district or the teacher in your practicum class to identify the kinds of exemplary language arts programs being provided. Secure permission to visit one of these programs and note in your journal how the practices promote learning for all children.

- *Building Cultural Bridges* (1997) by Robinson, Bowing, and Ewing. This book provides teachers with interactive lesson plans aimed at helping adolescents deal with cultural differences and prejudices.

- *From Rage to Hope: Strategies for Reclaiming Black and Hispanic Students* (1997) by Crystal Kuykendall. This book, written by the former Executive Director of the National Alliance of Black School Educators, focuses on the underachievement and social problems experienced by African American and Hispanic youth. There are strategies for working with discipline problems in the classroom and involving parents, among other activities.

- *Achievement for African-American Students: Strategies for the Diverse Classroom* (1997) by Gary Reglin. Providing meaningful classroom instruction with greater sensitivity to the needs and expectations of African American students in grades K–12 is the focus of this book. There are strategies for resolving conflicts in the classroom, involving parents, and improving social interactions.

- *Teaching in the Diverse Classroom: Learner-Centered Activities That Work* (1997) by Tonya Huber. The focus of this book is on 29 quality learning experiences aimed at teaching specific content areas, such as reading, writing, and science, in multicultural classrooms. Teachers and students alike learn to appreciate racial, ethnic, and cultural diversity while learning the basic subjects.

- *Effective Strategies for Teaching Minority Students* (1997) by Howard Hill. This book provides teachers with the theory and ethnic history background they will need to work successfully with minority students. The focus is on connecting theory to practice while motivating students to achieve in the classroom.

Meeting Special Needs: Cultural Factors in the Classroom

The societal changes of the 1990s are reflected to a great extent in the public schools. Schools have generally been assumed to transmit societal norms and values. While education helped assimilate the immigrants of the late 1800s and early 1900s, societal needs have taken a sharp turn away from the melting-pot mentality of that period.

Sometime in the early 1970s, educators began to realize the importance of ethnicity and the need to teach their students how to understand and accept cultural differences (Banks, 1979). For a variety of reasons, emphasis began to be placed on the strength of diversity. Evidence of such changes can be found in school-reform policies and teacher-effectiveness literature. Concern has been shown for

> particular needs of children who are poor, who are a minority, who live in the big cities, and who, if educational policies continue to be developed in the future in the same manner as they have in the past, are likely to end up labeled as educational failures. (Valdes, 1990, p. 31)

Questions are being raised about what kind of schools this country should have and what activities are most productive for teachers and students.

CLASSROOM CLIMATE AND CULTURE

At the beginning of this century, the majority of students in American schools were from Western European countries; thus the Anglo-Americans were the macroculture. As the century ends, the Anglo-American population in many schools is now the minority; however, the majority of American teachers are Anglo-Americans. All teachers must strive to understand and accept the cultures of their students. Students from various cultures must not feel that their behavior is wrong, strange, or unacceptable. They deserve an environment that respects their individual culture and helps them adapt to the dominant cultural patterns (Irujo, 1989). The chart found in Figure 11.1 is not intended to stereotype any culture but rather to give teachers insight into behaviors seen in the classroom that are often misinterpreted.

The broad titles given to each of the five "macro" cultures represent people from many different countries/cultures. For example, the term *Anglo-Americans* is used to represent people who come from or descend from many Western European countries, each of which holds its own cultural beliefs. The term *Hispanic-American* is applied to individuals immigrated or descended from many different countries; for example, Spain, Puerto Rico, Cuba, Mexico. Natives and descendants of each one of these countries may hold differing beliefs and customs. The term *Asian-Americans* is used to refer to individuals from or descended from such countries as Japan, Korea, China, Vietnam, Pacific Islands and Taiwan. The cultures of each of these countries is unique; their languages are also very diverse, and within the languages various dialects exist. The term *African-American* is used to refer to individuals from or descended from countries on the African continent. Finally, the term *Native Americans* is used to describe peoples from hundreds of individual tribes, and each tribe has very different customs. Therefore, it is important that a teacher see and recognize students as individuals and not assume that all students grouped within one of these "macro" cultures will act the same.

Figure 11.1 *A broad overview of cultural beliefs.*

ATTRIBUTES, CULTURES	FAMILY	VALUES	WORK ETHIC	RELIGION	COMMUNICATION	EDUCATION
Anglo-American	Extended family unlikely to live in same house Future lies with children. Children's activities dominate family's life.	Success may be measured by status in community, workplace, and number of possessions. Being competitive; looking out for self. Being sophisticated (connoisseur of many things) reflects success.	Work hard to keep climbing. "Hitch wagon to a star!"	Religious practices are individualistic.	It is important to look opponent in the eye and persuade, convince, and proselytize. When speaking, one does not invade personal space.	Learning takes place in schools. Advanced degrees are key to success. Teacher is not always right.
Native American	Elders are highly respected and honored. Children are discouraged from questioning elders. Extended families often live together as one.	Worldly possessions hold little meaning. Live for the moment. Share everything with everyone. Accept others as they are.	Work only for what you need. Manual work is sacred.	Everything belongs to Mother Earth. Mother Earth surrounds its Spirits. Dance is a part of religious ceremonies.	Take pride in native tongue; it is passed on orally. To look elders in eye is considered disrespectful.	Learning comes from studying the past.
Asian-American	Male tends to be head of household and make decisions. Parents may arrange marriages. Children often take care of older parents; they live together.	Position is very important and honored. Harmony is important and honored. Humility is important; compliments are difficult to accept. Kindness is highly regarded. One does not question anyone in high position.	High positions are desired. Wisdom is more important than work.	Many are Buddhist, who believe that spirits of dead ancestors rest on one's head; therefore, it is disrespectful to put hands on their heads.	Formal names are used unless you are close friends. Each culture has its own language, with many dialects. It is disrespectful to look someone with position in the eye. Greetings range from bowing to handshakes.	It is important. Teachers have position and are respected. Students tend not to question teachers. They are more comfortable with lectures than small groups. Work to please teacher. Like to work independently. Poor grades bring disgrace to family.

(continued)

Figure 11.1 *Continued.*

ATTRIBUTES, CULTURES	FAMILY	VALUES	WORK ETHIC	RELIGION	COMMUNICATION	EDUCATION
Hispanic-American	Male tends to be dominant. Children tend to respect parents' wishes. Children may work to support family. Extended family may live together.	Playing, enjoyment, and relationships are important. Sharing and cooperation are important, creating interdependency. One derives self-identity by the company one keeps. Believe in social hierarchy. Live for the present; enjoy now!	Work to share with family. Money is used for social purposes. Enjoy working together.	Catholicism is dominant.	Tend to be polychronic: They can do many things at one time. Tend to stand very close when speaking to one another. Touching is a part of interaction. A smile replaces many words (e.g., hello, please, thank you). When being disciplined, children are taught to lower their eyes.	Working to support family comes before education.
African American	Head of house is major breadwinner. Children are the future.	Clothes tend to be a powerful statement of identity. Time is approximate. Prefer people over objects.	Employment affords respect, whatever the job.	Practice many religions. Church tends to be center of social life for many.	Nonverbal communication is very effective. May use home language even though they understand Standard English.	May seek aid from other students before asking teacher. For the majority, education is very important.

*These observations are intended to provide a broad overview of beliefs that may hold significance to people of various cultures. Of course beliefs and values differ tremendously among individuals of any culture.

Source: Information for Anglo-Americans is based on Irujo (1989), Van Anderson (nondated), and Spigner-Littles (1992). Information for Native Americans is based on Irujo (1989). Information for Asian-Americans is based on Van Anderson (nondated). Information for Hispanic-Americans is based on Irujo (1989). Information for African-Americans is based on Spigner-Littles (1992).

LEARNING STYLES OF THE FIVE MACROCULTURES

The following list contains generalizations of the various learning preferences of the five major cultures in American schools. It is important to remember that teachers are responsible for helping each individual student and must attempt to understand the learning preference of each student. The list is given so that teachers have some insight concerning various learning preferences (Anderson, 1995).

A child miseducated is a child lost.

JOHN F. KENNEDY

NATIVE AMERICAN

Tend to:

- be visual learners
- remember through visual images instead of words
- be global learners—focus on whole rather than on parts

AFRICAN AMERICAN

Tend to:

- be global learners—focus on whole rather than parts
- prefer inferential reasoning to deductive or inductive reasoning
- approximate rather than exact
- be proficient in nonverbal communication; prefers an animated teacher

ASIAN-AMERICAN

Tend to:

- prefer quiet, well-structured class
- set well-defined goals
- prefer constant reinforcement from teacher
- refrain from expressing personal opinions
- enjoy rote memorization
- do less well with creative or analytical writing
- not questions teacher
- work to please teacher

HISPANIC-AMERICAN

Tend to:

- work best in cooperative learning groups
- desire to keep native language
- like close contact with and individualized attention from teacher
- avoid looking teacher in the eye if reprimanded
- be global learners
- benefit from well-defined goals

ANGLO-AMERICAN

Tend to:

- prefer independent activities because of competitive spirit
- uses deductive and inductive reasoning
- enjoy expressing own opinions or ideas
- be either global or analytical learners

BEYOND THE CLASSROOM

Interview several general education teachers. Ask them how they make a new child feel welcome. Then ask them what—if any—differences occur when they are trying to make a student with a disability or a child from a minority culture feel welcome. Reflect upon their answers, and determine what you would do through language arts to achieve a sense of welcome for a student with a disability or from a minority culture.

IN & BEYOND THE CLASSROOM

Visit a classroom in which the teacher has a reputation for providing a strong, positive classroom climate. Ask to observe or volunteer to participate in activities. Observe the dynamics of the classroom; try to identify three activities that show the children that they belong to a supportive classroom. An alternative activity is to select a section of interest from *The Whole Language Catalog* (Goodman, Bird, & Goodman, 1991) and identify characteristics of the whole language approach associated with developing a positive classroom climate.

THE CURRICULUM AND CULTURALLY DIVERSE CHILDREN

Educators have long been challenged to design curriculum models that facilitate self-actualization of students. Focus must be on the student as an individual who brings a wide variety of traditions and knowledge to the subject matter. With the myriad of cultures in our schools, this advice must be taken seriously, with emphasis placed on the student as a person.

One of the simplest and most easily modifiable content areas to lend focus to the student as an individual is language arts. Novels such as *Farewell to Manzanar* by Houston and Houston, *House Made of Dawn* by Momaday, and *Bless Me Ultima* by Anaya draw students into the cultures of Japanese-Americans, Native Americans, and Mexican-Americans. Poems such as "I Am Joaquim" by Gonzales and *Mother to Child* by Langston Hughes all expand students' sense of oneness. Holidays and celebrations such as Tet, a Vietnamese festival, can set the stage for discussing birthday customs (Vietnamese people consider Tet everyone's birthday because on Tet everyone is one year older). Reading, writing about, and discussing such books, plays, poems, and other significant events are a natural way to mirror the plurality of today's culture. See Figure 11.2 for more books on cultural diversity.

Figure 11.2

Children's literature that reflects a variety of cultures.

AFRICAN AMERICAN

Adedjouma, D. (ed.). (1996). *The Palm of My Heart: Poetry by African American Children.* Illustrated by G. Christie. New York: Lee & Low.

Angelou, M. (1996). *Kofi and His Magic.* Photos by M. Courtney-Clark. New York: Crown.

Belton, S. (1994). *May'naise Sandwiches and Sunshine Tea.* Illustrated by G. G. Carter. New York: Four Winds.

Bloom, V. (1997). *Fruits: A Caribbean Counting Poem.* Illustrated by D. Axtell. New York: Holt.

Cooper, F. (1994). *Coming Home: From the Life of Langston Hughes.* New York: Philomel.

Curtis, C. P. (1995). *The Watsons Go to Birmingham—1963.* New York: Delacorte Press.

Fenner, C. (1995). *Yolonda's Genius.* New York: Simon & Schuster.

Highwater, J. (1985). *Eyes of Darkness.* New York: Lothrop, Lee & Shepherd Books.

McKissack, P., & McKissack, F. (1992). *Sojourner Truth: Ain't I a Woman?* New York: Scholastic.

Mitchell, R. (1997). *The Talking Cloth.* New York: Orchard Books.

Mohr, N. (1988). *Going Home.* New York: Bantam.

Moodie, F. (1997). *Nabulela: A South African Folk Tale.* New York: Farrar Straus & Giroux.

(continued)

Figure 11.2

Continued.

Myers, W. D. (1997). *Harlem.* Illustrated by C. Myers. New York: Scholastic.

Paulsen, G. (1993). *Nightjohn.* New York: Laurel-Leaf.

Polacco, P. (1994). *Pink and Say.* New York: Philomel.

Schroeder, A. (1996). *Minty: A Story of Harriet Tubman.* Illustrated by J. Pinkney. New York: Doubleday.

Taylor, M. (1990). *Mississippi Bridge.* New York: Dial.

ASIAN-AMERICAN

Brown, T. (1995). *Konnichiwa! I Am a Japanese-American Girl.* New York: Holt.

Chin-Lee, C. (1997). *A Is for Asia.* Illustrated by Y. Heo. New York: Orchard.

Demi. (1997). *One Grain of Rice: A Mathematical Folktale.* New York: Scholastic.

Garland, S. (1992). *Song of the Buffalo Boy.* New York: Harcourt Brace Publishers.

Hamanaka, S. (1995). *Bebop-a-Do-Walk!* New York: Simon & Schuster

Ho, M. (1996). *Hush! A Thai Lullaby.* Illustrated by H. Meade. New York: Orchard.

Jiang, J. L. (1997). *Red Scarf Girl: A Memoir of the Cultural Revolution.* New York: HarperCollins.

Lee, M. (1997). *Nim and the War Effort.* Illustrated by Yangsook Choi. New York: Frances Foster Books/Farrar Straus & Giroux.

Rattigan, J. K. (1996). *The Woman in the Moon: A Story from Hawaii.* Illustrated by C. Golembe. Boston: Little Brown.

Salisbury, G. (1994). *Under the Blood-red Sun.* New York: Delacorte.

Uchida, Y. (1978). *Journey Home.* New York: Athenean.

Uchida, Y. (1996). *Jar of Dreams.* Boston: Houghton Mifflin.

Wells, R. (1996). *The Farmer and the Poor God.* Illustrated by Yoshi. New York: Simon & Schuster.

Yep, L. (1994). *Dragon's Gate.* New York: HarperCollins.

Yep, L. (1997). *The Case of the Goblin Pearls.* New York: HarperCollins.

Yep, L. (1997). *The Khan's Daughter: A Mongolian Folktale.* Illustrated by J. Tseng and M. Tseng. New York: HarperCollins.

HISPANIC-AMERICAN

Ada, A. (1997). *Gathering the Sun: An Alphabet in Spanish and English.* Illustrated by S. Silva. New York: Lothrop, Lee & Shepherd.

Bunting, E. (1996). *Going Home.* Illustrated by D. David. New York: Harper-Collins.

Dorros, A. (1995). *Isle.* Illustrated by E. Klevev. New York: Dutton.

Eversole, R. (1995). *The Flute Player/La Flautisa.* Illustrated by G. B. Karas. New York: Orchard.

Gershator, D., & Gershator, P. (1995). *Bread Is for Eating.* Illustrated by E. Shaw-Smith. Austin, TX: Holt.

Herrera, J. F. (1995). *Calling the Doves/El canto de los Palomas.* Illustrated by E. Simmons. New York: Children's Book Press.

(continued)

Figure 11.2

Continued.

Kleven, E. (1996). *Hooray, a Pinata!* New York: Dutton.

Lomas, G., & Carman, C. (1990). *Family Pictures: Cuadros de Familia.* San Francisco: Children's Book Press.

Lopez, L. (1997). *The Birthday Swap.* New York: Lee & Low Books.

Mohr, N. (1986). *Going Home.* New York: Bantam.

Presilla, M. E., & Soto, G. (1996). *Life Around the Lake: Embroideries by the Women of Lake Patzcuaro.* New York: Henry Holt.

Reiser, L. (1998). *Tortillas and Lullabies.* Illustrated by C. Valientes. New York: Greenwillow.

Soto, G. (1997). *Snapshots from the Wedding.* Illustrated by S. Garcia. New York: Putnam.

Van Laan, N. (1996). *La Boda: A Mexican Wedding Celebration.* Illustrated by A. Arroyo. Boston: Little, Brown & Company.

NATIVE AMERICAN

Ancona, G. (1995). *Earth Daughter: Alicia of Acoma Pueblo.* New York: Simon & Schuster.

Bruchac, J. (1993). *The First Strawberries: A Cherokee Story.* Illustrated by A. Vojtech. New York: Dial.

Bunting, E. (1995). *Cheyenne Again.* Illustrated by I. Toddy. New York: Clarion.

Duncan, L. (1996). *The Magic of Spider Woman.* Illustrated by S. Begay. New York: Scholastic.

Heinz, B. (1996). *Kayuktuk: An Arctic Quest.* Illustrated by J. Van Zyle. San Francisco: Chronicle Books.

Highwater, J. (1985). *Eyes of Darkness.* New York: Lothrop, Lee & Shepherd.

Hulpach, V. (1996). *Ahaiyute and Cloud Eater.* Illustrated by M. Zawadzki. Translated by P. Hejl. San Diego: Harcourt Brace.

Keams, G. (1995). *Grandmother Spider Brings the Sun: A Cherokee Story.* Illustrated by J. Barnardin. Flagstaff, AZ: Northland.

Nex, R. T. (1995). *Forbidden Talent.* Flagstaff, AZ: Northland.

Roessel, M. (1995). *Songs from the Loom: A Navajo Girl Learns to Weave.* Minneapolis: Lerner.

Watkins, S. (1997). *White Bead Ceremony: Mary Greyfeather Gets Her Native American Name.* Tulsa, OK: Council Oak Books.

Wood, T., & Wanbi Numpa Afraid of Hawk. (1992). *A Boy Becomes a Man at Wounded Knee.* New York: Walker.

We must see that every child has equal opportunity, not to become equal, but to become different—to realize the unique potential he or she possesses.

JOHN FISCHER

Language arts programs should be extended to include the experiences of many different ethnic groups. Such groups include Greek-Americans, Italian-Americans, and Anglo-Saxon Protestants as well as Native Americans, African Americans, and Hispanic-Americans. A comparative approach to cultural diversity through language arts activities allows students to enjoy the challenges, joys, and humanity shared by one people of the world while diminishing ethnocentric bias or stereotyping. (Refer back to the literature bibliographies in Chapter 10 for some ideas on books to use.)

By utilizing language arts materials and activities that represent the cultures of children in the classroom, the teacher demonstrates the value of diversity as well as the value of individuals in the room. Presentation of language arts materials based on ethnic diversity enhances students' beliefs that they are recognized, esteemed, and valued as part of a network of shared communication and commitment by peers and teachers.

Children with Language Differences

As discussed in Chapter 4, language acquisition is a normal and exciting developmental process in all children. Children are surrounded by language and interact with the language—or languages—of their environment. They naturally gain facility in talking, gesturing, intonation, listening, singing, and all other forms of social communication.

No precise timeline or specific sequence of skills is appropriate for describing language development in all children (Peregoy & Boyle, 1997). Children proceed at their own rates through a process that in many ways remains a mystery. However, they do appear to follow a general developmental sequence building from simple to more and more complex use of communication: Sounds, for example, precede words; words precede phrases; and phrases precede sentences. Children of all cultures appear to follow this developmental sequence, beginning with prelinguistic abilities and culminating in mastery of complex language rules.

> **BEYOND THE CLASSROOM**
>
> Visit your local children's library. Make a list of books and tapes that describe how children and teachers help each other to feel like they belong to part of a social group. An alternate activity is to identify three biographies or storybooks that reflect various cultural groups and that can be used in conjunction with particular science, math, and social studies topics.

BLACK ENGLISH VERNACULAR, OR EBONICS

Author Lisa Delpit says, "I can be neither for Ebonics or against Ebonics any more than I can be for or against air. It exists. It is the language spoken by many African American children."

On December 18, 1996, the school board of Oakland, California, adopted a resolution that has come to be known as the *Ebonics Resolution*, which concerns the use by a majority of African American children of their home/community language (often referred to as Black English or Ebonics) in the public school classrooms.

Ebonics is not a new term; it was actually coined in 1973 from two words, ebony and phonics, at a conference on Language and the Urban Child to describe the dialect spoken by many African Americans (Smith, 1997). However, until the Oakland Resolution of 1996, terms such as African American English, Black English Vernacular, Black Language, or simply Black English remained more popular in the media press and literature.

The resolution further stated that teachers in the Oakland school district need to acquire knowledge about the nature and history of Ebonics in order to help their students become more successful in the classroom. This echoed a famous 1979 case involving a group of African American students from the Martin Luther King Jr. Elementary School in Ann Arbor, Michigan. Attorneys for the children argued that the Black English vernacular spoken by these youngsters was so different from standard English as to constitute a separate language. Therefore, they contended that the children should be entitled to separate and special instruction. The judge in the case agreed with this argument and ordered the Ann Arbor teachers to attend special training sessions in dialect awareness (Yellin, 1980). Nearly 20 years later, the teachers of Oakland faced a similar situation.

Issues Related to the Ebonics Controversy

To fully understand the significance of the Oakland Ebonics Resolution for the education of African American children, teachers must be aware of the various issues related to this controversy. The following is just a summary of those issues.

Language or dialect? Is Ebonics a legitimate separate language, or is it a dialect variation of standard English? This question continues to plague the discussion surrounding the use of Ebonics in the classroom. As far back as 1972, the linguist William La Bov argued that Black English was a distinct language because it possessed a systematic, rule-governed grammar and vocabulary that distinguished it from standard English. In 1997, the linguist Wayne O'Neil similarly argued for defining Ebonics as a language, but for social and political reasons in response to the wishes of the majority of the African American population (O'Neil, 1997)—in spite of the fact that newspapers reporting on the Oakland controversy characterized Ebon-

ics as a substandard dialect variation lacking consistent spelling, pronunciation, or rules. Stanford University's John Rickford also takes the position that whether a speech form is described as a separate language or dialect depends more on social and political climate than on linguistic arguments (Rickford, 1997). For example, Norwegian and Swedish share many vocabulary terms yet are considered different languages. But Mandarin and Cantonese are regarded as different dialects of the same language yet are mutually incomprehensible. Rickford concludes that although Ebonics is best described as a dialect, "it is the most distinctive dialect in the U.S. and the one that has gotten the attention of linguists more than any other for the last 30 years" (Rickford, 1997, p. 12).

Issues of power and identity. Underlying the arguments, complexities, and issues surrounding Ebonics is the notion of power and identity. For many African American children, life in America is one of powerlessness, a feeling that they have less and are less than their white peers. The acclaimed novelist James Baldwin, writing in 1979 in response to the Ann Arbor case, put it this way: "It goes without saying, then, that language is also a political instrument, means and proof of power. It is the most crucial key to identity: It reveals the private identity, and connects one with or divorces one from the larger public or communal identity" (Baldwin, 1997, p.16).

Like Baldwin, researcher/writer Lisa Delpit (1997) contends that there is a wealth of information linking children's identity and self-esteem to their local dialect. For example, research among the Pima Indian children of Arizona showed that in grades 1 through 3 the children were approximating the standard English speech of their teachers. One would expect that as they grew older, their standard English proficiency would improve. This was not the case. By grade 4, their language moved more toward the local dialect of the community. That is, these children chose to use their local dialect over the standard form of school talk. By ages 8 and 9, children become aware that they are members of a group; that group identity, in turn, influences their identity of self. Delpit argues that the language form African American children bring to school is an expression of themselves, their family, and their community and must be respected as such by the teachers who teach them.

Some Characteristics of Ebonics (or Black English)

Many aspects of Ebonics, such as vocabulary terms, verb tenses, inflections, and grammatical constructions, differ from standard English and often cause confusion among teachers and other students who may not be familiar with these differences. Phonologically, for example *jump* is pronounced /jum/, *desks* is pronounced /desses/, *they* is pronounced /dey/, *tooth* is pronounced /toof/, *sister* is pronounced /sistuh/, *pig* is pronounced /pick/, and *hundred* is pronounced /hundret/ (Fashold & Shuy, 1970).

Syntactically, Ebonics also differs from standard English in many ways, most prominently in the verb "to be" (Smith, 1997). Examples of grammatical structures in Ebonics include "He be doin' that," "They be tired," or "They tired." Other nonstandard examples commonly used in Ebonics speech include, "That teacher she mean," "That girl she smart," "They done came," or the use of double and triple negatives as in "I ain't never had no trouble wit none of them" (Fashold & Shuy, 1970; Hoover, 1997; Smith, 1997).

Geneva Smitherman, professor of English at Michigan State University and one of the foremost scholars on the characteristics of Ebonics, describes many of these characteristics in her now-classic 1977 book, *Talkin and Testifyin: The Language of Black America.* Smitherman includes, for example, the expression, "The Brotha be lookin good"; Brotha refers to an African American male. "Lookin good" refers to an attractive style but not necessarily physical beauty. The verb tense to be is often misunderstood among non-Ebonics speakers. "He be lookin good" is a continual or habitual state, whereas "He lookin good" refers to the present moment only (Smitherman, 1997).

Smitherman (1997) explains that Ebonics is also much more than phonological differences or grammatical changes. Ebonics also includes a style of speaking that differs from standard English. For example, **signifyin** is a "form of ritualized insult in which a speaker puts down, talks about, needles—signifies on—other speakers" (1997, p. 9). One type of signifyin', called "playin' the dozens," involves linguistic insults at a person's mother or other relatives, as in this exchange between two women about a hairstyle. First woman: "Girl, what up with that head?" Second woman: "Ask yo momma" (i.e., It's none of your business). Another example would be this exchange between two males. First male: "Yo momma wear combat boots and concrete drawhs." Second male: "Yo momma so ugly, she scare the white offuh rice." Signifyin', playin' the dozens, and other humorous retorts reveal a person's language skills in the African American community yet are often viewed negatively by the majority white community. See Figure 11.3 for features of Ebonics.

Figure 11.3

Features of Ebonics.

	STANDARD ENGLISH	EBONICS
Final consonant sounds	send, sent	sen
	six	sic
	asked	asc
	walked	walk
	five cents	five cent
	running, going	runnin, goin
Consonant sounds /l/ and /r/	school	schoo
	teacher	teachuh
	help me	hep me
"Th" sounds as /d/, /v/, or /f/	this, that, these	dis, dat, des
	with	wid
	brother	brovah
	death	deaf
Articles a, an	an apple	a apple
	an egg	a egg
Double negative	I don't have any money.	I ain't got no money.
Tense marker	He is playing over there.	He playing der.
	Pete has four dogs.	Pete have four dog.
	She works every day.	She work every day.
Present tense used for both present and past	he said	he say
	he got	he get
Verb to be	She is busy now.	She be busy now.
	They are busy now.	They be busy now.
Helping verbs	John is coming at 6:00 P.M.	John come at 6:00 P.M.
	Mary has gone away.	Mary gone away.
Pronouns	That's mine.	That mines.
	He did it himself.	He did it hisself.
Subject noun and pronoun	John said that.	John, he say dat.
	Miss Jones always says.	Miz Jones, she alway be saying.

Source: Adapted from J. Lindfors (1987), *Children's Language and Learning* (2nd ed.).

Classroom Implications for Teachers

It was once believed by linguists that television, radio, and movies would have a homogenizing influence on language in the United States (Stevens, 1985). That is, the media should provide to all children, regardless of their background, a common tongue with which to enter the classroom. That has not been the case. In fact, as we approach the twenty-first century, the linguistic and comprehension gap between many minority children and their standard English–speaking teachers has actually widened, with the result that many African American children are struggling without success in our schools (Rickford, 1997).

Classroom teachers cannot ignore the issue of nonstandard speech in their classrooms, nor can they pretend it will take care of itself. To do so only dooms thousands of African American children to years of frustration and failure and ultimately leads to the high dropout rates we currently witness among minority students. Instead, teachers must address the controversies and issues surrounding nonstandard speech with sensitivity and innovative approaches.

Lisa Delpit (1997) has reviewed the research on classroom practices that have been successful with minority students. Here is a summary of some of her suggestions:

- Make the study of language diversity an actual part of the school curriculum. Even young children can discuss the way different television characters or people from different cultures speak.
- Audiotape stories narrated by speakers from different cultures, including stories that contain Ebonics speech such as "Flossie & the Fox" by Patricia McKissack.
- Have your students become "language detectives," where they interview different people, listen to different speech variations on the radio and television, and identify similarities and differences in talking.
- Help your students to create bilingual dictionaries of their own language forms and those of standard English. Teacher and students work together to decide which appropriate translations to include in the dictionaries.
- Many teachers have successfully used role playing and other dramatics activities to get students to switch back and forth from one language form to another. Memorizing dramatic parts in another dialect or in standard English is a good way to practice language skills without fear of constant correction.
- Along with drama, some teachers videotape student presentations and then use them in self-critique class lessons to develop awareness of and improvement in standard English.
- Students use a tape recorder in class during ordinary lessons. Afterwards, upon listening to the tape, students note how often and under what circumstances they switch between Ebonics and standard English.
- Young children can create puppet shows or role plays using cartoon characters to address issues of Ebonics or standard English in the classroom. As with other forms of dramatic play, puppetry allows students to use and deal with various language forms without fear of corrections or negative reactions from the teacher.
- In New York City, some teachers have their students present daily news reports to their classmates modeling their favorite newscaster, such as Tom Brokaw or Dan Rather. Television newscasters are often held up as good examples of standard English speakers because regardless of their sex, age, or race they must communicate clearly with a wide and varying audience.
- Use children's literature to develop students' awareness of dialect and cultural differences among characters. For example, in "Flossie & the Fox" by Patricia McKissack, lessons could include translations of Flossie's speech into standard English identifying the wordplay and humor in the book, role-playing scenes from the book, and writing extensions of the story.
- Use children's books to identify specific contrasting language patterns between standard English and Ebonics. For example, in *Millions of Cats* by Wanda Gag, children will encounter the pattern "hundreds of cats, thousands of cats, millions and billions and trillions of cats." This pattern is repeated throughout the story, providing children with a model for the use of the standard English plural form *s*, which is often omitted in Ebonics. Oral repetitions of the plural *s* pattern can be supplemented with other activities, such as acting out parts of the story, retelling the story into a tape recorder, or retelling the story using puppets (Tompkins & McGee, 1983).

Vignette in the classroom

Carrie Secret teaches fifth grade in Prescott Elementary School in Oakland, California. Prescott was one of the few schools where a majority of the teachers adopted the Standard English Proficiency (SEP) program. This is the statewide initiative that uses systematic instruction in Black English while at the same time has as its goal that children learn standard English.

Mrs. Secret has been at Prescott, a troubled inner school, for 31 years. She has seen teachers come and go, but she herself has elected to remain in this school. As she puts it, "I've never desired to do anything but teach. I have never desired to leave the classroom for any other position. Teaching is my passion."

She is a strong believer in the SEP program, which uses many strategies from second-language learning programs. In SEP, there are three emphases: culture, language, and literacy. "Our program," she states, "is not just a language program that stresses how well you acquire and speak English. We emphasize the learning of reading by incorporating a strong literacy component. Another crucial issue is that we push students to learn the content language of each area of the curriculum."

In explaining her approach to instruction, Mrs. Secret explains, "In fifth grade, I encourage the students to practice English most of the instructional time. I say encourage because required is a word that sends a message that if you don't use English, then you are operating below standard."

Some days Carrie Secret announces to her class, "While you are working, I will be listening to how well you use English. In your groups, you must call for translation if a member of your group uses an Ebonics structure." Other days she tells her children they are attending Spelman or Morehouse College (historically African American colleges) and that they are expected to use the language the professors use, which is standard English.

Carrie Secret also believes in reading aloud to her students regularly, particularly when she taught in the younger grades. She would read to them first thing in the morning, after recess, and again after lunch. She still reads aloud to her fifth-graders and stresses not only reading for information but also for pleasure. She also shares poetry aloud each day and has the whole class singing songs such as "I Believe I Can Fly" and "Step by Step."

Source: Adapted from "An Interview with Carrie Secret," in *The Real Ebonics Debate*, Theodore, AL: Beacon Press, 1997.

ENGLISH AS A SECOND LANGUAGE (ESL)

Background of ESL

"For the rich, learning a second or foreign language has always been valued and expected, whereas for the poor, speaking a language other than English has been seen as a deficit to be remediated, replaced or eradicated" (Nancy Lemberger, 1997).

One of the most interesting and controversial aspects of American education is the proliferation of students who do not speak English or who speak another language in addition to English. Much has been written about this under the headings of Second-Language Acquisition and Bilingual Education. This section is intended to give you an overview of the whole area of bilingual education and make you aware of some of the issues, along with their complexities.

One thing is for certain: The demographics of America since the 1960s have changed and are continuing to change, and these changes are readily seen in the classrooms. In 1987, estimates of the number of new immigrants who came to the United States since 1977 ranged from 6 to 15 million (Bouvier & Agresta, 1987; Haney, 1987). The number of students whose native language is not English increased by 51.3 percent between 1985 and 1991 (Schirmer, Casbon, & Twiss, 1996). Over 2 million of those new immigrants were school-age children. Particularly in America's large urban areas, the minority populations skyrocketed to the point where in many cities the minorities had become the majority (Kellogg, 1988). The English-as-a-second-language (ESL) student population represents 327 different languages (Schirmer, Casbon, & Twiss, 1996). The number of immigrants is expected to increase two and one-half times the rate of English-speaking students between 1995 and 2000 (Clair, 1995). Obviously, linguistic diversity abounds and is an issue that cannot be ignored in schools.

In 1968, the first **Bilingual Education Act,** which provided federal funds to school districts to help them in teaching children whose native language was not English, was passed by Congress. The Bilingual Education Act also provided that the child's native language should be used for instructional purposes in the classroom. In practice, however, the latter provision was ignored; most teachers simply were not qualified to teach their children in Spanish, Chinese, Vietnamese, Cambodian, or whatever other language was spoken. In effect, the act was ignored.

In 1974, the issue of bilingual education again came to the fore with the famous *Lau v. Nichols* Supreme Court decision. Lau was a Chinese-American living in the San Francisco Bay area. His child was enrolled in a public school and was expected to perform in English even though he did not speak English. Many Chinese-American children were in a similar situation. As a result, lawyers for Lau and others brought a class-action suit against the school system, claiming that the bilingual nature of these children was not being respected because their own language was ignored in the schools. In ruling in their favor, the Supreme Court mandated that a truly bilingual education program be provided; the Department of Health, Education, and Welfare was charged with developing guidelines to help the school implement truly bilingual programs. These so-called *Lau* guidelines require that a school meet the linguistic needs of the students, regardless of the languages they speak. Thus, Chinese could and would be used for instructional purposes in the San Francisco school system, and the burden to provide such bilingual instruction fell on the schools. The *Lau* case has since been used to justify the use of Spanish for instruction in many public schools in California, Arizona, Texas, and Florida.

Throughout the period of the 1970s and 1980s, while various approaches and programs were being tried all under the umbrella terms of bilingual education, the stream of immigrants from Mexico, Latin America, and Asia to America became a flood. Making the adjustment from their native language to English often took six to seven years of participation in a bilingual education program. During that time, many of these students dropped out of school. Predictably, a conservative, antibilingual reaction emerged. Its most vocal proponent was California's U.S. Senator and former professor of linguistics, S. I. Hayakawa. In 1981, Senator Hayakawa went so far as to introduce an amendment to the U.S. Constitution to make English the official language of the United States. During the 1980s, this English-only movement gained great momentum. In 1985, Secretary of Education William Bennett declared bilingual education a "failed path" and called for its dismemberment in favor of English-only curriculums in America's public schools. Bilingual education as we had known it since 1974 was under attack from all sides.

In June 1998, voters in the state of California passed **Proposition 227,** called the English for the Children initiative, which for all practical purposes ended bilingual education in the California public schools (Beck, 1998). It provided that after one year of intensive English instruction, all of California's non-English–speaking students would be mainstreamed into regular English instruction classes. Almost immediately a new storm arose. School districts with a majority of non-English–speaking students served by the current bilingual programs said they would not stop teaching just because of the proposition. Clearly the issue of bilingual education is just as much a political issue as an educational issue.

California's Proposition 227 attacking bilingual education as a whole has been roundly criticized by many professional educators and their representative organizations. For example, in 1998 the National Council of Teachers of English issued its National Research Council (NRC) report in which they came out strongly in favor of bilingual education programs (Kaufman, 1998). Furthermore, the report recommended that children who speak a language other than English and who are in schools where there are appropriate materials and fluent teachers be taught to read in their native language while they are acquiring proficiency in spoken English. This is the position of the NRC and the learned research communities; this refutes the direction in which California and other states are going.

Second Language Acquisition

It is easy to recognize the incredible difficulties that bilingual programs present to the individual elementary classroom teacher who might be expected to provide instruction in math, science, and social studies to her students who speak three, four, or as many as half a dozen different languages. In response to this need, the entire field of second-language acquisition research took on a new urgency. Leading the way was the work of Stephen Krashen.

Krashen's (1981, 1982, 1985) model of second-language acquisition provides the theoretical foundation for understanding the many approaches to bilingual education; at the same time, it raises questions about many of the negative practices associated with bilingual education programs in America. First, Krashen distinguishes between language learning and language acquisition. Learning another language is associated with school; it involves memorizing new vocabulary terms, studying grammar rules, and translating passages from one language to another. But as Constance Weaver (1996) points out, knowing about a language is not the same as knowing a language. The latter is more of a subconscious process that enables one to function in a given environment.

To better understand this notion, let's break Krashen's theory down into its components. First, to know language requires what Krashen calls *comprehensible input,* or the ability to understand the general language patterns of what is heard or read and to attach meaning to form in a language environment. Second is Krashen's notion of the *low affective filter,* which refers to the learner's openness to learning as well as a willingness to take risks and make mistakes. Finally, the *monitor hypothesis* is the way in which learners edit or correct their use of the new language based on their conscious understanding of the rules of that language. In sum, Krashen believes that knowing a language begins with indirect, unconscious experiences and later precedes to direct instruction. Elley's (1991) review of nine major studies of second-language acquisition supported Krashen's belief in indirect instruction in which children were exposed to the English language through oral experiences and high-interest storybooks.

There are two levels of language proficiency. **Basic interpersonal communication (BIC)** is the ability to orally communicate with native speakers at a comfortable level on most topics. It takes the average second-language learner two years to obtain BIC. The second level is **cognitive academic language proficiency (CALP);** this is the ability to read and write academic materials that native speakers of the same chronological age can do. It takes the average second-language learner five to seven years to obtain CALP (Cummins, 1989; Peregoy & Boyle, 1997). At any given time in any given classroom, a teacher may encounter a number of factors that will influence the teaching environment: multiple languages, various levels of literacy, varying background experiences, and various levels of self-esteem (Chamot & O'Malley, 1994).

Following Krashen's work and that of others in the field of second-language acquisition, a number of different program models emerged in the schools. Three main types that emerged were based on three educational theories—behaviorist, innatist, and interactionist (Peregoy & Boyle, 1997).

Programs based on the Behaviorist Theory are **pull-out programs,** in which students leave their regular classroom and go to another room where a specialist works with them for a certain amount of time each day. These programs emphasize repetition of simplified phrases; designers of these programs believe a controlled, simplified vocabulary is the quickest way for the student to acquire English. In these programs, students study English for part of the day until they are proficient in English and can function in the regular classroom for all subjects. These programs have declined somewhat in popularity both because of cost and because research indicates that students learn English best through social interaction with other English-speaking students, not by simplifying some aspect of the language (Goodman & Freeman, 1993).

Programs based on the Innatist Theory use **total submersion programs,** based on the belief that language is naturally learned when it is heard and used (Chamot & O'Malley, 1994; Edelsky, Altwerger, & Flores, 1991). In a total immersion program, students spend the entire day in the regular classroom because proponents believe the quickest way for the student to learn English is in a regular classroom, learning alongside other students their age. An example would be in some places in Canada where students learn French and English (Cummins, 1989).

The third type of program, based on the Interactionist Theory, states that language is acquired through **nature and nurture.** These programs, which have various names, emphasize the importance of comprehensible input (Krashen, 1989) and social interaction (Vygotsky, 1962). If only one language other than English is being spoken in the classroom, it is possible to find a bilingual teacher or a bilingual paraprofessional. In such cases, the teacher explains the concept in English, checks for understanding in English, and then repeats the concept in the other language. The English-speaking students also benefit from this type of teaching because they learn another language.

Today's ESL Programs

Today the goals for most bilingual educational programs are to provide ESL students access to the core curriculum and to give them the opportunity to become proficient in English while maintaining a high self-esteem (Altwerger & Ivener, 1994). According to Peregoy and Boyle (1997), the best learning environment (1) permits ESL students to use their first language while learning or expressing themselves when necessary; (2) prepares ESL students to learn content in English; (3) provides ESL students comprehensible but challenging materials, tailored to the individual; and (4) provides ESL students with many literacy opportunities.

Code Switching

Code switching is a linguistic expression that often occurs with ESL students. **Code switching** is typically defined as the alternate use of two or more languages in the same word, phrase, clause, sentence, or conversation. The following are examples of code switching between Spanish and English (Valdes-Fallis, 1978):

- La consulta era eight dollars. (The office visit was eight dollars.)
- Well, I keep starting some. Como por un mes todos los dias escribo y ya dejo. Last week empece otra vez. (Well, I keep starting some. For about a month I write every day and then I stop. Last week I started again.)

Code switching occurs in both fluent and emerging bilinguals. It seems to be learned at a very early age, and it can be used to clarify meaning or attract or retain attention. Code switching is grammatically and functionally derived from standard language principles (McClure, 1977). In all respects, code switching is deliberate and linguistically appropriate.

Sometimes teachers and other adults have negative attitudes toward code switching. They tend to classify code switching as a "grammarless mixture of two languages, a jargon or gibberish that is an insult to the monolingual's own rule-governed language" (Grosjean, 1982, p. 146). Pejorative terms used to describe code switching include *Tex-Mex* and *Spanglish* for a mixture of Spanish and English and *Franglais* for a combination of French and English. Even the term *limited english proficient* (LEP) has negative connotations. The mistaken belief behind these terms is that children employing code switching really speak neither of the languages.

The false notion that code switching is a sign of an alingual or nonlingual speaker must be replaced with accurate information. Negative biases can influence how a teacher responds to a child: If a teacher views code switching as a sign of low intelligence, she or he might treat children who code-switch as unlikely to achieve in school. Negative biases can lower the teacher's expectations of success for such children and result in de facto segregation within the classroom if such students are automatically placed in lower reading groups.

Once a teacher understands that code switching represents a combination of the linguistic rules of both languages, a more accurate assessment of the child's language arts needs can be made. Alfonso is no longer viewed as an unskilled language learner but as a child learning to handle two disparate linguistic systems—an intellectual challenge that his monolingual teachers

---

IN & BEYOND THE CLASSROOM

Many school systems have developed both bilingual and English as a second language (ESL) programs. Ask the teachers in these classes to define bilingual and ESL programs for you. Visit each of these programs and observe how language arts instruction is conducted. Reflect on how the techniques you observed could be applied in the general classroom. If it is not possible for you to visit such rooms, read the article "Learning About Language Learning" (Piper, 1986) and compare the information found in this article with the information you've read in this chapter.

have not met. Developmental literature suggests that while Alfonso is acquiring two languages, one of the languages may surge ahead or lag behind the other, or both may develop simultaneously (Garcia, 1983). Instead of being somehow inferior in language skills, young Alfonso is teeming with language learning—perhaps to a greater extent than any of his monolingual peers.

Language Arts Instruction for ESL Students

So what kind of language arts instruction should students such as Alfonso receive while they are becoming fluent bilinguals? In general, the instruction should be the same as for fluent bilinguals: language arts concepts, information, and skills taught in the language of greater linguistic comfort. While many classroom teachers are not bilingual, language arts instruction for emergent bilinguals can easily incorporate the cultural heritage associated with the native language and focus on development of self-esteem.

A balanced language arts program includes a melding of both whole language and direct instruction practices. For children who are learning English as a second language, Gersten and Dimino (1990) have said, "the rate at which they learn is directly dependent on how clear our explanations and examples are, how careful our instructions are, how much practice we provide, and the wording of the feedback provided to students" (p. 24).

To provide this approach, classroom teachers use a number of strategies. Inquiry-based instruction permits students to study concepts that interest them by viewing videos if they cannot read, and later reading books that are at their reading level. Inquiry-based instruction results in small-group learning or buddy learning, which is less threatening to these students. Second, the teacher modifies the lesson so the ESL student will feel successful. Third, the teacher encourages and permits ESL students to use their native language in speech and writing when they cannot find the appropriate English term. At first, the student may only be able to draw his or her understanding of the concept. Fourth, the teacher respects their culture by learning something about it and sharing the information with the class. Finally, the teacher provides time for cooperative learning groups and socialization (Peregoy & Boyle, 1997; Schirmer, Cashon, & Twiss, 1996).

Peregoy and Boyle (1997) suggest that a teacher, while giving instruction, should remember the 11 following points:

1. Don't shout! They're not deaf; they just do not understand English.
2. Speak at a somewhat slower rate, but keep it natural.
3. Speak clearly.
4. Avoid figures of speech and idioms.
5. Repeat key phrases or vocabulary.
6. Use descriptive language.
7. Use many visuals—pictures, charts, videos, manipulatives.
8. Use gestures, but be conscious of gestures that offend some cultures.
9. Teach phrases or sentences instead of isolated words.
10. Relate a new concept to some concept they already know.
11. Give models or examples of how to complete the assignment.

> ### IN & BEYOND THE CLASSROOM
>
> Identify a child with a learning disability, a communication disorder, or a mental disability who is mainstreamed for all or part of the day in a class in your practicum school. Discuss the child's individual education plan (IEP) as related to language arts instruction with the special education teacher. Discuss how the language arts objectives are being achieved both in the special setting and in the general education classroom.

There are other factors that accelerate second-language learning: (1) The teacher makes reading, writing, and speaking applicable to daily living (Chamot & O'Malley, 1994); (2) the teacher celebrates approximations and progress (Altwerger & Ivener, 1994); (3) the parents become involved in the student's education (Peregoy & Boyle, 1997); (4) the holistic approach is used (Goodman & Freeman, 1993); and (5) portfolios are used to reflect the student's progress because it is encouraging for them to see their growth (Garcia, 1994).

Here are 13 specific practices that teachers can use for second-language learners:

1. Use LEA (an activity that has the student dictate to the teacher as the teacher writes exactly what the student says), which permits students to see the words that they can speak in print; it also helps them become aware of the letter/sound relationships (Chamot & O'Malley, 1994). (See Chapter 9 for further discussion of LEA.)

2. Expose the students to print even if they are not proficient speakers (Chamot & O'Malley, 1994; Goodman & Freeman, 1993).

3. Read to the students as you point to the text so they can follow along; they also get to hear the new language (Peregoy & Boyle, 1997).

4. Use the writing process approach when writing because it has manageable parts (Farnan, Flood, & Lapp, 1994; Peregoy & Boyle, 1997).

5. Permit students to keep learning logs in their native language as long as necessary (Peregoy & Boyle, 1997).

6. Use small-group discussions so students can try out the language in a nonthreatening setting (Chamot & O'Malley, 1994).

7. Permit the student to work with a partner (Peregoy & Boyle, 1997).

8. Use dialogue journals with the teacher (Farnan, Flood, & Lapp, 1994).

9. Be sure the students are doing academic work and not busy work such as coloring pictures from a coloring book (Peregoy & Boyle, 1997).

10. Emphasize comprehension over pronunciation (Chamot & O'Malley, 1994).

Vignette *in the classroom*

The students in Mr. Decker's class are planting seeds and later will write about the experience in their journals. The teacher is having a conversation with Sergio, an emergent bilingual English–Spanish speaker. The teacher is a monolingual English speaker.

Sergio asks, "Teacher, where is my *semilla*?"

The teacher holds up a seed and says, "Are you asking for your seed?"

"Yes, my seed. I'm going to *plantarla*."

In order to facilitate Sergio's ability to use words in context, the teacher picks up a seed and a cup, and as he hands them to Sergio, he says, "Sergio, here is your seed. You also need dirt and a cup."

Sergio plants his seed in the cup and then goes back to his teacher and says, "Teacher, I'm done. Where's *mi diario*?" Mr. Decker responds, "I don't understand. What is a *diario*?"

Sergio points to another student's journal and says, "This." The teacher replies, "Oh, OK, I see. *Diario* means 'journal.' Thanks for teaching me a new word. Your journal is on the counter."

Sergio collects his journal, returns to his work space, and happily begins to write about planting seeds. His teacher assists other students in the class. Both Sergio and his teacher have enjoyed another positive language learning experience together.

11. Use books with a wide range of reading levels as well as multiple books on one topic (Farnan, Flood, & Lapp, 1994).
12. Connect prior knowledge to new content (Farnan, Flood, & Lapp, 1994; Goodman & Freeman, 1993).
13. Use books that are linked to students' culture (Allen, 1994).

Using literature in combination with systematic instruction and feedback is clearly an important means of unifying reading, writing, speaking, and listening. Books of children's literature not only enhance children's self-esteem but can also provide excellent models of the English language. Take, for example, the book *The Very Hungry Caterpillar* by Eric Carle. Through this story, children are exposed not only to a beautifully illustrated and interesting account of a caterpillar's metamorphosis but also to number, time, and color concepts. For students learning English as a second language, it provides an excellent example of what the English language looks and sounds like—an example that can aid them in their own reading, writing, and speaking.

Children with Disabilities

Today any teacher at any one time may have students who may be learning-disabled, low-achievers, emotionally disturbed, mentally retarded, hearing impaired, visually impaired, have attention deficit hyperactivity disorder, some level of autism, or a speech impairment or any other speech problems. For each special need, the teacher is required by law to have an individualized educational plan (discussed below) if the parent consents that his or her child receive special education.

In this chapter, only some of the special needs are addressed. It is important to remember that when these children are in your classroom, you are their teacher, not just their babysitter. It is important that they be given learning experiences that fit their needs and abilities.

LEGISLATION AND INDIVIDUALS WITH DISABILITIES

In 1975, Congress passed the *Education of All Handicapped Children Act*, also called **PL 94-142,** which required that "a free and appropriate education and related services be provided in the least restrictive environment" and that an **individualized educational plan (IEP)** be written for each qualifying student. Since 1975, the law has been amended several times.

IN & BEYOND THE CLASSROOM

There is much disagreement among researchers, educators, and parents whether full inclusion is appropriate for all disabled students and for the nondisabled students. You may want to take some time and reflect on the pros and cons of full inclusion. We recommend that you visit some classroom teachers who have full inclusion in their rooms and ask if you may observe the classroom. While you are there, focus on the interaction between the children with special needs and the other students. Are all students actively engaged in appropriate activities? Are some students shy around students with special needs? Ask the teacher if you may also see the IEP form that the school uses.

In 1983, the amendments emphasized that schools provide transitional services for secondary students and that schools provide parents some training in helping their child. In 1986, amendments were passed to extend appropriate education for ages three to five and to provide early intervention programs for children two years old and younger. In 1990, Congress renamed the act *Individuals with Disabilities Education Act.* This change also gave children with autism and traumatic brain injury the special services they needed, such as therapeutic recreation, assistive technology, and necessary counseling. In 1994, Congress recommended that children with special needs be included in the regular classroom.

BEYOND THE CLASSROOM

Arrange to observe a general education classroom in your practicum school in which a child with a sensory or physical impairment is mainstreamed for all or part of the day. Observe the child and how the environment has been modified to assist that student in learning language arts material. Discuss your observations with the child's special and general education teacher. An alternate activity is to describe a real or hypothetical child with a physical or health impairment receiving language arts instruction in the general education classroom. Using a minimum of three current journals as your knowledge base, describe the kinds of modifications you would make for this student. See Figure 11.4 for a list of special education journals.

Figure 11.4

Special education journals.

- *Behavioral Disorders: Journal of the Council for Children with Behavioral Disorders*
- *Exceptional Children*
- *Journal of Learning Disabilities*
- *Remedial and Special Education*
- *Teacher Education and Special Education*
- *Teaching Exceptional Children*

ATTENTION DEFICIT HYPERACTIVITY DISORDER (ADHD)

Many teachers believe that all students in their class have ADHD because of all the wiggles, movement, and calling out. However, wiggles and the true symptoms of ADHD are quite different. Johnson (1992) compiled the following list of symptoms that the classroom teacher may observe in the child with ADHD. She cautions against two incorrect conclusions—a child does not have to demonstrate all the symptoms in order to have ADHD and a child with two or three of the symptoms does not necessarily have ADHD. **Attention deficit hyperactivity disorder (ADHD)** is manifested in these ways:

- *Disorganization.* These children often have messy desks, papers, and backpacks.
- *Impulsive reading.* They often make quick guesses. They do not stop to think whether a letter has a line or a hump, and they often do not read past the first or second letter.
- *Impulsive writing.* Their papers are often messy because of writing over letters to make corrections or because they erase so hard that the paper tears. Often they do not stay on the line and crowd their words when they get to the end of the line.
- *Math difficulty.* They often copy inaccurately and will quickly do the math problem without checking to see if the sign indicates addition, subtraction, multiplication, or division.
- *Undetailed drawings.* Drawings are usually done quickly with stick figures and no details. The coloring is usually messy and outside the lines.
- *Impatient with classroom pace.* The pace of the classroom is usually too slow for them; therefore, they talk out of turn about topics that are not being discussed. They cannot stay on task for a long period of time. They are very restless and constantly move around the room, bothering other children. Waiting in line is a difficult task for them.
- *Touching troubles.* They often touch classmates' hair, clothes, and other belongings. They are quick to accidentally hit others.
- *Frequent outbursts.* Because these children feel out of control, they often are bossy and not liked by their peers. This results in low self-esteem.

There are some practical tips for classroom teachers to use with students who have ADHD. Shima and Gsovski (1996) suggest these four:

1. Whether in small groups or with individual work, use creative hands-on activities.
2. Give directions in small pieces and restate them often.
3. Help the student organize and monitor his or her homework by providing contracts and notebook folders with pockets.
4. Insist on high levels of participation by giving the children small jobs and calling on them often.

Armstrong (1996) suggests that the teacher engage these children in physical, outdoor exercise and sports with no competition. In this way, they can release some of their energy without fear of failure. He also suggests the use of personal contracts so the child can see accomplishments. Computers help students with ADHD feel successful by eliminating the messy handwriting. Johnson (1992) found that quiet classical music had a calming effect on students with ADHD and that tutors were useful because the children received one-on-one attention, which they crave.

AUTISM

Autism is an umbrella term describing a syndrome or cluster of behaviors exhibited by children whose characteristics and needs are actually heterogeneous. Autistic behaviors have been described along a continuum of severity. Definitions of **autism** and autistic disorders generally include the following six behavioral characteristics:

1. Profound failure to relate to or emotionally bond with significant people in their environment
2. Impaired language acquisition and comprehension; muteness or echolalia (repeating what is said by the other person)
3. Under- or overresponsiveness to sensory stimulation
4. Inappropriate or flat affective trait (which is speaking without emotions)
5. Preoccupation with stereotypical, repetitive, self-stimulatory behaviors, such as body rocking or hand tapping
6. Profound resistance to environmental change, including modifications in daily routines

Not all children described as autistic or autistic-like exhibit all these behavioral characteristics, nor do they demonstrate these behaviors to the same degree. Nonetheless, autism is one of the most disruptive and severe childhood disabilities.

The cause for autism and autistic-like behaviors is not clearly known. At one time, theory held that something in the parenting behaviors created this condition. This idea has been substantially refuted, and parents are now being recruited to facilitate therapy in many treatment programs (Bristol, 1985; Lovaas, 1987). The hunt for causal agents in autism has now led to genetic links, none of which has been identified as definitive (Rutter & Shopley, 1987).

Some children described as autistic are educated in the regular classroom for all or part of the school day. Since autistic behaviors are idiosyncratic, educational provisions should focus on individual children and their particular behaviors.

With respect to language arts instruction, techniques and materials should be modified according to the behavior of the particular child. For some students, the need to maintain a strict routine is critical; for others, participation in group activities is likely to aggravate negative social tendencies. Some children can participate in all language arts activities with no major modifications but might become highly agitated by environmental factors, such as the sound of a fire engine siren or the sight of popcorn popping. Certain topics found in storybooks may also set off delusional behaviors, and excessive preoccupation with spelling or handwriting style may be observed.

Regardless of the instructional topic, the general educator needs to create a reasonably appropriate educational

Listen rather than lecture. Show the road but expect the child to reach his destination on his own.

HAIM GINOTT

Figure 11.5

Questions for assisting autistic children.

- Which teaching strategies have been successful with this student in the past?
- Which procedures can be applied in the classroom without extensive support?
- What is the expected effect of any medications prescribed for the child?
- To what degree have the following behaviors been observed in an education setting: unresponsiveness to social stimuli, gaze aversion, overselective response, language disorders, and excessive fantasy and delusions? How disruptive were these behaviors?

environment for autistic children. Answers to questions posed in Figure 11.5 should be helpful in establishing a positive learning environment for students with autistic behaviors.

The answers to the last of these questions are particularly helpful when preparing other students in the classroom to accept their autistic classmate in a positive way. The other children need to be prepared for some atypical behaviors and to know how to depersonalize their occurrence. When gaze aversion happens during a conversation, for example, the inattention or lack of willingness to enter into this social activity should be taken no more personally than an interruption of conversation caused by a sneeze or hiccup. The other students also need to realize that delusional or fantasy behaviors are part of their classmate's problem, not a deliberate attempt to be dishonest with them. Preparation of the other children in the classroom is as important as understanding the needs of the child with autism if a successful social and learning climate is to be established.

> *Start a program for gifted children, and every parent demands that his child be enrolled.*
>
> THOMAS BAILEY

Academically Gifted Children

Most educators today recognize that students who are academically gifted have special needs and fall under PL 94-142. However, there are differing opinions among educators on how to meet these special needs. Some believe that the "least restrictive environment," which is promised to all children in PL 94-142, is a pull-out program, while other educators believe gifted students belong in the inclusive classroom (Sapon-Shevin, 1994/1995). Both groups have reasons for their stance.

Advocates for pull-out programs argue that the traditional **scope-and-sequence curriculum** (a curriculum that stresses that certain concepts

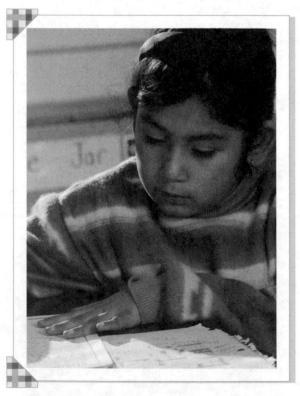

must be mastered in a specific sequence and that emphasizes repetition) is restrictive and does not permit a gifted student to grow cognitively. They believe that the scope-and-sequence curriculum includes unnecessary review with no higher-level thinking activities (Winebrenner, 1992). Tomlinson (1994/1995) found that (1) large class size hinders the regular classroom teacher from giving needed time to the gifted; (2) teachers feel that these students will succeed without any extra help; and (3) many classroom teachers lack the skills for designing and implementing appropriate curriculum for the gifted. Gallagher, Harradine, and Coleman (1997) found in a study of 871 academically gifted students that these students considered core subjects unchallenging, regular classrooms boring, and cooperative learning groups in regular classrooms unfair because they were held back and had to do all the work. There is also the possibility that gifted students choose not to succeed under the regular curriculum because they desire to "belong." To alleviate this problem, proponents of gifted education believe that gifted students need opportunity to excel with other gifted students with an appropriate curriculum that (1) permits the gifted student to reach his or her potential; (2) gives opportunity for in-depth study of concepts that interest the student; (3) allows for divergent thinking; and (4) permits students to solve real-life problems (Lewis, 1996).

Educators who favor the inclusive classroom for all students believe that gifted students belong in the regular classroom because it reflects society and there students learn to accept the differences of individuals. They believe that the pull-out programs make it more difficult to promote a positive response to differences by labeling gifted students and making them leave the regular classroom.

It is worth noting that there is no federal mandate for gifted education programs; however, most states have legislation that provides for the funding of gifted programs because they see the special needs for students with a high IQ (Doina, 1997). Across states and within states, these programs vary greatly because there are no national guidelines. Some have two-day pull-out programs for the entire district, while other districts may have only one hour per day in individual buildings.

The discussion that follows will include characteristics of the gifted student and some strategies that are affective with the gifted student. Also listed are resources that are useful to the classroom teacher.

CHARACTERISTICS OF GIFTED CHILDREN

The National Foundation for Gifted and Creative Children (1996) classifies students as gifted who (1) have an IQ of 130 or above, (2) have a score on an intelligence test of two standard deviations above the mean on group or individual measures, (3) have a score of 97th percentile or higher on standard achievement tests, (4) have high levels of leadership ability, or (5) have extraordinary talent in visual or performing arts. Clark (1993) states that gifted students are divergent thinkers, have advanced vocabulary, are fast thinkers, are unusually sensitive to exceptions, are idealistic, and seek justice. Figure 11.6 is a list of additional characteristics of the gifted student that was compiled by the teachers of the Gifted Education Program in Yukon, Oklahoma, schools (1995).

1. Asks lots of questions.
2. Possesses lots of information on specific things.
3. Is very curious; wants to know "Why?" or "How?"
4. Has concern and is sensitive about social, political, and global issues.
5. Has own ideas about how something should be done.
6. Enjoys debating.
7. Has a better reason for not doing something than you have for doing it.
8. Becomes impatient with work that is not perfect.
9. Expects others to be perfect.
10. Finds assignments unchallenging.
11. Thinks deeply and differently about things.
12. Enjoys exploratory levels of learning.
13. Loves abstract ideas.
14. Has a sense of humor.
15. Has a passionate interest in a specific area.
16. Has many interests and hobbies.
17. Can make personal application of concepts.
18. Has high level of energy.
19. Sees relationships between ideas.
20. Has a good memory.
21. Does not begin a task if there is a possibility of failure.
22. Easily sees subtle cause-and-effect relationships.
23. Prefers to work alone.

Figure 11.6

Characteristics of giftedness.

Source: Adapted from the Gifted Education Program in Yukon, Oklahoma.

BEYOND THE CLASSROOM

Take some time to reflect on your stance. Permit yourself to list the advantages and disadvantages of pull-out programs. Maybe you were in such a program and can give some insight on how you felt about the program while you were in it. If you were not in a gifted program, you may want to research the subject in order to validate your stance. Telephone some districts around your university and ask how they meet the needs of gifted students. If they have a pull-out program, ask for permission to visit it.

The national educational movement is toward inclusion (Sapon-Shevin, 1994/1995) and extending the pedagogy of gifted education to all students (Reis, Gentry, & Park, 1996). Therefore, classroom teachers are given more of the responsibility to meet the needs of gifted students.

REGULAR CLASSROOM ACTIVITIES FOR GIFTED STUDENTS

It is evident that gifted students need appropriate educational opportunities. Whatever type of special program they receive, the majority of the school time is spent in the regular classroom. Therefore, two types of activities that can be used by the classroom teacher in the regular classroom are the enrichment triad model and curriculum compacting. Both of these programs provide the following goals, which professionals agree would be at the heart of all activities that the academically talented students encounter (Doina, 1997):

- Flexible rate at which to work
- Student choice of topic
- Studies based on broad themes with in-depth study on one aspect of theme
- Open-ended tasks
- Alternative assessment

Enrichment Triad Model

Renzulli and Ries (1985), two nationally recognized researchers and leaders in gifted education, designed the **enrichment triad model,** which has three types of enrichment activities. This model, originally designed for gifted programs, is now used for schoolwide enrichment programs (Renzulli, 1994).

Type I enrichment activities are designed to expose students to new topics that they may wish to investigate later in greater detail. Type I activities include outside speakers, videos, assemblies, field trips, interest centers, and Bloom's taxonomy tasks (see Figure 11.7 for the levels of Bloom's taxonomy).

Figure 11.7

Bloom's taxonomy: Type I activity.

Knowledge:	Simple recall of learned facts. Student will bring to mind what was read, seen, or heard.
Comprehension:	Translating or interpreting material from one form to another. Student explains or predicts what did or will happen.
Application:	Ability to use learned material in personal life. Student applies rules, concepts, or theories to daily life.
Analysis:	Ability to break down material into its components. Student will identify the parts, be able to see the relationships among parts, and recognize the organization of all parts.
Synthesis:	Ability to put parts together to form a new whole. Student will research various materials, recognize similarities and differences, and be able to give an oral or written presentation.
Evaluation:	Ability to judge the value of the material studied. After studying the material, student will give a value statement with clearly defined criteria.

Source: Adapted from Bloom, *Taxonomy of Educational Objectives, Handbook I: Cognitive Domain* (1956).

Bloom's taxonomy task cards can be on any topic or book. The student begins with the first task and continues to the last one. A Bloom's taxonomy task card example on Ruth Heller's *Color* is found in Figure 11.8. After reading *Color*, a concept book about how printers apply color to the pages of a book, the students would individually complete the task folder. All Type I activities are enrichment activities and are not part of the ordinary curriculum.

1. Explain the four stages used by a printer when applying color to a page in a book.
2. Explain the magic of creating secondary colors.
3. Using the supplies on the table, mix colors to create your own color wheel.
4. Explain which primary or secondary colors create black.
5. Using four transparencies, draw a picture by using each of the transparencies as part of the entire picture; then place the transparencies over each other to show your complete picture.
6. Survey your classmates to find out which color is their favorite and create a bar graph to show the results of the survey.

Figure 11.8

Type I activity: Bloom's taxonomy task on Color by Ruth Heller.

Type II enrichment activities focus on the development of higher-level thinking skills. Type II activities include research projects that develop library skills, problem-solving puzzles, mind-benders, and community projects that focus on helping and serving others or promoting pride within one's community.

Type III enrichment activities involve real-life problems. The activities are in-depth independent or small-group projects in which a real-life problem is addressed. The goal is to find possible solutions to a real-life problem. Projects may include going to city officials to present a possible solution to a traffic problem around the school, inventing a new product, or writing and illustrating a new storybook or concept book about a favorite topic.

The enrichment triad model can be implemented in the regular classroom. All three types of activities are used, beginning, of course, with Type I. Teachers who use the enrichment triad model set aside special time each week for the activities. When working with Type II and Type III activities, students with similar interests are permitted to work together. In a Type III activity, the activity may be a group or individual project.

Compacting for the Gifted

Many teachers are challenged by gifted students. These students are easily bored and can present behavioral problems if they are not challenged. One way to accommodate these students is through **curriculum compacting:** "Curriculum compacting is a flexible, research-supported instructional technique that enables high-ability students to skip work they already know and substitute more challenging content" (Reis & Renzulli, 1992, p. 51).

The most frequently compacted areas are math, reading, language arts, science, and social studies. Compacting is done for individual subjects and for individual students. It is an individualized educational program for the gifted student. A student may be strong in one subject area and be able to compact most of that subject; however, in another content area that same student may not be able to do any compacting. Usually compacting is done by chapter or units and is done for the entire school year.

There are three steps to curriculum compacting. First, the teacher must articulate the goals and outcomes for the chapter or unit. While doing this, the teacher makes note of whether the material is review material or new content. The second step is to identify all students who have already mastered the objects or goals. One way to identify these students is to check the students' scores on standardized tests. Then the teacher gives the targeted students the posttest for that chapter or unit that is going to be studied. From the test, the teacher analyzes exactly which skills the student can perform and which concepts the student knows. Next the teacher lists the skills and concepts that the student has not mastered. If the student is weak in a skill or concept, the teacher will write specific parts of the chapter that the student must complete and will determine how the student will demonstrate mastery of the skill or concept.

The third step states the project, research, or self-directed activities that the student will accomplish while the class is working on the curriculum. The decision is agreed upon by the student and teacher and is often written as a contract. The student and teacher list specific materials to be read, documents to write, videos to view, or projects to complete. Most schools will use the compactor form that Renzulli and Smith (1978) designed (see Figure 11.9).

Figure 11.9

Sample compactor form.

The Compactor

Student's name _____ Age _____ Teachers _____

Conference date _____ Grade _____ Parents _____

Topics to be covered; tests used to prove competency	Parts of chapter to be completed to ensure competency	Enrichment tasks to be completed

Source: Adapted from J. Renzulli and L. Smith (1978), *A Guidebook for Developing Individualized Educational Programs for Gifted and Talented Students.* Copyright © Creative Learning Press, Mansfield Center, CT.

Besides the gifted students, there may be other students in the classroom who could benefit from curriculum compacting. Starko (1986) listed some behaviors of students for whom compacting may be of benefit: (1) finish tasks quickly, (2) appear bored, (3) have test scores that are consistently high despite average class work, (4) have advanced vocabulary, and (5) ask higher-level thinking questions.

The regular classroom teacher who uses both the enrichment triad model and curriculum compacting will be catering to at least some of the needs of gifted students. A list of resource materials that can be used with gifted students is found in Figure 11.10.

Figure 11.10

Resources for gifted and enrichment education materials.

Challenge Magazine: Reaching and Teaching the Gifted
Good Apple
Box 299
Carthage, IL 62321
(217) 357-3981
www.goodapple.com
(ready-to-photocopy enrichment activities)

Creative Learning Press
P.O. Box 320
Mansfield Center, CT 06250
(203) 281-4036
www.creativelearning.com/
(publisher of Renzulli's materials)

Creative Publications
5040 W. 111 Street
Oaklawn, IL 60453
1-800-624-0822
www.creativepublications.com
(excellent source for logical thinking, brainteaser books)

Critical Thinking Press & Software
P.O. Box 448
Pacific Grove, CA 93950-0448
1-800-458-4849
www.criticalthinking.com
(excellent source for a wide variety of critical thinking materials)

Engine-Unity, Ltd.
P.O. Box 9610
Phoenix, AZ 85068
(602) 997-7144
(packets for learning centers using Bloom's taxonomy)

Free Spirit Publishing Ind.
400 First Avenue, North, Suite 616
Minneapolis, MN 55401
1-800-737-7323
www.freespirit.com
(life skills material; special emphasis on gifted)

Future Problem Solving
315 W. Huron, Suite 140-B
Ann Arbor, MI 48103-42013
(313) 998-7377
(national contests for teaching creative problem solving)

Games Magazine
575 Boylston Street
Boston, MA 02116
1-800-950-6339
(puzzles and mind-benders)

Interact
P.O. Box 997-H91
Lakeside, CA 92040
1-800-359-0961
www.interact.simulations.com
(wide variety of simulations on many topics)

Summary

Many students in elementary schools are at risk of failing in a school system geared toward white, middle-class students who possess "normal" learning abilities. The diverse needs of certain children derive from language and cultural differences, physically based linguistic discrepancies, social and behavioral disorders, and various academic activities.

Effective teachers are concerned about meeting the diverse needs of each student in their ever-changing classroom. Because many classrooms have students from various cultures, teachers must understand and embrace all students' cultures. Teachers must understand and accept individual students who do not have English as their native language nor speak it in their homes. Since teachers cannot be expected to speak all the languages that are represented in their classroom, they need effective strategies to work with students as they become proficient in English.

Students who are academically talented also need special attention as they reach their potential. Using the enrichment triad model and the curriculum compacting strategy permits these students to work at their level and rate within the regular classroom.

Schools provide students with a context and climate for developing self-concepts. The teacher as the classroom leader sets the tone for acceptance or rejection of class members. Effective teachers minimize labels and look beyond categories to the students they are teaching. They celebrate their students *con cariño y amor* (with affection and love), for they may not pass their way again.

With Children *activities*

LIVING LANGUAGES

Children often learn the meanings of new words through contextual language cues. One way to heighten children's awareness and appreciation of languages is to give students five or six sentences written in English with a non-English word embedded. This word can be printed in any type of script appropriate to the language (Korean symbols for Korean terms). Allow the children to work in small groups and list meanings and how they arrived at these meanings. The students can illustrate their new words or begin a class dictionary.

MONEY, MONEY, MONEY!!!

The day before this activity, ask the children to bring money of any type from home to share with the class. You also bring money from at least three countries to class. Locate the lands represented by the money on the map. Have the students compare sizes, shapes, and value relative to currency from the United States. Next, have the children plan a shopping trip to the land of their choice, real or imagined. They describe what they will buy and how much purchases will cost in the currency of the United States and the country of their choice. If a student chooses an imaginary country, then currency will need to be invented.

STORY TREK

On a VCR, play the opening credits of the TV series "Star Trek" that includes the phrase "Dare to go where none have gone before!" Involve the class in a discussion about this phrase. Then select a story or book that takes place across time and in a foreign land. As students listen to this historical or fictional account, they plot the sequence of events on a timeline. Illustrations by the students would be fun to include on the timeline.

WALK IN ANOTHER'S SHOES

This writing activity engages children's imagination, prior knowledge, and creativity while building on cultural awareness. Write the sentence *Never judge a person until you have walked two days in his or her moccasins* on the board. Have the students discuss possible meanings of this sentence. Next have the children form small groups; give each group a picture of a kind of "moccasin": a wooden shoe from Holland, a sandal from Guatemala. Ask them to imagine that they are the person who owns the "moccasin" and to write a story about experiences they've had with their "moccasins." Students can share their stories by acting them out, reading them aloud, or placing them in a notebook in the learning center.

WHAT HAPPENS WHEN . . .

In this activity, children are helped to appreciate the strengths of their physically or sensory impaired peers. One-half of the class adopts a physical or sensory impairment while the others become their recording partners. For one full day, the "disabled" child completes routine tasks. The child's partner records the "disabled" person's feelings either on paper or through a tape recorder. The next day, write the term *handicapable* on the overhead. Have the partners write a story about experiences they've had with their "disability" and how the term *handicapable* applies. Stories can be collected and made into a class book.

technology *Creating a Web Page*

There are a number of reasons for your students to create a Web page. First, it is an easy, informal way to share information about your class with the entire world. What your students consider commonplace in your area of the country (e.g., trout farms, marine life, peanut farms, or the Grand Canyon) may be new, interesting information to other children. Second, the Web page is a fun way to share students' written work, such as stories, riddles, book reviews, projects, puzzles, and mind-benders, with parents, the community, and the world. Third, it is a means for students to display their creative work, such as artwork, cartoons, and graphic designs. Fourth, if the class includes an opportunity for others to e-mail comments back to them, the Web page is the means for building friendships or for creating partnerships in projects. Finally, a Web page can be a means of communicating a newsletter to parents and the community about upcoming events or posting a list of materials the class needs for a science project.

It is not difficult to create a Web page if you use a Web publishing tool. Two common ones used in education are Claris Home Page and Microsoft's Front Page. Both of these use *HTML* (HyperText Markup Language), which is the language used on the Internet. Some terms you may want to know are *URL* (Uniform Resource Locator, or the Web page address), *GIF* or *JPEG* (electronic formats for photographs or images), and *Java* (a programming language that facilitates use of special features such as animation). If you use a publishing tool to create your Web page, you do not need to learn HTML and the other technical terms; you only need to know how to use a word processing program.

Once you create your Web page, you need to (1) find an Internet provider, (2) upload the Web page (the publishing tool tells you how to upload), (3) edit the Web page, and (4) test your links so they are "live" and do not link to inappropriate material.

When you publish a Web page, there are some points to consider:

1. Create a Web page that loads quickly. To load quickly, consider the following:
   A. If you include photographs (digital cameras are discussed later) or graphics, do not make them too large.
   B. Use the same background for all the pages because once it is loaded, it does not need to reload for each page.
   C. Use "thumbnails," which permit pictures to be enlarged when the audience is viewing your page.
2. Design your page carefully so it is appealing; a good font is Times New Roman.
3. Map your sites carefully and thoroughly by doing the following:
   A. Be sure navigational tools are consistent (where to return to main menu, submenu, etc.).
   B. Be sure menus and submenus are comprehensive and understandable.
   C. Be consistent (e.g., frame all pictures in the same manner).
   D. When linking to other sites, include only the information you want to include.
4. Check copyright laws; one good way is to view the Stanford copyright site.
5. The home page should be visible without scrolling.

One way to personalize your home page is to include photographs of you, subjects that interest you, or objects you are attempting to explain. There are two ways to include photographs. One way is to take any favorite picture that was taken with your regular camera and scan it onto your Web page. The one extra piece of equipment you will need is a scanner.

The second way to include pictures is to use a digital camera, which records the image directly onto computer chips. Instead of film, digital cameras have either a removable memory card or a regular disk. With the first digital cameras that were on the market, one needed connection cable and transfer software, which were included with the camera. However, with the newer digital camera, one transfers the disk from the camera into the computer without any extra cables and software.

Two advantages of the digital camera are that (1) one does not have to pay for film processing and (2) one can edit the software in order to touch up pictures. Most digital cameras come with Adobe PhotoDeluxe, which is an image-editing program that is quite easy to use. Two disadvantages of the digital camera are that (1) it is expensive (however, the price is lowering as more companies are making them) and (2) the computer needs a lot of memory (usually 100 MB is recommended).

A good introduction to the use of the digital camera is Julie Adair King's book *Digital Photography for Dummies*, published in 1997 by IDG Books Worldwide in Foster City, CA.

websites   *E-learning*

ENGLISH AS A SECOND LANGUAGE

www.educ.wsu.edu/esl/esl.html
This site is rich in ESL lesson plans, thematic units, and hyperlinks to other language resources.

www.eslcafe.com
This site offers discussion forums, idioms, quotes, and writing ideas for teachers.

www.aitech.ac.jp/~iteslj/
This is the home page for the Internet TESL Journal.

www.aitech.ac.jp/~iteslj/quizzes/
This site contains self-study quizzes for ESL students.

www.aitech.ac.jp/~iteslj/cw/
This site has fun puzzles for ESL students in a number of categories on various levels of difficulty.

www.aitech.ac.jp/~iteslj/th
This is an Internet treasure hunt for ESL students. It gives practice in retrieving information from the Internet TESL Journal.

EBONICS

www.cal.org/ebonics/
This site disseminates information about Ebonics.

www.geocities.com/CapitolHill/3070/ebonics.html
This site gives opinions against the Oakland decision.

linguist.emich.edu/topics/ebonics
This site explains Oakland's resolution and links to other sites on the topic.

members.tripod.com/~cdorsett/ebonics.htm
This site includes topics on Ebonics, African American issues, and information on other dialects.

putwest.boces.org/StSu/Social.html
This site is the National History Standards home page.

www.yahoo.com/Arts/Humanities/History/Genealogy/
This site gives information about the histories of many cultures.

www.philaedfund.org/wedweb/html/mlk.html
This site has information about Martin Luther King Day and the civil rights movement.

www.geocities.com:80/Athens/Forum/9061/afro/afro.html
This site is full of information on African American history.

www.nara.gov/education/teaching/teaching.html
This gives the National History Standards for U.S. history.

www.nara.gov/education/teaching amistad/home.html
This site has documents of the *Amistad* case.

lcweb.loc.gov/exhibits/african/intro.html
This site documents immigration in American history.

Related Readings

BOOKS

Banks, J. A., & Banks, C.A. (1993). *Multicultural education: Issues and perspective* (2nd ed.). Boston: Allyn & Bacon.

> This book discusses many topics of diversity—race, class, gender, disability, religion, language, and exceptionalities. The emphasis is on reforming the schools in order that there may be effective education for all students.

Gonzalez, V., Brusca-Vega, R., & Yawkey, T. (1997). *Assessment and instruction of culturally and linguistically diverse students with or at-risk of learning problems: From research to practice.* Needham Heights, MA: Allyn & Bacon.

> This book focuses on the assessment of the various disabilities and how to provide the appropriate classroom for each type of disability. It also gives great information on how the school can work with the parents.

Johnson, D. A. (1992). *I can't sit still: Education and affirming inattentive and hyperactive children.*

> This book offers practical suggestions for parents, teachers, and other care providers of children up to age 10 who have ADHD.

Spangenberg-Urbschat, K., & Pritchard, R. (eds.) (1994). *Kids come in all languages: Reading instruction for ESL students.*

> This book is a collection of essays written by researchers and educators who have worked with ESL students. The chapters cover three main topics—issues concerning ESL, organizing for instruction for ESL, and instructional practices that work with ESL.

Winebrenner, S. (1992). *Teaching gifted kids in the regular classroom: Strategies and techniques every teacher can use to meet the academic needs of the gifted and talented.* Minneapolis: Free Spirit Publishing.

> This book has prepared learning contracts, conference record sheets, and other prepared assessment sheets that can be used by the teacher. The book also gives great strategies to use with gifted students in the regular classroom.

PROFESSIONAL JOURNALS

Educational Leadership, December 1994/January 1995, 52(4).

> This issue, titled The Inclusive School, has articles that give reasons for full inclusion and other articles that argue against full inclusion.

Educational Leadership, February 1996, 53(5).

> This issue, titled Students with Special Needs, has articles about the various special needs that are found in the classroom.

References

Allen, V. (1994). Selecting materials for reading instruction of ESL children. In K. Spangenberg-Urbschat & R. Pritchard (eds.), *Kids come in all languages: Reading instruction for ESL students.* Newark, DE: International Reading Association.

Altwerger, B., & Ivener, B. (1994). Self-esteem: Access to literacy in multicultural and multilingual classrooms. In K. Spangenberg-Urbschat & R. Pritchard (eds.), *Kids come in all languages: Reading instruction for ESL students.* Newark, DE: International Reading Association.

Anderson, W. (1995, July). Learning styles of the various cultures. Class lecture presented in the Education Department at the University of Central Oklahoma, Edmond, OK.

Armstrong, T. (1996). A holistic approach to attention deficit disorder. *Educational Leadership, 53*(5), 34–36.

Baldwin, J. (1997). If Black English isn't a language, then tell me, what is? Reproduced from a 1997 *New York Times* letter to the editor in "The real Ebonics debate" (T. Perry & L. Delpit, eds.). *Rethinking Schools: An Urban Educational Journal, 12*(1), 16.

Banks, J. (1979). *Teaching strategies for ethnic studies* (2nd ed.). Boston: Allyn & Bacon.

Banks, J. (1993). Multicultural education: Characteristics and goals. In J. Banks & C. Banks (eds.), *Multicultural education: Issues and perspectives* (2nd ed.). Boston: Allyn & Bacon.

Banks, J., & Banks, C. (1993). *Multicultural education: Issues and perspectives* (2nd ed.). Boston: Allyn & Bacon.

Beck, J. (1998, June 13). English the only choice. *Tulsa World*, p. A17.

Benning, V., & Nakashima, E. (1998, September 16). Schools strive to raise test scores of minorities. *The Washington Post*, p. 7.

Bloom, B. (1956). *Taxonomy of educational objectives: Handbook I: Cognitive domain.* New York: David McKay Co.

Bouvier, L. F., & Agresta, A. J. (1987). The future Asian population in the United States. In J. T. Fawcett & B. Carino (eds.), *Pacific bridges: The new immigration from Asia and the Pacific Islands.* New York: Center for Migration Studies.

Brisk, M. E. (1998). *Bilingual education: From compensatory to quality schooling,* Mahwah, NJ: Lawrence Erlbaum Publisher.

Bristol, M. N. (1985). Designing programs for young developmentally disabled children: A family system approach to autism. *Remedial and Special Education 64*(4), 46–63.

Chall, J., & Curtis, M. (1991). Children at risk. In Flood, J., Jensen, M., Lapp, D., & Squire, J. (eds.), *Handbook of research on teaching the English language arts.* New York: Macmillan.

Chamot, A., & O'Malley, J. M. (1994). Instructional approaches and teaching procedures. In K. Spangenberg-Urbschat & R. Pritchard (eds.), *Kids come in all languages: Reading instruction for ESL students.* Newark, DE: International Reading Association.

Clair, N. (1995). Mainstream classroom teachers and ESL students. *TESOL Quarterly, 29,* 189–196.

Clark, B. (1993). *Growing up gifted* (4th ed.). Columbus, OH: Charles E. Merrill.

Cummins, J. (1988). Second language acquisition within bilingual education programs. In L. M. Beebe (ed.), *Issues in second language acquisition: Multiple perspectives.* New York: Newbury House Publishers.

Cummins, J. (1989). *Empowering minority students.* Sacramento, CA: CABE.

Cummins, J. (1994). The acquisition of English as a second language. In K. Spangenberg-Urbschat & R. Pritchard (eds.), *Kids come in all languages: Reading instruction for ESL students.* Newark, DE: International Reading Association.

Delpit, L. (1988). The silenced dialogue: Power and pedagogy in educating other people's children. *Harvard Educational Review, 58*(3), 280–298.

Delpit, L. (1997). Ebonics and culturally responsive instruction. In "The real Ebonics debate" (T. Perry & L. Delpit, eds.). *Rethinking Schools: An Urban Education Journal, 12*(1), 6–7.

Doina, R. (1997). Evaluation of gifted programs. *Gifted Child Today* (Sept./Oct.), 38–40.

Edelsky, C. (1986). *Writing in a bilingual program. Habia una vez.* Norwood, NJ: Ablex.

Edelsky, C., Altwerger, B., & Flores, B. (1991). *Whole language: What's the difference?* Portsmouth, NH: Heinemann.

Elley, W. (1991). Acquiring literacy in a second language: The effect of book-based programs. *Language Learning, 41,* 375–411.

Farnan, N., Flood, J., & Lapp, D. (1994). Comprehending through reading and writing: Six researched-based instructional strategies. In K. Spangenberg-Urbschat & R. Pritchard (eds.), *Kids come in all languages: Reading instruction for ESL students.* Newark, DE: International Reading Association.

Feldhusen, J. (1996). How to identify and develop special talents. *Educational Leadership, 53*(5), 66–69.

Gallagher, J., Harradine, C., & Coleman, M. (1997). Gifted students in the classroom. *Roper Review, 19*(3), 132–136.

Garcia, E. (1983). Bilingual acquisition and bilingual instruction. In T. H. Escobedo (ed.), *Early childhood bilingual education.* New York: Teacher's College Press.

Garcia, G. (1994). Assessing the literacy development of second-language students: A focus on authentic assessment. In K. Spangenberg-Urbschat & R. Pritchard (eds.), *Kids come in all languages: Reading instruction for ESL students.* Newark, DE: International Reading Association.

Garibaldi, A. M. (1992). Educating and motivating African-American males to succeed. *Journal of Negro Education, 61*(1), 4–11.

Gersten, R., & Dimino, J. (1990). Reading instruction for at-risk students: Implications of current research. *Oregon School Study Council Bulletin, 33*(5).

Goodman, K. (1986). *What's whole in whole language?* Portsmouth, NH: Heinemann.

Goodman, K., & Freeman, D. (1993). *What's simple in simplified language?* In M. L. Tickoo (ed.), *Simplification: Theory and application. Anthology series 31.* ERIC Document Reproduction Service No. ED 371 578.

Grosjean, F. (1982). *Life with two languages.* Cambridge, MA: Harvard University Press.

Hahn, A. (1987). Reaching out to America's dropouts: What to do? *Phi Delta Kappan, 69*(3), 256–263.

Haney, W. (1987). *An estimation of immigrant and immigrant student populations in the United States as of October 1986.* Boston: Immigrant Student Project, Boston College.

Hoover, M. R. (1997). Ebonics: Myth and realities. In "The real Ebonics debate" (T. Perry & L. Delpit, eds.). *Rethinking Schools: An Urban Education Journal, 12*(1), 17.

Institute for Educational Leadership. (1989). School dropout: Everybody's problem. Washington, DC: Institute for Educational Leadership.

Irujo, S. (1989, May). Do you know why they all talk at once? Thoughts on cultural differences between Hispanics and Anglos. *Equity and Choice,* pp. 14–18.

Johnson, D. D. (1992). *I can't sit still.* Santa Cruz, CA: ETR Associates.

Kaufman, F. (1998). Reading report encouraging: Report supports variety of methods, bilingual education. *The Council Chronicle. The NCTE 7*(5), 1, 6.

Kellogg, J. B. (1988). Forces of change. *Phi Delta Kappan, 31,* 199–204.

Krashen, S. (1981). *Second language acquisition and second language learning.* Oxford: Pergamon Press.

Krashen, S. (1982). *Principles and practice in second language acquisition.* New York: Pergamon Press.

Krashen, S. (1985). *The input-hypothesis: Issues and implication.* New York: Longman.

Krashen, S. (1989). *Language acquisition and language education.* Englewood Cliffs, NJ: Prentice-Hall.

Krashen, S. (1993). *The power of reading: Insights from the research.* Englewood, CO: Libraries Unlimited.

Lemberger, N. (1997). *Bilingual education: Teachers' narratives.* Mahwah, NJ: Lawrence Erlbaum Publisher.

Lewis, B. A. (1996). Serving others hooks gifted students on learning. *Educational Leadership, 53*(5), 70–75.

Lichtenstein, S. J. (1987). A study of selected post-school employment patterns of handicapped and non-handicapped graduates and dropouts. Unpublished doctoral dissertation, University of Illinois.

Lovaas, O. I. (1987). Behavioral treatment and normal educational and intellectual functioning in young autistic children. *Journal of Counseling and Clinical Psychology, 55,* 3–9.

Maring, G., & Furman, G. (1985). Seven "whole class" strategies to help mainstreamed young people read

and listen better in content area classes. *Journal of Reading, 28,* 694–700.

McClure, E. F. (1977). *Aspects of code-switching in the discourse of bilingual Mexican-American children.* Urbana, IL: Center for the Study of Reading. Technical Report No. 44.

McInerney, D., & McInerney, V. (1998). The goals of schooling in culturally diverse classrooms. *The Clearinghouse, 71*(6), 363–366.

Nadeau, A., & Miramontes, O. (1988). The reclassification of limited English proficient students: Assessing the interrelationship of selected variables. *The Journal for the National Association for Bilingual Education, 12*(3), 219–242.

National Foundation for Gifted and Creative Children. (1996). Characteristics of gifted/creative children. [Online]. 1008. Available HTTP: http://www.eskimo.com/~user/zbrief.html.

Ogbu, J., & Gibson, M. (eds.) (1991). *Minority status and schooling.* New York: Garland Press.

Ogbu, H., & Simons, H. (1994). *Cultural models of literacy: A comparative study.* Berkeley, CA: National Center for the Study of Writing and Literacy.

Oklahoma State Department of Education. (1993). Regulations for gifted and talented education. Oklahoma City, OK: Oklahoma State Department of Education.

O'Neil, W. (1997). If Ebonics isn't language, then tell me, what is? In "The real Ebonics debate" (T. Perry & L. Delpit, eds.). *Rethinking Schools: An Urban Education Journal, 12*(1), 17.

Perry, T. (1997). "I'on know why they be trippin.'" In "The real Ebonics debate" (T. Perry & L. Delpit, eds.). *Rethinking Schools: An Urban Education Journal, 12*(1), 3–4.

Peregoy, S., & Boyle, O. (1997). *Reading, writing and learning in ESL: A resource book for K–12 teachers.* New York: Longman.

Reis, S., & Renzulli, J. (1992). Using curriculum compacting to challenge the above-average. *Educational Leadership, 49*(2), 51–57.

Reis, S., Gentry, M., & Park, S. (1996). Extending the pedagogy of gifted education to all students. [Online]. (1998). Available HTTP: http://www.http://www.eskimo.com/~user/zbrief.html.

Rickford, J. (1997). Holding on to a language of our own. In "The real Ebonics debate" (T. Perry & L. Delpit, eds.). *Rethinking Schools: An Urban Education Journal, 12*(1), 12–13.

Rickford, J. (1997, December). Suite for Ebony and phonics. *Discover Magazine,* pp. 82–87.

Renzulli, J. (1994). *Schools for talent development: A comprehensive plan for total school improvement.* Mansfield Center, CT: Creative Learning Press.

Renzulli, J. (1994/1995). Teachers as talent scouts. *Educational Leadership, 52*(4), 75–81.

Renzulli, J., & Reis, S. (1985). *The schoolwide enrichment model.* Mansfield Center, CT: Creative Learning Press.

Renzulli, J., & Smith, L. H. (1978). *A guidebook for developing individualized educational programs for gifted and talented students.* Mansfield Center, CT: Creative Learning Press.

Rumberger, R., & Larsen, K. (1998). Toward explaining differences in educational achievement among Mexican-American language-minority students. *Sociology of Education, 71*(1), 68–92.

Rutter, M., & Shopley, E. (1987). Autism and pervasive developmental disorders: Concepts and diagnostic issues. *Journal of Autism and Developmental Disorders, 17*(1), 159–186.

Salvia, J., & Ysseldyke, J. (1998). *Assessment* (7th ed.). Boston: Houghton Mifflin.

Sapon-Shevin, M. (1994/1995). Why gifted students belong in inclusive schools. *Educational Leadership, 52*(4), 64–67.

Schifini, A. (1994). Language, literacy, and content instruction: Strategies for teachers. In K. Spangenberg-Urbschat & R. Pritchard (eds.), *Kids come in all languages: Reading instruction for ESL students.* Newark, DE: International Reading Association.

Schirmer, B., Casbon, J., & Twiss, L. (1996). Diverse learners in the classroom. *The Reading Teacher, 49*(5), 412–414.

Shade, B., & New, C. (1993). Cultural influences on learning: Teaching implications. In J. Banks & C. Banks (eds.), *Multicultural education: Issues and perspectives.* Boston: Allyn & Bacon.

Shima, K., & Gsovski, B. (1996). Making a way for Diana. *Educational Leadership, 53*(5), 37–40.

Singham, M. (1998). The canary in the mine: The achievement gap between Black and White students. *Phi Delta Kappan, 80*(1), 8–17.

Smith, E. (1997). What is Black English? What is Ebonics? In "The real Ebonics debate" (T. Perry & L. Delpit, eds.). *Rethinking Schools: An Urban Education Journal, 12*(1), 14–15.

Smitherman, G. (1977). *Talkin & Testifyn.* New York: Houghton Mifflin.

Smitherman, G. (1997). Black English/Ebonics: What it be like? In "The real Ebonics debate" (T. Perry & L. Delpit, eds.). *Rethinking Schools: An Urban Education Journal, 12*(1), 14–15.

Spigner-Littles, D. (1992). Learning styles of African-American (Black) students. Oklahoma City, OK: Oklahoma State Department of Education.

Stahl, S. L., & Miller, P. D. (1989). Whole language and language experiences approaches for beginning reading: A quantitative research synthesis. *Review of Educational Research, 59*(1), 87–116.

Starko, A. (1986). *It's about time.* Mansfield Center, CT: Creative Learning Press.

Stevens, W. (1985, March 15). Black and standard English held diverging more. *New York Times,* sec. 1, p. 14.

Strickland, D., & Morrow, L. (1988). Creating a print-rich environment: Emerging readers and writers. *Language Arts, 42*(2), 156–157.

Temple, C., & Gillet, J. (1989). *Language arts: Learning processes and teaching practices* (2nd ed.). Glenville, IL: Scott, Foresman and Co.

Tomlinson, C. A. (1994/1995). Response: Gifted learners too: A possible dream? *Educational Leadership, 52*(4), 68–71.

Tompkins, G., & McGee, L. (1983). Launching non-standard speakers into standard English. *Language Arts, 60*(4), 463–469.

Tunnell, M., & Jacobs, J. (1989). Using "real" books: Research findings on literature-based instruction. *Reading Teacher, 42,* 470–477.

Valdes, G. (1990). Unrealistic rhetoric and realistic reform in education: A critical perspective. In H. Romo (ed.), *Latinos and Blacks in the cities.* Austin: University of Texas Press.

Valdes-Fallis, G. (1978). Code switching and the classroom teacher. *Language in education theory and practice 4.* Arlington, VA: Center for Applied Linguistics.

Van Anderson, T. (nondated). Cultural behavior of Asians. Oklahoma City, OK: Oklahoma State Department of Education.

Vygotsky, L. S. (1962). *Thought and language.* Cambridge, MA: MIT Press.

Wang, M., Reynolds, M., & Walberg, H. (1995). Serving students at the margins. *Educational Leadership, 52*(4), 12–17.

Weaver, C. (1996). *Teaching grammar in context.* Portsmouth, NH: Boynton-Cook.

Winebrenner, S. (1992). *Teaching gifted kids in the regular classroom: Strategies and techniques every teacher can use to meet the academic needs of the gifted and talented.* Minneapolis: Free Spirit Publishing.

Wolman, C., Brunicks, R., & Thurlow, M. L. (1989). Dropouts and dropout programs: Implications for special education. *Remedial and Special Education, 10*(5), 6–19.

Yellin, D. (1980). The Black English controversy: Implications from the Ann Arbor case. *Journal of Reading, 24*(2), 150–154.

Self-Diagnostic Instrument

This short (38-item) test is designed to help you determine the basic skill areas in the language arts in which you are weak. Any errors that you make here should be seen as areas that require your review.

Write your responses on the indicated lines. When you have finished, check your answers against the correct choices listed at the end of this appendix.

STRUCTURAL ANALYSIS AND PHONETICS

1. A morpheme placed at the beginning of a word to alter the meaning of that word is called a _____.
2. A _____ comes at the end of a word and alters its meaning.
3. The root word in *redevelopment* is _____.
4. The underlined portion of the word <u>p</u>raying is called a _____.
5. The common phonetic element in *chop, ship, moth,* and *when* is called a _____.
6. The common phonetic element in *hoist, round, gown,* and *boy* is called a _____.
7. The correct syllabication and accent for *coconut* and *cogitate* are _____.
8. Which of the following words contains a prefix?

   a. record   c. recruit

   b. realize   d. recover

1. _____   5. _____
2. _____   6. _____
3. _____   7. _____
4. _____   8. _____

SPELLING AND VOCABULARY

Select the *synonym* of the underlined word in each sentence.

9. Jake is the most <u>ingenious</u> person in our family.

   a. sincere   c. sociable

   b. modest   d. clever

10. Examination determined that the tumor was <u>benign.</u>
   a. noncancerous
   b. kind
   c. malignant
   d. bestial

11. She reportedly suffered from <u>chronic</u> head colds.
   a. constant
   b. bellicose
   c. painful
   d. perceptible

12. The <u>mendicant</u> approached them on the street.
   a. merchant
   b. police officer
   c. beggar
   d. salesperson

Select the *antonym* of the underlined word in each sentence.

13. His <u>nefarious</u> character was well known to all.
   a. clever
   b. kindly
   c. wicked
   d. generous

14. He made a <u>lucrative</u> investment last year.
   a. fortunate
   b. rewarding
   c. unprofitable
   d. fraudulent

15. The boy was called a <u>dolt</u> by his teachers.
   a. clever fellow
   b. delinquent
   c. prankster
   d. doll

9. _____ 13. _____
10. _____ 14. _____
11. _____ 15. _____
12. _____

Choose the word in each pair spelled correctly and write it on the line below.

16. Sarah (recieved, received) a sweater for her birthday.
17. The boys found (their, there) books where they had left them.
18. Today the natural (environment, enviroment) is threatened by industrial pollution.
19. Try to use correct (grammar, grammer) in your composition.
20. The stars were (shining, shinning) brightly in the sky.
21. We will (definately, definitely) meet you at eight o'clock.
22. The city was (fourty, forty) miles from the airport.

16. _____ 20. _____
17. _____ 21. _____
18. _____ 22. _____
19. _____

PROOFREADING

One word in each line is spelled or used incorrectly. Write the correct word on the line below.

23. There are too main points to

24. be considired. First, the cost
25. of the entire operation must be less then
26. the transpertation of the various materials.
27. Second, the sight of the building
28. should depend on the advise of an expert.

23. _____   26. _____

24. _____   27. _____

25. _____   28. _____

PUNCTUATION, CAPITALIZATION, AND PARTS OF SPEECH

29. Which of the following sentences is punctuated correctly?
    a. The lake which is calm, is not deep
    b. She ran down the steps, and across the street.
    c. The road stretched forever, we drove on until midnight.
    d. "I'll never see you again," she said.

29. _____

Indicate on the line below which word (or words) in each line should be capitalized.

30. They lived on hester street for
31. ten years before moving to michigan,
32. where her husband taught english at the college.

30. _____   32. _____

31. _____

Write the name of the part of speech for the underlined word in each line.

33. There were seventy <u>large</u> elephants
34. in the parade. They walked, <u>slowly</u>
35. swinging their heavy <u>trunks.</u>
36. <u>Around</u> the square they trudged
37. for hours. <u>However,</u> their pace never changed.
38. Which of the following sentences is punctuated correctly?
    a. They gathered up their coats, hats scarves and left.
    b. Where have all the flowers gone!
    c. Today, unlike previous days, the weather is clear.
    d. I will leave now: but tomorrow I shall return.

33. _____   36. _____

34. _____   37. _____

35. _____   38. _____

ANSWERS

1. prefix
2. suffix
3. develop
4. blend
5. digraph
6. diphthong
7. co´co-nut, cog´i-tate
8. d (recover)
9. d (clever)
10. a (noncancerous)
11. a (constant)
12. c (beggar)
13. b (kindly)
14. c (unprofitable)
15. a (clever fellow)
16. received
17. their
18. environment
19. grammar
20. shining
21. definitely
22. forty
23. two, *not* too
24. considered, *not* considired
25. than, *not* then
26. transportation, *not* transpertation
27. site, *not* sight
28. advice, *not* advise
29. d
30. Hester Street
31. Michigan
32. English
33. adjective
34. adverb
35. noun
36. preposition
37. conjunction
38. c

Index